Interventions

EVIDENCE-BASED BEHAVIORAL STRATEGIES FOR INDIVIDUAL STUDENTS

Randy Sprick, Ph.D.
Mickey Garrison, Ph.D.

2ND EDITION

PUBLISHED IN THE UNITED STATES BY PACIFIC NORTHWEST PUBLISHING 2451 WILLAMETTE ST. EUGENE, OREGON 97405

11 10 09 08   5 4 3 2

ISBN: 978-1-59909-017-7

COVER DESIGN: HANNAH BONTRAGER

TABLE OF CONTENTS

Randy Sprick, Ph.D., has worked as a paraprofessional, teacher, and teacher trainer at the elementary and secondary levels. Author of a number of widely read books on behavior and classroom management, Dr. Sprick is director of Safe & Civil Schools, a consulting company that provides inservice programs throughout the country. Each year, he conducts workshops for more than 20,000 teachers and administrators. As director of Safe & Civil Schools, he and his trainers work with numerous large and small school districts on longitudinal projects to improve student behavior and motivation. Dr. Sprick was the recipient of the 2007 Council for Exceptional Children (CEC) Wallin Lifetime Achievement Award.

Mickey Garrison, Ph.D., has been a teacher, administrator, and consultant. As a principal, her school was awarded national recognition and received attention from the George Lucas Foundation, which created a documentary about the school's accomplishments in mathematics (see www.glef.org/magic-of-math). She is currently the school improvement director for a joint venture among the Oregon Department of Education, Oregon's Education Service Districts, Oregon's K–12 system, and higher education. Under Dr. Garrison's leadership, districts are advancing school improvement from being an event to becoming an integral part of how their schools operate. As a consultant, Dr. Garrison specializes in training school teams to increase student achievement and improve behavior. She has coordinated numerous statewide and school district change initiatives. Dr. Garrison is currently developing training materials that support difficult-to-reach students in grades K–10.

ACKNOWLEDGMENTS

W E WOULD like to give special thanks to the authors of specific chapters and sections. Their names also appear on the respective chapters they contributed to, and we wish to recognize their efforts and thank them for their time and expertise.

- Marilyn Sprick: "Intervention B: Academic Assistance"

- Shawn Reaves: "Intervention G: Managing Physically Dangerous Behavior," specifically the Managing Threats section

- Geoff Colvin: "Intervention I: Managing the Cycle of Emotional Escalation"

- Leanne S. Hawken and Sarah L. Adolphson: "Intervention N: Functional Communication"

- Barbara Gueldner and Ken Merrell: "Intervention R: Internalizing Problems and Mental Health"

Daniel Gulchak provided extensive and very helpful feedback, including some additional monitoring forms for "Intervention K: Self-Monitoring and Self-Evaluation."

We would like to thank Jessica Sprick, Lisa Theobold, Matthew Treder, Betsy Norton, Natalie Conaway, Michelle Nicolson, and Sara Ferris for help in editing and shaping the content. Thanks also to Matt Sprick and Caroline DeVorss at Pacific Northwest Publishing. We would also like to thank the following people for providing revision suggestions and help with citations:

Barbara Bachmeier, Melissa Bergstrom, Chris Borgmeier, Angelisa Braaksma, Kim Bronz, Erin Chaparro, Emily Chow, Kelli Cummings, Chrissy Davis, Laura Feuerborn, Hank Fien, Kevin Filter, Brian Gaunt, Kristi Hagen-Trujillo, Keith Herman, Diane Hill, Rachell Katz, Travis Laxton, Moira McKenna, Nicole Nakayama, Michelle Nutter, Lana Putnam, Wendy Reinke, Marianna Rocha, Lisa Sterling, Dave Van Loo, and Jennifer Watson.

TESTIMONIALS

A WONDERFUL BOOK on evidence-based practices that every teacher and related services specialist working in schools should have. It provides an invaluable guide for navigating the difficult challenges that so many of today's students present during the teaching-learning process. All school staff should familiarize themselves with this material. I especially like Randy's RTI distinction between early-stage and highly structured intervention approaches that address prevention goals and outcomes at different levels.

"Randy's book provides comprehensive coverage of the tools and techniques that are so necessary in setting up, managing, and teaching in today's classroom environments. I can think of no better resource for addressing these critical tasks that are so influential in achieving school success for all students."

Hill Walker, Ph.D., Professor of Special Education, University of Oregon
Co-Director, Institute on Violence and Destructive Behavior, University of Oregon
Director, Center on Human Development

"*Interventions* is an easy-to-use guide for planning and implementing behavior management with interventions based on the latest research and time-tested strategies; is organized logically; speaks in a relaxed and clear voice; and provides specific actions, tools, and reproducible forms for a teacher, school psychologist, counselor, or behavior specialist to use every day.

"Randy Sprick—an exceptional educator and presenter—and his colleague Mickey Garrison have provided what is needed to support student behavior through a positive, respectful, and logical continuum of schoolwide, classroom, and individual interventions."

Susan Gorin, CAE, Executive Director, National Association of School Psychologists

"Randy understands the complexity of today's classroom and translates research-based practices into user-friendly, efficient, and effective tools that are manageable in today's school environment. He is a pioneer in developing systems and sustaining their efforts in producing a positive culture that honors and respects students and staff. Anyone in my district who has heard Randy speak knows that he is a master at transforming the beliefs of even the most resistant and guiding them to research-based tools and practices."
Sally LaRue, Ph.D., Director of Educational Support Services, Humble ISD

"Dr. Sprick has provided a practical 'how-to' guide with evidence-based strategies for helping staff effectively intervene with students who have challenging behaviors. He has again provided a timely and rich resource to guide us through the challenges of RTI for behavior that synthesizes current best practices with step-by-step procedures [that move] from prevention to [intensive] intervention."
Mike Box, LCSW, Behavior Response Team Coordinator, Pasadena ISD

"Dr. Sprick's extensive experience as an educator and purveyor of best practices is apparent in the revised edition of *Interventions*. He has the unique talent of deconstructing complex ideas into workable, understandable, and useful components that translate into teachable processes. With increased efforts to address RTI across the nation, *Interventions* successfully integrates the best of evidence-based practices with practical, easy-to-use approaches to RTI. This revised edition couldn't have come at a better time! All school intervention staff, especially teachers, will undoubtedly benefit."
Jose Luis Torres, Ph.D., Executive Director, Parent Services, Dallas ISD
Former Dallas ISD Director of Psychological Services and districtwide implementator of SCS *Foundations*, *START*, and *Interventions* programs

"This book is a how-to manual which guides the reader through step-by-step instructions for implementing function-based interventions that are positive and preserve the dignity of students. StaRTIng with early-stage interventions and then moving to more highly structured interventions, this book follows the Response to Intervention model with an emphasis on Positive Behavior Supports. This book is a must for anyone working with struggling students who wants practical, positive, and research-based interventions."
William R. Jenson, Ph.D., Professor of Educational Psychology, University of Utah
Coauthor of the *Tough Kid* series

"In my work supporting best practices in schools nationwide, the work of Dr. Randy Sprick represents, by far, the best of some really great work in behavior support. This book, like his other efforts, provides a foundational tool that while scientifically based, translates positive behavior support in a clear, understandable language with implementable and effective interventions for practitioners."
Mark R. Shinn, Ph.D., Professor of School Psychology, National-Louis University

SAFE & CIVIL SCHOOLS

Overview

THE SAFE & CIVIL SCHOOLS SERIES is a comprehensive, integrated set of resources designed to help educators improve student behavior and school climate at every level—districtwide, schoolwide, within the classroom, and at the individual intervention level. The findings of decades of research literature have been refined into step-by-step actions that teachers and staff can take to help all students behave responsibly and respectfully.

The difference of the *Safe & Civil Schools* model is its emphasis on proactive, positive, and instructional behavior management—addressing behavior *before* it necessitates correction, collecting data before embarking on interventions, implementing simple corrections before moving to progressively more intensive and time-intrusive ones, and setting a climate of respect for all. As a practical matter, tending to schoolwide and classwide policies, procedures, and interventions is far easier than resorting to more costly, time-intrusive, and individualized approaches.

Resources in the series do not take a punitive approach to discipline. Contrary to popular notions, managing students ought never to come down to an "I say it, you do it" formula. Direct ultimatums from authority figures constitute only a small part of a student's overall experience. To the students who receive them the most, such statements fade like background noise into insignificance. Ultimately, neither the teacher nor even the school principal has the power to "make" a student behave—or even pay attention. The variables many teachers feel are the only tools in their arsenal—commands and corrections—are, in fact, among the least effective.

Instead, *Safe & Civil Schools* addresses the sources of teachers' greatest power to motivate: through structuring for student success, teaching expectations, observing and monitoring student behavior, and, above all, interacting positively. Because experience directly affects behavior, it makes little sense to pursue only the undesired behavior (by relying on reprimands, for example) and not the conditions (in behavioral theory, the *antecedent*) that precipitate experience and subsequent behavior.

Safe & Civil Schools acknowledges the real power teachers have—not in controlling students, but in affecting every aspect of the students' experience while they are in the classroom: the physical layout, the way time is structured, arrivals and departures, and the quality of time spent in the intervening interval.

The core beliefs of the *Safe & Civil Schools* approach are consistent with the latest behavioral and teacher-effectiveness research, cultivated through more than 25 years of in-the-field teaching and consulting experience:

- School is important to a student's success in life (although some students and families may not believe this).
- All students should be treated with dignity and respect.
- Student misbehavior represents a learning opportunity.

THIS BOOK was originally published in 1993. Since that time, research has continued to confirm that the proactive, positive, and instructional approaches suggested in the original edition are far more effective in managing and motivating students than traditional authoritarian and punitive approaches. From the literature on schoolwide behavior support, classroom management, and interventions with individual students, we know at a minimum that students are most likely to thrive with educators who:

- maintain and communicate high expectations for student success

- build positive relationships with students

- teach students how to behave successfully

- create consistent, predictable classroom routines

- provide consistent monitoring and supervision

- provide frequent positive feedback

- correct misbehavior in a calm, consistent, logical manner

This revised edition translates these broad ideas about behavior management and interventions into specific actions you can take to improve the behavior of individual students. The previous edition offered 16 specific interventions, along with a procedural manual delineating how to provide schoolwide coordination for delivery of intervention services. Those interventions have been combined, revised, and expanded for this edition, and several new additions bring the total to 19 interventions. This book is intended to furnish everything necessary to design and implement customized individual interventions in the classroom. The information on schoolwide coordination (and one of the interventions, "Mentoring") from the earlier edition has been revised and expanded and is now in a new book entitled *Behavioral Response to Intervention* (B-RTI): *A Schoolwide Approach*. B-RTI provides information for administrators, psychologists, counselors, and behavior specialists on how to organize the resources within a school to ensure that no students fall through the cracks and that students and teachers receive the support they need. This revised version of *Interventions* is a companion resource to B-RTI and contains specifics about how to plan evidence-based interventions. If B-RTI is the background information administrators and school leaders need to set up a system for individualized intervention, *Interventions* is the how-to manual, with step-by-step instructions for teachers, school psychologists, administrators, and anyone working directly with students and their families.

This book fits into a continuum of behavior support products in the *Safe & Civil Schools Series*, a comprehensive resource designed to help school personnel make all school settings physically and emotionally safe for all students. In implementation projects throughout the country, my colleagues and I have learned that when expectations are clear and directly taught to students, much as you would teach writing skills, the vast majority of students will strive to be cooperative and meet those expectations. By implementing the preventive aspects of the *Safe and Civil Schools Series*, teachers can spend less time dealing with disruption and resistance and more time teaching.

However, some students will need more. Sometimes you will need to work one-to-one with a student on a behavioral intervention plan targeted to meet his or her individual needs—a plan made up of one or more of the interventions in this book.

While individualized interventions are important, they are much easier to carry out in a school with a well-designed and fully implemented schoolwide behavior plan. *Foundations: A Positive Approach to Schoolwide Discipline* provides a broader overview of effective policies at the building and district level that can help ensure that school is a physically and emotionally safe place for students and staff; that policies and procedures are clear, reasonable, and equitably enforced; and that staff actively strive to build relationships with students that inspire them to do their best. If your school does not have a proactive and positive schoolwide approach, we urge you to involve the whole staff in a continuous effort to implement and sustain such policies. There is no more effective way to reduce the need for individual interventions.

INTRODUCTION

STUDENT MISBEHAVIOR is one of the leading frustrations of educators. Any major misbehavior that is engaged in chronically—insubordination, disruption, disrespect, or refusal to do work—can make even highly skilled teachers feel helpless, frustrated, and angry. This book gives teachers and all educators more tools to correct any and all chronic problems—overt misbehavior, lack of motivation, anger and hostility, and even chronic internalizing behaviors such as shyness, depression, or anxiety. This book is built on the understanding, well founded in the research literature of the last 70 years, that behavior can be changed. Using positive and respectful intervention procedures, problem behavior can be shaped and modified to become productive behavior. One important and unavoidable job of educators is to use these intervention procedures to help students learn to be successful students and, eventually, successful and productive citizens.

The basis for this book is a set of well-researched behavioral principles:

- Behavior is learned.

- Behavior can be changed.

- Lasting behavioral change is more likely with positive, rather than punitive, techniques.

- No student should be intentionally or unintentionally humiliated or belittled.

> Note: Each chapter includes a reference section that cites examples documenting the efficacy of each intervention.

As vast as the body of research literature regarding behavior change is, its key findings can be summed up in a simple acronym: STOIC. Each letter in this acronym represents one category of intervention types that have a proven track record.

Structure for Success

Identify any changes in physical arrangements, scheduling, procedures, supervision patterns, and other factors that may have a positive effect on behavior.

Teach Expectations

Identify a plan to teach students to function successfully in the structure you have created. This can be as simple as a goal discussion or as involved as daily modeling and rehearsal of responsible behavior. The intervention plan must address when, where, and how these positive expectations will be taught to the students.

Observe and Monitor

In the short term, continuously circulate and visually scan. In the longer term, collect data to determine progress (or lack of progress) across time.

Interact Positively

Build positive relationships with students by greeting and showing an interest in them, and provide frequent positive feedback on behavioral and academic efforts when students are meeting your expectations, following your procedures, and engaging appropriately in academic tasks.

Correct Misbehavior Fluently

React to misbehavior calmly, briefly, consistently, and immediately. Avoid power struggles that distract from the instructional activity, and as soon as possible after the student begins behaving responsibly, begin interacting positively with that student.

/sto•ic/ adj. Definition 1: Tending to remain unemotional, especially showing an admirable patience and endurance in the face of adversity.

Definition 2: Unruffled, calm, and firmly restraining response to pain or distress.

Stoic is the perfect definition of educators who understand behavioral intervention practice—they are relentless in striving to find interventions that will help troubled students and continually demonstrate their high positive regard for all students. They do not "tolerate" misbehavior but are endlessly patient in experimenting with different interventions until they find some combination of strategies to help their students become successful.

Those with training in behavior analysis will recognize an *Antecedent-Behavior-Consequence* (ABC) analysis of behavior embedded in the STOIC acronym. With ABC analysis, any behavior can be viewed as a function of the antecedents (those stimuli that precede a behavior) and the consequences that naturally follow from the behavior. This simply means that people learn from their environment.

STOIC is a way of thinking about intervention—you can change aspects of the antecedents by changing the *structure* of the setting, and you can *teach* the student new behaviors to replace old behaviors in those settings. An example of this would be a basketball coach who devises a new play and then teaches the team to execute that play during a game. A person can also affect another person's behavior by *observing*. For example, a person may suck in his or her stomach while walking on the beach past a member of the opposite sex. Similarly, most drivers slow down to the legal speed limit when a police officer is in sight. The simple act of active observation goes a long way to curtail many behavior problems. Both *interacting positively* and *correcting fluently* are responses that follow behavior. They positively reinforce desirable behavior and calmly discourage problem behavior. This increases likelihood that students will choose to engage in positive behaviors in the future.

Any behavior a person engages in repeatedly serves some function or meets some need for the individual exhibiting it. A student may be trying to get something, such as attention from teachers or peers, or *avoid* something, such as an embarrassing or stressful situation. It's important to grasp that all student behavior has a purpose and that most behavior is not employed with malevolent intent. Behavior that seems illogical, mean-spirited, and unproductive from the teacher's point of view may seem logical, reasonable, and even smart from the student's perspective, which is made up of past experience and current perceptions. Understanding what motivates unwanted or self-defeating behavior is the first key to finding an appropriate planned response.

Intervention is the word educators have devised for this planned response to a behavior (or set of behaviors) that is interfering with a student's success in school. An effective intervention addresses the function of the behavior. So, for example, with a student who seeks attention, the interventionist will attempt to reduce the amount and intensity of attention the student receives for disruptive behavior while increasing the amount and intensity of attention the student receives for productive academic behavior. *Function-based intervention*, which is the framework for many of the interventions in this book, simply means that the intervention should be designed to help the student get his or her needs met by exhibiting responsible and appropriate behavior rather than through misbehavior.

Although this book will be helpful to an individual teacher, it works best when it is implemented schoolwide as part of a *behavioral response to intervention* (B-RTI) approach. B-RTI is a fancy term for some simple concepts:

- Prior to using more complicated and costly interventions, you should try the easiest, cheapest, and least time-consuming intervention that has a reasonable chance of success.

- You cannot know that a simple intervention will not work unless you try it and implement it well.

- If a student with a behavioral problem is resistant to simple interventions, progressively more detailed and intensive interventions should be attempted until the problem is resolved.

- To be considered, an intervention should have a long track record of success—evidence and research literature documenting that it is effective in a variety of settings, with varied student populations, and without being coercive or humiliating to the student.

BOOK ORGANIZATION

THE BOOK is organized to be easy to use by individual teachers, counselors, psychologists, behavior specialists, and collaborative teams. The 19 specific interventions are arranged into chapters, and each intervention meets several prerequisites:

- Multiple studies have demonstrated its effectiveness.

- It allows students dignity and respect.

- It can be implemented by classroom teachers who do not possess highly specialized training (such as training in clinical psychology).

- It achieves relatively quick, measurable results (as compared with treatments that take much longer—even years, as do some forms of psychotherapy).

The book is divided into three sections. The first, *Pre-Intervention: Classroom Management Strategies*, focuses on classroom management—the art and skill of ensuring that most students behave responsibly on most days. Here's one way to look at this section: The best and simplest intervention is the one you don't have to implement—prevention. Going into the school year, every teacher should anticipate the kinds of behavior problems he or she can expect from students. Teachers should structure their classroom and overall management plan according to the age and maturity of their students and the nature of the curriculum. This section can help every teacher develop a classroom management plan that clearly addresses expectations, rules, and routines.

The next section of the book, *Early-Stage Interventions*, contains six chapters, Interventions A through F. Each chapter provides guidance to classroom teachers on how to implement a specific intervention that is designed to be a starting place in intervening. These interventions involve trying the easiest first and are tools that any (and, hopefully, every) teacher can keep in his or her "bag of tricks."

The final section of the book contains 12 chapters, Interventions G through R. These *Highly Structured Interventions* are a powerful group of tools that may be more time-intensive to plan and more time-consuming to implement. A general education teacher with responsibilities for teaching many children may find these interventions more involved or complicated than is possible or realistic to implement without some assistance. Highly Structured Interventions are well worth knowing and understanding, but the assumption is that intervention design and implementation will be a collaborative endeavor among teams of school professionals. In this way, school resources are directed to the students who need the most intensive interventions and will benefit from them the most.

> Note: The only absolute rule about behavior management is that belittlement of students has no place in any educational setting—all behavioral interventions must treat children with dignity and respect. To have a positive and lasting impact, interventions must attempt to build up student strengths and expand skills for replacing problem behavior, rather than simply squelching or containing problem behavior.

Following is a description of each chapter.

Pre-Intervention: Classroom Management Strategies

This section is provided to help teachers self-assess their strengths and possible areas of improvement in general classroom management. If more than a few students are engaged in chronic misbehavior, changes in the general classroom management plan are probably needed before working up individualized intervention plans for each student. For a general education teacher with 20, 30, or more students, planning individualized interventions for more than one or two students is not reasonable and should not be expected.

Early-Stage Interventions

"INTERVENTION A: Planned Discussion" is designed to make the student aware of the teacher's perception of the problem and what the teacher wants the student to be doing instead. This simple intervention is often a logical starting place, potentially resolving any behavioral issues that may be a function of the student's not knowing or understanding the teacher's expectations.

"INTERVENTION B: Academic Assistance" helps the teacher identify whether the student's acting out is strictly behavioral in nature or if it is compounded by, and perhaps even caused by, academic deficits. The chapter includes information on how to perform informal academic assessments. If the student suffers from hidden academic difficulties, a variety of differentiation strategies—adaptations and accommodations—are provided to help the student become more academically successful as she works on learning necessary academic skills. These strategies will often eliminate or reduce the troubling behavior.

"INTERVENTION C: Goal Setting" provides suggestions on how to frame correcting the problem behavior as a positive goal to strive toward—something to achieve. Forms are provided to guide both long-term and short-term goal-setting processes.

"INTERVENTION D: Data Collection and Debriefing" assumes that the behavior in question is chronic, since the student has not responded to the simplest interventions. Data collection starts with defining the problem in measurable terms. The teacher is then guided in how to collect and report data on the problem and how to involve the student and parents in reviewing the data, discussing progress, and becoming "shareholders" in the student's process of improvement. Data Collection and Debriefing alone will often resolve a problem. Even when it does not, subsequent interventions will make use of this data as the intervention process becomes more objective and analytical.

"INTERVENTION E: Increasing Positive Interactions" helps ensure that the student is receiving far more attention for positive behavior than for negative behavior. Research has repeatedly demonstrated that most students respond optimally to instruction when the teacher's ratio of positive to negative interactions is significantly skewed in the positive direction. By focusing more on a student when he is engaged in positive behavior and less on any undesired behaviors, the teacher communicates high expectations and high positive regard for the student. The teacher also avoids inadvertently reinforcing attention-seeking behavior and, in many cases, increases the student's motivation to continue to exhibit positive behavior. For the teacher, periodic self-monitoring of the ratio of positive to negative interactions, both with the target student and with the whole class, can help identify areas where the student might be responsive to increased encouragement and recognition.

"**INTERVENTION F**: STOIC Analysis and Intervention" is the final Early-Stage Intervention—the last to try before moving to more intensive interventions. It is also the last in the collection of interventions that might reasonably be implemented by a classroom teacher without requesting outside assistance. It guides the teacher in analyzing the function of a particular misbehavior— why might this behavior be occurring? From this working hypothesis, a multi-faceted intervention to address the function of the behavior can be designed, incorporating each of the five variables of classroom management over which the teacher has control (Structure, Teach, Observe, Interact, Correct). The STOIC framework encourages thinking about function as comprehensively as possible. For example, if the function of the misbehavior is attention seeking, the intervention plan would address that function within each of the STOIC variables—exploring structural changes, teaching expected behavior, closely observing and monitoring, stepping up efforts to interact positively with the student, and revising procedures for correcting fluently.

Highly Structured Interventions

The first two Highly Structured Interventions deal with *Code Red* situations— so named because behaviors are either so dangerous or so disruptive that classes cannot continue. These interventions should be carefully planned, discussed, and understood by all building administrators, teachers, and support staff. The procedures should be revisited and reevaluated on a consistent (no less than annual) basis. Teachers and administrators should think of Code Red interventions as a necessary last resort, not as a convenient fallback for troublesome or unruly students. While they may be effective in the short term, Code Red interventions in and of themselves are unlikely to produce the long-term outcomes desired, either for the student or the classroom teacher.

"**INTERVENTION G**: Managing Physically Dangerous Behavior and Threats of Targeted Violence" is a reactive intervention to help staff design a plan for dealing with intense misbehavior that creates a risk of physical injury. In this intervention, guidance is provided for making decisions about when and how to clear a room or use physical restraint. Data regarding dangerous incidents will be collected, charted, and analyzed to determine whether progress is being made. Above all, the primary intent of this intervention is to keep students and staff safe; consequently, other interventions will be needed to help the student learn alternative productive behaviors.

"INTERVENTION H: Managing Severely Disruptive Behavior" is another reactive intervention that is designed to prevent one student's behavior from infringing on her classmates' ability to learn. This intervention involves developing agreements between the teacher and the school administrator about what behaviors are severe enough to warrant removal of the student from the room and what procedures will be instituted if the student refuses to leave. Since the Code Red interventions G and H are strictly reactive, other interventions should be implemented concurrently to help the student learn more responsible behaviors.

"INTERVENTION I: Managing the Cycle of Emotional Escalation" describes a predictable cycle of escalation that occurs with emotional behavior such as tantrums, refusal to comply with instructions, aggression, and confrontation. Understanding the stages of this cycle will allow school personnel to analyze patterns in a student's acting-out behavior, identify when the student is beginning to escalate, and intervene quickly and appropriately before the student reaches the boiling point. Learning to interrupt the cycle in a fluent manner can bring a student back to a calm state without the student reaching the kind of peak, out-of-control behavior that might otherwise portend a potentially explosive Code Red situation.

"INTERVENTION J: Cueing and Precorrecting" is simple but powerful. Cueing involves increasing the student's own awareness of the negative behaviors in which he tends to engage. For example, a teacher and student may work out a system by which the teacher can covertly signal the student that she is bragging in ways that may be alienating other students. Precorrection is similar to cueing, but instead of reacting to a student's problem behavior, a teacher will remind the student not to exhibit the problem behavior *before it happens*. Precorrection is most effective when the teacher has a good idea of which situations are likely to trigger the unacceptable behavior, as in the case of a student who habitually argues with the teacher when directions are presented.

"INTERVENTION K: Self-Monitoring and Self-Evaluation" can help students gain control over their own behaviors. A commonplace example of self-monitoring would be the "things-to-do" list that many adults write daily and then check off as each item is completed. Self-monitoring can be used to reduce misbehavior, such as disruptions, or it may be used to increase positive behavior, such as work completion. Self-evaluation procedures are designed to improve the quality or consistency of a particular behavior, such as cooperation, participation, or neatness of written work, by having the student rate the behavior on a scale with descriptors for each item on the scale. Self-evaluation can also stimulate discussion and help a student and teacher reconcile differing views of the student's behavior and performance.

"INTERVENTION L: Positive Self-Talk and Attribution Training" can reduce chronic negativity. If the negativity is directed toward other people, things, and events (as compared to merciless self-criticism), simply teaching the student positive statements to say to replace the negative ones can change the student's behavior. Eventually, this intervention may also lead to changes in the student's attitude and self-talk (the words people silently say to themselves). If the individual's negativity is primarily directed inward (self-criticism), the problem may be one of *attribution*—that is, do you attribute successes and failures to things within your control or things that are out of your control? Attribution training (or retraining, as it is sometimes known) helps the student learn to attribute successes to herself ("I got a good grade because I studied hard") rather than to external forces or happenstance ("I got a good grade because the test was too easy"). By the same token, this intervention can help the student learn to ascribe mistakes, difficulties, and "failures" to things outside herself or outside of her control ("I forgot about band rehearsal, so I didn't give myself the time I needed to do a great job on my homework" as opposed to "I always do badly at homework because I am stupid"). Refocusing self-talk and reframing attribution can profoundly change a student's confidence level, sense of self-efficacy, motivation, and, in some cases, tendencies toward depression or anxiety.

"INTERVENTION M: Teaching Replacement Behavior" can be a useful component of almost any behavior intervention plan. It is based on the idea that behaviors can be learned. Just as a coach knows with certainty that ongoing teaching, practice, and feedback will help a team improve, a teacher can also help a student improve his behavior by teaching more positive and responsible behaviors to replace the problem behavior. More than simply "telling" a student to exhibit a particular behavior, this chapter explains how to teach a student to master a particular behavior and incorporate it into daily life.

"INTERVENTION N: Functional Communication" is useful for any student who does not know how to get his needs met by communicating those needs verbally or nonverbally, but instead tries to get those needs met through misbehavior. In conjunction with a multidisciplinary team and with the guidance of a school psychologist, speech/language clinician, and/or occupational therapist, the teacher must first ascertain that the problem is communication-based and then design an alternative communication system for the student to get her needs met in positive and responsible ways instead of by misbehaving.

"INTERVENTION O: Structured Reinforcement Systems" is useful when a student lacks intrinsic motivation to want to improve a particular behavior. By creating a structure of points, tokens, or other age-appropriate means of tracking positive performance, the teacher can introduce incentives and rewards for positive behavior. By earning points or tokens, the student can accumulate enough to "spend" them on desired interactions, activities, or other tangible items. This chapter also addresses concerns parents and educators may voice about reward systems, such as "I've heard you shouldn't have to bribe students to do what is expected of them." While it is important for students to learn to behave appropriately without external rewards, this is a temporary intervention designed to move students in a more positive direction.

"INTERVENTION P: Defining Limits and Establishing Consequences" acknowledges that reasonable consequences for misbehavior are both appropriate and necessary for the well-being of all students and staff, although most interventions should focus on providing positive support. A range of consequences with pros and cons are presented so you can decide which consequence to apply to various situations. With this chapter, the teacher will learn how to define the problem behavior by delineating limits—that is, by clarifying the lines between behavior that is always appropriate (and always encouraged), behavior that is acceptable only to a point or at certain times, and inappropriate behavior that will always receive a clearly defined consequence. Setting clear limits is the only way to ensure that consequences will be applied fairly, consistently, and equitably, which greatly increases the likelihood consequences will be effective.

"INTERVENTION Q: Relaxation and Stress Management" is geared toward the teacher rather than the student. If a student's misbehavior is making a teacher tense, angry, or frustrated, it can be difficult, if not impossible, for the teacher to calmly and consistently implement the other interventions in this or any program. By learning to physically relax, mentally decompress, and keep the student's behavior in perspective, the teacher can more positively and effectively instruct her students—not just the challenging students, but all students.

"INTERVENTION R: Internalizing Problems and Mental Health" addresses those quiet problems that often go undetected, such as students who may be anxious or depressed. Even without previous training in counseling, teachers and other school personnel can try several effective strategies for helping troubled students. These techniques may be of help in working with a student who is sad, withdrawn, worried, or nervous. At the same time, this chapter also provides guidance in identifying when a problem is severe enough to warrant referral to a mental health professional.

HOW TO USE THIS BOOK

To the classroom teacher:

IF A particular misbehavior is exhibited by several or many students, work carefully through the suggestions in *Pre-Intervention: Classroom Management Strategies*. For problems with individual students, start by implementing Early-Stage Interventions A through F, usually in that order. Try each intervention for a couple of weeks. In implementing these or any other interventions, do not be discouraged if the behavior gets worse for a few days after the initial implementation before beginning to improve.

If you are unsure how to proceed with selecting an intervention, see the intervention Decision Guide (Reproducible Form Intro 1) on the following page for a reference of the problem behavior that is best addressed in each intervention. Remember that you should always attempt the easiest and least time-intensive interventions first.

Reproducible Form Intro 1: *Decision Guide*

Decision Guide

Presenting Behavior	Check if true	Intervention	Date of implementation	Effectiveness (+/−)
Several or many students in class misbehave.		**Preintervention:** *Classroom Management*		
The student may not know what is expected.		**Intervention A:** *Planned Discussion*		
The student may have an underlying academic problem.		**Intervention B:** *Academic Assistance*		
The student has difficulty with motivation and may not understand how to reach a goal.		**Intervention C:** *Goal Setting*		
The student's behavior appears to be chronic and resistant to simple intervention.		**Intervention D:** *Data Collection and Debriefing*		
The student gets a lot of attention from adults or peers for misbehavior or failure.		**Intervention E:** *Increasing Positive Interactions*		
The reason the behavior is occuring chronically needs to be analyzed and incorporated into the intervention plan.		**Intervention F:** *STOIC Analysis and Intervention*		
The student's escalating behavior is physically dangerous, or poses a threat to physical safety.		**Intervention G:** *Managing Physically Dangerous Behavior and Threats of Targeted Violence*		
The behavior is so severe that the teacher cannot continue to teach.		**Intervention H:** *Managing Severely Disruptive Behavior*		
The student is impulsive and has difficulty maintaining emotional control.		**Intervention I:** *Managing the Cycle of Emotional Escalation*		
The student seems to be unaware of when he/she engages in inappropriate behavior.		**Intervention J:** *Cueing and Precorrecting*		
The student has some motivation to change or learn new behaviors.		**Intervention K:** *Self-Monitoring and Self-Evaluation*		
The student makes negative comments about him- or herself and others.		**Intervention L:** *Positive Self-Talk and Attribution Training*		
The student does not know how to meet expectations.		**Intervention M:** *Teaching Replacement Behavior*		
The student cannot or will not communicate verbally.		**Intervention N:** *Functional Communication*		
The misbehavior is a firmly established part of the student's behavior.		**Intervention O:** *Structured Reinforcement Systems*		
It is difficult to be consistent with the student because it is not always clear when the student has crossed the line between appropriate and inappropriate behavior.		**Intervention P:** *Defining Limits and Establishing Consequences*		
Consequences for misbehavior seem necessary but do not seem to work.				
Teacher feels anxious, worried, discouraged, or angry about one or more students.		**Intervention Q:** *Relaxation and Stress Management*		
The student seems anxious, lethargic, or depressed.		**Intervention R:** *Internalizing Problems and Mental Health*		

EARLY STAGE / *HIGHLY STRUCTURED*

Note: A copy of this form and other introductory forms are also provided on the CD. (The reproducible forms for each chapter will similarly be included within each chapter and on the CD.) Some chapters feature additional forms that are not referenced in the text—these appear at the end of the chapter.

Throughout this book, permission is given for individual classroom teachers to reproduce any forms labeled "Reproducible" for classroom use. Reproduction of these materials for an entire school system is prohibited without the express permission of the publisher.

Read each statement in the far left column, labeled "Presenting Behavior." If the statement about the student's behavior is true, place a checkmark in the next column. The checkmarks will indicate interventions that may be worth considering as you design an intervention plan. The middle "Intervention" column provides a guide to the chapters in this book— that is, which specific interventions to consider. The column labeled "Date of Implementation" allows you to indicate any interventions that have already been implemented, and the final column allows you to record if that particular intervention was successful or unsuccessful. Once you have filled out the Decision Guide, choose from among the interventions that have not been tried but are worth considering (those interventions with a checkmark that do not have an implementation record)—or, better yet, select a logical combination of interventions to use when designing the next phase of the intervention plan. To create a logical intervention plan, you might skim the chapters that seem most appropriate, and then choose one or two interventions to work through step-by-step as you design, implement, and monitor the intervention plan.

In choosing interventions, remember to always try the easiest thing first, moving to more complex interventions only if needed. This book contains a general classroom management section labeled "Pre-Intervention," which means try these basic management strategies first. This "Pre-Intervention" chapter contains essential strategies that will benefit your entire classroom, often eliminating many of the behaviors that might have warranted individual intervention. If these general strategies have already been implemented, then consider the Early-Stage Interventions, A through F.

Interventions often work best in combination. Try combining "Intervention B: Academic Assistance" with "Intervention C: Goal Setting." As an alternative, "Intervention D: Data Collection and Debriefing" and "Intervention E: Increasing Positive Interactions" also work well together.

Before leaving the Early-Stage Interventions, spend some time creating a comprehensive STOIC-based plan (Intervention F). At least four interventions or combinations of interventions over a period of at least six weeks should be tried and implemented with fidelity before moving to the Highly Structured Interventions. All interventions should be practiced with the expectation that the student's behavior will improve in response.

If the Early-Stage Interventions are ineffective or inconclusive, move to Highly Structured Interventions. This normally requires the involvement of one or more colleagues in designing and implementing a more intensive intervention. Note that collaboration on Early-Stage Interventions may also be a successful strategy if staffing is sufficient to support that option. Also note that if Intervention D is implemented, you will have at least four weeks of data documenting two or three different interventions that were ineffective. This data will be the basis for all subsequent interventions, and you will continue data collection throughout the rest of the intervention process. With your colleagues, review the background information you have accumulated on the problem and all data collected to date. Then use the intervention Decision Guide (Reproducible Form Intro 1) to decide which interventions to consider next.

To the administrator, psychologist, counselor, staff developer, and others:

This book is designed to facilitate efficient staff development. It is our hope that all classroom teachers in both general and special education will be trained in how to implement the Pre-Interventions and Early-Stage Interventions A–F. To reduce the staff development burden on general education teachers, they need only be trained in these general management and early intervention practices. Special education teachers and all those charged with working with chronic behavioral issues (e.g., school psychologists, counselors, behavior specialists, and problem-solving team members) should be trained in the Highly Structured Interventions, G through R.

If everyone is trained in the Pre- and Early-Stage Interventions, a common language and practice will emerge in the school/district about what should be tried first with misbehavior. It can become standard practice that all teachers will examine and adjust their classroom management plan in a similar fashion. If this is not sufficient to solve a behavior problem, teachers will implement easy interventions such as "Planned Discussion," "Academic Assistance," and/or "Goal Setting." If the problem still exists, "Intervention D: Data Collection and Debriefing" will be implemented and continued throughout any further interventions. Thus data-driven decision-making can become part of the culture of a school (or, even better, of an entire district) in the early stages of any chronic behavior problem. The two other early-stage interventions, E and F, ensure that teachers will work on increasing positive interactions and designing function-based interventions. By training all the teachers in your school/district in these procedures, you create an expectation or protocol that one should implement Early-Stage Interventions prior to asking for assistance from a counselor, psychologist, or problem-solving team.

When a student's behavioral difficulties are not responsive to the Early-Stage Interventions, a teacher can ask for assistance from a specialist or problem-solving team. The teacher will then be asked, "Do you have any data on the problem?" and "What interventions have you already implemented?" The collaborative process will begin with an examination or the data and a discussion about the efficacy, or lack thereof, of previous intervention. The data that the teacher has collected will serve as baseline data for all subsequent interventions. Then the specialist or problem-solving team can assist the teacher in choosing, designing, and implementing a Highly Structured Intervention or combination of interventions.

This protocol of Pre-Intervention, moving to the Early-Stage Interventions if needed, and finally moving into collaborative Highly Structured Interventions when earlier strategies have failed, is the basis for a Response to Intervention (RTI) process for behavior. An RTI approach essentially means try the easiest thing first. In RTI, universal practices such as effective classroom management are often described as Tier 1. The Early-Stage Interventions in this book correspond to a Tier 1 approach in that they represent universal practice in a district—the practices all teachers would implement at the first signs of behavioral or motivational difficulties in one student or a small group of students. Highly Structured Interventions are implemented at the Tier 2–Targeted and the Tier 3–Intensive levels. The structure of this book is designed to facilitate efficient problem-solving and can serve as a basis for staff development for a district's implementation of RTI.

Note: One of the central premises of this book is that educators will work with the student and the student's family as active partners in all aspects of problem identification, goal setting, intervention design, and intervention implementation. However, in referring to a student's family, we have chosen to use the term *parents* throughout the majority of this resource to refer to a student's major care provider. We know that caretakers of students are often single parents, grandparents, foster parents, or other such guardians. We mean no disrespect to anyone by using the term *parents*, but simply felt that one term would be less distracting than listing the multiple possibilities of caregivers repeatedly with each reference. By the same logic, when referring to a student who is the target of an intervention or referring to those implementing the intervention, the examples throughout each chapter are sometimes male and sometimes female. We have done our best to alternate, but we mean no disrespect if some chapters are weighted more heavily with male or female references. We are simply trying to avoid the potential annoyance and distraction of the repeated "s/he" and "him/her" references.

To all users of this book:

Including a student's parents in all aspects of behavioral intervention is essential. When school personnel work collaboratively with parents, the student perceives a united front of significant adults who have her best interests at heart. We know that in some cases parents may be unwilling or unable to be active partners in intervention processes, but an ongoing effort to invite them to be active partners is essential. Throughout this book, each

Reproducible Form Intro 2: *Parental Permission Form*

Parental Permission Form

Dear _____ :

Parent or Guardian Name

We would like to develop a plan to support _____

Student Name

To assist us in developing the most useful plan possible, we would like your permission to informally assess your child's behavior and work habits. This process may include any or all of the following:

_____

_____

_____

_____

_____

_____

After we gather preliminary information, we will ask to meet with you to discuss the information and how to proceed to ensure that your child is successful in school. We hope to work with you as partners in creating a positive school experience for your child.

Please sign the slip below and return it to school by _____ . As soon as the assessment has been completed, we will be in touch.

Thank you for your assistance.

Sincerely,

- -

_____ has my permission to informally assess _____ 's academic skills and work habits, and to develop a plan of assistance.

_____   _____

Signed (Parent or Guardian)   Date

intervention assumes and requires that educational professionals are actively reaching out to include parents. As such, be sure that you are following your district's expectations (and, of course, any state or federal requirements) in regard to keeping parents informed and seeking parental permission for collecting information and designing interventions. If your district does not currently have a "Parental Permission" form, consider using Reproducible Form Intro 2.

 # Reproducible Materials

The following reproducible materials appear in the *Interventions* Introduction. Copies are also provided on the CD. Permission is given for individual classroom teachers to reproduce any forms labeled "Reproducible" for classroom use. Reproduction of these materials for an entire school system is prohibited without the express permission of the publisher.

Reproducible Form Intro 1: Decision Guide, p. 14
Reproducible Form Intro 2: Parental Permission Form, p. 19

Ⓟre-Intervention:

CLASSROOM MANAGEMENT STRATEGIES

THIS ONE-CHAPTER SECTION focuses on classroom management. Effective classroom management will ensure that most students behave responsibly on most days. Here's one way to look at this section: The best and simplest intervention is the one you don't have to implement—prevention. Classroom Management Strategies will help teachers assess their strengths and suggest possible areas of improvement in general classroom management. If more than a few students engage in chronic misbehavior, changes in the general classroom management plan are likely needed before working up individualized intervention plans for each of the students.

The chapter is organized around the STOIC framework. That is, the teacher is encouraged to assess, and revise as needed, a number of procedures and techniques for each of the following categories:

- *Structure*/organize the classroom for success.

- *Teach* students the routines and expectations.

- *Observe*/monitor student behavior.

- *Interact positively* with students.

- *Correct* misbehavior fluently.

Note: The only absolute rule about behavior management is that belittlement of students has no place in any educational setting—all behavioral interventions must treat children with dignity and respect. To have a positive and lasting impact, interventions must attempt to build up student strengths and expand skills for replacing problem behavior, instead of simply squelching or containing problem behavior.

Classroom Management Strategies

| *Several or many students in class misbehave*

CLASSROOM MANAGEMENT is a major concern for all educators, and for decades, discipline has ranked as the general public's first or second greatest concern for public schools. Classroom management represents a first-year teacher's most serious challenge, and discipline problems continue to be a major factor in stress and burnout for all teachers.

Despite these concerns, classroom management and discipline are often neglected in training programs for teachers. Citing the 1997 Farkas & Johnson Public Agenda Survey of attitudes among professors who teach in schools of education, Jean Johnson (2005, p. 3) reports that there is:

> a substantial gap between the attitudes of teachers in the classroom and those of the professors who prepare them for their careers. While virtually all classroom

Discipline problems continue to be a major factor in stress and burnout for all teachers.

teachers (97%) say that good discipline is "one of the most important prerequisites" for a successful school, fewer than 4 in 10 education professors (37%) consider it absolutely essential to train "teachers who maintain discipline and order in the classroom." Only 30% say that their teacher education program places a lot of emphasis on teaching prospective teachers how to handle a rowdy classroom.

So, if you struggle with behavior and discipline issues in the classroom, you are not alone.

RATIONALE

Although the purpose of the entire *Interventions* book is to help you help students improve their behavior, most of this book is about designing specific plans for individual students—one student at a time. This chapter on general classroom management strategies is designed to help you improve the behavior of an entire class—for lack of a better phrase, crowd control. If only one or two students are continually exhibiting problem behavior or chronically lack motivation, you can probably skip this chapter and go directly to the individual interventions. On the other hand, if three or more students are chronically misbehaving, plan to work through this chapter prior to, or along with, designing plans for one or two individual students.

Teachers can do many things to prevent problems with students. This chapter delineates these strategies, or pre-interventions, in a manner that will allow you to identify both your current strengths and those areas that need improvement in your current classroom management plan.

If three or more students are chronically misbehaving, plan to work through this chapter prior to, or along with, designing plans for one or two individual students.

PRE-INTERVENTION SECTIONS

The first section of this chapter includes a template that will help you design a comprehensive behavior syllabus that clarifies your classroom policies, procedures, and routines. This syllabus is best composed during the summer or during a major break, when you have some relaxed planning time to prepare your comprehensive plan.

The second section contains a quick checklist of essential classroom management components. This checklist can be used while facing the day-by-day pressures of the classroom as you reevaluate your management plan. This checklist is organized around the STOIC acronym, which was presented in the book introduction. Each question corresponds to one of the STOIC components (*Structure, Teach expectations, Observe, Interact positively, Correct fluently*), and procedural suggestions are offered. Consider having a copy of the checklist in front of you as you work through this chapter. Evaluate which of the checklist items you have in place and which you do not. For those items you do not have in place, read the corresponding explanation and decide whether implementing the suggestions would help improve your students' behavior and motivation.

Section 1: Comprehensive behavior syllabus that delineates classroom policies, procedures, and routines

This section will be especially useful if you are reading this book prior to the start of a new semester and you have time to engage in extensive planning. Figure Pre-Int 1 shows a template for an extensive behavior syllabus that defines what students need to know about your behavioral expectations and their responsibilities. (This template is reprinted with permission from *Discipline in the Secondary Classroom: A Positive Approach to Behavior Management*, by R. S. Sprick). Once completed, the information on the syllabus must be communicated directly to students—teaching students exactly what is expected for them to be successful in the classroom. High school teachers of upperclassmen can simply duplicate this information and distribute it to all students on the first day of class. Teachers of 9th- and 10th-grade students can divide this information into three or four logical sections and distribute reproduced copies of the first section to all students on the first day of school, the second on the second day, and so on. Either way, this syllabus will serve as the basis for direct instruction on expectations during the first week of school, which is an essential element of effective classroom management. Plan to reteach essential aspects of the syllabus before and after vacations, prior to major exams, and any time behavior is beginning to become problematic.

Elementary and secondary teachers may or may not want to distribute a written copy of this information; you do not want to overwhelm young students. However, all the information needs to be communicated to students in age-appropriate ways across the first month of school. Distributing lessons across time, with gentle repetition, will allow you to communicate the information without overwhelming students.

Figure Pre-Int 1 (1 of 2): *Syllabus Template*

(Page 1 of 2)

Syllabus Template

Teacher: _____

CLASSROOM GOALS

Write your classroom goals in the form of what students will be able to do successfully at the end of the year or semester.

GUIDELINES FOR SUCCESS

Write your list of attitudes and traits that you believe will ensure your students' success.

CLASSROOM RULES

Outline the important student behaviors that will ensure that your class runs efficiently.

ACTIVITIES

Outline the activities in which students will be engaged during a typical week.

GRADES

Grading scale

Outline the percentage cutoffs for A's, B's, and so on.

Relative value

Outline the relative weight of homework, quizzes, tests, papers, behavior, and effort on the final grade.

CLASSROOM PROCEDURES

Entering the classroom

Outline exactly what students should do from the time they enter the room until the bell rings for class to begin.

Tardy to class

Provide your definition of on time and tardy, and identify the consequences of being tardy.

Pen or pencil

Identify whether students should write with a pen or pencil. In addition, specify what a student should do if he or she does not have this and what, if anything, you implement as a consequence.

Tracking daily assignments

Identify where and how students turn in classwork and homework. Specify if students are to check off completed work they have turned in.

Returning assignments to students

Detail your policies on how you will return completed work to your students.

Figure Pre-Int 1 (2 of 2): *Syllabus Template*

CLASSROOM PROCEDURES (CONTINUED)

Finding out grade status

Review your grading system, and explain whether you will give students a weekly grade report or if you expect them to track their grades themselves. Also identify when and how a student can approach you to discuss his or her current status in the class.

Student responsibilities after an absence

Outline what students will need to do when returning after an absence.
- How to find out what they missed
- How long they have to make up assignments
- What to do if they miss a test

Late, missing, or incomplete assignments

Outline the maximum number of late assignments you will accept, along with penalties and time limits for the work.

Communication procedures with parents and families

Identify whether you will initiate any regular communication with families. Provide information on when, where, and how family members can get in touch with you.

Ending class

Specify how you will end class, any responsibilities your students may have at the end of class, and how you will dismiss the students.

CONSEQUENCES FOR CLASSROOM RULE VIOLATIONS

List the range of corrective consequences that you may assign if rules are violated.

CONSEQUENCES FOR CODE-OF-CONDUCT VIOLATIONS

Inform students that you must follow through with disciplinary referrals for violations of schoolwide rules, including dress code, unexcused absences, threats, and so forth. Make sure to get this information from your principal or assistant principal.

Note: For more comprehensive and detailed help with long-term planning, see the following resources. This chapter has pulled heavily from these resources and provides a summary of their key points, but does not include all of the detail that they provide.

For grades K–8:

Sprick, R. S., Garrison, M., & Howard, L. (1998). *CHAMPs: A Proactive and Positive Approach to Classroom Management.* Eugene, OR: Pacific Northwest Publishing.

For grades 9–12:

Sprick, R. S. (2006). *Discipline in the Secondary Classroom: A Positive Approach to Behavior Management* (2nd ed.). San Francisco: Jossey-Bass.

Section 2: STOIC checklist of essential classroom management considerations

Make a copy of the Classroom Management STOIC Checklist shown in Reproducible Form Pre-Int 1 to have in front of you as you read through this section. Read each question on the checklist and the corresponding explanatory text on the next few pages, and make a judgment about whether that feature is firmly in place in your classroom. If it is not in place, circle *N*. After completing the checklist, use the items marked *N* to set up a prioritized list of things to work on in revising your management plan. Organize by items that have the greatest potential for improving student behavior. Implement changes to a few of the items on the list each week until student behavior has improved to the point that only one or two students engage in chronic misbehavior.

Note: A copy of this form and other Pre-Intervention forms are also provided on the CD.

Reproducible Form Pre-Int 1: *Classroom Management STOIC Checklist*

Classroom Management STOIC Checklist

Variables	Questions to guide discussion	Y	N	Comments
Structure/ Organize the classroom for success.	1. Is the room arranged so you can get from any part of the room to any other part of the room relatively efficiently?	Y	N	
	2. Can you and your students access materials and the pencil sharpener without disturbing others?	Y	N	
	3. Does the schedule create consistency, variety, and opportunities for movement?	Y	N	
	4. Do you have effective beginning and ending routines?	Y	N	
	5. Have you defined clear expectations for instructional activities?	Y	N	
	6. Have you defined clear expectations for transitions between activities?	Y	N	
Teach students how to behave responsibly in the classroom.	1. Have you created lessons on expectations and explicitly taught them for classroom activities and transitions?	Y	N	
	2. Have you created lessons and explicitly taught expectations for classroom routines and policies?	Y	N	
	3. Have you provided teaching and reteaching as needed? (Think about a basketball coach reteaching particular plays or patterns.)	Y	N	
Observe student behavior (supervise!).	1. Do you circulate and scan as a means of observing/ monitoring student behavior?	Y	N	
	2. Do you model friendly, respectful behavior while monitoring the classroom?	Y	N	
	3. Do you periodically collect data to make judgments about what is going well and what needs to be improved in your management plan?	Y	N	
Interact positively with students.	1. Do you interact with every student in a welcoming manner (e.g., saying hello, using the student's name, talking to the student at every opportunity)?	Y	N	
	2. Do you provide age-appropriate, non-embarrassing feedback?	Y	N	
	3. Do you strive to interact more frequently with every student when he is engaged in positive behavior than when he is engaged in negative behavior?	Y	N	
Correct irresponsible behavior fluently— that is, in a manner that does not interrupt the flow of instruction.	1. Do you correct consistently?	Y	N	
	2. Do you correct calmly?	Y	N	
	3. Do you correct immediately?	Y	N	
	4. Do you correct briefly?	Y	N	
	5. Do you correct respectfully?	Y	N	
	6. Do you have a menu of in-class consequences that can be applied to a variety of infractions?	Y	N	
	7. Do you have a plan for how to respond to different types of misbehavior fluently?	Y	N	

STOIC: **STRUCTURE/organize the classroom for success**

A. Is the classroom arranged so you can get from any one part of the room to any other part of the room relatively efficiently?

The arrangement of a classroom should allow you to move around quickly and easily. All students should be easily accessible. If a student requires immediate corrective feedback and the physical layout does not allow you to move quickly to the student, one of two things may happen: (1) you correct the student loudly and publicly, embarrassing the student and drawing attention to the inappropriate behavior; or (2) you have to work your way around obstacles to reach the student, wasting time and delaying consequences.

When the room is arranged in such a way that you can interact easily with students, the following important aspects of classroom management are facilitated:

- your ability to respond consistently to minor misbehavior

- your ability to respond to misbehavior before it escalates

- your ability to engage more frequently in positive interactions with all students

- a reduction of stress because a barrier to effective student-teacher interactions has been removed

B. Can you and your students access materials and the pencil sharpener without disturbing others?

Try to arrange the room so that natural traffic flow is the least distracting to instructional activities. If you assign seats, place the most responsible students near the areas that have the highest potential for distraction, such as near where students turn in their in-class work.

C. Does the schedule create consistency, variety, and opportunities for movement?

Although students need a schedule within each class that is reasonably consistent from day to day, they also need variety each day. Effective teachers plan the day to include a balance of activities and a change of pace for students. Lessons should alternate between teacher-directed activities and student-directed activities, quiet times and active times, and independent work and cooperative work. To determine whether your schedule provides sufficient variety, ask yourself the following questions:

Do students become fidgety because they are expected to stay seated for long periods of time?

Primary-age students should not be expected to sit still longer than 30 minutes without some form of activity that gets them out of their seats. Older students should not be expected to be in their seats longer than an hour at a time. Within that hour, there should be varied activities to actively involve the students.

Is the amount of teacher-directed instruction adequate?

Teacher-directed instruction is absolutely critical to a well-run classroom. However, teacher-directed instruction does not mean that students should have to listen passively to lectures all day. Lessons should be structured in such a way that students are kept actively participating throughout. A rough guide for structuring class time should include about 50 percent of class time for teacher-directed instruction with strategies for active student participation (this includes large- or small-group instruction); 25 percent of class time for independent work; and 25 percent of class time for students to work in cooperative groups.

Note: Appropriate length of time for any given activity will vary from group to group based on the maturity of students, the nature of the subject, and the time of day or year.

D. Do you have effective beginning and ending routines?

How you start and end each school day (or class period) will have a significant influence on the climate of your classroom. Effective and efficient beginning and ending procedures create an inviting, supportive atmosphere and communicate that time will not be wasted. These things, in turn, will make a difference in student behavior. Some of the specific items below may be more applicable to elementary classes, while others are more appropriate for secondary classes.

1. Entering class

When students enter the classroom, they should feel welcome and should immediately go to their seats and start working on a productive task.

Effective and efficient beginning and ending procedures create an inviting, supportive atmosphere and communicate that time will not be wasted.

Greeting students as they enter your classroom helps them feel welcome and reduces classroom behavior problems. In general, you should greet students at the door. In addition to greeting students as they enter your classroom, you should have a task prepared that students can work on after they sit down. Having students work on a daily task communicates to them that you value instructional time and plan to use every minute as efficiently as possible.

2. Opening activities

Opening activities should be efficient and orderly and should ease students into the school day.
Effective teachers vary widely in the way they deal with the beginning of the school day. Because there is no single correct way to start the day, what follows are a few considerations to keep in mind:

- Opening activities should include accurate recording of attendance, lunch count, and so on.

- Opening activities that take more than a few minutes should have an educational objective.

- Opening activities should keep students actively engaged. If students are expected to sit and do nothing, you will have behavior problems.

If your procedures for opening activities address the preceding considerations, there is no reason to change them. If they don't address the considerations, you can talk to other teachers about what they do first thing in the morning and how long it usually takes.

Students should be instructionally engaged while you take attendance.
When the bell rings and students continue to work on the assigned task, use a seating chart to take attendance rather than calling out names and having students reply. This will allow students to stay focused on their daily task.

Announcements and other housekeeping tasks should not take up too much time.
Begin instructional activities as soon after the beginning of the period as possible. Try to spend no more than a minute or two on announcements and housekeeping.

Students should understand that school attendance and punctuality are important.

Periodically (every two weeks or so), have a brief discussion with your class about the importance of consistent attendance and punctuality. When punctuality and regular attendance are not high priorities for students or their families, having teachers regularly emphasize that coming to school and being on time are important will help the students develop these values.

If either absenteeism or tardiness becomes a significant problem, one effective technique is to calculate and publicly chart the percentage of students who come to school and/or who arrive on time each day. If necessary and appropriate, you might also set up a small reward system for promptness. (For example, when everyone is on time, the class gets a point. When the class collects ten points, the class gets to go to recess five minutes early.)

Tardiness should be dealt with efficiently, without disrupting instructional time.

Procedures for dealing with tardiness should ensure that tardy students do not disrupt class or take your attention away from teaching, let you keep accurate records of excused and unexcused tardies, and allow you to assign consistent correction consequences for unexcused tardies. If tardiness is a problem, reducing the frequency of tardies can:

- increase academic engagement

- reduce disruption to the flow of instruction and increase instructional time

- create better connections between opening activities and later content of the lesson

Note: If tardiness is a problem throughout the school, consider adopting a schoolwide approach to reducing tardiness. *Start on Time!*, a tardiness program published by Pacific Northwest Publishing, has reduced tardiness by as much as 95 percent in many secondary schools.

3. Being prepared with materials

Procedures for dealing with students who do not have materials or who are unprepared should:

- ensure that a student who does not have the necessary materials to participate in class can obtain them in a way that does not disrupt instruction

- include reasonable penalties that will reduce the likelihood of the student forgetting materials in the future

- reduce the amount of time and energy that you spend dealing with this problem

First of all, clearly communicate to students exactly what materials you expect them to have in class each day. Communicate this verbally to students and in writing to students' families (as part of the syllabus that goes home on the first day of school). At the end of each class period during the first week of school, remind students what materials they should have when they return to class the next day.

Next, develop procedures that allow a student to obtain what he or she needs to participate in the lesson and that result in a mild consequence to reduce the probability that the student will forget materials again.

During the first couple days of school, inform students how you will respond if they do not have the required materials. After a couple days, start conducting periodic spot checks. If any students are missing required materials, provide a gentle but firm reminder about the importance of being responsible. After the first few weeks, start conducting unpredictable, intermittent spot checks of materials. Any students who do not have what they need should receive a minor corrective consequence, while students who have all materials might receive a bonus point. If you plan to do this, be sure to inform students during the first week of school that you may conduct spot checks one or twice a week for the first few weeks of school.

4. Returning after an absence

Students who have been absent should be able to find out what assignments they missed and get any handouts and/or returned papers in a way that does not involve a large amount of your time and energy.

After the first few weeks, start conducting unpredictable, intermittent spot checks of materials.

One way to manage receiving and returning work to a student who has been absent is to set up two baskets—one for "Absent, What You Missed" and one for "Absent, Assignments In"—that you keep in a consistent location. Any time you give students an assignment, homework, and/or graded papers, put the material in an individual folder for any student who is absent. Write the student's name, date, and class period on the folder. Some teachers pair students in a buddy system. When one of the students is absent, it is the responsibility of his or her partner to copy any assignments and collect any handouts and graded papers, place them in a folder, and put them in the "Absent, What You Missed" basket.

The basket marked "Absent, Assignments In" can be used in two ways. When a student returns on Tuesday from a Monday absence, she can turn in any assignment that was due on Monday to the "Absent, Assignments In" basket at the same time she is picking up her folder from the "Absent, What You Missed" basket. In addition, when the student completes the work that was assigned on Monday, she should also turn in that work by putting it in the "Absent, Assignments In" basket.

This type of system can save you lots of time and interruptions, but it will work only if you keep the baskets up to date by checking them daily and reminding students who return from an absence to collect what they missed and hand in anything that was due.

5. Wrap up/cleanup at the end of day or class period

Your procedures for wrapping up the day/class period/activity should ensure that:

- students don't leave the classroom before they have organized their materials and completed any necessary cleanup tasks
- you have enough time to give students both positive and corrective feedback and set a positive tone for ending class

You want to leave enough time at the conclusion of an activity/period/day to ensure that students leave your classroom on a relaxed note. The amount of time for wrapping up will vary depending on the grade level and activity. When students have finished organizing and cleaning up, give the entire class feedback on things they are doing well and things that may require more effort on their part. This is

PRE-INTERVENTION

especially important during the first six weeks of school, but it is also useful intermittently through the school year.

6. Dismissal

Students should not leave the classroom until you (not the bell) dismiss them.

On the first day of school, and periodically thereafter, remind your students that they are not to leave their seats when the bells rings. Excuse the class only when they are reasonably quiet and all wrap-up tasks have been completed. If you let students bolt for the door when the bell rings, it will set a precedent that your instructional control ends when the bell rings. By reserving the right to excuse the class, you can make judgments about whether you should excuse the whole class at once, by rows, or by table clusters. As a general rule, primary students should be excused by rows and older students can be excused as a class.

The beginning and ending of the day or class period play major roles in setting the climate of the classroom. Opening and dismissal routines that are welcoming, calm, efficient, and purposeful will demonstrate to students that you are pleased to see them and that you care so much about class time that not a minute will be wasted.

E. Have you defined clear expectations for instructional activities?
Successful teachers are very clear with students about exactly how they expect them to behave during the school day. If you don't communicate your behavioral expectations to students, they will have to guess what constitutes responsible behavior.

Successful teachers are very clear with students about exactly how they expect them to behave during the school day.

The CHAMPs acronym can help you define your expectations by having you ask and answer specific questions about how you want students to behave during major classroom activities.

C **Conversation**

H **Help**

A **Activity**

M **Movement**

P **Participation**

Prior to applying the CHAMPs acronym, make a list of the major types of activities in which your students will engage on a daily (or regular) basis. Your list may include:

- opening/attendance routines
- class meetings
- teacher-directed instruction
- tests/quizzes
- small-group instruction
- centers/lab stations
- independent work
- peer-tutoring sessions
- sustained silent reading
- cooperative groups
- cushion activities (what students do when they have finished assigned work and time still remains in the work period)

Make sure you identify specific activities and/or categories of activities for which you will have *different* behavioral expectations. For example, your expectations for independent work will greatly differ from those for cooperative groups. Then, for each activity or category you identify, make a copy of the CHAMPs Classroom Activity Worksheet (Reproducible Form Pre-Int 2). Use the form as you define *detailed* behavioral expectations for how students should behave in each activity by asking and answering each question.

F. Have you defined clear expectations for transitions between activities?

In addition to defining expectations for classroom activities that take place during the school day, you should define your expectations for transitions or times when students are moving from one task to another. Transitions are often problematic in terms of student behavior, and poorly managed transitions are troublesome both because of their potential for student misbehavior and because they end up consuming valuable instructional time. Clearly define and communicate your expectations for these times to create well-managed and efficient transitions.

As with classroom activities, the first step in defining behavioral expectations for transitions involves listing the major transitions that typically occur during your school day or class period. Be sure to identify all the specific transitions and/or categories of transitions for which you will have *different* behavioral expectations. A list of transitions might include the following:

- time before the bell rings
- time after the bell rings

CHAMPs Classroom Activity Worksheet

Activity: _____

CONVERSATION

Can students engage in conversation with each other during this activity?

If yes, about what?

With whom?

How many students can be involved in a single conversation?

HELP

How do students get questions answered? How do students get your attention?

If students have to wait for help, what should they do while they wait?

ACTIVITY

What is the expected end product of this activity? (Note: This may vary from day to day.)

MOVEMENT

Can students get out of their seats during the activity?

If yes, acceptable reasons include: Pencil   Restroom

Drink   Hand in/Pick up materials

Other:

Do they need permission from you?

PARTICIPATION

What behaviors show that students are participating fully and responsibly?

What behaviors show that a student is not participating?

- getting out paper and pencil
- getting a book out and opening to a particular page
- moving to and from a small-group location
- leaving and entering the classroom
- putting things away
- handing in work
- trading papers for corrections
- cleaning up after projects
- leaving the classroom at the end of day or class period
- moving as a class to a different location (e.g., library, playground)
- handing materials out
- handing materials back
- opening and dismissal routines (expectations for these transitions were discussed previously in the chapter)

Once you have a list of transitions, use CHAMPs as a guide for defining your behavioral expectations for the important issues. Make copies of the reproducible CHAMPs Classroom Transition Worksheet (Reproducible Form Pre-Int 3) for all transitions on your list. The Transition Worksheet differs from the Activity Worksheet mainly in the "A–Activity" section, which specifies the details of the transition and the anticipated length of the transition. Complete one worksheet for each type of transition. Be thorough—remember that the more detailed you are, the more clearly you will be able to communicate your expectations to students and the more consistent you are likely to be in implementing your expectations.

The more structure your class requires, the more specific and tightly orchestrated you need to make your expectations for transitions. For example, with a class that can function with less structure, you probably don't need to specify the routes students are to take to the small-group instruction area. On the other hand, for students needing high structure, you should explain to students the expectation that they need to quietly take the most direct route and that they must keep their hands, feet, and objects to themselves so they do not disturb students who are working at their seats.

After you have defined your expectations of students during major activities and transitions, you must clearly and effectively communicate them to your students. The next section—the *T* in *STOIC*—provides detailed information on how to do this effectively.

The more structure your class requires, the more specific and tightly orchestrated you need to make your expectations for transitions.

CHAMPs Classroom Transition Worksheet

Transition: _____

CONVERSATION

Can students engage in conversation with each other during this transition?

If yes, clarify how (so that they are keeping their attention on completing the transition).

HELP

How do students get questions answered? How do students get your attention?

ACTIVITY

Explain the transition. What will be different afterward (e.g., change in location, use of different materials, etc.)? Include time criteria (i.e., how long it should take).

MOVEMENT

If the transition itself *does not* involve getting out of seats, can students get out of their seats for any reason during the transition?

If yes, what are acceptable reasons?

If the transition itself involves out-of-seat movement, can a student go elsewhere (e.g., to sharpen a pencil)?

PARTICIPATION

What behaviors show that students are participating in the transition fully and responsibly?

What behaviors show that a student is not participating appropriately?

STOIC: **T**EACH students how to behave responsibly in the classroom.

A. Have you created lessons on expectations and explicitly taught them for classroom activities and transitions?

After you have defined your expectations, develop a preliminary plan and prepare lessons for teaching your expectations to students. Use the three-step process outlined in the following illustration:

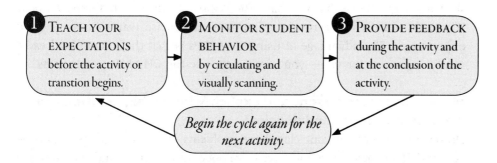

1 TEACH YOUR EXPECTATIONS before the activity or transition begins.

2 MONITOR STUDENT BEHAVIOR by circulating and visually scanning.

3 PROVIDE FEEDBACK during the activity and at the conclusion of the activity.

Begin the cycle again for the next activity.

Your plan for how you will teach your expectations should address three basic questions:

- How detailed do your lessons need to be?

- How long do you anticipate having to actively teach the lessons?

- What is the best way to organize the "content"?

Consider the complexity of your expectations, your teaching style, and the age and sophistication of your students when answering these questions. In a setting with mature and responsible students, it may be sufficient simply to verbally describe your expectations on the first day of school and provide occasional reminders thereafter. However, if your class includes students with behavior problems, you may need to teach your expectations using visual displays, demonstrations, and perhaps actual practice every day for at least the first two weeks of school.

If a verbal presentation alone will suffice for your students, you may not need to prepare any lessons—you can just have your CHAMPs worksheets handy for your reference. However, if your class needs high structure and repeated teachings will be necessary, you should vary the instructional approach you use and prepare lessons with maximum variety to keep these activities interesting. Include activities with student participation to reduce the probability that students will get bored and ensure that they fully understand your expectations.

Organize the content of your teaching plan so that students can see the consistency regarding what they have to know and how to behave responsibly. You may find the CHAMPs acronym useful, particularly for second- through sixth-grade students, in helping them realize that for each classroom activity and transition, you have specific expectations about each category. For very young students (prekindergarten to first grade), the CHAMPS acronym may not be meaningful, as some students may not yet know the alphabet. On the other hand, mature secondary students may find the acronym corny or babyish. Without an anchor such as the CHAMPs acronym, however, students may believe that you have thousands of unconnected expectations. If you do not use the acronym, plan another concise way to convey your expectations. The advantage of using CHAMPs is that the content is already neatly organized for you—you can simply use the CHAMPs worksheets.

B. Have you created lessons and explicitly taught expectations for classroom routines and policies?

Do several students in your class have problems with certain classroom procedures? If so, make sure you have developed clear policies and then reteach these policies a couple of times per week until you see that most students are improving. Refer to the syllabus template in Figure Pre-Int 1.

C. Have you provided teaching and reteaching as needed? (Think about a basketball coach reteaching particular plays or patterns.)

Be aware that teaching your expectations at the beginning of the year does not mean that students will continually follow through on meeting those expectations. Coaches of team sports and symphony conductors—or anyone responsible for coordinating groups of people—know that they must continually reteach and re-inspire the individuals in the group.

During the year, there are particular times when you can predict that students' behavior will deteriorate unless you reteach and re-inspire students to follow your behavioral expectations, including:

- several days before major vacations
- immediately after major vacations
- times of high stress (e.g., just before major high-stakes testing such as state-level testing)
- times of high excitement (e.g., Halloween in elementary school)
- the last month of school

It is easy to make assumptions about what students would know in regard to appropriate behavior. Teaching behavioral expectations ensures

Coaches of team sports and symphony conductors know that they must continually reteach and re-inspire the individuals in the group.

that students understand exactly what the teacher expects of them and increases the likelihood they will act in appropriate ways.

STOIC: **O**BSERVE student behavior (supervise!).

A. Do you circulate and scan as a means of observing/ monitoring student behavior?

Once your classroom has been arranged to allow easy movement, you need to circulate among the students as much as possible. When presenting instruction, move through the classroom. Close physical proximity encourages student eye contact and attention as you are able to engage each student in both verbal and nonverbal interactions. Maintaining responsible classroom behavior through continued close contact is called *proximity management.*

Proximity management is important during teacher-directed lessons, and it's even more critical when students are working independently or in cooperative groups. When you move about the room, you provide an ongoing reminder to students that they are expected to be responsible, do their best, and work cooperatively to accomplish certain tasks.

Identify times or activities in which proximity management might be effective to reduce problem behavior. Then, during those times or activities, plan to move around the room in an unpredictable pattern.

Another way to monitor student behavior is to scan the room, visually examining different locations. Teachers who scan frequently and provide acknowledgement to students when they are behaving responsibly tend to experience fewer behavior problems. Teachers who scan frequently also tend to notice and correct minor misbehaviors before they accelerate into major problems.

Scanning during teacher-directed instruction is relatively easy to do, although it is easy to fall into the habit of looking primarily at the first two rows or only to one side of the room. When presenting a lesson, periodically make eye contact with each student and occasionally scan quickly across the entire classroom. Scanning provides information about how well students are paying attention. You're more likely to notice when students begin getting restless and can adjust your instruction accordingly.

Scanning while you are not directing instruction is more difficult. When students are working independently, involved in group work, or working at learning centers, teacher interactions tend to focus on one student or a small group of students at a time. While these interactions are essential, it is important that you occasionally scan the classroom while continuing to work with individuals and/or small groups. This is one of the most difficult aspects of teaching—doing several things at one time while keeping your attention focused.

B. Do you model friendly, respectful behavior while monitoring the classroom?

As you are circulating and scanning, you should portray an air of confidence and positive regard. You want to communicate with your body language and eye contact that you are enjoying being among the students and that you are hoping to "see" them at their best. Contrast this with the teacher of old, who stands at the front of the classroom with a stern expression, ruler in hand, waiting in anxious anticipation for the next student she can "catch" doing something wrong. Instead, you want to convey that you are ready to help and ready to notice all the good work students are doing. Obviously, you will occasionally be correcting behavioral errors. However, you should be engaging in positive interactions far more often.

C. Do you periodically collect data to make judgments about what is going well and what needs to be improved with your management plan?

In addition to your subjective perception about how your management plan is working, consider periodically (every three to four weeks) collecting some form of objective data. The following forms can be used:

• CHAMPs Versus Daily Reality Rating Scale

• Ratio of Interactions Monitoring Form

• Misbehavior Recording Sheet forms

CHAMPs versus Daily Reality Rating Scale

The CHAMPs Versus Daily Reality Rating Scale (Reproducible Form Pre-Int 4) allows you to examine each major activity and transition during your day and evaluate (on a five-point scale) how well students are meeting your CHAMPs expectations for that activity or transition. With this information, you will be able to decide whether you need to reteach your CHAMPs expectations to individuals or the whole class and/or modify the level of structure you have selected as most appropriate for your students.

To use the form, identify the major activities and transitions that occur during a typical school day (using your planning book or daily schedule).

As you are circulating and scanning, you should portray an air of confidence and positive regard.

Reproducible Form Pre-Int 4: *CHAMPs Versus Daily Reality Rating Scale*

CHAMPs Versus Daily Reality Rating Scale

Teacher _____

Date _____

Ratings:
5 = All students met expectations
4 = All but one or two students met expectations
3 = Most students met expectations

2 = About half the class met expectations
1 = Most students did not meet expectations

CONVERSATION	1 2 3 4 5
HELP (TEACHER ATTENTION)	1 2 3 4 5
ACTIVITY:	
MOVEMENT	1 2 3 4 5
PARTICIPATION	1 2 3 4 5

CONVERSATION	1 2 3 4 5
HELP (TEACHER ATTENTION)	1 2 3 4 5
ACTIVITY:	
MOVEMENT	1 2 3 4 5
PARTICIPATION	1 2 3 4 5

CONVERSATION	1 2 3 4 5
HELP (TEACHER ATTENTION)	1 2 3 4 5
ACTIVITY:	
MOVEMENT	1 2 3 4 5
PARTICIPATION	1 2 3 4 5

CONVERSATION	1 2 3 4 5
HELP (TEACHER ATTENTION)	1 2 3 4 5
ACTIVITY:	
MOVEMENT	1 2 3 4 5
PARTICIPATION	1 2 3 4 5

CONVERSATION	1 2 3 4 5
HELP (TEACHER ATTENTION)	1 2 3 4 5
ACTIVITY:	
MOVEMENT	1 2 3 4 5
PARTICIPATION	1 2 3 4 5

CONVERSATION	1 2 3 4 5
HELP (TEACHER ATTENTION)	1 2 3 4 5
ACTIVITY:	
MOVEMENT	1 2 3 4 5
PARTICIPATION	1 2 3 4 5

CONVERSATION	1 2 3 4 5
HELP (TEACHER ATTENTION)	1 2 3 4 5
ACTIVITY:	
MOVEMENT	1 2 3 4 5
PARTICIPATION	1 2 3 4 5

CONVERSATION	1 2 3 4 5
HELP (TEACHER ATTENTION)	1 2 3 4 5
ACTIVITY:	
MOVEMENT	1 2 3 4 5
PARTICIPATION	1 2 3 4 5

CONVERSATION	1 2 3 4 5
HELP (TEACHER ATTENTION)	1 2 3 4 5
ACTIVITY:	
MOVEMENT	1 2 3 4 5
PARTICIPATION	1 2 3 4 5

CONVERSATION	1 2 3 4 5
HELP (TEACHER ATTENTION)	1 2 3 4 5
ACTIVITY:	
MOVEMENT	1 2 3 4 5
PARTICIPATION	1 2 3 4 5

Write each activity and transition on the "Activity" line in the center of one of the form's rating boxes. Before each activity or transition, briefly review your CHAMPs expectations with students (if necessary). Immediately after completing the activity/transition, rate the degree to which students met your expectations. Finally, review the data and determine which activities or transitions require reteaching of your expectations.

Ratio of Interactions Monitoring Form

If you believe you are responding negatively more often than positively to a particular student or the class as a whole, you can use the Ratio of Interactions Monitoring Form to evaluate whether you have fallen into the "criticism trap" and whether you need to increase the number of inter- actions you have with students when they are behaving appropriately. (See "Intervention E: Increasing Positive Interactions" for a copy of this form and more information on how to use it.) It may be helpful to use this

Reproducible Form E1: *Ratio of Interactions Monitoring Form*

A full-size version of this form is available in "Intervention E: Increasing Positive Interactions," on p. 268.

Intervention E:
Increasing Positive Interactions

Ratio of Interactions Monitoring Form

Student _____ Grade/Class _____ Teacher _____ Date _____

Coding system used (e.g., to indicate specific activities or transitions): _____

Directions: Tally _every_ interaction you have with the student.

Attention to Positive Behavior	Attention to Negative Behavior
(Praise and/or noncontingent attention)	

Analysis and plan of action:

form periodically, even when you believe your interactions are generally positive. This will reduce the chance that you have or will unconsciously slip into patterns of negativity.

Misbehavior Recording Sheet forms

The Misbehavior Recording Sheet forms (Reproducible Forms Pre-Int 5 and Pre-Int 6) can be used to determine whether you need to implement an intervention plan or plans to deal with specific types of student misbehavior. These forms can help you identify how often and for what reasons you are intervening with students. They can also help you detect patterns of student misbehavior; help provide specific, objective information about individual student behavior; and help you decide whether you might need a classwide management system to increase students' motivation to behave responsibly.

Choose one of the two reproducible recording sheet forms and make a copy. The first form is a daily record of misbehavior by hour, organized by student name. This form is appropriate for elementary teachers who may have the same group of students for a longer portion of each day. Note that you can change the headings (e.g., 1st hour, 2nd hour) to reflect particular activities (e.g., math, reading). The second form is a weekly record of misbehavior by day, organized by student name. This form is most appropriate for secondary teachers, who would use one form for each class being monitored.

1. Keep the form close by for the entire day (if you are an elementary teacher) or for five days of a particular class period (if you are a secondary teacher).

2. Explain to students that for the entire day (or next five class periods), you will be recording any time you have to speak to someone or the whole class about inappropriate behavior.

3. Whenever you speak to a student about misbehavior, note the specific misbehavior on the form using a coding system such as the following:

> o = off task   h = hands/feet/objects bothering others
> t = talking   d = disrupting class
> a = arguing   s = out of seat at wrong time

Build your code so that there is a different letter for each type of major misbehavior you think you might encounter.

Reproducible Form Pre-Int 5: *Misbehavior Recording Sheet (Daily)*

Misbehavior Recording Sheet
(Daily by Student Name)

Date _____   Reminders _____

Name	1st Hour	2nd Hour	3rd Hour	4th Hour	5th Hour	Total

Reproducible Form Pre-Int 6: *Misbehavior Recording Sheet (Weekly)*

Misbehavior Recording Sheet
(Weekly by Student Name)

Date _____   Reminders _____

Name	Mon.	Tue.	Wed.	Thur.	Fri.	Total

Analyze the data and determine a plan of action. If behavior improves because you are keeping records, consider using a recording form on an ongoing basis. Also, make a subjective decision regarding your level of concern about the amount of misbehavior occuring in your class. If you are not concerned, do not bother making changes. If you are concerned, analyze the data further. Determine whether just a few students are exhibiting a particular misbehavior. If so, identify the three students who had the most frequent incidents of misbehavior and calculate the percentage of the total class misbehavior that could be attributed to those students.

Once you calculate the percentage of total classroom misbehavior that can be attributed to the three individual students, use the following guidelines to determine your plan of action:

90 percent
Keep your level of structure and procedures as they are. Consider individual behavior management plans for the three students whose behavior is most problematic.

60–89 percent
Review your level of classroom structure and consider setting up an extrinsic reward system to enhance the motivation of the class to meet your behavioral expectations (see "Intervention O: Structured Reinforcement Systems" for more details). Also consider individual behavior management plans for the three students whose behavior is most problematic.

Less than 60 percent
Review and implement all the suggestions for high-structure classrooms.

Note: See the following for more information:

For grades K–8:

Sprick, R. S., Garrison, M., & Howard, L. (1998). *CHAMPs: A Proactive and Positive Approach to Classroom Management.* Eugene, OR: Pacific Northwest Publishing.

For grades 9–12:

Sprick, R. S. (2006). *Discipline in the Secondary Classroom: A Positive Approach to Behavior Management* (2nd ed.). San Francisco: Jossey-Bass.

STOIC: **I**NTERACT positively with students.

A. Do you interact with every student in a welcoming manner (e.g., saying hello, using the student's name, talking with the student at every opportunity)?

It is very important for you to make an effort to provide every student with attention that is not contingent on any specific accomplishment. This kind of interaction shows students that you notice and value them as people and not because they "earned" your attention. When students feel valued, they are more likely to be motivated to engage in appropriate behaviors. The benefits to you include a more connected feeling to your students; a model for students of pleasant, supportive social interactions; improved student behavior; and an improved and more pleasant classroom climate.

Showing an interest and acting friendly does not mean trying to be a friend or a peer. You are the teacher, and you do not want to be so friendly that you seem like an equal. You are the authority figure who needs to intervene if rule violations occur. However, as the person in authority, you want to communicate that you value and are interested in every one of your students as individual people. You can give students noncontingent attention in several ways, including but not limited to the following:

- greeting students as they arrive

- showing an interest in students' work

- inviting students to ask for assistance

- having a conversation with a student or group of students, as time permits

- making a special effort to greet or talk to any student with whom you've had a recent interaction regarding misbehavior

B. Do you provide age-appropriate, nonembarrassing positive feedback?

Among the most important practices of an effective teacher is letting students know about behavioral and academic progress and/or success. Providing positive feedback is a powerful way to encourage responsible behavior. When done well, positive feedback confirms for students that they are on the right track and increases the probability that they will strive to demonstrate the same behaviors in the future. Incorporating the following five hallmarks of effective positive feedback into the feedback you give your students will significantly increase the probability that they will be encouraged and motivated to behave more responsibly in the future:

When students feel valued, they are more likely to be motivated to engage in appropriate behaviors.

- Feedback should be accurate.
- Feedback should be specific and descriptive.
- Feedback should be contingent.
- Feedback should be age-appropriate.
- Feedback should fit your style.

Feedback should be accurate. Positive feedback *must* be true to be effective. If you give a student positive feedback about something he did not actually do, the feedback is basically meaningless.

Feedback should be specific and descriptive. Be sure to tell a student exactly what she did correctly when giving positive feedback. Specific, descriptive feedback lets the student know which aspects of her behavior encouraged your comment. By being specific and descriptive, you can avoid the following common mistakes:

- The "Good job" syndrome: Don't fall into the trap of simply repeating a phrase, such as "Good job," "Nice work," or "Fantastic," over and over again. These phrases don't convey any useful information and become nothing more than background noise for the student after repeated use.

- Making judgments or drawing conclusions about the student: Don't make broad statements about the intelligence or ability of students, such as "You're smart," "You're so clever," or "You can do anything." These statements don't convey any specific information about what the student has done and may imply the opposite is true about the student if he doesn't behave in the same way the next time.

- Calling attention to yourself: Don't praise with phrases that start with, "I like the way you . . . ." The student shouldn't get the idea that he must behave to "please" you. The goal should be for the student to behave because it will help him become a successful learner. Some students might also get the idea that you "like" them when they behave, which in turn could imply you don't like them when they misbehave. Keep the focus on the student's action, not on your likes and dislikes.

Feedback should be contingent. Feedback should follow behavior that has some level of importance. If you give positive feedback for overly simple behavior, the student may feel insulted. For example, if you said, "Great job of sitting in your chair" to a high-school student, he would probably think you're trying to insult him because sitting in a chair is such an easy task and something he has done successfully countless times before. Three major circumstances contribute to positive feedback being contingent: (1) the feedback occurs when a new skill or behavior is being learned; (2) the feedback refers to a behavior that requires effort; and (3) the feedback concerns a behavior about which the individual is proud.

Feedback should be age-appropriate. Make sure your feedback fits the age and sophistication of the student. Clearly, you wouldn't offer the same feedback to a kindergartener and an eighth-grade student; both your vocabulary and tone of voice would differ. Feedback that is appropriate for a young student would most likely embarrass an older student, and feedback that is appropriate for an older student might be difficult for a younger student to understand and fully appreciate.

At different stages of development, some kids may become embarrassed by any kind of attention or praise. If a student seems to be uncomfortable when you give positive feedback, consider experimenting with one or more of these suggestions:

- Use a quiet voice.
- Be brief.
- Be somewhat businesslike.
- Avoid pausing and looking at the student after you praise.

Feedback should fit your style. There is no single right way to give positive feedback. Even if you incorporate all these recommendations when you offer feedback, there is plenty of room for your individual style. Make sure that when you give feedback, you do so in such a way that it fits your personality and feels natural. If you feel like you're being fake or insincere, students will feel that way too.

C. **Do you strive to interact more frequently with all students when they are engaged in positive behavior rather than when they are engaged in negative behavior?**

Ratio of Interactions is one of the most powerful behavior management strategies in a teacher's repertoire. You should plan on interacting *at least* three times more often with each student when he is behaving appropriately than when he is misbehaving (i.e., at least a 3:1 ratio). It's important to note that interactions are considered positive or negative based on the *student's* behavior, not *your* behavior, at the time of the interaction. For example, if a student is off task and the teacher pleasantly asks if she

Feedback should fit your style. There is no single right way to give positive feedback.

needs any help, this is considered negative—not because the teacher was negative, but because the student was engaged in negative behavior at the time of the interaction. The student is getting attention for misbehaving rather than behaving. It's important to realize that just because an interaction is negative does not mean it is wrong. A negative interaction may be the most useful way to get the student back on task at the time. However, because some students are starved for attention of any kind, unless you make an effort to interact more often with the student when he is on task, he may learn that it is easier to get your attention by engaging in misbehavior than by behaving responsibly.

Although it's not always easy to remember to pay attention to a student who is behaving responsibly, it may be even more difficult to remember *not* to pay undue attention to a student who is misbehaving. The consequences of dwelling on misbehavior could mean you are inadvertently reinforcing your students' misbehavior. You risk teaching students that if they are quiet, well behaved, and responsible, you will not even notice they are in the room—all your attention is directed at the students with behavior problems. See "Intervention E: Increasing Positive Interactions" for more information on positive interactions and for how to use the Monitoring Ratios of Interactions form.

STOIC: **C**ORRECT irresponsible behavior fluently—that is, in a manner that does not interrupt the flow of instruction.

A. Do you correct consistently?

Implement consequences for rule violations in a manner that is predictable and does not vary from day to day, hour to hour, and student to student. This sounds easier to do than it actually is. One of the best ways to determine whether you are being consistent is to collect data using a Misbehavior Recording Sheet form (see Reproducibles Forms Pre-Int 5 and 6). When you collect this data, reflect on whether your responses to misbehavior are consistent and predictable.

B. Do you correct calmly?

Emotional reactions to misbehavior demonstrate to students that they have power and influence and are able to "push your buttons." On the other hand, calm reactions demonstrate to students that they must live with the consequences of their actions, and how the teacher "feels" about it does not matter. Calm reactions also show students that they, like their teacher, can stay calm and composed in difficult situations.

C. Do you correct immediately?

When misbehavior occurs, let the student know *at that time* that the behavior is unacceptable. Although some delay may occur before you can actually implement the consequence, let the student know at the time of the infraction what that consequence will be: "Adrian, that was disruptive, and you will owe me 15 seconds at the end of the class period."

D. Do you correct briefly?

Most of us have a tendency to talk too much when we're correcting misbehavior. Remember that you are correcting violations of expectations that you have taught and retaught. Therefore, at the time of the infraction, simply state the misbehavior and the consequence and get back to teaching.

E. Do you correct respectfully?

As you correct, speak quietly; you are not trying to put the student on public display. Avoid using put-downs, criticisms, or labels. Simply state the misbehavior and the consequence.

F. Do you have a menu of in-class consequences that can be applied to a variety of infractions?

It is important to enter a classroom prepared with a wide variety of corrective consequences so you can select a consequence that adequately addresses the nature and severity of the misbehavior. This menu is somewhat like a mechanic's toolbox, containing many different tools to fit a variety of jobs. Just as a mechanic would not apply a hammer to every repair, a teacher should not apply the same consequence to every infraction. The following section, "A Menu of Classroom-Based Corrective Consequences," contains descriptions of effective corrective consequences that can be implemented in a classroom setting. Each description includes a brief explanation of the consequence and how to use it. Remember that when you're using corrective consequences, assign them consistently, calmly (that is, unemotionally), immediately, respectfully, and by interacting with the student as briefly as possible.

Note: Never use a corrective consequence that involves humiliation or ridicule of the student, and avoid using academic tasks as corrective consequences.

A Menu of Classroom-Based Corrective Consequences

Time owed

When a student misbehaves and you must intervene, some of your time is wasted. Therefore, a reasonable corrective consequence would be to have the student lose time from an activity she values. Time owed is an appropriate and effective corrective consequence for misbehaviors that occur frequently and for behaviors that tend to involve duration. In both of these situations, the time a student "owes" should equal the time the student spent misbehaving.

To use this corrective consequence, you must decide when the time owed will be paid back. It needs to occur during a time that the student values. For example, with an elementary student who likes recess, time owed from recess would be an easy and logical choice. It is important that the time not be paid back in such a way that it interferes with the student's time with another teacher, however. Thus, if keeping a middle-school student after class for more than one minute would mean that the student would not be able to get to his next class on time, you should not keep the student for more than one minute.

You will also need to decide how much time will be owed for each infraction. As a general rule, you should keep the amount of time short enough that you will not hesitate to implement the consequence each time the student misbehaves. Also keep in mind how much time you have access to that can be used as a penalty. Elementary teachers might have students owe one minute per infraction, or if only one recess per day is offered, perhaps 30 seconds per infraction is appropriate. Secondary teachers (who can't keep students after class for more than one minute) may use 15 seconds owed for each infraction. Although a consequence of only 15 seconds may sound almost silly, it is a pretty long time for an adolescent who wants to be in the hall talking with friends. The short time period also makes it possible for you to assign the consequence for up to four infractions. Secondary teachers may need to establish a policy such as "Each infraction will cost 15 seconds of time owed, and if more than four infractions occur, the student will be assigned after-school detention." When dealing with behaviors that last for a longer period of time, establish a minute-to-minute correspondence rule—the number of minutes owed corresponds directly to the number of minutes in which the student engages in the misbehavior.

Your final decision regarding this corrective consequence is what activity the student should do when repaying the time owed. As a general rule, the student should do nothing. However, during the first consequence of time owed, you may wish to discuss the misbehavior and ways the student could behave more responsibly in the future. Do not do this regularly, however, as the one-to-one interaction time with you may become reinforcing to the student and may actually serve to perpetuate the misbehavior.

Timeout

Many people think that the purpose of a timeout is to send the student to an adverse setting. That is not necessarily the case. The actual purpose is to remove a misbehaving student from the opportunity to earn positive reinforcement. The goal is to communicate to the student that if she engages in misbehavior, she will not get to participate in the interesting, productive, and enjoyable activities from which she has been removed. The obvious implication is that instruction and classroom activities need to be interesting, productive, and enjoyable.

Following are descriptions of five types of timeouts that are appropriate for different logistical situations and different student ages.

a) **Timeout from a favorite object (primary level)**

When developing your intervention plan, you might ask the student if he would like to bring a favorite object, such as a stuffed animal, to class to watch the student work and follow the rules. Initially, the object is placed on the student's desk. If the student misbehaves, the object is removed and placed on the teacher's desk, facing away from the student. When the student begins behaving appropriately, the object is returned to the student's desk. Bill Jenson describes this as a "Bumpy Bunny Time-Out" in the *Tough Kid* series. If you are concerned that the student might play with the object, explain to the student that playing with the object will mean that the object will go to timeout on your desk. Another option is to initially place the object near the student (e.g., on a bookshelf near the student's seat). If the student misbehaves, the object is taken to a different part of the room and placed facing away from the student. When the student begins to behave responsibly again, the object is returned to the shelf near the student so that it can "watch the student behaving responsibly."

b) **Timeout from small-group instruction (elementary level)**
If a student misbehaves during small-group instruction, you can have him push back his chair so that he is not physically part of the group. You should conduct the next minute or two of instruction in as fun and as reinforcing a manner as you possibly can. You want the student to feel that he is missing out on the privilege of participating in something that is enjoyable and beneficial.

c) **Timeout at desk (elementary level)**
If a student misbehaves, ask him to put his head down on his desk and close his eyes for a short period of time (e.g., two minutes). This form of timeout is very mild but can be effective for relatively minor problems (such as minor disruptions during instructional periods or during independent seat work).

d) **Timeout in class—isolation area (elementary and secondary levels)**
Using this option, establish a "timeout area" in a low-traffic part of your classroom. It can be as simple as a chair that is pushed off to the side of the room, or it can be more involved, such as an area behind a screen that is arranged so that you can see the student, but he cannot see the majority of his classmates.

e) **Timeout in another class (elementary or secondary levels):**
For a student who is likely to misbehave during an in-class timeout (e.g., the student clowns around to get other students to laugh at him), it may be necessary to assign the student to a timeout in another class. To do this, you need to find a teacher with a room near yours who has a class with fairly mature students. The students in this class should probably not be at the same grade level as your student. If the student misbehaves in your room, he would be sent to the "timeout teacher's room." This teacher should have a prearranged spot for the student (such as a chair in a low-traffic area of the room) and should preteach his or her class to ignore the student when he enters. The "timeout teacher" should not have to stop teaching or do problem-solving with the misbehaving student. The idea behind this procedure is simply that the student is less likely to "show off" for students in a different class (especially with students at a different grade level).

With any of these options, you should keep the length of the timeout brief, and you should not allow the student to take work to the timeout area. The purpose of the timeout is for the student to notice the enjoyable class activities he is missing. Assigning the student to do work defeats that purpose and increases the chance the timeout will lead to further conflicts if the student refuses to do the work. For primary students, a two- or three-minute timeout is best; for intermediate and secondary students, the optimal timeout is about five minutes. When using this consequence, you should instruct a student to go to timeout each time he misbehaves. The timeout period does not begin until the student is seated in the area and quiet.

If you think the student is unlikely to go to timeout and the student is old enough to understand time owed, establish that when instructed to go to timeout, he has one minute to get there and get settled. If it takes more than one minute, the student will owe the amount of time beyond the one minute during his recess or after school. If the student is unlikely to understand time owed (as in the case of a kindergarten student or a student with cognitive deficits), plan to conduct a few private "practice sessions" in which you model and have the student role-play going to timeout. If you conduct practice sessions in this way, be sure the student knows he has not done anything wrong and that you are just pretending so that he can learn how to go to timeout when he is asked to do so.

Restitution

Restitution (or compensation) can be effective for chronic purposeful misbehaviors if they involve damage to property or to social relationships. If a student engages in behavior that causes damage, a logical consequence would be that the student has to repair the damage. For example, if a student makes a mess in the restroom (e.g., using paper towels to plug a sink so water runs all over the floor), requiring the student to use a mop to dry the floor is a logical restitution, rather than having the custodian clean up the mess. When used with ongoing misbehavior, the "amount" of restitution should increase with successive instances of misbehavior. Thus, if a student wrote on her desk, you would have her wash the desk. If she did it a second time, you would have her wash all the desks in the class.

Positive practice

Positive practice (or overcorrection) is an appropriate corrective consequence when having the student practice the responsible behavior

*A Menu of
Classroom-Based
Corrective Consequences
(continued)*

might be effective. For example, you could make a student who runs in the halls stop, go back, and walk. A student who runs in the halls repeatedly might be required to spend time during recess or after school "practicing" walking in the halls.

Response cost—loss of points

If you use any kind of point system in your class, you might want to make certain infractions result in point "fines." If you do not use a point system, disregard this consequence; however, if your class is extremely challenging, you should consider setting up a point system. For more information, talk to colleagues about types of systems they use or have used in the past and see "Intervention O: Structured Reinforcement Systems."

Note: For more detailed information on how to use point systems as a management tool, see "Module 8: Classwide Motivation Systems" in *CHAMPs: A Proactive and Positive Approach to Classroom Management* (Sprick, Garrison, & Howard, 1998). For grades 9–12, consult the chapter "Behavioral Grading" in *Discipline in the Secondary Classroom: A Positive Approach to Behavior Management* (Sprick, 2006).

A simple way to use a point system as a corrective consequence is to start each student with 20 points at the beginning of the day or class. Every time you have to speak to a student about misbehavior, deduct a point from the individual's 20 points. At the end of the day, write the number of remaining points on a special note that goes home with the student. Each remaining point will equal ten minutes of television/video game time or some other privilege the student enjoys at home. The less the student misbehaves, the more points he will have at the end of the day, and the more television time he will get. Obviously, this system depends on family cooperation. Also, because your main interaction within this system is to give the student attention when he has misbehaved, you will need to make a concerted effort to pay attention to the student when he is not misbehaving.

Response cost lottery

This is a variation on a response cost consequence that can be used for situations when three or four students in class exhibit challenging behaviors. Give those students, or perhaps every student in the class, a certain number of tickets—say, ten—at the beginning of each day (or each week for secondary level). Each time a student misbehaves, he or she loses a ticket. At the end of the day (or week), the students write their names on all their remaining tickets and place them in a container for a drawing. The name of the student on the ticket drawn gets a treat or a small reward. The more tickets a student has, the greater the student's chances of winning.

Detention

Detention is usually a schoolwide system that involves assigning a student to spend a set amount of time (e.g., 40 minutes) in a non-stimulating setting. Most schools that use detention schedule these periods after school, before school, and/or during lunch. When used as a schoolwide procedure, any teacher can assign any student to detention. Detention is often structured so that the students in detention are required to work on academic tasks during the detention period. One problem with detention is that students may find the time reinforcing if their friends are assigned to the same detention. As with any corrective consequence you try, keep records. If you are repeatedly assigning the same student to detention across a period of weeks, then this particular corrective consequence is not working for this student and you should modify your correction plan to include a more effective consequence.

Demerits

Demerits essentially represent negative points that, when accumulated, result in the loss of a privilege or the imposition of a negative consequence. Demerits can be used to soften a predetermined consequence that might otherwise be overly harsh for a single example of misbehavior. For example, if the consequence for talking in class is after-school detention, which seems rather harsh for a single instance, you may be likely to respond to that behavior inconsistently—sometimes ignoring the behavior, sometimes threatening, and perhaps finally assigning detention. The use of demerits allows you to set up a more consistent policy. For example, a secondary teacher might tell students that each time he has to speak to a student about talking in class or has to deal with other minor disruptions from a student, that student will get a demerit. If a student gets four demerits within

A Menu of Classroom-Based Corrective Consequences (continued)

one week, it will equal one after-school detention. This teacher will be more likely to intervene every time a disruptive behavior occurs because the response for each single incident is reasonable, meaning more consistency.

Another way to use demerits, which may be especially useful for elementary teachers, is to specify that all students who have no more than five demerits get to participate in a free-time activity at the end of the day, but students with six or more demerits do not get to participate. You could even up the ante by arranging to give a special treat to each student who had no more than one demerit.

Office referral

Referring a student to an administrator should be used only in cases involving the most severe misbehaviors (i.e., physically dangerous behaviors and/or illegal behaviors). If you think you might want to send a student to the office for other types of behaviors, you should discuss these circumstances with the administrator ahead of time, so that he or she can coordinate a plan for when the student is sent to the office.

G. Do you have a plan for how to respond to different types of misbehavior fluently?

Once you have determined a wide array of possible classroom consequences, determine how various types of misbehavior will be handled in the classroom, using the following procedures:

1. Brainstorm a list of all the misbehaviors that could potentially occur each day.

List all the misbehaviors that might occur in your classroom, ranging from severe to trivial. List misbehaviors that involve individual students as well as groups of students. Consider misbehaviors that occur in different settings and during different kinds of activities. Following are some common misbehaviors you might see:

- teasing
- off-task behavior
- bad habits
- pounding on the desk
- tattling
- pencil tapping
- pushing, poking, hitting
- refusing to follow directions
- sarcasm
- shouting in class
- being cruel to others
- annoying others

Ask questions such as the following until the list is exhaustive:

- Do any problems occur as students enter the room in the morning?
- Do any problems or annoying misbehaviors occur during attendance-taking?
- Are students doing too much tattling?
- How is student behavior after recess?
- Are students respectful?
- What do particular students do to annoy or frustrate you?
- How do students treat each other?

Review the list to make sure each item is an observable behavior. The way to determine if a behavior is observable is if it can be measured, such as counting the frequency of a behavior or recording the duration. If you cannot measure the behavior, it is probably not observable and needs to be further clarified. Some misbehaviors may be listed as general descriptions of negative traits, such as "Jessie annoys the other students" or "Many students are cruel to others." Identify specifically what students are doing to lead to these conclusions. This will provide you greater clarity and consistency in designing a plan for reducing these problems. For example, explain *how* Jessie annoys the other students. "During work times and cooperative groups, Jessie wanders around the room, touching

If you cannot measure the behavior, it is probably not observable and needs to be further clarified.

Figure Pre-Int 2: *Behavior Categories*

Behavior Requiring Information	Behavior to Ignore	Behavior Requiring In-Class Consequences	Behavior Requiring Out-of-Class Consequences
• Teasing • Off-task behavior • Bad habits • Sarcasm	• Blurting out answers • Smart comments • Minor disruptions (i.e., chair noise, brief pencil tapping) • Asking silly question • Tattling	• Pushing, poking, minor hitting • Disruptive behavior (i.e., pounding on the desk, shouting in class) • Refusal to follow directions	• Severe intrusions • Insubordination to teacher

students and calling them names. During instruction, she tries to engage students in conversation when they should be listening or participating. On the playground, Jessie runs through games, pushes other students, and kicks balls into the street." Also describe how students are cruel to others. "Students frequently put each other down. They make sarcastic comments like, 'Good one, Tasha' or 'What's the matter, retard?'"

2. Determine whether misbehavior should be handled with correction information, ignored, or corrected with consequences.

Once a list of misbehaviors has been developed, determine how to respond. When consequences are determined in advance, it will be possible for you to respond calmly and consistently with appropriate consequences. Various misbehaviors can now be categorized using a chart similar to that shown in Figure Pre-Int 2.

3. Identify which consequences might be appropriate.

For behavior requiring in-class or out-of-class consequences, determine specific consequences. The chart in Figure Pre-Int 3 shows various consequences that you could use for particular behaviors.

Figure Pre-Int 3: *Behavior Consequences*

Behavior Requiring Consequences	Selected Consequences
• Pushing, poking, minor hitting • Severe intrusions • Refusal to follow directions • Disruptive behavior (e.g., pounding on the desk, shouting in class) • Insubordination to teacher	• One minute per infraction off recess • Office referral/parental contact • Time owed from recess and/or after school until compliance • Five-minute time-out • Behavior Improvement form/ parental contact • Written apology

4. Mentally or verbally rehearse how to handle different situations.

Once consequences have been selected and behavior categorized, it is helpful to rehearse ahead of time how you will handle different situations. Think about what you will do if the following occurs:
   • A student blurts out an answer without raising his hand.
   • A student hits someone.
   • A student teases another student by sticking out her tongue.
   • A student calls someone a name.
   • A student is tardy to class.
   • A student swears accidentally.

Note: For more detailed information regarding classroom consequences, see "Intervention P: Defining Limits and Establishing Consequences."

CONCLUSION

When only one or two students chronically misbehave, Interventions A–F, the Early-Stage Interventions, represent good starting points to help those students. However, when three or more students are chronically misbehaving, individual interventions are extremely time consuming and difficult for the teacher to manage. If this is the case, continue working on classroom management—crowd control—until the vast majority of students are behaving appropriately the vast majority of the time.

PRE-INTERVENTION

REFERENCES

Alberto, P., & Troutman, A. (2003). *Applied behavior analysis for teachers* (6th ed.). Upper Saddle River, NJ: Prentice Hall.

Bear, G. G. (1998). School discipline in the United States: Prevention, correction, and long-term social development. *School Psychology Review, 27,* 14–32.

Brophy, J. E. (1999). Perspectives of classroom management: Yesterday, today, and tomorrow. In H. J. Freiberg (Ed.), *Beyond behaviorism: Changing the classroom management paradigm* (pp. 43–56). Boston: Allyn & Bacon.

Cook, B. G., Landrum, T. J., Tankersley, M., & Kauffman, J. M. (2003). Bringing research to bear on practice: Effecting evidence-based instruction for students with emotional or behavioral disorders. *Education and Treatment of Children, 26,* 345–361.

Doyle, W. (1986). Classroom organization and management. In M. C. Wittrock (Ed.), *Handbook of research on teaching* (3rd ed., pp. 392–431). New York: Macmillan.

Emmer, E. T., Evertson, C. M., & Worsham, M. E. (2003). *Classroom management for secondary teachers* (6th ed.). Boston: Allyn & Bacon.

Evertson, C. M., Emmer, E. T., & Worsham, M. E. (2003). *Classroom management for elementary teachers* (6th ed.). Boston: Allyn & Bacon.

Evertson, C. M., & Weinstein, C. S. (Eds.). (2006). *Handbook of classroom management: Research, practice, and contemporary issues.* Mahwah, NJ: Lawrence Erlbaum Associates.

Farkas, S., & Johnson, J. (1997). *Different drummers: How teachers of teachers view public education.* New York: Public Agenda.

Hall, R. V., Lund, D., & Jackson, D. (1968). Effects of teacher attention on study behavior. *Journal of Applied Behavior Analysis, 1,* 1–12.

Hall, R. V., Panyan, M., Rabon, D., & Broden, M. (1968). Instructing beginning teachers in reinforcement procedures which improve classroom control. *Journal of Applied Behavior Analysis, 1,* 315–322.

Horner, R. H. (2002). On the status of knowledge for using punishment: A commentary. *Journal of Applied Behavior Analysis, 35,* 465–467.

Johnson, J. (2005). Isn't it time for schools of education to take concerns about student discipline more seriously? *Teachers College Record*, Retrieved February 14, 2005, from http://www.tcrecord.org.

Kauffman, J. M., Mostert, M. P., Trent, S. C., & Pullen, P. L. (2006). *Managing classroom behavior: A reflective case-based approach* (4th ed.). Boston: Allyn & Bacon.

Kounin, J. S. (1970). *Discipline and group management in classrooms*. New York: Holt, Rinehart, and Winston.

Maag, J. W. (2001). Rewarded by punishment: Reflections on the disuse of positive reinforcement in schools. *Exceptional Children, 67*, 173–186.

Nelson, C. M. (1981). Classroom management. In J. M. Kauffman & D. P. Hallahan (Eds.), *Handbook of special education* (pp. 663–687). Upper Saddle River, NJ: Prentice Hall.

Rhode, G., Jenson, W. R., & Reavis, H. K. (1992). *The tough kid book: Practical classroom management strategies*. Longmont, CO: Sopris West.

Sprick, R. S. (2006). *Discipline in the secondary classroom: A positive approach to behavior management* (2nd ed.). San Francisco: Jossey-Bass.

Sprick, R. S., Garrison, M., & Howard, L. (1998) *CHAMPs: A proactive and positive approach to classroom management*. Eugene, OR: Pacific Northwest Publishing.

Walker, H. M. (1995). *The acting-out child: Coping with classroom disruption* (2nd ed.). Longmont, CO: Sopris West.

Walker, J. E., Shea, T. M., & Bauer, A. M. (2004). *Behavior management: A practical approach for educators*. Upper Saddle River, NJ: Prentice Hall.

White, M. A. (1975). Natural rates of teacher approval and disapproval in the classroom. *Journal of Applied Behavior Analysis, 8*, 367–372.

Reproducible Materials

The following reproducible materials may be used in conjunction with this chapter. Copies are also provided on the CD. Permission is given for individual classroom teachers to reproduce any forms labeled "Reproducible" for classroom use. Reproduction of these materials for an entire school system is prohibited without express permission of the publisher.

Early-Stage Interventions:

THIS SECTION OF THE BOOK, Early-Stage Interventions, contains six chapters, Interventions A through F. Each chapter provides guidance to classroom teachers on how to implement a specific intervention that is designed to be a starting place in dealing with student misbehavior. Always try the easiest intervention first. These interventions are tools that any (and, hopefully, every) teacher can keep in his or her bag of tricks.

Although not a rigid sequence, the order of interventions in this section is quite intentional. It is always best to start with "Intervention A: Planned Discussion" (p. 71) to ensure that the student and parents are aware of the teacher's concern. If that does not solve the problem, the next step is to determine whether the problem is a behavior/motivation problem, an academic deficit, or a combination of both—thus the next intervention is "Intervention B: Academic Assistance" (p. 93). "Intervention C: Goal Setting" (p. 185) is designed to make expectations and goals more clear and attainable. If these very early stage efforts do not solve the problem, it is time to use data to drive subsequent intervention design and implementation, so next we include "Intervention D: Data Collection and Debriefing" (p. 223). If these strategies are not sufficient, two other interventions are well worth experimenting with in the early stages. "Intervention E: Increasing Positive Interactions" (p. 257) has great potential for changing problematic behavior by building a positive relationship with the student and ensuring that the student is getting more attention for goal behaviors than for problem behaviors. "Intervention F: STOIC Analysis and Intervention" (p. 305), the final chapter in this section, provides information on how to analyze the "function" of the misbehavior and design a comprehensive (Structure, Teach, Observe, Interact, Correct) and individually tailored plan that addresses that function.

If the student with the problem behavior does not respond to these early-stage interventions, it is probably worth asking for assistance from a school counselor, psychologist, behavior specialist, or problem-solving team. This is analogous to a medical model in which a general practitioner tries some basic treatments to treat the early stages of a problem. If those are not effective, he or she will collaborate with a specialist on subsequent diagnosis and treatment. In a school environment, this collaborative relationship may involve the implementation of one or more of the Highly Structured Interventions found in Section III of this book.

Note: The only absolute rule about behavior management is that belittlement of students has no place in any educational setting—all behavioral interventions must treat children with dignity and respect. To have a positive and lasting impact, interventions must attempt to build up student strengths and expand skills for replacing problem behavior, instead of simply squelching or containing problem behavior.

Planned Discussion

*The student may not know what is expected or may
be unaware of the teacher's concern*

PURPOSE

Pᴌᴀɴɴᴇᴅ ᴅɪsᴄᴜssɪᴏɴ with a student is just what it
sounds like. One or more adults confer with a student
about a particular concern and develop a plan for resolving
it. As simple as it sounds, this intervention has a reasonable
chance of success, so it represents a good starting place—
remember to always try the easiest thing first.

THIS INTERVENTION IS APPROPRIATE FOR:

Minor but potentially annoying misbehavior
- tattling
- hypochondria
- immaturity
- perfectionism
- disorganization
- sloppy work

Moderate misbehavior in the early stages
- poor listening skills
- dependency
- arguing
- disruptive behavior
- tardiness
- inaccurate or incomplete work

Chronic or severe concerns (as part of a comprehensive plan)
- destroying property
- aggression/fighting
- tantrums
- stealing
- cheating
- absenteeism

Even if a problem will require more intensive intervention, engaging in discussion is usually worth the time.

Planned Discussion has the potential to have a positive impact on just about any behavior. With any child whose language skills are sufficient, discussion should be an integral part of every intervention plan. For a minor concern or in the early stages of a moderate problem, this intervention may be sufficient in and of itself. Even if a problem will require more intensive intervention, engaging in discussion is usually worth the time. It will almost certainly improve the results of other interventions you try.

Planned Discussion should not take place in the immediate aftermath of an incident. Determine a neutral time, schedule the discussion time in advance, create an agenda for the discussion, and keep the time free from distractions and interruptions. Don't let the busyness of school, however legitimate, affect how a student perceives her importance or your intentions when you bring up a concern.

RATIONALE

- Behavior problems may result from a lack of information.
- This is the easiest, quickest intervention.
- Planned Discussion is a respectful and potentially empowering way to address problem behavior.

Because it is such a simple intervention, discussion is often overlooked. In busy classrooms, teachers are continually interacting with students—praising, reprimanding, instructing, refereeing, and counseling. When problems occur, teachers may believe that they have already discussed their concerns with students: "Kaelyn, leave Sam alone and get back to work . . . . Kaelyn, keep your hands to yourself . . . . It is very important for you to keep your hands and your feet to yourself . . . . Kaelyn, if you are going to pick on the other children, you will need to stay in during recess . . . ." Though the teacher may believe that she has sufficiently discussed her concerns with Kaelyn, Kaelyn may not realize she's been a part of any discussion. In fact, she may actually be unaware of any concern at all on the teacher's part! Suppose Kaelyn is from a home where interactions (if they even occur) are relentlessly negative. Perhaps she has a long history of behavior problems (and in all likelihood, she does). What effect will a teacher's constant reprimands and consequences have on her?

The truth about students like Kaelyn is that constant corrections and reprimands at school will not have a great effect because they represent just another day in another unpleasant environment. Even if a teacher could temporarily affect her behavior, these kinds of interactions probably wouldn't change Kaelyn's behavior in the long run because she hears reprimands so often they are almost like background noise. This is not to discount the uses of fluent correction when appropriate. But for students who have built up a tolerance or resistance to corrections, you may be better off trying alternative strategies first.

The preceding example provides a few clues as to why a Planned Discussion may be necessary. The purpose of this intervention is to demonstrate your concern in such a way that the student truly understands it, to involve the student in brainstorming solutions to her own problems, and to let that student know with certainty that you are there to help her learn and grow. Low in structure, high in potential, Planned Discussion should be one of your first steps in designing an intervention. Often, the need for more intensive interventions can be circumvented.

Meeting individually with students

Many teachers think, "I don't have time to meet with individual students!" However, with only a few exceptions, teachers can create a daily window of opportunity to talk to students individually. The first five to ten minutes of independent work periods can be used to briefly meet with a few students one-to-one. Exceptions would include teachers of very young children (kindergarten and early-year first graders) and potentially dangerous settings such as shop or chemistry, where a teacher's extra vigilance is necessary for everyone's safety.

Inform your class in advance that you will be meeting individually with students. Let them know that you want to get to know them and help every student be successful. Sometimes you may talk to a student about

Let that student know with certainty that you are there to help her learn and grow.

INTERVENTION

A

grades and look at the grade book; at other times you might talk about a concern, discuss goals, or ask the student how school is going.

At the end of instruction, before starting independent or cooperative group activities, give the class final directions: "If you have any questions about how to get started on this task, ask now, because for the next five minutes I will be at my desk talking with one or two students. Any questions?"

Meet with students on a regular basis so that these meetings will not stand out as odd and you will not appear to be singling out particular students. Even better, you will have set aside discrete times of the day into which you can easily fit planned discussions. Keep a record of the students with whom you meet. You want to ensure that you meet with all of your students at least once a semester (secondary) or once a month (elementary).

Discussing a one-time event

If you would like to discuss an isolated event with a student, address it without breaking the flow of instruction, keep your correction brief, and immediately set a time with the student to follow up. Following up on a one-time event differs from Planned Discussion in that it does not address a repeated behavior; note, however, that you can also apply the principles of this intervention to your discussion of a one-time event.

Teacher:	Elaina, I am very concerned about what you just said to your group. I am writing down what you said, and in a few minutes, after I make sure the other groups are doing okay on the assignment, you and I will need to discuss this.

When you meet, show the student the What Happened? form (Reproducible Form A1) with your description of what occurred (in this case, what Elaina said).

Give the student a chance to describe her view of the event. Note if and how the student's account differs from yours. Let the student know what action you plan to take—assigning a detention, contacting a parent, writing a referral, keeping the form on file so you have a record of the event, or another consequence.

Reproducible Form A1: *What Happened?*

Intervention A:
Planned Discussion

What Happened?

Student _____   **Date** _____

Teacher _____   **Grade/Class** _____

Teacher's description of problem _____

_____

_____

_____

Student's description of problem _____

_____

_____

_____

Teacher actions   Student actions

_____   _____

_____   _____

_____   _____

_____   _____

_____   _____

_____   _____

Does there need to be a follow-up meeting?   ❑ yes   ❑ no

_____ _____ _____
Date   Time   Participants

IMPLEMENTATION STEPS
Step I: Prepare to meet with the student.

A. Identify the central concern.

Before meeting with the student, go through a mental list of behavioral concerns about the student and define for yourself the primary concern. How pervasive is the problem? What other factors should be considered? Where does the issue occur? When and how often? Is the problem more likely to occur in particular situations or with certain people? Keep this information in mind as you go through the planning steps.

Mr. Anderson is concerned about Joey, a fourth-grade student in his class. Joey is easily distractible, rarely able to concentrate longer than five or ten minutes on any assignment. He talks to other students, plays with anything he can find, taps his pencil, and gets in and out of his seat. Mr. Anderson decides to talk with Mrs. Gaske, the consulting teacher in the building. Perhaps Joey has an attention deficit disorder.

During their discussion, Mr. Anderson and Mrs. Gaske identify things that have already been tried. Mr. Anderson has tried gentle reminders, praising Joey for responsible behavior, keeping him in at recess to finish his work, and calling his parents. They also establish that Joey's poor work habits seem to be pervasive in all academic subject areas.

In talking with the parents, Mr. Anderson learns that Joey has an older sister who does very well in school, and Joey seems to believe he can't compete. His parents are worried and help him with his homework.

Mr. Anderson thinks Joey's ability is at least average and that he is capable of doing his work but just won't stick with it. When Mr. Anderson stands next to Joey, the boy completes his assignments, and the quality of the work is satisfactory. Mr. Anderson and Mrs. Gaske decide that it would be worthwhile to discuss the concern with Joey and his parents. If no improvement is seen, they can meet again to consider a more intensive intervention.

B. Establish a focus.

Isolating your target concern may be relatively simple—off-task behavior, work completion, interactions with other students, problems with authority, and similar issues. Sometimes, however, a student presents an interrelated set of misbehaviors. In this case, constrain the scope of what you hope to accomplish with Planned Discussion. Use the information you developed about your primary concern for the student (who, what, when, where, and how often) to narrow the focus of your discussion. Introducing too many concerns at once may increase the student's sense of inadequacy and reduce the likelihood of success.

Most importantly, identify some of the student's strengths. When you share your concerns, you want to be able to begin and end with valid information on the student's positive behaviors. Doing so demonstrates interest, perceptiveness, and authentic concern. When a student hears positive attributes from a voice of authority—even an authority the student professes not to heed—such comments often register more deeply than even the student is aware of.

C. Determine who should participate in the discussion.

Inform the student's parents that you will be meeting with their child to discuss a concern and invite them to participate. However, if the issue is relatively mild or early-stage, you can meet only with the student. If you are distressed or angry about the situation, ask a consulting teacher or interventionist to facilitate the discussion. With severe concerns such as physically dangerous acts or open defiance, an administrator should also be included in the discussion.

Don't overwhelm the student with too many adults at the meeting. Including more than three adults other than the student's parents can backfire because the student may feel picked on and become defensive. The student should feel like a partner in the discussion, rather than the focus of an inquisition.

Joey's teacher decides to have a discussion with Joey and his parents. Though he is grateful that Joey's parents are concerned, Mr. Anderson has difficulty communicating with them. Mr. Anderson believes that including Mrs. Gaske in the meeting might help facilitate the discussion.

INTERVENTION

A

The discussion is not just a reaction to an immediate concern, but a time to work on a plan for the future.

D. Schedule the discussion for a neutral time.

There is a natural tendency to initiate a discussion with a student immediately following a behavioral incident. Generally, however, such an interaction with the student takes the form of a reprimand rather than a productive discussion. Emotions may be high, and the conversation is more likely to be defensive and argumentative. A better strategy is to put enough distance between yourself and the incident for emotions to cool, but schedule the meeting close enough in time for the concern to still be relevant. It is reasonable to correct the misbehavior immediately with a very brief reprimand and a statement that you would like to discuss the incident at a later time. Schedule a Planned Discussion meeting for a time that can be private, unhurried, and free from interruption. The higher the level of your concern, the longer you should make the interval between the misbehavior and the discussion. For minor or infrequent concerns, this might be 20 minutes or an hour afterward. For a major issue, it should be no sooner than the next day, which also affords you time to invite the student's parents to participate.

E. Make an appointment with the student to discuss the concern.

Make an appointment with the student. Let the student know who will be present and why you will be meeting. Invite the student to think about the concern in advance. By arranging the discussion for a neutral time, it is obvious that the discussion is not just a reaction to an immediate concern, but a time to work on a plan for the future.

Mr. Anderson: (Teacher)	Joey, I have a concern that I need your help with. I am very concerned about the difficulty you have getting your work completed. I thought you, your mom, and I could talk about ways to help you become more responsible for your work. I've set up an appointment tomorrow after school. Between now and then, let's both think about ways that we can work on this. I've also asked Mrs. Gaske to join us. She has helped a lot of other students, and I'm sure she'll have some ideas for us. I am looking forward to this session because I'm sure that we can all come up with a plan.

F. Plan to keep a written record of the discussion.

Summarizing the discussion in writing (Reproducible Form A2) serves two functions:

1. It provides documentation of what is discussed. This will be needed for subsequent interventions if the student is not responsive to this effort.

2. The student is more likely to take the situation seriously.

> **Note:** The Discussion Record (Reproducible Form A2) is an optional form for conducting discussions that may help to keep the discussion focused and provide a record of the discussion. It is not essential to keep such a record, but even some form of informal notes will assist in keeping the discussion focused.

Step 2: Meet with the student.

A. Work with the student to define your concerns.

Throughout your meeting, maintain a future orientation. When you refer to past problems, make it clear that you are not attaching blame, but rather looking for better ways to handle situations in the future. Furthermore, continually treat the student "as if" he were a highly responsible person. If anything, act slightly surprised that someone as responsible as the student would have such a problem.

> "Treat people as if they were what they ought to be, and you help them become what they are capable of being."
>
> –Goethe

Clarify your concerns and encourage the student to share his perspective. From the beginning of the discussion, the student should understand that this is a joint problem-solving session, not a lecture about what the student must do differently. Help the student understand that you are working together by stating the concern from your perspective. Starting with "I have a concern . . ." tends to work better than "You have a problem . . ." When you avoid statements that might appear to lay blame, the student will be less defensive and it will be easier to engage in a productive discussion.

Reproducible Form A2: *Discussion Record*

Discussion Record

_____   _____   _____
Student   Teacher   Date

_____   _____
Participants   Grade/Class

Describe the problem. _____

_____

_____

_____

Establish a goal. _____

_____

_____

Brainstorm.

_____

_____

_____

_____

_____

Select actions.
- Check selected actions from the list.
- Identify who will be responsible for taking each action.

Set up next meeting:

_____   _____   _____
Date   Time   Participants

Mr. Anderson: (Teacher)	Thank you for joining me today. The reason we're meeting is to help me with a concern. Before we get into it, though, I want you to know I respect you very much. You are liked by other students and you do a fine job on the work you turn in. One of my jobs is to help students learn to be good workers and to complete their assignments. I'm not sure how I can help you with finishing assignments, Joey, so I thought we could all work on this together. Mrs. Gaske is experienced at helping with these kinds of concerns, so she will be guiding our discussion today.
Mrs. Gaske: (Consulting Teacher)	I am very happy to be here. Joey, you are an important part of our school. I appreciate that you always have a big smile for me when I see you. Can you help us figure out why you have trouble getting your work done?
Joey:	I don't know.

Sometimes a student will have difficulty entering into the discussion. If you notice a student fidgeting, visually casing the room for exits, or otherwise looking genuinely uncomfortable, try giving the student a specific task. This may relieve some of the tension and help the student direct his attention.

Mrs. Gaske:	Joey, why don't you look in Mr. Anderson's grade book and help us figure out how many assignments you are missing. I have covered the names of the other students for privacy. How many missing assignments did you count?
Joey:	Eight.
Mrs. Gaske:	Do you know which assignments they are?
Joey:	Well, some are in math and others are in reading.
Mrs. Gaske:	Joey, can you help us figure out why you didn't get your assignments turned in?
Joey:	I didn't have time to get them done.
Mrs. Gaske:	Why do you think that is?
Joey:	I just don't have time.
Mrs. Gaske:	Mr. Anderson, perhaps you can help us. Do you think Joey has enough time in class to get his work done?
Mr. Anderson:	Yes. In fact, Joey works very hard sometimes and does get his work in. He accomplishes this about half the time, and he does very well. Joey, other times you tend to find

INTERVENTION

A

	all kinds of things to do instead of your work. You get up and down, play in your desk, and chat with the other kids.
Joey's mother:	We really want Joey to do well in school. This has been a concern every year. All of his teachers believe that he is capable, but he just doesn't seem to be motivated. One thing I noticed is that Joey doesn't like to sit still. Even when he is watching TV, he is up and walking around or fidgeting.
Mr. Anderson: (Teacher)	Joey, during my many years of teaching, I've known a lot of kids who like to move around a lot. I'm actually not worried about that. What I am worried about is your getting your work done. If you had one thing that you would like to change, what would it be?
Joey:	I guess I'd like to be smarter.
Mr. Anderson:	Smart is kind of an interesting thing. What is smart?
Joey:	I don't know.
Mr. Anderson:	Do you think it means doing well in school?
Joey:	My sister's smart.
Mr. Anderson:	Does your sister do well in school?
Joey:	Yeah.
Mr. Anderson:	You can be smart, too, by learning to work. We can start by finding ways to get your work done.

B. Brainstorm actions that each participant in the discussion can take to help the student resolve the concern.

Brainstorming can help a student understand that many things can be done to help him become more successful, and it's a great way to open a dialogue (particularly among people with very different agendas, such as teachers, students, their parents, and school administrators). Clarify that the goal at this stage is to develop ideas, not to finalize a plan: These are things we might do, not necessarily things we will do.

Mrs. Gaske: (Consulting Teacher)	Now we can get to the fun part. Let's make a list of all the things that you, Mr. Anderson, and your mom might do to help you stay on task during independent work times. When we brainstorm, we all come up with as many ideas as we can. Even if they are silly ideas, we will write them down. When we are done brainstorming, we'll look over

the list and pick some things we can do. Let's see. Joey, your mom said that it was hard for you to sit still for long periods of time. Maybe we could move your desk to the side of the room so you can stand up while you are working if you feel like it. Does anyone else have some ideas? Joey, think about some things you could do that would help you get to work and keep working.

Joey: I guess I could sharpen my pencil before class.

Mr. Anderson: I could give Joey a checklist, and he could keep track of **(Teacher)** the work he finishes each day.

Mrs. Gaske: You could work on talking to other kids only at recess and not talking during your work times.

Joey: I could go to the bathroom after recess.

Mrs. Gaske: Mr. Anderson could give you a little signal that no one else would know about if he sees you off task.

Mr. Anderson: Joey's mother could go through his papers with him once each week and put his best work in a scrapbook. This would help Joey see how well he does on the work he completes.

Mrs. Gaske: We could send a daily report card home.

At this level of intervention, the best actions generally do not require an exorbitant amount of time on anyone's part.

C. Set up an informal action plan.

After a number of ideas are on the table, pick a few actions that seem manageable and likely to increase student success. At this level of intervention, the best actions generally do not require an exorbitant amount of time on anyone's part. Simply helping the student find strategies to focus his attention, and on your part, demonstrating some level of commitment to the student's success, is a good place to start.

Mrs. Gaske: This is a great list of things to do. Let's identify the things **(Consulting** that would be fairly easy to do. Joey, this is not a big problem, **Teacher)** and you came up with some terrific ideas to help us manage this. You are growing up! Let's put checks by things that any of us could do that would help.

The group selects the following actions:

- Move Joey's desk to side so that he can stand while he does his work if he chooses to.
- Joey will sharpen two pencils before class.

> • Joey will make a checklist of work completed each day.
> • Joey will talk to other students at recess, not during independent work times.
> • Joey will go to the restroom after recess.
> • Joey's mother will go through Joey's papers with him and start a scrapbook of his best work.

D. Schedule a follow-up meeting.

The simple act of scheduling another meeting increases the likelihood that all participants will work on their part of the action plan. It's easy to focus on solving a problem for a short time (say, the length of a planned discussion) but then forget all about it. Knowing there will be a sustained effort to resolve the problem may bring the student a greater sense of accountability. Of course, the same is likely true for you, the teacher, and for the parents. Follow-up also assures that student efforts are recognized and that the plan will be revised, if necessary. The follow-up meeting should take place a couple of days to a week after the initial meeting.

E. Conclude the meeting with words of encouragement.

Mr. Anderson: (Teacher)	Joey, I am very encouraged by your participation today. I know that you have had trouble getting your work done in the past and that has been very frustrating. I think you have demonstrated today that you can get your work done. You had great suggestions, and I know you are willing to work with me.

F. If appropriate, share a copy of the written record of the meeting with the student and parents.

Step 3: Follow up with the student.

A. Encourage student efforts.

After you have met with the student and clearly defined your expectations, the student's effort should be recognized on a daily basis. It is not uncommon to see immediate improvement following a discussion, which is then followed by a loss of momentum. Your encouragement is important. Think of the lengths to which professional sports teams go to motivate athletes—who are already paid millions for their efforts! Realize how important it must be, then, to motivate the student who is paid nothing and who hasn't yet grasped the impact that seemingly small efforts today will have on future dreams and aspirations. Sometimes it may be necessary to provide encouraging reminders about actions from the discussion that the student is forgetting. Make a conscious effort to give the student feedback on successes and even the small steps that lead toward success.

Mr. Anderson: (Teacher)	Joey, this morning I noticed several times that you were working hard. I know Karen stopped by your desk, and when she moved on, you went right back to work. You also had your pencils ready and finished your math.

Your encouragement is important. Think of the lengths to which professional sports teams go to motivate athletes.

B. Meet once a week with the student to discuss progress and adjust the action plan as necessary.

Periodic meetings keep momentum going. If the student's efforts are paying off, he deserves recognition. If things have improved but additional progress is needed, you can discuss ways to continue growing and learning. If the situation has not improved, discuss the option of more structured interventions.

C. Determine whether more structured interventions are required.

If you, the student, or the student's parents aren't seeing the progress you anticipated, it's time to consider more intensive intervention. You can maintain a positive focus by viewing this next step as a logical extension of the discussion-based problem-solving process, not as a failure.

Mrs. Gaske: (Consulting Teacher)	I'm happy that we could all get back together again. We had a great session last time, and I am looking forward to reviewing how things have been going. Joey, tell us what you were working on.
Joey:	Getting my work done.
Mrs. Gaske:	Can you tell us how you're doing?
Joey:	OK, I guess.
Mr. Anderson: (Teacher)	We've seen some good improvements in some things. Joey has been remembering to use the restroom after recesses, and he sharpens his pencils each morning. Joey, can you tell us how you are doing with your work?

INTERVENTION

Joey:	(Shrugs)
Mr. Anderson: (Teacher)	Let's have you look at the grade book again. Do you see missing assignments?
Joey:	Yeah.
Mr. Anderson:	I would like us all to be aware that Joey has made improvements. After our discussion, he got all of his work in. I was very impressed. Unfortunately, since then he has gotten less and less work completed, almost by the day.
Mrs. Gaske: (Consulting Teacher)	In some ways that seems a little discouraging, but in other ways I am very hopeful. Joey, you have demonstrated that you do care about your work and that you can get it done. I think it's just hard to keep it up day after day. Let's see if we can do some other things to help you accomplish your goals.

The consulting teacher, teacher, and parent meet later to consider designing a more in-depth plan that may involve one or more additional interventions:

    Intervention B: Academic Assistance

    Intervention C: Goal Setting

    Intervention J: Cueing and Precorrecting

    Intervention K: Self-Monitoring and Self-Evaluation

    Intervention M: Teaching Replacement Behavior

    Intervention O: Structured Reinforcement Systems

D. Provide continued follow-up, support, and encouragement.

Whether or not the student is able to improve his behavior solely through Planned Discussion, follow-up discussions play an important role in keeping the student involved. If other interventions are needed, Planned Discussion will play a continuing role. If successful, the student needs to know that his efforts and successes are recognized. Without continued support, the student may return to old and established patterns of behavior. Though follow-up is generally composed of short, informal discussions with the student, some discussions should be scheduled so they are not forgotten.

INTERVENTION
A

Note: When several students exhibit the same behavior of concern, you can consider implementing this intervention with a small group—but note that should these students compete, ridicule one another, or otherwise give each other a hard time, small-group format may backfire. If you have concerns about your students' maturity or level of structure, you may be better off working individually with one student at a time.

If successful, the student needs to know that his efforts and successes are recognized.

If the behavior of concern is exhibited by five or more students, consider intervening with the entire class. Steps in this chapter can easily be modified to apply to a whole class. Parents may not need to be invited to a classwide Planned Discussion, though you might consider informing them of your concerns, goals, and your class's collective strengths through a newsletter or notes home.

CONCLUSION

A Planned Discussion can be as formal as the goal-setting procedure in Intervention C or as informal as a family discussion. Though a sensible and logical first step, this intervention does not necessarily come naturally to teachers who are busy attending to the needs of dozens of students, and you should not be discouraged if your first attempts feel awkward or forced. Time is the biggest barrier to Planned Discussions, and finding the time to implement this intervention will likely be your most important key to success. You may need to schedule discussions before school, during recess, or after school. With a colleague's consent, you might be able to schedule a discussion during another activity or class, such as music, PE, or library. (Never take a student out of another class without prior approval.) As a last resort, you could ask a colleague to manage your classroom while you meet with a student.

If the concern is still in its early stages or is relatively simple, Planned Discussions may also be conducted during class time. When the teacher has provided effective instruction, individuals can be pulled aside for brief discussions while other students work independently or in small groups.
Because a Planned Discussion requires setting time aside, it can seem

Through discussion, the student can learn to take an active role in the process of growing and maturing.

hard to justify—especially during a busy school day. However, the time you spend on Planned Discussion will more often than not result in an early resolution to a brewing problem, saving everyone time, effort, and frustration.

A well-conceived discussion may help a student understand the situation from your perspective and will help the student know that you are interested in him individually—you are not an adversary. Through discussion, the student can learn to take an active role in the process of growing and maturing. In some cases, this intervention may be sufficient to motivate a student to change his behavior. Even when Planned Discussion alone is insufficient to resolve a problem, it reinforces the power of other concurrent or subsequent interventions. Planned Discussion is a natural launch pad for interventions and should be an integral part of any further planning that you do.

REFERENCES

Bruce, M. A. (1995). Fostering resiliency in students: Positive action strategies for classroom teachers. *Teacher Educator, 31*(2), 177–188.

Camp, B. W. (1977). Verbal mediation in young aggressive boys. *Journal of Abnormal Psychology, 86,* 145–153.

Cormier, W. H., & Cormier, L. S. (1991). Interviewing strategies for helpers: Fundamental skills and cognitive behavioral interventions. Pacific Grove, CA: Brooks/Cole.

Durlak, J. A. (1983). Social problem solving as a primary prevention strategy. In R.D. Felner, L. A. Jason, L. N. Moritsugu, & S. S. Farber (Eds.), *Preventive psychology: Theory, research, and practice* (pp. 31–48). New York: Pergamon Press.

Fagen, S. A. (1981). Conducting LSI: A process model. *The Pointer, 25*(2), 9–11.

Gardner, R. A. (1971). *Therapeutic communication with children.* New York: Science House.

Graham, N., & Singer, M. (Eds.). (1981). Life space interviewing [special issue]. *The Pointer, 25*(2).

Heuchert, C. M. (1983). Can teachers change behavior? Try interviews. *Academic Therapy, 18,* 321–328.

Hindle, D. (1996). Planning together: Positive classroom environments. In *Diversity of the classroom series, Number four*. Saskatchewan, Canada: Saskatchewan Professional Development Unit.

Jensen, A. R. (1966). Verbal mediation and educational potential. *Psychology in the Schools, 3*, 99–109.

Muscott, H. S. (1995). Techniques for avoiding counter-aggressive responses when teaching youth with aggressive behavior. *Journal of Emotional and Behavioral Problems, 4*(1), 41–44.

Rathvon, N. (1999). *Effective school interventions: Strategies for enhancing academic achievement and social competence* (Guilford School Practitioner Series). New York: Guilford Press.

Redl, F. (1959). The concept of the life space interview. *American Journal of Orthopsychiatry, 29*, 1–18.

Simon, H. (1980). Problem solving in education. In D. T. Tuma & R. Reif (Eds.), *Problem solving and education: Issues in teaching and research*. Hillsdale, NJ: Lawrence Erlbaum Associates.

Skyrms, B. (1986). *Choice and chance: An introduction to inductive logic* (3rd ed.). Belmont, CA: Wadsworth.

Sugai, G., & Colvin, G. (1997). Debriefing: A transition step for promoting acceptable behavior. *Education and Treatment of Children, 20*(2), 209–221.

Thurman, R., & Kenton, W. (1999). *Improving academic achievement of underachieving students in a heterogeneous classroom*. Unpublished master's project. Saint Xavier University, Chicago, Illinois.

Van de Werfhost, F. H. (1986). Temperament and teacher child interactions. In G.A. Kohnstamm (Ed.), *Temperament discussed: Temperament and development in infancy and childhood* (pp. 141–147). Leiden, The Netherlands: University of Leiden.

VanGundy, A. B. (1987). *Creative problem solving: A guide for trainers and management*. New York: Quorum Books.

Winn, J. A. (1991). *An investigation of implementation and student outcomes of instruction for self-regulation through mediated collaborative problem solving*. Unpublished doctoral dissertation, Michigan State University, East Lansing, MI.

Reproducible Materials

The following reproducible materials appear in "Intervention A: Planned Discussion." Copies are also provided on the CD. Permission is given for individual classroom teachers to reproduce any forms labeled "Reproducible" for classroom use. Reproduction of these materials for an entire school system is prohibited without the express permission of the publisher.

INTERVENTION

A

INTERVENTION  A

PLANNED DISCUSSION

Step-by-Step Summary

Following is a summary of the steps involved in Intervention A. It is important to use professional judgment, adjusting procedures to meet the needs of the situation and the individual. See the chapter "Intervention A: Planned Discussion" for a detailed description of this intervention.

STEP 1   Prepare to meet with the student.

A. Identify the central concern.

B. Establish a focus.

C. Determine who should participate in the discussion.

D. Schedule the discussion for a neutral time.

E. Make an appointment with the student to discuss the concern.

F. Plan to keep a written record of the discussion.

STEP 2   Meet with the student.

A. Work with the student to define your concerns.

B. Brainstorm actions that each participant in the discussion can take to help the student resolve the concern.

C. Set up an informal action plan.

D. Schedule a follow-up meeting.

E. Conclude the meeting with words of encouragement.

F. If appropriate, share a copy of the written record of the meeting with the student and parents.

Reproducible Step-by-Step Summary (2 of 2)

INTERVENTION

STEP 3   Follow up with the student.

A. Encourage student efforts.

B. Meet once a week with the student to discuss progress and adjust the action plan as necessary.

C. Determine whether more structured interventions are required.

D. Provide continued follow-up, support, and encouragement.

INTERVENTION B

Marilyn Sprick, M.S.

Academic Assistance

The student may have an underlying academic problem

PURPOSE

WHEN A student's misbehavior has become chronic or resistant to other interventions, conduct one or more of the assessment procedures described in this intervention. Often, what appears to be a behavior problem has an academic component.

THIS INTERVENTION IS APPROPRIATE FOR:

- incomplete or late work
- class clown behaviors
- attention problems
- shy or withdrawn behavior
- cheating
- poor motivation
- disruptive behavior
- tantrums
- anger or hostility
- lying
- complaints about health
- stealing
- poor self-concept
- lack of energy

INTERVENTION

B

ASSESSMENT STRATEGIES

Determine whether the student is able to:

- decode assigned reading material with reasonable rate and accuracy based on fluency tables
- retain information that has been read
- make inferences and engage in other higher order thinking skills from material that has been read
- understand and retain information from written directions
- complete assignments independently
- stay on task for extended periods of time
- demonstrate basic organizational skills for keeping track of assignments, budgeting time, completing homework, studying for tests, etc.

ADAPTATION STRATEGIES

Academic Assistance provides several informal ways to assess a student's academic needs and a menu of adaptation strategies to assist the student in achieving greater academic success. This chapter details how to:

- construct and use framed outlines
- design and use interactive graphic organizers
- build cumulative review of essential objectives into subsequent units
- identify and preteach essential vocabulary
- highlight textbooks and printed material
- transcribe or summarize highlighted text
- provide two-column study guides
- focus assignments on essential course content
- focus test items on essential course content
- provide framed writing assignments
- teach the student to manage homework or other organizational strategies

RATIONALE

Students who fail to thrive academically are often frustrated. When their performance fails to match their aspirations, they may feel inadequate and engage in any number of inappropriate behaviors to mask a sense of incompetence. Such students may become withdrawn, seem unmotivated, clown around, or be uncharacteristically sarcastic, distractible, or hyperactive. They can be endlessly resourceful in covering for their lack of ability, making it hard to gauge how much their academic difficulties may be contributing to their behavioral problems.

Academic problems are not always obvious. This intervention may help expose academic problems that are mild enough to contribute to behavioral problems but not so severe as to have drawn attention in the past.

> Dylan is a fourth grader whose academic skills are low enough that he has been referred for special education. Though his skills are low, Dylan tests too highly to qualify as mildly developmentally delayed and does not qualify as learning disabled. Dylan's parents and teachers are concerned. In the primary grades, Dylan's parents were told that Dylan was just slow to develop and that his time would come, but Dylan still struggles with every task. As Dylan is now entering fourth grade, his parents fear he isn't going to pop into gear. They think that his lack of competence has resulted in Dylan's becoming more belligerent, sullen, and uncooperative as time has passed. Dylan's behavioral problems are obviously related to academic issues, so Dylan's teachers opt to intervene, with Academic Assistance as the top priority.

> Note: Academic Assistance may be a useful intervention when academic difficulties persist but are not so pervasive that referral to special education is warranted. Academic Assistance may also be useful as a pre-referral intervention—an interim plan while a referral to special education is being considered—or as a resource in developing an Individualized Education Plan (IEP) for a special education student.

They can be endlessly resourceful in covering for their lack of ability, making it hard to gauge how much their academic difficulties may be contributing to their behavioral problems.

INTERVENTION

B

Cynthia, a seventh-grade student, is a different story. She is verbal, articulate, and witty. Cynthia is referred to the Intervention Planning Team (IPT) not for academic problems, but for her "attitudinal" problems—disrespect, flippant comments, and clowning around during work times. When asked about Cynthia's academic abilities, one teacher comments, "Cynthia doesn't have an academic problem. She often doesn't get her work turned in, but she can do the work if she wants to. She's just more interested in giving teachers a hard time." Cynthia's standardized test scores confirm that she should be a very capable student. Though this problem seems to be primarily behavioral, the IPT decides that academic problems haven't been ruled out. Cynthia may mask a minor academic problem by being mouthy and off task. Academic Assistance is considered as a potential intervention for Cynthia, despite the primarily behavioral nature of the referral.

Motivation

Academic difficulties often appear to be due to the lack of motivation. Students who fail to perform often seem to lack either extrinsic motivation or intrinsic motivation. Comments such as "She just doesn't care about grades" or "He just doesn't like to read" ascribe poor motivation to a lack of desire or value.

First articulated by Feather (1982), motivation can be understood by looking at the interaction of two variables—expectancy for success and value. The theory can be understood as an equation: Motivation = Expectancy x Value. The first variable, expectancy, is how successful a person thinks he or she will be on a given task. A straight-A student will have a high expectancy for success. A student who struggles academically year after year will have a low expectancy. The second variable in the equation, value, is how much a person wants something. Value can be extrinsic—how much someone wants a good grade, an award, money, or attention. It can also be intrinsic—how much someone enjoys a sense of accomplishment, a job well done, or the task itself. If both factors are high, you will have a highly motivated individual. If either factor is low, you will have an individual who is not very motivated.

"Intervention O: Structured Reinforcement Systems" may be useful for suggestions on how to successfully implement and fade extrinsic motivation systems. Academic Assistance provides you with a menu of strategies for helping students succeed academically and in the process develop a stronger expectancy for success—an "I can do it" attitude.

Behavior and academics

Behavior and academic success are intricately interwoven: Academic frustration leads to behavioral problems, and poor behavioral choices often result in academic problems. Ascertaining which issue started first is like the chicken or egg dilemma. Regardless of which comes first, Academic Assistance is often a powerful behavioral intervention. If academic performance can be improved, a student's sullen or disruptive behaviors often dissipate, as motivation is fueled by a sense of growing competence. Students who manifest behavioral problems often benefit from Academic Assistance. Academic Assistance shifts attention away from misbehavior while providing an opportunity for positive interactions with adults and increased academic learning.

Before implementing academic assistance

Before embarking on this intervention, discuss your specific concerns and general goals for improvement with the student. Gather any relevant background information that may help in designing and implementing the intervention. As with any intervention, be sure you have contacted the student's parents to discuss the problem and have invited them to participate. Keep them informed of all aspects of the intervention plan.

While this intervention is laid out in a step-by-step format, it is important to use your professional judgment in adapting procedures to the situation and the needs of the student.

If academic performance can be improved, a student's sullen or disruptive behaviors often dissipate, as motivation is fueled by a sense of growing competence.

IMPLEMENTATION STEPS
Step 1: Identify concerns and establish a focus.

Defining the nature and scope of the concern provides essential information for developing a successful intervention.

A. Talk with staff members.

Aaron is an eighth-grade student who has been referred frequently to the after-school detention program. Aaron's English teacher, Mrs. Graham, has finally gone to the assistant principal, noting that she has never before had a student who made teaching so difficult. She indicates that Aaron pushes her buttons so hard she can barely tolerate him in class. Though Aaron is never openly defiant, he skirts the edge of insubordination constantly. He makes wisecracks at her expense. He disrupts class. He fidgets when he should be working, asks inappropriate questions at inopportune times, and does anything else but his assignments.

The assistant principal, Mr. Wagner, checks with his other teachers and learns that Aaron is a "Dr. Jekyll and Mr. Hyde" type. Two of his teachers see Aaron as a major problem, while four teachers find Aaron to be a "character"—"Oh, Aaron. He's got a mouth, but he's actually kind of fun to have in class." Mr. Wagner asks Mrs. Graham if Aaron could have an academic problem. Mrs. Graham replies, "He's just too bright for his own good. He'd rather cause problems than try to do the work. The work he does turn in isn't outstanding, but it's certainly acceptable."

B. Contact the student's parent(s) or guardian.

Before working with the student, take the following steps:

1. Discuss the problem.

Aaron's parents are contacted by Mr. Wagner. Aaron's mother indicates that her son's behavior has always been a source of complaints.

2. Discuss goals for improvement.

Mr. Wagner: (Asst. Principal)	What goals do you see for Aaron?
Aaron's mother:	I'd like to see him happier at school. He talks about wanting to go to Stanford, but at this rate we'll be lucky if he graduates from high school. Since Aaron was little, I've worried about his reading. I know his test scores are OK, but when he reads to his little sister, it's almost painful to listen to him. We just keep telling him how smart he is and how he could do better. I think he's frustrated.
Mr. Wagner:	Has Aaron ever been tested for help in reading?
Aaron's mother:	I've asked several times, but his other schools said that he reads too well to get any help.

Mr. Wagner notes that Aaron's behavioral difficulties seem to be chronic. With Aaron's aspirations to go to Stanford, Mr. Wagner knows that Aaron places a surprisingly high value on academic success. Mr. Wagner wonders if Aaron's aspirations are in conflict with possible reading problems.

3. Request parental permission to conduct an informal assessment of the student's academic needs and to develop a plan of assistance.

Academic Assistance may or may not involve instruction from a certified special education teacher. Whoever is involved in Academic Assistance, the plan will resemble an informal Individualized Education Plan (IEP). Out of general respect for the rights of families, it is important that parents be as involved in the process as they want to be. District or school policy should dictate whether parental permission is required for academic assessment. If in doubt, err on the side of clear communication and written permission from the parents. A sample completed permission form is shown in Sample Reproducible Form B1 on the following page.

Before meeting with parents, review Step 2: Develop a plan for conducting an informal academic assessment and identify the specific assessment strategies you plan to use. List these strategies on the form before obtaining parental permission to conduct an academic assessment.

> *Out of general respect for the rights of families, it is important that parents be as involved in the process as they want to be.*

Note: A copy of this form and other Academic Assistance forms are provided in the *Reproducible Materials* section at the end of this chapter and on the CD.

| **Mr. Wagner:** (Asst. Principal) | I appreciate the information you've shared. I'd like to help Aaron work on two goals: improving his grades and getting along better with his teachers. With your permission, I'd like to do a little informal academic assessment, and then we can plan from there. |

Step 2: Develop a plan for conducting an informal academic assessment.

A number of methods can be used to informally assess a student's ability to complete school-related tasks. Although standardized testing allows schools to evaluate the overall effectiveness of their programs, testing may not provide useful information for analyzing an individual student's ability to meet academic expectations in a particular classroom. Does the student know how to study for a test? Can the student monitor his own homework? Can the student

Sample Reproducible Form B1: *Parental Permission Form*

Parental Permission Form

Dear _Mrs. Mathison_ :

We would like to develop a plan to support _Aaron in his attempts to improve_ _his academic performance and interactions with teachers during_ _class._

To assist us in developing the most useful plan possible, we would like your permission to informally assess your child's academic skills and work habits. This process may include any or all of the following:

1. _conducting a teacher inventory_
2. _analyzing work samples_
3. _determining Oral Reading Fluency_
4. _working with Aaron one-to-one_

Please sign the slip below and return it to school by _November 10_ . As soon as the assessment has been completed, we will be in touch.

Thank you for your assistance.

Sincerely,

Mr. Wagner
Assistant Principal

- -

Jackson Middle School has my permission to informally assess _Aaron Mathison_ 's academic skills and work habits and to develop a plan of assistance.

_____   _____
Signed (Parent or Guardian)   Date

read assigned materials in a timely fashion? Does the student have needed skills, or does he compensate for deficiencies? These questions are better answered through informal academic assessments.

The following procedures are not intended to be a thorough diagnostic battery, but they can help determine whether a student has the skills and strategies needed to complete academic tasks. Select procedures that are relevant for the age and needs of the student as well as the requirements of the classroom.

A. Analyze information from Student Status Reports.

Teachers' perceptions are an invaluable part of an informal academic assessment. How often does the student complete his work? (Always? Usually? Sometimes? Rarely? Never?) Is the quality of the work satisfactory? Does the student perform well in one subject but struggle in another? Gather enough information to develop a clear picture of the student's daily performance (as measured in different classes at the secondary level, or different subjects or activities at the elementary level). Use the Student Status Report (Reproducible Form B2, p. 102) to identify the student's strengths and goals for improvement.

The Student Status Report can be customized with different variables. For example, instead of Period or Subject Area at the elementary level, you may wish to gather student performance information in traditional subjects, such as social studies, science, and PE. At a primary level, you may wish to gather information on how a student performs during math center work, project work, writing, and so on. Two versions of the form are provided in the reproducibles at the end of this chapter. Student Status Report, Version 2 (Reproducible Form B3 at the end of the chapter) is blank to allow customizing.

If the student has several teachers, give each teacher a separate form to maintain student confidentiality and to avoid having teachers influence one another. Consolidate all of the individual responses and analyze them. Can you identify specific subjects that cause difficulty? Do specific skills present roadblocks for the student? Does the student have problems with homework? Does the student have difficulty with tests? Does the student fail to participate in class? Is attendance or tardiness a continuing problem? Does the student have special difficulty in classes that require a lot of reading or writing? Does the degree of academic success seem to be related to behavior in class?

INTERVENTION

B

Reproducible Form B2: *Student Status Report (Version 1)*

Student Status Report (Version 1)

Student _____ Grade/Class _____ Staff Member Requesting Information _____ Date _____

Please complete performance ratings for this student. The information you provide will be used to help develop an individualized plan of assistance and match the student with appropriate interventions.	Period or Subject Area						
	1	2	3	4	5	6	7

Key: 5 = Always   Note:
      4 = Usually   A rating of 3 or below
      3 = Sometimes   indicates a problem or
      2 = Rarely   concern that warrants
      1 = Never   further follow-up.
  N/A = Not applicable

Student Performance	1	2	3	4	5	6	7
Academic Standing — List student's current grade using the values assigned on the report card (letter grades, ✓/+/-, etc.)							
Attends class regularly							
Punctual							
Cooperative							
Participates in class activities							
Stays on task							
Completes in-class assignments							
Completes homework							
Quality of work is satisfactory							
Passes tests							

Student strengths (list at least three):

List areas of concern:

Note: Please attach a representative sample of student work.

B. Analyze student work samples.

Ask teachers to attach a sample of the student's work to the inventory. If you are unfamiliar with the course content or the degree of competency the teacher expects from students, ask the teacher to include work samples by an excellent student and an average student for comparison.

Work samples can provide the interventionist with information that may not be evident from standardized tests. For example, the student may read and comprehend well enough to pass multiple-choice reading tests but lack the organizational skills to summarize a passage in writing. The student may have the skills to research and write a report, but she may lack time-management strategies for completing the work on schedule. A work sample may indicate that the student lacks basic skills. For example, the student may perform well verbally but have trouble putting thoughts down on paper due to poor handwriting or typing skills.

C. Collect oral reading fluency data.

As a multidimensional skill, reading can be assessed in many ways and at many levels. It is beyond the scope of this intervention to outline a detailed diagnostic battery; however, you should test oral reading fluency as a preliminary step toward determining whether reading problems contribute to an academic problem.

Though constrained in scope, oral reading fluency as a measure of both the rate and the accuracy of a student's reading is an extremely powerful screener: "The most salient characteristic of skillful readers is the speed and effortlessness with which they seem able to breeze through text" (Adams, 1990, p. 409). Although fluency alone is not sufficient for reading with understanding, it is clearly a necessary prerequisite for understanding, interpreting, and responding to print.

- Fluency allows but does not guarantee that readers can construct meaning. If students must search for appropriate words—self-correcting, inserting, omitting, misreading, and sounding out words—comprehension suffers. When mental energy is heavily invested in figuring out the words, readers have a difficult time understanding and responding to text.

- Fluency allows but does not guarantee that readers will be motivated to read. If a student reads accurately but laboriously, it is difficult for her to grasp important concepts and ideas. If text moves slowly, it's much like watching a movie in slow motion: the message becomes distorted and attention tends to wander. Students who lack fluency often become bored with reading.

If students must search for appropriate words—self-correcting, inserting, omitting, misreading, and sounding out words—comprehension suffers. When mental energy is heavily invested in figuring out the words, readers have a difficult time understanding and responding to text.

INTERVENTION

B

- Fluency allows but does not guarantee that readers can read strategically (i.e., adjusting the way they read depending on the purpose and the type of material being read).

Fluent readers quickly skim through text when material is familiar and read deeply when new, important, or difficult information is presented. Students who haven't developed into fluent readers are unable to adjust their reading strategies to the materials and the purpose of their reading.

Thus, though fluency does not guarantee good comprehension, it certainly plays a critical role in facilitating timely completion of assignments.

Choose passages representative of the level of difficulty normally encountered in the class.

INTERVENTION

B

Oral Reading Fluency, Assessment Procedures

DIBELS

If your school or district makes use of DIBELS (Dynamic Indicators of Basic Early Literacy Skills), examine the student's DIBELS data to determine whether the student is meeting benchmark. DIBELS is a set of standardized, individually administered measures of early literacy development—short (one-minute) fluency measures used to regularly monitor the development of pre-reading and early reading skills. The measures build on the essential early literacy domains discussed in reports by the National Reading Panel (2000) and National Research Council (1998) and assess phonological awareness, alphabetic understanding, and fluency. To learn more about DIBELS, visit the program's home page at the University of Oregon web site, http://dibels.uoregon. edu.

Curriculum Based Measurement Procedures

Curriculum Based Measurement procedures can also be used to collect oral reading fluency data. This data can help you determine whether the student has adequate basic reading skills.

1. Select two passages, each approximately 250 words in length, from grade-level reading. The passages may be taken from a basal reading text or from other reading material that will be used in the class. Choose unpracticed passages—passages that the student hasn't yet read. Choose passages representative of the level of difficulty normally encountered in the class. Choose cohesive passages that have a

clear beginning point and a reasonable message. Avoid passages with an unusual number of difficult words or hard-to-pronounce names.

2. You will need a stopwatch and two copies of each passage—a clear copy from which the student can read and a scoring copy. Time the student for one minute on each passage, marking any incorrect words on the scoring copy. When assessing the student, follow the procedures listed on the following page for each of the two passages.

3. Score each of the passages by counting only the words read correctly in one minute and then averaging the two scores.

4. To interpret student performance scores, use the curriculum-based norms shown on page 107. These norms were derived in 2004 from thousands of students in grades 1 to 8. The sample included students from general education programs and students who were participating in compensatory, remedial, and special education programs.

The norms provide rough guidelines for determining adequate reading fluency. As shown, a student who reads about 50 words correct per minute or better from beginning second-grade materials in the fall of second grade is making adequate progress. However, a third-grade student who reads about 50 words correct per minute from third-grade materials has fairly severe reading difficulties.

Unfortunately, norms are not available for older students; however, some liberty can be taken in extrapolating from the norms that do exist. One can safely assume that by high school, students should read somewhere above 150 words per minute. (There is a point at which the rate of oral reading is no longer relevant. Due to rate of speech, some variance in acceptable oral reading rates above 150 words per minute is likely.) If in doubt, it may be useful to assess two or three capable students for comparison with the target student.

Note: Students scoring below the 50th percentile using the average scores of two unpracticed grade-level materials need a basic decoding and fluency program.

INTERVENTION

B

Oral Reading Fluency
Procedures
(continued)

Curriculum Based Measurement Procedures for Assessing and Scoring Oral Reading Fluency

Say to the student: "When I say 'start,' begin reading aloud at the top of this page. Read across the page (demonstrate by pointing). Try to read each word. If you come to a word you don't know, I'll tell it to you. Be sure to do your best reading. Are there any questions?"

Say, "Start."

Follow along on your copy of the story, marking the words that are read incorrectly. If a student stops or struggles with a word for 3 seconds, tell the student the word and mark it as incorrect.

Place a vertical line after the last word read and thank the student.

The following guidelines determine which words are to be counted as correct or incorrect:

1. *Words read correctly*. Words read correctly are those words that are pronounced correctly given the reading context.
   a) The word "read" must be pronounced "reed" when presented in the context of "He will read the book," not as "red."
   b) Repetitions are not counted as incorrect.
   c) Self-corrections within 3 seconds are counted as correctly read words.

2. *Words read incorrectly*. The following types of errors are counted: (a) mispronunciations, (b) substitutions, and (c) omissions. Further, words not read within 3 seconds are counted as errors.
   a) Mispronunciations are words that are misread: "dog" for "dig."
   b) Substitutions are words that are substituted for the stimulus word; this is often inferred with a one-to-one correspondence between the word orders: "dog" for "cat."
   c) Omissions are words skipped or not read; if a student skips an entire line, each word is counted as an error.

3. *Three-second rule*. If a student is struggling to pronounce a word or hesitates for 3 seconds, the student is told the word, and it is counted as an error.

Source: Reprinted with permission from Shinn, M.R. (Ed.).(1989). Curriculum-based measurement: Assessing special children (pp. 239-240). New York: The Guilford Press.

2005 Hasbrouck & Tindal Oral Reading Fluency Data

This table shows the oral reading fluency rates of students in grades 1 through 8 as determined by Hasbrouck and Tindal's data.

Grade	Percentile	Fall WCPM*	Winter WCPM*	Spring WCPM*
1	90		81	111
	70		47	82
	50		23	53
	25		12	28
	10		6	15
2	90	106	125	142
	75	79	100	117
	50	51	72	89
	25	25	42	61
	10	11	18	31
3	90	128	146	162
	75	99	120	137
	50	71	92	107
	25	44	62	78
	10	21	36	48
4	90	145	166	180
	75	119	139	152
	50	94	112	123
	25	68	87	98
	10	45	61	72
5	90	166	182	194
	75	139	156	168
	50	110	127	139
	25	85	99	109
	10	61	74	83
6	90	177	195	204
	75	153	167	177
	50	127	140	150
	25	98	111	122
	10	68	82	93
7	90	180	192	202
	75	156	165	177
	50	128	136	150
	25	102	109	123
	10	79	88	98
8	90	185	199	199
	75	161	173	177
	50	133	146	151
	25	106	115	124
	10	77	84	97

*WCPM = Words Correct Per Minute

From Hasbrouck, J., & Tindal, G. (2005). *Oral reading fluency: 90 years of measurement* (Technical Report No. 33). Eugene, OR: University of Oregon, College of Education, Behavioral Research and Teaching.

Working one-to-one with a student makes it easier to identify the student's strengths and weaknesses.

D. Use an informal reading inventory.

If a more detailed assessment seems necessary, consider administering one of the many published inventories available, such as the Analytical Reading Inventory (ARI) by Woods and Moe (2006). The ARI helps ascertain whether the student can retain information that has been read, determine the meaning of vocabulary, and engage in higher-order thinking about information presented in both narrative and expository passages. The ARI includes an array of subtests that examine general levels of word recognition, word recognition strategies, and comprehension strategies through retellings and questions. ARI terms for oral and silent reading performance and listening comprehension are reported as "independent, instructional, and frustration levels." Used with an oral reading fluency measure, inventories such as the ARI can provide valuable assessment information.

E. Work one-to-one with the student on an assignment.

When a student has difficulty completing assignments or completing assignments satisfactorily, have the student work on an assignment one-to-one with an adult. It may be useful to have the student redo an assignment that was not completed satisfactorily or was incomplete. Working one-to-one with a student makes it easier to identify the student's strengths and weaknesses. Hesitation or avoidance will make it more apparent when the student is unsure of how to proceed. One-to-one assistance provides the opportunity to observe closely and ask the student to clarify his understanding of expectations and strategies for working through the task.

When working one-to-one with the student, keep the following questions in mind:

Does the student understand the instructions?

For an assignment involving written instructions, try to determine whether the student understands the instructions without further clarification from an adult.

Does the student possess the prerequisite skills necessary to complete the assignment?

If the assignment involves writing, consider whether the student possesses the skills necessary to complete the assignment. Does the student have the handwriting and spelling skills he needs to write fluently without losing his train of thought? If the assignment involves three-digit multiplication, determine whether the student is able to line up numbers accurately, whether the student knows multiplication facts, whether he accurately records numbers in the correct place, and so on.

Does the student have effective strategies for completing the assignment?

If the student is studying for a spelling test, determine whether the student has a strategy for systematically learning how to spell words. If the assignment involves math story problems, determine whether the student possesses strategies for writing and solving equations. If the assignment includes essay questions, try to determine whether the student has the required knowledge, knows how to find the required knowledge, and can articulate and write a reasonable response.

Is the student able to stay on task for extended periods of time?

When the student appears to have the needed skills but simply lacks the ability or motivation to stay on task, see "Intervention M: Teaching Replacement Behavior" or "Intervention O: Structured Reinforcement Systems."

F. Select procedures that are useful, manageable, and age appropriate.

The more information obtained from various sources, contexts, and informal assessments, the greater the likelihood that a clear picture will emerge of the student's abilities and weaknesses. However, the need for information should be balanced with the importance of creating an intervention plan as quickly as possible. Select procedures that will provide enough information to develop an appropriate plan of Academic Assistance within a reasonable period of time.

Mr. Wagner decides that the Student Status Report (Reproducible Form B2) is an important tool because Aaron has several teachers. He also decides to collect work samples, conduct an oral reading fluency assessment, and set up a one-to-one work period.

INTERVENTION

B

G. Prepare or collect any materials necessary to complete the assessment.

> Mr. Wagner selects two passages for Aaron to read—one from his geography text and another from a novel used in his English class. Aaron has not previously read either passage. Mr. Wagner also obtains a blank copy of a geography assignment that Aaron did not complete.

Step 3: Conduct the assessment.

First complete the components of the informal assessment that do not require working directly with the student.

> Mr. Wagner routes copies of the Student Status Report to each of Aaron's teachers, along with a brief note of explanation. Once the surveys are returned, he compiles one master copy with everyone's responses (see Sample Reproducible Form B2).

Once the master version of the Student Status Report is completed, analyze responses to determine any patterns of specific strengths and weaknesses.

> Given the varied responses from Aaron's teachers, Mr. Wagner notes the following:
> 1. Aaron cooperates only in classes in which his grades are good.
> 2. Participation in class seems to be good across subjects.
> 3. Homework seems to be a problem in all classes.
> 4. Quality of work is a problem only in geography and English.
> 5. Tests present a minor problem.
>
> Aaron does fairly well in Spanish, physical science, math, and PE. However, he has major academic and behavioral difficulties in geography and English. These classes have the heaviest reading and writing requirements. Work samples confirm that Aaron seems to have difficulty handling assignments that require writing. Work is incomplete and nearly illegible when extensive writing is required. Mr. Wagner suspects that Aaron is a capable student with underdeveloped skills.

Sample Reproducible Form B2: *Student Status Report (Version 1)*

Student Status Report (Version 1)

Aaron Mathison	*8*	*Mr. Wagner*	*11/15*
Student	Grade/Class	Staff Member Requesting Information	Date

Please complete performance ratings for this student. The information you provide will be used to help develop an individualized plan of assistance and match the student with appropriate interventions.

Key: 5 = Always
4 = Usually
3 = Sometimes
2 = Rarely
1 = Never
N/A = Not applicable

Note: A rating of 3 or below indicates a problem or concern that warrants further follow-up.

Student Performance	Period or Subject Area						
	1 Math	2 Geography	3 P.E.	4 Lunch	5 English	6 Spanish	7 Physical Science
Academic Standing — List student's current grade using the values assigned on the report card (letter grades, ✓/+/-, etc.)	B-	D-	A-	NA	F	C	B
Attends class regularly	5	5	5	NA	5	5	5
Punctual	5	5	5	NA	5	5	5
Cooperative	5	3	5	NA	2	4	5
Participates in class activities	4	3	5	NA	3	4	5
Stays on task	4	2	5	NA	2	4	4
Completes in-class assignments	5	2	5	NA	2	4	5
Completes homework	3	1	NA	NA	1	1	4
Quality of work is satisfactory	5	1	5	NA	1	5	5
Passes tests	5	3	5	NA	3	5	5

Student strengths (list at least three):

Math: Aaron is very good conceptually in math. He could be getting an "A" in math; however, he got a "C" last term because he didn't turn in his math notebook. All he had to do was keep his papers throughout the term.
Geography: Aaron participates well during class discussions.
P.E.: Aaron does well in P.E. He cooperates and often helps other students.
Spanish: Aaron does well in Spanish. He participates and is cooperative.

List areas of concern:

Geography: Aaron needs to improve his classroom behavior, to work on homework completion, and to improve his test scores. English: Aaron has to work on his behavior so that he can get his work done, both in class and at home. Cooperation is his biggest problem. Spanish: The only reason he doesn't have a better grade is missing homework. Physical Science: Aaron has a good conceptual understanding and participates in class. He could easily get an "A" if he does well on the next couple of tests.

Note: Please attach a representative sample of student work.

A blank version of this form is available on p. 102.

A. Meet with the student to complete the assessment.

I. Review the concerns and overall goals with the student.

Mr. Wagner: **(Asst. Principal)**	Aaron, thanks for coming today. Do you remember the problem we talked about a few weeks ago?
Aaron:	Yeah, "Mrs. Grammar" had some problems about my mouth.
Mr. Wagner:	Right. Since then I've spoken with your mother and teachers. I'd like to see if we can help you figure out why you're having problems in some of your classes. Then we can work on some things to help you get along better and also improve your grades.

2. Conduct the assessment.

When conducting the informal assessment, help the student relax as much as possible.

Mr. Wagner: **(Asst. Principal)**	Aaron, I understand that you do very well in most of your classes. We need to figure out what's going on in the others. I'd like to listen to you read, and then I'll work with you on a geography assignment. The assignment won't be graded, but when we're done, I'll do some thinking about things we might work on. Then we'll get back together to work out a plan.

B. Analyze the results.

Mr. Wagner finds that Aaron reads 101 words correctly per minute on average with the two passages. Mr. Wagner compares Aaron's rate to the Oral Reading Fluency Norms (p. 107) and notes that Aaron is reading at a rate between other eighth graders at the 10th percentile and 25th percentile. This score suggests that Aaron is an inadequate reader. Mr. Wagner also notes that Aaron's reading does not sound fluent. Though they were not counted as errors, Aaron makes 11 self-corrections in one passage and 8 in the second, and he frequently repeats himself. (To double-check his perceptions, Mr. Wagner has another student read the same passage. This straight-A student averages 192 words correct per minute with a clear qualitative and quantitative difference.)

Working with Aaron on the geography assignment, Mr. Wagner notes that Aaron becomes very distracted when the task is introduced. Though the textbook is provided, Aaron does not use it. His written answers are poorly developed in somewhat illegible printing. Aaron forms the letters correctly; however, he begins writing at the end of each letter, and from the bottom rather than the top. After Aaron has completed four of the eight questions in writing, Mr. Wagner asks Aaron if he would like to dictate his answers to the last four questions. Mr. Wagner notes that Aaron's verbal answers are fully developed and reflect higher order thinking.

C. Summarize student strengths and weaknesses using the Academic Assistance Form.

Using information from the Student Status Reports, the oral reading assessment, work samples, and the one-to-one work with Aaron, Mr. Wagner summarizes Aaron's strengths and weaknesses on part A of the Academic Assistance Form, as shown on Sample Reproducible Form B4 on page 114.

D. Target specific areas in which assistance can be provided.

After completing the informal academic assessment, Mr. Wagner consults with Aaron's mother by phone. They decide that Aaron needs more help with English and geography. Homework completion is targeted as a short-range goal, and two long-range goals include improving reading fluency and handwriting.

Step 4: Consider and plan for remediation options.

Basic skills or tool skills are abilities that students need to access content and demonstrate knowledge. Tool skills allow students to function as independent learners. Adaptation strategies may be necessary to help students who lack these basics. Unfortunately, adaptation strategies alone will not provide students with the means to function independently. Some form of remediation is often required.

Tool skills include:
- **Reading fluency.** Though reading fluency alone is not sufficient for understanding text, without adequate reading fluency a stu-

Sample Reproducible Form B4: *Academic Assistance (One-Page Form)*

Academic Assistance (One-Page Form)

Aaron Mathison	*8*	*Mrs. Thompson*	*12/7*
Student	Grade/Class	Teacher	Date

A. Informal assessment information

1. Oral Reading Fluency: ___*101*___ words correct per minute

   Materials: *Geography text, The Red Pony*

2. Strengths and weaknesses:

	Subjects	Abilities	Behavior
Strengths	Math P.E. Physical Science Spanish	Verbal Strong conceptually Comprehension	Cooperation and partici- pation in subjects he is doing well in
Weaknesses	Geography English	Writing Handwriting Reading Fluency Homework	No cooperation in class- es he is not doing well in

B. Remediation

1. *Reading fluency tutorial during homeroom: Corrective Reading Decoding B Program*

2. *Daily handwriting practice (at home, supervised by his mother) with district-developed program*

C. The Adaptation Process

Use the outline below as an optional framework for developing a plan of Academic Assistance.

1. Identify assignments or activities that haven't yet been given.
2. Anticipate problems that the student (and other students) may encounter.
3. Design whole-class instruction to prevent anticipated problems.
4. Consider making assignments more manageable by providing additional assistance.
5. Consider alternative ways for the student to demonstrate knowledge or ability.
6. Gradually fade the adaptations as the student gains competence.

D. The Adaptation Menu

Adaptation involves a never-ending variety of procedures. The strategies that follow are provided as suggestions but are not exhaustive. Discuss and brainstorm other possibilities.

1. Focus assignments on essential course content and skills.
2. Focus test items on essential course content and skills.
3. Build cumulative review of essential objectives into subsequent units of instruction.
4. Construct and use framed outlines.
5. Design and use interactive graphic organizers.
6. Identify and preteach essential vocabulary words.
7. Highlight textbooks and printed materials.
8. Transcribe or summarize highlighted text.
9. Provide two-column study guides.
10. Provide framed writing assignments.
11. Teach the students to manage their homework.

E. Attach a summary of the Academic Assistance Plan.

F. Schedule a follow-up meeting.

12/8, 3:15--to review highlighting
12/12, 3:15--to review the plan

dent cannot adequately access meaning, nor keep up with the quantity of reading that may be required.

- Spelling. When a student must frequently interrupt writing to struggle with or invent spelling, he has difficulty maintaining his train of thought.

- Handwriting. Difficulties with handwriting present a major obstacle for many classroom assignments and activities. Even note-taking is a burden. While other students are writing and thinking simultaneously, the student with handwriting problems falls behind and is soon lost.

If tool skills are a problem, remediation should be considered. Consult with a special education teacher or reading specialist. Sometimes this is appropriate as part of an Individualized Education Plan. However, when a student is not eligible for special education services, other possibilities, such as small-group instruction in the classroom or a tutorial, should be explored. By discussing the possibilities with building or district specialists, it may be possible to set up programs that not only help the student to be successful through greater assistance and adaptation, but also provide the student with skills needed to become independent.

Mr. Wagner decides to discuss Aaron's fluency problems with the special education teacher and school psychologist. After reviewing Aaron's records, they both agree that Aaron will not qualify for special education. They also agree that without specific work on reading fluency and handwriting, Aaron will continue to struggle academically. The special education teacher suggests that Aaron work in Science Research Associates' (SRA) *Corrective Reading Decoding B* program. Because Aaron's academic problems are relatively minor, the special education teacher believes that she can train a student to work with Aaron, but stresses that he will need to work in the program five days a week. Mr. Wagner decides to try to set up tutoring with an older student during Aaron's advisory period. The special education teacher agrees to teach Aaron and the tutor how to work in the program. It is also decided that Aaron's handwriting can be improved by using a district-developed program. As practice is presented systematically, they decide to see whether Aaron's mother can supervise his daily handwriting practice.

Step 5: Consider adaptation options.

When students are struggling in general education courses, adaptations should also be considered. Appropriate adaptations do not water down the curriculum. Ideally, adaptations benefit many students—not only the student who has been targeted for assistance. Any adaptations you make for one student may be useful to do with a small group.

Adaptation focuses students' attention on the essentials of a course. The teacher adjusts instruction and the pacing and content of assignments so that all students can learn. Adaptation is a problem-solving process rather than a specific set of procedures, as it is applicable to a multitude of content areas, grade levels, and student skill levels.

If a student has experienced academic failure that is related to skill deficits, some form of adaptation will be necessary. Adaptation may be useful with students who have been identified as needing special education services as well as those who have not. While working with students on curriculum adaptations, provide instruction on skills needed for long-term success.

While working with students on curriculum adaptations, provide instruction on skills needed for long-term success.

A. Familiarize yourself with the Adaptation Process.

1. Identify assignments and activities that will be assigned in coming weeks.

   All too often, assistance comes to students after they have already failed. By then, students may be burdened by negative emotional responses to the learning activity. Knowing in advance what students must master creates an opportunity to prevent student failure and the concomitant negative associations.

2. Anticipate problems that the targeted student (and other students) may encounter.

   Targeting potentially difficult assignments and activities in advance allows education professionals to anticipate likely problems. For example, there are usually some students who fail to complete a long-term project on time—some have difficulty selecting a manageable project, while others have difficulty seeing the project through to completion. Worksheet assignments may pose problems, as some students may have difficulty following instructions, lack the reading skills to understand the questions, or lack the skills to find the answers.

3. Design whole-class instruction to prevent anticipated problems.

Whole-class instruction can often prevent anticipated difficulties. For example, if several students do not take useful class notes, structured lessons on note-taking can increase the skill proficiency of all students while teaching lower-performing students to take adequate notes. If several students are unable to write a report, have the whole class collectively complete brief reports prior to working independently on a longer report. In Math, 5 to 10 minutes spent each day "thinking out loud" and working through a problem-solving process can help all students become more proficient with word problems. Whole-class instruction can be very powerful for all students in a classroom. Involve students actively by creating frequent opportunities for them to respond. Students should be active participants, not passive recipients. Ask questions, present practice problems, give ungraded quizzes, have students work with a partner—these are just a few examples of keeping all students actively engaged in whole-class instruction.

4. Consider making assignments more manageable by providing additional assistance and/or adjusting the length and complexity of assignments.

Assignments that are worthwhile to most students may be threatening to the student who is falling behind. While a well-trained marathon runner might eagerly face the challenge of a 26-mile run, most armchair athletes would know better than to attempt it—or would drop from sheer exhaustion on the course. For students prone to procrastinating, quitting, or simply running out of steam, adapting assignments may provide enough support so that their internal response when approaching a task is, "Oh, I can do that," rather than, "It's hopeless. I'm frustrated. I hate it." Assignments are productive only if they are manageable for all students.

One way to make assignments more manageable is to provide additional assistance. Extra support and guidance can make assignments and activities easier for a student. Additional assistance is provided when the teacher works with a small group of students while others work independently. Additional assistance can also be attained through partner work, or with help from tutors, assistants, volunteers, and parents.

Adjusting the length and complexity of assignments can also make them more manageable. The teacher can make a task manageable by narrowing the focus of student efforts to the most essential skills and knowledge. The goal is to reduce the demands of the task without losing the most important aspects of the assignment. For example, if students are required

Whole-class instruction can often prevent anticipated difficulties.

INTERVENTION

B

to write a report using three sources, an adjusted assignment might require only one source. If a story-writing assignment includes a prewriting activity, a rough draft, editing, and a final draft, it could be simplified by having someone type the final draft. Adjusting a worksheet assignment might mean having students complete only 8 of 10 items, selected for their importance to the unit of study.

5. Consider alternative ways for the student to demonstrate knowledge or ability.

Alternative response forms are often necessary for students with specific disabilities. For example, students who are sight impaired or reading disabled might require voice-recorded texts and oral exams. Alternative response forms may also be necessary when a student shows a deficiency in a basic skill. For students capable of learning a skill, adjust the way they will demonstrate their knowledge and abilities until remediation allows them to handle the regular assignment.

Though alternative response forms enable students to succeed, they should not be considered sufficient. For example, students who lack the handwriting and spelling skills to answer essay questions in writing might be allowed to dictate responses until their skills improve. These students should also receive spelling instruction and remedial handwriting or keyboarding instruction to help them improve in those areas.

6. Gradually fade the adaptations as the student gains competence.

Fading can be accomplished by slowly reducing special supports and adjustments. Maintain gains by frequently emphasizing the student's accomplishments and periodically revisiting strategies learned.

B. Consider selecting or modifying strategies from the Adaptation Menu.

Following are suggested adaptation strategies to help students meet the academic requirements of the regular classroom. The Adaptation Menu (Reproducible Form B4 or B5, Part D, and Figure B1) is by no means exhaustive, but it provides a place to start. Each strategy suggested must be tailored to the course content as well as to the age and ability level of the students. Many other options can arise from the Adaptation Process and the teacher's specific expectations.

Figure B1: *The Adaptation Menu*

> Adaptation involves an endless variety of procedures. Discuss adaptations that may be applicable and brainstorm other possibilities.
>
> 1. Focus assignments on essential course content and skills.
> 2. Focus test items on essential course content and skills.
> 3. Build cumulative review of essential objectives into subsequent units of instruction.
> 4. Construct and use framed outlines.
> 5. Design and use interactive graphic organizers.
> 6. Identify and preteach essential vocabulary words.
> 7. Highlight textbooks and printed materials.
> 8. Transcribe or summarize highlighted text.
> 9. Provide two-column study guides.
> 10. Provide framed writing assignments.
> 11. Teach students to manage their homework.

Adaptation Strategy 1: Focus assignments on essential course content and skills.

Description

Not all instructional content is equally important. Plan to target content that is most important for student success, elements of which are probably defined by state or district standards. This strategy involves marking the essential content of assignments to separate it from nonessential content. Eighty percent of an assignment should reflect what students must know and be able to do. Once assignments are marked, teach students to complete the marked items first and finish the remainder of the assignment as time allows. Although students should be required to complete the entire assignment and should be graded accordingly, focusing students on the most important parts of an assignment can increase students' opportunity for success. (This procedure assumes that 90% to 100% is an A grade, 80% to 89% is a B, and so on. If the school uses a different scale, such as 92% to 100% is an A, 84% to 91% is a B, and so on, the procedures should be adjusted.)

Rationale and uses

The process of identifying the 80 percent of the assignment that focuses on essential course content and skills provides teachers with a tool for analyzing the usefulness of the assignment. Sometimes assignments place a heavy emphasis on nonessential objectives. If this occurs, the assignment can be partially rewritten so that at least 80 percent of the assignment reflects the teacher's learning expectations.

Marking the most important part of the assignment can also be used to reduce a task for students at risk of failure. Even though the assigned work load may be reduced, the strategy allows students the opportunity to earn a legitimate grade. An 80 percent focus includes room for error but does not preclude the option of doing well. Some students build enough positive momentum on the first 80 percent of an assignment to keep them motivated through the full assignment. Should students run out of time or effort, their energies will have been spent on the most important part of the assignment.

Procedures

- On selected assignments, circle the 80 percent of the items that represent essential course objectives.

- If more than 20 percent of the items represent nonessential learning, revise items or consider an alternative assignment.

- Teach the students who have difficulty completing assignments to begin with the circled items and to finish the remainder as time allows.

Additional adaptations

If students are not able to read or write answers, consider having these students dictate their responses to another student, a teacher assistant, or classroom volunteer. Unless disabled, students should be graded on the full 100 percent of assignments. If a student is identified as a special education student, consult the student's IEP.

Example: INTERMEDIATE AND SECONDARY LEVELS

Figure B2 shows a worksheet on animal behavior. In this example, the teacher found that only 13 out of 20 points (65 percent of the assignment) was congruent with essential course objectives. When assignments do not align, revise the assignment by reallocating the point distribution of various items, revise selected items, or create a new assignment by using only selected items. In Figure B2 the teacher has replaced items 1c and 2d with new questions. With these revisions, the circled items represent 16 out of 20 points, or 80 percent of the assignment.

Conclusion

By marking the 80 percent of an assignment that represents the most essential course content and skills, teachers offer at-risk students manageable assignments that focus their attention on the most important course objectives.

Figure B2: *Focused Assignment*

Animal Behavior Assignment

Name: _____

1. **Write a sentence using the following words. Each sentence is worth 2 points.**

   2 (a.) behavior

   2 (b.) acquired behavior

   2 (c.) ~~cochlea~~ *change to "reflex"*

   2 (d.) conditioning

   2 (e.) inborn behavior

2. **Multiple Choice. Underline the correct word. Each item is worth 1 point.**

   1 (a.) A(n) (*reflexact, instinct, conditioned response*) is one kind of acquired behavior.

   b. The (*optic nerve, auditory nerve, spinal cord*) connects the eye to the brain.

   c. The (*color, body structure, migration*) of birds is controlled by an internal living clock.

   Replace with "(Reasoning, Conditioning, Instinct) is the ability to
   1 (d.) ~~A (queen, drone, worker) produces eggs that develop into new bees.~~
   remember past experience and use it to solve a problem."

   e. If an animal population becomes too large, the individual's territory will likely (*increase, decrease, remain the same*).

3. **Completion. Each item is worth 1 point.**

   1 (a.) Saliva produced in the mouth of a dog at the sound of a bell is a(n) _____ response.

   b. Eardrums in a grasshopper are located on the insect's _____.

   1 (c.) Training a dog to sit on command is an example of _____ behavior.

   1 (d.) _____ is a change in behavior that results from experience.

   1 (e.) A rat may learn not to eat poison through trial and _____.

Adaptation Strategy 2: Focus test items on essential course content and skills.

Description

Mark tests to identify the 80 percent of items that represent the most essential course objectives. Teach students at risk of poor grades to begin with the identified items and to complete the remainder of the test as time allows.

Rationale and uses

When students begin a test by answering items that assess essential course objectives, it increases the likelihood that they will be successful. When students begin successfully, they build positive momentum to complete the remainder of the test.

The process of identifying essential course content and skills allows the teacher to evaluate whether the test places too much emphasis on nonessential objectives. If it does, the test can be partially rewritten or an alternative test developed.

Procedures

- Select or develop a test in advance of instruction.

- Identify the 80 percent of the test that reflects essential course objectives.

- The remaining 20 percent of the test can be composed of items that reflect nonessential learning and challenge questions.

- If 80 percent of the test does not test important objectives, rewrite the test to weight important items more heavily, or select an alternative test.

- Create many opportunities to master important course information and skills during instruction and through assignments.

- Teach students who have difficulty taking tests to begin with the identified items and then complete the remaining items as time allows.

Additional adaptations

If students are not able to read or write answers, they may be given an oral test. Unless disabled, students should be graded on the full 100 percent of tests. If a student is identified as a special education student, consult the student's IEP.

Example

In Figure B3, the teacher has underlined 16 points out of 20, or 80 percent of the test. These items evaluate objectives the teacher has emphasized during class time and through assignments.

Figure B3: *Focused Test*

Quiz: Compromise of 1850

Name: _____ Date: _____

| 18-20 points = A | 16-17 points = B | 14-15 points = C | 12-13 points = D |

Write "North" or "South" by each of the statements below.

1. (**1**) _____ There were many small farms where farmers raised grain, hay, and livestock.

2. (**1**) _____ There were very few large cities or factories.

3. (1) _____ People wanted to put a tax on imported goods.

4. (**1**) _____ Threatened to leave the Union.

Short answer (on your own paper)

5. (**2**) You would like to get a dog. Your parents do not want a pet. Write a compromise to this problem.

6. (**1**) What event forced Congress to deal with the differences between the North and the South over slavery?

7. (**2**+1) List three things the North won in the Compromise of 1850.

8. (**1**+1) Explain why the North and South differed over the issue of slavery.

9. (1) Why was Webster willing to compromise over the issue of slavery?

10. (**1**) What did the Fugitive Slave Law require?

Fill in the blank and short answer.

11. (**1**) Southerners threatened to _____ from the Union over the issue of slavery.

12. (**1**) The Compromise of 1850 allowed the North and South _____ years to settle their differences.

13. (**1**) What was likely to happen if a state had tried to secede in 1850?

14. (**2**) Why is compromise important?

15. (**1**) Is compromise always the best answer to a problem? Why or why not? (Opinion)

Courses that include cumulative review are structured for success.

Conclusion

Marking the 80 percent of a test that reflects important course objectives helps to ensure that, if students have completed their assignments and participated in class, they have an opportunity for success. This simple procedure helps teachers focus their instruction and assignments and helps students demonstrate their knowledge and abilities.

Adaptation Strategy 3: Build cumulative review of essential objectives into subsequent units of instruction.

Description

When course content requires maintenance of skills, knowledge, and concepts, cumulative review is a critical factor in academic success—especially for those at risk of academic failure. Courses that include midterms and finals as well as certain subject areas, such as beginning reading, math, or a foreign language, require maintenance of skills, knowledge, and concepts across time. For these courses and subject areas, review should be cumulative—frequent, systematic, and planned.

Rationale and uses

Courses that include cumulative review are structured for success. When students need academic intervention, the structure of these courses makes it possible for a parent, tutor, or interventionist to help a student gradually prepare for midterm and final exams.

Procedures

- Identify essential course objectives for a unit, a term, then a semester.

- Develop or modify unit tests to reflect the cumulative review schedule.

- Develop or modify assignments to reflect the cumulative review schedule.

- Develop midterms and final exams such that 80 to 85 percent of the point value covers essential objectives from the course.

Additional adaptations

After each unit, all students can be given a review sheet that lists the unit's essential objectives. If a student is receiving assistance from someone other than the classroom teacher, review outside of class time can be targeted and productive.

Example: SECONDARY LEVEL

A possible schedule of review for tests and assignments is shown below. In this high-school example, the schedule includes new objectives for the unit, advanced objectives for the unit, and cumulative review of previously learned objectives. An elementary Math example might include only new and review objectives.

High School Cumulative Review Schedule

Unit 1:   80% of the point value covers essential objectives from Unit 1

20% of the point value covers advanced objectives from Unit 1

Unit 2:   60% of the point value covers essential objectives from Unit 2

20% of the point value covers advanced objectives from Unit 2

20% of the point value cumulatively reviews essential objectives from Unit 1

Unit 3:   60% of the point value covers essential objectives from Unit 3

20% of the point value covers advanced objectives from Unit 3

20% of the point value cumulatively reviews essential objectives from Units 1 and 2

Unit 4:   60% of the point value covers essential objectives from Unit 4

20% of the point value covers advanced objectives from Unit 4

20% of the point value cumulatively reviews essential objectives from Units 1 through 3

Continue the pattern with subsequent units.

When learning can be distributed across time and is continuously reviewed, all students have a high probability of success.

INTERVENTION

B

Conclusion

Once teachers have clearly identified essential course objectives and a classroom system for ongoing review, larger numbers of students can be successful without further adaptation. When learning can be distributed across time and is continuously reviewed, all students have a high probability of success. Students at risk of academic failure have an opportunity to improve.

Adaptation Strategy 4: Construct and use framed outlines.

Description

A framed outline provides students with a tool for understanding, recording, and reviewing important course content. A framed outline organizes information, while providing students with a tool for taking notes. Framed outlines can be used across grade levels with all students who are skilled enough to write. As instructional tools, these materials can also be used to increase student engagement in combination with almost any class activity—lectures, discussion, demonstrations, video, role plays, brainstorming sessions, simulations, reading assignments, and so on.

Rationale and uses

Framed outlines serve many purposes for teachers and students. A framed outline provides an organizing tool for course information. When lively, but divergent, conversations occur in class, a framed outline can help instructors bring the focus of instruction back to essential course objectives.

Framed outlines are also a valuable tool for students. The interactive outline increases engagement and focuses attention on important learning during class time. Outside of class time, the outline can be reused to retrieve and review essential learning.

Framed outlines may also be used by parents, teaching assistants, specialists, interventionists, and tutors to recover, review, and reteach what was taught during class time.

Procedures

- Identify references, texts, assignments, curriculum guides, and other materials that will be used in a unit of study. From these materials, identify essential concepts and processes to be learned in the unit and develop a unit outline.

- Identify class activities that might be used in conjunction with the outline. (Include structured and open-ended activities.)

- Modify the course outline by providing blanks and spaces for students to write notes.

- Have students fill in information during instruction. After instruction, have students teach someone else the information, summarize the information orally or in writing. Have students illustrate the outline or create study guide questions.

- Provide the outline to tutors, mentors, parents, teaching assistants, or specialists so that assistance can be targeted and productive.

Additional adaptations

For students who have difficulty keeping up in class, partially completed outlines can help the student keep up with the class by reducing the writing load.

Example: PRIMARY LEVEL

Though an outline can organize instruction, many activities can occur between the writing frames. Figure B4 and the script demonstrates how a framed outline can be used even in the early primary grades.

Figure B4: *Primary Framed Outline*

Matter

A. Matter is anything that:

takes up space.

B. Things that are matter:

1. my dog

2. this paper

3. you

Teacher:	Class, today we're going to review what we know about the scientific word *matter*. Who can tell me what *matter* is? Everyone read the sentence starter on your outline.
Class:	Matter is anything that ...
Teacher:	That's right. Now help me finish the sentence. Matter is anything that ...
Class:	... takes up space.
Teacher:	Yes. Class, write that definition on your outline. Matter is anything that takes up space. Today we're going to look at the posters you made showing things that are made of matter. Later, you will write three things that are made of matter on your outline. Alicia, show us what you put on your poster.
Alicia:	(Shows her poster) I made a picture of a book, me, and my cat, Pickles.
Teacher:	Class, how do we know Pickles is made of matter?
Class:	He takes up space.
Teacher:	Yes, Pickles takes up space, so Pickles must be made of matter. I'm going to write "Pickles" on the board.

Next, the teacher has students pair off and record on their framed outlines three things that are made of matter. The teacher then continues her lesson with a demonstration of the three types of matter.

This teacher has two English Language Learners and another child with special needs in her class. Each child has been targeted for Academic Assistance. Goals for each include developing academic language and increased participation in classroom activities. The teacher decides to instruct with framed outlines in her science or social studies lessons every Wednesday. She also sets up a volunteer to work with her three students the last 15 minutes of school on Wednesdays. Using their framed outlines, the students will take turns teaching the volunteer what they learned that day. After the first few sessions, the teacher notices that participation in class has improved for all three students.

Example: INTERMEDIATE LEVEL

Use of framed outlines with older students also focuses student attention in important concepts, processes, and information, provides a permanent record for later review, and helps organize more sophisticated course content. The following outline, Figure B5, and the accompanying script demonstrates how this tool might be used to introduce a history unit covering the years 1800 to 1860.

Figure B5: *Intermediate and Secondary Framed Outline*

America: _1800–1860_

I. What you know about the early 1800s:

    A. _Transportation: walking, horses, covered wagons, stagecoaches_

    B. _Communication: Pony Express, mail, talking, no cells, newspapers_

    C. _Work: farming, hunting (American Indians), slaves—working cotton_

II. Questions about the 1800s:

    A. _When were the railroads built and where did they go?_

    B. _____

    C. _____

III. Many historians feel the 1800s were _a time of great change_ .

    A. _____

    B. _____

    C. _____

INTERVENTION

B

Teacher:	We're going to begin studying the years 1800 to 1860. Please write those years in at the top of your outline. Work with your study partner and tell me how many years ago the year 1800 was. Bart, what did you and Jared come up with?
Bart:	We figured out that it was 208 years ago.
Teacher:	How did you come up with that figure?
Jared:	We took this year, 2008, and subtracted 1800 to get the difference.

Teacher:	Nice job. Historians would say this period of time began about 200 years ago. People were heading west in covered wagons. What else do you know about the 1800s? Devon.
Devon:	It was kind of primitive. There were no cars, no phones.
Teacher:	That's right. There was no technology back then. How do you think people got from place to place?
Juan:	They had horses, and they walked.
Teacher:	Yes, some people rode horses, and people walked—a lot. We're going to take a deep look at that time period and explore how it affected how we live now. Look at my overhead. Roman numeral I says, "What you know about the early 1800s." Under that I've listed three topics "transportation, communication, and work." You're going to write the topics on your outline. Then you'll work with your partners and fill in what you know about transportation, communication, and work in the 1800s. Use nice handwriting as we'll be using these outlines for a couple of weeks. You have 10 minutes to work together. (After ten minutes of partner work) Let's hear what you came up with. I'm going to jot some of your ideas on my outline. Add to yours as we go. What do you have about transportation?
Joshua:	We have "walked, covered wagons, stage coaches, and, horses." We weren't sure about trains.
Teacher:	What's a question we might ask about the railroads?
Keisha:	When were they invented?
George:	And where could you go on them?
Teacher:	Excellent.

During this course of study, students will engage in a variety of activities—discussions, reading assignments, making a cartoon of life in the 1800s, viewing a video . . . The interactive course outline will be used throughout the unit to provide a permanent record of course content and to provide cohesion across the multiple activities.

Conclusion

Framed outlines create many opportunities for student-teacher interaction. These tools provide all students with a system for understanding a course while concurrently providing students at risk of failure with a method for retrieving course content.

Adaptation Strategy 5: Design and use interactive graphic organizers.

Description

Graphic organizers visually show how important concepts and information are related. Graphic organizers can take many forms—flow charts, Venn diagrams, cycle charts, timelines, matrices, and story maps.

Rationale and uses

Some students have difficulty understanding important concepts because they view the information as isolated, non-meaningful facts. Graphic organizers provide a visual framework for comparing and contrasting, sequencing events, seeing part/whole relationships, and understanding classification schemas.

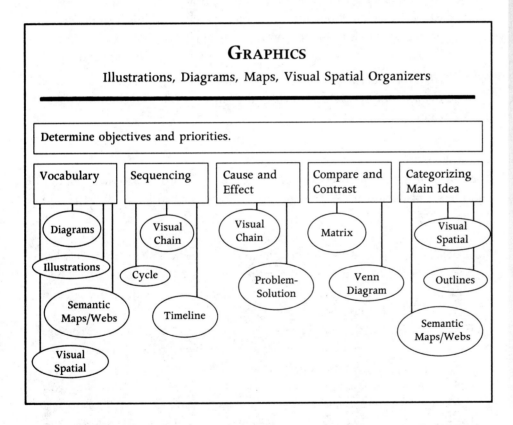

Graphic organizers encourage students to engage in higher order thinking skills as they categorize, illustrate, and sequence information. Graphic organizers can be used in a variety of ways, in combination with other activities, to focus students on important relationships. With these tools, student engagement is increased.

Outside of class time, the organizers can be reused to retrieve and review essential learning. Graphic organizers may also be used by parents, teaching assistants, specialists, interventionists, and tutors to recover, review, and reteach what was taught during class time.

Procedures

- Identify the essential concepts and processes to be learned in a unit of study.

- Identify important relationships that students should understand.

- Select or develop graphic organizers to show the relationships as simply as possible. Reproducible forms are widely available or can be made with a simple computer program.

- Have students fill in information during instruction. After instruction, have students teach someone else the information, or summarize the information orally or in writing. Have students illustrate the graphic organizer or create study guide questions.

- Provide the organizer to tutors, mentors, parents, teaching assistants, or specialists so that assistance can be targeted and productive.

Example: MIDDLE SCHOOL LEVEL

The use of graphic organizers can enhance many classroom activities. Figure B6 and the script demonstrates how a graphic organizer can be used in the middle grades.

Teacher:	Yesterday, we talked about compromises. Shanna, what happens in a compromise?
Shanna:	Well, first there's a problem. Then each side wins and each side loses.
Teacher:	That's right. We discussed several different compromises that you might make in your lives. What was an example of a compromise?
Abe:	Buying expensive shoes. My mom would say they cost too much, so we'd split the difference.
Teacher:	Yes, that was a great example. Today, we are going to talk about the Compromise of 1850. It happened about 150 years ago. A compromise long ago was much like a compromise today. Look at your graphic organizer. What do you know about the North and South already?
Sasha:	Each side is going to win something and each side is going to give something up.

Figure B6: *Intermediate Graphic Organizer*

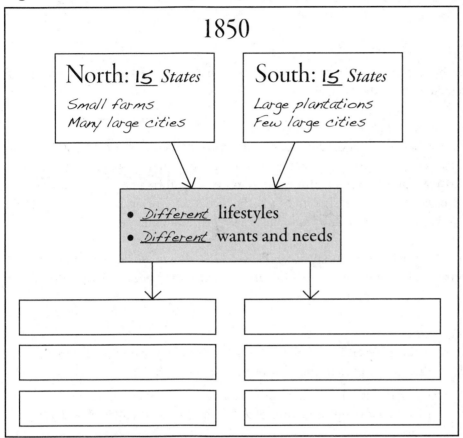

> *These tools provide all students with a system for understanding advanced concepts while concurrently providing students at risk of failure with a method for retrieving course content.*

Teacher:	That's right. Please turn to page 58 in your text. Partner 1s, please read the first two paragraphs out loud. Partner 2s, your job will be to follow along. At the end of paragraph 1, summarize what the North was like. At the end of paragraph 2, summarize what the South was like.
	Work in partners to fill in the first part of your graphic organizer. Identify how many northern and southern states there were. Then jot down at least two descriptions of the North and two of the South.

Conclusion

Graphic organizers enhance course content by helping students see relationships that allow them to categorize, infer, draw conclusions, and defend positions. These tools provide all students with a system for understanding advanced concepts while concurrently providing students at risk of failure with a method for retrieving course content.

Directly teaching essential vocabulary words allows all students to develop a conceptual foundation, which in turn provides the necessary background for ever-increasing opportunities to learn.

Adaptation Strategy 6: Identify and preteach essential vocabulary words.

Description

Teach essential vocabulary directly—words that are central to understanding and communicating knowledge.

Rationale and uses

The smaller a student's vocabulary, the more difficult it is for the student to learn new vocabulary. For students who have difficulty paying attention or who read poorly, opportunities to acquire and store new vocabulary words are often lost. These students lack the skills and prior knowledge to build new vocabulary at a rate commensurate with academic demands.

Directly teaching essential vocabulary words allows all students to develop a conceptual foundation, which in turn provides the necessary background for ever-increasing opportunities to learn.

Procedures

- Identify essential vocabulary—high-frequency words and terms that are central to the unit of instruction.

- Use student-friendly definitions of the vocabulary words. Dictionary or glossary definitions are often difficult for students to understand.

- Introduce the words in manageable amounts. Rather than introducing 15 words on the first day of instruction, start with two to four new words. Gradually add new words as the unit continues.

- Have students use the essential vocabulary words many ways, in different contexts.

Student practice of essential vocabulary words should occur across several days. Possible student activities include the following:

- making a concept map
- illustrating what the word means
- finding a picture that illustrates what the word means
- acting out the word
- defining the word
- using the word when speaking
- writing a sentence using the word

- writing a paragraph using the word

- playing "Concentration" (matching the definition with the word)

- catching someone using the word

- assigning a "fill in the words" worksheet as review

- reviewing the words in a crossword puzzle

- checking definitions in a glossary or dictionary

- making a vocabulary log: entering the word, defining it, and writing a sentence using the word

Example: SECONDARY LEVEL

Have students use vocabulary words many times, in many ways, in many contexts. The following secondary example and script demonstrates how to begin developing deep vocabulary knowledge of the word "democracy."

First, the class develops a concept map. Then students complete an entry in a vocabulary log. With vocabulary logs, students define vocabulary words in their own terms, write a meaningful sentence, and draw a picture. Each step requires that the student comprehend the word. Each part of the vocabulary log requires students to demonstrate understanding that goes beyond rote memorization.

A high school civics teacher begins a unit on democracy by having students brainstorm words and phrases related to democracy. The students then build a concept or semantic map, define the word "democracy" in their own terms, and check the glossary or dictionary definition.

Teacher:	Today, we are going to begin a unit on democracy. I'm sure "democracy" is a word you've heard before. In the next three minutes, I'd like you and your partner to come up with as many words or phrases as you can think of when you hear the word "democracy."
Teacher:	John, what did you and Oleta come up with?
John:	Freedom of speech, freedom to bear arms, voting, choices ...
Teacher:	Excellent. I'm going to start a concept map for the word "democracy." After we finish up here, I'm going to have you fill in your own concept maps. I've got a blank copy on the overhead. Let's see, the first two things you thought of were freedom of speech and the freedom to bear arms. I'm going to draw a line from the word "democracy."

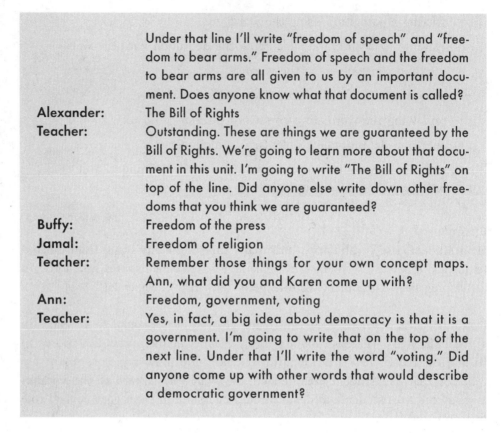

	Under that line I'll write "freedom of speech" and "freedom to bear arms." Freedom of speech and the freedom to bear arms are all given to us by an important document. Does anyone know what that document is called?
Alexander:	The Bill of Rights
Teacher:	Outstanding. These are things we are guaranteed by the Bill of Rights. We're going to learn more about that document in this unit. I'm going to write "The Bill of Rights" on top of the line. Did anyone else write down other freedoms that you think we are guaranteed?
Buffy:	Freedom of the press
Jamal:	Freedom of religion
Teacher:	Remember those things for your own concept maps. Ann, what did you and Karen come up with?
Ann:	Freedom, government, voting
Teacher:	Yes, in fact, a big idea about democracy is that it is a government. I'm going to write that on the top of the next line. Under that I'll write the word "voting." Did anyone come up with other words that would describe a democratic government?

Figure B7: *Vocabulary Concept Map, Secondary*

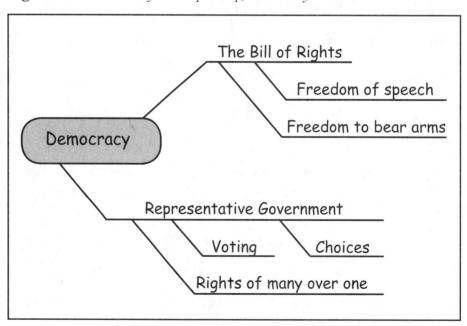

Following the class discussion, the teacher turns off the overhead, has students read from their text, and complete a concept map for the word "democracy." The assignment requires students to identify four big ideas, each with three subordinate ideas. Students on adapted assignments are given the four big ideas and must write the supporting details. The next day students begin class by defining democracy and checking the glossary definition. Homework later in the week includes a vocabulary log of four words, one of which is democracy.

Sample Reproducible Form B6: *Entry from Vocabulary Practice Log, Secondary*

Vocabulary Practice Log

Tanya Joneson — History — Mar. 5
Student ——— Class ——— Date

Word	Definition	Sentence	Pictu
democracy	A form of government in which the people vote for their leaders.	People in a democracy have many freedoms.	

A blank full-page version of this form is available in the *Reproducible Materials* section at the end of the chapter.

Example: ELEMENTARY LEVEL

Concept maps and vocabulary logs can be used across grade levels. Because younger students have less background knowledge, the teacher might start with a read aloud on the topic being studied. For example, if students are studying inventions and learning related words, the teacher might read aloud, "Marvelous Mattie: How Margaret E. Knight Became an Inventor." Students can complete a vocabulary log by defining the word "inventor" on Day 1, write a sentence on Day 2, and draw a picture on Day 3. On the fourth day, the class can make a concept map.

INTERVENTION

B

Figure B8: *Vocabulary Log and Concept Map, Primary*

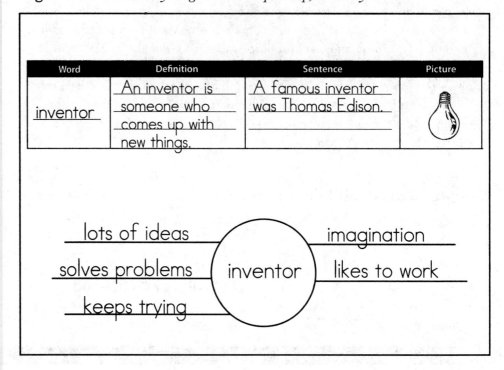

Additional adaptations

Once completed, vocabulary assignments become a permanent record of required learning. For students who need additional practice, the vocabulary log can be used to repeat practice orally or in writing. Those assisting can model and guide practice as needed.

Teaching Assistant:	Here's my definition of inventor. An inventory is a person who thinks of new ways to do things. Your turn. Finish the sentence. An inventor is someone who ...
Student:	An inventor is someone who makes new things.
Teaching Assistant:	Great. I like the way you used your own words. An inventor is someone who makes new things—things that have never been made before.

Conclusion

Deep knowledge of vocabulary words requires multiple repetitions in a variety of contexts. Enhanced vocabulary instruction can be of benefit to all students, not just those at risk of academic failure. Once basic procedures or tools are in place, there are many ways to increase practice for those who most need to build vocabulary.

Adaptation Strategy 7: Highlight textbooks and printed materials.

Description

For courses that rely heavily on reading, highlight classroom reading materials—in both expository and narrative text.

Rationale and uses

Teachers can use highlighting to identify essential course objectives in any text assigned to students and secondly as an adaptation to help poor readers focus on what is most important. Highlight portions of the text that support course requirements—central ideas, important concepts, and critical facts. Once materials have been highlighted, they can be used to make reading manageable for slow and dysfluent readers.

> Note: A student who reads slowly may require two to three times as much time to read an assignment than an able reader.
>
> A one-hour assignment can quickly turn into three of drudgery.
>
> When this occurs, effort is hard to sustain.

Highlighted text may also be used by parents, teaching assistants, specialists, interventionists, and tutors to preview, review, and reteach as needed. By targeting what a student must know and understand to pass a course, extra assistance becomes targeted and affords students the opportunity to succeed.

Procedures

Ideally, highlighted texts should be created by the regular classroom teacher in advance, during lesson planning. This prompts the classroom teacher to identify important concepts and information that need to be emphasized during instruction. It also ensures that another person, such as a teaching assistant or volunteer, does not incorrectly guess what the teacher might think is important. If someone other than the classroom teacher does the initial highlighting, it should be double-checked by the classroom teacher before the materials are used for instruction. (Additional copies of highlighted texts can be made by students or volunteers.)

- Preview the text.
- Underline the text in pencil to determine what may be highlighted. Underlined portions should read like a condensed story. Though sentences may be shortened by leaving out clauses,

By targeting what a student must know and understand to pass a course, extra assistance becomes targeted and affords students the opportunity to succeed.

INTERVENTION

B

the underlined version of the text should make up complete sentences. Sometimes, complete sentences may be formed by combining parts of sentences.

- Read the text to determine whether the underlined text is both comprehensive and cohesive enough to stand alone. Revise as necessary.

- After all the revisions have been completed, use a highlighter to make a final version. Underlined texts can be difficult to follow, but students can track a highlighted version with their fingers.

- Highlighted texts may be given to (or checked out by) students who have comprehension or reading fluency problems. Some classrooms maintain a set of four or five highlighted texts that are provided each year to students with reading difficulties, then reused in following years.

- Highlighted texts may be distributed to tutors, mentors, assistants, parents, or specialists. The highlighted texts can assist others as they help students review essential course objectives.

Additional adaptations

If students are unable to read the highlighted text, someone can read it to them, or a voice-recorded version of the highlighted text may be provided.

Example: SECONDARY LEVEL, NARRATIVE MATERIAL

Mrs. Jones teaches an eighth grade literature class. The English staff is required to teach Frank Stockton's classic short story, "The Lady, or the Tiger." Though the syntax and vocabulary are difficult, the plot provides great debates and discussions about character, conflict, and decisions.

Mrs. Jones knows that several of her students will have difficulty reading the text. She considers reading the text aloud, but knows that she does not have a sufficient amount of class time to do so. She also worries that her lowest performers will have difficulty following the story even if it is read aloud. Rather than assign an alternative story, Mrs. Jones decides to highlight the story so that all her students can enjoy the rich discussions that this story can provoke.

The first portion of the highlighted text follows. When Mrs. Jones finishes highlighting the text, she is surprised at how cohesive the shortened text is. For a transcribed version of the entire text, see Adaptation Strategy 8.

INTERVENTION

B

Figure B9: *Highlighted Narrative Text*

THE LADY, OR THE TIGER?
by Frank R. Stockton

In the very olden time there lived a semi-barbaric king, whose ideas, though some-what polished and sharpened by the progressiveness of distant Latin neighbors, were still large, florid, and untrammeled, as became the half of him which was barbaric. He was a man of exuberant fancy, and, withal, of an authority so irresistible that, at his will, he turned his varied fancies into facts. He was greatly given to self-communing, and, when he and himself agreed upon anything, the thing was done. When every member of his domestic and political systems moved smoothly in its appointed course, his nature was bland and genial; but, whenever there was a little hitch, and some of his orbs got out of their orbits, he was blander and more genial still, for nothing pleased him so much as to make the crooked straight and crush down uneven places.

Among his borrowed notions by which his barbarism had become semified was that of the public arena, in which, by exhibitions of manly and beastly valor, the minds of his subjects were refined and cultured.

But even here the exuberant and barbaric fancy asserted itself. The arena of the king was built, not to give the people an opportunity of hearing the rhapsodies of dying gladiators, nor to enable them to view the inevitable conclusion of a conflict between religious opinions and hungry jaws, but for purposes far better adapted to widen and develop the mental energies of the people. This vast amphitheater, with its encircling galleries, its mysterious vaults, and its unseen passages, was an agent of poetic justice, in which crime was punished, or virtue rewarded, by the decrees of an impartial and incorruptible chance.

When a subject was accused of a crime of sufficient importance to interest the king, public notice was given that on an appointed day the fate of the accused person would be decided in the king's arena, a structure which well deserved its name, for, although its form and plan were borrowed from afar, its purpose emanated solely from the brain of this man, who, every barleycorn a king, knew no tradition to which he owed more allegiance than pleased his fancy, and who ingrafted on every adopted form of human thought and action the rich growth of his barbaric idealism.

Example: SECONDARY LEVEL, EXPOSITORY MATERIAL

Mr. Jones teaches a high school earth science course. Students are preparing essays on how changes have occurred on the Earth's surface across geologic time. Students are required to use a variety of sources, including government documents available on the web. As part of a schoolwide effort to improve academic learning for all student, Mr. Jones has received a list of six students whose reading fluency levels are at or below the 25th percentile. Mr. Jones has decided he will assist these students by assigning them essays on the ice age, by providing transcribed versions of highlighted text, and by meeting regularly with them to teach them how to take notes.

A sample of the highlighted text is shown below. See Adaptation Strategy 8, Condensed Text, for a sample of how the same text reads when transcribed.

Figure B10: *Highlighted Expository Text*

The Great Ice Age
by Louis L. Ray

The Great Ice Age, a recent chapter in the Earth's history, was a period of recurring widespread glaciations. During the Pleistocene Epoch of the geologic time scale, which began about a million or more years ago, mountain glaciers formed on all continents, the icecaps of Antarctica and Greenland were more extensive and thicker than today, and vast glaciers, in places as much as several thousand feed thick, spread across northern North America and Eurasia. So extensive were these glaciers that almost a third of the present land surface of the Earth was intermittently covered by ice. Even today remnants of the great glaciers cover almost a tenth of the land, indicating that conditions somewhat similar to those which produced the Great Ice Age are still operating in polar and subpolar climates.

Much has been learned about the Great Ice Age glaciers because evidence of their presence is so widespread and because similar conditions can be studied today in Greenland, in Antarctica, and in many mountain ranges where glaciers still exist. It is possible, therefore, to reconstruct in large part the extent and general nature of the glaciers of the past and to interpret their impact on the physical and biological environments.

During the long course of Earth history, the climate has fluctuated, just as the general character of the Earth's surface has changed. In fact, there is evidence that glaciations occurred long before the Great Ice Age.

After a period of warm and equable climate, a worldwide climatic refrigeration initiated the Great Ice Age glaciers. At times during the Great Ice Age, the climate was cooler and wetter and at times warmer and drier than today. Many attempts have been made to account for these climatic fluctuations, but their ultimate cause remains unclear. Although we cannot predict a period of climatic cooling, another Ice Age in the future is a possibility.

Source: U.S. Department of the Interior (n.d.). *The great ice age*. Retrieved March 7, 2008, from http://pubs.usgs.gov/giplice_agelice_age.pdf.

Conclusion

Adapting grade-level text by highlighting is not a sufficient strategy for struggling readers. Students should also receive systematic daily instruction in a program designed to remediate their reading problems. However, while students are receiving this intensive instruction, reading assignments throughout the day are often unmanageable for them. Highlighted texts provide students who have reading difficulties with a text that focuses their attention on the most important information.

Adaptation Strategy 8: Transcribe or summarize highlighted text to create condensed text.

Description
Retype or type a summary of small but critical portions of the text for student use. (Caution: Federal copyright laws must be followed.)

Rationale and uses
Condensed texts can be used to provide poor readers with important information in bite-sized portions. Condensed texts can be used by tutors, parents, teaching assistants, and specialists as they preview and review important course objectives.

These texts are easier to use than highlighted versions. Condensed text may also be used by parents, teaching assistants, specialists, interventionists, and tutors to preview, review, and reteach as needed. By targeting what a student must know and understand, extra assistance becomes targeted and affords students the opportunity to succeed.

Procedures
- Highlight a text as described in Adaptation Strategy 7.
- Delete all portions of the text that are not highlighted or type a summary of the highlighted portions. Add appropriate punctuation.

Additional adaptations
If students read the condensed text poorly, someone can read it to them or a voice-recorded version can be provided.

Once the condensed text for "The Lady, or the Tiger" has been prepared, Mrs. Jones is surprised at how well it reads. Knowing that oral reading will take longer than silent reading, Mrs. Jones decides to have her class read "The Lady, or the Tiger?" independently while she meets with a small group of students for an oral reading of the condensed text. With the small group, Mrs. Jones directs the reading. She stops to discuss vocabulary and has students summarize the text periodically. Throughout the reading, Mrs. Jones monitors comprehension and scaffolds questions to help students with inferences. The next day, Mrs. Jones conducts a discussion of "The Lady, or the Tiger" with her class. She is amazed at the participation of the students who worked in her small group and decides that she will continue the process in the future.

Figure B11: *Full Adapted Narrative Text*

THE LADY, OR THE TIGER?
by Frank R. Stockton

In the very olden time there lived a semi-barbaric king. At his will, he turned his varied fancies into facts. Whenever there was a little hitch, nothing pleased him so much as to make the crooked straight and crush down uneven places.

When a subject was accused of a crime of importance to the king, the fate of the accused person would be decided in the king's arena. When all the people had assembled, and the king sat high up on his throne, a door beneath him opened, and the accused subject stepped out. Directly opposite him were two doors, exactly alike and side by side. It was the duty of the person on trial to walk to these doors and open one of them. He could open either door he pleased. If he opened the one, there came out of it a hungry tiger which immediately sprang upon him and tore him to pieces as a punishment for his guilt.

But, if the accused person opened the other door, there came forth from it a lady, the most suitable to his years that his majesty could select, and to this lady he was immediately married, as a reward of his innocence. It mattered not that he might already possess a wife and family, or that his affections might be engaged.

This semi-barbaric king had a daughter. As is usual in such cases, she was the apple of his eye. Among his courtiers was a young man. He was handsome and brave, and she loved him.

This love affair moved on happily until one day the king happened to discover its existence. The youth was immediately cast into prison. Never before had a subject dared to love the daughter of the king.

The tiger cages of the kingdom were searched for the most savage beasts, from which the fiercest monster might be selected for the arena. The ranks of maiden youth and beauty throughout the land were carefully surveyed in order that the young man might have a fitting bride.

The day arrived. From far and near the people gathered. All was ready. The signal was given. A door beneath the royal party opened, and the lover of the princess walked into the arena. Tall, beautiful, fair, his appearance was greeted with a low hum of admiration.

As the youth advanced into the arena, his eyes were fixed upon the princess. Had it not been for the barbarism in her nature it is probable that lady would not have been there. But, she had thought of nothing, night or day. She had done what no other person had done; she had the secret of the doors. She knew in which of the two rooms, stood the tiger, and in which waited the lady. And not only did she know in which room was the lady, but she knew who the lady was. Often had she seen this fair creature throwing glances upon her lover, and sometimes she thought these glances were even returned. The princess, with all the intensity of savage blood, hated the woman who trembled behind that silent door.

When her lover turned and looked at her, and his eye met hers, he saw, that she knew behind which door crouched the tiger, and behind which stood the lady.

Then it was that his glance asked the question: "Which?" She raised her hand, and made a slight, quick movement. No one but her lover saw her.

He turned and walked across the empty space. Every eye was fixed upon that man. Without the slightest hesitation, he went to the door on the right, and opened it.

Now, the point of the story is this: Did the tiger come out of that door, or did the lady?

She had known she would be asked, she had decided what she would answer. Without the slightest hesitation, she had moved her hand to the right. The question of her decision I leave it with all of you: Which came out of the opened door, the lady, or the tiger?

The End

While Mr. Jones's earth science class is at the computer lab, Mr. Jones meets with the six students who read poorly. He decides to have each student read a paragraph aloud. Even with the condensed text, Mr. Jones is surprised at the number of words the students stumble over. As they discuss the text, Mr. Jones realizes his students are able to get the gist of the condensed passage, but feels that without his assistance even this text would be too difficult. Mr. Jones decides that he will continue to meet with this small group of students for the remainder of the term. He also decides to join the high school's committee on reducing academic risk. Mr. Jones wonders how these students have been able to get by in their academic classes.

Figure B12: *Full Adapted Expository Text*

The Great Ice Age
by Louis L. Ray

The Great Ice Age began about a million or more years ago. Mountain glaciers formed on all continents. Vast glaciers spread across northern North America and Eurasia. Almost a third of the present land surface of the Earth was intermittently covered by ice. Even today remnants of the great glaciers cover almost a tenth of the land.

During the long course of Earth history, the climate has fluctuated. The Earth's surface has changed. After a period of warm climate, a worldwide refrigeration initiated the Great Ice Age glaciers. At times during the Great Ice Age, the climate was cooler and wetter and at times warmer and drier than today.

Many attempts have been made to account for these climatic fluctuations, but their cause remains unclear. Although we cannot predict a period of climatic cooling, another ice Age in the future is a possibility.

Source: See p. 142.

Conclusion

When students are poor readers, time is often the greatest barrier to improvement. By cutting down the amount of reading, in effect, the playing field is evened. The shorter reading assignment may take as much time for a poor reader to read as the longer assignment requires of a capable reader. Carefully highlighted or condensed text keeps the most important concepts intact while reducing the amount of reading. Students who read poorly also require a reading intervention to become self-sufficient students.

Adaptation Strategy 9: Provide two-column study guides.

Description

The two-column study guide is a variation of the traditional study guide. Questions are presented on the left side of the page, and students write the answers on the right. Students are taught to quiz themselves by folding the paper in half, asking themselves a question, and then checking their answer.

Rationale and uses

Study guides can help direct attention to the important information presented in the text or in class. Study guide questions prompt students to think comprehensively and critically about what they are learning in class and reading in their texts. Often students do not have effective study strategies; they simply read and reread their text. Two-column study guides provide students with an organizational method for quizzing themselves. Although some students can remember information they have heard or read and written down, others need additional rehearsal.

Two-column study guides provide students with an organizational method for quizzing themselves.

Procedures

- Identify the most important concepts, skills, processes, and information from the unit of study.

- Write study guide questions. Eighty percent of the questions should correspond to essential course objectives. The remaining 20 percent should include questions that students generate or that represent less important details and challenge questions.

- If working from a text, sequence questions in the order that information is presented in the text. If textbooks have been highlighted, many of the questions should correspond to the highlighted text.

- Relate questions to the text or class discussions.

- Assign small sections of the study guide questions for students to answer in class. Check the answers. Then have students make corrections.

- Teach students how to study from the guide by folding the paper in half and quizzing themselves.

- Assign small-group or paired practice for continuous cumulative review.

- Use the study guide before and after instruction. Possible activities include:
    - previewing information with low-performing students
    - having students quiz each other
    - making games from study guide questions
    - assigning practice from the study guide as homework
- Provide study guides to tutors, mentors, parents, assistants, and specialists who might assist students. Parents can sign the study guides to indicate that someone has quizzed the students.

Additional adaptations

Students who are unable to read can be given a voice-recorded study guide. A reader records the question, pauses for the student to think about or verbally state his answer, and then provides the correct answer. Answers can also be framed for students who have writing difficulties.

Example: ELEMENTARY LEVEL, SCHOOLWIDE

Following is an illustration of how an elementary staff teaches their students how to use a study guide. The same process can be used with secondary students who do not have adequate test preparation strategies.

Washington Elementary School has a schoolwide goal of sending their students to middle school ready for academic challenges. As part of this effort, staff has agreed to begin teaching students how to use a two-column study guide to prepare for quizzes and tests.

At the beginning of third grade, teachers provide students with a four item, two-column study guide. Each week in health, social studies, or science, students learn how to write answers and quiz themselves using the two-column study guide. By the second semester, students have also learned how to write two of their own questions.

By the end of fourth grade, students have learned how to use a 10-item study guide. By the end of fifth grade, students have learned to locate information, write answers, and study from a 20-item study guide.

The following script demonstrates how students at the fifth grade level are reviewing how to study from a two-column guide.

Teacher:	Fold your study guide in half (Sample Reproducible Form B7). To study from your guide, first read the question to yourself. Think about the answer. Now turn your paper over and check the answer. "A microorganism is a living creature that can only be seen with a microscope." Did you have to stop and think about the answer? If yes, put a circle around question 1. That tells you that you need to keep reviewing the question.

Sample Reproducible Form B7: *Study Guide*

Intervention B:
Academic Assistance

Study Guide

Aisha Washington   *Science*   *Mr. Mendoza*   *4/6*
Student   Grade/Class   Teacher   Date

Questions	Answers
1. Describe a microorganism. (page 168-1)	*A microorganism is a living creature that can only be seen with a microscope.*
2. What is a communicable disease? (page 169-2)	*It is a disease you can get from someone else.*
3. Identify three things people do to avoid harmful microorganisms. (class)	*1. Collect garbage* *2. Treat water* *3. Drink pasteurized milk*
4. Write a question of your own. *What is an antibiotic?*	*It is a medicine that kills harmful bacteria.*

 A blank version of this form is available in the *Reproducible Materials* section at the end of the chapter.

Conclusion

Teaching students to rehearse from a two-column study guide is a powerful study strategy that can be used across disciplines and into advanced study at any age.

Adaptation Strategy 10: Provide framed writing assignments.

Description

Give students writing prompts—sentence or paragraph starters—to help them begin a writing assignment.

Rationale and uses

Framed writing assignments that provide students with prompts often stimulate thinking. Some students have knowledge and thoughts that they are unable to communicate in writing. Prompts may allow these students to take part in the writing process. Framed writing assignments can reduce the handwriting burden for students who have difficulty with fine motor skills.

Procedures

- Determine when the writing demands of the regular classroom might overwhelm a student with writing problems.
- Create frames, such as an open-ended outline structure.

Additional adaptations

If students are unable to read or write, writing prompts can be read to the students, and the students can dictate their responses.

Example: ESSAY QUESTION

Figure B13 shows a framed response for an essay question. This type of frame would be useful for a student who has reasonably good reading skills but poor handwriting, spelling, or composition skills.

Figure B13: *Framed Writing Assignment*

8. (1+1) Explain why the North and South differed over the issue of slavery.

The North and South differed over the issue of slavery because

_____

The North had _____

While the South had _____

The South needed _____

Example: STORY SUMMARY

Figure B14 shows a framed story summary. A story summary could be used in a similar manner to the essay question frame.

Figure B14: *Framed Story Summary*

This story took place _____

There were three main characters: _____

_____, and _____

In these times, justice _____. When a person was

accused of crime, he _____

_____

Behind one door was _____

_____

This created a problem for the young man and the princess. They _____

_____

Because this was _____

the young man _____

Conflict arises when _____

_____

_____

_____

Conclusion

Writing frames will assist students who have difficulty writing. Frames also help students get started on an assignment and organize their thoughts.

Adaptation Strategy 11: Teach students to manage their homework.

Description
Teach systematic procedures such as using notebooks or folders and standard assignment sheets. When age-appropriate, teach students to monitor their own grades using these methods.

Rationale and uses
Chronic disorganization is a major factor in poor academic performance. Only some students need to be taught how to keep track of assignments systematically, but all students can benefit from the consistent use of this strategy. Systematic tracking of things to do is an important life skill that can benefit the student not only in school, but in the student's future in college, work, or the general management of daily life.

When all students are required to follow standard procedures and use a common format for logging assignments, it is easier to use guided practice and partner checking to increase the likelihood that all students use the system. Teaching students to track grades helps them take control of their grades. Students who earn poor grades often think that grades are something the teacher does to them. Bad grades just happen—no matter what the student does. When students learn to monitor their own grades and can identify specific things they can do to earn acceptable grades, they learn to assume responsibility. Tracking grades is not appropriate in the early grades, as students may not yet understand grading systems and how they relate to their long-term performance. However, as students begin moving into a formal grading system, it is important to teach them how the system works.

Procedures
- Establish a schoolwide notebook or folder requirement.
- Have students use a standard assignment sheet.
- Actively teach students how to use the assignment sheets through modeling, guided practice, and partner checks.
- Teach students how to monitor their grades (optional).
- Teach students how to complete a daily homework plan (optional).

Example: PRIMARY GRADES
The primary staff at Washington Elementary School has agreed to use the form shown in Sample Reproducible Form B8 on the following page. All students are given folders with the form printed on the outside. Each evening's homework assignment is placed in the folder, and parents sign the form

Systematic tracking of things to do is an important life skill that can benefit the student not only in school, but in the student's future in college, work, or the general management of daily life.

INTERVENTION

B

when the task is completed. In kindergarten, students will have homework every Monday and Wednesday. Homework for young children will involve such tasks as telling parents about pictures they've made, playing a game, or telling a story from a picture. First- through third-grade students will have homework every Monday, Tuesday, Wednesday, and Thursday. Their homework will involve reading a short story to parents, completing a short math worksheet, and other tasks. The goal is to teach students to get in the homework habit while they are young. The emphasis of instruction is on teaching students responsibility with easy, manageable tasks.

Each evening, students hold up their homework folders before going home so the teacher can help students develop the habit. Parents are taught to have students put their homework folders by the door so they aren't forgotten in the morning. Teachers check off and acknowledge returned homework folders when they take roll.

Additional adaptations

If a young student is not having success with homework routines, have the student do homework with a parent helper or older student before going home. The student should still take the homework folder to and from school to develop the habit of taking materials back and forth.

Sample Reproducible Form B8: *Entry, Grades K-2 Homework Log*

Intervention B:
Academic Assistance

Homework Log (Signature/Comments)

Brian Smith
Student

6
Homeroom

Due	Parent/Guardian Signature and Comments
9/10	*M. Smith—Enjoyed listening to Brian! Great story!*

 A blank full-page version of this form is available in the *Reproducible Materials* section at the end of the chapter.

Example: INTERMEDIATE GRADES

The fourth- and fifth-grade teachers at Washington Elementary School decide to have students log their assignments and the dates they are due. Because the staff at Washington believes parent involvement is essential in developing good homework habits, students continue to obtain parent signatures when they complete their homework. The following scenario illustrates how a teacher might teach students to use the assignment sheet shown in Sample Reproducible Form B9 on the next page.

Teacher:	I am going to give you your math assignment. Show me what you need to do. (Students get out their notebooks and turn to the assignment pages. Partner checking ensures that all students complete this task successfully and efficiently.)
	Great. Your assignment is due tomorrow, September 10. Your assignment is to complete page 10 and is written on the overhead. Please copy it and then check your partner's homework log. Tell your partner when you plan to get your assignment done. (Students tell their partners.)
	Now tell your partner what you will do with your homework when you finish your assignment. (Students tell their partners.)
	That's right. You will have your parent look at your assignment and sign your assignment sheet. Tell your partner where you will put your notebook after the assignment is finished so you won't forget it in the morning. (Students tell their partners.) Everyone, tell me what you need to take home tonight.
Class:	Notebooks and math books.
Teacher:	(Just before students leave for home.) Show me what you are taking home this evening. (Students hold up their math books and notebooks.)
	Now review with your study partner when you will get your math assignment done. (Students tell their partners.)

Homework Log (Assignment/Signature)

Kara Logan   Kessler

Due	Assignment	Parent/Guardian Signature
9/10	Page 10	S. Logan

 A blank version of this form is available in the *Reproducible Materials* section at the end of the chapter.

Example: UPPER-INTERMEDIATE GRADES

The sixth-grade staff at Washington Elementary School decides that students should learn to keep track of their assignments and grades in different subject areas to prepare for middle school. The following scenario illustrates how a teacher might teach students to use the grade-tracking assignment sheet shown in Reproducible Form B10.

Teacher: This year, you will have an assignment sheet for the different subjects we study—math, reading, social studies, science and health . . . The assignment sheets will help you get ready for middle school. It will also show you how to track your grades. We're going to start by using the assignment sheet in math.

Everyone, open your notebooks to the first section of your notebook. Label the divider "math." While you're doing that, I'm going to pass out your Assignment and Grade Tracking sheets.

It looks like you all have your assignment sheets in the right place. Look at my overhead sample. Your first job is to write your name, my name above "Homeroom," and "Math" above "Subject." Please write neatly. Partner's check each other's work.

Sample Reproducible Form B10: *Grades 6-12 Grade Tracking Log*

Assignment and Grade Tracking Log

Jonah Sampley
Student

Mrs. Moss
Homeroom

Math
Subject

Due	Assignment	Points Earned	Points Possible	Total Points Earned	Total Points Possible	Current Grade
9/15	Worksheet 1	10	10	10	10	A
9/16	Worksheet 2	8	10	18	20	A
9/17	Worksheet 3	~~8~~ 6	10	~~18~~ 24	30	~~D~~ B

A blank version of this form is available in the *Reproducible Materials* section at the end of the chapter.

Teacher:	I just gave you your first math assignment. Everyone, when is it due?
Class:	At the end of class today
Teacher:	That's right. Look at my overhead sample. Under "Due" you're going to write "9/15." Under "Assignment," you're going to write "Worksheet 1," under "Points Possible," you're going to write "10," and under "Total Possible Points" you're going to write "10." When you're done, partners check. After your first assignment is graded, I'll show you how to enter your score.
	(The next day) Everyone, get out your notebooks and turn to your math assignment sheet. I've returned your math worksheets from yesterday. You did a nice job partner checking and correcting errors before you turned in your papers. Everyone got 9 or 10 correct. Write the number of points you earned on Worksheet 1 under points earned. Now write "9" or "10" under "Total Points Earned."
	With each assignment we're going to add points, and then you can look at the board to see what your grade is. If you are not happy with your grade, we can talk about ways to improve it. Look at the board. What grade do you have now?
Class:	An "A"
Teacher:	Everyone, look at my overhead. It shows Jonah Sampley's Assignment and Grade Tracking sheet. Of course, Jonah isn't real. We're going to look at what happens to his grades when he doesn't turn in an assignment. What's Jonah's grade on Worksheet 1?
Class:	An "A"
Teacher:	(pointing to each item on the sample) On Worksheet 2, Jonah missed two out of ten. How many points did he earn?
Class:	Eight points
Teacher:	That's right. He had 10 points from Worksheet 1. He got eight points on Worksheet 2. He has 18 out of 20 points. What grade does that give him?

Class:	An "A"
Teacher:	OK, let's look at Worksheet 3. Jonah forgot to turn his assignment in. He did it, but he didn't turn it in. How many points did he earn?
Class:	Zero
Teacher:	When we add zero to the 18 points Jonah had, he ends up with 18 out of 30 total possible points. Everyone, look at the board . . . What does that drop his grade to?

90% to 100%	27 to 30 = A
80% to 89%	24 to 26 = B
70% to 79%	21 to 23 = C
60% to 69%	18 to 20 = D
50% to 59%	17 or less = F

Class:	A "D"
Teacher:	Oh, oh! What do you think Jonah should do?
Sally:	Panic . . .
Teacher:	Yes, then he should talk to me. A mistake is an opportunity to learn. I would have Jonah turn in his assignment. He would lose two points because it was late. Let's assume Jonah got eight correct, so he would still earn six points. That would give him a total of 24 points. Look at the grading scale on the board. With 24 points out of 30, what would Jonah's grade jump back up to?
Class:	A "B"
Teacher:	Yes, and a "B" is much better than a "D."

Example: SECONDARY

A middle school staff decides to implement a schoolwide notebook policy and is systematically teaching all students to log and track their grades. All staff members are using the same procedures outlined in the upper elementary school example on page 155. By the third week of school, teachers agree that homework completion has improved over previous years. More importantly, teachers feel that students are taking a more active interest in their grades and assuming more responsibility. When students have difficulty, the special education staff and the counseling staff feel that they are better able to assist.

INTERVENTION

B

Additional adaptations

Some students may also need to make a daily homework plan before going home.

By the third week of school, Greg is referred to the counselor to work on homework completion. First the counselor does long-term goal setting. (See "Intervention C: Goal Setting.") The counselor learns that Greg hopes to go to college and has him work on a Daily Homework Plan (Reproducible Form B11).

Counselor:	I think your goal of going to the University is very doable. Right now, the University is accepting students with a 3.0 G.P.A. That's a straight B average. Right now you have "A's" in Band, Spanish, and P.E. so I think a "B" average is possible, but not unless you do better with homework. What do you think the problem is?
Greg:	Well, sometimes I don't have the right books I need, and sometimes I turn on the TV. I think I'll get around to the homework, but . . . I get involved. Mom thinks I'm addicted to TV. Besides, It's eighth grade. Grades don't count yet.
Counselor:	I'd like you to think of this as your high school prep year. It will be very difficult for you to develop new habits all of a sudden next year.

At the end of the day, I want you to stop by here and write a homework plan. We'll write up your class schedule on a Homework Plan and I'll run copies for you. Each day, you'll go through your assignment sheets, list what you have due, the materials you'll need, and then you can plan when you will do it. You can reward yourself with a favorite TV show. |
| **Greg:** | I think it's hopeless. I've already got zeroes in math and history. |
| **Counselor:** | Here's what we'll do. First, you need to demonstrate that you are working on this. Then we can talk to your math and history teachers and see if there is something you can do to get partial points for missed work. You were referred by both teachers. Those referrals mean they want things to change for you. It's still early in the term so I don't think it is too late. |

Sample Reproducible Form B11: *Homework Plan*

Daily Homework Plan

Greg Poe
Student

Sept. 15
Date

List of Things to Do:

Class/Period	Assignment	Materials	When
Spanish	Verb conjugations	Spanish Book	4:30-4:45
Band	Practice	Music - horn	4:45-5:15
Math	Worksheet 10	NA	5:15-5:45
PE	NA		
Lunch	NA		
English	Ch 1 Red Badge of Courage	Book	7:00-7:15
US History	Project - Notes	Handout	7:15-7:30

A blank version of this form is available in the *Reproducible Materials* section at the end of the chapter.

Conclusion

Homework problems can be prevented and corrected by teaching students strategies for managing homework. The more systematic and consistent staff are in their policies and procedures, the greater the chance they have to help students who need to develop positive homework habits.

IMPLEMENTATION STEPS *(continued from p. 118)*

To this point, you've read about the following implementation steps:

Step 1: Identify concerns and establish a focus.
Step 2: Develop a plan for conducting an informal academic assessment.
Step 3: Conduct the assessment.
Step 4: Consider and plan for remediation options.
Step 5: Consider adaptation options.

The final steps in putting a plan in place are as follows:

Step 6: Set up a plan to review with staff members.
Step 7: Meet with staff.
Step 8: Finalize the plan.
Step 9: Implement the plan.

Step 6: Set up a plan to review with staff members.

The format for discussing Academic Assistance will vary depending on the staff members' prior experience with adaptation strategies. The Academic Assistance Form (Reproducible Form B4 or B5) provides a framework for discussing possible adaptation strategies and may be particularly useful if staff members are unfamiliar with adaptation strategies.

> Mr. Wagner decides to use the one-page format of the Academic Assistance Form (see p. 114) to help him present Aaron's strengths and weaknesses to the staff members and to discuss the remediation plan for improving Aaron's reading fluency and handwriting. Mr. Wagner will also use the information on the form to review the Adaptation Process and to explore the possibility of adapting materials for Aaron while concurrently working on his skill deficits and homework problems.

Step 7: Meet with staff.

Meet with appropriate staff members to discuss the student's strengths and weaknesses and to develop a manageable plan of Academic Assistance. Plan to take notes to keep track of the roles and responsibilities of all individuals involved in the intervention.

> Because Aaron has the most difficulty in English and geography, Mr. Wagner meets with Mrs. Graham, the English teacher, and Mr. Baxter, the geography teacher. Mrs. Elliot, the special education teacher, offers to join the group as an additional resource person. Mr. Wagner also thinks the Student Status Reports (Reproducible Form B2) that were previously filled out by each teacher have provided a good profile of Aaron's strengths and weaknesses.

A. Review student information from the Academic Assistance Form.

> Mr. Wagner provides each teacher with a copy of Aaron's Academic Assistance Form (Sample Reproducible Form B5 on p. 114). After summarizing his findings, he explains the tutorials that are being set up to improve Aaron's reading fluency and handwriting.
>
> **Mrs. Graham:** I'm glad that Aaron will be getting some help, though
> **(English Teacher)** I'm surprised to hear that he has a reading problem.
> **Mr. Wagner:** As you know, Aaron is bright and articulate. I think he
> **(Asst. Principal)** compensates for his reading problem when he can. When he can't, he misbehaves.
> **Mr. Baxter:** That explains a lot. I think I have a lot of kids with the same problem.

B. Review and discuss the Adaptation Process and possible strategies that might be implemented.

> **Mr. Wagner:** Aaron clearly has a pattern of being obnoxious when he isn't being successful, but he is also consistently well behaved when he is successful. I'm hopeful that we can bring some relief to everyone, including Aaron, if we can

	help him improve his academic record. I've been reviewing how to adapt his instruction, and I think we might be able to work out some possibilities. Let's look at "C, The Adaptation Process" on Aaron's Academic Assistance Form. It might help stimulate some ideas and discussion.
Mrs. Elliott:	The process is pretty logical, but I'm going to talk you through it. First, we're going to have you think about assignments or activities that you haven't given out yet and then try to anticipate problems. Next, we're going to see if there are some things you can do with the whole class that will also help Aaron. Finally, we'll look at making assignments more manageable and perhaps even consider alternative ways that Aaron can demonstrate his competence.

There are also several adaptation strategies listed under item D. There's always a lot that can be done for these kids, but we also want to find strategies that are doable for you and worthwhile for other students as well as Aaron.

C. Identify a manageable plan of assistance.

After going through the Adaptation Process and discussing a few of the strategies from the Adaptation Menu, the group decides to help Aaron manage his homework by requiring him to use a notebook and teaching him to log his assignments and record his grades.

As they discuss Aaron's difficulties, Mrs. Graham and Mr. Baxter become convinced that they probably have several students in each class who have reading problems. Mrs. Elliott agrees to show the teachers how to give oral reading fluency assessments and how to highlight written references.

The teachers also agree to look at alternative ways for Aaron to submit written work. For example, Mr. Baxter will accept a final report typed by a parent or volunteer, and Mrs. Graham will let Aaron give her an oral book report.

INTERVENTION

B

D. Identify ways to determine whether the intervention is helping the student reach his goals.

At least two independent means of evaluating progress should be used. Because academic success takes time, small improvements may go unnoticed unless you can determine whether the intervention is having a positive impact. Evaluation might include subjective assessments by the teacher, student, and parent; monitoring work completion, grades, or office referrals; or comparing work samples.

> Because Aaron will be using an assignment system that includes daily monitoring of grades, his plan has a built-in evaluation system. Mr. Wagner also decides to check informally with Mrs. Graham and Mr. Baxter once each week to see how things are going and offer assistance as necessary.

E. Review staff responsibilities.

> **Mr. Wagner:**
> (Asst. Principal)
>
> Let me review what we are doing here. I've been jotting down some notes, and I'll send everyone a written summary.

F. Schedule a follow-up meeting.

> **Mr. Wagner:**
>
> I appreciate everyone's cooperation. I'll meet with Aaron and his mother to go over everything and do some goal setting. I'd also like to schedule a follow-up meeting.
>
> I know you are really busy, but I would like to make sure that we give you enough support to see this through.

Step 8: Finalize the plan.

Before implementing any remediation, meet with the student to discuss and finalize the plan.

Because academic success takes time, small improvements may go unnoticed unless you can evaluate whether the intervention is having a positive impact.

INTERVENTION

B

A. Review the problem and goal.

> Mr. Wagner meets with Aaron and his mother. Because Aaron is very sophisticated, Mr. Wagner goes through the assessment results, treating Aaron as an adult. As they talk, Aaron agrees that the goals Mr. Wagner and his mother have discussed seem reasonable.

B. Discuss the possible Academic Assistance plan.

Mr. Wagner: (Asst. Principal)	First let's talk about reading and handwriting. This is what we would like to propose. (Mr. Wagner explains the tutoring and handwriting programs he wants to implement.) What do you think?
Aaron:	I don't mind doing it, but who will I work with for reading?
Mr. Wagner:	We have Evie Collins in mind. She's a senior and looking for a volunteer project.
Aaron:	Will she blab to everyone that she's helping me?
Mr. Wagner:	We thought of Evie because she would protect your feelings. We would explain to her why you are doing this and that it is a very mature decision on your part. We'll also explain that you are very bright, but that somehow you just missed out on this one skill. What do you think?
Aaron:	I guess it'd be OK.
Mr. Wagner:	Good. Now, I want to talk about what Mrs. Graham and Mr. Baxter are willing to do. This will take some negotiating occasionally, but both teachers are willing to help you as long as you are willing to help yourself.

C. Make revisions to the plan as necessary.

D. Schedule a time to teach the strategies or skills.

Mr. Wagner: (Asst. Principal)	Aaron, you'll be reporting to the counseling center during your advisory period. We'll start tomorrow. I'll review the homework sheet you'll be using and get you started on the handwriting exercises. Next week we'll begin work on the reading fluency.

E. Schedule a time to meet regularly with the student to discuss progress.

Mr. Wagner: (Asst. Principal)	Once we've got you going, why don't we meet every Wednesday during advisory? You can keep me informed, I can listen to you and Evie work on reading, and we can see if you need help with anything.

F. Review everyone's roles and responsibilities.

Mr. Wagner:	I'd like to go over everything again. I know there are a number of things we need to remember . . .

G. Conclude with words of encouragement.

Mr. Wagner:	Aaron, I'm very excited about this plan. I think you've had to hobble along until now, and I can understand your frustration because you are a very bright student. Once your handwriting and reading problems are fixed up, I think you'll fly. You are giving yourself a great present. Nothing will change overnight, but I know that you'll begin seeing a change in things. Overall, I want you to know that Mrs. Graham, Mr. Baxter, myself, and your mom are all willing to help you.

Step 9: Implement the plan.

A. After getting started, be sure to provide the student with ongoing support and encouragement.

B. Evaluate the impact of the intervention, making revisions and adjustments as necessary.

Academic Assistance may require many variations on a theme as the demands of the classroom change and student skills grow. If possible, teachers should read all of Step 4 (Consider and plan for remediation options). Knowledge of the Adaptation Process can help classroom teachers alter procedures as necessary.

Because behavior and academic difficulties are often interwoven, consider other interventions:

> Intervention C: Goal Setting (p. 185)
> Intervention L: Self-Talk and Attribution Training (p. 535)
> Intervention M: Teaching Replacement Behavior (p. 567)
> Intervention O: Structured Reinforcement Systems (p. 639)

During the first two weeks of the intervention plan, Mr. Wagner is very pleased with Aaron's progress. Both Mr. Baxter and Mrs. Graham report improved behavior by Aaron.

In the third week, Aaron begins having problems remembering to take home materials to complete his homework. Mr. Wagner decides to implement a daily homework plan (Reproducible Form B11).

At the end of the first month of the intervention, Mr. Wagner and Aaron jointly decide that things are going better. Aaron's grades have improved to C's in both geography and English. Aaron's reading fluency is also clearly improving. The suggestion of the special education teacher to practice word families and accurate reading and re-readings of easy-to-read passages from SRA's *Corrective Reading Decoding B* seem to be paying off. Mr. Wagner can tell that Aaron is beginning to let go of his habit of rushing and bumbling through text. Though Mr. Wagner recognizes that this intervention will be a long-term process and that other interventions may be necessary, he knows that it may make a big difference over the years—one less kid in detention, and one more graduate.

CONCLUSION

Regardless of how supportive adults might be, when students are unable to meet academic expectations, they must deal with their own sense of failure and frustration on a daily basis. Some students respond with apathy. Some become irritated or angry. Some students will do anything to avoid feeling incompetent, including misbehaving to distract from their academic needs. Though Academic Assistance tends to be work-intensive, it gives students a chance to survive in and become competent members of the learning community.

Note, Secondary Schools: If staff is interested in comprehensive staff development in effective instruction and remediation, you may wish to learn more about the Strategic Instruction Model (SIM) and the Content Enhancement Series developed by Don Deshler and his colleagues at the University of Kansas Center for Research and Learning. For more information, go to www.ku-crl.org/sim.

REFERENCES

Adams, M. J. (1990). *Beginning to read: Thinking and learning about print.* Cambridge, MA: MIT Press.

Baumann, J., & Kame'enui, E. (1991). Research on vocabulary instruction: Ode to Voltaire. In J. Flood, J.M. Jensen, D. Lapp, & J.R. Squire (Eds.), *Handbook of research on teaching the English language arts* (pp. 604–632). New York: Macmillan.

Beidel, D. C., Turner, S. M., & Taylor-Ferreira, J. C. (1999). Teaching study skills and test-taking strategies to elementary school students: The Testbusters program. *Behavioral Modification, 23*(4), 630–646.

Bergerud, D., Lovitt, T. C., & Horton, S. (1988). The effectiveness of textbook adaptations in life science for high school students with learning disabilities. *Journal of Learning Disabilities, 21*, 70–76.

Black, H., & Black, S. (1990). *Organizing thinking: Book II.* Pacific Grove, CA: Midwest Publications.

Bryan, T., Burstein, K., & Bryan, J. (2001). Students with learning disabilities: Homework problems and promising practices. *Educational Psychologist, 36*(3), 167–180.

Carnine, D., Silbert, J., Kame'enui, E., & Tarver, S. (2004). *Direct instruction reading* (4th ed.). Upper Saddle River, NJ: Pearson.

Coyne, M. D., Kame'enui, E. J., & Simmons, D. C. (2001). Prevention and intervention in beginning reading: Two complex systems. *Learning Disabilities Research and Practice, 16*(2), 62–73.

De La Paz, S., & Graham, S. (2002). Explicitly teaching strategies, skills, and knowledge: Writing instruction in middle school classrooms. *Journal of Educational Psychology, 94*(4), 687–698.

Engelmann, S., Johnson, G., Becker, W., Meyers, L., Carnine, L., & Becker, J. (2008). *Corrective reading decoding B1: Decoding strategies.* Chicago, IL: Science Research Associates.

Engelmann, S., Johnson, G., Becker, W., Meyers, L., Carnine, L., & Becker, J. (2008). *Corrective reading decoding B2: Decoding strategies.* Chicago, IL: Science Research Associates.

Feather, N. T. (Ed.) (1982). *Expectations and actions.* Mahwah, NJ: Erlbaum.

Gerstein, R., & Dimino, J. (1990). *Reading instruction for at risk students: Implications of current research.* Eugene, OR: Oregon School Study Council, University of Oregon.

Gettinger, M., & Seibert, J. K. (2002). Contributions of study skills to academic competence. *School Psychology Review, 31*(3), 350–365.

Hasbrouck, J., & Tindal, G. (2005). *Oral reading fluency: 90 years of measurement* (Tech. Rep. No. 33). Eugene, Oregon: University of Oregon, College of Education, Behavioral Research and Teaching.

Heimlich, J. E., & Pittelman, S. D. (1986) *Semantic mapping: Classroom applications.* Newark, NJ: International Reading Association.

Hofmeister, A., & Lubke, M. (1990). *Research into practice.* Boston: Allyn and Bacon.

Hughes, C. A., Ruhl, K. L., Schumaker, J. B., & Deshler, D. D. (2002). Effects of instruction in an assignment completion strategy on the homework performance of students with learning disabilities in general education classes. *Learning Disabilities Research and Practice, 17*(1), 1–18.

Kachgal, M. M., Hansen, S., & Nutter, K. J. (2001). Academic procrastination prevention/intervention: Strategies and recommendations. *Journal of Developmental Education, 25*(1), 14–24.

Lovitt, T. C. (1991). *Preventing school dropouts: Tactics for at risk, remedial and mildly handicapped adolescents.* Austin, TX: Pro-Ed.

INTERVENTION

B

Mallinson, G., Mallinson, J., Smallwood, W., & Valentino, C. (1985). *Silver Burdett science*. Morristown, NJ: Silver Burdett Company.

Ness, E. (1967). *Sam, Bangs and moonshine*. New York: Henry Holt and Company.

Noel, G. H., Freeland, J. T., Witt, J. C., & Gansle, K. A. (2001). Using brief assessments to identify effective interventions for individual students. *Journal of School Psychology, 39*(4), 335–355.

Northwest Regional Educational Laboratory. (1990). *Effective schooling practices: A research synthesis, 1990 update*. Portland, OR: Author.

Sakelaris, T. L. (1999). Effects of a self-managed study skills intervention on homework and academic performance of middle school students with attention deficit hyperactivity disorder (ADHD). *Dissertation Abstracts International, 60*(2-A), 0337.

Salend, S. J., & Gajria, M. (1995). Increasing the homework completion rates of students with mild disabilities. *Remedial and Special Education, 16*(5), 271–278.

Santa, C. M., Havens, L. M., Nelson, M., Danner, M., Scalf, L., & Scalf, J. (1988). *Content reading including study systems: Reading, writing, and studying across the curriculum*. Dubuque, IA: Kendall Hunt Publishing.

Shinn, M. R. (Ed.). (1989). *Curriculum-based measurement: Assessing special children*. New York: Guilford Press.

Skinner, C. H. (2002). Empirical analysis of interspersal research evidence, implications, and applications of the discrete task completion hypothesis. *Journal of School Psychology, 40*(4), 347–368.

Snow, C.E., Burns, S., & Griffin, P. (Eds.). (1998). *Preventing reading difficulties in young children*. Washington, DC: National Research Council.

U.S. Department of Education. (1987). What works: Research about teaching and learning (2nd ed.). Washington, DC: Author.

U.S. Department of Health and Human Services. (2000). Report of the National Reading Panel: Teaching children to read. Washington, DC: Author.

Woods, M., & Moe, A. J. (2006). *Analytic reading inventory* (8th ed.). Saddle River, NJ: Prentice Hall.

Reproducible Materials

The following reproducible materials may be used in conjunction with "Intervention B: Academic Assistance." Copies are provided here and on the CD. Permission is given for individual classroom teachers to reproduce any forms labeled "Reproducible" for classroom use. Reproduction of these materials for an entire school system is prohibited without express permission of the publisher.

INTERVENTION

B

INTERVENTION  B

ACADEMIC ASSISTANCE

Step-by-Step Summary

Following is a summary of the steps involved in Intervention B. It is important to use professional judgment, adjusting procedures to meet the needs of the situation and the individual. See the chapter "Intervention B: Academic Assistance" for a detailed description of this intervention.

STEP 1   Identify concerns and establish a focus.

A. Talk with staff members.

B. Contact the student's parent(s) or guardian.
   1. Discuss the problem.
   2. Discuss goals for improvement.
   3. Request parental permission to conduct an informal assessment of the student's academic needs and to develop a plan of assistance.

STEP 2   Develop a plan for conducting an informal academic assessment.

A. Analyze information from Student Status Reports.

B. Analyze student work samples.

C. Collect oral reading fluency data.

D. Use an informal reading inventory.

E. Work one-to-one with the student on an assignment.

F. Select procedures that are useful, manageable, and age appropriate.

INTERVENTION B

STEP 3 Conduct the assessment.

A. Meet with the student to complete the assessment.
   1. Review the concerns and overall goals with the student.
   2. Conduct the assessment.
      When conducting the assessment, help the student relax as much as possible.

B. Analyze the results.

C. Summarize student strengths and weaknesses using the Academic Assistance Form.

D. Target specific areas in which assistance can be provided.

STEP 4 Consider and plan for remediation options.

STEP 5 Consider adaptation options.

A. Familiarize yourself with the Adaptation Process.
   1. Identify assignments and activities that will be assigned in coming weeks.
   2. Anticipate problems that the targeted student (and other students) may encounter.
   3. Design whole-class instruction to prevent anticipated difficulties.
   4. Consider making assignments more manageable by providing additional assistance and/or adjusting the length and complexity of assignments.
   5. Consider alternative ways for the student to demontrate knowledge or ability.
   6. Gradually fade the adaptations as the student gains competence.

B. Consider selecting or modifying strategies from the Adaptation Menu.
   Adaptation Strategy 1:   Focus assignments on essential course content and skills.
   Adaptation Strategy 2:   Focus test items on essential course content and skills.
   Adaptation Strategy 3:   Build cumulative review of essential objectives into subsequent units of instruction.
   Adaptation Strategy 4:   Construct and use framed outlines.
   Adaptation Strategy 5:   Design and use interactive graphic organizers.
   Adaptation Strategy 6:   Identify and preteach essential vocabulary words.
   Adaptation Strategy 7:   Highlight textbooks and printed materials.
   Adaptation Strategy 8:   Transcribe or summarize highlighted text to create condensed text.
   Adaptation Strategy 9:   Provide two-column study guides.
   Adaptation Strategy 10: Provide framed writing assignments.
   Adaptation Strategy 11: Teach students to manage their homework.

Reproducible Step-by-Step Summary (3 of 3)

INTERVENTION **B**

STEP 6   Set up a plan to review with staff members.

STEP 7   Meet with staff.

A. Review student information from the Academic Assistance Form.

B. Review and discuss the Adaptation Process and possible strategies that might be implemented.

C. Identify a manageable plan of assistance.

D. Identify ways to determine whether the intervention is helping the student reach his goals.

E. Review staff responsibilities.

F. Schedule a follow-up meeting.

STEP 8   Finalize the plan.

A. Review the problem and goal.

B. Discuss the possible Academic Assistance plan.

C. Make revisions to the plan as necessary.

D. Schedule a time to teach the strategies or skills.

E. Schedule a time to meet regularly with the student to discuss progress.

F. Review everyone's roles and responsibilities.

G. Conclude with words of encouragement.

STEP 9   Implement the plan.

A. After getting started, be sure to provide the student with ongoing support and encouragement.

B. Evaluate the impact of the intervention, making revisions and adjustments as necessary.

Intervention B:
Academic Assistance

Parental Permission Form

Dear _____ :

We would like to develop a plan to support _____

_____

_____

To assist us in developing the most useful plan possible, we would like your permission to informally assess your child's academic skills and work habits. This process may include any or all of
the following:

_____

_____

_____

_____

_____

_____

Please sign the slip below and return it to school by _____ . As soon
as the assessment has been completed, we will be in touch.

Thank you for your assistance.

Sincerely,

- -

_____ has my permission to informally assess _____'s
academic skills and work habits and to develop a plan of assistance.

_____   _____
Signed (Parent or Guardian)   Date

Reproducible Form B3: *Student Status Report (Version 2)*

Intervention B:
Academic Assistance

Student Status Report (Version 2)

Student	Grade/Class	Staff Member Requesting Information	Date

Please complete performance ratings for this student. The information you provide will be used to help develop an individualized plan of assistance and match the student with appropriate interventions.

Key:
5 = Always
4 = Usually
3 = Sometimes
2 = Rarely
1 = Never
N/A = Not applicable

Note:
A rating of 3 or below indicates a problem or concern that warrants further follow-up.

Period or Subject Area						
1	2	3	4	5	6	7

Student Performance

Academic Standing
List student's current grade using the values assigned on the report card (letter grades, ✓/+/-, etc.)

Student strengths (list at least three):

List areas of concern:

Note: Please attach a representative sample of student work.

Reproducible Form B4 (1 of 2): *Academic Assistance (Two-Page Form)*

Academic Assistance (Two-Page Form)

Student _____   Date _____

Teacher _____   Grade/Class _____

A.   Informal assessment information

1. Oral Reading Fluency: _____ words correct per minute
    Materials:

2. Strengths and weaknesses:

	Subjects	Abilities	Behavior
Strengths			
Weaknesses			

B.   Remediation

C.   The Adaptation Process

Use the outline below as an optional framework for developing a plan of
Academic Assistance.

1. Identify assignments or activities that haven't yet been given.
2. Anticipate problems that the student (and other students) may encounter.
3. Design whole-class instruction to prevent anticipated problems.
4. Consider making assignments more manageable by providing additional assistance.
5. Consider alternative ways for the student to demonstrate knowledge or ability.
6. Gradually fade the adaptations as the student gains competence.

Reproducible Form B4 (2 of 2): *Academic Assistance (Two-Page Form)*

D.   The Adaptation Menu

Adaptation involves an endless variety of procedures. The following strategies are provided as suggestions, but are not an exhaustive list. Discuss adaptations that may be applicable and brainstorm other possibilities.

1. Focus assignments on essential course content and skills.
2. Focus test items on essential course content and skills.
3. Build cumulative review of essential objectives into subsequent units of instruction.
4. Construct and use framed outlines.
5. Design and use interactive graphic organizers.
6. Identify and preteach essential vocabulary words.
7. Highlight textbooks and printed materials.
8. Transcribe or summarize highlighted text to create condensed text.
9. Provide two-column study guides.
10. Provide framed writing assignments.
11. Teach the students to manage their homework.

E.   Attach a summary of the Academic Assistance Plan.

F.   Schedule a follow-up meeting.

Reproducible Form B5: *Academic Assistance (One-Page Form)*

Academic Assistance (One-Page Form)

| Student | Grade/Class | Teacher | Date |

A. Informal assessment information

1. Oral Reading Fluency: _____ words correct per minute

   Materials: _____

2. Strengths and weaknesses:

	Subjects	Abilities	Behavior
Strengths			
Weaknesses			

B. Remediation _____

_____

C. The Adaptation Process

Use the outline below as an optional framework for developing a plan of Academic Assistance.

1. Identify assignments or activities that haven't yet been given.
2. Anticipate problems that the student (and other students) may encounter.
3. Design whole-class instruction to prevent anticipated problems.
4. Consider making assignments more manageable by providing additional assistance.
5. Consider alternative ways for the student to demonstrate knowledge or ability.
6. Gradually fade the adaptations as the student gains competence.

D. The Adaptation Menu

Adaptation involves a never-ending variety of procedures. The strategies that follow are provided as **suggestions but are not exhaustive**. Discuss and brainstorm other possibilities.

1. Focus assignments on essential course content and skills.
2. Focus test items on essential course content and skills.
3. Build cumulative review of essential objectives into subsequent units of instruction.
4. Construct and use framed outlines.
5. Design and use interactive graphic organizers.
6. Identify and preteach essential vocabulary words.
7. Highlight textbooks and printed materials.
8. Transcribe or summarize highlighted text.
9. Provide two-column study guides.
10. Provide framed writing assignments.
11. Teach the students to manage their homework.

E. Attach a summary of the Academic Assistance Plan.

F. Schedule a follow-up meeting.

Reproducible Form B6: *Vocabulary Practice Log*

Intervention B:
Academic Assistance

Vocabulary Practice Log

Student _____ Class _____ Date _____

Word	Definition	Sentence	Picture	Page

Reproducible Form B7: *Study Guide*

Study Guide

Student _____ Grade/Class _____ Teacher _____ Date _____

Questions	Answers
1.	_____ _____
2.	_____ _____
3.	_____ _____
4.	_____ _____
5.	_____ _____
6.	_____ _____
7.	_____ _____
8.	_____ _____
9.	_____ _____
10.	_____ _____

Reproducible Form B8: *Homework Log (Signature/Comments)*

Homework Log (Signature/Comments)

Due	Parent/Guardian Signature and Comments

Reproducible Form B9: *Homework Log (Assignment/Signature)*

Homework Log (Assignment/Signature)

Student _____   Homeroom _____

Due	Assignment	Parent/Guardian Signature

Reproducible Form B10: *Grade Tracking Log*

Assignment and Grade Tracking Log

Student _____   Homeroom _____   Subject _____

Due	Assignment	Points Earned / Points Possible	Total Points Earned / Total Points Possible	Current Grade

Intervention B:
Academic Assistance

Daily Homework Plan

Student _____   Date _____

List of Things to Do:

Class/Period	Assignment	Materials	When

Goal Setting

The student has difficulty with motivation and may not understand how to reach a goal

PURPOSE

GOAL SETTING can assist students with just about any behavior- or motivation-related problem.

THIS INTERVENTION IS APPROPRIATE FOR:

Minor misbehavior
- tattling
- disorganization
- perfectionism
- sloppy work

Annoying habits
- nose picking
- gum chewing
- pencil tapping
- leaning back in chair

INTERVENTION

C

Goal Setting helps the student find the motivation and steps necessary to change.

Conduct
- disruptive behavior
- insubordination
- rambunctious behavior

Attitude
- complaining
- negativity
- criticism
- bossiness

Authority
- arguing
- talking back
- disrespect

Neglect
- deprivation
- lack of positive role models
- lack of positive interactions with adults
- poor self-esteem

This intervention, Goal Setting, helps students identify what they hope to accomplish and what actions they can take to reach their goals. Goal Setting is effective when it is implemented in the early stages of a student's problem behavior, reducing the likelihood that more intensive interventions will be required later. In chronic or severe cases, Goal Setting helps the student find the motivation and steps necessary to change. In later-stage intervention, Goal Setting can be implemented in conjunction with other interventions to increase the likelihood students will change their behavior in the long term. Interventions that work well with Goal Setting include "Intervention M: Teaching Replacement Behavior," "Intervention K: Self-Monitoring and Self-Evaluation," and "Intervention O: Structured Reinforcement Systems."

Note: Whether the process of identifying achievement targets is called *goal setting* or *contracting* is largely a matter of semantics. Informal verbal agreements are often referred to as goal setting, and formalizing goals with a written agreement is often called contracting. Since the difference between these terms is hazy, this intervention will use the term *goal setting* to refer to both processes.

RATIONALE

Students with behavior problems frequently lack a sense of direction and purpose. Though they often have the same long-range aspirations as "good" students, they may have difficulty doing what is necessary to develop the habits and skills required for success. They may know they should "try harder" and "be more responsible," but they often do not know how to take action to move toward those ends. As their perceived failures multiply, many of these students begin to view themselves as "bad" and incapable of success.

When goals are clear and within reach, students can begin taking control of their actions.

Students who experience repeated failure or lack positive guidance also often have difficulty setting realistic goals. They tend to select goals that are too easy, so they experience no pride in accomplishment. Or they select goals so challenging that they set themselves up for failure. These students often believe that their efforts are futile. This intervention can give students the direction and confidence they need to become more successful in school.

Goal Setting also has many positive side benefits. It increases both the clarity and specificity of the teacher's expectations, provides extra opportunities for the student to receive positive adult attention, and communicates (and fosters) high expectations.

Goal Setting helps students and adults identify goals that are specific, attainable, and worthy. When goals are clear and within reach, students can begin taking control of their actions. Adults can acknowledge accomplishments, and errors can be used to help students learn how to get back on track.

> "Students can hit any achievement target they can see and that will sit still for them."
>
> – Richard Stiggins, Assessment Training Institute

Some students lack motivation and need a structured problem-solving process like Goal Setting in order to make changes. For example, Keisha is a third-grade student who annoys adults and is shunned by peers. She is a chronic tattler. If two students have an argument on the playground, Keisha has to tell the teacher. If a student accidentally bumps into Keisha, she immediately lodges a complaint with the teacher. She promptly tells the lunchroom supervisor if another student cuts in line. Not a day goes by that Keisha doesn't tattle several times. Her teacher has tried discussing the problem with Keisha, but Keisha continues to demonstrate tattling behaviors. Because Keisha is an irritation to those around her and is clearly unhappy about her social status, her teacher decides to try Goal Setting. This process can help Keisha identify a personal goal and actions that can be taken to reach the goal. Through Goal Setting, Keisha may learn to make friends and to determine when adult help is really needed.

Similarly, Caden can benefit from setting goals. This ninth-grade student is at risk of dropping out of school. Though he maintains passing grades, Caden has begun cutting classes and associating with kids who have already dropped out. The counselor decides that Caden might still have a chance of completing school if someone intervenes immediately. By establishing goals for Caden's future and then providing the support he will need to reach them, the counselor hopes to help Caden redirect himself before it is too late.

Goal Setting can be a useful process to help resolve problems that range from trivial to severe for people of all ages, abilities, and walks of life. Learning to set and achieve realistic goals is a lifelong skill that allows students to develop purpose and control.

IMPLEMENTATION STEPS
Step 1: Develop a plan.

Gather any relevant background information that may help with designing and implementing the intervention. In addition, keep parents or guardians informed about your concerns and all aspects of any intervention plans being considered.

A. Review the problem and overall goals for the student.

1. Identify the student's strengths.

> Every intervention should start with a review of the student's strengths. By acknowledging a student's positive traits and skills, you can frame the goal discussion in terms of building on those qualities—and avoid sounding overly critical.

2. Determine the outcome you hope to achieve.

One of the surest ways to get where you want to go in life is to know the destination from the start. This is the central point of Goal Setting. Identify the outcome you hope to achieve with the student, considering in advance what you want to address with this intervention and why. Do you want to reduce a problem behavior? In this case, think about positive behaviors the student might be asked to substitute for the unwanted behavior. Do you want to increase a particular behavior or trait? To increase a positive quality such as motivation, consider a few questions: What would a more highly motivated student look like? How would you (and the student) determine whether the student was in fact becoming more motivated? Would you see outward signs? To intervene effectively with a student to set effective goals, you should have a good idea where you're heading before you perform any further steps.

3. Review information gathered from previous interventions.

If you are working in sequence through this book, you may have already tried "Planned Discussion" and/or "Academic Assistance" interventions, in which case you already have a record of the prior actions taken with this student. Examine that information and decide whether you want to capitalize on the previous interventions or whether it might be more productive to move in a different direction for Goal Setting. Reviewing the student's data can help you determine whether her problem is one of ability, motivation, or some other factor that might influence the goals you set with the student.

4. Decide whether to focus on short-range or long-range goals.

Short-range goals can generally be accomplished within the year. Long-range goals, with or without immediate targets for achievement, help spur a student's thinking about aspirations and the future. With planning for long-range goals, you typically start at the desired end result or outcome and work backward. ("Here is where you would like to see yourself in 10 years. What would you have to do to get to that point? What would you have to work for to get to that?") Of course, you may elect to try a combination of long-range and short-range goals.

5. Consider whether corrective consequences should be part of the plan.

If consequences for rule violations are already in play, perhaps continue with them as a standard part of your classroom management plan. You may

As a general principle, it's best not to include rewards as part of an intervention plan, at least initially.

also want to explore whether a different set of consequences or a different type of consequence would be more conducive to the goal-setting process. It's important that you let the student know in advance what corrective consequences (if any) you will implement if the goal target is not met so the student does not feel blindsided if and when consequences are leveled. Consequences should be mild enough that you know you can consistently follow through. Think through consequences before the meeting with the student so that you can explain the consequences at the meeting. Refer to "Intervention P: Defining Limits and Establishing Consequences."

6. Decide whether rewards should be part of the plan.

Consider whether you will offer the student rewards for attaining her goals. As a general principle, it's best *not* to include rewards as part of an intervention plan, at least initially. It may be worthwhile to wait and see if Goal Setting itself is sufficient to improve behavior. If behavior does improve, you still have the option of foregoing structured rewards in favor of positive feedback, with its accompanying (and research-documented) benefits to student motivation, morale, and outcomes. Rewards in and of themselves are not bad and are sometimes necessary, but the danger is that the student may come to expect rewards and regress to previous behavior patterns when the intervention has faded.

If you are fairly confident that a student will not be intrinsically motivated to work toward a goal, consider whether the goal can be reframed to be more compelling to the student. If you do decide to use structured rewards with Goal Setting, it may be useful to combine this intervention with "Intervention O: Structured Reinforcement Systems."

If rewards will not be part of the intervention plan, have a ready response for the natural question, "What's in it for me?" You might mention the satisfaction of achieving a goal, discovering the ability to accomplish things the student hasn't done before, pride in a job well done, or the extra attention the student will receive from you and other teachers as a direct result of making an effort and improving.

7. Decide whether you will be directive (unilateral) or collaborative in negotiating goals with the student.

As much as you can, make the student an integral part of the goal-setting process. Involving a student in negotiating goals makes the student feel like an active participant with an investment in the intervention process. You may choose to direct the conversation more actively in a couple of situations. For example, if the student is a chronic attention-seeker and you would like the student to appeal for attention appropriately instead of demanding it in inappropriate ways, you may be directive in suggesting goals, at least initially. After introducing your concern, explain why the student's current strategies are disruptive and not the best way to get attention. With as much specificity as you can, outline some behaviors you would prefer to see and explain why they may be better, easier, and more effective ways to get your attention or the attention of peers. Then stress how you'll work to notice the student's efforts and how proud you'll be when the student's goals are met.

Another type of student with whom you may need to be more directive is the withdrawn, passive student who rarely volunteers more than a one-syllable response or contributes actively. If you envision a one-sided conference where you do all the talking and the student responds monosyllabically, think through your preferred goal contract in advance so that you can move right into that phase of the discussion: "A couple of goals that I would like to see you working on are . . . "

Negotiating goals can offset a power struggle with a strong-minded, articulate student. Instead of trying to one-up the student, appeal to the student's strengths: "Here's the problem that I have when you do these things in the classroom. I'm open to your ideas on this, because I know you are smart and articulate and have good ideas. Let's work on goal-setting together so that we can get your needs met, and I can continue to teach and be effective." By engaging in some give-and-take, you can have a spirited interaction that takes advantage of the student's own problem-solving abilities. The more you can use what that student says in the goal conference, the more the student will feel a level of ownership as a result.

Caden is a high school freshman. He has been identified as a high-risk student due to a 1.5 GPA in the first quarter of school. Caden has already been sent to detention twice for being "mouthy" with two different teachers. Because of the school's policy of "red-flagging" any students who fails two or more classes in a quarter, Caden's situation has come to the attention of Mr. Williams, the counselor for the freshman class.

Mr. Williams has spoken with Caden, Caden's mother, and the counselor from Caden's middle school. Caden's mother and the middle school counselor indicate that Caden has a long history of disruptive behavior and

Goal Setting may involve short-range goals, long-range goals, or both, and goals may be behavioral, academic, or social.

fighting and a poor academic record. School records show that Caden has been referred to special education for academic assistance, but he fails to qualify. An informal reading inventory shows good fluency in reading and adequate comprehension skills. Work samples show marginal writing skills. Teacher comments frequently mention that Caden is very capable when he tries, but he continually fails to complete both in-class and out-of-class work.

Caden is an only child in a single-parent home. Caden's mother says his behavior at home is also disruptive and she doesn't know what to do with him. Though adult supervision is limited, shouting matches seem to occur frequently.

Caden's mother is pleased that he has made it through the first nine weeks of school without a major behavioral problem. She says that she will consider joining a parent support group sponsored through the school, but she probably won't bother to attend—she is "tied up with AA and all." She says she would be happy to have the school try anything, but "Caden is just a bad kid" and she doesn't have time to come to school "to bail Caden out all the time."

Mr. Williams decides that intervention is critical if Caden is going to complete high school, so he submits Caden's name for intervention through the team of teachers who work with Caden's group. This team meets regularly to talk about their students who are struggling.

After discussing Caden's general background, the team selects Goal Setting to implement. Mr. Williams agrees to work with Caden on goal setting and to meet with him regularly to monitor progress.

B. Select a goal-setting format.

Goal Setting can be formal or informal. It may involve short-range goals, long-range goals, or both, and goals may be behavioral, academic, or social. The actual goal-setting format will depend on the age and sophistication of the student and the student's degree of readiness to improve. To select an appropriate goal-setting format, review the reproducible goal-setting forms in this chapter. These forms include a range of options that allows for flexibility in designing an intervention plan. Included are forms that focus on long- or short-range goals as well as forms that specify both. In addition, the forms vary in the amount of detail, who will sign them, and their degree of formality. After looking through the possibilities, choose the forms that will best assist in the goal-setting process. You may wish to alter the basic formats or design your own. Try to envision a goal-setting session with your student. This will help you in determining a format that is appropriate for the situation and the student.

> Note: Not all reproducible forms are shown throughout this chapter. You should skim through the *Reproducible Materials* section at the end of this chapter to determine which goal-setting format is best suited to the student's needs.

Because of Caden's age and sophistication, Mr. Williams decides to help him look at long-range job and personal goals first. This will allow them to establish a reason for setting short-range goals that are focused on improving school success.

C. Determine who will meet with the student.

Invite parents to the goal-setting meeting. Parents or guardians should always be welcomed to participate. Most parents appreciate the opportunity to be involved, and they can provide context regarding the student's prior school history, behavior at home, and family values and aspirations. Even when parents are not overtly supportive, their participation can be important. For example, a parent who encourages his child to fight with others should hear that this cannot be tolerated in the school setting. The parent who associates negative experiences with school should know what school staff members are doing to support the student in a positive way.

In the early stages of a minor problem, Goal Setting may involve an adult and student working one-to-one. The more serious the behavior, the more adults may be involved. A counselor may be necessary to help facilitate and mediate the conversation, and a building administrator should be on hand if the student has major behavioral problems. For the most productive goal-setting conference, try to include people who know the student well and can convey a sense of support and teamwork. Though some students may be overwhelmed by too many adults, in the most severe or chronic cases you may need to involve as many as three adults (not including the student's parents) and produce a detailed written contract.

INTERVENTION C

The goal-setting conference should be scheduled at a neutral time—not as an immediate response to misbehavior.

Mr. Williams calls Caden's mother and describes the intervention planning team's (IPT's) plan to help Caden. During the phone conversation, Caden's mother reiterates that she has no objections to the school trying anything it wants, but she is not interested in being directly involved.

In talking with Caden's teachers, Mr. Williams hears consistently that Caden tends to be passive-aggressive and discourages friendly interactions with his teachers. Based on these considerations, Mr. Williams decides to work alone with Caden during the goal-setting session. He senses that involving other teachers may make Caden feel that the goal-setting session is designed to push the school's agenda rather than to help Caden establish his own goals.

D. Set up a goal-setting conference.

Prearrange the goal-setting conference with the student and all adults who will be involved. Whether it's designed to assist with minor or severe problems, the goal-setting conference should be scheduled at a neutral time—not as an immediate response to misbehavior. If a student is asked to engage in Goal Setting immediately following a major problem with a teacher or with other students, he is likely to feel angry, afraid, or defensive. In these situations, it is difficult for adults and students to think objectively about the future. Once the immediate situation has passed, Goal Setting can be used to help the student prevent future problems.

The atmosphere of the conference needs to be as supportive and as upbeat as possible, with enough time reserved to explore options with the student.

Note: As a general rule, plan to actively involve the student in planning goals the student will work on, as it increases the likelihood that he will strive to reach them. However, if the student tends to be very passive, be prepared to move the conference along. You may also need to be more directive if the student is highly attention seeking, as you will want to clarify how the student should be getting your attention in a productive manner.

Step 2: Meet with the student.

Introduce the concept of goal setting to the student. The student needs to understand that setting goals will help him take control. It isn't something that is being "done to" him, but is a process that can help him learn to grow and mature.

Mr. Williams: (Counselor)	Caden, I am glad to be meeting with you. We have a large high school here, and sometimes we feel that we are losing touch with some of our students. I asked you to meet with me today because we are worried about you and hope that we can help you get a good education at this school.

Note: The text follows a step-by-step progression. However, the order in which these steps occur will vary depending on the situation. Read through the procedures to determine whether to begin with Step 2A, 2B, or 2C. Step 2A is optional and may be inappropriate for younger students.

A. Help the student establish long-range goals (optional).

1. Encourage the student to think about the kind of life he or she would like to have in the future.

   What kind of residence, car, job, and family can the student envision? If the student has ideas on the type of lifestyle he would like in the future, determine whether the student has any idea of the cost and effort it will take to attain the vision. If not, provide some assignments (for you and the student) to collect information. For example, you could have the student look up car prices on the Internet or at local lots, and you could get information on housing costs in different areas of the city.

   If the student has no idea about any type of future job, learn about the student's interests and try to help the student explore job options that would capitalize on those interests. It might be useful at this point to have a career counselor join you, or at the very least to do Web searches.

If the student has no aspirations, identify someone you could invite to the next conference who might serve as an inspiration. For example, if the student is a "gang wannabe," you could try to find a community group comprised of former gang members who talk to youth. Or perhaps you could identify a local pastor, sports personality, or anyone else who might be able to spark interest in life goals—and invite him or her to join you and the student.

2. Help the student determine qualifications for the types of jobs that are of most interest.

This may require more research, such as calling employers. Between the student's efforts and your efforts on the student's behalf, gathering more information about future career paths could potentially take a month or two.

3. Identify immediate actions the student can take to move toward this goal.

This step may move you toward short-range Goal Setting. Once you have established some typical qualifications for pursuing the student's ideal job, start working in reverse chronological order. That is, work backward from the ideal situation to where the student is now to determine logical steps the student will need to take to reach the goal. If the job skills require a trade school or some college education, what would it take for the student to get into that kind of institution? Finding out what GPAs, curricular mileposts, and extracurricular activities these schools look for would be a good next step.

This "backward plan" will end at the student's current situation. How many credits will the student need to graduate? How many credits does the student currently have? Does the student need help with passing particular classes? The conversation can naturally move into the area of short-range Goal Setting: determine what the student can do right now and in the near term to start taking conscious control of his immediate future and begin heading toward his long-range goals.

If the goal-setting meeting is with an elementary or middle school student, the discussion can be much more cursory. You can sketch the general outline without going into the level of detail that you would with a high school student. You might talk about what the child will need to accomplish to get into high school and be successful there. Consider sitting down with a high school counselor to talk about what it takes to get through the higher grade levels and how other students have achieved it.

The goal-setting process is almost as important as the outcome. Introduce goal-setting strategies as skills that will help the student be more successful in the future. Many students have difficulty setting realistic goals. It is not uncommon to find at-risk students who aspire to be basketball stars—though they do not play on a basketball team—or rock stars— though they can barely play a guitar. Likewise, it is not uncommon to find at-risk students who aspire to get straight As even though they are failing several classes. By setting unrealistic goals, these students set themselves up for failure. Goal Setting helps students learn to establish goals that are not only attainable, but worthy of their personal pride.

In the long range, Goal Setting helps the student envision what he will be doing in the future. The Long-Range Goal Setting form (Reproducible Form C1) guides the student to identify an age at which he would like to be independent and the type of job and personal life he hopes to enjoy.

> *The goal-setting process is almost as important as the outcome.*

> **Note:** A copy of this form and other goal-setting and behavioral contract forms are provided in the *Reproducible Materials* section at the end of this chapter and on the CD.

If a student's long-range goals seem unrealistic, it is generally best to acknowledge the goals and encourage the student to include other job possibilities. "You would like to be a famous actor. That's great! When we look at your short-range goals, we'll need to think about ways to get you into some drama classes. Actors draw on a lot of real-life experiences to create their roles, so you should be thinking about the kinds of experiences you can choose at school to help you. I'd also like you to do some thinking about other things you'd like to do. Adults who have major difficulties are often people who haven't left themselves many options. Think of other things you enjoy and the types of jobs that might be possible."

If the student can't identify what he wants, he probably hasn't thought much about it. Provide the student with a variety of options. For example, on the Long-Range Goal Setting form, the student is asked to describe the kinds of people he wishes to spend his time with as an adult. If the student doesn't know where to begin, generate a list of options. "Let's make a list of the characteristics of people we know. Then you can look at that list and identify words that describe the kind of people you would like to spend time with when you are older."

After long-range goals have been established (Step 2A), have the student identify actions to take and actions to avoid to reach the goal (Step 2B). In Step 2C, have the student establish short-range goals. This three-step process helps the student connect his current actions with the future. The process may need to be repeated again and again, not unlike the natural goal-setting process that occurs incidentally in many family settings.

After long-range goals have been established, have the student identify actions to take and actions to avoid to reach the goal.

INTERVENTION C

Mr. Williams: (Counselor)	Caden, I'd like to help you set some goals. We'd like to know what you need to accomplish during the four years you attend West Lincoln High.
Caden:	So . . . ?
Mr. Williams:	So, first we need to look at what you would like to do when you are no longer in school.
Caden:	What difference does that make?
Mr. Williams:	It makes a lot of difference. Let's think ahead. Think about what you might like to be doing when you are 22. That's a time when you will be on your own. More than likely, you won't be living with your mother any longer.
Caden:	She's made that clear. Eighteen and out . . . .
Mr. Williams:	I know it's kind of hard to think about now, but by the time you are 18, you may be glad to be on your own. We need to do three things today. First, I'd like to work with you on what you'd like to do as an adult, and then we can begin identifying what you can do now so you'll be able to accomplish those things. Finally, I'd like to help you put together some short-range goals that you can actually work on in the next nine weeks.
Caden:	If it'll make you happy.
Mr. Williams:	Yes, it will make me happy. But more importantly, this may help you take control of your own life.
Caden:	This is all pretty stupid. I'm going to be in a band. If my mom would just buy me a new amp, I'd be set.
Mr. Williams:	Caden, music is a wonderful thing, and I hope that you are able to keep it up. Let's not forget that you have that goal. In the meantime, I also want you to think about how you will support yourself while you are waiting for your big break—what you'll do to support yourself, who you will want to be around, and so on. Some musicians make it when they're still very young, but most have to support themselves by other means.
Caden:	(No response)

| Mr. Williams:
(Counselor) | Let's get started, then. Caden, long-range goal setting is a process that you will need to do over and over again. It's part of being an adult. It can be adjusted over time, but it will help you get a handle on what you want for yourself. |

Mr. Williams is able to assist Caden in identifying long-range goals (Sample Reproducible Form C1).

Once long-range goals are clarified, Mr. Williams guides Caden through a process of identifying situations to avoid and things he can do to reach his long-range goals. This leads to short-range goal setting to help Caden begin making a connection between his current actions and his future goals.

Ask the student to think of the types of problems that are roadblocks to success.

Note: For younger students, Goal Setting should generally begin with Step 2B, the process of identifying actions to avoid and actions to take, or with Step 2C, identifying short-term goals.

B. Brainstorm actions to avoid and actions to take—what the student can do to find greater success in the school setting.

If problems triggered the need for the goal-setting conference, the conference should include brainstorming and identifying things to avoid as well as goals to strive for. Ask the student to think of the types of problems that are roadblocks to success—hitting, fighting, poor grades, talking back, arguing, putting others down, and so on. If the student uses blanket statements such as "I get sent to the office because I cause trouble" or "I get on the teacher's bad side," help translate these value-laden generalizations to specific and observable behaviors. If the student denies having had behavioral problems, gently provide evidence.

At the same time, brainstorm specific actions that the student can take to be more successful. Set a ground rule for all members of the conference that all ideas will be written down and will not be evaluated at this time. Identifying actions to take and actions to avoid is a major step in Goal Setting. The student needs to know that he can take specific actions to be "good," "better," "more responsible," "smarter," and generally more successful. Figure C1 provides an example list of ideas

Sample Reproducible Form C1: *Long-Range Goal Setting*

Long-Range Goal Setting

<u>Caden Martinez</u>   <u>9</u>   <u>Mr. Williams</u>   <u>9/30</u>
Student   Grade/Class   Teacher   Date

At the age of __22__ , I hope to have or be doing the following.

Self-Sufficiency

I would like to support myself in a job that pays _about $30,000 per year._

I would like a job where I work _outside a lot or play music. I would like to work in the woods._

A job I might like to have is _working with the State Fish and Wildlife Commission._

Personal Life

I hope that my family is _kind, caring, and generous. I would like to be married and hope to have one kid (with another later on)._

I would like to spend time with people who are _friendly to others, considerate, and don't think only of themselves._

During my free time, I would like to _hunt, fish, and travel._

for a student who has difficulty with peer interactions. It lists the actions she should avoid and actions she should take.

Figure C1: *Brainstormed Actions*

Actions to Avoid	Actions to Take
Hitting	Stop, think, get help
Calling names	Treat everyone respectfully
Spitting	Respect school property

If the goal-setting conference has included long-range Goal Setting, help the student determine behaviors that create roadblocks to achieving long-range goals—and positive actions that can be taken to reach them.

Mr. Williams: (Counselor)	Caden, we need to identify the things that might make it hard to reach your goals. You said that you might like a job with the state Fish and Wildlife Commission and that you'd like to be around people who are friendly and considerate of others. Let's make a list of actions you can take to make those goals happen (Figure C2).

Figure C2: *Caden's Brainstormed Actions*

Job Goal Actions to Take	Personal Goal Actions to Take
Graduate from high school	Make friends
Go to college	Not be an idiot
"B" average	Listen
Work hard	Think about others
Pay attention	Be considerate of others
Get my work done	Help people out
Pass tests	

Job Goal Actions to Avoid	Personal Goal Actions to Avoid
Getting suspended	Picking fights
Fighting	Thinking about just me
Smart mouthing the teacher	Trying to get even
Procrastinating	
Getting mad	

Though Goal Setting is especially effective with at-risk students, the process can benefit all children.

Brainstorm things that adults who are present might do to assist the student in reaching goals. Get the student's input on which actions adults can take to give the greatest assistance. Then proceed to Step 2C to help establish what the student can do to create and reach short-range goals.

C. Help the student establish short-range goals.

Short-range goals help the student establish a target to achieve in the near future. Goals should be positively stated and reachable. Too often students are asked to reach a goal like "not hitting others." Because the goal is stated negatively, the student cannot take pride or satisfaction in reaching it. Moreover, the student must "fight" the natural human tendency to gravitate *toward* the subject of a statement. When you say, "Don't think about a pony," a pony will often be the next image that springs to mind. Similarly, if a student has difficulty with hitting and aggression, the goal "don't hit other students" may have the opposite effect and tempt the student to hit others. A better goal might be to "play cooperatively with other students." If a student is impulsive, the goal might be to "practice self-control." If a student has difficulty sitting still and listening during class discussions, the goal might be to "listen respectfully and contribute responsibly to class discussions."

Short-term Goal Setting can help the student learn to work for specific goals, such as improving grades, or it can help the student work to develop positive traits, such as being responsible, organized, respectful, tolerant, self-reliant, cooperative, flexible, hardworking, or creative. Short-range Goal Setting can help a student learn to be a problem-solver or risk-taker. Though Goal Setting is especially effective with at-risk students, the process can benefit all children.

TIP: *Attach a label (a positive attribute or trait) to the goal for easy reference.*
Attach a positive attribute or trait that creates an umbrella for the specific behaviors you would like the student to work on. Umbrella statements could be something like "be independent" or "persevere with a difficult task." You will use this label to both teach and inspire the student to achieve and exhibit the specific behaviors that are subsumed under this broad umbrella statement.

Reproducible Form C2 is a useful tool for setting short-range goals. Use this form or another format to guide you and the student in determining short-range goals and procedures. The goal statement on Reproducible Form C2 begins, "My personal goal is . . ." and should finish with the trait or positive action that is the focus of the goal conference, such as the following:

Reproducible Form C2: *Goal Setting (Version 1)*

Goal Setting (Version 1)

_____   _____   _____   _____
Student   Grade/Class   Teacher   Date

My personal goal is _____

_____

I can show that I am working on this goal by _____

_____

_____

_____

_____

Student signature _____

. . . .

I can help you reach this goal by _____

_____

_____

_____

_____

Teacher/Mentor signature _____

- to get along with other students
- to treat others respectfully
- to be self-reliant
- to be independent
- to read a book from start to finish
- to be more creative in my writing
- to get a B in science
- to show self-control
- to persevere with difficult tasks
- to make one new friend

After Caden and Mr. Williams have identified actions to take and actions to avoid, Mr. Williams assists Caden in short-range Goal Setting. In discussing his long-range goal of working with the Fish and Wildlife Commission (while playing in a band on weekends), Caden decides that he needs to go to college. This statement logically brings the discussion to grades. Caden learns that his 1.5 GPA would make it next to impossible to get into a four-year college. However, he also finds out that since he hasn't received his first semester grades in high school, he still has time to turn things around.

Caden:	So what kind of grades do I need to get into a college?
Mr. Williams: (Counselor)	Things are getting tighter in our state. You might want to think about going to the community college here in town.
Caden:	Mom says it isn't any good. I should go to the university.
Mr. Williams:	I know some people think that way. Many of our students go to the community college first and then move on to the university. It's something I'd like you to keep an open mind about. The community college is also a lot less expensive. Another thing to think about is that freshman classes at the university are huge—imagine 150 to 200 students in one classroom. At the community college, you can get your basics out of the way in smaller classes and then move on to the university for more specialized courses.
Caden:	Maybe.
Mr. Williams:	You've got four years here, so there's a lot of time to think about it. The important thing to recognize is that you can make it possible to do what you want or you can make it impossible.

Caden:	What kind of grades do I need for the university?
Mr. Williams:	Well, they just raised the entrance requirement to a 3.0 GPA.
Caden:	That's what I want to do.
Mr. Williams:	Good. Let's work on a short-range goal that gradually gets you to that goal.
Caden:	Yeah, right! You don't think I can do it.
Mr. Williams:	Right now, you have a 1.5. It would be pretty hard to get to a 3.0 by the end of the semester. But maybe you could try for a 2.0 for this semester and then a 2.5 or 3.0 by third quarter. Caden, you have been very mature through this session. It's important that you are learning how to set goals you can reach. Some of our students are always unhappy because they set themselves up for failure. I don't think you need to do that. You are too wise.
Caden:	So, OK. I need to get a 2.0.
Mr. Williams:	Yes. Work for a 2.0. If you do better, that's great. Then we can work toward your next goal. If you get the 2.0, you will know that you can set a goal and reach it. If you don't reach the 2.0, we will work together to find other strategies to help you reach that goal.

D. Help the student identify specific actions he is willing to take to reach his short-range goals.

Once a short-range goal has been established, help the student select specific actions that he is willing to take to reach that goal. Go over the list of actions to take and actions to avoid that were brainstormed in Step 2B. (If this step hasn't been completed yet, work on it now.) Next, assist the student in selecting actions that are most likely to bring the student success.

E. Identify ways that adults can help the student reach his goals.

Adults can help the student in his efforts to reach short- and long-range goals. This step is important so that the student knows he is not alone. Another brainstorming exercise that involves the adults and student may assist in this portion of the goal-setting conference. Once members have brainstormed a list of adult support activities, have the student work with you to pick the items that would be most helpful. Some ideas follow:

INTERVENTION

C

- Give positive feedback when the student makes an effort to meet the goal.

- Call the student's parents on good days.

- Send home a daily report card of some sort.

- Let the student have lunch with the principal or a favorite teacher when things are going well.

- Give the student reminders about the goal.

- Correct the first problems on an assignment immediately.

- Provide a tutor.

In many cases, the student and adult should also clarify consequences for problem behavior.

F. **If using rewards, a structured reinforcement system, or corrective consequences, make sure the student understands all of the contingencies.**

The need for external motivators or consequences varies with the age, willingness, and sophistication of the student. Goal Setting combines well with "Intervention O: Structured Reinforcement Systems" and "Intervention P: Defining Limits and Establishing Consequences."

Goal-setting conferences are generally positive, designed to create an atmosphere and expectation of success. However, if Goal Setting is initiated due to a severe and chronic problem, a 180-degree turnaround is unlikely to result from this single intervention alone. In many cases, the student and adult should also clarify consequences for problem behavior. In all parts of the conference, the student should be involved in advancing this process (even a young student). "Monique, if you forget about your goal to treat others respectfully and you call other children names, what should I do?" Explore different aspects of the problem behavior and identify consequences for inappropriate behavior that cannot be ignored.

Avoid setting up overly harsh consequences. When severe consequences are laid out, adults are often unwilling to implement them—especially if the student has been showing signs of improvement. Consequences should be prearranged so that adults can implement them consistently. Once consequences are determined, ask *what-if* questions to ensure that everyone understands when and how consequences will be implemented. (See "Intervention P: Defining Limits and Establishing Consequences" for more information.)

Some goal-setting plans will also require structured reinforcement, but it's best to avoid these systems if the plan has a high probability of success without external rewards. Although there is nothing wrong with or unethical about using reinforcement systems, they take a great deal of time and effort to establish and maintain, and they may decrease the likelihood the student will continue to exhibit positive behavior as the intervention is faded. In addition, if the student strives to achieve goals without a reinforcement system, it is easier for the student to attribute success to his own commitment and efforts. However, if the student needs additional motivation to work toward the goal, implement "Intervention O: Structured Reinforcement Systems" along with this intervention. The positive aspects of a reinforcement system generally outweigh the negative. The sooner the student begins practicing successful behavior, the better.

If the problem is severe or the student is very young, brief once-a-day conferences may be necessary.

Mr. Williams believes that Caden's goals will be inherently reinforcing, and because Caden established the goals, Mr. Williams decides that an external reinforcement system may not be necessary. If Caden can improve his grades and develop some positive relationships with adults and other students, reinforcement will come from attaining his goal.

Mr. Williams: (Counselor)	Caden, at this point I sometimes talk with students about consequences for not engaging in appropriate behavior, but I think you already know the consequences. If you fail to get your work in, what will happen?
Caden:	I'll flunk.
Mr. Williams:	And if you argue with the teachers, what will happen?
Caden:	They'll kick me out.
Mr. Williams:	Now that you are in high school, the rules have changed a bit. Teachers have high expectations. You will be treated like the adult you are becoming.

G. Set regular times to follow up and discuss progress.

This step is an important key to making Goal Setting an effective intervention. Adults need to show an active interest in the student's progress, as Goal Setting is rarely a quick, one-shot intervention. Schedule the first follow-up meeting no later than one week after the initial conference and plan to meet regularly thereafter, both formally and informally.

These progress conferences can be conducted by classroom teachers, counselors, administrators, teaching assistants, or anyone who serves as a mentor to the student. In most cases, the student should meet with an adult at least once each week. If the problem is severe or the student is very young, brief once-a-day conferences may be necessary.

Mr. Williams: (Counselor)	Caden, now that you've got a couple of great goals, you'll need to select a few things that you want to do to reach your goals. Then I'll see if I can help you with some of them. I would like to meet with you once a week to discuss your progress. I'm wondering if we can meet briefly every Monday at the end of sixth period. We can keep it short so you will not miss your bus.

H. Review responsibilities and sign the Goal Setting form.

Summarize the information developed in the goal-setting conference. When completed, have all involved parties sign the Goal Setting form that was used. (See Sample Reproducible Form C2 for a completed sample of Caden's Goal Setting form.)

Rarely, a student will refuse to sign. Ask the student to identify changes that could be made so he would be willing to sign. If the student still refuses, it is important not to turn the situation into a power struggle. Simply let the student know that the adults will carry out their end of the plan to help the student achieve his goals. If the student makes some progress, he may be willing to sign the form in a subsequent goal-setting session.

I. Conclude the goal-setting conference with words of encouragement.

Mr. Williams: (Counselor)	I am very glad that I will have an opportunity to work with you. You have a good future ahead of you. We can work together to get you where you want to go. Thanks for coming in, Caden. I'll meet with you on Friday so we can set up a grade-monitoring system.

Step 3: Provide ongoing support and encouragement.

Like an athletics coach, recognize progress—even if it is seemingly minute—and encourage the student to keep striving. With the student's permission, share his goals with parents and other staff members who have contact with the student. For example, if a student has difficulty with peer relationships, playground supervisors should be informed of the student's goal-setting plan so that they can recognize the student's efforts. "Deke, I noticed that you were sharing the ball with Samantha today, even though you were the first to get it. I'm impressed!"

Mr. Williams: (Counselor)	Caden, I would like to share your goals with your mom and your teachers. I think it will help you if they know what we are working on. I've looked at the list of your teachers, and I believe they will all try to help. I realize that you aren't comfortable with all your teachers, but they do want you to succeed. Is that OK?
Caden:	I guess.
Mr. Williams:	Good.

Mr. Williams sends a letter to each of Caden's teachers (Figure C3). The letter requests assistance and identifies specific actions that staff can take to provide support. A copy of Caden's goal plan is attached to the letter.

Figure C3: *Letter to Caden's Teachers*

West Lincoln High School

Dear Staff:

I have just completed a goal-setting conference with Caden Martinez.
He is a freshman in your _____ class, _____ period.
Caden's goal-setting form is attached.

Caden is very nervous around adults. He has good aspirations, but a long history of failure. Your assistance is needed.

PLEASE
1. Review Caden's goals
2. Fill out our weekly rating sheet for Caden. (I will send it around every Friday.)
3. Say hello quietly to Caden each day.
4. Ignore any talk-backs by immediately turning to another student.
5. Keep in touch with me regarding progress and problems.

THANKS! Let me know if there are questions or concerns.

Sincerely,

Brad Williams
Brad Williams

Sample Reproducible Form C2: *Goal Setting (Version 1)*

Goal Setting (Version 1)

Caden Martinez	9	Mr. Williams	9/30
Student	Grade/Class	Teacher	Date

My personal goal is _to earn a 2.0 G.P.A. for the next grading period and to get along with others--including the teachers._

I can show that I am working on this goal by _____

1. _Turning in all homework._

2. _Studying for tests._

3. _Not arguing with teachers._

4. _Being friendly and acknowledging others._

Student signature _Caden Martinez_

· ·

I can help you reach this goal by _____

1. _Getting you into the homework club._

2. _Helping you set up a system for tracking your assigments and grades._

3. _Helping you set up a system for studying for tests._

4. _Setting up some sessions to practice dealing with anger-provoking situations._

Teacher/Mentor signature _Mr. Williams_

A blank version of this form is available on p. 203.

A. Provide ongoing support and frequent positive feedback when the goal behaviors are exhibited, linking them to the broad label or trait.

It is important to provide continued support and feedback in order to help motivate the student and monitor progress. Using the umbrella statement (the broad positive label or trait) you identified in Step 2C will help the student remember to achieve and exhibit the specific behaviors that are subsumed under a label, such as "be independent" or "persevere with a difficult task."

B. When the student is not successful, correct calmly; avoid sounding disappointed or reproachful.

C. Evaluate the impact of the intervention, making revisions and adjustments as necessary.

When evaluating the impact of the intervention, make changes as needed. If Goal Setting involves long-range goals, have the student periodically rework his short-range goals. When goals are relatively simple and attained quickly, conferences can be held less frequently and through informal check-ins by classroom teachers.

D. Encourage the student to keep striving toward his goals.

During subsequent interactions with the student, cheerfully acknowledge large- or small-scale improvements. Whereas some interventions do produce overnight turnarounds, you will be more likely to see gradual change over time with Goal Setting as the goal behaviors become integrated into the student's self-picture. As this intervention is faded, continue to refer to the goal. If one or more goals have been attained, acknowledge the student's accomplishment and prompt the student to set new goals. Reminding a student how far he has come is a great way to demonstrate your continued interest. Moreover, progress that is self-evident to you as a teacher may not be obvious or even apparent to the student. The student should know that his continued efforts will not be taken for granted.

As this intervention is faded, continue to refer to the goal. If one or more goals have been attained, acknowledge the student's accomplishment and prompt the student to set new goals. Reminding a student how far he has come is a great way to demonstrate your continued interest.

CONCLUSION

Goal Setting is frequently overlooked when planning interventions for at-risk students, yet it offers these students an opportunity to learn how to take control of their own actions. Many students fail to make the connection between their behavior and their experiences—how their daily actions help or hinder their ability to realize a personal goal. Short-range Goal Setting shows students how they can set meaningful achievement targets and attain them. Setting long-range goals can help drifting students connect to their long-term aspirations and futures.

At-risk students generally do have goals and aspirations comparable with those of their peers, but they may need adult assistance in determining realistic and attainable goals. Goal Setting is a powerful tool for helping these students establish a purpose and the means to achieve it.

REFERENCES

Anderman, E. M., Anderman, L. H., & Griesinger, T. (1999). The relation of present and possible academic selves during early adolescence to grade point average and achievement goals. Elementary School Journal, 100, 3–17.

Conte, K. L., & Hintze, J. M. (2000). The effects of performance feedback and goal setting on oral reading fluency within curriculum-based measurement. *Diagnostique, 25*, 85–98.

Copeland, S. R., & Hughes, C. (2002). Effects of goal setting on task performance of persons with mental retardation. *Education and Training in Mental Retardation and Developmental Disabilities, 37*, 40–54.

Dardig, J. C., & Heward, W. L. (1981). *Sign here: A contracting book for children and their parents* (2nd ed.). Bridgewater, NJ: Fournies & Associates.

Doud, J. (1986). A nonintrusive intervention for acting out behavior. *Teaching Exceptional Children, 19*, 38–41.

Graziano, A. M., & Mooney, K. C. (1984). *Children and behavior therapy.* Hawthorne, New York: Aldine de Gruyter.

Kanfer, F., & Goldstein, A. P. (Eds.). (1986). *Helping people change: A textbook of methods.* New York: Pergamon Press.

McKinnon, A. J., & Kiraly, J. (1984). *Pupil behavior, self-control and social skills in the classroom.* Springfield, IL: C. C. Thomas.

Miller, D. L., & Kelley, M. L. (1994). The use of goal setting and contingency contracting for improving children's homework performance. *Journal of Applied Behavior Analysis, 27*(1), 73–84.

Rosen, J. M. (1982). Self-help approaches to self-management. In K. R. Blankstein & J. Polivy (Eds.), *Self-control and self-modification of emotional behavior.* New York: Plenum.

Ruth, W. J. (1996). Goal setting for students with emotional and behavioral difficulties: Analysis of daily, weekly, and total goal attainment. *Psychology in the Schools, 33*, 153–158.

Sprick, R. S. (2006). *Discipline in the secondary classroom: A positive approach to behavior management* (2nd ed.). San Francisco: John Wiley & Sons.

Sprick, R. S., Garrison, M., & Howard, L. (1998). *CHAMPs: A proactive and positive approach to classroom management.* Eugene, OR: Pacific Northwest Publishing.

Sprick, R. S., & Howard, L. (1995). *The teacher's encyclopedia of behavior management: 100 problems/500 plans.* Eugene, OR: Pacific Northwest Publishing.

Walker, H. M., & Fabre, T. R. (1987). Assessment of behavior disorders in the school setting: Issues, problems, and strategies revisited. In N.G. Haring (Ed.), *Measuring and managing behavior disorders* (pp. 198–243). Seattle, WA: University of Washington Press.

Wielkiewicz, R. M. (1986). *Behavior management in the schools.* New York: Pergamon Press.

Reproducible Materials

The following reproducible materials may be used in conjunction with "Intervention C: Goal Setting." Copies are provided here and on the CD. Permission is given for individual classroom teachers to reproduce any forms labeled "Reproducible" for classroom use. Reproduction of these materials for an entire school system is prohibited without express permission of the publisher.

INTERVENTION **C**

GOAL SETTING

Step-by-Step Summary

Following is a summary of the steps involved in Intervention C. It is important to use professional judgment, adjusting procedures to meet the needs of the situation and the individual. See the chapter "Intervention C: Goal Setting" for a detailed description of this intervention.

STEP 1   Develop a plan.

A. Review the problem and overall goals for the student.
   1. Identify the student's strengths.
   2. Determine the outcome you hope to achieve.
   3. Review information gathered from previous interventions.
   4. Decide whether to focus on short-range or long-range goals.
   5. Consider whether corrective consequences should be part of the plan.
   6. Decide whether rewards should be part of the plan.
   7. Decide whether you will be directive (unilateral) or collaborative in negotiating goals with the student.

B. Select a goal-setting format.

C. Determine who will meet with the student.

D. Set up a goal-setting conference.

STEP 2   Meet with the student.

A. Help the student establish long-range goals (optional).
   1. Encourage the student to think about the kind of life he or she would like to have in the future.
   2. Help the student determine qualifications for the types of jobs that are of most interest.
   3. Identify immediate actions the student can take to move toward this goal.

B. Brainstorm actions to avoid and actions to take—what the student can do to find greater success in the school setting.

C. Help the student establish short-range goals.

INTERVENTION **C**

D. Help the student identify specific actions he is willing to take to reach his short-range goals.

E. Identify ways that adults can help the student reach his goals.

F. If using rewards, a structured reinforcement system, or corrective consequences, make sure the student understands all of the contingencies.

G. Set regular times to follow up and discuss progress.

H. Review responsibilities and sign the Goal Setting form.

I. Conclude the Goal Setting conference with words of encouragement.

STEP 3 Provide ongoing support and encouragement.

A. Provide ongoing support and frequent positive feedback when the goal behaviors are exhibited, linking them to the broad label or trait.

B. When the student is not successful, correct calmly; avoid sounding disappointed or reproachful.

C. Evaluate the impact of the intervention, making revisions and adjustments as necessary.

D. Encourage the student to keep striving toward his goals.

Reproducible Form C1: *Long-Range Goal Setting*

Long-Range Goal Setting

Student   Grade/Class   Teacher   Date

At the age of _____ , I hope to have or be doing the following.

Self-Sufficiency

I would like to support myself in a job that pays _____

I would like a job where I work _____

A job I might like to have is _____

Personal Life

I hope that my family is _____

I would like to spend time with people who are _____

During my free time, I would like to _____

Reproducible Form C3: *Goal Setting (Version 2)*

Goal Setting (Version 2)

Student _____ Grade/Class _____ Teacher _____ Date _____

Description of the problem _____

_____

_____

_____

Goal _____

_____

_____

_____

Student responsibilities for achieving the goal _____

_____

_____

_____

Teacher support responsibilities _____

_____

_____

_____

Evaluation procedure _____

_____

_____

_____

Date of goal evaluation _____

Student Signature _____ Date _____ Teacher Signature _____ Date _____

Reproducible Form C4: *Goal Setting (Version 3)*

Goal Setting (Version 3)

_____   _____   _____   _____
Student   Grade/Class   Teacher   Date

I plan to work on the following goals:

Long Term	Short Term

Student Responsibilities

Things I will do to reach my goals _____

_____

_____

Teacher Responsibilities

Things my teacher will do to help me reach my goals _____

_____

_____

Evaluation

How we will know if I have reached my goals _____

_____

Follow-Up Meeting

We will meet again on _____ to discuss my progress.

_____   _____   _____   _____
Student Signature   Date   Teacher Signature   Date

Reproducible Form C5: *Goal Setting (Version 4)*

Goal Setting (Version 4)

Student _____ Grade/Class _____ Teacher _____ Date _____

Goals

Long-range goals _____

_____

_____

_____

_____

Short-term goals _____

_____

_____

_____

_____

Actions

Things I will do in the next week to begin reaching my goals _____

_____

_____

_____

_____

Evaluation _____

_____

_____

_____

_____

Goal Setting (Version 5)

Student _____ Grade/Class _____ Teacher _____ Date _____

Statement of student responsibilities _____

_____

_____

_____

Statement of teacher responsibilities _____

_____

_____

_____

Statement of student advocate responsibilities _____

_____

_____

_____

Agreement _____

_____

_____

_____

Signatures

_____   _____
1st period   6th period

_____   _____
2nd period   7th period

_____
3rd period

_____   _____
4th period   Advocate

_____   _____
5th period   Student

Reproducible Form C7 (1 of 2): *Goal Setting (Version 6)*

Goal Setting (Version 6)

_____   _____   _____   _____
Student   Grade/Class   Teacher   Date

_____   _____
Classroom Teachers   Previous Teachers

_____   _____   _____   _____
Parent/Guardian   Address   Email   Phone

I. Student target behaviors and expectations

1. _____
2. _____
3. _____
4. _____

II. What alternative behaviors can you use?

1. _____
2. _____
3. _____
4. _____

III. Plan implementation

Who is responsible?	What needs to be done?	When will it happen?	How will it be evaluated?

IV. Student choices

Responsible choices	Consequences	Irresponsible choices	Consequences

Reproducible Form C7 (2 of 2): *Goal Setting (Version 6)*

V. Evaluation criteria

1. _____
2. _____
3. _____
4. _____

VI. Interagency support

Who was contacted?	Suggestions	Follow-up or support
_____	_____	_____
_____	_____	_____
_____	_____	_____

VII. Student agrees to

1. _____
2. _____
3. _____
4. _____

VIII. Family agrees to

1. _____
2. _____
3. _____
4. _____

IX. Interventionist agrees to

1. _____
2. _____
3. _____
4. _____

_____ _____ _____ _____
Student Signature   Date   Parent/Guardian Signature   Date

_____ _____ _____ _____
Interventionist Signature   Date   Other Signature   Date

Contract review date _____   Contract review date _____

Data Collection and Debriefing

| *The student's behavior appears to be chronic and resistant to simple intervention*

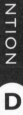

PURPOSE

Dᴀᴛᴀ COLLECTION AND DEBRIEFING has the potential to advance almost any student's behavioral goal. It is appropriate for virtually any concern about a behavior that appears to be chronic. Whether to increase a positive behavior or decrease a negative behavior, a systematic approach to gathering data usually pays dividends. Even if no improvement results from this intervention alone, subsequent interventions will require ongoing collection of data to gauge their efficacy.

THIS INTERVENTION IS APPROPRIATE FOR ANY:

- chronic behavior of concern
- chronic misbehavior

INTERVENTION

D

It's part of human nature to "shape up" when we know we're being watched.

RATIONALE

Data collection in the treatment of behavior problems is somewhat like the modern practice of medicine—both involve empirically based, data-driven decision making. If you have a headache and you take an aspirin as the first intervention, one of two things will happen: It will go away, in which case you won't think about it again, or it will persist, prompting you to try a new course of action. You might take another aspirin, or even two. You might try a different pain reliever, bed rest, or hot liquids and a cold compress. If your follow-up treatment works—if the headache goes away and doesn't become chronic—then you won't need data. But if you still have the headache, you will begin gathering progressively more systematic data to help you understand the problem, what's triggering it, and what to do about it.

If a student's problematic behavior persists after several corrections, you are faced with a similar choice. Like taking a pain reliever, you might implement a simple first intervention with the reasonable expectation that it may succeed and the student's behavior will improve. If it doesn't work, little effort has been expended, and you might try a second and possibly third intervention without worrying too much about data. But if the student still isn't responding, your approach should become more methodical, just as it would if your headache did not respond to basic remedies. You can conserve precious resources—your valuable time and effort—by learning more about the nature, scope, and size of the problem. Matching the data to progressively more intensive interventions will increase the likelihood of success.

WHY IS GATHERING DATA IMPORTANT?

Gathering data often solves the problem all by itself.

How can this be? The simple answer is that it's part of human nature to "shape up" when we know we're being watched. This is as true for adults as it is for children. People tend to do their best when they're being observed by someone important to them—a boss, a girlfriend, a teacher, or a mentor. You can probably find examples like this in your own life. When is your home at its cleanest and neatest? If you're like most people, it's when you're having company over. Similarly, the only time many people drive exactly the speed limit on an uncrowded interstate highway is when a police officer is in view.

Teachers can take advantage of this natural human tendency to "put the best foot forward" simply by recording the behavior of a student. This lets the student know she is being watched and allows meaningful data to be collected. Observation is a key variable in the repertoire of effective teachers, borne out by decades of educational research. By making the act of observation overt and intentional, Data Collection and Debriefing most directly address the *O* for *Observe student behavior* in STOIC.

The *modus operandi* of this intervention is to collect data in a manner conspicuous to the student but subtle enough to be respectful of the student in front of his peers. The act of collecting data may make things better, not because of any special intervention strategy such as a structured reward system, but simply because of Data Collection and Debriefing in and of itself. In other words, many students shape up when they sense they are being sized up. This effect, though it can be frustrating to those doing research because it can skew the results of a study, is a free bonus for teachers implementing an intervention with a child. You need not be concerned with *why* a student's behavior is getting better—just that it is!

The modus operandi *of this intervention is to collect data in a manner conspicuous to the student but subtle enough to be respectful of the student in front of his peers.*

A True Story

One special education coordinator found herself challenged trying to reach an eighth-grade student who had become "one of the most disrespectful students" she had ever seen. "Jacob had a very troubled home life and a very troubled past at the age of 12," she wrote. "He stole money off my teacher aide's desk. The next week he wrote very crude writing on the bathroom door. His behavior went downhill from there. Not that he wasn't before, but he became the absolute king of backtalk in that bad-behavior time."

She decided to try data collection using a behavior counting card.

"I started last Friday and told him up front what was going on. The behavior chart looked something like this:

Friday	18
Monday	15
Tuesday	8
Wednesday	2
Thursday	1

This worked so well that on Wednesday and Thursday he would even stop himself while talking back to me and apologize! What a difference a week can make! It was so easy. The first two days were tough, but he knows the reason I am doing this is because I care. The report has even improved. He cheated on an assignment and just confessed. All I can say is WOW! Who would think something so easy would work so well?"

Note: One of the strengths of this procedure is that it gives the teacher something to do in response to the misbehavior that is brief, calm, and consistent. It also demonstrates to the other students that some action is being taken.

Data will form the basis of all subsequent intervention planning.

If collecting data does not solve the problem on its own, it is still a necessary step to assist in other interventions. Up to this point in the book, systematic data hasn't been a requirement for intervening. If a problem can be solved easily, collecting systematic data isn't crucial to the success of the intervention or follow-up. This intervention represents a turning point. From this point on, what you do next with any interventions will depend on the data you collect. Should an intervention be maintained? Faded? Replaced with a different intervention? Data gives collaborating teachers, administrators, and interventionists a common point of reference for looking at the issue constructively and making decisions about how to proceed.

Using data is the only way to determine objectively whether interventions are working.

Without data to evaluate an intervention's effectiveness, teachers have to rely on subjective perception, which is a notoriously cloudy barometer. Emotions, preconceptions, distractions, being busy with teaching—all of these diminish the usefulness of subjective impressions.

The previous example of using a simple home remedy for a headache is analogous to the first three interventions in this book. These interventions can be easily enacted and do not require the systematic collection of data. However, if you had a headache that turned into a fever, you would begin a more methodical approach that would continue throughout the diagnosis and treatment of your condition. This intervention also marks a turning point in which objective data will now be collected to guide decisions throughout the remainder of the intervention process. For a fever, data gleaned from checking your temperature a few times would inform further decisions, including whether you need to see a physician. At the doctor's office, your temperature, pulse, and blood pressure would be routinely checked. Your doctor may order additional tests or blood work. The amount of data collected will correspond with the complexity and seriousness of your condition, which is similar to the increased intensity of Data Collection with increasingly complex and serious behavior problems.

Don't Abandon Successful Interventions

One of the most compelling reasons for collecting and analyzing data on a chronic problem is that incremental but significant improvements in a student's behavior may go unnoticed without seeing data on a chart that summarizes progress. Figure D1 shows the duration (more on how to collect this kind of data later) regarding a student's nonparticipation in a full-day kindergarten classroom. Note that early in the intervention process, the student is in excess of 100 minutes of nonparticipation per day, but by the time eight weeks have gone by (40 days), the student has made about a 70 percent improvement. Without this chart, the teacher may have become so discouraged that she threw out the intervention because the behavior still seemed pervasive. The teacher's subjective perception may be that the intervention was unsuccessful, but with the chart, the teacher can see that the student is continuing to make great progress.

Figure D1: *Nonparticipation Scatterplot*

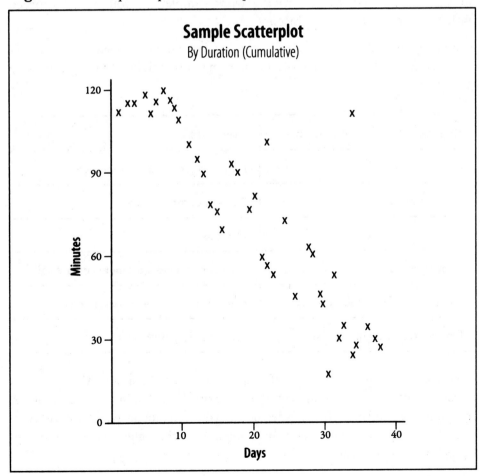

Because discussions and setting goals usually solve most simple problems, you know this is a chronic and possibly serious problem.

BEFORE YOU BEGIN

If you are considering this intervention, you have probably already tried "Intervention A: Planned Discussion" and "Intervention C: Goal Setting" and found them to be ineffective in resolving your concerns with the student. Because discussions and setting goals usually solve most simple problems, you know this is a chronic and possibly serious problem.

The most basic intervention for all chronic behavior problems is Data Collection; the reasons will become clearer as you progress through the book. But the principal reason right now is this: Collecting data requires that you identify the problem in an objective manner, which allows you to measure in a way that will enable you to assess progress. As you think about what behavior to measure, you will determine whether you have defined the problem in an observable way.

Imagine that you are concerned about a student's progress relative to the rest of the class. Are you thinking about the student's work completion—a measurable behavior—or are you worried about the student's flagging motivation? A student's lack of motivation is not measurable. Until you define an objective clearly, such as improving work completion, you cannot proceed with Data Collection and Debriefing.

The following table compares measurable behaviors to some common behavioral descriptors that need to be more narrowly defined before anything can be measured.

Unmeasurable (Too Broad)	Measurable
Bad attitude	Makes disrespectful comments
Unmotivated	Doesn't complete work
Off in his own world	Off task
Poor self-image	Makes negative statements about self
Attention deficit problems	Fidgets and makes tapping noises
Emotional problems	Makes angry outbursts

If you are having trouble identifying the problem in a way that you can measure, keep an anecdotal record for a few days. Using a voice recorder, computer, or notepad, be as specific as you can about what you've been seeing—what happened, when it happened, and what might have caused it to happen (see Figure D2).

Figure D2: *Anecdotal Record*

Notes on Jin-Luen —10/2	
8:25	Jin-Luen told the class that her father is a pilot in the Navy and that he is away on a secret mission. (Untrue--Her father is unemployed and lives out of the state.)
9:30	Jin-Luen told me that she did not have her homework because some boys stole it from her this morning. (True?)
10:45	Jin-Luen was quietly crying at her desk.
12:30	Jin-Luen claimed that she could not participate in PE because she sprained her ankle at lunch. It was not swollen, but I sent her to the nurse to get it checked out. The nurse didn't know for sure, so we let her sit out PE. (True?)
1:10	She said she didn't want to do her work.
2:15	When I was collecting the reading assignments, Jin-Luen said she already turned in the completed assignment. I asked her to find it in the stack and she couldn't. She claimed I lost it. (Untrue--I happened to see the incomplete assignment hanging out of her book. She then denied lying and said she was just confused.)

If you haven't narrowed the scope of your goal to an observable behavior that can be transformed into metrics or data, a confidential journal or several days of anecdotal notes will help you wrangle the major issues and pin down the specific behaviors you want to target for Data Collection. Zero in on one or two observable behaviors that you can monitor by counting the frequency, recording the duration, or grading on a rating scale that you create, such as a 1–5 scale with 1 being *never does* _____ and 5 being *always does* _____ .

For example, Jin-Luen has a problem with lying. Unsure of where to start, her teacher begins the Data Collection and Debriefing process by taking careful notes (Figure D2). Based on these observations and a few more days of notes, Jin-Luen's teacher decides to focus on the true vs. untrue statements, measuring incidents of lying.

After a few days of taking notes, you'll begin to notice some emerging patterns that you hadn't noticed before. As you come to understand these patterns, you can narrow the focus of your Data Collection to one aspect of the student's behavior that can be counted or recorded. Pick what you consider to be the most important and start keeping data on that behavior.

IMPLEMENTATION STEPS
Step 1: Choose an objective data collection method.

In this first step of Data Collection and Debriefing, you will identify what kind of data will be useful to assist with the student's situation and problem, and you will choose the tools and techniques to collect it, using an objective method. Obviously, the easiest sources of data to gather will be the ones you already have:

- grade book
- attendance record
- tardiness record
- class record

If your concern is work completion, you probably already have a good source for data in your grade book—the number of assignments completed versus the number you have given. From this data you can calculate the percentage of work completed week-by-week or overall. Attendance and tardiness are other problem behaviors for which you may have a similar existing record.

Data on student behavior can be collected in many ways. If your concern centers on something for which you do not have a preexisting source, consider using one of the following tools to collect data. The following sections summarize the most common types of data on student behavior and provide descriptions and tools. Read through these to find a method that fits the nature of the problem and your teaching style.

A. Weekly Misbehavior Recording Sheets

These recording sheets can be used to track the frequency of rule violations and other misbehaviors with the entire class. If you're already using a record-keeping form such as one of the Misbehavior Recording Sheets (Reproducible Forms D1 and D2) to track the misbehaviors of all students in the class, it should be easy to convert the information into useful data on a particular student. For example, if you are tracking the disruptions and off-task behavior of the entire class, you can easily track those two behaviors for a particular student and add a tally of her true vs. untrue statements.

Reproducible Form D1 is a daily form that is useful for teachers who have the same group of students for the entire day, such as elementary or special education teachers.

Reproducible Form D2 is intended for a full week of data collection and is useful for secondary teachers who have students for only one class period. In the following sample Misbehavior Recording Sheets, Scott Henry is the focus of a Data Collection and Debriefing intervention. His teacher tracks misbehavior by week using the weekly Misbehavior Recording Sheet (Sample Reproducible Form D2). A frequency count of his misbehaviors from this form is placed on a weekly chart to track his misbehavior. For the week of November 3, eight misbehaviors were tallied. On days where an escalation in problem behavior is anticipated, such as a field trip day, the teacher chooses to record behavior with more detail using the daily Misbehavior Recording Sheet (Sample Reproducible Form D1).

B. Basic frequency count

The most common type of behavioral data collected is a frequency count—simply the number of occurrences of a positive or negative behavior.

The simplest way to keep a frequency count for an individual student is with a tally of hash marks, which can be kept on a card in your pocket or on a sheet of paper on your clipboard. The nice thing about structuring a frequency count this way is that you can add columns as you notice different behaviors you would like to record. You might have a column for disruptions, another for the number of times the student remembers to raise his hand, and a third for the number of times he gets out of his seat inappropriately.

This method does require that you carry materials with you. If that's not your style, you can use alternatives. A golf counter or hand tally counter can work. Another alternative is to put a handful of paper clips in one pocket. Each time the student exhibits the behavior you are monitoring, move a paper clip to a different pocket. The disadvantage of these methods, however, is that you may be limited to counting only one behavior for a single student.

Some interventionists recommend always counting the positive behaviors you want to increase rather than any negative behaviors you are trying to decrease. This is a nice idea, but it's not always easy to do. You could, for example, count the frequency of a student raising his hand instead of counting the frequency that he blurts out answers, but opportunities for hand-raising vary from day to day. This means your count may actually show a positive increase in hand-raising, masking the negative reality that the student is also blurting out more often. In this example, you may want to count both behaviors, which gives you the ability to compute and display a percentage (appropriately raising hand versus blurting out).

The most common type of behavioral data collected is a frequency count— simply the number of occurrences of a positive or negative behavior.

Sample Reproducible Form D1: *Misbehavior Recording Sheet (Daily)*

Misbehavior Recording Sheet
(Daily by Student Name)

11/12
Date

Art museum field trip
Reminders

Name	1st Hour	2nd Hour	3rd Hour	4th Hour	5th Hour	Total
Anderson, Chantel				T		1
Baker, Ruben						0
Bell, Justin						0
Cabrezza, Melinda		T		T	T	3
Cummings, Teresa						0
Demalski, Lee			T			1
Diaz, Margo						0
Etienne, Jerry						0
Fujiyama, Kim						0
Grover, Matthew						0
Henry, Scott	DDT	DO		DT	T	8
Isaacson, Chris						0
Kaufman, Jamie						0
King, Mark						0
LaRouche, Janel				T		1
Morales, Marie Louisa				T		1
Narlin, Jenny						0
Neely, Jacob	D					1
Nguyen, Trang						0
Ogren, Todd	TT			T		3
Pallant, Jared						0
Piercy, Dawn				O		1
Reaes, Myra						0
Thomason, Rahsaan		T			T	2
Vandever, Aaron						0
Wong, Charlene						0
Yamamoto, Junko				O		1

Codes: D – Disruption
O – Off task
T – Talking

A blank version of this form is available in the *Reproducible Materials* section at the end of the chapter.

Sample Reproducible Form D2: *Misbehavior Recording Sheet (Weekly)*

Intervention D:
Data Collection and Debriefing

Misbehavior Recording Sheet
(Weekly by Student Name)

Week of 11/3
Dates

On Wed. remind about Fri. test
Reminders

Name	Mon.	Tue.	Wed.	Thur.	Fri.	Total
Anderson, Chantel				T		1
Baker, Ruben						0
Bell, Justin						0
Cabrezza, Melinda		T		T	T	3
Cummings, Teresa						0
Demalski, Lee			T			1
Diaz, Margo						0
Etienne, Jerry						0
Fujiyama, Kim						0
Grover, Matthew						0
Henry, Scott	DDT	DO		DT	T	8
Isaacson, Chris						0
Kaufman, Jamie				D		1
King, Mark						0
LaRouche, Janel				T		1
Morales, Marie Louisa				T		1
Narlin, Jenny						0
Neely, Jacob			O	O		2
Nguyen, Trang						0
Ogren, Todd	TTD	D	OO	T		7
Pallant, Jared						0
Piercy, Dawn			T	O	T	3
Reaes, Myra						0
Thomason, Rahsaan	TT		T	T	TT	6
Vandever, Aaron						0
Wong, Charlene						0
Yamamoto, Junko		T		OT		3

Codes: D – Disruption
O – Off task
T – Talking

 A blank version of this form is available in the *Reproducible Materials* section at the end of the chapter.

Sample Reproducible Form D3: *Behavior Counting Form*

Behavior Counting Form

Logan Firth	6	Jean Polese	Apr. 20
Student	Grade/Class	Teacher	Week of

Monday

1	2	3	4	5	6	7	8	9	10	11	12	13	14	15	16	17	18	19	20	21	22	23	24	25

Tuesday

1	2	3	4	5	6	7	8	9	10	11	12	13	14	15	16	17	18	19	20	21	22	23	24	25

Wednesday

1	2	3	4	5	6	7	8	9	10	11	12	13	14	15	16	17	18	19	20	21	22	23	24	25

Thursday

1	2	3	4	5	6	7	8	9	10	11	12	13	14	15	16	17	18	19	20	21	22	23	24	25

Friday

1	2	3	4	5	6	7	8	9	10	11	12	13	14	15	16	17	18	19	20	21	22	23	24	25

A blank version of this form is available in the *Reproducible Materials* section at the end of the chapter.

In some cases, it is not feasible to count a positive behavior. If classroom disruptions are your concern, for example, it would be very difficult to count the absence of those disruptions or the times when a student is not being disruptive! The simplest solution would probably be just to count the number of disruptions the student causes, as shown in Sample Reproducible Form D3.

The Happy Cat/Sad Dog form (Reproducible Form D4) is a basic frequency count for monitoring the behavior of younger students. Note that the top half of Reproducible Form D4 show shows happy cats, while the bottom half shows happy dogs, giving both cat fanciers and dog lovers among your primary-age students equal opportunity to indicate positive behavior with the animal pal of their choice.

C. Advanced frequency count

You can get even more sophisticated with frequency counts, so long as the extra effort doesn't overtax your resources. For example, if a student continually argues with you and your teaching assistant, you could divide

Reproducible Form D4: *Happy Cat/Sad Dog, Happy Dog/Sad Cat*

Happy Cat/Sad Dog

Name _____   Behavior _____

Each time you remember, color the smiling cat. When you forget, color the sad dog.

Happy Dog/Sad Cat

Name _____   Behavior _____

Each time you remember, color the smiling dog. When you forget, color the sad cat.

Figure D3: *Advanced Frequency Count (Example 1)*

	Notes on Alexa's Arguing —11/4 Frequency		
	WITH TEACHER	WITH ASSISTANT	
	AA PPPP	AAAA PPPPP PPPP	
	NOTES:		
9:05	Mr. Yarborough (assistant) told Alexa that she needed to clean up the Science Center when she finished. Alexa argued that it was a mess before she got there. They went back and forth several times until Alexa was almost shouting. I went over to find out what was going on, and Alexa told me to stay out of it and then started to argue with me.		
9:50	When I was collecting the science papers, Alexa told me that I did not give her enough time to finish. I reminded her that she should take the work home as homework just like anyone else, but she kept demanding that I explain why I never give enough time to finish assignments.		
1:00	I told the students that they needed to hand in their long-term project proposals. Alexa asked why I didn't remind them yesterday. I told her that I had reminded them yesterday, but she kept insisting that I hadn't. After a few back-and-forth exchanges, several other students told her I was right. That silenced her.		
3:15	This afternoon was typical. Alexa didn't think that she should have to do the art project, she didn't want Mr. Y to correct her work, she didn't know that we had given out book order forms, and on and on.		

your tally into two columns representing you and the aide. To refine the data further, you could use one-letter codes to indicate more specific information about the arguing, such as *A* for a.m. and *P* for p.m. Without taking any more time than a simple frequency count, your count can yield more granular data.

Figures D3 and D4 are examples of frequency counts that use anecdotal notes and do not require the use of a dedicated form.

Figure D4: *Advanced Frequency Count (Example 2)*

	Colin's Bothersome Behavior —4/3 Frequency Count		
	Type of Activity + When		
	INDEPENDENT WORK	COOP. GROUPS	TRANSITIONS
	AAAAAA AAAPP	PPPPP PPPPP	AAAAA PPP PPPPP
	PPPPP PP		PPPP
	NOTES:		
8:40	Transition--As Colin is moving to join his cooperative group, he pokes Blaine		
	in the arm, knocks Belinda's books off her desk, and pulls Maria's hair.		

D. Countoons/public posting

A "countoon" can be used to count positive behavior, negative behavior, or both. This method of recording data is most appropriate with younger students. The countoon will be publicly posted, so you need to make sure that it is OK with the student or students involved, and you may want to consider counting only positive behaviors. Data reporting should never be embarrassing to a child. A natural use would be in resource rooms or special education classrooms in which most, if not all, students have a behavioral or academic goal that is being recorded and charted. In this way, the countoon doesn't stand out as odd or appear to single out one particular student.

The top countoon in Reproducible Form D5 is for a student who makes frequent negative comments. Once you've seen a countoon in action, you can be creative and devise ones of your own. Reproducible Form D5, available here and on the CD, includes a template for you to create your own.

E. Duration recording

When a behavior does not occur regularly but tends to last a long time when it does occur, you may want to perform a duration count. Instead of counting the frequency of the behavior, time the duration of the behavior. You can do this using a stopwatch or wristwatch, or by jotting down the time of day each occurrence begins and ends. If you are using a stopwatch, don't reset it after each instance. Simply stop the time and restart it if the behavior begins again. At the end of the day, you will have recorded the cumulative amount of time the student engaged in the behavior. Divide this accumulated time by the number of behavioral episodes that occurred to get the average duration of the behavior. Duration recording is another statistic that may add to your understanding of the problem.

Data reporting should never be embarrassing to a child.

Reproducible Form D5: *Countoon Behavior Counting Form*

Countoon Behavior Counting Form

Name _____ Grade/Class _____ Teacher _____ Date _____

Positive Comments

Negative Comments

Countoon Behavior Counting Form

Name _____ Grade/Class _____ Teacher _____ Date _____

F. Interval recording or scatterplot

Sometimes, the behavior you want to understand is situational, happening more in some situations or at particular times. Interval recording involves marking whether the behavior occurs during a particular time interval. A *scatterplot* is a fancy name for a data collection form that shows the inter-relationship between two variables, such as the occurrence or lack of a behavior during a particular activity in a particular time interval. A sample scatterplot, shown in Sample Reproducible Form D6, combines interval recording and frequency counts by recording a tally of the number of targeted behaviors that occur each day during each activity and transition. In this case, two weeks of observation show Mondays to be problematic and demonstrate that reading, lining up, and hallway behaviors are problematic across all days. This detailed information has tremendous potential for aiding the design of a very targeted intervention plan.

Reproducible Form D7 is an interval/scatterplot for one week that you can use to record the time of day behaviors occur.

> *Interval recording involves marking whether the behavior occurs during a particular time interval.*

> Note: Not all reproducible forms are shown in this chapter.
> You should skim through the Reproducible Materials section
> at the end of the chapter to determine which Data Collection
> and Debriefing format is best suited to the student's needs.

G. Rating scale

You can rate the quality or intensity of a behavior on a simple scale. Though more subjective than the other methods, a rating scale can be made more objective by your application of judgments consistently over time and across activities. You could, for example, use three behaviors a student exhibits during different activities as a measure to build an overall picture of the student's behavioral pattern and identify possible points of intervention.

The following sample of Reproducible Form D10 shows a rating scale in which a student receives a point for each of three behaviors and whether she exhibited that trait appropriately during an activity. A blank template of this form is available at the end of this chapter and on the CD. One week's worth of data can be recorded on one page.

INTERVENTION

D

Sample Reproducible Form D6: *Interval Chart (Activity/Transition)*

Interval Chart (Scatterplot)

Tristan Russell	*5*	*Ms. Byers*	*October*
Student	Grade/Class	Teacher	Date

Disrespectful Comments
Behavior

Put a tally mark in the corresponding box each time the student engages in the targeted behavior.

		Week: 10/6					Week: 10/13					Week:					Week:				
		M	T	W	Th	F	M	T	W	Th	F	M	T	W	Th	F	M	T	W	Th	F
Activity	*Opening*	II					II														
	Reading	III	II	II	III	I	IIII	I	I	II	I										
	Writing/Spelling	II			I		I		I												
	Math																				
	Lunch	II	I				I				I										
	Science	I					I				I										
	Health	II			I		II		I												
	Recess	III		I			I				I										
	Social Studies	I					I														
Transition	*Entry*	IIII					II	I													
	To/From ??	II	I	I			IIII														
	Lining Up	III	I	I	I	II	IIII		I		I										
	Hallway	II		I	I	I	II		I	I	II										
	Cleanup	I					I														

Reproducible Form D7: *Interval Chart/Scatterplot*

Interval Chart/Scatterplot

Student _____   Grade/Class _____   Teacher _____   Week of _____

Goal _____

Rating (+/−)	Monday	Tuesday	Wednesday	Thursday	Friday
8:00 – 8:30					
8:30 – 9:00					
9:00 – 9:30					
9:30 – 10:00					
10:00 – 10:30					
10:30 – 11:00					
11:00 – 11:30					
11:30 – Noon					
Noon – 12:30					
12:30 – 1:00					
1:00 – 1:30					
1:30 – 2:00					
2:00 – 2:30					
2:30 – 3:00					

Sample Reproducible Form D10: *Rating Scale*

Rating Scale

Alita	3	Mr. Johns	6
Student	Grade/Class	Teacher	Period/Time

	Monday	Reading	History	Lunch	Math	Music	Language
Behavior	Uses only appropriate language	① 0	① 0	① 0	① 0	① 0	① 0
	Cooperates with others	① 0	1 ⓪	① 0	① 0	① 0	① 0
	Problem-solves positively	① 0	1 ⓪	① 0	① 0	① 0	① 0

A blank version of this form is available in the *Reproducible Materials* section at the end of the chapter.

Another example of a rating scale would be ranking a particular behavior on a scale of 1 to 5. If the ratings have a specific descriptor, this type of form is called an *anchored rating scale*. A partially anchored scale may have descriptors for only the first and last numeral ratings, but a fully anchored scale may be more objective. As described in "Intervention K: Self-Monitoring and Self-Evaluation," rating scales may be completed by a teacher, the student, or both. Though any rating scale is admittedly more subjective than data collected by other methods, this body of information can provide another useful window into a student's behavior over time. Sample Reproducible D11 shows an anchored scale regarding a student's class participation.

Step 2: Select a way to display the data.

How you display data may dictate the quality of your analysis and interpretation and will affect everyone's understanding of the data's meaning. Give some thought to how you will display the data. You should think about whether a table, bar graph, pie chart, or scatterplot will make trends and patterns apparent to you as well as to the student.

Sample Reproducible Form D11: *Participation Evaluation Record*

Participation Evaluation Record

Justin	*I I*	*Mr. Mathison*	*1 2/6*
Student	Grade/Class	Teacher	Date

Rating Scale: 0 = Did not participate verbally and did not take notes
1 = Participated verbally at least once but did not take notes
2 = Took notes but did not participate verbally
3 = Participated verbally at least once and took notes

Directions: For each subject, circle the number that best describes your level of participation.

Subject	Monday	Tuesday	Wednesday	Thursday	Friday
Science	0 ①2 3	0 ①2 3	0 1 ②3	0 1 2 3	0 1 2 3
Health	⓪1 2 3	⓪1 2 3	0 1 2 3	0 1 2 3	0 1 2 3
English	0 1 ②3	0 1 2 ③	0 1 2 3	0 1 2 3	0 1 2 3
Math	⓪1 2 3	0 ①2 3	0 1 2 3	0 1 2 3	0 1 2 3
Art	⓪1 2 3	0 ①2 3	0 1 2 3	0 1 2 3	0 1 2 3
History	0 ①2 3	0 1 ②3	0 1 2 3	0 1 2 3	0 1 2 3

 A blank version of this form is available in the *Reproducible Materials* section at the end of the chapter.

Display changes across time so that when meeting with the student, you can illustrate the progress the student is making. You may want to employ statistical techniques such as drawing the "line of best fit," either by hand or automatically using a spreadsheet application such as Excel. Software allows you to automate the charting and can help in keeping a record of your data and generating meaningful statistics.

Decide where to record and keep the data so you don't lose it. If you are the type who jots notes on slips of paper rather than forms, be sure to enter the data on a master chart, preferably on a daily basis. Slips of paper are easily lost, and you don't want to negate several days of work by being careless with your data.

Ask yourself whether the data you have collected can show trends across time. This generally depends on the format in which the data was entered in the first place. Data collected on separate sheets of paper is of little use for conducting a cogent analysis. These should be brought together in one place as a chart. Frequency counts, duration records, and rating scales should be summarized on a chart to help you and others make sense of their significance across time. On the other hand, interval recording and scatterplot forms steadily reveal more information as you enter your observations—the relationships between the variables on the X and Y axes will become clearer as more data points are filled in. These forms may be fine without transferring the data to a separate chart, but by the time you have collected data for more than a week or two, you will probably need to display the trend on some kind of chart. For example, charting the number of intervals each day that the student was successful allows you to see progress over two or three months and perhaps correlate anomalies in the graph with events that occurred in class, at school, or in the student's life.

Data collected on separate sheets of paper is of little use for conducting a cogent analysis.

Step 3: Meet with the student.

Set up a meeting with the student. The student's parents should be given the option to join you.

A. Explain the data you plan to collect.
Explain to the student that you will be collecting data, not as a punishment, but to help both of you understand the significance of the problem (the magnitude or severity) and what everyone involved might do to try to make things better.

Explain how you will communicate the data to the student as you are collecting it—neither your actions nor the data you collect should be a secret. For example, if you are counting the frequency of disruptions, you might tell the student, "Paul, that's disruptive," when he is causing a disturbance and then mark the record form. Both of these actions provide feedback that can help the student self-regulate future behavior. Moreover, you want to be as overt as you reasonably can without causing embarrassment. This overtness is part of what might make the intervention work all by itself.

Thereafter, perhaps once a week, you can show the student how he is doing using a summary graph or chart to reinforce your shared understanding of the behavior and to monitor the student's progress in modifying it. Remember that it is not unusual for a behavior to get worse before it gets better. Seeing your data from different angles and making distinctions will help you detect positive signs, which you can then share with the student as encouragement.

Above all, meetings with the student and the student's parents about the data should be encouraging. Even if the numbers you're collecting appear to be getting worse, your focus should be on ideas from you, the parents, and the student that might improve the situation. Make suggestions—or better yet, ask the student, "Is there anything I can do to help you make this better, to help turn this around?" By putting yourself on the student's side, you are taking on the essential role of a coach—"Yes, we may have lost a couple of close games, but I know you have what it takes to do it. This next week can be our best yet, and I'm committed to helping you make that happen."

B. Meet regularly with the student to discuss the data and debrief.

Plan to meet at least once a week to review the data, discuss trends, set improvement targets, celebrate progress, and so on. Invite the student's parents to join you at any of your regularly scheduled meetings.

CONCLUSION

Data Collection and Debriefing represents a turning point in the nature and classification of the student's behavioral problem—you have already tried the simplest and least time-consuming interventions (Pre-Intervention through Intervention C), indicating that the student's problem is chronic and possibly serious. Data Collection and Debriefing may help to solve the problem when it is used alone because of the natural human tendency to improve behavior when we are being observed. However, if this intervention is not sufficient in and of itself to improve the problem behavior, the data collected will serve as the foundation for any subsequent intervention plans. You will use the accurate and objective data gathered in Data Collection and Debriefing to make decisions and implement any of the later Highly Structured Interventions.

Meetings with the student and the student's parents about the data should be encouraging.

INTERVENTION

REFERENCES

Alberto, P., & Troutman, A. (2003). *Applied behavior analysis for teachers* (6th ed.). Upper Saddle River, NJ: Merrill/Prentice-Hall.

Baer, D., Wolf, M., & Risley, T. (1968). Some current dimensions of applied behavior analysis. *Journal of Applied Behavior Analysis, 1,* 91–97.

Broussard, C. D., & Northup, J. (1995). An approach to assessment and analysis of disruptive behavior in regular education classrooms. *School Psychology Quarterly, 10,* 151–164.

Davies, S., & Witte, R. (2000). Self-management and peer-monitoring within a group contingency to decrease uncontrolled verbalizations of children with attention-deficit/hyperactivity disorder. *Psychology in the Schools, 37,* 135–147.

Fantuzzo, J., & Polite, K. (1990). School-based behavioral self-management: Review and analysis. *School Psychology Quarterly, 5,* 255–263.

Fox, J., & Gable, R. A. (2004). Functional behavioral assessment. In R .B. Rutherford, M. M. Quinn, & S. R. Mathur (Eds.). *Handbook of research in emotional and behavioral disorders* (pp. 143–162). New York: Guilford Press.

Gresham, F. M., Quinn, M. M., & Restori, A. (1999). Methodological issues in functional analysis: Generalizability to other disability groups. *Behavioral Disorders, 24,* 180–182.

Quinn, M. (2000). Functional behavioral assessment: The letter and the spirit of the law. *Preventing School Failure, 44,* 147–151.

Rhode, G., Jenson, W. R., & Reavis, H. K. (1992). *The tough kid book: Practical classroom management strategies.* Longmont, CO: Sopris West.

Sulzer-Azaroff, B., & Mayer, G. R. (1991). *Behavior analysis for lasting change.* Fort Worth, TX: Holt, Rinehart & Winston.

Walker, H. M. (1995). *The acting-out child: Coping with classroom disruption* (2nd ed.). Longmont, CO: Sopris West.

INTERVENTION

D

Reproducible Materials

The following reproducible materials may be used in conjunction with "Intervention D: Data Collection and Debriefing." Copies are provided here and on the CD. Permission is given for individual classroom teachers to reproduce any forms labeled "Reproducible" for classroom use. Reproduction of these materials for an entire school system is prohibited without express permission of the publisher.

Reproducible Step-by-Step Summary

DATA COLLECTION AND DEBRIEFING

Step-by-Step Summary

Following is a summary of the steps involved in Intervention D. It is important to use professional judgment, adjusting procedures to meet the needs of the situation and the individual. See the chapter "Intervention D: Data Collection and Debriefing" for a detailed description of this intervention.

STEP 1   Choose an objective data collection method.

A. Weekly Misbehavior Recording Sheets

B. Basic frequency count

C. Advanced frequency count

D. Countoons/public posting

E. Duration recording

F. Interval recording or scatterplot

G. Rating scale

STEP 2   Select a way to display the data.

STEP 3   Meet with the student.

A. Explain the data you plan to collect.

B. Meet regularly with the student to discuss the data and debrief.

Reproducible Form D1: *Misbehavior Recording Sheet (Daily)*

Intervention D:
Data Collection and Debriefing

Misbehavior Recording Sheet
(Daily by Student Name)

Date _____   Reminders _____

Name	1st Hour	2nd Hour	3rd Hour	4th Hour	5th Hour	Total

Intervention D:
Data Collection and Debriefing

Misbehavior Recording Sheet
(Weekly by Student Name)

Dates _____   Reminders _____

Name	Mon.	Tue.	Wed.	Thur.	Fri.	Total

Reproducible Form D3: *Behavior Counting Form*

Behavior Counting Form

Student _____ Grade/Class _____ Teacher _____ Week of _____

Monday

1	2	3	4	5	6	7	8	9	10	11	12	13	14	15	16	17	18	19	20	21	22	23	24	25

Tuesday

1	2	3	4	5	6	7	8	9	10	11	12	13	14	15	16	17	18	19	20	21	22	23	24	25

Wednesday

1	2	3	4	5	6	7	8	9	10	11	12	13	14	15	16	17	18	19	20	21	22	23	24	25

Thursday

1	2	3	4	5	6	7	8	9	10	11	12	13	14	15	16	17	18	19	20	21	22	23	24	25

Friday

1	2	3	4	5	6	7	8	9	10	11	12	13	14	15	16	17	18	19	20	21	22	23	24	25

Monday

1	2	3	4	5	6	7	8	9	10	11	12	13	14	15	16	17	18	19	20	21	22	23	24	25

Tuesday

1	2	3	4	5	6	7	8	9	10	11	12	13	14	15	16	17	18	19	20	21	22	23	24	25

Wednesday

1	2	3	4	5	6	7	8	9	10	11	12	13	14	15	16	17	18	19	20	21	22	23	24	25

Thursday

1	2	3	4	5	6	7	8	9	10	11	12	13	14	15	16	17	18	19	20	21	22	23	24	25

Friday

1	2	3	4	5	6	7	8	9	10	11	12	13	14	15	16	17	18	19	20	21	22	23	24	25

Monday

1	2	3	4	5	6	7	8	9	10	11	12	13	14	15	16	17	18	19	20	21	22	23	24	25

Tuesday

1	2	3	4	5	6	7	8	9	10	11	12	13	14	15	16	17	18	19	20	21	22	23	24	25

Wednesday

1	2	3	4	5	6	7	8	9	10	11	12	13	14	15	16	17	18	19	20	21	22	23	24	25

Thursday

1	2	3	4	5	6	7	8	9	10	11	12	13	14	15	16	17	18	19	20	21	22	23	24	25

Friday

1	2	3	4	5	6	7	8	9	10	11	12	13	14	15	16	17	18	19	20	21	22	23	24	25

Reproducible Form D6: *Interval Chart (Scatterplot)*

Interval Chart (Scatterplot)

Student _____ Grade/Class _____ Teacher _____ Date _____

Behavior _____

Put a tally mark in the corresponding box each time the student engages in the targeted behavior.

	Week:					Week:					Week:					Week:				
	M	T	W	Th	F	M	T	W	Th	F	M	T	W	Th	F	M	T	W	Th	F

Activity

Transition

Reproducible Form D8: *Scatterplot Data Collection*

Scatterplot Data Collection

Student _____ Grade _____ Teacher _____ Dates _____

Behavior _____

Activity	Time	Day 1	Day 2	Day 3	Day 4	Day 5	Day 6	Day 7	Day 8	Day 9	Day 10

Reproducible Form D9: *Interval Chart/Scatterplot*

Interval Chart/Scatterplot

Student _____ Grade/Class _____ Teacher _____ Period/Time _____

Behavior:			Week:					Week:				
Activity		**Time**	Mon	Tue	Wed	Thu	Fri	Mon	Tue	Wed	Thu	Fri
Transition		**Time**	Mon	Tue	Wed	Thu	Fri	Mon	Tue	Wed	Thu	Fri

Behavior:			Week:					Week:				
Activity		**Time**	Mon	Tue	Wed	Thu	Fri	Mon	Tue	Wed	Thu	Fri
Transition		**Time**	Mon	Tue	Wed	Thu	Fri	Mon	Tue	Wed	Thu	Fri

Reproducible Form D10: *Rating Scale*

Rating Scale

Student _____ Grade/Class _____ Teacher _____ Period/Time _____

Subject

Monday

Behavior	___	___	___	___	___	___
	1 0	1 0	1 0	1 0	1 0	1 0
	1 0	1 0	1 0	1 0	1 0	1 0
	1 0	1 0	1 0	1 0	1 0	1 0

Tuesday

Behavior	___	___	___	___	___	___
	1 0	1 0	1 0	1 0	1 0	1 0
	1 0	1 0	1 0	1 0	1 0	1 0
	1 0	1 0	1 0	1 0	1 0	1 0

Wednesday

Behavior	___	___	___	___	___	___
	1 0	1 0	1 0	1 0	1 0	1 0
	1 0	1 0	1 0	1 0	1 0	1 0
	1 0	1 0	1 0	1 0	1 0	1 0

Thursday

Behavior	___	___	___	___	___	___
	1 0	1 0	1 0	1 0	1 0	1 0
	1 0	1 0	1 0	1 0	1 0	1 0
	1 0	1 0	1 0	1 0	1 0	1 0

Friday

Behavior	___	___	___	___	___	___
	1 0	1 0	1 0	1 0	1 0	1 0
	1 0	1 0	1 0	1 0	1 0	1 0
	1 0	1 0	1 0	1 0	1 0	1 0

Participation Evaluation Record

Student _____ Grade/Class _____ Teacher _____ Period/Time _____

Rating Scale: 0 = Did not participate verbally and did not take notes
1 = Participated verbally at least once but did not take notes
2 = Took notes but did not participate verbally
3 = Participated verbally at least once and took notes

Directions: For each subject, circle the number that best describes your level of participation.

Subject	Monday	Tuesday	Wednesday	Thursday	Friday
	0 1 2 3	0 1 2 3	0 1 2 3	0 1 2 3	0 1 2 3
	0 1 2 3	0 1 2 3	0 1 2 3	0 1 2 3	0 1 2 3
	0 1 2 3	0 1 2 3	0 1 2 3	0 1 2 3	0 1 2 3
	0 1 2 3	0 1 2 3	0 1 2 3	0 1 2 3	0 1 2 3
	0 1 2 3	0 1 2 3	0 1 2 3	0 1 2 3	0 1 2 3
	0 1 2 3	0 1 2 3	0 1 2 3	0 1 2 3	0 1 2 3

Subject	Monday	Tuesday	Wednesday	Thursday	Friday
	0 1 2 3	0 1 2 3	0 1 2 3	0 1 2 3	0 1 2 3
	0 1 2 3	0 1 2 3	0 1 2 3	0 1 2 3	0 1 2 3
	0 1 2 3	0 1 2 3	0 1 2 3	0 1 2 3	0 1 2 3
	0 1 2 3	0 1 2 3	0 1 2 3	0 1 2 3	0 1 2 3
	0 1 2 3	0 1 2 3	0 1 2 3	0 1 2 3	0 1 2 3
	0 1 2 3	0 1 2 3	0 1 2 3	0 1 2 3	0 1 2 3

Increasing Positive Interactions

The student gets a lot of attention from adults and peers for misbehavior or failure

PURPOSE

INCREASING POSITIVE INTERACTIONS may be effective with any chronic misbehavior or problem with self-concept. Any time the function of a student's behavior is attention seeking, this intervention is especially useful.

THIS INTERVENTION IS APPROPRIATE FOR:

Chronic attention-seeking behavior
- disruptive behavior
- arguing
- tattling
- creating excuses for every mistake
- teasing
- negotiating
- off-task behavior
- distractibility

Poor self-concept
- the clingy child
- helplessness

You can help a child who "fishes" for attention through misbehavior by teaching and showing that responsible behavior is an effective way to get adult attention and by demonstrating that responsible behavior in your class results in more desired attention than misbehavior. Though the idea behind Increasing Positive Interactions is deceptively simple, in practice it is among the most powerful interventions used to change student behavior.

By reducing the *frequency, duration,* and *intensity* of the attention you pay to students' misbehavior and focusing more of your time and attention on responsible behaviors, you can rebalance your *ratio of interactions*—the number of positive interactions with students to the number of negative interactions—and try to make the ratio primarily positive. Redirecting a student's ingrained pattern of behavior through increased positive interactions requires patience and consistency on your part, but the results are worth your effort. Outcomes may include markedly improved student behavior and self-esteem, students who feel valued (and hence more motivated), and an increase in the time you can devote to instruction rather than correction.

> Note: While this intervention, like the others in this book, is structured as a one-to-one framework, Increasing Positive Interactions—and in particular, improving your ratio of positive to negative interactions—is equally effective and important with a whole class. A teacher's ratio of interactions should be predominantly positive with students of all grade levels and abilities.

RATIONALE

Students enter your classroom with a diversity of needs and backgrounds. Some children have received a lot of positive attention since infancy, and some have received little attention of any kind from adults. Unfortunately, a few children may have received primarily negative attention all their lives.

However, all children want and need attention of some sort. Recognizing the needs of your students as individuals is essential to building authentic relationships with them, tailoring your help to meet their needs, and intervening appropriately and effectively with students whose needs may be different from those of their classmates.

Students want and need adult attention. They therefore tend to engage in whatever behaviors seem to get them the most attention. This is ordinarily not a bad deal for a teacher. Imagine how nice it would be if every child wanted and sought your approval, did A+ work, turned it in on time, and greeted you with a beaming smile. In this scenario, you are happy for the students, happy to see such good progress, and happy that your day is going so well. So you smile, say something pleasant, maybe positively recognize the students a little more throughout the day. It feels natural to radiate "good vibes" that pour forth in the form of compliments, smiles, warmth, jocularity, and cheerfulness. So much is going right! In this imaginary classroom, all is well in the world, or at least in your little corner of it. The positive interactions flow naturally. You don't have to strain to think of something positive to say or plan how and when you will initiate positive interactions with difficult students.

It is easy to believe that having a classroom full of positive interactions springs from having responsible students who are exceedingly well behaved and responsible. Many skilled educators work from similar assumptions, and yet this belief is exactly backward.

In truth, positive interactions are more like the fuel that drives good behavior and personal responsibility. Unfortunately, some students with chronic behavior problems have learned it is easier and more reliable to get attention by doing things wrong than by following the rules. Positive interactions are even more important with these students who tend to provoke or draw out negative interactions from their teachers and peers—those who exhibit chronic behavior problems, have a poor self-image, or underperform academically. These students have found that responsible behavior goes unnoticed, while behavior that annoys the teacher or disrupts the class results in riveted attention from the entire class, including the teacher, almost every time. If you're considering this intervention, your student of concern probably matches this description.

Unfortunately, some students with chronic behavior problems have learned it is easier and more reliable to get attention by doing things wrong than by following the rules.

Ericka is a student in Mr. Chang's sixth-grade class. She comes from a home where interactions are primarily negative. Both parents have strenuous work schedules and are often very tired and impatient by the time they get home. In class, Ericka engages in a lot of little annoying behaviors—clicking her fingers loudly enough to be distracting, being in the wrong place at the wrong time, failing to follow directions, and asking irritating questions all day long: "Mr. Chang, do we have to do the whole assignment?" "Mr. Chang, are my math problems lined up straight enough?" Ericka's problem is not related to academic difficulties. Her work is always of high quality; however, her behavior wears the teacher down. Though Mr. Chang has the reputation of being one of the most caring and positive staff members, he finds himself very irritated with Ericka. Before she drives him crazy, Mr. Chang will need to teach Ericka how to get his attention through responsible behavior.

This student may have found that if she behaves and acts responsibly, she runs the risk of you not even noticing she is in the room.

For students like Ericka, the form that the adult attention takes (whether positive or negative) doesn't matter; the critical variables are intensity and frequency. What matters to Ericka is the intensity of the interaction—and the fact that someone notices her at all. This student may have found that if she behaves and acts responsibly, she runs the risk of you not even noticing she is in the room. When too much attention is paid to negative behavior, you may unconsciously send the message that students who behave inappropriately will be rewarded with all of your attention, whereas students who exhibit positive behavior will be ignored.

Other students may not misbehave to get attention, and they may not seek any attention at all—the passive, quiet kids. In this case, the problem is not one of a negatively skewed ratio of interactions, but one of no interactions at all. Increasing the amount of attention you give to these students' positive behavior may be a powerful intervention to increase these students' motivation as well as to demonstrate to other students that positive behavior is a better way to gain your attention and praise.

In increasing your positive interactions with students, you are teaching them that not only is it easier to engage in appropriate behavior, it's simply more enjoyable. In time, the rewards of good behavior and interacting positively become intertwined, and a new habit is born.

INTERVENTION

E

COMMON CONCERNS ABOUT INCREASING POSITIVE INTERACTIONS

Is it appropriate to give even more time and attention to students who misbehave?

Students who misbehave can usurp unfair amounts of teacher time. When a student is constantly demanding your attention through misbehavior, it may be difficult to imagine giving that student *more* of your time. The trick is to give that extra time and attention when the student is *not* acting up. Increasing Positive Interactions does not mean that you give a misbehaving student more attention. It means you will work to reduce the amount of attention the student gets for misbehavior as you increase the amount of attention the student receives for behaving responsibly and respectfully. Instead of saying, "Quit making those noises. You are disturbing those around you," take advantage of opportunities to say hello to the student, ask how she's doing, and compliment her at appropriate times.

What you're aiming for is a shift in focus. This can be difficult when a student is acclimatized to a deeply entrenched pattern of interacting with teachers only when she misbehaves. By focusing on the student's positive qualities and responsible behavior, you are helping her do the same.

Do problem students deserve extra positive attention?

It isn't a question of what students "deserve." You should have already set consequences for unacceptable behavior, which you should be applying calmly and consistently. "Less positive attention" shouldn't be one of them! All students flourish in the rays of extra positive attention.

But some students do not know how to invite a positive interaction—how to look at someone, nod, smile, and in other ways initiate the positive interactions they want. These students may rarely or never experience the normal positive interactions others enjoy—simple pleasantries and quiet exchanges that let them know they are valued. These students do not deserve any less than others to hear you say, "Hi, Ericka. How are you today?" or "Ericka, I appreciated your use of class time today." Whether these students show it or not, the lack of positive interactions with others leaves a void that they struggle to fill. If they have not learned appropriate ways of doing this, you will be dealing with their inappropriate attempts for some time to come. With a student who does not know how to gain attention appropriately or interact positively, you need to take the lead.

Isn't selectively granting extra attention unfair to the other students?

Treating students "fairly" does not necessarily mean treating students "equally." Some students have a greater need for adult attention and may misbehave in order to get that need met. Those students who are striving to do their best and behave appropriately are telling you through positive behavior that their needs for attention and recognition are being met. Any time a student's behavior begins to deteriorate, this intervention can be a promising experiment to determine if the deterioration is a function of the student needing more attention and recognition.

Won't the student think that the positive attention is phony?

Making a conscious effort to change your ratio of interactions with a student may initially feel phony. However, practicing over time will lessen any awkwardness. When you first greet the student, she may not know how to respond. However, positive interactions eventually become the "new norm," and the student is likely to invite positive interactions herself: "Hi, Mr. Chang. How did your softball game last night go?"

There's little likelihood of overdoing it, but if the possibility concerns you, think of the number of positive interactions you typically have with your favorite students—those who are socially and academically successful. If you can match that with a student who has difficulties, the frequency and tone of your interactions will not seem phony—because they won't be.

What can I do when I just don't like the student?

Because teaching involves people and people have feelings, it is possible to have a student in your class who is difficult for you to like. However, liking or disliking a student should have nothing to do with the quality of professional effort given to the student. Physicians cannot give patients they do not like a substandard quality of care, and retail store owners don't reserve courtesy and service just for patrons they like. Teaching is no different. All students, like all patients, should be guaranteed the best possible care. The venerable educator Siegfried Engelmann was once asked, "What do you do when you just don't like a student?" He replied, "You can't dislike kids on company time." In teaching, as in any profession, professionalism means keeping personal feelings separate from work; ratios of positive to negative interactions should have nothing to do with your personal feelings about a student.

Doesn't changing ratios of interactions give a misbehaving student her own way?

Some students are desperate for adult attention. If you are not providing more positive attention, the student will demand attention the only way she knows how—through misbehavior. Though making an effort to improve your ratio of interactions with the student might feel like caving in or giving the student her own way, the opposite is true—you are changing your behavior on your terms, initiating positive interactions when you "catch" the student being friendly, responsible, considerate, or engaged in any behavior you would like to see more of, rather than on the student's terms, initiating interactions only when the student acts out.

DEFINING TERMS FOR INCREASING POSITIVE INTERACTIONS

Before we discuss with ways to increase your positive interactions with students, the following are a few definitions to clarify the differences between types of interactions. Although *positive* and *negative interactions* may seem relatively straightforward, there are important distinctions that you should be aware of before proceeding with the intervention process.

Interactions

Classroom interactions occur any time an adult pays attention to a student. The interaction can be verbal (making a comment or discussing something with the student) or nonverbal (smiling, frowning, moving closer, tensing up, or nodding to a student). An interaction may be as subtle as a shrug or as intense as physical restraint, and an interaction occurs whether you indicate approval, disapproval, or simply recognize a student. For the purposes of intervention, consider any attention directed to an individual student an interaction.

Whether an interaction is considered positive or negative is determined by *what the student is doing* in the moments immediately before and during the interaction. To determine whether an interaction in which you have just engaged is positive or negative, ask yourself what the student was doing immediately prior to it. For example, if you say to a student during an independent work time, "How are things going, James? Do you have any questions?," you have clearly initiated an interaction.

Was the interaction positive or negative? Without more contextual information, you have no way of knowing. It depends entirely on what James was doing when you initiated the interaction. If he was following directions, it was a positive interaction. If he was off task and you were asking the question as a gentle way to reengage him, it was a negative interaction.

Note that "negative" in this sense does not connote bad or wrong; it is negative only because it involves interacting with the student when he is demonstrating a negative behavior. Classify interactions based on the student's

Whether an interaction is considered positive or negative is determined by what the student is doing *in the moments immediately before and during the interaction.*

INTERVENTION

E

behavior at that moment, not your tone or intent. The difference is in the timing (what was James doing?), not the tone (how did I sound?).

Positive interactions

As it turns out, James was busy checking answers on his assignment. When you asked James how things were going, your interaction was positive—you paid attention to a student who was appropriately engaged in the task (good for you!). Although you may have made no attempt to reinforce James and did not specifically praise him, count the interaction positive.

Negative interactions

A negative interaction has nothing to do with the tone or substance of what you say. It has everything to do with the inappropriate, irresponsible, or incorrect behavior in which the student is engaged just before you interact. Negative interactions can be as extreme as restraining a student or as mild as a gentle verbal reminder.

Suppose you now realize—(oops!)—that James was actually checking over his assignment *after* you explicitly told your class to put away their schoolwork and line up by the door. No matter how kindly and gently you said, "How are things going, James? Do you need any help?," you must now classify the interaction—the exact *same* interaction—as negative. The context has changed, so the classification of the behavior has also changed.

Although the interactions that follow may be quite pleasant and supportive, each represents a negative interaction:

- A student is off task, and the teacher says, "Kris, you need to get back to work or you won't have time to finish."

- A student in a cooperative learning group is getting angry, and the teacher reminds the student, "Josh, try to state your opinion in a less emotional way."

- A student ignores a teacher's direction to put away her art project. The teacher says, "Shawna, I am looking at my watch. If it takes you longer than one minute to get the project put away, you will owe me that much time after school."

- A student is off task, and the teacher redirects her by saying, "Amy, just a few minutes ago you were working very hard. Let's get back to it."

- A student is disruptive, and the teacher says, "Kareem, we have discussed this before. You need to go to the timeout area and think about how to work quietly without disturbing others at your table."

The goal is not to eliminate negative interactions. Gentle corrections are as much a part of instruction as negative interactions are a fact of life. However, if you interact more frequently with your students when they misbehave, you run the risk that the attention itself will reinforce the student's misbehavior. Improving your ratio of interactions so that the positives significantly outnumber the negatives will ensure that your students learn it is easier (and more gratifying) to get your attention by behaving responsibly than by misbehaving.

Note: We recommend striving for at least a 3:1 ratio of positive to negative interactions, both with individual students and your class as a whole. Although this number may seem high or difficult to achieve, many other behavior specialists recommend up to a 9:1 ratio of interactions with individual students.

The goal is not to eliminate negative interactions.

IMPLEMENTATION STEPS
Step 1: Plan more positive interactions.

A. Review the problem and overall goal for the student.
Defining the nature and scope of the problem provides critical information for developing a successful intervention.

Duane is a second-grade student who is often disruptive. He wanders around the room, frequently disturbing other children. During instruction or large-group discussions, Duane makes rude and inappropriate comments. He fidgets and makes annoying noises. Duane's teacher, Mrs. Saltzman, finds Duane hard to manage, and by the end of each day, Mrs. Saltzman finds herself wishing that Duane was no longer in her classroom.

In her efforts to improve a deteriorating situation, Mrs. Saltzman mentions to the principal, Mr. Umaki, that she would like to ask Duane's parents to have him evaluated by a physician to determine if he might have attention deficit/hyperactivity disorder (ADHD).

Mrs. Saltzman: (Teacher)	There is obviously something wrong. Duane is worse now than he was at the beginning of the year. I believe that he is out of control and that he probably has ADHD. I think he should be placed in special education or given medication.
Mr. Umaki: (Principal)	I know you have Duane's best interests at heart, but we need to try some other measures before we take this kind of drastic step. We should see if there are factors in the classroom we can manipulate to improve Duane's behavior without medication. We would also need to consult our school psychologist before we even consider talking to his parents about ADHD.

Mrs. Saltzman agrees that it would be good to explore all options before considering more intrusive interventions. In checking with Mrs. Saltzman, Mr. Umaki finds that Duane is doing well academically, although his behavior is out of control. Mr. Umaki know that sometimes teachers and children fall into poor patterns of behavior with one another, so he offers to do what he can to help out. Mr. Umaki checks with Duane's previous teachers. Duane's kindergarten teacher indicates that Duane was a bit impulsive, but not so difficult that she saw a problem. Duane's first-grade teacher indicates that Duane was a challenge, but also a pleaser.

First-Grade Teacher:	Oh, Duane. Once I won him over, we had a great year. He needs to know his limits, but he is very responsive. Duane is a bright boy. He performs above average in both math and reading.

Note: It is never the teacher's place to diagnose problems such as ADHD or recommend that parents consider medication. Speak to your administrator, school psychologist, or behavior specialist if you are concerned about these types of issues. Remember, always try the simplest, most noninvasive interventions first.

B. Self-assess or have an observer monitor your ratio of interactions.

Monitoring and analyzing your interactions with students can provide important objective information. Though subjective evaluation is valid, subtle patterns of behavior do not lend themselves to detection and often go unnoticed by teachers who are busy teaching. The following sections include information on how an observer can help gather information, as well as a variety of ways that a teacher can self-assess his or her ratio of interactions with a student.

1. Set up an observation by an interventionist.

The teacher and interventionist should agree on a time, purpose, and format for the observation. Observations should be scheduled during times when the student is most likely to misbehave. This will yield the most useful information.

The purpose of the observation is not to evaluate, but to assist in designing an intervention to improve student behavior. Teachers should act as normally as possible to facilitate the problem-solving process.

Before the observation, determine a method to record interactions between the teacher and student, which will be analyzed at a later meeting. Information can be recorded on the Ratio of Interactions Monitoring Form (Reproducible Form E1), the Observation Form (Reproducible Form E2), or another format of your choice.

Ratio of Interactions Monitoring Form
This form can be used any time to assess whether a teacher is interacting with a student (or group of students) at least three times more often when the student is behaving responsibly than when he is misbehaving—to determine if the teacher is maintaining at least 3:1 positive to negative ratio of interactions.

An outside observer, such as an interventionist, or a teacher who wishes to self-monitor his or her own interactions can use the Ratio of Interactions Monitoring Form (Reproducible Form E1). To self-monitor, keep the form on a clipboard and mark a tally whenever an interaction with the target student(s) occurs. Another method is to audio record or videotape classes and record interactions at a later time. (These self-monitoring procedures are described later in this step and can be explored in more detail in "Intervention K: Self-Monitoring and Self-Evaluation.")

INTERVENTION

E

Reproducible Form E1: *Ratio of Interactions Monitoring Form*

Ratio of Interactions Monitoring Form

_____   _____   _____   _____
Student   Grade/Class   Teacher   Date

Coding system used (e.g., to indicate specific activities or transitions):

Directions: Tally <u>every</u> interaction you have with the student.

Attention to Positive Behavior	Attention to Negative Behavior
(Praise and/or noncontingent attention)	

Analysis and plan of action:

Whenever the teacher interacts with the student, mark a tally in the corresponding "Attention to (Positive/Negative) Behavior" box. Review the definitions at the beginning of this chapter to ensure that you are accurately categorizing positive and negative interactions. For example, if a teacher interacts with a student in response to misbehavior, the interaction is counted as negative, regardless of whether the interaction carries a positive tone or intent. An instruction to an individual student might also be considered negative if the student is off-task at the time of the interaction. For a more detailed record, create a coding system to include more information about each interaction (e.g., type of instructional activity [I = Independent Work, G = Group Work], specific type of attention, severity of the misbehavior, etc.).

After the tallying record is complete, calculate the ratio of positive to negative interactions, using separate ratios for each category if the interactions are coded. If overall interactions do not reflect at least a 3:1 positive to negative ratio, use the strategies in this chapter to decrease attention to negative behavior and increase attention to positive behavior. After approximately two weeks, monitor interactions again to see if the desired 3:1 ratio is achieved.

If overall interactions do not reflect at least a 3:1 positive to negative ratio, use the strategies in this chapter to decrease attention to negative behavior and increase attention to positive behavior.

> **Note:** A copy of this form and other Increasing Positive Interactions forms are also provided on the CD.

Observation Form

As an alternative to the tallying method used with the Ratio of Interactions Monitoring Form, keep a scripted log of interactions to provide an anecdotal record of positive and negative interactions between the teacher and student. The Observation Form (Reproducible Form E2) can be used for this purpose with an individual student, a group of students, or a whole classroom. Although a scripted log may be more time-consuming to implement and analyze, it may yield important information about the nature of interactions with students. On the Observation Form, column 1 is used to note the time of an interaction. Column 2 is used to log what the student or students are doing immediately before the interaction or during the time of the interaction, and column 3 is used to record exactly what the teacher does or says during the interaction. This anecdotal record may be kept by an outside observer or by a teacher who is self-monitoring through use of an audio or video recording.

Reproducible Form E2: *Observation Form*

Observation Form

Student _____   Grade/Class _____   Teacher _____   Date _____

Observer _____   Subject _____   Activities _____

Time	Description of Student Behavior	Description of Teacher Interaction

Mr. Umaki: (Principal)	If it's OK with you, I would like to schedule an observation.
Mrs. Saltzman: (Teacher)	That would be fine, but you should know that Duane can be different when others are in the room.
Mr. Umaki:	That's good for me to know. The observation may help us learn what Duane is able to do to improve his behavior. I know that it will be difficult, but it will help if you act pretty much as if I'm not in the room.
Mrs. Saltzman:	I've always been a little unnerved during observations.
Mr. Umaki:	Let me go over the form that I'll be using. Keep in mind that this has nothing to do with our formal teacher evaluation. Our purpose is to help Duane learn to behave in ways that are more productive and enjoyable. I know observations can yield slightly "unnatural" information, but we can often detect patterns that aren't apparent while you are busy teaching. I'll record whatever Duane does and what you say or do when you interact with him. Later, we'll go over the form to analyze what Duane does to get attention. Let me show you the form I will be using.

Mr. Umaki and Mrs. Saltzman schedule two half-hour observations—one during math in the morning and another during a less structured afternoon activity.

2. Conduct the observation.

Decide whether or not to introduce the observer/visitor to the class based on what will be the least disruptive to instruction.

Mrs. Saltzman:	Class, Principal Umaki is here to visit during our math class.
Mr. Umaki:	Thank you for letting me join you. Part of my job is to visit classes. Your job as students will be to carry on as if I weren't here. I appreciate your letting me visit. I know I will enjoy watching you work.

3. Analyze interactions.

See the sample filled-out version of Reproducible Form E2 at right for examples of teacher/student interactions. Once the interactions have been recorded, the teacher and interventionist should meet, review the interactions to determine the ratio of positive to negative interactions, and discuss the quality of interactions.

Notes about the student's behavior, even when there is no interaction with the teacher, may still provide useful information. Note that several of the descriptions of Duane's behavior indicate that no corresponding teacher interaction occurred.

During the post-observation conference, Mr. Umaki and Mrs. Saltzman examine the Observation Form. Mr. Umaki acknowledges how challenging Duane's behavior must be.

By examining the Observation Form, Mr. Umaki helps Mrs. Saltzman identify negative and positive interactions. Initially, there is some confusion over the first interaction, when Mrs. Saltzman said, "Yes, Duane. That's correct and that was a hard problem." Though Mrs. Saltzman complimented Duane, Mr. Umaki explains that the interaction was actually negative. Duane blurted out the answer rather than following the class expectation of raising his hand and waiting to be called on. Mrs. Saltzman's positive comment was given when Duane engaged in a minor misbehavior; therefore, the interaction gave attention to negative behavior.

From the observation, Mr. Umaki and Mrs. Saltzman find that Duane received attention from the teacher seven times in 30 minutes. Only one interaction occurred when Duane engaged in positive behavior. Thus the ratio of interactions was one positive to six negative, or 1:6.

Mr. Umaki: (Principal)	This is very interesting. It looks like Duane has gotten into a habit of demanding and receiving attention by misbehaving. That's probably why you have been feeling so frustrated.
Mrs. Saltzman: (Teacher)	I'm very surprised. I always thought I was very positive with Duane.
Mr. Umaki:	I think you are positive, but what we need to do is teach Duane to get attention when he is engaging in positive behavior, rather than misbehavior.

Sample Reproducible Form E2: *Observation Form*

Observation Form

Duane Williams	*2*	*Mrs. Saltzman*	*11/2*
Student	Grade/Class	Teacher	Date
Mr. Umaki	*Math*	*Teacher demo, discussion, guided practice*	
Observer	Subject	Activities	

Time	Description of Student Behavior	Description of Teacher Interaction
10:30	*(When I arrived, Duane immediately came over. I told him I could not talk with him as I had work to do, but that I'd stop by to see him when I left. Duane returned to his seat.)*	*(None.)*
10:32	*Listening and participating in lesson.*	*(None.)*
10:35	*Blurts out answer.*	*"Yes, Duane. That's correct and that was a hard problem."*
10:36	*Begins to fidget and tap pencil like a drum.*	*"Duane, you need to listen, not play the drums."*
10:37	*He ceases tapping and appears to listen.*	*(None.)*
10:39	*Gets out of seat and goes and draws on board.*	*"Duane, get back to your seat."*
10:39	*Starts back to seat, but stops and talks to James.*	*Stares at Duane and motions him back to his seat.*
10:40	*Gets back to his seat and begins to work on the problems assigned.*	*(None.)*
10:43	*Continuing to work.*	*Circulating, looks at Duane's work and says, "Nice job on these problems, Duane."*
10:47	*Gets out of his seat while the teacher is presenting and goes to the pencil sharpener, but taps kids on the way.*	*"Duane, that is not fair to the other students. Keep your hands to yourself."*
10:50	*Duane is still at the pencil sharpener.*	*"That is enough, Duane. Get back to your seat."*
10:51	*Duane takes his seat and appears to participate in lesson.*	*(None.)*
10:58	*As the lesson concludes, Duane takes the completed (?) paper to hand in, but on the way pokes students, drums on desks, and talks to other students.*	*(None.)*
11:00	*Still bouncing around the room.*	*(None.)*

A blank version of this form is available on p. 270.

> After discussing the ratio of interactions in more depth, Mr. Umaki and Mrs. Saltzman agree that it would be worthwhile to explore increasing the ratio of positive to negative interactions with Duane. Though Mr. Umaki concedes that this intervention alone is not guaranteed to be successful, he explains that it has fewer long-term ramifications than referring Duane to special education or suggesting that a physician medicate the student. Thus, Increasing Positive Interactions should be tried first.

Audio recording is an easy way to monitor and improve your classroom interactions.

INTERVENTION

E

4. Consider self-monitoring classroom interactions (optional).

Once teachers begin analyzing classroom interactions, they often find it useful to continue the process with individual students or with the whole class. Because observations are often difficult to schedule, self-monitoring can become a valuable classroom tool. Self-monitoring can be accomplished by audio recording or videotaping class sessions or by keeping a frequency count of positive and negative interactions.

AUDIO RECORDING. Audio recording is the least intrusive method of self-monitoring interactions. Simply record a class session and later transcribe and analyze your exchanges with students using an the Ratio of Interactions Monitoring Form (Reproducible Form E1) or the Observation Form (Reproducible Form E2). Audio recording is easy to set up but somewhat limited, as you can record only verbal interactions. What the student was doing at the time of an interaction often has to be reconstructed by memory, and such reflection is invariably less accurate than data recorded in the moment by a third-party observer. Even so, audio recording is an easy way to monitor and improve your classroom interactions.

VIDEOTAPING. To conduct videotaped monitoring, set up a stationary camcorder and record a class session. You can later transcribe and analyze the video using one of the monitoring forms (Reproducible Form E1 or E2). Videotaping often captures interactions that go unnoticed by busy classroom teachers. After the initial novelty wears off and students are accustomed to having a camera in the classroom, behavior tends to be natural. Because you can see as well as hear your interactions, the accuracy of your observations will be pretty good, almost on par with a direct observation. You will also be able to observe your body language, facial expressions, and the activity students are engaged in at the time of an interaction.

KEEPING A FREQUENCY COUNT OF POSITIVE AND NEGATIVE INTERACTIONS. Use the Ratio of Interactions Monitoring Form (Reproducible Form E1) or even a note card in your pocket to keep an ongoing tally of positive and negative interactions.

C. Decide how you will respond to misbehavior.

This step is important because what you decide will impact your ratio of positive to negative interactions. Your aim will be to decrease (not eliminate) the attention you pay to negative behavior. Following are some possible strategies.

1. Brainstorm negative behaviors.

List every negative behavior of the student that comes to mind. Include every behavior that has been annoying you or disrupting class, regardless of how trivial. These questions are a good place to start:

- What does the student do that is annoying or disruptive when he first arrives at school?

- What does the student do that is annoying or disruptive as the day progresses?

- What does the student do during different types of activities?

- Does the student need frequent reminders about anything?

- Do problems occur in other places—on the playground, in the hallways, in the cafeteria, or in other classes?

2. Categorize the behaviors.

Examine the list to determine whether some misbehaviors can be lumped together. For example, if your list includes tapping pencils, screeching chairs, and making animal noises, combine these into a category called "noisemaking." Continue consolidating similar or redundant items on the list until you have completed a comprehensive set of categories.

3. Decide whether to ignore the misbehavior or impose a consequence.

By grouping behaviors together, you have reduced the complexity of your plan. You can now decide how each misbehavior category should be addressed. In this way, you will ensure that your expectations with respect to this student remain consistent, even as you begin changing your approach—for instance, ignoring certain behaviors that you would have corrected in the past. (Of course, in keeping with your existing classroom management plan, you will not necessarily ignore the same behaviors when they come from other students.)

None of this should be a secret from the student. When you meet with the student to discuss your concerns, tell the student what behaviors you are going to ignore and why. You and the student will be working from clear and unambiguous expectations, and this will reduce stress all around.

In some cases, you may be able to address misbehavior *before* it occurs, thereby sidestepping the need to reprimand or ignore. You can employ one or both of the following strategies:

- Identify aspects of the physical setting, schedule, and class organization you might modify to reduce the likelihood of misbehavior. If the student sometimes pushes others in the rush to get out the door, excuse students by rows or table groups.

- Try *precorrecting*. If you anticipate that students will push each other while leaving the classroom, give a prompt like, "Remember to keep your hands and feet to yourself as you are leaving the room when I excuse the class."

If it is necessary to ignore or reprimand the student, determine in advance the categories of behavior that will warrant each response.

CATEGORIES THAT SHOULD BE IGNORED. These can include behaviors that do not get in the way of teaching or in the way of other students' learning. Though ignoring misbehavior is sometimes uncomfortable, no consequence can be dispensed without giving the student at least some attention. If attention is what the student wants, each consequence may actually be reinforcing the misbehavior, and withholding attention may be the most effective consequence you can implement.

The use of ignoring is counterintuitive to many adults and therefore difficult to implement. However, constant nagging, repeated corrections, and increasingly severe consequences will not improve misbehavior that is fueled by the need for attention and may in fact be reinforcing to an attention-starved student.

To ignore misbehavior effectively, you must act as though you have not seen or heard the misbehavior. This means you must stay calm and physically relaxed. A rigid body response or even shooting a look might be reinforcing.

Consistency is the key to ignoring effectively. If the plan calls for you to ignore Harvey for blurting out responses, then he must be ignored every time he blurts out a response. If you ignore Harvey the first two or three times he blurts out answers and then apply a consequence, your previous ignoring will not be effective and intervention fidelity will be compromised. Harvey will soon learn that persistence pays when he wants to get attention through misbehavior—and you'll be hearing a lot more from Harvey.

CATEGORIES THAT REQUIRE A SPECIFIC CONSEQUENCE. Some categories of misbehavior cannot go unaddressed. For misbehavior that disrupts learning and for which ignoring would not be appropriate, establish a mild consequence that can be implemented quickly and easily as well as calmly and consistently.

As with ignoring, consistency is the key to the effective use of consequences. For example, if you have a plan that calls for you to implement a consequence with Sophie for disturbing other students, apply the consequence every time Sophie disturbs another student. If Sophie's behavior is overlooked the first few times she disturbs another student and then consequences are resumed later in the day, the effect of this lack of consistency is predictable. Sophie learns that it's OK to disturb students—sometimes. Now you are dealing with a challenge. Sophie may find ever more creative ways to test the limits: "What can I get away with today?"

Implement consequences with as little attention to the student as possible. Keep emotion out of your interaction, and save that speech you've been building up to. Students who are in desperate need of attention are often more reinforced by the intensity and length of the interaction than by its content. If you appear to be angry when implementing a consequence, the student may be reinforced for the misbehavior. Avoid emotional confrontations and consequences that take time to enact. Spare your long explanation when a word will do. If you must have a negative interaction, keep it unremarkable and nonintrusive—in a word, boring.

When possible, select consequences that have some logical association with the inappropriate behavior. If the student is usurping class time, it might be appropriate to have the student owe time from recess or after school. If the student is bothering another student, it might be appropriate to have the offending student move to a different location.

Implement consequences with as little attention to the student as possible.

INTERVENTION

E

Classroom consequences should also be mild. If you are at all reluctant to implement severe consequences, don't put yourself in a position that will force you to do so when you honestly don't believe "the punishment fits the crime." This will improve the consistency of how you implement consequences and increase the likelihood the student will understand the correlation between his behavior and the consequence.

Progressive Versus Fixed Consequences

Some teachers in our school assign each student a set of colored cards, with each card representing a step in a progression of consequences— green is a warning, yellow means the student loses recess, orange means a parental contact, and red lands the student in the office.

This system of colored cards is considered progressive, as consequences become more severe with each subsequent infraction. There is no set rule that one system of consequences (progressive or fixed) is better than the other. However, when evaluating any disciplinary intervention in your classroom, ask yourself two questions. First, does the intervention treat children with dignity and respect? Second, is the intervention working? Is it helping in your efforts to motivate students to be responsible and actively engaged in instruction?

If the answer to both questions is yes with the system you use, you have a disciplinary plan—no sense "fixing" what isn't broken.

However, though it is possible for a teacher to assign progressively more serious consequences and do it respectfully, progressive consequences have inherent drawbacks. (These are discussed further in "Intervention P: Defining Limits and Establishing Consequences.") The biggest drawback is that it is difficult to be consistent in handing out progressively harsher penalties, especially if you have the same children for the entire day.

You've no doubt come across "Johnny" in your classroom. Johnny absentmindedly taps his pencil on his desk. He is not doing this purposefully to cause trouble. It's a habit, and he is virtually unaware he does it. However, his action is disruptive to the lesson. You issue a warning and pull out the green card. Johnny stops immediately.

INTERVENTION

E

Twenty minutes later, Johnny starts tapping again. You genuinely like Johnny, but you pull his yellow card anyway. Now he's lost his recess. But he does stop.

Ten minutes go by. Johnny starts up again without even realizing it. What do you do now? Pull the orange card and call his parents? What if he does it again? To the office?

How silly will you feel telling Johnny's parents that their son tapped his pencil, so you're going to need a parental conference? How happy will your administrative support be if they have to deal with something so trivial?

Maybe you could overlook the offense. *Poof*!—there goes your consistency. Maybe you could bargain—look Johnny straight in the eye and say, "Don't make me pull this card!" Oops!—you've just announced to Johnny that he has the power to make his teachers do things they don't want to do. Or you could level with him and say, "I really don't want to pull this card," leading Johnny to wonder what it is you *do* want to do—and start in tapping again just to find out.

In a system of progressive consequences, all misbehavior is painted with the same brush, and the brush gets wider with each application. However, misbehaviors are not equivalent. Tapping a pencil is not the same as pushing someone. If law enforcement treated parking tickets the same way it does DUIs, most of us would be doing hard time! Fortunately for us, the law draws distinctions between parking tickets, speeding tickets, and DUIs. We can and should do the same in our classrooms.

Thus, a progressive system such as the colored cards may be suitable for certain serious behaviors but inappropriate as a blanket consequence. Carefully consider the various responses you plan to use, from minor to severe misbehavior, to ensure that you can implement consequences calmly, consistently, and while treating all students with dignity and respect.

Making progressive consequences work

Recognizing that misbehavior can be minor or serious, set up a two-pronged system of consequences. On one side are the "parking ticket" misbehaviors. These will be treated with fixed consequences that

Progressive Versus Fixed Consequences (continued)

are comparatively mild. On the other side are the "speeding ticket" misbehaviors. These will receive progressively more serious consequences with each infraction.

Now, when Johnny taps his pencil, you can tell him he loses 15 seconds on the computer. If he does it again, you assign another 15 seconds. If Johnny misbehaves 12 times, he still has lost only three minutes of computer time. That may not seem like a lot, but guess which three minutes will be the longest of Johnny's day? Don't underestimate the power of small consequences that are consistently applied. On the other hand, if Johnny refuses to follow a direction, the teacher could pull a card for refusal.

It is important that you clearly and explicitly teach your students which misbehaviors will warrant fixed consequences, which will receive progressive consequences, and what those consequences will be.

Using fixed consequences

It is easy and useful to develop a four-category system of nonprogressive, or fixed, consequences. Consider various misbehaviors you encounter, and then visualize four distinct categories.

The first is misbehavior that receives no consequences at all, just reminders. In kindergarten, for instance, your youngest pupils will simply forget that they are not supposed to shout out answers. There is no need to issue a consequence when a simple reminder will do.

Misbehavior that receives a minor consequence falls into the second category—like Johnny with his pencil. As with parking tickets, the consequences remain the same. Every time Johnny taps, he owes 15 seconds. Sound too simple to be effective? If you apply it consistently over time, you'll find this approach is too effective to be so simple. These two minor-misbehavior categories will cover 90 to 95 percent of the misbehaviors you encounter.

In the third category are more serious infractions that earn more serious consequences—displays of disrespect, use of bad language, and so forth. Create a menu of consequences that all of your students know about and understand. When a student commits one of these misbehaviors, select one of the consequences from the menu, trying for maximum consistency—for example, time owed, timeout, detention, parental contact, or parent conference.

The fourth category is reserved for those misbehaviors that violate your school's code of conduct or involve physical or emotional violence. For these and only these, you reserve the school's ultimate consequences (office referral or suspension). The four-category system allows some flexibility between classrooms in all categories except this one. Consequences for these severe misbehaviors should be consistently applied throughout the entire school.

Once again, you must make sure that your students understand the system. Teach them exactly what consequences apply to which behaviors.

Classroom teachers can use the following onsequences:

- **Have the student owe time.** Keeping a student in from recess, one minute per infraction, is appropriate when the student has usurped class time.

Mrs. Saltzman: (Teacher)	Duane, you have wasted class time by wandering around. You owe one minute of recess.

- **Assign an in-class timeout.** An in-class timeout may be appropriate if the student is not able to participate appropriately in a class activity. A brief timeout—15 seconds to a minute or two—demonstrates that it is a privilege to be a part of class activities.

Mrs. Saltzman:	Duane, you have disrupted your reading group by making noises. You need to go to the quiet corner for one minute to think about how to be a cooperative member of your group.

- **Assign the student to a different seat.** Assigning the student to a different seat may be appropriate if the student is bothering other students. The move may set the student apart from others, but it should not be permanent. The consequence might move the student during the remainder of an activity but allow him to return to his normal seat with the next activity. This demonstrates that it is a privilege to sit with peers, but it gives the student an opportunity to try again after a short period of time. A permanent move to an isolated spot implies that the student is "bad" all the time.

Mrs. Saltzman: (Teacher)	Duane, you need to learn to work without poking other students. Please take the seat by my desk. You may return to your own seat when we come back from recess.

- Have the student fill out a Behavior Improvement Form. This consequence helps the student learn from his misbehavior by thinking about what happened. The Behavior Improvement Form (Reproducible Form E3) has the student reflect on his actions and identify what he will do in the future to avoid a similar problem.

If the misbehavior is so severe that it cannot be handled with classroom consequences, see "Intervention G: Managing Physically Dangerous Behavior" or "Intervention H: Managing Severely Disruptive Behavior." These interventions provide in-depth planning for dealing with dangerous, illegal, severely disruptive, and insubordinate behavior while concurrently teaching the student to get attention and needs met through responsible behavior.

After brainstorming a list of Duane's misbehaviors and categorizing them, Mrs. Saltzman and Mr. Umaki decide that Duane engages in a lot of minor misbehaviors. He isn't physically threatening, nor is he overtly defiant. Duane never disrupts the class so much that Mrs. Saltzman is unable to teach. Mr. Umaki and Mrs. Saltzman develop the following plan for ignoring some misbehaviors and implementing mild classroom consequences for others (see Figure E1).

Reproducible Form E3: *Behavior Improvement Form*

Behavior Improvement Form

Name   Grade/Class   Teacher   Period/Time

1. What did you do? _____

_____

2. Why did you do it? _____

_____

3. What else could you have done? _____

_____

Figure E1: *Consequences for Duane's Misbehavior*

Probable Misbehavior	Teacher Reaction
• Talking out loud	• Ignore
• Wandering around the room	• Ignore
• Poking other students	• In-class timeout
• Making smart-aleck remarks and inappropriate comments	• Ignore
• Making noises	• Ignore
• Being disrespectful of other students during cooperative groups	• In-class timeout
• Being off task during cooperative groups—hard on group members	• Time owed (no penalty for group)
• Pushing other students	• In-class timout
• Arguing with the teacher	• Time owed until follows instructions
• Threatening to leave the classroom	• Ignore
• Refusing to go to in-class timeout	• Time owed until goes to timout area

4. Verbally rehearse how to handle each misbehavior.

> Make adjustments if any part of the plan feels unworkable. The teacher should feel that she can and will implement the procedures every time a misbehavior occurs.

Mr. Umaki: (Principal)	Let's pretend Duane is making burping noises. What will you do?
Mrs. Saltzman: (Teacher)	Ignore him.
Mr. Umaki:	When Duane finds he can't get your attention with burps, he switches to loud coughing. What will you do?
Mrs. Saltzman:	Ignore him.
Mr. Umaki:	Now he switches to . . .
Mrs. Saltzman:	I know. Now he begins giggling loudly. I may crack up, but I'll give it my best shot.
Mr. Umaki:	What if he makes disrespectful comments to another student in class?
Mrs. Saltzman:	I will give him an in-class timeout.

A structured plan for responding to misbehavior removes the stress of making constant judgment calls when the student misbehaves.

D. Develop a plan to increase positive interactions.

In addition to reducing the amount of attention the student gets for misbehavior, the success of this intervention is dependent upon increasing attention to responsible behavior. Adults must clearly demonstrate that students have a higher probability of getting adult attention when they behave than when they misbehave.

1. Brainstorm a list of noncontingent positive interactions.

Noncontingent positive interactions occur simply because the student is part of the class community, meaning that the student does not have to *do* anything to get this attention. Noncontingent positive interactions are nonevaluative and simply tell students that they are important. Here are some examples:

- Say hello to a student who is entering the classroom.

- Walk with a student in the hall when escorting the class to the cafeteria.

- Greet a student returning from lunch or recess.

- Wish a student a happy vacation.

- Say things like, "I look forward to seeing you tomorrow," at the end of the day.

- Ask how things are going.

- Chat about a shared interest.

All students need and deserve noncontingent positive interactions. Though it may feel awkward at first to increase friendly interactions, students respond to them. Eventually, these interactions become second nature. As the running dialogue between you and your students becomes more positive, the student who wasn't very likable becomes more likable. Time that you spent nagging, scolding, and reprimanding can be diverted to more enjoyable and productive interactions.

Mr. Umaki and Mrs. Saltzman develop a list of times that Mrs. Saltzman might provide Duane with noncontingent positive interactions. They start their list with the beginning of the day:

- Greet Duane as soon as he enters the door in the morning.

- Give Duane a job during opening circle.

- Have Duane sit front and center during opening circle.

Adults must clearly demonstrate that students have a higher probability of getting adult attention when they behave than when they misbehave.

INTERVENTION

E

Contingent positive feedback gives a student the attention he craves and information that describes what the student was doing responsibly, which helps the student learn what responsible behavior is.

- Make friendly eye contact with Duane during opening circle.
- Ask Duane one question during sharing time.
- Between reading groups, check that Duane is where he needs to be.
- Have Duane listen to other students read when he is finished with his work.
- Whenever Duane is in line, chat and walk with him to recess.

A list of possible noncontingent positive interactions prompts adults to try interacting positively with a student who has behavior problems. As the teacher and student engage in these kinds of interactions, the student learns that he doesn't have to misbehave to get attention. With each positive interaction, the student's need for attention is momentarily fulfilled, and the student will begin to demonstrate appropriate behavior. In turn, the teacher will have more opportunities to provide the student with contingent positive feedback.

2. Plan to provide contingent positive feedback.

In addition to providing the student with noncontingent positive interactions, teachers need to consciously give students attention when they behave appropriately. Contingent positive feedback gives a student the attention he craves and information that describes what the student was doing responsibly, which helps the student learn what responsible behavior is. Students who have had difficulty consistently engaging in responsible behavior need to learn that it is an easier and more satisfying way to get attention than irresponsible behavior.

The following guidelines may assist teachers in providing contingent positive feedback:

- Provide positive feedback to all students as a routine part of instruction. While presenting information to the class, the teacher can transition from one concept to another with short bursts of positive feedback.

> **Mrs. Saltzman:** Joanne, Duane, Leah, thank you for actively listening. I
> **(Teacher)** can see that you have been following along on your
> diagrams. Now, class, the next thing we are going to
> do is . . . .

- Provide positive feedback in all settings and activities. Opportunities for positive feedback exist in all classroom settings and activities. Here are some examples:

  - While groups work on projects, the teacher can put her hand on Duane's shoulder and say, "This group is working together respectfully. Keep going."

  - While working independently, the teacher might go to different individuals, including Duane, and say, "You are hard at work. May I look at what you have done so far?"

  - During discussions, the teacher might say, "Students, I can tell by your comments that you are listening respectfully to your classmates. Duane, your comment about whales eating plankton is very knowledgeable."

- Provide honest feedback. If the student is tapping his pencil, it would not be appropriate to praise the student for sitting in his seat. Praise is not appropriate if the student is misbehaving. If a positive comment is triggered by inappropriate behavior, the interaction is negative because the teacher is responding to misbehavior. Misbehavior should be ignored or a consequence implemented according to the consequences that were previously set. Honest positive feedback can be given by catching the student when he is legitimately demonstrating responsible behavior.

> **Mrs. Saltzman:** Duane, you started the morning very responsibly. You
> **(Teacher)** put your attendance card in its pocket. You got out
> your reading book and started reading independently.
> I am impressed.

Note: An exception to this guideline may be made when behavior is so severe that it needs to be gradually shaped. In this case, it might be appropriate to provide positive feedback on an appropriate behavior while the student is engaged in an unrelated misbehavior. For example, if a student is developmentally delayed, it may be appropriate to praise her for working with her peers without touching, poking, or pushing—even though the student is making inappropriate noises.

- Link your positive feedback to a student's goals or general class rules. By linking specific behavior to the student's goal or to classroom rules, students will begin to understand how their actions are related to more global or sophisticated expectations.

Mrs. Saltzman: (Teacher)	Duane, by lining up quickly and keeping your hands and feet to yourself, you are demonstrating cooperation and a sense of responsibility.

- Recognize important behavior and avoid praising overly simple behavior. If a student is working on improving self-control, saying something like, "Good sitting," is not meaningful and is actually potentially demeaning. Appropriate and relevant feedback might be, "You demonstrated self-control by listening patiently while I was giving instructions." Praise should be given for tasks or behavior that are new or difficult so that feedback is meaningful. It is important to remember that the same behavior may be simple for one student but new and complex for another. If the behavior is difficult, it would be appropriate to provide the student with positive feedback when he is engaging in the behavior.

- Avoid the "good job" syndrome. One of the most difficult aspects of teaching is that teachers must focus on numerous variables at one time. While thinking about instruction and a class full of students, it is natural to fall into an automatic pattern of nonspecific rote comments such as "terrific," "super," or "nice job." When this happens, positive comments become background noise. Students may not even notice the attention because no usable information is being provided. Students need to know how their specific actions translate into being "responsible," "on task," "polite," and so on. Positive feedback is meaningful only when students are aware of what they did well.

- **Provide positive feedback in a way that does not embarrass the student.** Be sure to recognize that every student responds differently to praise, and structure your interactions accordingly. Some students will misbehave simply to avoid receiving compliments they find embarrassing or patronizing. Some students respond well to private comments but are embarrassed when comments are public. Others respond better when comments are emotionally neutral. "Ellen, you have produced a very creative story" may be more acceptable than, "Oh Ellen! I loved your story about the sea monster. It was so imaginative! I enjoyed it so much!" Some students respond well to nonverbal signals that can be worked out in advance. The teacher can look the student in the eye, give a prearranged signal such as a nod of the head, and then resume teaching. If the teacher has discussed the signal with the student, eye contact and a nod of the head will clearly communicate the message, "That was a good example of self-control." While specific feedback is important, it should always be delivered in a way that is acceptable to the student.

Some students respond well to private comments but are embarrassed when comments are public.

You may want to develop a list of possible contingent feedback to give to your student of concern, taking the previous guidelines into consideration.

Mr. Umaki and Mrs. Saltzman make a list of contingent comments that might be given to Duane if he is behaving appropriately.

Mrs. Saltzman: Duane, you are cooperating by:
(Teacher)
- working quietly at your seat

- keeping your hands to yourself

- going directly to the pencil sharpener, sharpening your pencil, and returning to your desk

- staying in your seat while someone was speaking

INTERVENTION

E

> - following directions immediately
>
> - waiting until the completion of the lesson to talk to other students
>
> - participating actively with a cooperative group and staying on task

3. Plan to conference informally with the student regarding his progress.

Contingent positive feedback should occasionally be given to the student during a one-to-one conference or informal conversation. This procedure takes time, but it is very powerful and should not be overlooked.

Mrs. Saltzman: (Teacher)	Duane, do you mind if I talk with you for a minute before you get on the bus?
Duane:	Am I in trouble?
Mrs. Saltzman:	No. In fact, just the opposite. I wanted to talk about what fine progress you are making in learning to cooperate and thinking before you act. Do you think that you are beginning to control your own behavior better?
Duane:	I guess.
Mrs. Saltzman:	Can you tell me a few examples of things that show cooperation and thinking before you act?
Duane:	Well, one thing I've been trying real hard to do is to keep from bugging other kids when they are working. (Pause) I guess I've been doing better at working in my reading group. Instead of making noises and stuff, I try to work hard.
Mrs. Saltzman:	Duane, that's great. I've noticed the exact same things. I think your parents would like to hear about the things you just shared with me. It's important for you to tell yourself that you are doing a good job. Do you have any questions or anything you wanted to mention to me?
Duane:	No, I don't think so.
Mrs. Saltzman:	OK. I'll see you tomorrow morning. Have a good day.

INTERVENTION

E

4. Involve other staff members in interacting positively with the student.

The impact of positive interactions can be increased by soliciting the help of other adults. PE and music teachers, the librarian, playground supervisors, cafeteria and custodial staff, bus drivers, office staff, and instructional assistants can all provide students with additional positive adult interactions. As the student experiences the support and recognition of adults throughout the school, the need for attention in the classroom will be reduced. The student will also feel a greater sense of connection and self-worth in the school community, which will often improve motivation.

Staff members who have contact with the student should be informed of the student's goals and encouraged to watch for opportunities to provide the student with additional positive interactions. Help from staff may be solicited individually, via a letter, or in a staff meeting. When the school is large, it is sometimes useful to show a picture of the student. Ask staff members to greet the student, make eye contact, nod to the student in recognition, and acknowledge the student in other specific ways.

As the student experiences the support and recognition of adults throughout the school, the need for attention in the classroom will be reduced.

E. **Continue to collect objective data to determine whether the intervention is helping the student's behavior improve.**
At least two independent means of evaluating the student's progress should be put in place. Because behavior is difficult to change, small improvements may go unnoticed unless you have established ways to determine whether the intervention is having a positive effect. If you have been implementing these interventions in order, you may already have begun collecting data using "Intervention D: Data Collection and Debriefing." If you have not used Data Collection, begin doing so now and continue through the rest of your intervention efforts. See Intervention D for details and sample forms.

Possible data sources include direct observation, periodic frequency counts of the desired behavior, or a self-monitoring system. Other methods of monitoring student progress might include tracking grades, work completion, time on task, and other similar actions. Evaluation systems will vary depending on the goal of the intervention, the sophistication of the student, and the time and personnel available to assist with monitoring.

INTERVENTION

E

Mr. Umaki: (Principal)	To monitor Duane's progress, I would like to schedule an-other observation in two weeks, and I think it would also be useful to have you and Duane's parents complete an anecdotal log and informal evaluation.
Mrs. Saltzman: (Teacher)	Good. Duane's parents need to be a part of this. I would also like to informally monitor my interactions with Duane using the tape recorder. I'll try to do that a couple of times in the next two weeks.

Note: For additional information and samples of self-mon-itoring systems, see "Intervention K: Self-Monitoring and Self-Evaluation."

F. **Determine who will meet with the student to discuss and finalize the plan.**

Use professional judgment to determine who will be present when the plan is discussed with the student. Some students are more responsive to a discussion when only one adult is present. In other cases, it will be important to include parents, an interventionist, or an assistant who will be working with the student.

Mr. Umaki:	We need to decide how to introduce what we are going to do with Duane. Duane should establish goals and identify what he needs to do to reach those goals. He also needs to know what you will ignore and the consequences for behavior that cannot be ignored.
Mrs. Saltzman:	Do we actually tell Duane that I'm going to ignore him when he wanders around the room?
Mr. Umaki:	Yes, and there are several reasons for telling Duane that he will be ignored when he engages in certain misbehav-ior. He needs to know that he is still valued—he's not a nonentity. We also need to communicate to him that by implementing this plan, we are telling him that we trust in his abilities and know that he can be more responsible. If we are right about Duane's seeking attention through

> misbehavior, you should be prepared for his behavior to worsen before it gets better. If you ignore his misbehavior, he is likely to try harder to get your attention.
>
> **Mrs. Saltzman:** Oh, great. I guess if I know that's coming, though, I can deal with it.
>
> **Mr. Umaki:** It will be hard for Duane to change, but once he sees you are determined, I think we can turn things around. I'd like to be in on the first conference with Duane, and I think Duane's parents would like to know what we are doing.
>
> **Mrs. Saltzman:** I don't think I feel comfortable with his parents yet. Would you explain the plan to them?
>
> **Mr. Umaki:** I think Duane's parents will be responsive. Would it work for us to meet with Duane and his parents at 9:30 tomorrow morning? I can have Miss Eisenger take your class for you.

Step 2: Meet with the student.

Begin the meeting with a quick review of the problem and goal so you can begin discussing and finalizing the plan.

> After welcoming Duane and his parents to the meeting, Mr. Umaki reviews Duane's positive kindergarten and first-grade years. He then helps Duane think about a happier second-grade year and establish goals.
>
> **Mr. Umaki:** Let's review what we've come up with. You are a good student, and we want you to have a great second-grade year. What are the goals you can work on?
>
> **Duane:** I guess I need to work on cooperating, and I need to think before I do things.

A. Help the student identify and rehearse specific actions he is willing to take to reach his goal.

Though this intervention focuses heavily on teacher behavior, the student needs to know how to meet the expectations of the classroom. Have the student brainstorm actions he can take to reach his goal, verbally rehearse what he will do to reach the goal, and/or actually practice the behavior he will engage in to reach the goal.

Mr. Umaki: (Principal)	Mr. and Mrs. Williams, thanks for being part of this meeting.
Father:	Duane, your mother and I expect you to be successful and responsible at school.
Duane:	OK.
Mr. Umaki:	Duane, let's see if we can figure out how you can meet your two goals from the very beginning of the day. What should you do when you enter the classroom?
Duane:	I need to hang up my coat. Then I need to put my name in my attendance pocket. If I'm early, I need to get a book and then sit down to read.
Mrs. Saltzman: (Teacher)	That's exactly right, Duane.
Mr. Umaki:	Let's see if we can figure out actions that would be cooperative and actions that would not be cooperative. Would throwing your coat on the floor be cooperative?
Duane:	No.
Mr. Umaki:	Would hiding someone else's coat be cooperative?
Duane:	No.
Mr. Umaki:	Would sitting down in the reading corner and looking through several books be cooperative?
Duane:	Yes.
Mr. Umaki:	Would yelling to Mrs. Saltzman across the room be cooperative?
Duane:	No.
Mrs. Saltzman:	What could you do instead?
Duane:	I don't know.
Mrs. Saltzman:	You could come over to me and stand by my side. I will know that you need my attention if you wait quietly.
Mr. Umaki:	Good. Duane, if you feel yourself starting to yell at Mrs. Saltzman, remember your second goal. Think before you act.

Duane, Mr. Umaki, and Mrs. Saltzman verbally practice how Duane might handle various activities that occur during the day and then role-play various situations. Duane's parents are invited to be active participants.

B. Discuss the plan for ignoring some misbehaviors and providing consequences for others.

The student should have a clear understanding of how the teacher will handle misbehavior. Clarity of the student's understanding and consistency in the teacher's actions will help to eliminate unnecessary testing to determine what is or is not acceptable under the new rules.

Go through all of the probable misbehaviors and teacher responses identified in Step C with the student.

Mr. Umaki: (Principal)	Duane, so far we have talked a lot about what you will do to make improvements. Mrs. Saltzman has also agreed to help you out. We have made a list of the kinds of things you've done in the past that got in the way of your being cooperative.
Mrs. Saltzman: (Teacher)	Yes, Duane. I wasn't sure what was going on in class. That upset me because I like you very much. Sometimes I thought I should call your parents. Sometimes I had you go stand in the hall, and sometimes I just nagged you. I don't think either of us liked that very much.
Duane:	(Nods)
Mrs. Saltzman:	I'd like to change that, so I want to share with you how I will handle behavior that isn't cooperative. One of the things I will do is to ignore you if you do things that aren't cooperative.
Mr. Umaki:	Do you know what ignoring means?
Duane:	Yeah, she won't listen to me.
Mrs. Saltzman:	Yes, Duane. In fact, I will pretend that I can't hear or see you when you aren't cooperating, but I will listen to you and see you when you are cooperating like you are now.

Mr. Umaki and Mrs. Saltzman go through the list, explaining to Duane how Mrs. Saltzman will respond to various misbehaviors. They do not worry about Duane knowing exactly how Mrs. Saltzman will respond for every single misbehavior, but they work with the list until Duane has a good general knowledge of misbehavior, ignoring, and consequences.

C. Review ways the teacher and student can engage in positive interactions.

Mrs. Saltzman: (Teacher)	You know, Duane, I think you and I got off to a funny start. You are a very good student. You have a wonderful imagination and a lot of energy. Mr. Umaki and I decided that it was going to be very nice for you and me to enjoy working with each other when you are being responsible. If you need my attention, I want you to come stand by my side or raise your hand. I am going to make a big effort to say "hello" in the morning and to notice you when you are being cooperative.

D. Set up a time to meet regularly with the student to discuss progress.

Mr. Umaki: (Principal)	Duane, I would like to meet with you once a week for a while to talk about how you're doing. It will be fun for me to see you more often.
Mrs. Saltzman:	Duane, I'll be checking in with you throughout the day. I know we can make this work. Mr. and Mrs. Williams, with your permission, I would like to send home a weekly progress report.
Mother:	Mrs. Saltzman, that would be very helpful. Can we contact you if we have questions?
Mrs. Saltzman:	Yes, please do. The best time to reach me is after 3:00.

E. Review the roles and responsibilities of all participants.

F. Conclude the meeting with words of encouragement.

Mrs. Saltzman:	Duane, I am very relieved that we have this plan. I like you very much, and I know that we can have a great year. Together, we can make it the best year you've ever had.

INTERVENTION

E

Step 3: Follow the plan.

Provide the student with a high ratio of positive to negative interactions by following your plan as faithfully as possible. Learning new patterns of behavior and discarding old patterns can be very difficult for some students. If the student has learned to get attention for misbehavior, learning to gain attention through responsible behavior can feel very risky or uncomfortable. Demonstrate to the student that he has the support and encouragement of the adults around him. High ratios of positive interactions will be critical, as will calmly and consistently implementing the procedures designed for responding to misbehavior.

A. Evaluate the impact of the intervention, making revisions and adjustments as necessary.

This plan may require several weeks of consistent implementation before changes in behavior are noted. If the student's behavior does not gradually improve over two to three weeks, schedule another observation to make sure that the teacher has been able to improve the ratio of positive to negative interactions. If the teacher is having difficulty interacting positively with the student, additional practice with positive interactions may help. The teacher may also use the Ratio of Interactions Monitoring Form (Reproducible Form E1) or the Observation Form (Reproducible Form E2) to self-monitor interactions. By frequently recording or videotaping herself and occasionally analyzing the tape for positive and negative interactions, the teacher can learn to interact in a positive manner more effectively.

If consistently ignoring misbehavior or implementing mild classroom consequences is a problem for the teacher, he or she may be having difficulty differentiating the line between appropriate and inappropriate behavior. If this is the case, see "Intervention P: Defining Limits and Establishing Consequences" for information on how to define the borderline between behavior that should be ignored and behavior that requires a classroom consequence.

Even if the student has not made progress despite an effective change in interactions, continue with this plan. Improved interactions alone may not be a strong enough intervention to change the student's behavior. However, increased positive interactions should be continued as a general management strategy—all students function better in a supportive environment where the teacher provides more attention to responsible behavior than misbehavior. Remember, ratios of interactions should always be predominantly positive (at least 3:1). Further, contingent and noncontingent positive interactions should be a natural part of every student's and teacher's day.

This plan may require several weeks of consistent implementation before changes in behavior are noted.

INTERVENTION

E

If changing the ratio of positive to negative interactions does not result in significant changes with an individual student, consider adding any of the following interventions:

Intervention B: Academic Assistance (p. 93)
Intervention K: Self-Monitoring and Self-Evaluation (p. 485)
Intervention M: Teaching Replacement Behavior (p. 567)
Intervention O: Structured Reinforcement Systems (p. 639)

B. When the student demonstrates consistent success, fade the intervention.

Self-monitoring systems and formal monitoring of student progress may be faded as the student demonstrates consistent success across several weeks. However, the Increasing Positive Interactions procedures should be continued to some extent even after student behavior changes. If the student has a long history of getting attention through misbehavior, or if the teacher begins decreasing positive interactions, the student's behavior is likely to regress.

C. Once the intervention has been faded, provide continued support, follow-up, and encouragement.

Because it is easy for teachers and students to slip back into long-established patterns of behavior, continue to follow up on an occasional basis throughout the year. Sometimes positive interactions gradually deteriorate. Periodic informal interviews or an occasional observation can help the teacher resolve or prevent problems from developing.

By working together, Mrs. Saltzman, Mr. Umaki, and Duane's parents are able to implement the Increasing Positive Interactions plan: to ignore a large percentage of Duane's attention-seeking misbehavior; to provide calm, consistent consequences for behavior that cannot be ignored; and to provide Duane with a lot of positive interactions from many adults—including his parents. Though the change is initially difficult, Duane begins to thrive on the new positive attention and encouragement.

Duane's parents support their son by talking with him each night about things he has done during the day to show he is cooperating and thinking before he acts. Both parents even visit Duane in the classroom to help reinforce his ability to cooperate.

Though Duane occasionally has setbacks, Mr. Umaki continues to meet with Mrs. Saltzman. They find that periodic monitoring of interactions helps keep Duane and Mrs. Saltzman on track. By winter break, everyone agrees that Duane's behavior has improved tremendously and that they should continue the plan. Referral to special education or a recommendation for medicating Duane are seen as unnecessary by everyone involved.

CONCLUSION

Teaching students to behave responsibly by increasing your ratio of positive to negative interactions seems almost too simple to be more than wishful thinking. But it works, and a mountain of evidence and research literature back it up. This is a powerful intervention that is a useful part of all classroom management and intervention plans.

If you can accept the idea that children reflect what they experience in the home (for better or worse), it takes no great mental leap to understand that children will also reflect what they see at school. If what they experience in your classroom is affirming, conscientious, and positive, most students will respond to that with similar behavior.

Improving your ratio of positive interactions with one student or a whole class teaches students that they can get attention through responsible behavior. As their pride in responsibility grows, small successes will beget new success.

REFERENCES

Ammons, T. L., Booker, J. L., Jr., & Killmon, C. P. (1995). *The effects of time of day on student attention and achievement*. Charlottesville, VA: University of Virginia, Curry School of Education.

Balsam, P. D., & Bondy, A. A. (1983). The negative side effects of reward. *Journal of Applied Behavior Analysis, 16*, 283–296.

Brophy, J. E. (1983). Classroom organization and management. *The Elementary School Journal, 83*, 254, 285.

Brophy, J. E., & Good, T. L. (1974). *Teacher-student relations: Causes and consequences*. New York: Holt, Reinhart & Winston.

Brophy, J. E., & Good, T. L. (1986). Teacher behavior and student achievement. In M. Wittrock (Ed.), *The third handbook of research and teaching* (pp. 328–375). New York: Macmillan.

Bryant, S., McNeil, M. E., & Van Houten, R. (1988). A principal's inservice training package for increasing teacher praise. *Teacher Education and Special Education, 11*(3), 79–94.

Catalano, R. F., Loeber, R., & McKinney, K. C. (1999). School and community interventions to prevent serious and violent offending. *Juvenile Justice Bulletin,* October 1999.

Colvin, G., & Sugai, G. (1989). *Managing escalating behavior.* Eugene, OR: Behavior Associates.

Colvin, G., Sugai, G., Good, R. H., & Lee, Y. (1997). Using active supervision and precorrection to improve transition behaviors in an elementary school. *School Psychology Quarterly, 12*(4), 344–363.

Dietz, S., & Repp, A. (1973). Decreasing classroom misbehavior through the use of DRL schedules of reinforcement. *Journal of Applied Behavior Analysis, 6,* 457–463.

Dusenbury, L., Falco, M., Lake, A., Brannigan, R., & Bosworth, K. (1997). Nine critical elements of promising violence prevention programs. *Journal of School Health, 67*(10), 409–414.

Elliott, S. N., Witt J. C., Galvin, G., & Peterson, R. (1984). Acceptability of positive and reductive behavioral interventions: Factors that influence teacher's decisions. *Journal of School Psychology, 22,* 353–360.

Good, T. L., & Brophy, J. E. (1987). *Looking in classrooms* (4th ed.). New York: Harper & Row.

Hass, M. R., Passaro, P. D., & Smith, A. N. (1999). Reducing aversive interactions with troubled students. *Reclaiming Children and Youth: Journal of Emotional and Behavioral Problems, 8*(2), 94–97.

Horcones, C. (1992). Natural reinforcement: A way to improve education. *Journal of Applied Behavior Analysis, 25*(1), 71–75.

Hunter, M., & Russell, D. (1981). *Increasing your teaching effectiveness,* Palo Alto, CA: The Learning Institute.

INTERVENTION

E

Jordan, A., Lindsley, L., & Stanovich, P. L. (1997). Classroom teacher's instructional interactions with students who are exceptional, at risk, and typically achieving. *Remedial and Special Education, 18*(2), 82–93.

LaVigna, G. W., & Donnellan, A. M. (1986). *Alternatives to punishment: Solving behavior problems with nonaversive strategies.* New York: Irvington Publishers.

Lounsbery, M. F., & Sharpe, T. (1999). Effects of sequential feedback on preservice teacher instructional interactions and students' skill practice. *Journal of Teaching in Physical Education, 19*(1), 59–78.

McDonnell, J., Thorson, N., McQuivey, C., & Kiefer-O'Donnell, R. (1997). Academic engaged time of students with low-incidence disabilities. *Mental Retardation, 35*(1), 18–25.

Mercer, C. D., & Mercer, A. R. (1998). *Teaching students with learning problems* (5th ed.). Upper Saddle River, NJ: Merrill/Prentice Hall.

Nelson, J. R., & Roberts, M. L. (2000). Ongoing reciprocal teacher-student interactions involving disruptive behaviors in general education classrooms. *Journal of Emotional and Behavioral Disorders, 8*(1), 27–37.

Piazza, C. D., Bowman, L. G., Contrucci, S. A., Delia, M. D., Adelinis, J. D., & Goh, H. (1999). An evaluation of the properties of attention as reinforcement for destructive and appropriate behavior. *Journal of Applied Behavior Analysis, 32*(4), 437–449.

She, H. (1997, March). *Gender difference in teacher-student interaction in high- and low-achieving middle school biology classes.* Paper presented at the 70th annual meeting of the National Association for Research in Science Teaching, Oak Brook, IL.

Thurlow, M. L., Ysseldyke, J. E., & Wotruba, J. W. (1988). *Student and instructional outcomes under varying student-teacher ratios in special education* (Research Report No. 12), Washington, DC: Office of Special Education and Rehabilitation Services.

Worrall, C., Worrall, N., & Meldrum, C. (1983). The consequences of verbal praise and criticism. *Educational Psychologist, 3*, 127–136.

INTERVENTION

E

Reproducible Materials

The following reproducible materials may be used in conjunction with "Intervention E: Increasing Positive Interactions." Copies are provided here and on the CD. Permission is given for individual classroom teachers to reproduce any forms labeled "Reproducible" for classroom use. Reproduction of these materials for an entire school system is prohibited without express permission of the publisher.

Reproducible Step-by-Step Summary (1 of 2)

INTERVENTION E

INCREASING POSITIVE INTERACTIONS

Step-by-Step Summary

Following is a summary of the steps involved in Intervention E. It is important to use professional judgment, adjusting procedures to meet the needs of the situation and the individual. See the chapter "Intervention E: Increasing Positive Interactions" for a detailed description of this intervention.

STEP 1 Plan more positive interactions.

A. Review the problem and overall goal for the student.

B. Self-assess or have an observer monitor your ratio of interactions.
1. Set up an observation by an interventionist.
2. Conduct the observation.
3. Analyze interactions.
4. Consider self-monitoring classroom interactions (optional).

C. Decide how you will respond to misbehavior.
1. Brainstorm negative behaviors.
2. Categorize the behaviors.
3. Decide whether to ignore the misbehavior or impose a consequence.
4. Verbally rehearse how to handle each misbehavior.

D. Develop a plan to increase positive interactions.
1. Brainstorm a list of noncontingent positive interactions.
2. Plan to provide contingent positive feedback.
3. Plan to conference informally with the student regarding his progress.
4. Involve other staff members in interacting positively with the student.

E. Continue to collect objective data to determine whether the intervention is helping the student's behavior improve.

F. Determine who will meet with the student to discuss and finalize the plan.

INTERVENTION E

STEP 2   Meet with the student.

A. Help the student identify and rehearse specific actions he is willing to take to reach his goal.

B. Discuss the plan for ignoring some misbehaviors and providing consequences for others.

C. Review ways the teacher and student can engage in positive interactions.

D. Set up a time to meet regularly with the student to discuss progress.

E. Review the roles and responsibilities of all participants.

F. Conclude the meeting with words of encouragement.

STEP 3   Follow the plan.

A. Evaluate the impact of the intervention, making revisions and adjustments as necessary.

B. When the student demonstrates consistent success, fade the intervention.

C. Once the intervention has been faded, provide continued support, follow-up, and encouragement.

STOIC Analysis and Intervention

The reason the behavior is occurring chronically needs to be analyzed and incorporated into the intervention plan

PURPOSE

STOIC ANALYSIS AND INTERVENTION is intended to assist students with any chronic misbehaviors that have not responded positively to simple interventions; it may be of benefit with any student whose behavior problem has been resistant to other Early-Stage Interventions:

Intervention A: Planned Discussion

Intervention B: Academic Assistance

Intervention C: Goal Setting

Intervention D: Data Collection and Debriefing

Intervention E: Increasing Positive Interactions

An intervention that takes into account why a misbehavior is occuring will be much stronger and more likely to succeed than one that does not.

RATIONALE

This intervention requires more planning and forethought than previous interventions because the problem is chronic and resistant to easy interventions. Though effective classroom management is a lifelong learning task, analyzing and planning subsequent interventions according to function will increase the efficacy of your future efforts, and understanding the variables over which you have control takes relatively little time.

A. Determine whether the misbehavior is chronic.

If Interventions A through E have not been successful, you are dealing with a chronic misbehavior. A behavior that has been resistant to early interventions is going to take a more thoughtful plan of action with more advance preparation to achieve a positive outcome. Function-based planning involves two processes: developing a hypothesis or a guess about why the behavior is happening (function-based thinking) and designing a multifaceted STOIC intervention based on that guess.

B. Think about the function of the misbehavior.

Chronic behaviors happen for a reason. They aren't random, and they don't come out of the blue. An intervention that takes into account why a misbehavior is occurring will be much stronger and more likely to succeed than one that does not. For example, changing the behavior of an attention-seeking student will require a plan in which the student gets far less attention for being defiant and disruptive and far more attention for being cooperative and for following the rules. Designing an intervention without thinking about function can produce results quite the opposite of what is intended. It would be very easy to design an intervention that focuses mainly on how to correct argumentative behavior, for example, with harsher corrections and increasingly punitive consequences for repeated offenses. However, such an approach could actually make the problem worse by feeding into the student's argumentative behavior. The student might see more opportunities to argue (worse yet, with the whole class as audience), ratchet up the emotional intensity and rhetoric, and reinforce negative perceptions of the class or himself.

Consider three broad categories when thinking about function:

1. The student lacks the ability or awareness to exhibit the expected behavior.

2. The student is trying to get something.

3. The student is trying to avoid or escape something.

C. Effective classroom management comprises just five variables.

There are five broad categories of variables that can be manipulated to change student behavior: prevention, expectations, monitoring, encouragement, and correction. These are the essential ingredients of every successful classroom management plan, and specific and practical suggestions for intervention in each variable will be provided later in this chapter. To more easily remember the variables, you can encapsulate them in the acronym STOIC (**S**tructure for success, **T**each expectations, **O**bserve and monitor, **I**nteract positively, **C**orrect fluently).

Regardless of function, think of all five STOIC variables when you are designing an intervention plan; the function will simply direct the emphasis. For example, if the function of the misbehavior is because the student lacks the ability or awareness to exhibit the expected behavior, **T**each expectations. If the student is trying to get something, **I**nteract positively and **C**orrect fluently. If the student is trying to avoid or escape something, **S**tructure, **I**nteract positively, and **C**orrect fluently.

STOIC: **S**TRUCTURE for success

Effective teachers *structure for success* (prevent misbehavior before it happens) by organizing their classrooms and activities to encourage engagement and discourage misbehavior, promote participation and minimize distractions, and motivate every student. The following should be considered:

- physical layout and environment
- logistical planning
- level of structure

Teachers may, at their discretion, modify the level of structure of their classes, taking into account age, maturity, independence, and self-motivation of their students. Even time of year and day can be a factor. Experienced teachers increase the structure of their classrooms during the first and last months of the school year, before and after vacations, and for the first and last period of the day.

STOIC: **T**EACH expectations

Effective teachers teach their students how to function successfully within the individualized structure of their classroom by teaching and reteaching their *expectations* for behavior. Students should know exactly what is expected of them in all settings and for every major instructional activity and transition.

STOIC: **O**BSERVE and monitor

Effective teachers know what is going on in their classrooms at all times. They do this using a host of complementary observation strategies.

Circulate. Teachers circulate throughout the classroom in unpredictable patterns. They visually scan the classroom and are aware of what's going on in the room at all times, seemingly having eyes in the back of their heads—Kounin (1970) calls this *withitness*.

Scan. Effective teachers visually scan all corners of their room.

Use proximity. They use physical proximity to students to prompt responsible behavior and nip early-stage misbehavior in the bud.

Collect data. Effective teachers collect data on the behavior of one or two individual students and occasionally on the entire class to spot trends and patterns of behavior.

STOIC: **I**NTERACT positively

Effective teachers *interact positively* with each student, knowing that students work harder and behave better when they perceive their teacher values them and cares about their success. They maintain at least a 3:1 ratio of positive to negative interactions with their students. Strategies for achieving this ratio include:

- increasing opportunities for positive interactions
  - contingent praise (specific and general praise)
  - noncontingent positive attention (greetings, showing an interest in students as individuals)
- minimizing the frequency, duration, and intensity of negative interactions

STOIC: **C**ORRECT fluently

Effective teachers *correct fluently* by responding to undesired behavior calmly, consistently, briefly, and immediately. A fluent correction is respectful, does not break the flow of instruction, and often goes unnoticed by students other than the one targeted.

Note: Those with extensive behavior analysis training will note that STOIC is simply a procedural description of an ABC (Antecedent-Behavior-Consequence) analysis. For a simple example, suppose your cell phone rings (an antecedent). When you answer (behavior), the caller is either someone you want to talk to (positive consequence) or somebody you'd rather not talk to (negative consequence). If the consequences of answering calls are usually positive, you're probably an avid cell phone user with a big minutes plan. If the consequences involve a lot of unwanted conversations, you may be much less likely to pick up or more prone to forgetting your cell phone. Student behavior in the classroom is affected in a similar way. STOIC analysis essentially manipulates as many aspects of the antecedents as possible to set the student up for positive consequences. Structuring for success and Teaching expectations deal with changing behavior before it occurs, Observing takes place concurrently with behavior, while Interacting positively and Correcting fluently occur after behavior occurs.

Historically, educators and early behavioral research has tended to place too much emphasis on the C (for Correct), which is now largely recognized as ineffective in changing behavior. By weighting intervention planning toward A and B and away from C, STOIC intervention planning can be uniquely proactive, positive, and instructional.

INTERVENTION

F

Characteristics of a fluent correction
- calm
- consistent
- brief
- immediate
- respectful

Figure 1: *STOIC—A procedural description of ABC analysis*

STOIC—A procedural description of ABC analysis		
A (Antecedent)	**B (Behavior)**	**C (Consequence)**
Structure for Success Teach Expectations	Observe and Monitor Interact Positively	Correct Fluently

This intervention has three main parts:

- initial information on the function of the behavior
- initial information on STOIC and the types of things that can be manipulated within each category
- planning steps for building a STOIC intervention that addresses the function of the problem behavior

IMPLEMENTATION STEPS
Step 1: Identify what function the behavior serves.

Behavior serves a function. Interventions that address that function have a much higher chance of success than interventions that do not. The function of every problem behavior fits in one of three broad categories.

A. The student lacks the ability or awareness to meet target expectations.

1. Ability-type problems

In classic behavioral theory, people exhibit behaviors either to get or to avoid something, which is true. But what is also true, particularly in a school setting, is that some students act inappropriately because they don't realize they're behaving badly or because they're incapable of exhibiting the expected behavior. Lack of awareness or ability should always be considered and ruled out before proceeding with an intervention. For example, if you went to see your dentist and were handed several forms to fill out, would you nod, sit down in the waiting area, and then proceed to do nothing for the next 20 minutes? You might, if the forms were written in Cyrillic! Or perhaps you filled out the exact same forms at the same dentist on Tuesday or looked up to witness a collision in the parking lot and forgot all about the forms. There might be any of a number of perfectly valid reasons for ignoring the forms, none of which would be at all apparent to a receptionist observing you. In none of these examples were you trying to get or avoid something, although it could appear to the receptionist that you were trying to get attention or avoid/delay going to the dentist's chair. In reality, you simply lacked the ability or awareness to complete the forms.

Not all students are aware that they are failing to meet expectations, and some students simply can't meet certain expectations. Here are a few examples, starting with one that is absurd, but illustrates the point:

- A paraplegic student violates the "Walk in the Halls" rule. The student is not trying to get or avoid something; she is physically unable to walk.

- A student with severe academic deficits does nothing during independent work times. This student who has no hope whatsoever of completing the assigned work may sit and do nothing, not to get out of doing the work but because she knows she cannot complete the work—just as you wouldn't attempt to fill out a form in Cyrillic to "look busy" when you knew you would be producing gibberish.

- A student with Tourette syndrome cannot control his actions. Not all individuals with Tourette syndrome exhibit tics or random outbursts, but for those who do, the successful intervention is likely to be pharmacological, not behavioral. Whenever the underlying condition is at least partly neurological or physiological, the intervening teacher must work closely with the student's physician to determine what behaviors might be reasonable to treat behaviorally as opposed to behaviors that should be tolerated and accommodated.

- The student who is identified as having ADHD or is in the process of being diagnosed with ADHD cannot stay seated. ADHD is a special case because some combination of modified expectations and accommodations may be the best course. Though the student who can't stay seated for long periods of time may have difficulty

Students, like anyone, may exhibit patterns of behavior about which they are almost completely unaware.

doing what comes easily to other students, it is not beyond that student's ability to learn how to sit still. It is perfectly reasonable to design a plan to try to help a student with ADHD practice and learn improved behavior. Some ADHD children will overcome the difficulties associated with their condition, while others will continue to struggle and may benefit from some adjustment of expectations while they are learning new skills such as self-control and impulse control, staying still, and keeping their attention focused on a task. Teachers, while making some reasonable accommodations, can still hold high standards and firm behavioral expectations for their students with ADHD.

Intervention strategies: Interventions should involve accommodating the situation and in some cases concurrently teaching new strategies. With many students, do not expect immediate or complete behavior change.

2. Awareness-type problems

Students, like anyone, may exhibit patterns of behavior about which they are almost completely unaware. Take, for example, a fidgety student who constantly taps his pencil on the desk. The only time this student is not tapping his pencil is when his knee is bobbing up and down, which he does with equal unawareness. Only when he consciously thinks about keeping his hands and feet still is he completely quiet. He isn't irritating his teacher to get attention—in fact, he's completely unaware that that his tapping and bobbing is having any effect at all on the teacher!

Consider another example: A child incessantly talks, and talks, and talks. This student never seems to stop jabbering except to take a breath—and sometimes not even then. You are unlikely to be successful in correcting this behavior if you have not first identified and addressed its likely source—unawareness. For whatever reason, this student is probably completely unaware that she is behaving this way. Bringing her to a conscious awareness of how much she talks will make any subsequent steps much more successful. You could do this by keeping a duration or frequency tally of her talking, prompting her with a visual cue, or playing back an audio recording of a typical interaction with her. Over time, she may learn how to become a better listener, pause before talking, cue herself to get to the point, be concise when she is talking, and eventually bring the behavior under control. (It may help to consider that the child in this example is not trying to monopolize or disrupt anything any more than a long-winded caller to a radio talk show. Unawareness of this sort is common; with the child, you at least have the opportunity to intervene early.)

The student who raises his voice and gets very loud when he feels strongly about something may also have an awareness problem. His pattern of speech may reflect the types of interactions that are common in his home, community, or circle of friends, or they may simply be a product of his temperament and physiological makeup. He may not realize that his behavior is perceived as rude or even threatening, and he may be genuinely confused when adults get angry with him or when teachers refer him for insubordination.

Similarly, the student who gestures aggressively, assumes threatening body postures, or makes "challenging" faces may not realize how his behavior may be viewed as hostile or threatening to people in authority.

Intervention strategies: Interventions may involve accommodation, but should also involve signals or prompts, teaching replacement behavior, self-monitoring, positive reinforcement, or other strategies to help behavior improve over time. Providing a Koosh ball to a fidgety student would be an example of an accommodation—giving the student something quiet to do with his hands to replace the distracting behavior—while also implementing some form of self-monitoring, positive reinforcement, or other strategy as a long-range intervention designed to change the behavior.

B. The student is trying to get something.

Sometimes a student is trying to get or achieve something, whether it be attention from an adult or fellow students, free time, power or control, positive reinforcement, or something else the student experiences as a reward.

1. Adult attention

Some students will seek positive attention in inappropriate ways; an example would be the student who chronically tattles on others. This child has learned to get attention from teachers by doing the "right" thing in the wrong way, at the wrong time, or way too much.

Then there's the student who is constantly seeking reassurance or validation: "Look at my work! Look what I did!" Again, the student's motive is positive, but the method quickly becomes trying for the teacher.

The student whose range of behaviors might be summed up as "annoying" may actually be trying to get negative attention from the teacher—a scolding, a reprimand, a threat of disciplinary action. He may have had little success getting positive attention in the past. He may be struggling academically. He may be trying to impress his friends or appease his antagonizers. He may argue or be belligerent. Whatever his reasons, negative consequences may be serving as positive reinforcers for him.

Intervention strategies: Interventions will involve giving far less attention to the misbehavior in terms of frequency, duration of attention, and emotional intensity of the attention, while increasing the frequency, duration, and emotional intensity of attention the student receives for positive behavior. See "Intervention E: Increasing Positive Interactions" for specific intervention strategies.

2. Peer attention

Some students may be seeking attention from their peers. The class clown is going for laughter and social approval. The show-off wants to be seen as talented and popular. Conversely, a student may want negative attention. Some students have found that they get attention from their peers only by annoying, arguing, or bullying them or sometimes even by positioning themselves as chronic victims of bullying.

Intervention strategies: Interventions will involve trying to increase the amount of attention the student receives from peers in prosocial ways, usually by teaching the student better social skills for interacting with peers and making friends. It may occasionally involve working directly with the peer group to reduce the amount of attention the student receives for acting out.

3. Power and control

This is an extreme form of attention-getting behavior in which the student truly seems to want to get adults angry. Instead of being satisfied with any type of attention, the student actively tries to "push the teacher's buttons" or "get the goat" of the adult. An emotional reaction from an adult is like fanning the flames of a fire and can be highly reinforcing to students who are deliberately trying to provoke such a response. (See "Intervention I: Managing the Cycle of Emotional Escalation.")

Intervention strategies: The intervention will often involve actually giving the student more control by putting the student in charge of some aspects of the classroom environment or of his own situation when he exhibits positive behaviors. At the same time, reduce any control (such as emotional reactions) that the student elicits from adults through misbehavior.

4. Competing reinforcers

This is a fancy name for a simple concept—the student would rather do something other than the assigned task or activity. An example would be a very young child who, instead of doing her work, walks around the classroom or does other activities.

Intervention strategies: When a student is seeking different stimuli than the activity at hand provides, intervention will involve reducing access to outside reinforcers so that the reinforcers inherent to the desired activity are the best and most accessible ones available.

C. The student is trying to avoid or escape something.

1. Overly difficult or overly simple work

Assigned work may be beyond the student's current ability. Case in point: Suppose that you set up a round-robin reading activity, with each student reading a paragraph in turn. A student who knows he is a very poor reader might misbehave to escape having to read aloud in front of his friends. In other cases, the assigned work may be just barely within the student's range, but difficult enough that the student takes measures to avoid facing it. At the other extreme, "boring" work could be the culprit that triggers misbehavior. If a student finds the assignment extremely dull or simple, he may misbehave to avoid boredom more than the work itself.

Intervention strategies: Adapt instruction to fit the student's academic abilities. If you know that a certain assignment will be too easy for the student, consider letting the student skip it and assign an alternative task instead. For example, if a student has been blowing off "boring" work, you might try to create more interesting assignments while letting her know that occasionally she'll just have to "suck it up" and do the work. You could add that she'll have access to more interesting assignments or activities if she completes the assignment quickly enough. Or if the student is trying to escape work that is too difficult, implement any of the adaptation strategies in "Intervention B: Academic Assistance." If you have already implemented the assessment and adaptation strategies from Intervention B and the student is still unsuccessful, this would be a reasonable time to recommend a referral for special education assessment.

The assigned work may be just barely within the student's range, but difficult enough that the student takes measures to avoid facing it.

INTERVENTION

F

2. Uncomfortable situations

If you can manipulate something in all five STOIC variables, the resulting behavioral plan will be much stronger than if you address and try to change only one variable.

Most students go to some length to avoid negative, harsh, or embarrassing situations. For example, knowing that the "tough" kids like to hang out in the restroom, a student might avoid going into the bathroom during passing times to escape harassment (or worse). At some point during the day, that student will demand to be excused from class or will perhaps do something extremely negative to get thrown out of class so he can use the restroom while other students are not present.

Some students avoid interactions with adults whom they find overly harsh, caustic, or critical. Even if the student isn't truly afraid of a particular teacher, the prospect of trying to explain the significance of the Emancipation Proclamation or why she is yawning in class or doesn't have her bookbag may be too much to handle, so she searches for some escape such as getting kicked out of class or chronic absenteeism.

Intervention strategies: Try to restructure the student's environment so that exposure to the anxiety-producing stimuli is minimized, while reducing ways the student can easily escape unpleasant but necessary situations. For example, if the teacher is being overly harsh and critical, the teacher could be encouraged to work on "Intervention E: Increasing Positive Interactions" and "Intervention P: Defining Limits and Establishing Consequences."

Always try to take into account what function a behavior serves for the student and why a particular misbehavior might be happening. Understanding this will shape the decisions you make about a STOIC intervention and greatly increase the plan's chances for success.

Step 2: Plan a STOIC intervention.

Use the STOIC framework to build a comprehensive intervention. If you can manipulate something in all five STOIC variables, the resulting behavioral plan will be much stronger than if you address and try to change only one variable.

Work through this step using the STOIC Intervention Planning Form (Reproducible Form F1). This form will help you formalize a comprehensive intervention by having you consider the problem and goal, previous interventions, and the five STOIC variables. Decide in advance who will participate in the planning stages and complete the planning form. You

Reproducible Form F1: *STOIC Intervention Planning Form*

STOIC Intervention Planning Form

_____	_____	_____	_____
Student	Grade/Class	Teacher	Period/Time

Step 1   Review the information you have collected to date.

Notes from planned discussions (dates, goals, outcomes): _____

_____

_____

_____

Academic assessment and adaptations: Oral reading fluency: _____ words correct per minute

_____

_____

Notes from goal-setting activities (dates, goals, outcomes):_____

_____

_____

_____

List all behaviors of concern on data that has been collected to date: _____

_____

_____

Are these same behaviors to be the continued focus of intervention? _____

If no, what behavior will be the new focus of intervention, and what data will be collected to determine progress? _____

_____

Develop a hypothesis about the function of the problem behavior—what might be the reason the problem chronically occurs? Check any that may be applicable.

____ Ability	____ Power/Control	____ Awareness	____ Avoid work
____ Attention from peers	____ Avoid something else	____ Attention from adults	____ Competing reinforcers

Reproducible Form F1: *STOIC Intervention Planning Form*

Step 2   Develop an intervention that

- takes into account your hypothesis about the function of the misbehavior.
- modifies some aspect of each STOIC variable.

This ensures that you will have a comprehensive plan tailored to help the student meet all of his or her needs in positive ways.

Structure

_____

_____

_____

_____

Teach
Expectations

_____

_____

_____

_____

Observe
and Monitor

_____

_____

_____

_____

Interact
Positively

_____

_____

_____

_____

Correct
Fluently

_____

_____

_____

_____

may do this yourself and then present the form to the student and parents, or you may want to actively involve them in the planning process.

A. Structure and organize the environment to set up the student for success.

1. Change assigned seating.

The easiest alteration of the physical environment is to change where a student sits in the room. If a student always talks when seated with certain peers, he can be moved away from them. If a student is highly distractible and you find it difficult to keep his attention focused on the task at hand, try to move him as far away as possible from high-traffic areas. If the student is angling for adult attention, move the student closer to you so that he gets more attention while he is on task. Likewise, if the student is trying for peer attention, moving him closer to you will make that student's peer interactions easier to monitor. You will be better able to intervene early in a sequence of misbehavior before peer attention is drawn to the student.

2. Change the work requirements.

You can alter or modify the curriculum to fit the student's needs. If the student frequently fails to complete work, arrange for her to get feedback on the first part of an assignment: "When I give an assignment, do the first five problems and then raise your hand, and I'll come over to correct those first five and help you." This is also a way for the student to reliably get attention in a positive way. Likewise, curriculum can be modified in many ways to fit a student's needs and set up more success. (See "Intervention B: Academic Assistance.")

3. Change the schedule.

Build breaks into the class routine. If students are expected to remain seated during a 30-minute work period and several generally fail to comply, give the whole class a chance to stand up and stretch halfway through. If only one student struggles to get through the work time, give the student a legitimate way to move about by asking him to run an errand or pass out some papers, thus permitting the student to move about without having to misbehave to get relief. If you know a student is being perpetually harassed in the hallway after class, excuse the student one or two minutes early to get to the next class and thus avoid the harassment and make his time in class more productive.

> Note: Avoid any activity that goes too long for the maturity level and attention span of your students. See "Pre-Intervention: Classroom Management Strategies" for tips on scheduling activities.

4. Change expectations or procedures.

If you are flexible about when and how your expectations can be met, many students will appreciate and respond to the extra freedom. For a young student, you could place a masking tape box on the floor around her desk and give her permission to stand and work if she wants, as long as she does not leave her "office."

You can modify a rule that a student has trouble following consistently if you judge that the student's learning (and your sanity) won't be negatively affected. And of course you should exempt a student from a rule altogether if the student can't possibly comply with it because of physical or other legitimate limitations.

5. Assign a duty or responsibility.

Giving a job or responsibility can be particularly helpful for a student who seeks power and control. If a student craves attention, a job that furnishes him with a lot of attention can help—trash can duty, for instance, or helping you pass out papers the students will need when they come back from recess. If the student likes technology, he could be asked to clean keyboards or computer enclosures, or reboot and maintain systems in the computer lab. Two minutes of positive time with an adult through these kinds of tasks may be enough to substantially reduce the times the student attracts attention in negative ways.

6. Give the student viable choices.

Sometimes students rebel when they believe they have no influence over their school experience. Giving these students a real sense of choice may help them see themselves as creators of their own experience and the authors of their own success. A viable choice—some element of control— over situations that agitate or set off the student can have a calming effect.

"Viable" means that you present the child with a *real* choice—not a choice between doing exactly what you want and a consequence if she doesn't. Teachers often think they're giving kids choices when they say, "You can either get your work done or you can stay in from recess." There's nothing wrong with that, but it not a *viable* choice; it's a choice between doing exactly what the teacher expects or facing the consequence. A viable choice means providing a range of options—"You can do this, this, or this, and they would all be perfectly acceptable. Which of them would you prefer?"

With that in mind, here are a few examples:

- Offer a choice of work locations.

- Allow a student to choose the order in which she completes a series of tasks.

- Set a self-initiated timeout: "You have my permission to go to the designated quiet area whenever you need to take a timeout and regroup." Train the student not to abuse the privilege, and explain that work must still be completed and turned in. The idea here is that any time the student wants to calm herself down, it would be better that she learn to do so herself before getting so upset that you would have to intervene anyway. "As long as you continue to get your work done, you can use that area any time you need to."

B. Teach expectations—teach the student how to behave responsibly within that structure.

1. Reteach classroom expectations.

If several students are having trouble exhibiting your CHAMPs expectations (introduced in the Pre-Intervention chapter at the beginning of this book), you should probably reteach the whole class. If everybody but Zach is doing well, however, individualize teaching your expectations to Zach. Explain to him one-to-one when he can talk, how he can get help, or any other concepts that seem to be unclear or unnecessary to him. Spending time reteaching your expectations will save you time—potentially a lot of it—later on.

2. Teach the "positive opposite" of a problem behavior.

Teaching the positive opposite means teaching a student how to practice a behavior that is incompatible with the problem behavior. For example, with a student who is unable to stay on task, teaching specific skills for concentrat-

Spending time reteaching your expectations will save you time— potentially a lot of it—later on.

ing and staying focused will reduce off-task behavior. For a student who goes ballistic when you correct his work, teach him a range of acceptable responses. You can teach the positive opposite of many behaviors, such as difficulty accepting a compliment, difficulty accepting feedback, and so on.

3. Teach a particular skill.

As a teacher, you may frequently be called upon to help fill in skill deficiencies. Perhaps a student has difficulty focusing because, like some students, she has never been taught how to focus. You can teach and show these students, in just a minute or two a day, how focused attention is something people can and do manage. The concept of being able to manage your attention—reminding yourself to get back to work, noticing when you're staring out the window, developing strategies to bring yourself back to what's happening right now—may be entirely foreign to some students, and consciously teaching the skill can make a difference in their behavior.

4. Teach social skills.

Many matters of simple politeness, consideration, manners, and etiquette can be taught when a student appears to be lacking in one or more of these skills, such as how to accept a reprimand or compliment.

Note: All these aspects of teaching expectations are dealt with in more detail in "Intervention M: Teaching Replacement Behavior." This intervention also includes a listing of several social skills and study skills curricula.

C. Monitor and observe the student's behavior.
In other words, supervise!

1. Circulate frequently.

Move unpredictably throughout the classroom and avoid spending time at your desk. In particular, think about spending more time standing near the targeted student than you have in the past.

2. Increase frequency of scanning.

Regardless of where you are, look to other areas of the classroom. Great teachers do not really have "eyes in the back of their heads"—they just seem to because they always know what is going on in all parts of the classroom. Try visually scanning areas close to the targeted student more frequently than other areas.

3. Collect data and debrief (Intervention D).

If you're considering a STOIC intervention, data collection is likely already involved, so continue with any procedures from Intervention D and debrief the student regularly on progress. Ask yourself if the data collection is working. Are you still focusing on exactly the same behaviors? Do you need to modify your focus? If you have not been systematically collecting data, begin implementing procedures from "Intervention D: Data Collection and Debriefing."

D. Interact positively with the student.

1. Increase frequency of noncontingent attention.

Strategies for ongoing positive rapport with students are covered in depth in "Intervention E: Increasing Positive Interactions." For any student with whom you still have concerns after covering Interventions A–E, redouble your efforts to greet the student frequently and cheerfully, offer assistance and encouragement often, and provide timely precorrections at critical points before the student veers off course. Try to give confidence to the student with support and encouragement—every child is motivated by something, but you may have to experiment, as motivators vary with each child.

Praise the student for any progress you see in data on the student's goal behaviors. Praise any attempt you see the student making toward achieving those goal behaviors. If you are doing precorrection, pouring on direct, specific praise is essential.

Great teachers do not really have "eyes in the back of their heads"—they just seem to because they always know what is going on in all parts of the classroom.

INTERVENTION

E. Correct fluently—calmly, consistently, briefly, and immediately.

1. Preplan responses so your reaction does not interrupt the flow of instruction.

After having given some thought to the possible function of a student's misbehavior, avoid inadvertently reinforcing the misbehavior. If you are taking into account what function the misbehavior serves, your planned response should not feed into it. If the student is looking for attention, long lectures and harangues, or even gentle and supportive corrections that go on too long, could be reinforcing the misbehavior.

> *After having given some thought to the possible function of a student's misbehavior, avoid inadvertently reinforcing the misbehavior.*

As you preplan, make sure that your chosen response is something you will be willing to do each and every time the student exhibits the problem behavior. Well-meaning educators sometimes set "tough" consequences for mild to moderate misbehavior and then find they aren't willing to go through with the consequences in all cases or with every student because they seem too harsh. If you decide to go with gentle reprimands, use them every time. Getting angry after issuing five gentle reprimands not only fractures the consistency that characterizes fluent correction, but it can potentially teach or reinforce a host of unwelcome behaviors as the student learns that persistence is the trick to getting the teacher riled up. Emotional responses from a teacher simply reinforce a student's feelings of power or control. "Intervention P: Defining Limits and Establishing Consequences" offers some tips on how and where to set limits for what you will and will not tolerate. This point is important enough to reiterate: *Your response should be something you can do each and every time the student exhibits the problem behavior.*

Sample corrective techniques
- gentle reprimand
- redirection
- record the behavior
- assign time-owed from a desired activity
- implement timeout
- restitution (For example, a student who writes on desks can be made to wash desks.)
- contact parent or guardian
- assign detention
- refer to the office

The following tips can assist you in being fluent with your corrective techniques.

Preplan

When a misbehavior occurs, what you don't want is to have to stop and figure out what you're going to do. Plan and practice your response in advance so it is automatic, instantaneous, and as devoid of emotional subtext as you can make it.

Prediscuss

As part of your planning, discuss with the student how you will react to a misbehavior before it occurs. Decide and tell the student whether you will issue consequences. If you will be using consequences, be clear and direct about exactly what they will be: "If you do *that*, the consequence will be *this*."

Be calm

Correcting calmly avoids reinforcing the behavior and demonstrates to other students that you are a positive and in-control teacher.

Be consistent

Consistency can't be part-time. Anything other than full-time implementation is inconsistent, and for most students, getting away with something part of the time is tremendously reinforcing.

Be brief

Keep corrections short; don't talk too much. The length of the interaction or the intensity risks reinforcing the misbehavior of some students. In addition, being brief helps you get back to a positive footing; it keeps the duration, emphasis, and focus of your time on positive interactions and instruction, not on student misdeeds or negativity. Preplanning and prediscussing your response with students will allow you to be briefer at the time of the infraction.

Be immediate

Correct closer to the moment of a misbehavior rather than later. The closer your correction is to the behavior that triggered it, the more likely it is to be effective. If a consequence must be delayed, as with assigning detention, you can still be immediate in assigning it—promptly and briefly describe what the student did, let the student know that you are assigning detention, then continue with instruction.

Any time you identify the function of a misbehavior, remember that you are not developing a diagnosis, but merely a guess or hypothesis about why the misbehavior is occurring.

Step 3: Meet with the student.

A. Discuss the intervention plan.

Begin the meeting with a quick review of the problem and goal. Then you can begin discussing the intervention plan. Explain any changes you will be making in the student's routine, such as changes in structure, adaptations, or correctional techniques. Provide brief explanations of what you plan to do with each of the STOIC variables, focusing more time and energy on the variables you identified as being most important according to your hypothesis regarding the function of the misbehavior. For example, if the student's problem may be one of awareness, you should focus the meeting on teaching expectations while briefly explaining other aspects of the plan. Model and rehearse any necessary skills or interactions and conclude the meeting with words of encouragement.

B. Meet regularly with the student to discuss the data and debrief.

Plan to meet at least once a week to review the data, discuss trends, set improvement targets, celebrate progress, and so on. Invite the student's parents to join you at any of your regularly scheduled meetings.

CONCLUSION

STOIC Analysis and Intervention is designed to help you address the function of any chronic misbehavior. When simple interventions, such as the Early-Stage Interventions in this book, have been unsuccessful in changing a student's behavior, function-based analysis is useful to determine *why* the misbehavior is occurring. Any intervention plan has a much greater likelihood of success when it is designed to address the reason behind the misbehavior. Any time you identify the function of a misbehavior, remember that you are not developing a diagnosis, but merely a guess or hypothesis about why the misbehavior is occurring. If the intervention plan based on that hypothesis is successful in changing the student's behavior, then your hypothesis was probably correct. If the behavior does not change, consider that your hypothesis about the function may have been incorrect.

If one or more function-based interventions is not successful after being implemented for a couple of weeks, consider asking for help from an interventionist—a psychologist, counselor, or behavior specialist.

REFERENCES

Cook, B. G., Landrum, T. J., Tankersley, M., & Kauffman, J. M. (2003). Bringing research to bear on practice: Effecting evidence-based instruction for students with emotional or behavioral disorders. *Education and Treatment of Children, 26,* 345–361.

Donnellan, A. M., & LaVigna, G. W. (1990). Myths about punishment. In A. C. Repp & N. N. Singh (Eds.), *Perspectives on the use of nonaversive and aversive interventions for persons with developmental disabilities* (pp. 33–57). Sycamore, IL: Sycamore.

Emmer, E. T., Evertson, C. M., & Worsham, M. E. (2003). *Classroom management for secondary teachers* (6th ed.). Boston: Allyn & Bacon.

Evertson, C. M., Emmer, E. T., & Worsham, M. E. (2003). *Classroom management for elementary teachers* (6th ed.). Boston: Allyn & Bacon.

Fabiano, G. A., & Pelham, W. E. (2003). Improving the effectiveness of behavioral classroom interventions for attention deficit-hyperactivity disorder: A case study. *Journal of Emotional and Behavioral Disorders, 11*(2), 122–128.

Fox, J., & Gable, R. A. (2004). Functional behavioral assessment. In R. B. Rutherford, M. M. Quinn, & S. R. Mathur (Eds.). *Handbook of research in emotional and behavioral disorders* (pp. 143–162). New York: Guilford Press.

Fyffe, C. E., Kahng, S. W., Fittro, E., & Russell, D. (2004). Functional analysis and treatment of inappropriate sexual behavior. *Journal of Applied Behavior Analysis, 37,* 401–404.

Gresham, F. M., Quinn, M. M., & Restori, A. (1999). Methodological issues in functional analysis: Generalizability to other disability groups. *Behavioral Disorders, 24,* 180–182.

Hall, R. V., Panyan, M., Rabon, D., & Broden, M. (1968). Instructing beginning teachers in reinforcement procedures which improve classroom control. *Journal of Applied Behavior Analysis, 1,* 315–322.

Heward, W. L. (2003). Ten faulty notions about teaching and learning that hinder the effectiveness of special education. *The Journal of Special Education, 36,* 186–205.

Horner, R. H. (2002). On the status of knowledge for using punishment: A commentary. *Journal of Applied Behavior Analysis, 35,* 465–467.

INTERVENTION

F

Hyman, I. A. (1995). Corporal punishment, psychological maltreatment, violence, and punitiveness in America: Research, advocacy, and public policy. *Applied and Preventive Psychology, 4*, 113–130.

Kauffman, J. M. (2004a). Foreword for H. M. Walker, E. Ramsey, & F. M. Gresham, *Antisocial behavior in school: Strategies and best practices* (2nd ed., pp. xix-xxi). Belmont, CA: Wadsworth.

Kauffman, J. M. (2004b). Introduction [to Part 1: Foundations of Research]. In R. B. Rutherford, M. M. Quinn, & S. R. Mathur (Eds.), *Handbook of research in emotional and behavioral disorders* (pp. 11–14). New York: Guilford Press.

Kauffman, J. M., Mostert, M. P., Trent, S. C., & Pullen, P. L. (2006). *Managing classroom behavior: A reflective case-based approach* (4th ed.). Boston: Allyn & Bacon.

Maag, J. W., & Kemp, S. E. (2003). Behavioral intent of power and affiliation: Implications for functional analysis. *Remedial and Special Education, 24*, 57–64.

Malone. J. C. (2003). Advances in behaviorism: It's not what it used to be. *Journal of Behavioral Education, 12*, 85–89.

O'Neill, R. E., Horner, R. H., Albin, R. W., Sprague, J. R., Storey, K., & Newton, J. S. (1997). *Functional assessment and program development for problem behavior.* Pacific Grove, CA: Brooks/Cole.

Powell, S., & Nelson, B. (1997). Effects of choosing academic assignments on a student with attention deficit-hyperactivity disorder. *Journal of Applied Behavior Analysis, 30*, 181–183.

Rhode, G., Jenson, W. R., & Reavis, H. K. (1992). *The tough kid book: Practical classroom management strategies.* Longmont, CO: Sopris West.

Scott, T. M., & Nelson, C. M. (1999). Functional behavioral assessment: Implications for training and staff development. *Behavioral Disorders, 24*, 249–252.

Sugai, G., Horner, R. H., & Sprague, J. R. (1999). Functional assessment-based behavior support planning: Research to practice. *Behavioral Disorders, 24*, 253–257.

Walker, H. M. (1995). *The acting-out child: Coping with classroom disruption* (2nd ed.). Longmont, CO: Sopris West.

Walker, J. E., Shea, T. M., & Bauer, A. M. (2004). *Behavior management: A practical approach for educators.* Upper Saddle River, NJ: Merrill/Prentice-Hall.

INTERVENTION

F

Reproducible Materials

The following reproducible form may be used in conjunction with "Intervention F: STOIC Analysis and Intervention." A copy is provided here and on the CD. Permission is given for individual classroom teachers to reproduce any forms labeled "Reproducible" for classroom use. Reproduction of these materials for an entire school system is prohibited without express permission of the publisher.

INTERVENTION F

STOIC ANALYSIS AND INTERVENTION

Step-by-Step Summary

Following is a summary of the steps involved in Intervention F. It is important to use professional judgment, adjusting procedures to meet the needs of the situation and the individual. See the chapter "Intervention F: STOIC Analysis and Intervention" for a detailed description of this intervention.

STEP 1   Identify what function the behavior serves.

A. The student lacks the ability or awareness to meet target expectations.
   1. Ability-type problems
   2. Awareness-type problems

B. The student is trying to get something.
   1. Adult attention
   2. Peer attention
   3. Power and control
   4. Competing reinforcers

C. The student is trying to avoid or escape something.
   1. Overly difficult or overly simple work
   2. Uncomfortable situations

STEP 2   Plan a STOIC intervention.

A. Structure and organize the environment to set up the student for success.
   1. Change assigned seating.
   2. Change the work requirements.
   3. Change the schedule.
   4. Change expectations or procedures.
   5. Assign a duty or responsibility.
   6. Give the student viable choices.

INTERVENTION F

B. Teach expectations—teach the student how to behave responsibly within that structure.
    1. Reteach classroom expectations.
    2. Teach the "positive opposite" of a problem behavior.
    3. Teach a particular skill.
    4. Teach social skills.

C. Monitor and observe the student's behavior.
    1. Circulate frequently.
    2. Increase frequency of scanning.
    3. Collect data and debrief (Intervention D).

D. Interact positively with the student.
    1. Increase frequency of noncontingent attention.

E. Correct fluency—calmly, consistently, briefly, and immediately.
    1. Preplan responses so your reaction does not interrupt the flow of instruction.

STEP 3   Meet with the student.

A. Discuss the intervention plan.

B. Meet regularly with the student to discuss the data and debrief.

Highly Structured Interventions:

THE FINAL SECTION of the book contains 12 chapters, Interventions G through R. These Highly Structured Interventions are a powerful group of tools that may be more time intensive to plan and more time consuming to implement. Unlike Section II: Early-Stage Interventions, there is no sequential order implied in these highly structured interventions. It is assumed that school counselors, school psychologists, behavior specialists, and problem-solving teams are aware of these strategies and have the ability to work with classroom teachers to analyze the nature of the problem (especially by looking at the data the teacher has collected and the early-stage behaviors that have been implemented) and then select one or more highly structured interventions that fit the circumstances.

A general education teacher with responsibility for teaching many children may find these interventions too involved or complicated to implement without some assistance. Highly Structured Interventions are well worth knowing and understanding, but the assumption is that intervention design and implementation will be a collaborative endeavor among teams of school professionals. In this way, school resources are directed to the students who need the most intensive interventions and will benefit from them the most. The Highly Structured Interventions in this section include:

Note: The only absolute rule about behavior management is that belittlement of students has no place in any educational setting—all behavioral interventions must treat children with dignity and respect. To have a positive and lasting impact, interventions must attempt to build up student strengths and expand skills for replacing problem behavior instead of simply squelching or containing problem behavior.

Information on threat assessment contributed by

M. Shawn Reaves, M.A.

Managing Physically Dangerous Behavior and Threats of Targeted Violence

Code Red—The student's escalating behavior is physically dangerous or poses a threat to physical safety

PURPOSE

THIS INTERVENTION, presented in two complementary sections, is recommended and may be necessary when any of the following behaviors makes continuing normal class routines impossible.

THIS INTERVENTION IS APPROPRIATE FOR:

Physically dangerous behavior
- fighting
- self-destructive behavior
    - head banging
    - hitting windows
    - self-biting
    - self-pinching
- assault
- out-of-control behavior

Threats of targeted violence
- threats to use weapons
- threats toward a person, "hit lists"
- writings or drawings of school violence
- threatening electronic communications (e-mail, Internet)
- direct threats of physical violence

When a student's actions pose an immediate or future threat to the physical safety of other students, adults, or the student himself, intervention must be decisive and intensive. Promptly implement this intervention or your school's prearranged procedures for dangerous situations. Above all, safety must be your first consideration.

Several important distinctions must be made between the concepts of *physically dangerous behavior* and *threats of targeted violence*. *Physically dangerous behavior* typically describes behaviors that are spontaneous or impulsive expressions of anger or frustration in response to a relatively recent set of circumstances. Examples include fighting, assault, or severe destruction of property, possibly triggered by peer conflicts, serious academic difficulties, or delayed gratification.

By contrast, the term *threats of targeted violence* describes a variety of behaviors, from inappropriate joking or outbursts in which threatening terminology is used to specific plans to carry out detailed threats of lethal violence. Examples range from a student inappropriately joking, "I wish I could blow up this school," to a vague threat to "wreak havoc on this asylum on the last day of school," to a serious direct threat such as "I'm going to get that gun out of my car so I can blow that teacher away!" Clearly, with such a broad spectrum of possible "threatening" behaviors, interventions will need to be tailored to each individual circumstance.

Managing Physically Dangerous Behavior comprises the first half of this chapter, and strategies for dealing with Threats of Targeted Violence can be found in the second half.

Managing Physically Dangerous Behavior

INTRODUCTION

In dealing with violent or potentially violent events, nothing can be done to make the situation pleasant. Intense incidents are stressful and exhausting for everyone concerned. The goal of this part of the intervention is to help staff respond swiftly and professionally in matters of physically dangerous behavior. You must strive toward objectivity and consistency to implement an intervention that will be in everyone's best interests, including the student causing the problem.

Physical danger exists if a student is involved in fighting or habitually engages in malicious or sadistic behavior such as pulling chairs out from under others. It may also be present if a student loses control and physically lashes out at others or engages in self-destructive behavior such as head banging or self-mutilation.

You must strive toward objectivity and consistency to implement an intervention that will be in everyone's best interests, including the student causing the problem.

Note: Verbal threats will be dealt with in the second half of this

chapter. See page 355.

Effective interventions for managing a student's physically dangerous behavior should include five major components, as shown in Figure G1.

Figure G1: *Components of Effective Intervention*

Component 1	Immediately implement procedures to ensure everyone's safety.
Component 2	Involve and notify the student's parents or guardians.
Component 3	Develop record-keeping and reporting procedures.
Component 4	Determine whether the student should be referred to special education, and whether other agencies should be involved.
Component 5	Develop a comprehensive plan to prevent future incidents and teach the student to manage her own behavior.

INTERVENTION

G

All five components need to be designed concurrently to increase the likelihood that every variable is being addressed and all possible resources explored. Each component is described in detail in this intervention, and a scenario is provided as an example of how this intervention can be implemented.

RATIONALE

Students who present a physical danger to themselves or others require time-consuming and intensive help. If the school system does not act swiftly to ensure the safety of everyone involved, the potential for injury can become a reality, with hurtful consequences and potential legal repercussions. It is important to remember that students who engage in physically dangerous behavior are desperate children. The earlier intervention is provided, the greater the likelihood that the problem will be resolved. Teachers should be encouraged to seek assistance for such students as early as possible. Successful intervention in cases of physically dangerous behavior will require the resources and cooperation of many.

If your district or building does not already have a policy for responding quickly and safely to physically dangerous behavior, plan to develop one.

When students engage in violent or dangerous acts, adults who have not been briefed on how to respond are at a disadvantage. Building and district administrators (or site-based teams) should establish policy guidelines to address as many contingencies as possible, and staff should be trained to implement the policies swiftly and effectively. Of particular importance are clear guidelines for if and when staff members should implement a room clear, attempt physical restraint, call for help, and/or notify police.

By knowing and adhering to a consistent schoolwide policy, staff can respond efficiently even in unpredictable emergency situations. There are no right or wrong answers, but here are some general guidelines:

- Restraint should be avoided if at all possible. If used, restraint should be used only to eliminate the immediate threat of physical injury, and only after verbal warnings or directions have been ignored by the student(s) involved.

- If room clears are recommended, the policy should address how to handle possible property damage by students and when and how staff members are expected to prevent property damage. Procedures might include requiring the violent student to repair or replace

Successful intervention in cases of physically dangerous behavior will require the resources and cooperation of many.

INTERVENTION

G

damaged property. If the student is unable to repair or replace the damaged items, she might be required to work before or after school at a reasonable hourly rate to compensate for the damage.

- The policy should provide staff with guidance to determine what types of situations are severe enough to involve the police. For example, the line between hitting and assault should be predetermined.

- The policy should guide the reactions of all staff members in responding to and managing physically dangerous behavior to reduce the chance of inconsistency from situation to situation.

Using this information, the history of violent situations in the school, and any other relevant information, the policy-making group should develop policy recommendations to fit the needs of the school. Recommendations should be examined to ensure that they are in compliance with board policy and state and federal statutes. The proposed policy should then be presented to the entire staff and revised if necessary. Once a written policy is accepted and finalized, staff must be trained on how to implement each of the identified procedures.

INTERVENTION COMPONENTS

Although this intervention is laid out in a step-by-step format, it is important to use your professional judgment, adapting procedures to the situation and the needs of the student.

Be sure that you have contacted the student's parents to discuss the problem, invited them to participate in planning the intervention, and informed them about all aspects of the intervention plan.

Component 1: Immediately implement procedures to ensure everyone's safety.

When a student escalates into physically violent or dangerous acts, staff members must act swiftly to ensure the safety of everyone involved. From a practical standpoint, usually only two immediate options are available when a physically threatening incident occurs: Get everyone out of the student's way and out of the classroom, referred to as a *room clear*, or have one or more adults physically restrain the student. Although the latter is the less preferable of the two options, it may be necessary in certain special cases.

INTERVENTION

G

In every case, you have three priorities:

- Reduce the likelihood of anyone getting hurt.

- Respond in such a way that the student is not reinforced for out-of-control behavior.

- See that everyone involved, including anyone who provoked or participated in the event, is treated with dignity and respect.

A. Use room clears.

Whenever possible, the preferred method for dealing with out-of-control behavior is to remove everyone else from the threat of violence. In a classroom situation, this would mean a room clear. On a playground, students in the vicinity should be moved away from the student who is out of control.

A room clear is preferable to physical restraint for a number of reasons:

- A room clear is the most direct way to ensure everyone's safety. When students clear the room, they are removed from immediate threats of escalation and physical injury.

- Physical restraint is more likely to result in injury to the student or the adult attempting to restrain the student than a room clear.

- Physical restraint may stoke the emotional intensity of the situation. For some students, the sheer intensity of resisting the restraint or fighting an authority figure may be reinforcing for out-of-control behavior.

- Physical restraint is sometimes not an option. It requires an adult who is larger and stronger than the student. Should the student resist strenuously and prolong the struggle, more adults may have to be summoned. Through it all, the risk of injury to others continues.

- A room clear removes the audience and the potential reinforcer of peer attention. If "performing" for other students is reinforcing to the out-of-control student, the attention is removed.

- When physical restraint is used, the entire class witnesses the altercation. The scene can be upsetting and distressing to students, or it can cause outrage and mutinous feelings among classmates sympathetic to the out-of-control student.

- A room clear may help the student learn to manage his own behavior. When physical restraint is used to control behavior, the student may mistakenly learn to depend on an adult, an "outside force," to bring his behavior under control. In the long term, this may result in the student believing that he is unable to change or control his own behavior. The individual may grow up afraid of what he might do, or he may continue to depend on others to stop him when he gets out of control or "goes off."

1. Identify where students will go and what they will do during a room clear.

When students must clear the room, routine provisions should be made so that the disruption is minimized. Students should be taken into the hallway until assistance can be summoned. As soon as another adult arrives, the class should be taken to a predetermined location. Relevant instructional tasks should be prepared in advance. For example, students might be taken to the school stage, where paper and pencils have been stored. If a room clear is necessary, the supervising adult might give students a writing assignment, have the students solve math problems, run a spelling bee, or have students write a class story.

2. Establish procedures for supervising the student who is engaged in physically dangerous behavior.

Establish procedures for summoning a trained staff person to the classroom immediately. When a student begins engaging in physically dangerous behavior, the classroom teacher will need immediate assistance. Procedures should be established for receiving additional help rapidly. This should include a prearranged signal indicating that a crisis is occurring. Some schools use their intercom system. Others use a specially designed red crisis card that can be given to a student messenger. The messenger can take the crisis card to the office, where an immediate preplanned response will be initiated.

Plans for providing an immediate response should include the following:

- who will respond
- a chain of command in case the first person is unavailable
- a communication process to ensure that everyone involved will be kept informed

These procedures should be carefully designed and occasionally rehearsed so that the process works smoothly and high-probability contingencies (such as the principal being out of the building) have been addressed.

When a student begins engaging in physically dangerous behavior, the classroom teacher will need immediate assistance.

Staff who may be responsible for emergency duty should be trained. Training should include learning which behaviors to ignore and which require intervention as dictated by building or board policy. Adults who will supervise an out-of-control student should be trained to stand at the door and determine what actions to take if the situation escalates. If physical restraint is recommended under specified conditions, adults should be trained in how to restrain a student safely.

3. Determine the consequences for out-of-control behavior in advance.

Consequences for out-of-control behavior tend to have little effect on preventing future incidents. It is far more important to teach students to control their own behavior. Nevertheless, fluent correction is part of a comprehensive plan and should thus be predetermined. Appropriate consequences might include owing time from recess or after school, restitution (repairing the damage or cleaning the mess created, apologizing, explaining the outburst in writing), timeout, or suspension.

If the instigator is an identified special education student, it is vital that you work directly with the building special education personnel and school district (to avoid possible violation of federal law). For example, suspension of a special education student may constitute a change of placement and cannot be instituted without due process.

B. Use physical intervention only if necessary.

Although a room clear is preferable to restraint, it is not always the appropriate response. If a student is about to stab someone with scissors, there may not be time for a room clear. If a student is engaged in self-injurious behavior such as head banging, some form of restraint or physical intervention may be necessary.

Sometimes a room clear can be paired with appropriate physical intervention. For example, if two students are involved in a violent fight, the teacher may need to get the other students out of the room, call for help, and, when help arrives, separate and restrain the two students until they calm down enough to be released.

Note: The following steps apply to two or more students fighting as well as to any individual student who is out of control.

1. Remove other students from the area.

    In the classroom, use a room clear; outside, students may be sent to another part of the playground. Use a firm voice to direct students to another location. "Everyone needs to move immediately to the other side of the blacktop. Jackson, Alissa, Sandra, Tom, move now!"

2. Always try verbal interventions before resorting to any procedures.

    Avoid shouting, but use a firm and loud command. "Jeremy, stop pounding on that window and move to this side of the room, now!" Using the student's name increases the chance that he will respond to the verbal instruction. If more than one student is involved, direct each student to a different location. "Rico, move over to the doorway! Zach, move over to the lockers!"

3. If at all possible, signal or call for help before beginning any sort of restraint.

    To avoid possible concerns regarding the use of undue force or even abuse during restraint, the adult involved should always summon assistance. The act of calling for help indicates that the presence of another adult was requested as quickly as possible and that the adult has made no attempt to engage in inappropriate physical contact. If the school staff does not currently have routines for signaling for adult assistance, such procedures should be devised for every school location, including all classrooms, hallways, playgrounds, cafeterias, bus waiting areas, and so on.

4. Decide whether restraint is necessary and helpful.

    If the student does not cease the dangerous behavior after verbal instructions are issued, the staff person must use professional judgment regarding whether to intervene physically before assistance arrives or wait until help comes. No set rule can be used for making a decision of this type. However, staff should understand that they are not required to put themselves in direct physical jeopardy. Staff members may mistakenly believe that they will be negligent if they do not intervene physically in a fight. However, staff should behave in a reasonably prudent manner to keep everyone physically safe, including themselves. What is reasonable and prudent may depend on several factors:

- the number of students involved
- the size of the student or students involved
- the size and strength of the adult
- the degree of violence taking place
- the presence of any weapons or potential weapons
- staff training in the use of nonviolent restraint methods

If a small child is pounding on a window, it would be reasonable and prudent to remove her. However, if the student is large and strong and the teacher is small, it would be neither reasonable nor prudent for the teacher to attempt restraint. The teacher should address the student calmly and wait for help to arrive so the student can be safely restrained.

Note: If a student of any size has a weapon, staff members should not to try to disarm the student. The police should be called, and all adults and children should be kept as far from the crisis situation as possible.

The less training a staff has received in the use of physical restraint, the more cautious a member of that staff should be in using restraint.

When two or more students are fighting physically, take into account that attempting to break up the fight by pulling one student off may actually increase the risk of injury for everyone involved. If you grab the arms of one of the combatants, you make that student more vulnerable to direct blows from the other. Unless both students are very small, you should probably wait for assistance before trying to physically break up an altercation.

The less training a staff has received in the use of physical restraint, the more cautious a member of that staff should be in using restraint. If you are not sure whether you can successfully restrain a student without injury, avoid attempting it. At a school where violent incidents occur frequently, staff should be well trained in methods of restraint and students should be regularly instructed in nonviolent conflict resolution.

Note: Training in uses and methods of physical restraint requires demonstrations, practice, and rehearsal. It is beyond the scope of this book to provide detailed guidelines. Local law enforcement, mental health organizations, state agencies, and schools with successful violence-prevention programs in place may be good resources for strategies and recommendations.

Component 2: Involve and notify the student's parents or guardians.

Parents must be involved whenever a student exhibits tendencies toward physically dangerous behavior. After the first incident, hold a conference and request that the parents attend so you can communicate the staff's willingness to help the student, determine the severity of the problem, and begin joint problem solving. Depending on the severity of the situation, representatives from other social agencies such as police, juvenile justice, social workers, or mental health professionals might be included to assist in developing a comprehensive plan.

Parents of a troubled student often do not know what to do: "What do you expect us to do? He does the same kinds of things at home and we can't stop him." Therefore, working with parents is an important step to improve student behavior both at home and at school.

Alienation of parents from the school staff can often be avoided if the staff communicates a desire to work collaboratively. Staff members should consciously avoid implying that a parent should be able to control a student's behavior at school. If a severe problem exists, initial contact with parents may be the key to beginning a successful cooperative effort to help a troubled student.

As part of the initial contact, set up a systematic plan for ongoing communication. This should include regularly scheduled progress reports that occur at least weekly. Determine the form these reports will take: a note sent home with the student, phone conference, or e-mail communication. In addition, set up a plan for immediate communication regarding any future incidents in which the student exhibits physically dangerous behavior.

Parents must be involved whenever a student exhibits tendencies toward physically dangerous behavior.

INTERVENTION

G

Make sure you have phone contact information—work, home, cell—for the primary guardians and at least one backup person suggested by the guardians.

Component 3: Develop record-keeping and reporting procedures.

Given the severity of behavior that is physically dangerous, systematic and detailed records must be kept for many reasons:

- Records will assist staff in developing and evaluating interventions.
- Records will be needed if a special education referral and evaluation are initiated.
- Records may be necessary if any legal issues arise relating to a student's behavior.

An inescapable reality of severe and dangerous behavior is that the problem can lead to legal actions through a number of routes. If a student injures someone, assault charges may be filed. If the student injures herself or someone else, the school may be sued for negligence. If a staff member confines a violent student, parents could object and even press charges against the school staff. If the student is of an ethnic or racial minority, school personnel may be accused of discriminatory practices. As unpleasant as these possibilities may be, ongoing documentation should demonstrate that school personnel have made every necessary effort to keep everyone safe, while concurrently providing help for the student.

A. Set up an anecdotal log of all incidents in which a student's behavior has been physically dangerous.

An anecdotal log can be used to design effective interventions and to help determine whether an immediate referral to special education should be initiated. In addition, anecdotal logs provide the information necessary for keeping the summary records as described in the next step. Logs should detail all past and current incidents of violent or physically dangerous behavior.

The following types of information should be included in each notation:

- date and time of day of the incident
- location of the incident
- adult(s) supervising at the time of the incident

- events that occurred prior to the incident
- a detailed description of the student's behavior during the incident, including duration of the incident and specific behavior observed
- action(s) staff took to prevent physical injury
- consequences given to the student (if any)
- action(s) taken to minimize future occurrences of the behavior

Reproducible Form G1 on the following page is an example of an anecdotal log that may be used to record incidents of physically dangerous or highly disruptive behavior.

> Note: Copies of this form and other Managing Physically Dangerous Behavior forms are also provided on the CD.

Anecdotal logs should generally be kept by the administrator. As the administrator logs information, the teacher has an opportunity to debrief and talk through events that were likely disturbing and stressful. Concerns can be expressed and future actions considered. All staff members should be instructed to report every incident of physically dangerous or violent behavior to the administrator so that records are accurate and complete.

B. Keep summary records.

Summary records indicate the number of incidents per week, the number of minutes per week that the student was out of control, and some indication of intensity. Intensity could be a simple 1–3 rating with 1 being "Refusal to participate and follow directions," 2 being "Verbally abusive or threatening," and 3 being "Physically violent."

Because the intensity of out-of-control behavior is emotionally draining to participants, it is frequently difficult to determine objectively whether a plan is helping a student. If a first-grade student reduces the number of tantrums from four or five times per week to once per week, that student is clearly making progress. However, if that single incident is sufficiently distressing, staff may not be aware that progress is being made. Similarly, if staff has been trained to restrain a student, restraint procedures may go more smoothly. They may believe that the procedure is working well when in fact the number of incidents has not been reduced. With

Reproducible Form G1: *Extreme Behavior Log*

Extreme Behavior Log

Student _____   Grade/Class _____   Teacher _____

Code Red: Record all incidents of physically dangerous or highly disruptive behavior.

Date	Start/Stop Time		Total Duration	Intensity	Anecdotal Notes

Intensity Key: 1 = Refuses to comply or participate   2 = Verbally abusive or shouting   3 = Physically violent

summary data that tracks frequency, duration, and intensity, the effectiveness of the intervention plan will be easier to judge.

Reproducible Form G2, the Severe Behavior Summary Chart, is designed as a master chart that will allow you to complete separate charts for each level of intensity you identify. For each level of intensity, you can track frequency, duration, and average duration per week. This in turn will allow you to create charts like the one shown in Sample Reproducible Form G2, which follows. By looking at this chart, you can see that even though the duration of Level 3 incidents remained the same or went up for the first several weeks of intervention, by the seventh week rapid and consistent progress was being made.

Component 4: Determine whether the student should be referred to special education and whether other agencies should be involved.

If the student is not currently identified as eligible for special education services, data collected as part of the formal record-keeping system should assist in determining whether a referral for evaluation should be initiated. If records indicate that the student has a significant history of severe violent or self-destructive behavior, the referral process should be started immediately. In most districts, a lag time exists between referral, evaluation, and placement. As the wheels of special education referral and evaluation are set in motion, the other components of this intervention should be implemented immediately. This will ensure that safety issues are dealt with and that the school has begun the process of teaching the student how to behave more appropriately, even as the referral process is taking place. If at a later date professional judgment indicates that the situation is now under control and everyone's needs are being met, the referral process can always be terminated or put on hold.

Staff should also begin immediately identifying whether other agencies should be brought into the planning process. If the student's behavior has been severe enough to be considered assault, the police or juvenile authorities should be contacted to determine whether interagency planning would be appropriate. Preplanning for the possibility of a next time will let the student, parents, and staff know exactly what the consequences will be for any subsequent incidents.

With summary data that tracks frequency, duration, and intensity, the effectiveness of the intervention plan will be easier to judge.

INTERVENTION

G

Sample Reproducible Form G2: *Severe Behavior Summary Chart*

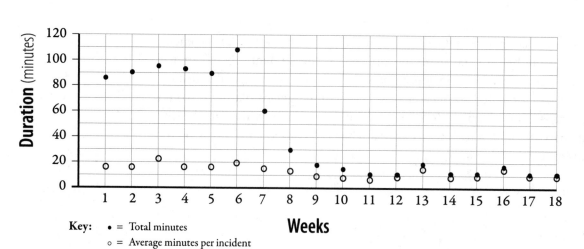

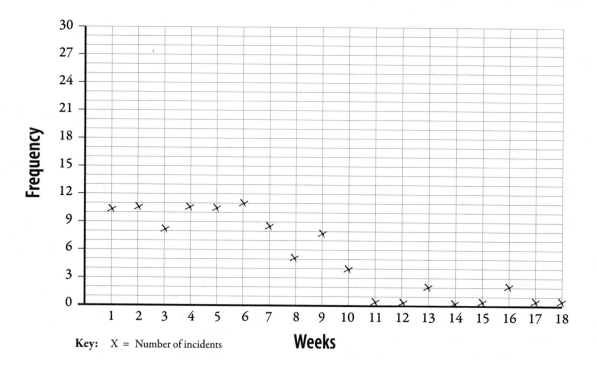

Intervention G:
Managing Physically Dangerous Behavior

Severe Behavior Summary Chart

Mike
Student

3
Grade/Class

Mr. Namel
Teacher

5/6
Date

Level of intensity (circle one):   1   2   ③

Key: X = Number of incidents

Weeks

Key: • = Total minutes
  ○ = Average minutes per incident

Weeks

A blank version of this form is available in the *Reproducible Materials* section at the end of the chapter.

Component 5: Develop a comprehensive plan to reduce future incidents and teach the student to manage her own behavior.

In addition to determining what to do in the event of another dangerous incident, methods should be developed to help the student handle situations without losing control. This component is an essential part of your plan as it will focus on helping the student develop strategies for preventing future violent or physically aggressive acts. Keep in mind that this intervention offers information about what to do *in a crisis*. Other chapters focus on how to prevent crisis situations from occurring in the first place. To develop procedures for teaching the student to manage her own behavior, "Intervention I: Managing the Cycle of Emotional Escalation" may be especially appropriate. In addition, consider implementing one or more of the other interventions in this book.

Several days after school began in the fall, Cynthia was registered at Adams School by her grandmother. Like many new students in this highly transient neighborhood, Cynthia arrived without any records from her previous school. Cynthia's grandmother promised to try to have her records sent.

Cynthia was placed in Mr. Carmody's fifth-grade classroom. The first two days, Cynthia did very little in class. She seemed sullen and quiet. She refused to participate in any activities, spending most of her time with her head down on her desk. On the third day, Mr. Carmody noticed a change. Cynthia seemed agitated from the moment she stepped into the classroom. By the middle of the morning, Cynthia was wandering around the room, poking and taunting the other students. When Mr. Carmody told Cynthia to take her seat and begin working, Cynthia responded loudly and angrily, "I don't have to do nothing you tell me to do!" Though Mr. Carmody tried speaking quietly to Cynthia, she became more and more agitated, yelling profanities. As Mr. Carmody tried to calm her down, Cynthia picked up a book and threw it. "Leave me alone! You leave me alone!" As Cynthia raged through the classroom, she overturned furniture and pushed students who were near her.

Mr. Carmody acted as quickly as possible, implementing previously developed building procedures for dealing with violent behavior. First, he instructed his class to leave the room and immediately report to Mrs. Zugliani's room across the hall. Mrs. Zugliani and Mr. Carmody had been paired as Crisis Partners at the beginning of the school year, agreeing to supervise one another's students in the event of a crisis.

INTERVENTION

G

Mr. Carmody then called the office and informed the office staff that a crisis was occurring. He asked for assistance but also indicated that the police were not needed. Mr. Carmody then went into the hallway and stood where he could observe Cynthia in case she hurt herself.

Meanwhile, because the secretary knew that the principal was out of the building, Ms. Alton, the counselor, was contacted. Ms. Alton went immediately to assist Mr. Carmody, who was watching Cynthia from the hallway to make sure that her out-of-control behavior had not escalated to the point of endangering her own safety. After turning over several desks, Cynthia eventually ran out of steam and sank to the floor, holding her arms over her head. When Cynthia was quiet for several minutes, Ms. Alton escorted Cynthia to her office. Twenty minutes had passed. The entire incident just seemed to have exploded. There hadn't been time to think.

When it was over, Mr. Carmody felt drained but relieved that he had known how to handle the situation.

Mr. Carmody took a few minutes to collect his thoughts and tidy up his classroom. Then he went to Mrs. Zugliani's room to get his students. The two classes were working on a choral reading of a poem. When they finished, Mr. Carmody thanked both classes for their cooperation. He explained that Cynthia had had a very difficult day, and that everyone would need to continue working as a community, welcoming Cynthia into the circle. He explained that Cynthia would probably feel very uncomfortable about what had happened and that it would be important for everyone to help her feel like a regular fifth grader. Mr. Carmody also explained that everyone had special goals to work on. He told the class that he himself was working on being more patient, and that Cynthia would be working on handling her angry feelings more constructively.

The principal, Mr. Feinberg, was contacted at the district office by the secretary and returned to the building immediately. As soon as he returned, he contacted Cynthia's grandmother, who came to pick her up. Before Cynthia and her grandmother left the school, the principal set up a conference for the next day with Cynthia and her grandmother to determine a plan for helping Cynthia learn to control herself.

After school that day, the principal, the counselor, and the classroom teacher met to establish a plan to present to Cynthia and her grandmother. They identified consequences for Cynthia's outburst. In this case, the

INTERVENTION

initial consequence consisted of having been sent home. In addition, Cynthia would need to spend one hour after school the next day to clean and organize the classroom, and she would be required to write an apology to Mr. Carmody.

In addition, they established modifications to the room clear procedure in case Cynthia had similar problems in the future. Mr. Carmody identified three responsible students whom he would train to get help in the event that he was unable to use the intercom. Two adults were also selected to contact for assistance in the event the principal was out of the building. The chain of command was as follows:

- Mr. Feinberg—the principal

- Ms. Alton—the counselor

- Mr. Black—the teacher next door

Together, Mr. Feinberg, Mr. Carmody, and Ms. Alton also clarified exactly how future out-of-control behavior would be handled:

- Students would be moved into the hallway (room clear).

- Mr. Carmody would call the office or instruct one of the trained student helpers to go immediately to the office for assistance.

- If the principal was available, he would immediately drop whatever he was doing and take Mr. Carmody's class to a prearranged location—the cafeteria or stage, where he would conduct prearranged lessons. (If the principal was unavailable, the office staff would contact the counselor. If both the principal and counselor were out of the building, the office staff would contact Mr. Black, the teacher next door.)

- After the room was clear, Mr. Carmody would remain in the doorway of the classroom to supervise Cynthia and make sure that she did not engage in behavior that could hurt herself.

- Once Cynthia calmed down, Mr. Carmody would quietly inform Cynthia of things that needed to be straightened up before the other students could return. When the room was restored to normal, Mr. Carmody would also show Cynthia any broken items that would be stored for later replacement. As Mr. Carmody, Mr. Feinberg, and Ms. Alton mapped out their plan for Cynthia, they found one of their most difficult decisions was what to do with Cynthia after an incident. Should there be consequences? Should she be suspended?

INTERVENTION

G

Mr. Carmody believed that Cynthia should be removed from the classroom and suspended from school for at least a week. Ms. Alton thought Cynthia should stay in the room—having to restore the room and face the other children when they entered was consequence enough. Ms. Alton feared that Cynthia might enjoy getting sent home. A middle-ground position was finally determined. Cynthia would be escorted to the office when she was calm enough to follow an adult without a physical confrontation. She would spend the remainder of that day in a timeout room off the front office. The next day she would return to the classroom.

It was also agreed that Ms. Alton would need to spend time with Cynthia investigating her academic abilities and conducting some preliminary self-control lessons (see "Intervention I: Managing the Cycle of Emotional Escalation" and "Intervention B: Academic Assistance"). Cynthia would spend 30 minutes per day with the counselor for at least a week. At the end of the week, the counselor would assess Cynthia's progress and continue meeting with her on a regular basis.

Temporary restraint was discussed in case Cynthia tried to attack someone before or during the time students were clearing the room. It was determined that Mr. Carmody would restrain Cynthia only to prevent an immediate injury to another student. Once the students were out of danger, Cynthia would be released and Mr. Carmody would go to his position in the hallway. These guidelines were created so that Mr. Carmody would never be put into the position of restraining Cynthia without witnesses and so that restraint would be used only as a last resort to prevent injury.

Mr. Feinberg also indicated that Mr. Carmody should begin keeping records. Ms. Alton, Mr. Carmody, and Mr. Feinberg agreed to meet whenever a room clear was required. Records would be kept on the duration and frequency of incidents, the events leading to the incident, and the outcome. It was decided that it was premature to begin special education referral or to involve the police or other agencies until Cynthia's records arrived.

As the plan was finalized, it was decided that both Cynthia and her grandmother should be invited to make suggestions on the proposed plan. Mr. Carmody, Ms. Alton, and Mr. Feinberg agreed that they would begin the conference with Cynthia and her grandmother by outlining two major goals. The first goal was to keep everyone safe, and the second was to help Cynthia learn how to deal with her anger.

Note: Physical restraint should occur only in the presence of witnesses to avoid any problems with accusations of impropriety.

CONCLUSION

Whenever students engage in physically dangerous behavior, the resulting scene is stressful and unpleasant for students and staff alike. However, if you, along with every member of the teaching, administrative, and support staff, plan how you will respond to a crisis situation before it occurs, everyone will know what to do immediately and will work quickly to ensure the safest and most professional response possible to a volatile situation.

After school staff members have trained for and rehearsed immediate responses to a crisis, they can direct their energies toward preventive strategies. While the immediate goal whenever you deal with physically dangerous behavior is to keep everyone safe, your long-range goal should remain focused on teaching skills that will give the student better options than having a blowup or a meltdown and that will allow the student to be successful. These skills will be explored more in "Intervention I: Managing the Cycle of Emotional Escalation."

Students, parents, and staff must know that everyone will respond swiftly to a crisis to ensure everyone's physical safety, and that staff will also work humanely to teach each student how to be a productive member of the school community.

Managing Threats of Targeted Violence

INTRODUCTION

Over the past two decades there have been many highly publicized acts of targeted violence in educational institutions. Although our collective awareness of possible violence has risen, many schools have found themselves ill-prepared to respond once warning signs have been observed. Unfortunately, the public outcry for "something to be done" to address school violence has led many districts to engage in misguided efforts to create "profiles" or checklists to identify potential school shooters, only to find that no such profile exists.

This intervention is designed to help schools recognize that, although there are no simple profiles or checklists to guide responses to threats of targeted violence, there are effective strategies that can be used to better recognize and respond to situations where students may pose a threat to others at school. Effective interventions for managing threats of targeted violence should follow a sequence of five major steps that focus on preparation, response, and recovery, as shown in Figure G2.

Figure G2: *Steps for Managing Threats of Targeted Violence*

Step 1	Adopt schoolwide policies, procedures and standards for record-keeping. (Preparedness)	
Step 2	Conduct training for threat assessment teams and awareness sessions for staff and students. (Preparedness)	
Step 3	Immediately implement procedures to respond to possible threats and ensure everyone's safety. (Response)	
Step 4	Involve parents and community agencies as appropriate. (Response)	
Step 5	Restore a sense of safety and security. (Recovery)	

Staff and students should be trained to identify and report threats of any kind.

Each step is described in detail in this intervention, along with strategies for recognizing, assessing, and addressing various types of threats.

Understanding the problem

For purposes of this intervention, a *threat* is defined as any expression of intent to harm another person. To create a safe and productive learning environment for all students, schools should be aware of and utilize a variety of methods for learning about potential threats so that warning signs of future violence and aggression can be dealt with before a situation escalates. Staff and students should be trained to identify and report threats of any kind so that school personnel can determine the seriousness of the threat and how to deal with it.

Threatening communications may come to schools in the form of writings, drawings, verbal statements, postings on Internet sites, and a host of other information technologies.

There are other ways in which concern about a student's future behavior may come to the attention of school personnel. Some students bring themselves to a school's attention by engaging in behaviors that raise concerns. Examples include a student writing a story for an English class in which one student shoots another student at school; a personal Web page in which a student sympathizes with others who have engaged in school shootings and fantasizes about mimicking that behavior; and a principal receiving an e-mail from a recently suspended student stating, "It's time for you to die!"

Another way students may come to your attention is through reports from others. Examples of such reports include a student sharing with the principal what appears to be a hit list that was written by a peer; a mother calling to report that her teenage son is ruminating over a breakup with his girlfriend and is preoccupied with violence, death, weapons, and seeking revenge; and a student reporting he saw what he believed was a switchblade in another student's backpack.

A third way possible threats may come to the attention of school authorities is through anonymous communication. A common way for this to occur in some communities is through anonymous "tip lines" that are operated by local schools, districts, or law enforcement agencies. Schools may also receive anonymous calls, letters, or e-mails with messages such as "Judgment Day is Here" or "This school is going down in flames!"

If schools can learn to identify and address warning signs and threatening communications in the early stages, it may prevent a student's violent thoughts or behaviors from turning into physical violence and will greatly increase the general sense of safety and security in the school.

Violence: A path from thought to action

Many individuals follow a discernible path from thought to action when considering or engaging in school violence. Although every situation is unique, many violent events that have occurred, or have been prevented, followed a basic path in which the individual:

1. experiences feelings of unresolved anger, resentment, hopelessness, frustration, vengefulness, perceived injustice

2. has vague, undifferentiated thoughts of "getting back" at individuals or institutions

3. imagines possible methods of violent retaliation

4. begins to research and consider options for an actual attack

5. adds details to plan such as location, date, and time

6. acquires materials that may be used in an attack

7. communicates plans to others

8. carries out the plan

Managing Threats of Targeted Violence is intended to help schools recognize when students may be moving down this path of violence and to respond accordingly should the need arise.

Determining the nature of a threat

This intervention is also intended to help schools distinguish between two types of situations:

- students who may have communicated a threat but have no actual or sustained intent to cause harm to others

- students who have made threatening communications and actually pose a threat to others

To help clarify this distinction, this intervention will use the terms *transient threat* and *substantive threat*. A transient threat is one in which there is no sustained intent to cause harm beyond the current situation. Transient threats are often impulsive acts, said in a moment of anger, or in a joking or sarcastic manner. Though these circumstances do not excuse threatening language, such situations should be handled differently from more serious threats.

In contrast, a substantive threat is one where there is ongoing intent to cause harm beyond the situation at hand. Substantive threats are typically more premeditated or thought out in advance of any communications or attempts to engage in a violent attack.

Finally, although not a distinct category, there are situations where a student's behavior raises concerns, but upon investigation, they turn out to be misunderstandings or false reports. This intervention is designed to help schools distinguish between the various types of threats and determine procedures for responding to them.

RATIONALE

Students who pose a threat of targeted violence are not only dangerous in the immediate sense of everyone's physical safety, but they are also potentially disruptive to the overall sense of safety and well-being in the school. Schools continually strive to create a safe, welcoming, and inviting

This intervention will use the terms transient threat *and* substantive threat.

INTERVENTION

G

climate in which teachers are able to teach and students are able to learn. In schools where students fear for their safety, whether from bullying, physically dangerous behavior, or threats of violence, they are less able to focus on academic matters than in schools where students feel safe.

Imagine, for example, that you are trying to read an interesting book while flying in a large jet over the Atlantic Ocean. Seemingly out of nowhere a violent storm erupts, and the plane begins to rock and shake in the turbulence. The plane quiets down, and although you were temporarily distracted, you soon return to your reading. Shortly thereafter, another wave of turbulence suddenly engulfs the plane. The lights flicker, and the pilot alerts passengers that the "fasten seat belt" light has been turned on. A baby in front of you is crying, and several rows back a couple starts to fight about why they chose this particular flight.

For the next 30 minutes this cycle of calm and turbulence is replayed many times. Each time the plane settles, you return to your reading. But after a while you find that you are not sure where you left off in your book. You scan through several pages and feel confident that you've already read them, but for some reason the content simply did not stick with you, and you have to read them again.

In this situation, you would likely have trouble focusing on and remembering what you read due to the anxiety or fear associated with severe weather, behavior of other passengers, and uncertainty for your own physical safety. The plane shakes, adults argue, a baby cries, and the pilot alerts passengers to stay in their seats with their seatbelts fastened. The bottom line is that when the environment in which you are trying to learn feels unsafe, you will not be able to function as well as you would in a setting where you feel safe and secure.

As you begin developing a plan for Managing Threats of Targeted Violence, ask yourself: Does my school feel any safer than that plane? Are there factors that impact the safe environment of school in the same way the storm affects the plane? Are there factors that make students fear for their safety? What strategies can I use to raise appropriate awareness of possible threats to safety, yet not cause undue stress and anxiety?

As with most complex problems, there are no quick fixes to address threats of violence in schools.

IMPLEMENTATION STEPS

Managing Threats of Targeted Violence is a unique intervention in that the intervention steps range from an individual student's response to school-wide preparedness. As with most complex problems, there are no quick

INTERVENTION

G

fixes to address threats of violence in schools. There are, however, rational steps schools can take to help prevent violent acts and to respond effectively when warning signs of violence arise. Consistent with standard emergency management planning, this intervention is a comprehensive approach to addressing possible threats of targeted violence. It includes preparedness, response, and recovery activities.

Step I: Adopt schoolwide policies, procedures, and standards for record-keeping—Preparedness.

Given the wide range of national, state, and local laws as well as the array of different policies and procedures in local school districts, it is beyond the scope of this intervention to provide specific language for your school or district to adopt regarding threat assessment. However, there are several guidelines for schools to consider when developing prevention and response plans to threats of targeted violence in schools.

A. Develop effective policies and procedures.

Policies and procedures to consider regarding threats of targeted violence in schools include the following:

- a clear statement that threatening communication of any kind is not appropriate or acceptable on school property or at school functions

- a list of types of communication that are unacceptable, such as verbal threats, written threats, gestures indicating intent to cause harm to others, creating a "hit list," making a bomb threat, and threats made through electronic communications

- procedures for investigating and responding to potential threats of violence, such as conferencing with the principal; threat assessment; interviews with the school psychologist, counselor, or other mental health professional; notification of law enforcement; notification of parents

- procedures for the possible removal of a student from classrooms and/or district transportation systems

- procedures for possible disciplinary action such as suspension, expulsion, or alternative placement

- procedures for possible legal action

Figure G3 is a sample of policies and procedures for dealing with assault and threats of violence.

Figure G3: *Sample Policy*

Sample Policy on Assault and Threats of Violence

(Adapted from Fayette County Public Schools, Lexington, KY. Used with permission.)

PUPILS

Any pupil who threatens, assaults, batters, or abuses another pupil shall be subject to appropriate disciplinary action, including suspension or expulsion.

SCHOOL PERSONNEL

Any pupil who threatens, assaults, batters, or physically or verbally abuses a teacher or other school personnel shall be subject to appropriate disciplinary action up to and including expulsion from school and/or legal action.

REMOVAL OF STUDENTS

School administrators, teachers, or other school personnel may immediately remove or cause to be removed threatening or violent students from a classroom setting or from the District's transportation system pending any further disciplinary action that may occur. Threatening or violent behavior shall include, but not be limited to:

1. Verbal or written statements or gestures by students indicating intent to harm themselves, others, or property.
2. Physical attack by students so as to intentionally inflict harm to themselves, others, or property.

- The Principal shall be notified immediately of such removal.
- Removal of students from a bus shall be made in compliance with state statutes.
- Each school shall designate the site(s) to which employees may remove students from a classroom setting and the employee(s) who will supervise the student at the site.
- When teachers or other personnel remove a student, they shall complete and submit a form to document the removal and the causes of the removal as soon as practicable. The Principal shall review the removal as soon as possible to determine if further disciplinary action is warranted or if the student is to be returned to the classroom.

REPORT TO LAW ENFORCEMENT AGENCY

When they have reasonable belief that a law violation has taken place, the Principal or building administrator shall immediately report the violation to law enforcement officials when the following conditions are met: 1) an act has occurred on school property or at a school-sponsored function; and 2) the act involves assault resulting in serious physical injury, a sexual offense, or kidnapping; or 3) the incident of assault involves the use of a weapon.

NOTIFICATION

Any District employee assigned to work directly with, or who comes in contact with, a student with a documented history of weapons violation and/or physical abuse of a school employee or of carrying a concealed weapon on school property or at a school function shall be notified in writing of the student's history by the Principal or designee, guidance counselor or other school official who has knowledge of the student's behavior prior to the assignment or contact.

Following the adoption of effective policies and procedures to address threats of violence, the school or district should make the information available to the public, including students, parents, the community, and the media. By sharing district policies on threatening communications and by teaching students expectations regarding what is and is not acceptable on school grounds and school functions, schools can significantly reduce the number of incidents of inappropriate joking, sarcasm, and figures of speech. Clear policies and procedures also increase the likelihood that threats will be reported to school personnel.

B. Develop a plan for documenting threatening incidents at the individual, school, and district level.

As with physically dangerous behavior, systematic and detailed records of threatening incidents must also be kept. Component 3 of Managing Physically Dangerous Behavior provides good strategies for documenting threats of targeted violence (see the first half of this chapter); however, additional record-keeping practices may be warranted.

Three categories of documentation should be considered. First, determine what information, if any, will be maintained in a student's cumulative records. This decision should not be made lightly. The goal for any student's permanent record should be to provide a valid representation of a student's behavior in order for his or her needs to be met in current and future educational settings. That said, it is essential that a student not be labeled as a "threat" simply because she made an inappropriate remark in a moment of anger, frustration, or joking.

Schools will also need to determine how internal records will be maintained at the school level. Typically, administrators will keep ongoing files or logs of all incidents that have occurred in the building. Schools will need to determine how these records will be stored, transferred, and destroyed, taking into account changes in administrative staff, the passage of time, and so on.

A final level of documentation that needs to be addressed is at the district level. Depending on the size of your district, you will need to consider what specific information will be kept in an electronic database or other central recordkeeping system and who will have access to those records. One approach to district-level documentation of threatening incidents would be to create a centralized electronic database that would allow designated individuals to access the information. For example, following threat assessments that are classified as serious and substantive, the principal and/or school psychologist would be expected to enter basic demographic information about the student and a brief summary of the incident. The complete file would be maintained in accordance with the school and district policies regarding student records (i.e., maintained at the school level, the district level, or both). After the database is established, these records could be accessed as needed by designated personnel to address possible future incidents of dangerous or threatening behavior.

> Note: Principals have a legitimate "need to know" status, as they will be dealing with potential threats within their school. They should have some level of access to a student's prior records, whether from an earlier grade or a prior school placement.

It is of critical importance to restrict access to a very limited number of people to effectively maintain such a database. No district should allow unlimited access to sensitive records of prior misbehavior, and any use of prior information should be with the intent of helping to meet the needs of the student while maintaining school safety. Examples of staff with limited access might include:

- designated district level staff
- school resource officers (if employed by the school or district)
- principals of the current school in which the student is enrolled
- principals of the school where threat assessment occurred

Conduct a thorough review of district policy as well as state and local laws, and consult with professional legal counsel before implementing any changes to documentation methods at the student, school, or district level. Schools must constantly balance privacy rights of students with the "need to know" of faculty and staff.

Step 2: Conduct training for threat assessment teams and awareness sessions for staff and students—Preparedness.

There are three major components to address when training the school community to prevent and respond to potential threats of targeted school violence:

INTERVENTION

G

- creating an identified threat assessment team with the training and expertise to respond quickly and effectively to potential threats

- awareness training for all faculty and support staff to help them understand early warning signs of violence and what to do should those warning signs be observed

- lessons for the entire student body to teach them what kinds of communication will be considered threatening, what the school's response to threats will be, and what students should do if they observe threatening communications from others

A. Conduct threat assessment team training.

Every school should have a designated team of professionals who are able to respond effectively when a threat of targeted violence is brought to the attention of school personnel. The purpose of the team is to guide the threat assessment process (Step 3 of this intervention) when the need arises. A building administrator should chair the threat assessment team because of his or her responsibility for the overall operations, safety, and security in the school.

Depending on your school's staffing practices, threat assessment teams might include the following representatives:

- seasoned principal or building administrator
- school psychologist or other mental health professional
- school resource office (SRO) or other police officer assigned to the school
- school counselor
- school social worker or resource center coordinator
- behavior specialist
- child guidance specialist
- special education specialist

Rather than assuming that individuals should simply know how to respond to threats of violence due to their profession or experience, schools should ensure that their teams have specialized training in threat assessment procedures. Ideally, the entire threat assessment team will participate in training together in order to form helpful working relationships and to clarify roles and responsibilities. Though

Ideally, the entire threat assessment team will participate in training together in order to form helpful working relationships and to clarify roles and responsibilities.

INTERVENTION

G

the entire team is concerned with providing for the safety and well-being of all students, each member will bring his or her own expertise to the threat assessment process. Multidisciplinary training allows professionals to understand and learn from the unique perspective of their counterparts on the team.

Mental health professionals, for example, are concerned not only with possible threats, but also with antecedent events, social contexts, risk factors, and precipitating events. Administrators, on the other hand, must be focused on maintaining safe and orderly operations of the entire school, whether school rules or board polices have been violated, and whether a student should be removed from school grounds. Finally, school resource officers are concerned with whether a crime has been committed, if an imminent danger is present, and if a perimeter needs to be established to protect a school campus.

Effective threat assessment team training should involve content in understanding warning signs, risk factors, precipitating events, and stabilizing factors of threats of targeted violence. *What-if* scenarios (also known as tabletop exercises) will allow team members to gain experience interpreting and responding to unfolding threats of violence. Strategies for conducting threat assessments and training continue throughout this chapter.

B. Develop and deliver awareness training for faculty and staff.

Having an identified threat assessment team is essential but insufficient to prevent or respond to possible threats of targeted violence. Awareness training should also be provided for all faculty and staff. In contrast to the detailed vignettes and practical application that will occur in the team training, faculty and staff training needs to be much more streamlined.

The focus of a faculty and staff orientation should include:

- school and district policy regarding threatening communications
- Student Code of Conduct regarding threatening communications
- how to recognize direct threats and behavioral signs of violence, rather than attempting to use profiles or checklists to identify at-risk students
- what actions to take with direct observation or reports of threats
- how to conduct lessons for students on school policies and procedures regarding threatening communications

It may be effective to have one or more members of the school's threat assessment team conduct the general staff training by developing a brief presentation for a faculty meeting. The session should address practical matters such as how to make a referral and when to seek immediate assistance. The primary focus of the training should be on the fact that the school is taking active steps to prevent school violence and preparing to respond should the need arise. If possible, the school should highlight prevention efforts such as social competency training and bully prevention programs, in addition to addressing how to respond to possible threats. In short, training for the faculty and staff at large should raise awareness and instill confidence but should not raise undue fears. Assure all staff that despite recent highly publicized events, incidents of targeted violence in schools remain very rare. However, staff should also recognize that their efforts may make the difference in preventing the escalation of threats to violence and might prevent threats themselves.

C. Create and conduct student lessons in school policy and student responsibility.

Teaching students the school's expectations regarding threatening communications is essential.

Countless students have found themselves facing administrative or legal consequences because they did not understand or appreciate the magnitude of a certain behavior, such as a joking, sarcastic, or "in the moment" threat. Many of these situations could have been avoided had students been taught clear expectations regarding what constitutes threatening communication. Therefore, teaching students the school's expectations regarding threatening communications is essential. Such awareness training should be developed and presented to the entire student body, although it is recommended that the content be delivered in small classroom settings rather than in large assemblies (in which students may be more likely to "zone out" or otherwise miss the information). Classroom orientation lessons should include:

- age-appropriate descriptions of behavior that will be considered threatening
- what actions will be taken by the school in response to threats of any nature
- what students should do if they observe a threat
- any additional information from your Student Code of Conduct

Sample lesson plans and student code of conduct forms are shown in Figures G4–G6 on the following pages and may be adapted to meet the needs of various grade levels of students. Note that Figure G4 is a sample lesson plan for teaching the school threat policies that are shown in Figure G5, the Policy on Verbal Threats.

In schools, we often do ourselves a disservice by not being as clear as possible regarding policies and procedures that address threats of violence. Standard practices of conducting at least annual lessons may eliminate a significant number of incidents, especially those involving jokes, figures of speech, and remarks made impulsively in anger.

Step 3: Immediately implement threat assessment procedures to respond to possible threats of targeted violence—Response.

When a possible threat of targeted violence is brought to the attention of any school staff, there should be clear procedures to follow to maintain everyone's physical and emotional safety. Though it is essential that all threats are taken seriously and investigated at least at some level, it is equally important to recognize that not all threats should be addressed in the same manner. A *threat assessment* approach is recommended and should be considered as an effective alternative to other models that may be currently in use.

A. Begin using a threat assessment approach.

Many schools that have implemented zero-tolerance policies have automatic responses to any and all behavior that could be considered a threat. This "one size fits all" approach tends to be problematic because it does not allow for interpretation of behavior in a context, does not allow for professional judgment, and often mandates specific consequences (such as suspension or expulsion) regardless of whether an individual actually posed a threat.

Additionally, schools that attempt to use student profiles or checklists have found two substantial deficits or concerns. First, the vast majority of students who meet established criteria for "school shooters" will never in fact make or pose a threat of targeted violence (false positives). Second, some students who do pose a threat of targeted violence will not be identified by profiles because they share no, or very few, characteristics of prior school shooters (false negatives).

Figure G4: *Sample Lesson Plan*

Model Lesson 1
Verbal threats will be taken seriously

- Students will be able to explain why school personnel must take action when aware of any threatening comments.
- Students will be able to identify the types of statements that coud be interpreted as threats.
- Students will be able to identify the range of consequences that can be applied by school personnel and law enforcement agencies for making threats.

TELL PHASE

- Give each student a copy of a document similar to the sample "Policy on Verbal Threats" found on the following page.
- Present and describe the concept that the rules and expectations regarding threats of violence have changed. (Section 1 of the sample "Policy on Verbal Threats" document.)
- Present and describe the types of statements that could be interpreted as threats. (Section 2 of the sample "Policy on Verbal Threats" document.)
- Present and describe the range of possible outcomes/consequences that could be imposed for making a threat. (Section 3 of the sample "Policy on Verbal Threats" document.)
- Make sure that students understand that the policy is nonnegotiable—all threats will be taken seriously.

- Allow questions and discussion on the policy.
- Ensure that students clearly understand all the components of the policy (i.e., threats are no joking matter, what constitutes a threat, and what the potential consequences are).
- Depending upon individual preference, discuss issues such as:
    - The relationship of free speech to making threats
    - If the students were school administrators, what types of threats or situations would lead them to contact police or other law enforcement agencies?
    - What students should do if they witness someone making a threat against someone else
    - What students should do if they are personally threatened; what they should do if there are no other witnesses to the threat

ASSIGNMENT

- Have students take the "Policy on Verbal Threats" document home. Tell them to discuss the document with a parent/guardian and to have their parent/guardian sign the document.
- Tell students when they will be expected to return the signed document.

Figure G5: *Sample Policy on Verbal Threats*

SAMPLE DOCUMENT: A document similar to this should be developed by staff ahead of time. Assistance with the specific content should be sought from the school district's attorney or legal department.

POLICY ON VERBAL THREATS

In the interest of ensuring that _____ School is a safe place for everyone, all threats will be taken seriously. Please read and discuss the information on this page with your student. Then sign the document, and have your student return it by _____ . If you have any questions/concerns about this policy, feel free to contact a school administrator.

1. The rules have changed. Threats are no joking matter!

The rules and expectations regarding language related to threats of violence have changed.

In the past, if someone said something like, "I am going to shoot those teachers and students who gave me a hard time," it may have been treated as a joke or idle threat. Due to violent incidents that have taken place in schools, any statement of this type now will be taken seriously.

"I was only joking" is not a reasonable explanation or defense. This type of comment will be treated as seriously in our school as it would be in an airport.

2. The types of behavior that will be considered threatening include:

- Stating that you have a weapon or bomb in your possession at school
- Stating that you plan to bring a weapon or bomb to school
- Stating that you plan to cause physical harm to a student or staff member
- Making a false statement that there is a bomb or other destructive device at school
- Any written or verbal indication that you intend damage to any person or property

3. In addition to parental notification, outcomes/consequences that may be imposed for making a threat include:

- Further investigation by school personnel
- Detention
- Suspension
- Expulsion
- Further investigation by law enforcement
- Prosecution for Disorderly Conduct, Criminal Mischief, Menacing

We have read and discussed the information in the "Policy on Verbal Threats."

_____   _____
Parent/Guardian Signature   Date   Student Signature   Date

Foundations: Establishing Positive Discipline Policies, Sprick, R.S., Garrison, M., and Howard, L.M. 2002

3

Figure G6: *Sample Student Code of Conduct*

<u>**Sample Entry from Student Code of Conduct**</u>
<u>**Threats of Violence, Assaults, and Terroristic Threatening**</u>

(Adapted from Fayette County Public Schools, Lexington, KY. Used with permission.)

The Fayette County Board of Education has adopted policies ensuring that students, teachers, and other school personnel are not subjected to assaultive or threatening behavior from other students. Any student who threatens, assaults, batters, or abuses another student shall be subject to appropriate disciplinary action, which may include suspension or expulsion from school and/or legal action.

Conduct and/or actions prohibited under this policy include, but are not limited to:

1. Verbal or written statements or gestures by students indicating intent to harm themselves, others, or property.

2. Physical attack by students so as to intentionally inflict harm to themselves, others, or property.

3. The act of threatening force or violence toward another person.

4. Making a threat that a bomb or chemical, biological, or nuclear weapon has been placed in or is about to explode in a school building, on school grounds, in a school bus, at a bus stop, or at any school-sponsored activity.

5. Creating a "hit list."

When a student is believed to have made a threat of harm toward another student, a teacher, or other school personnel, the school shall take appropriate steps to investigate the alleged incident and enact appropriate disciplinary and/or legal action. Procedures for investigating and responding to potential threats of harm may include, but are not limited to:

1. Removal of the student from the classroom setting or from the District's transportation system pending further disciplinary action that may occur.

2. Investigation of the alleged incident by the Principal or designee.

3. Threat Assessment, as detailed in the *FCPS School-Centered Emergency Management and Recovery Guide* "Threat of Harm" protocol. The Threat Assessment may include the student being interviewed by the School Psychologist, School Counselor, other qualified school personnel, and/or District personnel as needed.

4. Notification of and possible further investigation by FCPS Law Enforcement.

By contrast, a threat assessment approach is an inquisitive process in which a team reviews behaviors and facts on an individual basis to determine if a student appears to be on a path of violence. The team determines what may be done to provide support to that student and protect the safety of others. The following scenario illustrates the advantage of a threat assessment team approach over zero-tolerance policies or relying on student profiles or checklists.

Mr. Sherrard, a sixth-grade teacher, overhears several boys talking about a "hit list" that a student named Alan wrote and was showing to peers. Mr. Sherrard, aware of high-profile school shootings and the school's protocol regarding possible threats of violence, reports the incident to his principal. Consider the approaches taken by three different schools in responding to such a report:

School Number 1:

The principal immediately has Alan brought to the office. Upon questioning, Alan acknowledges writing the list. In accordance with the Board of Education's zero-tolerance policy, which mandates suspension for all threats of violence, the principal suspends Alan for the remainder of the school year.

School Number 2:

The principal questions Alan, who admits writing the hit list. Recalling a recent checklist developed to help profile potentially violent students, the principal and Mr. Sherrard note characteristics that appear to match Alan's behavior. Some of these characteristics are: "has low interest in school," "tends to blame others for difficulties," "history of discipline problems," and "has previously been truant from school." The principal and Mr. Sherrard conclude that Alan meets the profile of a possible school shooter and recommend that he be immediately transferred to an alternative setting.

School Number 3:

The principal receives the report and talks with Alan, who admits to writing the list. In further interviewing, Alan responds to a number of additional questions from the principal, such as "Why did you write the list?" "What can you tell me about people whose names are on the list?" "What were you hoping to accomplish by writing this list?"

INTERVENTION

G

Under the supervision of front office staff, Alan waits as the principal consults with Dr. Burcham, the school psychologist, and other members of the school's threat assessment team. Dr. Burcham interviews Alan while team members talk individually with Alan's peers and Mr. Sherrard.

The team convenes to share information and discovers several common themes. Mr. Sherrard, Alan, and the other students all reported that Alan had been teased and bullied to some degree by other students. Alan appeared to have no intent to cause harm and no real plan whatsoever to engage in violence. He said he had hoped the list would make him look "tough" or "cool" in front of the other students so he would no longer get teased. Alan expressed remorse at causing fear in others and apologized for his actions, but he also shared his frustration that, from his point of view, no one had done anything to stop other students from bullying him. To resolve the incident for the short term and long term, the following plans were enacted:

- Alan was suspended for one day for making the hit list.
- The school resource officer fulfilled "duty to warn" requirements.
- The administration set about implementing a number of plans to assess bullying.
- Staff immediately increased adult supervision in areas identified as in need of it.
- The school counselor began helping Alan:
  - learn to express anger and strong feelings in a nonthreatening way
  - appropriately seek help in the event he is teased or bullied in the future
  - learn a variety of other social competencies to improve peer relations

This scenario illustrates how a threat assessment should focus on behaviors, evidence, and facts rather than traits or characteristics, which often do not provide an accurate view of the situation. Those in charge of examining behaviors of concern when responding to a threat (administrators or threat assessment team members) should make judgments on an individual student basis, rather than using blanket assessments and consequences. Examples of behaviors of concern include (but are not limited to):

- communications of direct or implied threats to harm others
- evidence of specific plans to enact a violent attack
    - drawings, diagrams, floor plans of buildings
    - naming a specific date, time, location, and method of enacting violence
    - journal entries or stories with specific threats of violence or descriptions of events leading to the deaths of teachers, classmates, etc.
    - Internet sites with details of plans to engage in violence at school
- an identified or identifiable target or targets
- acquisition of, or attempts to acquire, materials that could be used in a violent incident
    - guns or knives
    - bomb-making materials
- warnings to certain individuals (such as to avoid a specified location in the building on a certain date because "all hell's gonna break loose")

To further understand threat assessment concepts, Figure G7 on the following page presents six fundamental principles of the threat assessment process as published by the U.S. Department of Education and the U.S. Secret Service. The Safe Schools Initiative was a project to study the "thinking, planning, and other pre-attack behaviors" of students who engaged in school shooting. The following six principles provide a good starting point regarding effective threat assessment.

B. Understand the fundamental difference between transient and substantive threats.

Not all threats are created equal; therefore, not all responses to threats should be equal. While some threats are clearly communications of a serious and plausible intent to cause harm, others clearly are not. The following section offers a more detailed description of transient versus substantive threats and the implications for threat assessment teams in real-world applications.

Figure G7: *Principles of Threat Assessment*

Six Principles of the Threat Assessment Process

(from *Threat Assessment in Schools: A Guide to Managing Threatening Situations and Creating Safe School Climates*, U.S. Secret Service and U.S. Department of Education, 2002)

- Targeted violence is the end result of an understandable, and oftentimes discernible, process of thinking and behavior.

- Targeted violence stems from an interaction among the individual, the situation, the setting, and the target.

- An investigative, skeptical, inquisitive mindset is critical to successful threat assessment.

- Effective threat assessment is based on facts, rather than on characteristics or "traits."

- An "integrated systems approach" should guide threat assessment inquiries and investigations.

- The central question in a threat assessment inquiry or investigation is whether a student poses a threat, not whether the student has made a threat.

---

1. Transient threats

Transient threats are communications that do not convey a real or lasting intent to cause harm to another person. Such statements are often made impulsively and may include angry outbursts, inappropriate jokes, insults, or figures of speech. Several examples follow, adapted from actual case studies, with a brief explanation of the actual intent of the communication:

- A kindergarten student says, "If you don't let me on that swing, I'm gonna kill you!" In reality, this student has no actual intent to cause harm to the other student; rather, he made an expression that demonstrated his poor frustration tolerance.

- Following a particularly frustrating class, a middle school student uses the word "kill" as a figure of speech, as in "That teacher made me so mad, I could have just killed her." There was no actual threat and no intent to cause harm to the teacher presently or in the future.

- Following the death of a teacher (an auto accident), a high school student insensitively jokes, "Let's take a poll to see which teacher we hope somebody will knock off next." The reality of the situation is the student was simply making a tasteless joke at the expense of teachers, but had no intent to cause physical harm.

- During a physical fight, one high school student yells to another, "After we get out of here, I'm gonna run your f***ing car off the road and wrap you around a tree!" Although this clearly *was* a threat, after the anger dissipated the student showed significant remorse and regret, and apologized for his actions. During an interview he said he was just trying to "save face" in front of peers and had no real intent to cause harm.

The most important characteristic of transient threats is that there is no sustained intent to cause harm beyond the current situation. That said, a clarifying explanation does not make such threats acceptable in our school settings. For example, even though the above high school student apologized and acknowledged why he made the threat, the fact remains that he made a threat and therefore may be subject to administrative or legal consequences.

If there is any doubt as to whether a reported behavior represents a transient threat, it should be addressed as a *possible* substantive threat, and the threat assessment process should begin.

2. Substantive threats

Substantive threats differ from transient threats in that there is an actual and sustained intent to cause harm beyond the current situation. Such actions are typically the end result of a series of thoughts and behaviors related to strong unresolved feelings, which may include social humiliation and torment, feelings of perceived injustice, inability to cope with significant losses, feelings of personal failure, etc.

Examples, adapted from actual threat assessment scenarios, include:

- An elementary school fifth grader asking, "Which one of these cars is Miss Hopkins'? When she gets in it, I'm going to drop a match in her gas tank." The student was found to have both matches and a lighter in his possession and repeatedly stated he was going to carry out his plan, "no matter what" anyone else did to him, and even if he blew himself up in the process.

The most important characteristic of transient threats is that there is no sustained intent to cause harm beyond the current situation.

INTERVENTION

G

- A series of writings entitled "Time for Them to Die" is found in a middle school student's English journal. Included is a paragraph expressing rage at "years of torment from those b****es" and detailing how she plans to push another girl in front of their school bus but to make sure it "looks like an accident."

- An Internet site is reported to school officials and law enforcement with the following specific sequence of events:

Tic 5—Get Josh to drive me to school, then kill him so he doesn't have to see what I'm going to do.
Toc 4—Leave bag outside of science lab window.
Tic 3—Walk in that f***ing school like everything's normal.
Toc 2—4th hour retrieve gun from bag.
Tic 1—Blast my way into the office to render MY Final Solution!
Toc 0—Die! Die!! Die!!!

The main defining characteristic of substantive threats is the intent to cause harm beyond the current situation.

Clearly the three substantive situations described above represent an entirely different level of concern than the examples of transient threats presented earlier. The main defining characteristic of substantive threats is the intent to cause harm beyond the current situation. Substantive threats also typically have a greater level of detail in the plan, such as time, place, identified target(s), and means of violence. Additionally, threats are often repeated over time, and often others are recruited as accomplices or to serve as an audience to the unfolding plan. Finally, with substantive threats there is often physical evidence of efforts to carry out the plan, such as detailed writings, acquisition of weapons or weapon-making materials, or a list of intended victims.

While is it imperative that schools acknowledge and address all threatening communications, distinguishing between transient and substantive threats is essential in determining appropriate responses to less serious versus more serious circumstances. Further, in terms of effectively managing staff resources, it is impractical and inadvisable to conduct a formal full-scale threat assessment in every situation that could remotely be considered a threat. Those situations with low need should involve a low-level response, and those with high need should receive a greater allocation of resources. Use the description above regarding transient versus substantive threats to make a judgment about whether a higher-level assessment is necessary. When in doubt, ask for input from other professionals (administrators, psychologists); if the situation is still uncertain, refer for a higher-level threat assessment.

INTERVENTION

G

C. Utilize the school-based threat assessment team (TAT).

Whenever a threat assessment is necessary, the threat assessment team (TAT) will gather the necessary information to determine the nature and consequences of the potential threat. A team process is recommended when conducting threat assessments to ensure that different perspectives are considered and that no one person has responsibility for responding to possible threats of violence. In broad terms, the basic purpose of the TAT is twofold:

- to develop a plan to manage possible threats of targeted violence

- to respond to and manage incidents of possible threats of targeted violence when the need arises

To achieve maximum effectiveness, TATs are encouraged to clarify their purpose as a team and to clarify their roles and responsibilities in preparing for and responding to possible threats of targeted violence. As noted in Step 2, the TAT should be led by a principal and should include a number of well-trained support staff such as a school psychologist, school counselor, school resource officer (SRO), etc. Recognizing the wide variation of job titles and roles across schools and districts, the following presents broad categories of how TAT roles may be defined and outlines a nonexhaustive list of responsibilities that may be associated with that role. You are encouraged to adapt these roles for the unique positions you have in your district as well as the expertise you have among individuals in those roles.

Building Principal(s):
- Lead the TAT process (both planning and response).

- Serve as initial contact for all referrals of potential threats of violence.

- Determine if there is imminent risk, and respond accordingly.

- Verify information by talking with the individual who reported the possible threat and the student of concern as well as consulting with faculty, staff, and parents as indicated.

- Determine whether the behavior should be considered a transient or substantive threat, and address as warranted.

- Convene TAT as needed.

- Prepare and deliver communications to students, staff, parents, and media as warranted.

- Document actions taken.

School Psychologist, School Counselor, School Social Worker:
- Assist principal in directing the efforts of the TAT.
- Conduct mental health interview with student.
- Gather information from records, parents, teachers, students, and others as needed.
- Serve as liaison between school and community agencies such as mental health centers, psychiatric hospitals, and child welfare.
- Assist in responding to the immediate situation at hand (short-term needs).
- Participate in safety planning meetings and implementation of safety plan (long-term needs).
- Document actions taken (forms, writings, drawings).

School Resource Officer (school based):
- For imminent risk, provide immediate assistance to school in response to threats of targeted violence in order to secure the facility.
- For nonimminent risk, collaborate with the TAT to determine the nature of a potential threat, whether a crime has been committed, and possible legal actions to be taken.
- Serve as liaison with local law enforcement agency, juvenile court, etc.
- Participate in safety planning meetings (short term) and implementation of safety plan (long term).

Others:
- Assist and participate with TAT to assess and respond to the immediate situation at hand and follow-up safety planning meetings as needed.
- Assist in implementation of safety plan, monitoring, and follow-up activities as needed.

D. Create and follow an effective flowchart or decision tree when responding to potential threats.

Figure G8 (p. 380), a model Threat Assessment Flowchart, can assist you in conceptualizing the threat assessment process. It may be modified as needed to suit the unique needs of your school. The first step in any flowchart involves school personnel becoming aware of a possible threat of violence and reporting that information to the principal. Administrator notification ensures that the individual who is ultimately responsible for the safety and security of the building is aware of what is going on and therefore able to activate the TAT and district resources as needed.

1. Determine whether or not there is an imminent risk.

Once notified of threatening behavior, the principal will determine if there is an imminent risk to anyone's safety. For purposes of this discussion, imminent risk is narrowly defined as when an individual is actively engaged in attempting to carry out a lethal threat of violence and has the means to do so. In other words, imminent risk goes beyond such acts as fighting, severe disruptive behaviors, and destruction of property. Rather, in the context of threats of targeted violence, an example of imminent risk would be a student brandishing a gun or knife and using it, or threatening to do so.

For imminent risk the principal does not go through the relatively time-intensive threat assessment process, but rather takes immediate action to ensure everyone's safety. Actions may include calling 911, initiating lockdown procedures, and securing or isolating the student who is attempting to engage in violence.

For nonemergency situations, the principal will verify the report and gather additional information from the student of concern, consult other support staff, interview possible witnesses, and contact parents. If, following this initial inquiry, the principal is confident that the reported behavior is not a threat or is a transient threat, then he or she would address it as appropriate through disciplinary action, referral to the school's intervention team, or clarifying and reteaching expectations. Although this places broad authority and discretion with the principal, this is consistent with the decisions and responsibilities faced daily regarding student discipline and building safety and security.

2. Convene the threat assessment team.

If, after interviewing the student and consulting with others as warranted, the principal determines the behavior cannot be addressed as a transient threat, he or she should notify and convene appropriate members of the school's TAT. Team members should meet to discuss relevant behaviors and facts that are known up to this point and then determine a course of action, which may include any or all of the following:

- a structured clinical interview with the student
- interviews with other students, teachers, and others who may have pertinent information
- contact with parents

Figure G8: *Threat Assessment Flow Chart*

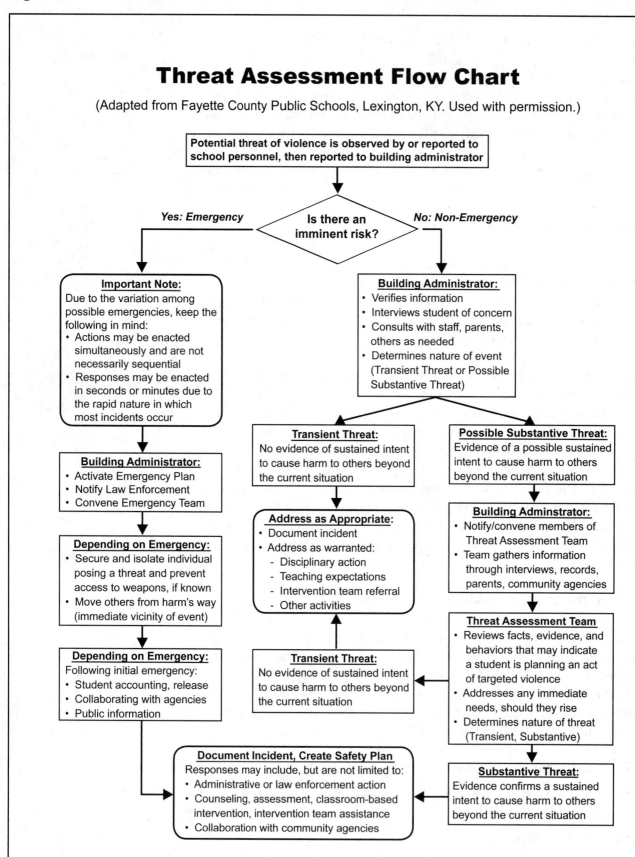

Threat Assessment Flow Chart

(Adapted from Fayette County Public Schools, Lexington, KY. Used with permission.)

Potential threat of violence is observed by or reported to school personnel, then reported to building administrator

Is there an imminent risk?

Yes: Emergency

No: Non-Emergency

Important Note:
Due to the variation among possible emergencies, keep the following in mind:
- Actions may be enacted simultaneously and are not necessarily sequential
- Responses may be enacted in seconds or minutes due to the rapid nature in which most incidents occur

Building Administrator:
- Activate Emergency Plan
- Notify Law Enforcement
- Convene Emergency Team

Depending on Emergency:
- Secure and isolate individual posing a threat and prevent access to weapons, if known
- Move others from harm's way (immediate vicinity of event)

Depending on Emergency:
Following initial emergency:
- Student accounting, release
- Collaborating with agencies
- Public information

Building Administrator:
- Verifies information
- Interviews student of concern
- Consults with staff, parents, others as needed
- Determines nature of event (Transient Threat or Possible Substantive Threat)

Transient Threat:
No evidence of sustained intent to cause harm to others beyond the current situation

Address as Appropriate:
- Document incident
- Address as warranted:
  - Disciplinary action
  - Teaching expectations
  - Intervention team referral
  - Other activities

Transient Threat:
No evidence of sustained intent to cause harm to others beyond the current situation

Possible Substantive Threat:
Evidence of a possible sustained intent to cause harm to others beyond the current situation

Building Administrator:
- Notify/convene members of Threat Assessment Team
- Team gathers information through interviews, records, parents, community agencies

Threat Assessment Team
- Reviews facts, evidence, and behaviors that may indicate a student is planning an act of targeted violence
- Addresses any immediate needs, should they rise
- Determines nature of threat (Transient, Substantive)

Substantive Threat:
Evidence confirms a sustained intent to cause harm to others beyond the current situation

Document Incident, Create Safety Plan
Responses may include, but are not limited to:
- Administrative or law enforcement action
- Counseling, assessment, classroom-based intervention, intervention team assistance
- Collaboration with community agencies

- review of school records
- criminal background check (school resource officer)
- collaboration with community agencies

During the initial TAT briefing, team members should designate who will be responsible for each action in order to ensure that all areas of need are addressed and that services are not duplicated. At the end of the meeting, the TAT should arrange specific "next steps" and when the group will reconvene.

3. Address short-term and long-term planning needs.

At the designated time, the TAT should meet again to review various findings and should then address the immediate short-term needs of the student and the school. As is outlined on the Threat Assessment Flowchart (Figure G8), it is possible, after conducting a more thorough investigation, to determine that the behavior is simply a transient threat. If this is the case, the incident will be addressed through disciplinary action, referrals for school-based services, clarifying expectations, the Student Code of Conduct, and other relatively low-level responses.

If, however, the TAT determines the threat is substantive, then short-term planning will involve containing the situation, providing support to identified targets, and taking action to reduce the possibility that a threat will be carried out. Depending on the severity of the situation and the results of the threat assessment, short-term planning may involve referrals for mental health evaluation, coordination of services with juvenile court or child welfare workers, or school-based counseling and support.

Long-term planning means taking measures to minimize the likelihood that the student who posed a threat will engage in threats of targeted violence in the future. Such measures vary widely from situation to situation, ranging from the extremely intensive approach of searching a student's backpack every day and escorting him from class to class to informal mentoring and relationship building. Long-term measures to ensure safety may be focused on the individual student who caused concern or may address broader matters such as bully prevention, effective supervision, and schoolwide discipline and classroom management.

INTERVENTION

G

Step 4: Involve parents and community agencies as appropriate— Response

It is in your school's best interest to establish positive working relationships with parents and community agencies before, during, and after any possible emergency situation. When a critical situation is at hand, your school will be better able to respond if there are open lines of communication, mutual levels of respect, and a climate of collaboration.

A. Establish positive partnerships with parents.

Whenever a student is suspected of expressing a threat of violence, parents must be notified and involved as quickly as possible. That said, there are circumstances where time is of the essence and rapid decision-making is required. Clearly, in serious situations (such as a student threatening to get a gun from his locker), the school should not wait until parental contact is made to take action. The school should prevent access to the weapon and strive to protect everyone's safety.

While responding to possible threats of targeted violence can be an emotional and draining experience for school employees, it is even more traumatic for parents. Schools are encouraged to work to develop positive relationships with all parents throughout the school year as part of an overall effort to establish a collaborative tone. When it is necessary to have interactions with parents because their student may have made a threat of targeted violence, you should always strive to reassure them that you are not working against them, but with them on behalf of their child. However, it is also strongly recommended that your school actively work to establish proactive working relationships with parents so your first interaction with them is not to report a serious incident.

B. Develop positive working relationships with local child and youth-serving agencies.

In far too many incidents of school violence, numerous child-serving agencies have found themselves with significant records indicating that a student was experiencing serious difficulties, but those records had not been shared with others. Though it would be inappropriate, and most likely in violation of federal laws, to recommend wholesale exchange of sensitive information across agencies, schools *are* advised to create formal and informal relationships with their counterparts in juvenile justice, child welfare, mental health centers, and other similar agencies.

Clearly there are important restrictions regarding the disclosing of information without obtaining signed releases; however, there are certain

It is in your school's best interest to establish positive working relationships with parents and community agencies before, during, and after any possible emergency situation.

Figure G9: *Information-Sharing Statutes*

Federal Statutes Regarding Information Sharing

(from *Threat Assessment in Schools: A Guide to Managing Threatening Situations and Creating Safe School Climates*, U.S. Secret Service and U.S. Department of Education, 2002)

Under existing federal law, a school's authority to release information about a student is governed by the Family Educational Rights and Privacy Act (FERPA). The intent of FERPA is to protect the privacy of "education records," a term that is defined as any records that contain information directly related to a student and that are maintained by the educational agency or institution or by a person acting for the agency or institution. Under provisions of FERPA, a school may not disclose personally identifiable information about a student from any education records without the prior written consent of the student's parent or, in the case of students who are 18 or older, the consent of the student.

FERPA does allow for various exceptions to privacy protections covering access to student records, specifying situations and conditions under which a school may disclose information from a student's education records without consent. A detailed analysis of these exceptions is beyond the scope of this Guide. However, there are two exceptions that are worth noting because of their specific relevance to accessing and sharing information for threat assessment inquiries:

- Health and Safety Emergencies: FERPA provides that schools may disclose information from a student's education records in situations where there is an immediate need to share that information in order to protect the health or safety of the student or others. Under this exception, schools must define the term "health or safety emergency" narrowly and are permitted to disclose information from education records only to those individuals who need the information in order to protect the student and others.

- Law Enforcement Unit Records: FERPA regulations draw a distinction between records created by a school law enforcement unit for law enforcement purposes, such as the enforcement of a local, state, or federal law, and records created by a school law enforcement unit for non-law enforcement purposes, such as the enforcement of school policies concerning behavior or disciplinary actions. FERPA also distinguishes between student information that school law enforcement unit officials gathered from education records, and student information that unit officials obtained from other sources. With respect to disclosure of student information contained in school law enforcement unit records, FERPA provides that:

  - Personally identifiable information about a student may be disclosed by school officials if that information is held in a school law enforcement unit record that was created to enforce a federal, state, or local law.

  - Information in school law enforcement unit records that was not obtained from a student's education records may also be disclosed without the consent of the student's parents or the student.

It is important to note that FERPA regulations govern the disclosure of student information from education records and any information about the student that is based upon information contained in education records. FERPA regulations do not restrict the authority of school officials to share other information about a student that is not contained in education records. For example, information such as a school official's personal observations about or interactions with a student that is not contained in education records may be disclosed.

instances where such disclosures are allowed. Figure G9 on the previous page provides a sound summary of the primary federal law related to maintaining and sharing a student's educational records, the Family Educational Rights and Privacy Act of 1970 (FERPA).

Step 5: Restore a sense of safety and security—Recovery.

To put it bluntly, threats of targeted violence, or even rumors thereof, have the potential to cause fear and panic in students, parents, staff, and the larger community. In this age of cell phones, e-mail, instant messaging, and a seemingly insatiable hunger for sensational "news," school districts must be prepared to deal with concerns as they arise. If a threatening incident happens on your campus, the news *will* get out, and you *will* have to address it. Therefore you should create guidelines regarding communication with students, parents, and the larger community during and following reported concerns.

Depending on the nature of the incident, information may change minute-to-minute and hour-to-hour. Principals should provide clear, concise, and prompt communications to appropriate internal and external audiences following a threat that affects the school community. Receiving direct information from the principal often reassures the staff and external community and prevents rumors from circulating.

While Step 4 deals with how to work with students, parents, and community agencies in *responding* to a potential threat, this step focuses on how to help restore a sense of safety and security in the immediate and longer term aftermath of the event.

Schools should be prepared to provide factual information to the parties who need it, while recognizing that different parties have different needs. Whether speaking to students, parents, concerned citizens, or the media, the following guidelines should be considered.

You will essentially be addressing three topics:

- Here is what happened.
- Here is what we are doing about it.
- Here is what we will do to see that it doesn't happen again.

If a threatening incident happens on your campus, the news will *get out, and you* will *have to address it.*

In answering questions:

- Be brief and to the point when explaining what happened.
- Correct inaccuracies.
- Use clear, simple terms.
- Reassure children and adults that their safety is the primary concern of the principal(s), school staff, and district staff.
- Discuss what is being done to keep people safe.
- Name a contact person if interested parties have questions.
- Send home a backpack letter with students affected by the situation.

Students, parents, teachers, and community members each have legitimate concerns and needs for information regarding possible threats of violence on school grounds. Taking proactive steps to familiarize yourself with the recommendations above can assist you in being better prepared to speak to these constituents' unique needs.

CONCLUSION

Preparing to respond to threats of violence in our schools is an emotion-filled, high-profile topic that has received a great deal of public attention in the past two decades. For school administrators and support staff, it can be frustrating, confusing, and even anxiety provoking to make sense of the myriad recommendations regarding how to respond to these possible threats. However, you and your staff can take measures that will ease anxiety and help staff feel empowered to respond, even in the event of a possible threat of violence. In order to facilitate this sense of preparedness, schools should take action at the district, school, teacher, and student level.

At the district level, clear policies and procedures should be developed detailing what will be considered threatening communication and what possible responses to such behavior will be. School-level actions include developing threat assessment teams and providing orientation training for all students and staff. The TAT should receive effective training in how to implement an effective threat assessment process in order to prepare for and respond to potential threats of targeted violence. Teachers and staff should participate in an orientation session to learn district policies and procedures regarding threatening communication and specific steps to follow should a threatening incident occur. Finally, students should participate in classroom lessons to address the Student Code of Conduct and/or district policies regarding threatening communication.

Schools should strive for positive working relationships with parents and community agencies and should strive to provide clear and concise communications should the need arise.

REFERENCES

Carr, E.G., & Durand, V. M. (1986). The social-communicative basis of severe behavior problems in children. In S. Reiss & R. Bootzin (Eds.), *Theoretical issues in behavior therapy*. New York: Academic Press.

Colvin, G. (1992). *Managing acting-out behavior: A staff development program*. Eugene, OR: Behavior Associates. (Distributed by Sopris West, Longmont, CO.)

Colvin, G., Ainge, D., & Nelson, R. (1997). How to defuse confrontations: Defiance, threats, and challenges. *Teaching Exceptional Children, 29*(6), 47–51.

Colvin, G., & Sugai, G. (1989). *Managing escalating behavior* (2nd ed.). Eugene, OR: Behavior Associates.

Cornell, D., Sheras, P., Kaplan, S., McConville, D., Douglass, J., Elkon, A., McKnight, L., Branson, C., & Cole, J. Guidelines for student threat assessment: Field-test findings. *School Psychology Review, 33*, 527–546, 2004b.

Cullinan, D., & Epstein, M. H. (1985). Behavioral interventions for educating adolescents with behavior disorders. *The Pointer, 30*(1), 4–7.

Dwyer, K., Osher, D., & Warger, C. (1998). *Early warning, timely response: A guide to safe schools*. Washington DC: U.S. Department of Education.

Fayette County Public Schools. (2001). *Policies and procedures: Students: 09.425: Assault and threats of violence*. Lexington, KY: Fayette County Public Schools.

Fayette County Public Schools. (2007a). *School-centered emergency management and recovery guide: Threat of harm protocol*. Lexington, KY: Fayette County Public Schools.

Fayette County Public Schools. (2007b). *2007-2008 Statement on rights and responsibilities and student code of conduct*. Lexington, KY: Fayette County Public Schools.

Fein, R., Vossekuil, B., Pollack, W., Borum, R., Modzeleski, W., & Reddy, M. (2002). *Threat assessment in schools: A guide to managing threatening situations and to creating safe school climates.* Washington, DC: U.S. Department of Education, Office of Elementary and Secondary Education, Safe and Drug-Free Schools Program and U.S. Secret Service, National Threat Assessment Center.

Goldstein, A. P. (1988). PREPARE: A pro-social curriculum for aggressive youth. In R. B. Rutherford Jr., C. M. Nelson, & S. R. Forness (Eds.), *Bases of severe behavior disorders in children and youth* (pp. 119–142). San Diego: College-Hill.

Goldstein, A. P. (1999). Aggression reduction strategies: Effective and ineffective. *School Psychology Quarterly, 14*(1), 40–58.

Goldstein, A. P., Glick, B., Reiner, S., Zimmerman, D., & Coultry, T. M. (1987). *Aggressive replacement training: A comprehensive intervention for aggressive youth.* Champaign, IL: Research Press.

Knapczyk, D. R. (1988). Reducing aggressive behaviors in special and regular class settings by training alternative responses. *Behavioral Disorders, 14,* 27–39.

Larson, J. (1998). Managing student aggression in high schools: Implications for practice. *Psychology in the Schools, 35*(3), 283–295.

LaVigna, G. L., & Donnellan, A. M. (1986). *Alternatives to punishment: Solving behavior problems with nonaversive strategies.* New York: Irvington Publishers.

Luiselli, J. K., & Slocumb, P. R. (1983). Management of multiple aggressive behaviors by differential reinforcement. *Journal of Behavior Therapy and Experimental Psychiatry, 14,* 343–347.

Matson, J. (1989). A 20 year review of punishment and alternative methods to treat problem behaviors in developmentally delayed persons. *Research in Developmental Disabilities, 10,* 85–104.

Meese, R. L. (1997). Student fights: Proactive strategies for preventing and managing student conflicts. *Intervention in School and Clinic, 33,* 26–29.

Morgan, S. R. (1994). *At-risk youth in crises: A team approach in the schools* (2nd ed.). Austin, TX: Pro-Ed.

Mulick, J. A., & Linscheid, T. R. (1988). Review of alternatives to punishment: Solving behavior problems with nonaversive strategies. *Research in Developmental Disabilities, 9*, 317–330.

Nelson, C. M., & Rutherford, R. B., Jr. (1988). Behavioral interventions with behaviorally disordered students. In M. C. Wang, M. C. Reynolds, & H. J. Walberg (Eds.), *Handbook of special education: Research and practice* (Vol. 2, pp. 125–153). Oxford, England: Pergamon Press.

Poland, S. (1994). The role of school crisis intervention teams to prevent and reduce school violence and trauma. *School Psychology Review, 23*(2), 175–189.

Rutherford, R. B., & Nelson, C. M. (1995). Management of aggressive and violent behavior in the schools. *Focus on Exceptional Children, 27*(6), 1–13.

Schechtman, Z. (2000). An innovative intervention for treatment of child and adolescent aggression: An outcome study. *Psychology in the Schools, 37*(2), 156–163.

Sprick, R., Sprick, M., & Garrison, M. (2002). *Foundations: Establishing positive discipline policies.* Eugene, OR: Pacific Northwest Publishing.

Stephens, R. D. (1994). Planning for safer and better schools: School violence prevention and intervention strategies. *School Psychology Review, 23*(2), 204–215.

Van Houten, R., Axelrod, S., Bailey, J. S., Favell, J. E., Foxx, R. M., Iwata, B. A., & Lovaas, O. I. (1988). The right to effective behavioral treatment. *Journal of Applied Behavior Analysis, 21*, 381–384.

Vossekuil, B., Fein, R., Reddy, M., Borum, R., & Modzeleski, W. (2002). *Final report and findings of the safe school initiative: Implications for the prevention of school attacks in the United States.* Washington, DC: U.S. Department of Education, Office of Elementary and Secondary Education, Safe and Drug-Free Schools Program and U.S. Secret Service, National Threat Assessment Center.

Watson, R. S., Poda, J. H., Miller, C. T., Rice, E. S., & West, G. (1990). *Containing crisis: A guide to maintaining school emergencies.* Bloomington, IN: National Education Services.

Reproducible Materials

The following reproducible materials may be used in conjunction with "Intervention G: Managing Physically Dangerous Behavior and Threats of Targeted Violence." Copies are provided here and on the CD. Permission is given for individual classroom teachers to reproduce any forms labeled "Reproducible" for classroom use. Reproduction of these materials for an entire school system is prohibited without express permission of the publisher.

INTERVENTION **G**

MANAGING PHYSICALLY DANGEROUS BEHAVIOR
& THREATS OF TARGETED VIOLENCE

Step-by-Step Summary

Following is a summary of the steps involved in Intervention G. It is important to use professional judgment, adjusting procedures to meet the needs of the situation and the individual. See the chapter "Intervention G: Managing Physically Dangerous Behavior and Threats of Targeted Violence" for a detailed description of this intervention.

Managing Physically Dangerous Behavior

COMPONENT 1   Immediately implement procedures to ensure everyone's safety.

A. Use room clears.
   1. Identify where students will go and what they will do during a room clear.
   2. Establish procedures for supervising the student who is engaged in physically dangerous behavior.
   3. Determine the consequences for out-of-control behavior in advance.

B. Use physical intervention only if necessary.
   1. Remove other students from the area.
   2. Always try verbal interventions before resorting to any procedures.
   3. If at all possible, signal or call for help before beginning any sort of restraint.
   4. Decide whether restraint is necessary and helpful.

COMPONENT 2   Involve and notify the student's parents or guardians.

COMPONENT 3   Develop record-keeping and reporting procedures.

A. Set up an anecdotal log of all incidents in which a student's behavior has been physically dangerous.

B. Keep summary records.

COMPONENT 4   Determine whether the student should be referred to special education and whether other agencies should be involved.

COMPONENT 5   Develop a comprehensive plan to reduce future incidents and teach the student to manage her own behavior.

INTERVENTION **G**

Managing Threats of Targeted Violence

STEP 1 Adopt schoolwide policies, procedures and standards for record-keeping—Preparedness.

A. Develop effective policies and procedures.

B. Develop a plan for documenting threatening incidents at the individual, school, and district level.

STEP 2 Conduct training for threat assessment teams and awareness sessions for staff and students—Preparedness.

A. Conduct threat assessment team training.

B. Develop and deliver awareness training for faculty and staff.

C. Create and conduct student lessons in school policy and student responsibility.

STEP 3 Immediately implement threat assessment procedures to respond to possible threats of targeted violence—Response.

A. Begin using a threat assessment approach.

B. Understand the fundamental difference between transient and substantive threats.
   1. Transient threats
   2. Substantive threats

C. Utilize the school-based threat assessment team (TAT).

D. Create and follow an effective flowchart or decision tree when responding to potential threats.
   1. Determine whether or not there is an imminent risk.
   2. Convene the threat assessment team.
   3. Address short-term and long-term planning needs.

STEP 4 Involve parents and community agencies as appropriate—Response.

A. Establish positive partnerships with parents.

B. Develop positive working relationships with local child and youth-serving agencies.

STEP 5 Restore a sense of safety and security—Recovery.

Reproducible Form G2: *Severe Behavior Summary Chart*

Severe Behavior Summary Chart

Student _____ Grade/Class _____ Teacher _____ Date _____

Level of intensity (circle one):   1   2   3

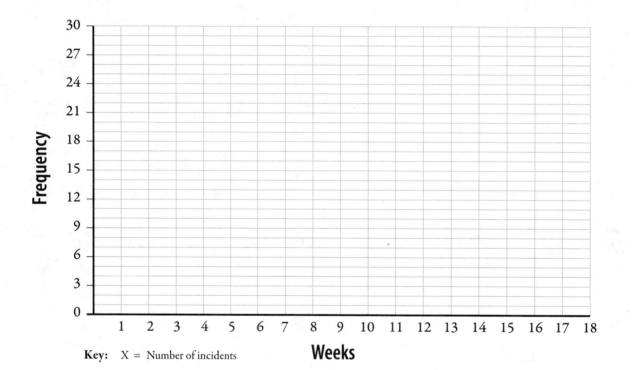

Key: X = Number of incidents

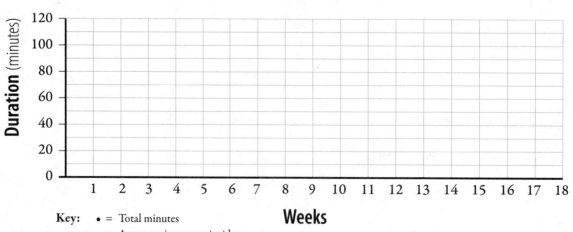

Key: • = Total minutes
         o = Average minutes per incident

Managing Severely Disruptive Behavior

| *Code Red—The student's behavior is so severe that the teacher cannot continue to teach*

PURPOSE

MANAGING SEVERELY DISRUPTIVE BEHAVIOR can be used to defuse and resolve behaviors that have escalated into a Code Red (a nonphysically dangerous situation in which the teacher cannot teach or class cannot continue).

THIS INTERVENTION IS APPROPRIATE FOR:

Overt defiance or flagrant disrespect toward adults
- cursing, yelling obscenities
- overt refusal to follow a direction

Loud, sustained disruptions
- pounding on a desk
- kicking chairs
- repetitive, loud noises
- screaming

Aggressive behavior
- persistent and highly intrusive behavior toward other children
- hair pulling
- grabbing

Note: Behaviors such as biting, kicking, and hitting are and should be viewed as physically dangerous. Follow the guidelines in "Intervention G: Managing Physically Dangerous Behavior and Threats of Targeted Violence."

Managing Severely Disruptive Behavior provides suggestions for responding to students when their behavior is highly disruptive but not physically dangerous to themselves or others around them. Severe misbehavior occurs when the teacher cannot teach and other students cannot learn. This intervention provides ways to respond effectively and appropriately to highly disruptive behavior. Managing Severely Disruptive Behavior is an immediate but temporary solution to a fairly pervasive problem and should be implemented concurrently with other interventions that are designed to help students learn more appropriate behaviors.

Students who engage in severe misbehavior present adults with particularly difficult choices.

RATIONALE

Students who engage in severe misbehavior present adults with particularly difficult choices. Because major student disruptions tend to be emotionally exhausting for everyone, teachers often find themselves purposefully trying to avoid triggering further disruptions by tiptoeing around students or accommodating them in ways that do not help the student learn more appropriate behaviors.

Anita is only in first grade, but her behavior has her teacher at wit's end. Mr. Black never knows what is going to happen. On the first day of school, Anita pulled down her pants and went to the bathroom on the playground. On the second day of school, she destroyed the block castle that some of the other girls were making during choice time. On the third day of school, Anita spit a mouthful of water at the other children who were in line at the drinking fountain, and then she dumped the pattern blocks out on the floor. Since

INTERVENTION

H

> the first day of school, the teacher has tried to interact positively with Anita, but Mr. Black finds himself feeling like he is walking on a tightrope: "I never know what is going to send Anita off into a frenzy. If I say the wrong thing or another student says the wrong thing or if she feels just plain ornery, you never know what she'll do!"

Dealing with a student who engages in severe misbehavior is highly stressful. The teacher must try to second-guess what the student is going to do and then try to figure out what to do when the student "goes off." This teacher may feel like he is at a loss, fighting the growing sense that it is impossible to teach while worrying about what is going to happen next.

It will come as no surprise to learn that early intervention with a student who exhibits severe misbehavior is essential.

> Note: Managing Severely Disruptive Behavior is a temporary intervention for responding immediately to severe misbehavior. More intensive planning in other interventions that are designed to teach students appropriate classroom behavior must follow this intervention.

IMPLEMENTATION STEPS
Step 1: Develop an immediate plan.

Quickly gather as much background information as possible. Defining the nature and scope of the problem will provide the critical information necessary to develop a successful intervention.

> Jeff Riley is in Mrs. Fogel's largely self-contained middle school classroom. Though school has been in session for only two weeks, Jeff has already been involved in two major disruptive incidents. The last one erupted unexpectedly when Jeff failed to follow directions to clear off his desk and Mrs. Fogel asked Jeff directly to put his papers away. Jeff pushed his papers onto the floor and shouted, "That's not fair. I hate this stupid school. You don't like me."

Mrs. Fogel responded, "Now, Jeff, you know that isn't true." As Mrs. Fogel moved toward Jeff to try to calm him down, Jeff ran to a corner, yelling, "I'm going to have my brother come down here, and he is going to beat you up. He won't take this kind of crap. You're a b****!"

At this point, Mrs. Fogel was unsure of what to do. The other children stared at Jeff as he began yelling at his classmates, "What are you staring at? My brother will beat the crap out of you, too."

Mrs. Fogel yelled back, "Jeff, STOP! Right now!" Quickly, Mrs. Fogel had her class line up as Jeff continued hurling obscenities at everyone. Luckily, this problem occured minutes before the students were to go to lunch, and although Mrs. Fogel felt uncomfortable sending her class to lunch with Jeff's screams ringing in their ears, she felt she had no other options.

With her class gone, Mrs. Fogel sat down at one of the children's desks, waiting for Jeff to quiet down. Within minutes, Jeff was silent. Even though he had wound down, Mrs. Fogel fought to control her emotions, vacillating between a sense of hopelessness and anger. "Jeff has no right to disrupt my class, but I can't make him stop. I don't know what will set him off next. What am I going to do?" Before lunch was over, Mrs. Fogel ushered Jeff to the office. There she filled out an office referral, noting at the bottom that Jeff was not to return to her classroom at that time.

As soon as the principal, Ms. Marshfield, had a chance, she quickly reviewed Jeff's records. Jeff's mother had been contacted after Jeff's first major outburst. The counselor noted that Jeff's mother could not come to school, and that Jeff had eventually been returned to his classroom. Jeff's name had been submitted for assistance with the Student/Staff Support Team (SST) with his mother's approval; however, the SST had not met yet to work out a plan for him. His records indicate that Jeff has had ongoing problems in school. He appears to be a bright, academically capable student with a long history of severely disruptive behavior. Most incidents seem to have involved insubordination with teachers and teaching assistants.

During Ms. Marshfield's talk with Jeff, Jeff remained impassive. When Ms. Marshfield indicated that she would need to contact Jeff's parents, Jeff looked up but made no response.

A. Contact the parents or guardian.

Parents must be involved whenever an incidence of seriously disruptive behavior occurs. Initially, contact should be made to let the student's parents know there has been a problem. Eventually, a conference should be held to begin the process of collaborative problem solving. Parents can provide valuable input as staff members determine how to help the student. Depending on the severity of the situation, assistance may include bringing in representatives from other social agencies to develop a comprehensive plan.

When working with parents, the staff needs to make professional judgments to determine how involved parents will be in any plan to assist the student at school. Adversarial stances can be avoided by letting parents know that staff members are committed to helping the student learn more successful behavior. Parents should not be asked to take full responsibility for problems that occur at school. Parents of students with severe misbehavior problems often do not know what to do at home, much less how to get the student to behave while at school. Instead, staff members should work proactively with parents to develop ways to encourage and support appropriate behavior both at school and at home, while teaching the student to avoid inappropriate behavior.

Noting Mrs. Fogel's request that Jeff not be returned to her classroom, Ms. Marshfield calls Jeff's mother to school. She arrives distraught and frightened. Ms. Marshfield lets Mrs. Riley know that the school is very concerned about Jeff's behavior and is committed to working with his family to improve the situation. Ms. Marshfield asks Mrs. Riley to provide background information about Jeff's home situation that might assist staff members. Mrs. Riley says that Jeff is the youngest child of three. His older brother and sister are teenagers. Both have dropped out of school and are living at home.

Mrs. Riley suggests in a roundabout way that her husband should not be involved. After a lengthy discussion with Mrs. Riley, Ms. Marshfield concludes that Jeff's mother is frightened both for herself and her son. Ms. Marshfield asks if the family needs any kind of assistance but is politely told to mind her own business. Mrs. Riley indicates that the counselor has already let her know about the SST, and she will try to make the meeting. Above all, she indicates that her husband should not be bothered, but that she will do whatever she can.

Before Mrs. Riley leaves, the principal asks if she would like to participate in an after-school meeting with Jeff's classroom teacher and the counselor to set up immediate, temporary measures for dealing with Jeff's disruptive behavior. Mrs. Riley thanks Ms. Marshfield for the invitation, but says that she has to be home when her husband returns from work.

Ms. Marshfield makes a note to have the counselor contact Mrs. Riley during morning hours to determine whether the school can help her get support from a local community program.

Jeff stays in the office for the remainder of the day and is told to report back to the office in the morning rather than going straight to his classroom.

B. Meet immediately with appropriate staff members to design temporary procedures.

When a student engages in highly disruptive behavior, the classroom teacher needs to be prepared to respond both immediately and calmly.

One of the most stressful aspects of working with a severely disruptive student is not knowing how to respond. When a student engages in highly disruptive behavior, the classroom teacher needs to be prepared to respond both immediately and calmly. If the teacher responds to disruptive behavior with anger, the student may actually be reinforced. "Wow, I can make the teacher lose it!" The student is in control because he can make the teacher go out of control. Similarly, if the teacher responds to disruptive behavior by panicking or acting like he or she doesn't know what to do, the student may be reinforced. Again, the student is in control of the situation. In either case, the student may find that disruptive behavior is a powerful way to control both the teacher and what happens in the classroom.

Early intervention is critical with problems involving severe misbehavior. The longer a problem continues, the greater the likelihood that the student is being reinforced for his inappropriate behavior and that the teacher will no longer be able to tolerate the student in the classroom. Early intervention can provide the teacher with a sense of relief by providing confidence that he or she knows how to respond appropriately and effectively. In combination with thoughtful long-term planning, early intervention may result in the student learning successful classroom behavior.

INTERVENTION

H

After school, Ms. Marshfield convenes an emergency meeting with the classroom teacher, the counselor (Mrs. Barron), and herself to develop an immediate intervention plan. The goal of this meeting is to establish a temporary plan until the SST can meet and develop a more comprehensive plan. The temporary plan will identify how to respond to disruptive behavior and establish a concurrent plan for encouraging more appropriate behavior.

Mrs. Fogel: (Teacher)	Ms. Marshfield, I've thought a lot about it. I don't think it's right to keep Jeff in my classroom. It's not good for the other kids to hear that kind of language, and it isn't fair to me. I was so upset after this morning that I couldn't teach, even with Jeff gone.
Ms. Marshfield: (Principal)	I understand that you are feeling very frustrated with this situation, but we don't have a lot of options right now. Jeff needs to be somewhere, and I'm not sure his behavior will improve if we simply move him. I would like to establish a two-week intervention phase, and then, if we don't see improvement, we can consider referral to special education. Jeff is already on the agenda for the SST, but I think we need to set up an immediate plan to implement right now.
Mrs. Fogel:	But I don't want Jeff back in my classroom. I have tried being positive with him, but I never know what's going to set him off. I can't spend all day tiptoeing around him.
Ms. Marshfield:	I know this is hard, but we're all here to try and develop a plan to help you out. I met with Jeff's mother this morning and that situation is very difficult. Let me fill you in on some of Jeff's background . . . .
Mrs. Barron: (Counselor)	Jeff is one of those kids who will need a lot of assistance from all of us. One of the first things we can do is to identify how to respond to him in an outburst. I think the hardest thing on all of us is not knowing what to do.

C. Identify positive student behavior, minor misbehavior, and severe misbehavior.

Students who exhibit severe misbehavior usually engage in a series of minor misbehaviors that culminate in disruptive behavior. When working with these students, it is critical for teachers to respond consistently and appropriately. Unfortunately, this is very difficult. It is easy to tolerate lots of minor misbehavior early in the day. Sometimes a teacher will avoid dealing with a minor misbehavior to avoid a more severe episode with a student. Sometimes, out of kindness, it seems easiest to give the student a break.

Unfortunately, as the day progresses, patience runs thin and irritation increases until relatively minor misbehavior is eventually viewed as severe misbehavior. This is the proverbial straw that breaks the camel's back, and the teacher imposes a consequence on the same behavior that had been ignored or tolerated earlier. When a student is treated inconsistently, he learns that it is OK to misbehave sometimes. Inconsistency sabotages efforts to teach the student to behave appropriately. When the teacher is inconsistent, the student will experiment to see what will happen.

Severe misbehavior involves screaming, streams of abusive language, defiant or disrespectful behavior, or behavior that physically interferes with other students. Mild misbehavior tends to be aggravating, but not overly disruptive. Because teaching involves hundreds of complex interactions with students, teachers sometimes view chronic mild misbehavior as severely disruptive behavior. Mild misbehavior should not be dealt with in the same manner as severe misbehavior. If behavior is not highly disruptive, the student should be taught appropriate behavior through the use of mild classroom consequences and proactive strategies for encouraging student responsibility.

To increase consistency in handling challenging students, a list of appropriate behaviors, mild misbehaviors, and severely disruptive misbehaviors should be developed, using these guidelines:

- Appropriate behavior reflects student responsibility, including special strengths and abilities.

- Mild misbehavior annoys but does not prevent the teacher from teaching.

- Severely disruptive behavior prevents the teacher from conducting a lesson and interferes with the learning of others.

1. Identify the student's strengths and positive, appropriate behavior.

This may be difficult when working with a very challenging student. However, it is important to recognize that every student has times when he behaves responsibly—no student is a problem 100 percent of the time. What does the student do well? When the student is not misbehaving, what is he doing? Are there activities in which the student participates appropriately? Think about a fairly good day and describe what makes it good. Identifying the student's strengths and positive behaviors will help staff capitalize on what the student has going for him, making it more likely an intervention can move forward instead of getting stuck by continually dwelling on his problems.

2. Identify every type of misbehavior the student has engaged in, regardless of how trivial.

This exercise should involve the teacher identifying any behaviors that may add to the teacher's feelings of annoyance and general irritation. What does the student do that is problematic besides the severely disruptive behavior? Does he disturb the class in other ways? What little things contribute to the problems?

3. Using the list of misbehaviors, categorize each one as either minor or severe.

It is sometimes difficult to view mild misbehavior as minor. However, if severe misbehavior receives the same response as minor misbehavior, students soon learn that severe misbehavior is no big deal. If consequences for making annoying noises are the same as those for overt defiance, the student learns that being defiant is no more severe than making annoying noises. Work to categorize each of the student's misbehaviors, keeping in mind that the fewer the types of behavior placed in the severe category, the easier it will be for staff to communicate to the student and parents that severe misbehavior will not be tolerated in the school setting. Lumping minor misbehavior in the same category as the severely disruptive behaviors waters down the message.

If severe misbehavior receives the same response as minor misbehavior, students soon learn that severe misbehavior is no big deal.

Ms. Marshfield: (Principal)	Unfortunately, a number of students in our building have had problems like Jeff's, but we've learned something helpful from each student. Sometimes we've had good luck taking care of the problem in the student's classroom. A few times we've had to refer a student to special education. I really hope that we can help Jeff. He's a young kid in a tough home situation. One of the things that's helped us in the past is to identify behavior as falling into three different categories. We'll identify appropriate behavior, mild misbehavior, and severe misbehavior. Probably the biggest distinction between mild and severe misbehavior is whether or not you can keep teaching.
Mrs. Fogel: (Teacher)	That won't be easy to do. It's hard for me to know when he's just fooling around. Things escalate so fast. This last time Jeff just exploded. The first time Jeff was pretty annoying all day long. It was like he was trying to push me into yelling at him.

> **Ms. Marshfield:** You are very perceptive. I'm sure you are probably right. Let's begin by trying to figure out what Jeff does right. Then we'll look at his misbehaviors and work together to categorize those as either minor or severe.

Figure H1 shows the results of the group's brainstorming and categorization of Jeff's behavior.

D. Establish procedures to focus on appropriate student behaviors and strengths.

When a student has severe behavior problems, it is often difficult to give him attention or recognition for appropriate behavior. Because the student usurps so much time and energy when he is misbehaving, it can be difficult to give him more attention when he is being responsible. Unfortunately, this results in the student learning again and again that adult attention is guaranteed during misbehavior and highly unlikely during appropriate behavior. When this occurs, misbehavior increases and responsible behavior decreases.

Once the list of the student's strengths and responsible behaviors has been generated, the classroom teacher will need to learn to focus attention on the things the student does well. Brainstorm a list of ways to focus attention on appropriate behavior and then check those items the teacher believes will be manageable. This is the beginning of a process to set up a long-range positive intervention plan. See Figure H4 later in this chapter for suggestions on other interventions within this text that may be useful in designing a comprehensive, proactive intervention for the student.

Figure H1: *Jeff's Behavior Categories*

Positive Behavior & Student Strengths	Minor Misbehavior	Severe Misbehavior
• Participates in music • Completes work • Stays on task • Acts pleased when praised • Strong in sports, athletic • Humorous • Imaginative writing	• Argues • Taps pencil to annoy • Pokes other students • Makes rude or snide comments • Disgusting noises • Tears up papers • Laughs inappropriately	• Yells obscenities • Will not stop arguing • Overtly defies the teacher by refusing to comply

Ms. Marshfield: (Principal)	Now that we've got a better idea of what Jeff does, we can think about how to respond. It's critical that we figure out what to do when he flips out, but first I want to think about directing our attention to things he does well so we can stay positive about creating a plan for Jeff. Let's brainstorm a list of things we might do to highlight the positive things this kid does.
Mrs. Barron: (Counselor)	I'm actually quite impressed with his strengths. Let's put on the list that he could be a tutor for the special education teacher.
Mrs. Fogel: (Teacher)	Jeff really likes sports, but I don't think he participates on any team. Do you think there's any chance of getting him on one?
Ms. Marshfield:	Let's put it on the list.

At the end of a few minutes, the group generates the following list. The teacher identifies things she is willing to do, and the principal and counselor mark things they would be willing to do.

- tutor for special education students—counselor will check into

- participation in after-school sports—principal will look into

- scrapbook of work well done—principal will get together with Jeff once each week to review academic work and to set up a scrapbook

- principal stopping by the classroom, with a stop at Jeff's desk when he's doing well—principal will do this once a week

- special job first thing in the morning—teacher will assign

- increase positive interactions—teacher will work on

- set up a special time to read jokes with Jeff—teacher will do once a week

- special recognition award for academic success—teacher will distribute

E. Arrange in-class consequences for minor misbehavior.

Using the list of minor misbehaviors, determine how the teacher should respond to each one.

Figure H2 shows the consequences identified by the teacher, principal, and counselor for responding to any of Jeff's minor misbehaviors.

Figure H2: *Responses to Minor Misbehavior*

Minor Misbehavior	Teacher Response
• Argues	• Ignore
• Taps pencil to annoy	• Ignore
• Pokes other students	• In-class timeout, not allowed to be around others
• Makes rude or snide comments	• Ignore
• Disgusting noises	• Ignore
• Tears up papers	• Redo
• Laughs inappropriately	• Give feedback

1. Misbehavior designed to get attention should be ignored if possible.

Attention-getting misbehavior is fueled when the teacher gives *any* attention, whether it is negative or positive. Ignoring this kind of behavior is often the best response, but to effectively ignore, the teacher will need to act as though he or she has not heard or seen the behavior. Sometimes this means that the teacher will have to work very hard at staying physically relaxed. A rigid body response, or even a look, can be reinforcing to a student who craves attention.

If student's misbehavior is being reinforced by peer attention, the other students may need to be taught to ignore inappropriate behavior.

If student's misbehavior is being reinforced by peer attention, the other students may need to be taught to ignore inappropriate behavior. If so, a classroom discussion should be held to discuss the importance of goals and how students need to help each other meet their goals. With this established as background, the teacher should share the target student's strengths and goals for the year and then define behavior that peers will need to ignore. Role-playing may be useful so students can practice how to ignore inappropriate behavior. Throughout the discussion, students need to be reminded that their cooperation and maturity are appreciated and that they should take pride in their ability to help each other.

Focusing a classwide discussion on the problems of one student must be handled with great care and sensitivity. If the students need to be taught to ignore the inappropriate behavior of an individual student, professional judgment should be used to determine whether that student should be present during the discussion. For some students, it would be appropriate to ask them if they would like to be present. For other students, this decision should be made by an adult. If the student is not to be present, he should be told that classmates will be helping him meet his goals by ignoring behavior that is not appropriate in the classroom. If the student has any questions or concerns about the class discussion, they should be answered truthfully. During the discussion, the student can be invited for an ice cream break

Figure H3: *Consequences for Severe Misbehavior*

Severe Misbehavior	Teacher Response
• Yells obscenities	• Intervene early • Stop, think, redirect • If needed, call the office for out-of-room timeout
• Will not stop arguing	• Intervene early • Stop, think, redirect • If needed, call the office for out-of-room timeout
• Overtly defies the teacher by refusing to comply	• Intervene early • Stop, think, redirect • If needed, call the office for out-of-room timeout

or something enjoyable with the principal or counselor. Time out of the classroom during a discussion should be pleasant and supportive.

2. Misbehavior that the student may not realize is unacceptable should be corrected with brief information.

If the student doesn't understand that a behavior is inappropriate, it is important to provide him with that information. If the student is unaware of making rude or critical comments, he will need feedback. "Jeff, that comment was hurtful." This type of feedback should be presented to the student in a calm, quick, and private manner.

3. Minor misbehavior that cannot be ignored should be dealt with by using an in-class consequence.

This demonstrates to the student that if he chooses to engage in inappropriate behavior, there will be a consequence for that choice. If the misbehavior cannot be ignored and is clearly understood by the student as inappropriate, identify a consequence that fits the misbehavior. For example, if the student tears up his own paper, he should have to redo it. If he tears up someone else's paper, he should repair the student's paper and write an apology. (The student whose paper was destroyed should be allowed to turn in his torn paper with no adverse consequences.) If the student destroys school property, he should be required to replace the materials or be given work to earn the funds necessary to replace the materials.

F. Arrange out-of-class consequences for severe misbehavior.

Using the list of severe misbehaviors, determine how the teacher should respond to each one. Figure H3 shows the consequences identified by the teacher, principal, and counselor for responding to Jeff's severe misbehavior.

1. Develop procedures to ensure that no one is in a physically dangerous situation.

   If such a situation exists, see "Intervention G: Managing Physically Dangerous Behavior."

2. Determine how the teacher should respond to the student who is engaging in severe misbehavior.

   When the student is out of control or beginning to escalate into out-of-control behavior, the teacher should calmly tell the student to stop and then direct him to do something else. If the student does not stop the misbehavior, the teacher should immediately summon help and direct the attention of the other students elsewhere.

Mrs. Barron: (Counselor)	Mrs. Fogel, now we need to determine what you will do if Jeff begins to exhibit severe misbehavior. If at all possible, intervene before he is totally out of control. For example, do you remember what happened first this morning?
Mrs. Fogel: (Teacher)	Yes, I asked Jeff to put his papers away, and he pushed them onto the floor and shouted something about hating school.
Mrs. Barron:	That's the point at which you want to intervene. As soon as he is moving into that highly charged behavior, you want to say very calmly, "Jeff, stop. Think about your choices here. I want you to ." You might give him the choice to pull out a book and read for ten minutes. You might ask him to get his notebook out and begin working on math. You could tell him to get a drink. The point is to get him to do something that would save him from humiliating himself. You want to try to get him to break the chain of increasingly agitated behavior.
Mrs. Fogel:	I can see your point. I tried to tell him to stop, but that was after he had already lost it.
Mrs. Barron:	Telling him to stop earlier and redirecting him may not work, but Jeff needs to hear the same consistent response as early as possible. We eventually hope to teach him to pull back before he is totally out of control.

Ms. Marshfield: (Principal)	If Jeff does not stop immediately, you should call the office and someone will come immediately to remove Jeff. So, our next job is to figure out who will help you and where Jeff will go.

3. Establish an out-of-the-room location where the student can be sent if severely disruptive behavior occurs.

When a student engages in severe misbehavior that is not physically dangerous, an out-of-class consequence is often necessary but still not desirable. The student must not be allowed to detract unduly from the activities and education of other students. On the other hand, removal of the disruptive student may increase the frequency of the severe misbehavior.

If an out-of-class consequence is required, carefully follow the remaining steps in this intervention to ensure that improvement occurs. Remember that *getting the student out of the classroom is a temporary measure that will not solve the problem in and of itself.* When selecting a location for an out-of-class consequence, carefully weigh the following three criteria:

- The location should be supervised. Unsupervised locations increase the risk of the student leaving the building, destroying property, or hurting himself.

- The location should be dull. A busy environment may provide a place that is more interesting to the student than the classroom.

- The location should allow a carefully orchestrated transition back into the classroom. Before the student returns, someone will need to help him identify what he did that was inappropriate and what he might do differently in the future.

Getting the student out of the classroom is a temporary measure that will not solve the problem in and of itself.

Advantages and disadvantages of various out-of-class consequences
Send the student to the hallway. Moving a disruptive student into the hallway is a very weak option because the student is unsupervised. While he is out in the hall, who is responsible for the student? What are the liability issues if the student runs away, is injured, or hurts another student?

Hallways are also not boring enough. If other students are in the hallway, the misbehaving student is on display. This can result in the student's being teased or ostracized, or it could result in the student's being able to set himself up as a negative hero—"Look how BAD I am. I got sent to the hallway."

Finally, if the teacher places a student who has engaged in severe misbehavior in the hallway, the teacher will need to transition the student back into the classroom. If the misbehavior is upsetting, it may be very difficult to ask the student calmly to clarify what he did and to identify how he might behave differently in the future.

Send the student home. At first glance, sending the student home may seem like a logical consequence and the best possible option when a student engages in severe misbehavior. In an ideal situation, a parent is contacted and immediately comes to the school to pick up the student. The student is then taken directly home and not allowed to watch TV, listen to music, read, draw, or play. The child is bored. Later that evening, the parents and child have a serious conversation about the importance of school. The parents let the child know the consequences for this and future problems. The child learns that his parents are deeply disappointed.

The office may be the most stimulating environment in the whole school.

Unfortunately, when a child has serious behavior problems, this scenario may be far from reality. It may not be possible to reach a parent immediately. Some parents will not or cannot supervise a student who has been sent home, and often students who are sent home are allowed to do something they would rather do than schoolwork, like playing a video game or watching TV. Some parents will sympathize with the child and talk about "those blankety-blank teachers and that principal—she doesn't know what she's doing." Other children may be physically abused as a punishment for their misbehavior.

Send the student to the office. The office meets the criterion of adequate supervision, but it is hardly a dull place. The office may be the most stimulating environment in the whole school. The student may thoroughly enjoy watching the secretary work, listening to the intercom, greeting the copy machine technician, and so on. These kinds of issues can sometimes be circumvented if a relatively quiet space can be created. For example, it may be possible to position a study carrel in the quietest corner of the office so that the student is visually shielded from high-traffic areas.

Send the student to another classroom. Another classroom may serve as an out-of-class placement. This choice is an option if the alternative classroom is composed of very mature students who are not easily distracted and who will ignore the student. If this option is selected, arrangements must be made in advance with another classroom teacher. The cooperating classroom teacher should tell his or her students that they may have another student join their class once in a while. If this occurs, their job will be simply to provide a quiet space. The class is expected to ignore the student and continue working. The teacher should explain that sometimes people need a place to get away and think. They will be helping others by providing that space.

If the student engages in severe misbehavior, he would be escorted to the alternative classroom and take a preassigned seat in an unobtrusive location. The other classroom teacher should continue teaching without interruption. This option is not intended to embarrass the student who has engaged in a severe misbehavior, so avoid sending an older student to a classroom of very young children.

Use a timeout room or in-school suspension. Timeout rooms can work very well if a school has the space as well as personnel to supervise the room. A timeout room is generally supervised by a trained assistant who does not interact with the student until he is ready to be transitioned back into the classroom.

Note: Though out-of-class placements have inherent problems, they may be necessary. When used, be aware that out-of-class placements are only temporary responses to misbehavior. It is highly unlikely that the consequence alone will change the behavior, and if they are used too often, consequences may actually reinforce the behavior.

Mrs. Barron: (Counselor)	We can begin by figuring out how to get Jeff out of the classroom if he loses it again. My waiting room is a possibility. It tends to be a busy place, but I'd be willing to give it a try.
Ms. Marshfield: (Principal)	I think there are too many kids coming and going. The office presents the same problem.
Mrs. Barron:	Maybe we could check to see whether the nurse would mind us using the health room.

INTERVENTION

H

Ms. Marshfield:	Let me check. If that isn't an option, we can see about using the supply room next to my office. It's pretty busy, but it might work.
Mrs. Barron:	I like the idea of having a place to send Jeff, but how do we get him there? I don't think he should go on his own when he's so out of control.

4. Establish a plan for receiving adult assistance immediately.

This plan should include a list of staff members who can go quickly to the classroom and escort the student to the appropriate location. The first person might be the principal. If the principal is out of the building, the next person might be the counselor. If the counselor is unavailable, it might be the teacher in the room next door, whose own room could be covered briefly by a member of the office staff. Each staff member should be trained to get the student's attention calmly and tell him that they will go together to the out-of-class placement. If the student fails to comply, the staff member should quietly ask the student if he will need assistance. If the student fails to respond or comply, a gentle physical prompt, such as taking the student by the arm, can be attempted if school and board policy permit. If the student does not respond appropriately, only three options remain:

- The student can be physically removed if the staff member is large enough and the student is small enough.

- Another adult can be called for assistance to remove the student physically.

- The other students can be removed from the room.

If any of these options are considered, staff should carefully study "Intervention G: Managing Physically Dangerous Behavior" and their school and board policies to develop contingency plans.

5. Develop procedures for transitioning the student back into the classroom.

How long should the student stay in the out-of-class placement? While the student is in the out-of-class placement, he should be directed to wait quietly. The length of time he will spend in the alternative setting should be predetermined. For example, from the time the student is calm, he may owe a certain number of minutes. Or if the infraction occurs in the early morning, he may need to wait in the out-of-class placement until the end of morning recess. If the severe misbehavior occurs after morning recess, he may need to eat his lunch in the out-of-class placement and remain there until lunch recess is over.

How will the student be returned to his classroom?

Determine who will discuss the severe misbehavior with the student and escort him back to class. At the designated time, the student should discuss with an adult what happened and how he can avoid future outbursts. This should be written down by the student if he has sufficient writing skills. If not, the adult should transcribe what happened and what the student could do differently in the future.

The student may also be required to fill out a Behavior Improvement Form (see Reproducible Form H1). If time permits, the adult might role-play the problem situation with the student and have the student act out appropriate responses. When the student reenters the classroom, he should give the teacher the written notes or the Behavior Improvement Form. The teacher should quietly acknowledge the student's return and act as though they were starting a new day.

6. As planning is completed, carefully explore what will be done in unforeseen circumstances by asking what-if questions.

The teacher should quietly acknowledge the student's return and act as though they were starting a new day.

For example, if the student is to go to another classroom and the teacher is absent, what will happen? Who will transition the student back to class if the responsible staff member is out of the building? A careful discussion of the plan can increase its probability of success.

G. Set up a record-keeping and monitoring system.

From the onset of the problem, situations involving major or severe misbehavior should be recorded. Include the following information:

- date and time of day the incident occurred

- location of the incident

- adult(s) who were supervising at the time of the incident

- events that occurred prior to the incident

- a detailed description of the student's behavior during the incident, including the duration of the episode and the student's specific behavior

Intervention H:
Managing Severely Disruptive Behavior

Behavior Improvement Form

Name _____ Grade/Class _____ Teacher _____ Period/Time _____

1. What did you do? _____

_____

_____

_____

_____

_____

2. Why did you do it? _____

_____

_____

_____

_____

_____

3. What else could you have done? _____

_____

_____

_____

_____

_____

- action(s) taken by staff

- consequences implemented (if any)

- action(s) taken to minimize future occurrences

The classroom teacher should be asked to provide his own account of each incident as soon as possible. This process can provide the teacher with an opportunity to talk through incidents that are likely to be disturbing, and notes from this debriefing can be recorded in an anecdotal log by the administrator. When the log is used over a period of time and several disruptions from a student are recorded, the information can be summarized to help determine the severity of the problem and whether the procedures being used are helping the student improve. (See Intervention G for an Extreme Behavior Log, Reproducible Form G1, which can be used to create a detailed anecdotal record of any incidents that involve severely disruptive, physically dangerous, or threatening events.)

H. Review the plan and identify the roles and responsibilities of all staff members involved.

Determine which staff members should be contacted about the intervention plan, training that may be needed, and who will assume responsibility for these tasks.

I. Determine who will meet with the student to discuss the temporary plan.

Determine who will discuss the plan with the student, who should be present, and when the discussion will take place. In most cases, the parents should be invited. The classroom teacher and at least one other staff member should be present.

The conference should be scheduled at a neutral time, not immediately following a disruptive incident. All parties need to be able to discuss problems and plans calmly. The conference should provide the student with the sense that he can be successful and that the plan will help him improve.

| Ms. Marshfield: (Principal) | I am very happy with our plan. You've all worked very hard on this, and I think it will give us a good start. We will all be doing things to help focus on Jeff's strengths and abilities, and we know what to do now when he misbehaves. Mrs. Fogel, I know that much of this is going to |

	fall on your shoulders and I truly appreciate your cooperation. Now we need to decide when we will discuss this plan with Jeff and who will participate in the discussion.
Mrs. Fogel: (Teacher)	I don't think Jeff should go back to his classroom until all of this has been cleared up.
Ms. Marshfield:	Yes, Jeff will report to the office in the morning. His mother said that she would bring him to me. Mrs. Barron, could you take Mrs. Fogel's class for her some time in the early morning? I think she needs to be part of the discussion.
Mrs. Barron: (Counselor)	Yes, I could take her class at 9:00.
Mrs. Fogel:	That's great. My class goes to electives at 9:30. I don't know how long this will take, but that would give us a buffer. I had a movie planned for the afternoon, but we could move it to the morning.
Mrs. Barron:	What about involving Jeff's mother?
Ms. Marshfield:	I'll ask her in the morning if she would like to be present. She is under a lot of stress, so I'll ask, but I won't push.

Step 2: Meet with the student to discuss the temporary plan.

Discuss the problem with the student. Calmly explain that everyone would like to help him be successful in the classroom. Review the student's strengths and positive behavior. Then have the student assist in describing the problem. During the discussion, gently try to help the student take ownership of the misbehavior.

Ms. Marshfield: (Principal)	Jeff, Mrs. Fogel agreed to meet with us this morning. She has shared with me that you are a very good student. I even have some of your work here, and I am very impressed with your writing. We see a lot of potential in you and would like you to have a successful seventh-grade year with us. What do you think?
Jeff:	(Shrugs)
Ms. Marshfield:	Can you tell us what happened yesterday?
Jeff:	I don't know.

Mrs. Fogel: (Teacher)	Can I help you, Jeff? Do you remember what you did when I asked you to clear off your desk and put your papers away?
Jeff:	Yeah, I threw them on the floor.
Mrs. Fogel:	Yes, and then what?
Jeff:	I yelled some things. Big deal.
Mrs. Fogel:	Yes, and the other kids looked at you. Did you feel embarrassed?
Jeff:	Yeah! They had no right to stare at me!
Mrs. Fogel:	You know, Jeff, we'd like to help you out. If you yell at people like that, they are going to stare. If you behaved like that on a city bus, what do you think would happen?
Jeff:	People would stare.
Mrs. Fogel:	Yes, I think so. Would you like some help? Yesterday, I was very upset and wanted you out of my class. But I talked with Ms. Marshfield and Mrs. Barron last night for a long time and finally came up with a plan to help you. I'm convinced it will work. We'll all have to work hard, but I think you are worth it. I want you to stay in my class, Jeff. You have a great sense of humor. You are good in music and writing. I like you and would miss you.
Jeff:	(Shrugs)
Ms. Marshfield:	Let me explain our plan. We made a list last night of things that you do very well, along with some minor misbehavior that Mrs. Fogel has noticed and severe misbehavior. Severe misbehaviors are ones that cannot be tolerated in a classroom. What do you think will happen if you use any of these severe misbehaviors?
Jeff:	You won't put up with it.
Mrs. Fogel:	Yes, that's right. Severe misbehaviors are things that you might do that would result in your having to leave our class. We have set up a place for you to go. This is how it will work if you do any of the things on the list . . .

The teacher, principal, and Jeff continue discussing the procedures for dealing with severe misbehavior, how mild misbehavior will be handled, and ways that they would like to help Jeff focus on the things he does well. Throughout the discussion, the adults try to engage Jeff as much as possible.

A. Review everyone's roles and responsibilities.

Before concluding the discussion, review everyone's responsibilities. Make sure the student understands the expectations and procedures. This can be accomplished by asking gentle questions, such as "What will happen if . . . ."

B. Conclude the meeting with words of encouragement.

Step 3: Implement the temporary plan.

When minor or severe misbehavior occurs, follow through with the predetermined procedures and consequences.

A. Set up a series of observations and conferences with the classroom teacher.

Once the temporary plan is in place, it is important to follow up with support for the classroom teacher and student. This should involve a series of observations and conferences for a more in-depth look at the severity of the misbehavior.

Because a teacher's perception of a student's behavior may be adversely affected by a personality conflict or amplified because of other stresses, it is generally recommended that the student be observed in the classroom environment by someone who can provide a more objective viewpoint. Though the problem may be perceived and initially described as severely disruptive behavior, it may ultimately be identified as something entirely different. It is critical to identify a problem correctly in order to select an appropriate and effective intervention. Consequently, involving other professionals is recommended at this stage. For example, the administrator, teacher, and counselor could work together to determine what behaviors are severe enough to warrant removal from the classroom. Observations from the counselor would be very useful within this discussion.

B. Provide ongoing support for the teacher.

The classroom teacher who is dealing with a student who exhibits severely disruptive behavior needs to know that other staff members will provide ongoing support and assistance. The temporary plan outlined previously suggests several procedures to provide such assistance. Entries in the anecdotal log, described in Step 1G, provide both a permanent record and a regular opportunity for the teacher to debrief about the student's progress and problems. Meeting with a Student/Staff Support Team (SST)

For example, the administrator, teacher, and counselor could work together to determine what behaviors are severe enough to warrant removal from the classroom.

to develop a more in-depth plan will also assist the teacher. Having staff members in place who are willing to remove the student if needed provides backup support and the comforting knowledge that the situation will never be entirely out of control.

Working on a daily basis with a severely disruptive student can be extremely stressful. The more others can assist, the less pressure the teacher will experience as she tries to help the student while continuing to teach a classroom of students. This in turn may automatically improve interactions between the student and teacher.

C. Provide ongoing support for the student.

Until a more comprehensive plan is developed, an adult should check in frequently with the student to see how things are going. Students who have problems with severe misbehavior need continual assurance that adults will be consistent and supportive, even when the student displays disruptive behavior.

D. Meet within one week to evaluate student behavior and establish a long-range plan.

This intervention provides temporary relief for a difficult situation while a more proactive plan is being developed. As soon as possible, conduct the series of observations and use all the information gathered to develop a more comprehensive, long-term plan. Consider asking for assistance from one or more behavior interventionists in your district.

As you explore how to design a comprehensive, ongoing intervention for severe disruption, consider the concept in Figure H4 that severely disruptive acts may be fundamentally different in how the cause of the chronic disruption is categorized. The type of disruption may influence what interventions may be most applicable. In the second column, proactive interventions are suggested for each type of disruption.

Analyzing disruption by type, as shown in the figure above, was first developed by Dr. Geoff Colvin. For a more detailed treatment of disruptive behavior, see Colvin, in press.

CONCLUSION

Even the most skilled teachers face stressful situations when their students are highly disruptive. Invariably, such a situation results in a teacher developing a negative emotional reaction to the student. Depending on the teacher's skill and tolerance levels, and on how long and frequently the

Figure H4: *Types of Disruption With Suggested Interventions*

Disruption Type	Interventions Within This Book to Consider
Emotional	"Intervention I: Managing the Cycle of Emotional Escalation"
Attention	"Intervention E: Increasing Positive Interactions" "Intervention P: Defining Limits and Establishing Consequences"
Relationships With Adults	"Intervention M: Teaching Replacement Behavior" "Intervention E: Increasing Positive Interactions" "Intervention P: Defining Limits and Establishing Consequences" "Intervention J: Cueing and Precorrecting"
Relationships With Students	"Intervention M: Teaching Replacement Behavior" "Intervention K: Self-Monitoring and Self-Evaluation" "Intervention L: Positive Self-Talk and Attribution Training"
Noncompliance	"Intervention B: Academic Assistance" "Intervention M: Teaching Replacement Behavior" "Intervention E: Increasing Positive Interactions" "Intervention P: Defining Limits and Establishing Consequences" "Intervention J: Cueing and Precorrecting"

disruptive behavior has been exhibited, a major barrier to a successful long-term intervention may be teacher burnout. By the time an intervention is discussed, the student may have openly challenged the teacher or embarrassed the teacher in front of the class. The student may have rejected the teacher's initial attempts to help. The student will have interfered with the learning of other students and at the very least contributed to a negatively charged classroom environment.

By the time help is requested for such a student, the teacher may be ready to be rid of that student. If the teacher hopes to get the student out of the room, it may be difficult to set up a plan that will keep the student in the classroom. Early intervention and a temporary plan, followed by more intensive planning, is critical. If early intervention has not been provided, it will be important to provide as much assistance to the teacher as possible so the temporary plan will have a chance of success.

Managing Severely Disruptive Behavior focuses on the initial steps to take when responding immediately to a crisis situation. The primary purpose of the intervention is to reduce classroom disruptions; thus, the intervention is geared toward helping the teacher and other students. For this reason, it is essential that long-range planning continue after this intervention is in place.

REFERENCES

Bauer, A. M., & Sapona, R. H. (1991). *Managing classrooms to facilitate learning.* Englewood Cliffs, NJ: Prentice Hall.

Charles, C. M. (1989). *Building classroom discipline: From models to practice* (3rd ed.). White Plains, NY: Longman.

Colvin, G. (1992). *Managing acting-out behavior: A staff development program.* Eugene, OR: Behavior Associates. (Distributed by Sopris West, Longmont, CO.)

Colvin, G. (In press.) *Managing non-compliance: Steps for teachers and specialists.* Thousand Oaks, CA: Corwin Press.

Colvin, G., & Sugai, G. (1989). *Managing escalating behavior* (2nd ed.). Eugene, OR: Behavior Associates.

Emmer, E. T., Evertson, C. M., & Worsham, M. E. (2003). *Classroom management for secondary teachers* (6th ed.). Boston: Allyn & Bacon.

Evertson, C. M., Emmer, E. T., & Worsham, M. E. (2003). *Classroom management for elementary teachers* (6th ed.). Boston: Allyn & Bacon.

Gregg, S. (1999). Creating effective alternatives for disruptive students. *The Clearing House, 73*(2), 107–113.

Jones, K. M., Drew, H. A., & Weber, N. L. (2000). Noncontingent peer attention as treatment for disruptive classroom behavior. *Journal of Applied Behavior Analysis, 33*(3), 343–346.

Keble, T. J., Bray, M. A., Theodore, L. A., Jenson, W. R., & Clark, E. (2000). A multi-component intervention designed to reduce disruptive classroom behavior. *Psychology in the Schools, 37*(5), 475–481.

Kerr, M. M., & Nelson, C. M. (1997). *Strategies for managing behavior problems in the classroom* (3rd ed.). Upper Saddle River, NJ: Prentice Hall.

Morgan, D. P. & Jenson, W. R. (1990). *Teaching behaviorally disordered students: Preferred practices.* Upper Saddle River, NJ: Prentice Hall.

Rhode, G., Jenson, W. R., & Reavis, H. K. (1992). *The tough kid book: Practical classroom management strategies.* Longmont, CO: Sopris West.

Robinson, T. R., Smith, S. W., Miller, D. M., & Brownell, M. T. (1999). Cognitive behavior modifications of hyperactivity-impulsivity and aggression: A meta-analysis of school-based studies. *Journal of Educational Psychology, 91*(2), 195–203.

INTERVENTION

H

Smith, S. W., Siegel, E. M., O'Connor, A. M., & Thomas, S. B. (1994). Effects of cognitive-behavioral training on angry behavior and aggression of three elementary-aged students. *Behavioral Disorders, 19*(2), 126–135.

Sprick, R. S. (1981). *The solution book: A guide to classroom discipline*. Chicago: Science Research Associates.

Sprick, R. S. (2006). *Discipline in the secondary classroom: A positive approach to behavior management* (2nd ed.). San Francisco: John Wiley & Sons.

Sprick, R. S., Sprick, M. S., & Garrison, M. (2002). *Foundations: Establishing positive discipline policies*. Eugene, OR: Pacific Northwest Publishing.

Stage, S. A. (1997). A preliminary investigation of the relationship between in-school suspension and the disruptive classroom behavior of students with behavioral disorders. *Behavioral Disorders, 23*(1), 57–76.

Reproducible Materials

The following reproducible form may be used in conjunction with "Intervention H: Managing Severely Disruptive Behavior." A copy is provided in the chapter and on the CD. Permission is given for individual classroom teachers to reproduce any forms labeled "Reproducible" for classroom use. Reproduction of these materials for an entire school system is prohibited without express permission of the publisher.

INTERVENTION

MANAGING SEVERELY DISRUPTIVE BEHAVIOR

Step-by-Step Summary

Following is a summary of the steps involved in Intervention H. It is important to use professional judgment, adjusting procedures to meet the needs of the situation and the individual. See the chapter "Intervention H: Managing Severely Disruptive Behavior" for a detailed description of this intervention.

STEP I   Develop an immediate plan.

A. Contact the parents or guardian.

B. Meet immediately with approprirate staff members to design temporary procedures.

C. Identify positive student behavior, minor misbehavior, and severe misbehavior.
1. Identify the student's strengths and positive, appropriate behavior.
2. Identify every type of misbehavior the student has engaged in, regardless of how trivial.
3. Using the list of misbehaviors, categorize each one as either minor or severe.

D. Establish procedures to focus on appropriate student behaviors and strengths.

E. Arrange in-class consequences for minor misbehavior.
1. Misbehavior designed to get attention should be ignored if possible.
2. Misbehavior that the student may not realize is unacceptable should be corrected with brief information.
3. Minor misbehavior that cannot be ignored should be dealt with by using an in-class consequence.

F. Arrange out-of-class consequences for severe misbehavior. and strengths.
1. Develop procedures to ensure that no one is in a physically dangerous situation.
2. Determine how the teacher should respond to the student who is engaging in severe misbehavior.
3. Establish an out-of-the-room location where the student can be sent if severely disruptive behavior occurs.
4. Establish a plan for receiving adult assistance immediately.
5. Develop procedures for transitioning the student back into the classroom.
6. As planning is completed, creafully explore what will be done in unforeseen circumstances by asking what-if questions.

G. Set up a record-keeping and monitoring system.

H. Review the plan and identify the roles and responsibilities of all staff members involved.

I. Determine who will meet with the student to discuss the temporary plan.

INTERVENTION H

STEP 2 Meet with the student to discuss the temporary plan.

A. Review everyone's roles and responsibilities.

B. Conclude the meeting with words of encouragement.

STEP 3 Implement the temporary plan.

A. Set up a series of observations and conferences with the classroom teacher.

B. Provide ongoing support for the teacher.

C. Provide ongoing support for the student.

D. Meet within one week to evaluate the student behavior and establish a long-range plan.

Geoff Colvin, Ph.D.

Managing the Cycle of Emotional Escalation

The student is impulsive and has difficulty maintaining emotional control

PURPOSE

THIS INTERVENTION IS DESIGNED to help manage any behaviors that are the result of emotional escalation.

THIS INTERVENTION IS APPROPRIATE FOR:

- tantrums
- out-of-control behavior
- buildup of angry behavior
- threats
- volatile behavior
- verbal outbursts
- physical outbursts
- aggressive actions
- sustained disruptions
- explosive behavior

> **Note:** If the student engages in highly violent or self-injurious behavior—*Code Red* behavior—immediately seek assistance from a school psychologist or certified behavior analyst (see "Intervention G: Managing Physically Dangerous Behavior"). Along with short-term emergency procedures, work with trained staff to implement this and other interventions to craft a proactive, long-term intervention plan.

Problem behaviors that escalate into serious acting-out behavior are often emotionally based and fueled by students' reactive responses to successive events—generally negative interactions with another person. These cases usually involve a cycle of behavior that follows a recognizable sequence of stages or phases, in which each behavior becomes more serious than the last. Learning to understand and manage this cycle of emotional escalation can be a powerful way for a teacher or specialist to intervene and defuse a potentially volatile confrontation. Managing the Cycle of Emotional Escalation can also be used to eventually teach the student to manage his or her own behavior and learn to stay in control without outside assistance.

RATIONALE

Managing the Cycle of Emotional Escalation is designed as a long-term intervention for students whose seriously disruptive or dangerous behavior warrants a Code Red intervention (Intervention G or H). The approaches in this intervention presume that you have already witnessed a student's behavior building to a serious level, or that you have seen lower-level behavior from the student on more than one occasion but you anticipate the student's impulsiveness may eventually lead to seriously disruptive or unsafe behavior. If you have reason to believe an outburst was a one-time event (perhaps caused by a current crisis, such as parents getting a divorce or going through a relocation), the structured analyses and detailed breakdown of behavioral phases in this intervention may not be necessary. In these cases, timely support and close supervision may be what is needed. If, on the other hand, you suspect the student's escalating behavior may be part of a recurring pattern, the strategies in this chapter can help you effectively manage the cycle.

Emotional escalation

A student throws some paper on the floor in the hallway, and a teacher asks him in passing to pick up the papers and throw them in the trash. The student says, "You are not my teacher," and keeps walking. The teacher repeats the direction more firmly, and the student shouts, "I don't have to do what you say!" It is easy to imagine how interactions such as this might continue to escalate in a destructive pattern.

The student's first behavior was throwing paper on the floor. This was followed by a disrespectful comment ("You are not my teacher") and noncompliance (leaving the paper on the floor and walking away). These negative behaviors reached a greater intensity when the student shouted.

This example of a cycle of behavior was escalatory in that the disrespectful remark was more serious than throwing the paper on the floor, the noncompliance was more serious than the disrespect, and the shouting noncompliance was still more serious. It is important to note that each successive response from the student was a stronger negative reaction to the teacher's requests and directions. These stronger student reactions are examples of emotionally escalated behavior. The key to understanding this kind of escalation is that it usually has an underlying emotional component. To break the cycle of escalation, you must first understand the relationship between underlying emotional responses, the role of successive interactions with the student, and the ratcheting up of student behavior.

Consider another example: Two students are arguing over whose turn it is to use the computer during break. The argument soon progresses to shouting and name calling, followed by pushing and shoving. Finally, the teacher intervenes, breaks up the conflict, sends the two students to their desks, and prevents a fight or major disruption.

The successive behaviors in this scenario begin with arguing, escalate to shouting and name calling, and intensify to the brink of a physical altercation with pushing and shoving. The pattern is escalatory in that each behavior ups the ante, being more serious and intense than the last, eventually leading to physical aggression (pushing and shoving). Had the teacher not intervened at this point, a fight might have broken out with potentially far more serious results than pushing and shoving.

In each of the previous examples, each successive student response was prompted or stimulated by an interaction with another person, and each interaction/response was more serious than the previous one. It is this back-and-forth pattern of action and reaction with increasingly serious behaviors that defines the cycle of emotional escalation.

The pattern is escalatory in that each behavior ups the ante, being more serious and intense than the last, eventually leading to physical aggression (pushing and shoving).

Defusion

It may be useful to examine the process of *defusion* to learn how to manage situations of escalation in the short term. Defusion is the immediate response to escalation and involves another person, generally the teacher, taking measures to interrupt the cycle. Defusion thereby prevents behaviors from worsening and helps the student settle down and resume class activities. Consider the earlier example of two students shouting at each other over who could use the computer. The teacher intervenes, asks them to cool it, and sends them to their desks. The students return to their desks and sit there scowling at each other, which is less serious than the previous behavior of a shouting match. Most importantly, the teacher has prevented the conflict from going further, defusing the situation for the time being. However, the students are still upset with each other, and the conflict may erupt at a later time, such as at recess. In this case, some conflict resolution work needs to be conducted with these two students to solve the problem.

> *Defusion is the immediate response to escalation and involves another person, generally the teacher, taking measures to interrupt the cycle.*

Note: Defusion is a short-term measure designed to prevent further escalation—it is not a long-term solution to the problem. Additional steps, which can be found in this and other interventions, are needed to solve the problem.

Key assumptions

Several key assumptions underlie this intervention's approach to managing emotionally escalated behavior:

1. Escalating behavior is expressed in many ways, but the cycle of emotional escalation and acting out is almost always accompanied by distinctive and readily identifiable behavioral patterns that you can learn to recognize and pinpoint.

2. Escalating behavior may occur with students of all ages and abilities.

3. Escalating behavior is rarely an isolated event. It tends to happen repeatedly over time as part of an established behavioral chain or pattern.

4. To be successful in the long term, analysis and intervention must address the entire chain—all phases of the cycle of emotional escalation in every setting.

5. As with any child who exhibits chronic problem behavior, helping a student who escalates may require a comprehensive schoolwide Behavior Support Plan, possibly including parental or community involvement.

6. The most effective intervention is to intervene early in the chain of the escalated cycle.

7. The procedures to manage escalating behavior usually involve two steps: first, an immediate response designed to defuse the situation, and second, a systematic plan to solve the problem and prevent it from occurring again.

The seven-phase model of escalating behavior

The cycle of emotional escalation generally progresses through seven distinct phases:

1. Calm
2. Triggers
3. Agitation
4. Acceleration
5. Peak
6. De-escalation
7. Recovery

Though behaviors in each phase may manifest differently from student to student, the "signature" of each remains readily identifiable. Once you can correlate a student's behavior with a specific phase, you can use the corresponding strategies to arrest the behavior before any further escalation occurs. Knowledge of the seven phases of emotional escalation will allow you to help the student settle down in the short term and develop a problem-solving plan in the long term. Each phase will be described in detail later in this chapter, followed by suggested strategies for managing the behaviors at each phase.

Figure I1: *Seven-Phase Model of Emotional Escalation*

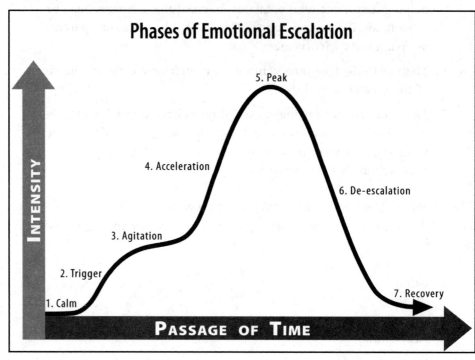

Phases of Emotional Escalation

The seven phases of escalation are depicted in Figure I1. Note that the graph rises as the interaction escalates and falls away as the student's behavior de-escalates.

The following is an example of a student who goes through the rising phases in the cycle of emotional escalation, illustrating how a student and teacher are both involved in the buildup of behavioral intensity. See if you can spot the ways in which each contributes to the growing confrontation.

> Note: The teacher in the following example and analysis gives responses that are common practice and effective with most students. However, with any student who has difficulty maintaining emotional control, certain responses often contribute to or exacerbate the situation, as you shall see.

Illustration: ESCALATING BEHAVIOR PATTERN

During independent work in math, students are expected to complete problems that were assigned in the previous class. One student, Michael, is sitting slouched in his seat, feet stretched out, head down, staring at the floor, and looking very serious.

Teacher:	Michael, it is time to get started with your math.
Michael:	What math?
Teacher:	The math you didn't finish this morning. Let me see your work, please. (Looks at the work.) Good, you have done four problems, but you need to do 10.
Michael:	I did finish it! (Michael leans back.) When did we have to do 10?
Teacher:	I announced that at the beginning of class yesterday. Michael, look at the board. See under assignment: one through ten.
Michael:	I don't remember that!
Teacher:	Look, Michael. This has gone far enough. You need to finish the rest of your assignment. So please get on with it.
Michael:	Well, that's the first time I've seen it.
Teacher:	OK. Here is your choice. Do the math now or you will have to do it in detention.
Michael:	No way. I'm done! F*** you!
Teacher:	Michael, that's verbal abuse. I'm going to give you an office referral.

Michael throws his book across the room.

Teacher:	All right. It's to the office. (Nudges Michael on the elbow)

Michael swings his arm in the teacher's direction and makes solid contact with the teacher's arm.

The teacher then follows emergency procedures and calls for help, resulting in the student being escorted to the office.

Review and analysis

The previous example highlights four common features of an escalating situation.

1. An expectation is placed on the student (Trigger—Phase 2).

   Michael is asked to engage in a task that is required of all the students and that he clearly does not want to engage in. He responds with a series of tactics aimed at avoiding the task. Avoidance or escape behaviors are common and can occur for any number of reasons. Ask yourself (or, when appropriate, the student) questions such as these to determine if task avoidance is a trigger for the student's acting-out behavior:

   - Does the student understand the directions?
   - Does the student have the prerequisite skills to carry out the task?
   - Does the student have any history of failure with the task or activity?
   - Has the student already mastered the skills called on by the task?

2. The student displays signs of being upset (Agitation—Phase 3).

   Michael's body language indicates that he is upset over something right from the beginning of the interaction. His initial posture and curt responses are strong indicators of agitation—signals that the situation is likely to worsen if not addressed effectively.

3. Both the teacher and student are fully engaged (Acceleration—Phase 4).

   Throughout this example, Michaels's behavior is preceded by a teacher-initiated comment or action inviting a response. There is a clear pattern of "My turn/Your turn." Suppose the teacher didn't respond in a way that invited a direct response? Or suppose the teacher refused to engage in turn taking, perhaps simply walking away after the initial interaction? This might have given the student time to respond in a productive manner—by completing his work. Often a teacher unwittingly escalates the situation by engaging in a "one-upmanship" game he or she may not even realize is happening.

4. A clear escalating progression or chain of behaviors occurs
(Peak—Phase 5).

In the example, the student behavior becomes progressively more serious with the successive teacher-student interactions. Michael's behavior
escalates from questioning and arguing to noncompliance, then defiance,
verbal abuse, and finally to assault.

You can see how each point of this analysis corresponds to one or more
phases in the cycle. The student appears to be out of sorts even before
the teacher's first interaction—Michael has already left Phase 1: Calm.
Had the teacher addressed Michael's agitation in the beginning, the ensu-
ing escalation might have been prevented. Instead, the teacher's initial
contact acts as a trigger for Michael (Phase 2): "Get started with your
math . . . the math you didn't finish . . . let me see your work." Once agitated, Michael becomes more belligerent and determined (Phase 3), and
it is not long before Michael and the teacher have staked out unyielding
positions. They become fully engaged (Phase 4), setting off a chain of
interactions that quickly ratchets up to peak behavior (Phase 5).

Characteristics of escalating behavior

The following section includes descriptions of each phase in the cycle of
emotional escalation. These descriptions can be used to help you determine
the typical behaviors your student of concern exhibits at each phase in the
cycle in order to appropriately respond and defuse the situation before it
escalates any further. Once you have identified a pattern of behavioral escalation, you are in a much stronger position to intervene early and interrupt
the cycle before it spirals into a seriously disruptive and unsafe situation.
Later in this chapter, Step 1 will help you develop a plan for managing
behavior in each phase.

Phase I: Calm—Overall behavior is cooperative and acceptable.

The student is to some degree able to exhibit behaviors essential to suc-
ceeding in class: staying on task, following rules and expectations, responding to praise, initiating appropriate behavior, and responding to goals and
success.

*Once you have
identified a pattern of
behavioral escalation,
you are in a much
stronger position to
intervene early and
interrupt the cycle
before it spirals into
a seriously disruptive
and unsafe situation.*

INTERVENTION

I

Phase 2: Triggers—Events or circumstance prompt emotional reactions.

Triggers are events that set off emotionally escalating behavior, propelling the student toward a tipping point. The student may be engaged appropriately in the first phase, and a trigger comes into play that sets the stage for problem behavior. Other names for triggers include antecedents, setting events, aversive stimuli, and negative circumstances. Triggers are classified either as school-based, arising from situations at school, or non-school-based, a catchall for all outside influences the student brings to class.

School-based triggers

Conflicts. Conflicts tend to arise at school when students who have limited impulse control are denied something they want or when something negative is inflicted on them.

Changes in routine. Students who are easily driven to escalating behavior will often react negatively to sudden changes in routine, especially if the current activity is something they enjoy or something that isn't quite finished.

Peer provocations. Unfortunately, classmates sometimes see easily triggered students as "fair game," enjoying "getting a rise" out of these students. In these situations, peers' antagonizing can predictably cause students to escalate and get into trouble.

Pressure. Students are expected to comply with a wide variety of directions and complete a number of complex tasks during the course of a school day. Students who exhibit escalating emotional behavior may not to have the necessary skills to meet these expectations; consequently, they may feel they are under constant pressure and react inappropriately.

Ineffective problem solving. Students who escalate generally have limited strategies for identifying the source of their antagonism, generating adaptive options, evaluating their choices, negotiating with others, or putting a plan into action.

Handling challenging work. When these students face new or challenging work, they often escalate to avoid facing difficulties and their perception of probable failure.

Facing correction. Easily triggered students often have problems receiving feedback that they have made errors and accepting assistance with the task.

Non-school-based triggers

The following triggers occur outside the school and result in the student coming to school already upset. These triggers are often called "setting events," in that the student is already roused—when another event at school serves as a trigger, the student often quickly escalates.

High-needs homes. Students who escalate often come from homes where many critical needs are not met.

Health problems. Easily triggered students may come to school with additional challenges that teachers may be unaware of. Students from low-income homes may not have health insurance or receive regular medical care. By necessity or by choice, students may be hungry or may not be having their nutritional needs met. Students may also be getting inadequate sleep, making it very difficult to behave or participate appropriately. Deficits in any of these areas, which are outside the school's control, not only impact the student's health and well-being, but can adversely affect student behavior.

Multiple diagnoses. In some cases, students may have been given various medical/psychological diagnoses, and the respective treatments may interact negatively with each other.

Substance abuse. Students who use drugs and alcohol often exhibit serious and unpredictable escalating behavior at school.

Gangs and deviant peer groups. Membership in gangs and deviant peer groups may set the stage for serious problems at school, especially when it comes to the authority of school personnel and relationships with other peers. Problem behavior, in this case escalated behavior, may be perceived as a "badge of honor" among the deviant peer group members.

Compound triggers. School-based and non-school-based triggers often act in combination to amplify escalating behavior. Students who are triggered in a mix of ways are often best supported by "wraparound" services that involve medical, psychological, behavioral, and academic interventions in combination. The key with wraparound services is that a team approach must be used, with all participants on the same page and informed about what each is doing to best serve the student.

Phase 3: Agitation—Overall behavior is unfocused and distracted.

Agitation is a general behavioral term that covers a range of emotional states such as being angry, upset, depressed, on edge, withdrawn, worried, disturbed, frustrated, or anxious. Students often display high outward levels of agitation as a function of their inability to control or manage emotional triggers. Agitation is often discernible either by *increases* in certain behaviors or *decreases* in behaviors.

Increases in behavior

Darting eyes. Students look here and look there with a certain level of intensity but with little focus or apparent purpose to their eye movements.

Busy hands. Students who are agitated often display a noticeable increase in hand movements that resemble those of a student with hyperactivity, except that the student does not exhibit these behaviors during the Calm phase. This behavior is prevalent among students with severe disabilities, especially in areas of language and communication deficits.

Moving in and out of groups. These students often want to join a group, but when they do, they quickly want to join another group or do something else.

Off-task and on-task cycle. Similarly, students in the agitation phase may start a task or activity, stop, and then start up again. There may appear to be little, if any, fixed or sustained attention to academic tasks or classroom activities, and the students may appear to be preoccupied.

Decreases in behavior

Staring into space. Students may stare into space and appear to be daydreaming or fixated on something, but their minds are somewhere else.

Veiled eyes. Students will often avoid eye contact by looking away, looking down, using a hat to cover their eyes, or pulling a jacket up and sinking as low into it as possible.

Nonconversational language. Agitated students respond in monosyllabic and noncommittal ways, making it difficult to build a conversation. Their body language and words communicate "I don't want to talk to you."

Contained hands. Where some students signal agitation with busy hands, other agitated students may hide their hands by sitting on them, folding their arms, or putting their hands behind their back.

Withdrawal. These students may withdraw from groups, shut down, show a clear preference for independent activities, or move to isolated areas. The implicit message is "Leave me alone."

Phase 4: Acceleration—"I want to engage you."

In this phase, the subtext to the student's behavior is "I want to engage you." The student's words, deeds, and body language all convey this message. The student may bait or otherwise try to pull the teacher in with behavior that is calculated to obtain a response and is usually quite predictable.

Typical engaging behaviors

Questioning and arguing. Some students need help or ask questions and then proceed to argue about the response they receive or continue to question details of the task at hand.

Noncompliance and defiance. Students may accelerate the situation by refusing to cooperate with instructions, classroom rules, or teacher expectations, setting up a confrontations or further negative interactions.

Off-task behavior. These students may stop working or deliberately stray off task, expecting that the teacher will respond.

Provoking others. Some students intentionally irritate or antagonize the teacher or another student, hoping to provoke a reaction. The stronger the reaction, the more positively reinforcing it may be to these students, setting the stage for further negative interactions.

Partial compliance. This behavior is a form of limit testing. It could be compliance accompanied by additional inappropriate behavior. Students complete tasks or follow stated directions, but also exhibit one or more additional social behaviors they know are unacceptable. Partial compliance has often been described as passive-aggressive behavior.

Criterion defiance. Another form of testing the limits occurs when students perform at standards clearly below the expected level and the teacher knows full well that they are capable of better performance.

Rule violation. Still another way students who have difficulty maintaining emotional control may test the limits is to break a rule deliberately—knowing that staff will have to respond with correction procedures that often involve established consequences. After provoking the desired response from staff, students are likely to instigate further negative interactions.

Whining and crying. By engaging in these behaviors, students hope to obtain immediate teacher attention or assistance. In some cases, students may seek to irritate or frustrate the teacher and provoke a confrontation.

Avoidance and escape. Students who aim at engaging may seek to avoid certain tasks or responsibilities, knowing that this behavior will usually result in securing a teacher response—often characterized with "You can't make me" comments and behaviors.

Threats and intimidation. By threatening staff members, students may hope to intimidate, but they may also have a secondary objective. If a targeted staff member responds in kind—that is, in any way that suggests a challenge—it is highly likely that students will swiftly escalate into a serious confrontation involving potentially unsafe or violent behavior.

Verbal abuse. Similarly, students who use offensive or abusive language toward staff may expect and want staff to address the behavior immediately—teachers typically react strongly to offensive language. This reaction sets the stage for the accelerating student to respond with more serious behavior.

Destruction of property. Some students may deliberately damage or deface property, expecting that staff will take immediate action and counting on further negative interactions as a result.

Phase 5: Peak—Behavior is out of control.

In this phase, the student's behavior is so dangerous or disruptive that class cannot continue or can continue only with great difficulty. Peak behaviors are the most serious in the whole chain of emotional escalation.

> **Note:** If a student is exhibiting peak behaviors or physically dangerous or severely disruptive behavior, immediately implement the emergency response procedures in "Intervention G: Managing Physically Dangerous Behavior and Threats of Targeted Violence" or "Intervention H: Managing Severely Disruptive Behavior."

Dangerous or disruptive behaviors

Serious destruction of property. Students who have reached the peak phase of the cycle of emotional escalation can cause substantial and costly damage to or defacement of property.

Physical attacks. Students may target others with the intent to cause physical harm (e.g. punching, kicking, throwing objects, hair pulling). Even more serious behaviors include attacks with objects or weapons.

Self-abuse. Peak behaviors may include self-directed harmful behaviors such as face slapping, hitting, pinching, hair pulling, head banging, and scratching.

Severe tantrums. These students may exhibit tantrum behaviors, including screaming, yelling, throwing objects, pushing desks over, and flailing on the floor.

Running away. Students who are out of control will often exhibit a fight-or-flight response, either continuing to escalate the situation or electing to escape it by running away. The departure may be accompanied by explosive behavior—yelling, cursing, banging doors, or kicking walls and furniture.

In the earlier example, Michael was successful in avoiding and escaping his math assignment by engaging in a full spectrum of escalating behavior. Had someone tried to contain him physically at the point at which he became out of control during the peak phase, he would likely have become more physical and might have caused further damage to school property or bodily harm to someone. Emergency procedures that come into effect when a student is out of control are designed to reduce the chances that anyone is injured during the crisis and to reduce, to the greatest degree possible, the disruption of the learning environment or property damage. See Interventions G and H for specific strategies to manage a student whose out-of-control behavior has become physically dangerous or severely disruptive.

Phase 6: De-escalation—Overall behavior shows confusion and lack of focus, perhaps appearing to vacillate between anger and calming down.

The phase might be thought of as a *reintegration process*. The student begins to disengage, with a corresponding reduction in intensity of behavior. However, the student remains generally uncooperative or unresponsive to adult social influence. In effect, the student is moving from out-of-control behavior to a phase of uncertainty and confusion. Think about times you have been very angry. Once you start to calm down, you do not immediately revert to a calm state. For a period of time between that emotional peak and complete calm, you are poised between the two states. It is almost like a balancing point in which, consciously or unconsciously, you are trying to figure out whether to hang on to the anger or allow yourself to return to normal functioning.

De-escalation responses

Confusion. Students who are coming down from an episode of out-of-control behavior often appear confused, displaying seemingly random behaviors or a lack of focus.

Reconciliation. Some students make peace overtures, attempt to make up, or try "testing the water" to see if the teacher still likes them.

Withdrawal. De-escalating students may drop their heads down and may even appear to be asleep. This can be a way to withdraw from the situation or a response of genuine fatigue. Students may also simply be buying time to pull themselves together after a prolonged behavioral episode.

Denial. These students may deny their recent behavior, especially regarding the most serious behaviors. They may genuinely not remember what sent them into this state or how they "ended up on the floor" or in the principal's office.

Blaming others. This is another form of denial, which is frequently accompanied by quite animated body language and an attempt to convey compelling conviction that the incident was caused by someone else.

Avoidance of discussion. In this phase, students may avoid discussion, debriefing, or invitations to problem solve. Consistent with reluctance to participate in class discussions or activities, students may obviously avoid talking about the episode, the behavior, or events leading up to the incident. In this case, postpone debriefing to Phase 7: Recovery.

Responsiveness to directions—specifically manipulative or mechanical tasks. For students who have just had an out-of-control behavioral episode, this is not the time for direct discussions. It is an excellent time to give them specific directions—especially regarding an activity to do. Many adult supervisors have found that students will cooperate, almost willingly, to concrete directions at this stage. Students often appear distracted in the de-escalation phase, and a clear, concrete direction can provide a needed focus. If possible, direct students to engage in tasks that

For a period of time between that emotional peak and complete calm, you are poised between the two states.

are physically manipulative or fairly mechanical—something that they can do easily, helping them focus on something unrelated to the incident and helping in the process of regrouping.

Phase 7: Recovery—Behavior shows an eagerness for busy work and reluctance to interact.

In the final phase, the student slowly returns to his original state, becoming progressively less agitated and more able to resume normal classroom activities. This phase is apparent by specific behavioral characteristics.

Typical recovery behaviors

Eagerness for independent work or activity. Students in the recovery phase become engaged in or actively seek some kind of relatively independent "busy work."

Subdued behavior in group work or class discussion. Activities that involve interactions with other students or staff may be very difficult for these students at this time.

Defensiveness. Students may display guarded behavior that is cautious and almost measured.

IMPLEMENTATION STEPS
Step 1: Develop a Behavior Support Plan for emotionally escalated behavior.

You should have an array of strategies for addressing and managing escalating behavior at each phase of the cycle. These strategies will help you map and defuse the cycle of problem behavior. In the following section, prevention strategies are introduced for the calm and trigger phases, defusion interventions are described for the agitation and acceleration phases, emergency crisis procedures are presented for the peak phase, debriefing strategies are given for the de-escalation phase, and redirection and reintegration techniques are described for the final recovery phase.

Look for opportunities to intervene as early as possible in the cycle before the onset of more serious behavior. In the event that you cannot head off disruptive or dangerous behavior, be prepared to move quickly into a Code Red intervention (Intervention G or H).

You should have an array of strategies for addressing and managing escalating behavior at each phase of the cycle.

Figure I2: *Strategies for Escalated Behavior*

Phase	Strategies
Phase 1: Calm	Early-Stage Interventions
Phase 2: Triggers	Cueing and precorrection
Phase 3: Agitation	Anxiety reduction
Phase 4: Acceleration	Diffusion
Phase 5: Peak	School emergency procedures
Phase 6: De-escalation	Debriefing
Phase 7: Recovery	Focus on Early-Stage Interventions

Even the most experienced behavior management teachers may experience an occasional behavioral flare-up. Therefore, you need to be ready to address these situations with strategies at each phase in the cycle. Figure I2 provides a general framework for developing an escalating Behavior Support Plan, which will then allow you to develop a list of preferred interventions that correspond to each phase.

This intervention involves *assessment*, in which the student's specific behaviors will be identified for each of the seven phases in the cycle of emotional escalation. You can use the previous breakdown of typical behaviors in each phase of the cycle to help identify which behaviors the student of concern exhibits at each point. Then determine *strategies* for managing each of the phases. Figure I2 shows each phase and corresponding strategies you can use when a student is in that phase.

Identify strategies for each phase.

The seven-phase conceptual model allows you to develop a list of preferred interventions that correspond to each phase. Reproducible Form I1 provides a framework for developing an escalating Behavior Support Plan. It is divided into Assessment, in which the student's specific behaviors are identified for each of the seven phases in the cycle of emotional escalated behavior, and Strategies for managing each of the phases. You might wish

Reproducible Form I1: *Behavior Support Plan*

Behavior Support Plan

Name _____

Date _____

Homeroom Teacher _____

Grade _____

Staff Present _____

Assessment	Strategies
Calm	Calm
Triggers	Triggers
Agitation	Agitation
Acceleration	Acceleration
Peak	Peak
De-escalation	De-escalation
Recovery	Recovery

to have this form in front of you as you work through the next section of this chapter. In the left column, you can describe the types of behaviors or events you see at each phase. In the right column, you can make note of strategies that may be useful to implement.

Phase 1: Calm

Your overriding aim in designing prevention strategies for this phase is first and foremost to keep students productively engaged with instruction. This is admittedly not simple, but this single goal can arrest a slew of problem behaviors down the road. Instruction that captivates and productively engages students will often prevent or overcome the conditions that lead to escalation—students who are on task, challenged, successfully engaged, and achieving academically are not likely to embark on the cycle of emotional escalation. See "Pre-Intervention: Classroom Management Strategies" at the beginning of this book for ways to keep students productively engaged and in Phase 1: Calm.

Phase 2: Triggers (prevention)

Once you have identified triggers, you are in a position to act beforehand to prevent these triggers from setting off the problem behavior.

Your best hope of avoiding escalation is to anticipate and proactively address triggers before escalation begins to snowball. Accordingly, you should take a systematic approach to prevention and precorrection. Once you have identified triggers, you are in a position to act beforehand to prevent these triggers from setting off the problem behavior. The following prevention plan is designed to systematically assist the student with addressing the triggers.

A. Identify contexts that trigger escalation.

Context can be any task, situation, setting, antecedent, or trigger that precedes the problem behavior. Look for a causal link among contexts, triggers, and the problem behavior. Can you identify specific contexts that set off the problem behavior? If so, take each context individually and decide whether to begin by modifying the context itself or working with the student on how to cope with the problem context. If the trigger is unavoidable and all students are expected to deal with it, implement "Intervention M: Teaching Replacement Behavior." If the triggering context can be manipulated directly, first try modifying the context (see the third step of this section).

B. Reteach expectations.

With the student, go over your expectations for desired behavior in an escalating situation. Clearly specify any relevant classroom behavioral expectations or rules and be sure that the student understands them. Consider revisiting "Intervention C: Goal Setting" to devise a set of goals for the student to engage in more productive behavior.

C. Modify the context.

The purpose of this step is to increase the chance that expected behavior will occur while decreasing the likelihood that problem behavior will occur. Examples of modifying the context are assigning the student to sit in the part of the room farthest from classmates who may tease the student or modifying assigned work to reduce frustration and increase task success. Again, these modifications are implemented before the student has an opportunity to respond. When the context is modified, careful planning needs to occur to eventually have the student progress systematically toward the original or the common context for all students.

D. Cue and precorrect.

Provide cues and precorrections when entering any contexts that seem to be a problem for the student. This will prompt the student to make behavioral adjustments as necessary. In other words, give the student some advance notice. For example, if the student has trouble with writing, you might say, "In a few minutes we will be switching to writing. I know you can do a good job."

E. Provide positive feedback when the student exhibits the expected behavior.

If, for example, the student correctly follows transition steps, which normally have been difficult, acknowledge the student's success and grant extra time on the computer or some preferred activity. With this prevention plan, you are trying to assist the student to replace a problem behavior with a more appropriate expected behavior. However, the new behavior will be in competition with a previously established problem behavior. Strong reinforcement (highly desired feedback, fun activities, things that the student wants to earn) will help tip the balance in favor of the new replacement behaviors.

F. Monitor and review the plan.

First, check to see if the plan has been implemented as designed, with fidelity. If so, begin collecting data on the student's performance. Track occurrences of the problem behavior, the replacement behavior, or both to determine what effect the plan is having.

INTERVENTION

I

Phase 3: Agitation (anxiety reduction strategies)

Once an easily escalated student is exposed to a trigger, it is often only a matter of time until the student exhibits agitated behavior leading to escalated behavior. Some students simply do not have the necessary skills to manage these triggers, resolve conflicts, or solve problems. In this phase, you can use *anxiety reducing* or *defusing* strategies to help the student settle down and regain control instead of embarking on a cycle of escalated behavior. The following strategies are essentially accommodations that involve slight departures from normal procedures. Because these accommodations are supportive in nature, they must be implemented *before* the onset of serious escalation to be effective; otherwise, the problem behavior may be reinforced. In a nutshell, timing is essential.

Teacher empathy

Perhaps the most powerful supportive strategy at your disposal is *empathy*. To show empathy, you must convey to the student that you understand or recognize the student's agitation and communicate your concern. Empathy will also be a much more effective strategy for defusing agitation if you have already created a good relationship with the student. Work to interact positively with the student in moments where the student is not agitated; this will help the student realize in moments of agitation that your concern and empathy are sincere.

Help the student focus

Agitated students often have difficulty focusing on their work, staying on task, and concentrating. Make use of strategies that assist a student in getting started or resuming work. For example, you could assist the student in getting out needed materials for the next task, or you could offer your assistance with the first step in the assigned task. In this way, the student's attention is shifted from the triggers to the specific tasks of the lesson.

Provide space

An agitated student usually wants to be left alone. Providing the student with some level of space or isolation from the rest of the class will often meet this need, allowing the student time to settle down and regain focus.

Provide assurances

In general, a student who is agitated on a frequent basis does not have effective problem-solving skills or strategies to deal with the trigger events (situations) that touch off the escalation cycle. Consequently, the student may panic and exhibit worse behavior. You can help offset this by providing assurances, offering after-class assistance, or allowing the student more time.

The goal is to reduce a sense of pressure the student may feel by helping the student realize that she has plenty of time to think about possible choices and that you are available to help.

Permit preferred activities

A student exhibiting agitation is often distracted and will find it difficult to concentrate on the tasks in the lesson. One way of helping a student refocus is to permit the student to engage in a preferred activity for a short amount of time. This is likely to help the student disengage from what is bothering her and become connected with the classroom activity without a sense of pressure. Be sure to set some parameters when this strategy is used; otherwise, the student may not leave the preferred activity or other students may want to participate.

Teacher proximity

Agitated students often feel insecure about their abilities, and a teacher standing near the student may provide reassurance. As with empathy, this strategy is more effective if you have already established a good relationship with the student.

Independent activities

In addition to serving several instructional opportunities, independent work provides a simple opportunity to help an agitated student become settled and focused. In addition, independent work provides the student with an opportunity to be left alone, allowing the student time to cool off before any other interactions further escalate the situation.

Passive strategies

Following high-stimulus events such as recess, gym class, or assemblies, the whole class may be overly excited, leaving some students in a state of agitation. Consider using passive strategies following these transitions for the whole class, such as watching a video, quiet reading, or reading out loud to the class. These activities require some attention from students but not much effort in terms of response, which can be useful in calming down both excited and agitated students.

Movement activities

Movement is a tool you can use to help a student who is agitated. Students who are agitated generally tend to move anyway, so when you direct them to do something that involves movement, such as distributing some materials, this movement helps them become more focused and calm.

Student self-management

Self-management is the long-term goal of any behavioral intervention program. Particularly with older students, it is important to involve students actively in devising a plan to control their own agitation. Students can often come up with (or may already have) their own strategies to reduce agitation. Actively soliciting and encouraging their participation also increases buy-in and personal commitment to creating positive results. Morevoer, these students are more likely to generalize self-chosen strategies to other settings.

Phase 4: Acceleration (defusion approaches)

Effective defusion approaches are critically important during this phase in the cycle of acting-out behavior. If behaviors are not managed successfully in this phase, the student is highly likely to escalate further and exhibit severe problem behavior. In effect, this is the last opportunity to defuse the situation prior to the onset of severe behavior. Although at first glance there may appear to be many complex steps, it can be summarized as: avoid prompting escalation, maintain calmness and detachment, approach the student in a nonthreatening manner, and use nonconfrontational limit-setting procedures. How to implement each of those suggestions is described below.

A. Avoid prompting escalation.

If a student has reached this phase in the cycle of escalation, his behavior has been characterized as *engaging*. In a sense the student is inviting you to engage in interactions that will lead to escalation. This student may challenge you, argue with you, and in many other ways try to draw you in and get you to respond. Should you "take the bait," you run a risk of reinforcing the behavior or inadvertently escalating the situation. A teacher response that results in more serious behavior from the student is called an *escalating prompt*. The root problem is that a student who is trying to bait the teacher may make comments or engage in actions that will be taken personally by staff. Consequently, staff may react, become agitated, and resort to "in-your-face" kinds of behavior, such as finger pointing, that are highly likely to escalate the student. To lessen the chance of further escalation, adults interacting with these students need to be very aware of the kinds of responses that are likely to worsen the situation and to deliberately avoid making them. Responses that may further escalate the situation include:

- engaging in agitated behavior, such as shouting or rapid speech
- cornering the student

> *This student may challenge you, argue with you, and in many other ways try to draw you in and get you to respond.*

- engaging in power struggles ("In my classroom you will...")

- encroaching on the student's space (leaning forward, exaggerating gestures, pointing directly into the student's face)

- touching, poking, or grabbing the student

- responding very quickly, half-cocked, or flippantly

- using statements that belittle, ridicule, or insult a student, such as "This is a high school, not a preschool." If such comments are made within earshot of the rest of the class, you may risk triggering escalation in other students as well

- engaging in defensiveness and arguing

- using body language such as rigid posture or clenched hands that communicates anger, frustration, or "losing your cool"

- implementing inconsistent consequences out of anger or frustration

B. Maintain calmness, respect, and detachment.

It is crucial that you interact with calmness, respect, and detachment when addressing students in this acceleration phase. This will greatly lessen the chance of escalation.

Calmness can be achieved by remembering that the student is "playing a game"—trying to engage you. The most powerful response you can make is to make no immediate response. Simply pause. Such a pause tells the student that her behavior is not getting to you personally. This also gives you a moment to think through an appropriate response to the behavior, greatly reducing the likelihood you will react emotionally and perpetuate the cycle. There is less chance of escalating the student if you can pause slightly and then inform the student in a calm, measured, and serious tone that the behavior is unacceptable and that some action will be taken. Moreover, you are serving as a good role model to this student and the class about how to respond in the face of problem behavior.

Respect for the student's dignity and rights must be a critical consideration when you respond to problem behavior. Any indication of disrespect will likely escalate the student to serious acting-out behavior. A useful guideline for you to use is to focus on the student's behavior instead of on the student himself. Similarly, in addressing a problem, you can communicate respect by beginning your statement with the student's name. Another respectful strategy is to speak to the student privately by taking the student aside. By emphasizing the privacy of the conversation, you are also lessening the chance of the student trying to "save face" in the presence of peers.

Detachment is a disposition used to communicate to the student that he is ultimately responsible for his behavior. In effect, the choice of how the interaction will proceed belongs to the student. While you may care about the student, it is very important not to communicate any degree of anxiety or any sense of coaxing and pleading for the student to behave appropriately. In this context, it is best to communicate in as matter-of-fact a manner as possible and to make it very clear to the student that the inappropriate engaging behavior needs to cease or there will be consequences. The choice lies with the student.

C. Approach the student in a nonthreatening manner.

Because there is a high probability that the student's behavior will escalate in this phase, your manner should be controlled, measured, and nonthreatening. There are several things to remember when approaching a student:

- **Move slowly and deliberately toward the problem situation.** Avoid giving signs of panic or anxiety. If possible, engage in some normal, on-task interactions with other students on the way to the target situation.

- **Speak privately.** When possible, take the student aside or ask the student to come to your desk. Talk quietly so as not to be overheard by other students.

- **Speak calmly and respectfully.** Use the student's name and speak in a neutral and businesslike voice. Avoid harsh, angry tones. Be as matter-of-fact as possible. Do not threaten or cajole.

- **Minimize body language.** Be as undemonstrative as possible. Avoid pointing or staring at the student.

- **Keep a reasonable distance.** Though proximity is important, do not get too close or invade the student's space. Don't crowd or "get in the student's face." It is also important to remember that a squared-off stance, directly facing the student, immediately signals that you are approaching the student in a confrontational manner. Try to speak to the student at an angle.

- **Match the student's eye-level position, if possible.** Some students react negatively to anyone towering over them. If the student is sitting, sit or squat beside her. If the student is standing, stand as well, perhaps taking a step back to show respect for the student's space. By meeting a student at her level, you are showing respect and you are less likely to risk escalation.

- **Be brief.** Keep the interaction brief and simple. Long-winded pronouncements or nagging will prompt negative reactions from some students.

- **Stay with the agenda.** Stay focused on your primary concern. Do not get sidetracked. Deal with lesser problems later.

- **Avoid power struggles.** Do not be drawn into "I won't" or "you will" types of engagement.

- **Withdraw if the situation begins to escalate toward Phase 5 peak behavior.** Immediately terminate the discussion—simply withdraw from the student and direct your attention to the other students. At the same time, keep a close eye on the troubled student. This simple act of withdrawing may stave off further escalation. However, if the student does escalate further, entering Phase 5 Peak behaviors, follow your school's emergency procedures for severely disruptive or physically dangerous behavior.

- **Acknowledge cooperation.** Whenever a student cooperates and disengages from an escalating situation, be sure to acknowledge this decision. At a later time or follow-up meeting, offer specific praise and congratulate the student, and perhaps mention the positive behavior to the student's parents as well.

The bottom line: Use common sense and approach the problem in a calm, unhurried, respectful, and preplanned manner. Remember that the student's behavior in this phase is intended to engage you. The less you allow yourself to be drawn in, the more effective you can be in defusing the situation.

D. Use nonconfrontational limit-setting procedures.
At the acceleration phase, you need to be prepared with strategies that are effective in arresting escalating behavior quickly and reliably to facilitate resumption of class activity as seamlessly as possible. The key lies in the delivery of your directions. You need to communicate clearly and unambiguously that the problem behavior needs to cease and that you are prepared to follow through with consequences, without being construed as confrontational or threatening. (See "Intervention P: Defining Limits and Establishing Consequences.") Furthermore, by demonstrating respect for the student and the student's personal view of the situation, you can negate some of the additional triggers that lead to escalation.

This strategy has three steps:

1. **Establish initial set-up.** The two critical steps in setting up the procedures are (a) rehearse the steps with the class and (b) establish a short list of negative consequences.

2. **Present the information as a decision.** It is helpful to use the following formula in the "heat of the battle":

   (a) Present the *expected behavior* and the *negative consequence* as a decision for the student to make.

   (b) Allow some time for the student to decide (usually less than a minute).

   (c) Withdraw from the student, and attend to other students or engage in some other task.

3. **Follow through.** The next steps are dependent on whether the student decides to follow the expected behavior or to maintain the problem behavior. Three common results are possible:

   (a) *Student exhibits expected behavior.* If the student decides to exhibit the expected behavior, acknowledge the choice *briefly* and continue with the lesson or activity. It is important to acknowledge the student's choice briefly and move to the other students. The student may still be somewhat agitated and aggravated by a lengthy praise statement.

   (b) *Student maintains problem behavior.* If the student does not choose the expected behavior— that is, he decides to maintain the current problem behavior—you will deliver the negative consequence.

   (c) *Student maintains the problem behavior and then switches to the expected behavior.* Once students become familiar with the teacher's follow-through procedure, it is common for them to try a delayed manipulation tactic. They will maintain the problem behavior, and after you tell them that they have chosen the negative consequence, they will then switch and follow the expected behavior. In these cases, you really need to *follow through* with the negative consequence to establish limits. It might be reasonable to have the student miss part of recess on the basis that the student did eventually begin work. Conduct a debriefing session after the student has been on task for some time and be sure to clarify that once the student makes his choice, you will act upon it. Be sure to clarify with the student in the preteaching session that the moment for the decision will be when the teacher returns. If there is some doubt whether the student understands the decision process, give the student the benefit of the doubt and reteach the procedures.

Phase 5: Peak (school emergency procedures)

Behavior in the peak phase of escalation often causes severe disruption and can result in physical harm to the involved student, the intervening adult, or others. Your primary objective must be to ensure the safety of all students and staff. Your secondary goal is to allow school and classroom activities to continue and to minimize damage to school property. Refer to "Intervention G: Managing Physically Dangerous Behavior" and "Intervention H: Managing Severely Disruptive Behavior" for information on when and how to invoke school emergency procedures.

Phase 6: De-Escalation (debriefing)

Though it is essential to be prepared with a variety of precorrection and defusion strategies to prevent the cycle of escalation, you should also have strategies to address de-escalation and recovery phases following a serious incident. These strategies should be designed to help the student process the serious incident with the intent of preventing future occurrences. In addition, the goal is to help the student resume regular classroom participation. In general, it is better for the teacher to conduct the debriefing session. The reason is that the incident may more than likely have occurred in the classroom. In this way the teacher is empowered by following through. For the students who have recurring problems, it may be better for the counselor or administrator to conduct the debriefing so that more time can be given to the process and the student may be more open to the process because of the disengagement from the classroom and classroom staff.

Be absolutely certain that the student has had enough time to calm down to prevent the risk of triggering more Peak behavior. Refer to the common signs of de-escalating behavior in Step 1, Phase 6 to determine whether the student has moved into De-escalation. This could be as soon as 10 minutes after an incident or as long as 90 minutes. It is also helpful to give a small direction such as "Would you sit over here, please?" or "Pass me that book, please." If the student cooperates with the direction, then follow though with the debriefing. If the student does not cooperate, that is clear information that the student is not ready to proceed and needs more time. A common

Your primary objective must be to ensure the safety of all students and staff.

Intervention I:
Managing the Cycle of Emotional Escalation

Behavior Improvement Form

Name _____ Grade/Class _____ Teacher _____ Period/Time _____

1. What did you do? _____

   _____

   _____

   _____

   _____

   _____

2. Why did you do it? _____

   _____

   _____

   _____

   _____

   _____

3. What else could you have done? _____

   _____

   _____

   _____

   _____

   _____

debriefing process consists of asking the student the following three questions (also on Reproducible Form I2: Behavior Improvement Form).

1. **What did you do?**
   Have the student label and describe all behaviors that occurred during the cycle of escalation, especially considering Acceleration and Peak behaviors (threw a chair, yelled at the teacher, threatened other students, etc.).

2. **Why did you do it?**
   Encourage the student to think about why he or she behaved in that way and identify the reasons or purposes behind it.

3. **What else could you have done?**
   Prompt the student to think of other behaviors that might meet the student's needs but would be more acceptable in a classroom.

Phase 7: Recovery (resumption of class activities)

Just because the student has regained composure and may have been cooperating in the previous phase, De-Escalation, doesn't mean that the student will maintain this cooperation when he's back in the classroom. The student now enters the setting where the problems began, and, in many cases, the initial triggers may still be present. This student will need carefully planned reintegration strategies to re-enter the classroom successfully. The following transition strategies build on the approaches in the previous phase to support the student's composure, focus, and cooperation:

- Provide a strong focus on normal routines.

- Provide a re-entry task that is simple for the student to complete successfully and that does not require immediate engagement with others. This will allow the student to gather himself and begin acting productively. Reinforce the student as soon as he is engaged with the re-entry task, and then transition the student to normal class activities.

- Do not negotiate with the student about consequences for the serious behavior.

- Strongly acknowledge occurrences of problem-solving behaviors.

- Communicate support and the expectation that the student can succeed with help.

- Establish a specific Behavior Support Plan, if necessary.

At this stage, you should have already implemented one or more Early-Stage Interventions. If you have, it may be worth re-analyzing the situation to determine whether a modified implementation of strategies from any of these interventions would be useful.

Resources

Additional information on these procedures can be found in the following resources developed by Geoff Colvin:

Colvin, G. (2004). *Managing the cycle of acting-out behavior in the classroom.* Eugene, OR: Behavior Associates.

Colvin, G. (2005). *Managing non-compliance: Effective strategies for K-12 teachers.* (Video). Eugene, OR: Iris Media.

Colvin, G. (2001). *Managing threats: A school-wide action plan.* (Video). Eugene, OR: Iris Media.

Colvin, G. (1999). *Defusing anger and aggression: Safe strategies for secondary school educators.* (Video). Eugene, OR: Iris Media.

These resources are available from Pacific Northwest Publishing Company.

The student's behavior plan should encompass all settings where problems occur and involve active participation by the supervisory staff in each of the target settings.

Step 2: Extend the Behavior Support Plan to multiple school settings.

A. Develop an expanded Behavior Support Plan.

Sometimes a student may exhibit serious problem behavior in several school settings, not just in the classroom. If escalating behavior extends to recess, the hallways, or the cafeteria, designing a classroom plan and hoping it will transfer to the other settings isn't likely to work. A systemic or schoolwide approach should be taken. In this case, the student's behavior plan should encompass all settings where problems occur and involve active participation by the supervisory staff in each of the target settings.

The details of an expanded Behavior Support Plan are essentially the same as for a plan designed for the classroom, the main difference being that planning needs to involve a group of staff members to better address occurrences of escalating behavior in multiple settings. Involving additional staff requires careful coordination and clearly defined roles:

INTERVENTION

1

1. Include a behavior support team, ideally comprising at least one classroom teacher, an administrator, specialist, and an area supervisor (such as the cafeteria or playground).

2. Designate a coordinator who is responsible for ensuring that everyone knows his or her role in the plan, all necessary materials are ready for use as needed, all necessary paperwork is completed, and meetings—especially review meetings—are scheduled. This coordinator could be the teacher, but will, in all probability, be the counselor, administrator, or behavior specialist.

3. Adapt the classroom Behavior Support Plan as needed for targeted settings.

4. Cueing and precorrection—reminders or rehearsal—must be integral parts of any plan, delivered just prior to times the student is entering targeted settings.

5. Develop a data collection plan to track the frequency of targeted incidents in each setting.

6. Familiarize all staff members who will interact with the student in targeted settings about the procedures of the Behavior Support Plan.

7. Have an administrator or specialist monitor target settings periodically to ensure that the plan is being carried out with fidelity.

8. Develop a communication system so members of the Behavior Support Plan team are apprised of the student's progress. For example, the classroom teacher should be informed of the student's performance in targeted settings outside the classroom.

9. Revise, maintain, or phase out the plan as data dictates.

Note: For an expanded support plan to be effective, every school should have a well-defined schoolwide discipline plan. This schoolwide plan will substantially reduce the number of students who engage in problem behavior and enable individual Behavior Support Plans to be more effectively implemented and maintained.

INTERVENTION

I

B. Develop a schoolwide discipline plan.

Following are the main general components involved in developing a positive schoolwide discipline plan:

1. Establish a school leadership team representative of the faculty.

2. Identify Guidelines for Success, the schoolwide behavior expectations for the school community to display in all school settings, such as, "Be responsible, be respectful, and be safe."

3. Specify expectations for student behaviors in each school setting.

4. Systematically teach these behaviors to students and develop reminder procedures. This is a crucial step in the process. If the student does not routinely demonstrate pro-social behaviors, assume the student doesn't have those skills and teach them.

5. Develop a schoolwide recognition plan for students who regularly act according to the school's expectations.

6. Implement an office referral system for managing serious problem behavior.

7. Develop a data management system to track information about disciplinary referrals and suspensions and use it for decision making.

8. Design procedures to ensure the plan is sustained over time.

Resources

A fuller description of these and similar procedures can be found in the following resources, which are available from Pacific Northwest Publishing Company:

Colvin, G. (2007). *7 Steps for developing a proactive schoolwide discipline plan: A guide for principals and leadership teams.* Thousand Oaks, CA: Corwin Press.

Sprick, R., Sprick, M., & Garrison, M. (1992). *Foundations: Developing school-wide discipline policies.* Eugene, OR: Pacific Northwest Publishing.

Sprick, R, Wise, B., Marcum, K., Haykim, M., & Howard, L. (2005). *Administrator's desk reference of behavioral management* (Vols. I–III). Eugene, OR: Pacific Northwest Publishing.

CONCLUSION

Serious emotionally escalated behavior can be described by a conceptual model composed of seven phases—each of which is characterized by specific, identifiable behaviors. Classifying behavior in this way can help educators understand the behavioral processes and emotional subtexts that drive escalating teacher-student or student-student interactions. By identifying the early behaviors in the chain, you can redirect the student toward appropriate behavior and preempt the cycle of acting out. Phases 1 through 4 emphasize effective teaching and proactive management practices. In the remaining phases, the emphasis is on safety, crisis management, and follow-up.

Knowing which problematic student behaviors to expect at each stage of a potentially explosive situation and being prepared with an array of strategies for each phase in the cycle can help you act immediately and decisively in a way that cools building acrimony rather than fanning the flames.

REFERENCES

Colvin, G. (1999). *Defusing anger and aggression: Safe strategies for secondary school educators* [Video]. Eugene, OR: Iris Media.

Colvin, G. (2001). *Managing threats: A school-wide action plan* [Video]. Eugene, OR: Iris Media.

Colvin, G. (2004). *Managing the cycle of acting-out behavior in the classroom*. Eugene, OR: Behavior Associates.

Colvin, G. (2005). *Managing non-compliance: Effective strategies for K-12 teachers* [Video]. Eugene, OR: Iris Media.

Colvin, G. (2007). *7 steps for developing a proactive schoolwide discipline plan: A guide for principals and leadership teams*. Thousand Oaks, CA: Corwin Press.

Sprick, R., Sprick, M., & Garrison, M. (2002). *Foundations: Developing school-wide discipline policies*. Eugene, OR: Pacific Northwest Publishing.

Sprick, R., Wise, B., Marcum, K., Haykim, M., & Howard, L. (2005). *Administrator's desk reference of behavioral management* (Vols. 1– 3). Eugene, OR: Pacific Northwest Publishing.

Reproducible Materials

The following reproducible materials may be used in conjunction with "Intervention I: Managing the Cycle of Emotional Escalation." Copies are provided here and on the CD. Permission is given for individual classroom teachers to reproduce any forms labeled "Reproducible" for classroom use. Reproduction of these materials for an entire school system is prohibited without express permission of the publisher.

INTERVENTION I

MANAGING THE CYCLE OF
EMOTIONAL ESCALATION

Step-by-Step Summary

Following is a summary of the steps involved in Intervention I. It is important to use professional judgment, adjusting procedures to meet the needs of the situation and the individual. See the chapter "Intervention I: Managing the Cycle of Emotional Escalation" for a detailed description of this intervention.

STEP I   Develop a Behavior Support Plan for emotionally escalated behavior.

A. Identify strategies for each phase.

- Phase 1: Calm

- Phase 2: Triggers (Prevention)
    A. Identify contexts that trigger escalation.
    B. Reteach expectations.
    C. Modify the context.
    D. Cue and precorrect.
    E. Provide positive feedback when the student exhibits the expected behavior.
    F. Monitor and review the plan.

- Phase 3: Agitation (Anxiety Reduction Strategies)
    - Teacher empathy
    - Help the student focus
    - Provide space
    - Provide assurances
    - Permit preferred activities
    - Teacher proximity
    - Independent activities
    - Passive strategies
    - Movement activities
    - Student self-management

- Phase 4: Acceleration (Defusion Approaches)
    A. Avoid prompting escalation.
    B. Maintain calmness, respect, and detachment.
    C. Approach the student in a nonthreatening manner.
    D. Use nonconfrontational limit-setting procedures.

INTERVENTION I

- Phase 5: Peak (School Emergency Procedures)
- Phase 6: De-Escalation (Debriefing)
- Phase 7: Recovery (Resumption of Class Activities)

STEP 2 Extend the behavior support plan to multiple school settings.

A. Develop an expanded behavior support plan.

B. Develop a schoolwide discipline plan.

Cueing and Precorrecting

The student seems to be unaware of when he is engaged in inappropriate behavior

PURPOSE

CUEING AND PRECORRECTING is used to help students control impulsive, excessive, habitual, or off-task behavior.

THIS INTERVENTION IS APPROPRIATE FOR:

Impulsive behaviors
- anger
- outbursts

Excessive behaviors
- bragging
- complaining
- put-downs
- whining

Habitual behaviors
- swearing
- nose picking
- masturbating
- arguing
- noncompliance

Off-task behaviors
- lack of attention to task
- misdirected attention

Cueing and Precorrecting are relatively similar in that each method is used to elicit a particular response in a particular situation, but they differ in their timing. *Cueing* is used to interrupt an inappropriate behavior that is already taking place. Cues typically take the place of reprimands or corrections that would be more verbose or lengthy and that the teacher would be obliged to issue on repeated occasions. *Precorrecting*, on the other hand, is an attempt to anticipate and prevent an inappropriate social or academic behavior by "correcting" the behavior *before* it occurs.

Cueing is used to interrupt an inappropriate behavior that is already taking place.

The goal with precorrection is that the student will "catch on" and begin engaging in appropriate or responsible behavior simply because of the verbal reminder. This will naturally produce more positive feedback and fewer negative interactions. For example, suppose you have a student who tends to get upset when you hand back work that needs to be corrected. If you have prediscussed with the student that it's OK to make mistakes and that the student can stay calm, fix the mistakes, and take notes about questions she wants to ask later, then you can precorrect by saying something to the effect of, "Here you go, Jeannine. You did a pretty good job on this, but a couple of items need to be corrected. Remember how we talked about how to handle that responsibly? Do you want to take a look at these now, or do you want me to come back in a couple of minutes?"

This example melds a precorrection ("Remember how . . .") with a viable choice for the student, as discussed in "Intervention F: STOIC Analysis and Intervention." By giving the student a "heads up" in a situation that tends to be problematic, you are allowing her a chance to handle the matter consciously and maturely without falling back into an automatic reaction or habitual negative response. By giving the student a viable choice—to look at the returned work now or in a few minutes—you are giving her some control over her school experience, which may prompt her to act in a more responsible way.

If you are teaching certain social skills to the class, you can introduce a physical gesture as a precorrection or cue. Thus, if you want to teach your class the skill of "not interrupting," you might devise and teach a nonconfrontational gesture such as a gentle stop sign with your hand. You could then cue members of the class when they interrupt others. The same holds true with individual students. If one student in particular tends to interrupt you when you're talking to other members of the class, you could first teach the hand signal and then precorrect that student by raising your hand in a nonaggressive way to signal that you see him but you're not ready to talk with him just yet, prompting him to wait rather than interrupt and induce a more time-intensive correction.

The signal needn't be physical, and it doesn't have to be overly obscure or clandestine. For a student who engages in habitual nose picking, you might signal the student by quietly saying the student's name and giving a subtle "no" shake of the head. If a student tends to blurt out obscenities impulsively, you might signal the student by discreetly modeling an alternative expression. If a student has problems with excessive behavior such as bragging or put-downs, you might cue the student by putting your finger to your lips. Cueing and Precorrecting is especially effective with students who already have the ability to behave appropriately, but tend to act first and think later. The purpose of the signal is to help these students become aware of their own behaviors.

For most students, simply teaching the appropriate response to a cue will be enough to change the behavior in time. If, however, an ingrained pattern of behavior appears resistant to simple cues or precorrections, this intervention may be effective when implemented with "Intervention M: Teaching Replacement Behavior."

RATIONALE

Cueing and Precorrecting is a fairly straightforward intervention that in a sense helps students help themselves—that is, it prompts students to change patterns of behavior they understand are undesirable, destructive, or self-defeating. Impulsive or habitual behaviors often go unnoticed by children who are unaware of their own propensities. All too often, students get stuck using behaviors that interfere with peer relationships or success in school. Students who brag excessively, argue, complain, or put others down may be unaware of the frequency or scope of their behavior, although they are probably aware of the adverse effects of such behavior. Cueing helps these students stimulate self-awareness, resulting in greater levels of self-management.

Precorrecting, on the other hand, is an attempt to anticipate and prevent an inappropriate social or academic behavior by "correcting" the behavior before it occurs.

INTERVENTION

J

Lance is a sixth-grade student from an upper–middle class neighborhood. Lance has many problems that make him stand apart from his peers. He is overweight, and he engages in behavior that makes him appear "weird." During class, he makes faces and swings his arms wildly around. Sometimes he makes goofy noises. Though Lance wants more than anything else to be accepted, numerous little behaviors separate him from his peers. Lance's teacher has discussed the weird behavior with him. Even though Lance wants to be "more like the other kids," he doesn't seem to be able to help himself. A thorough medical and neurological exam has ruled out physiological problems that might cause Lance to act impulsively. His physician has suggested school-based behavioral interventions. Lance's teacher decides Cueing and Precorrecting may help Lance learn to manage his inappropriate behavior.

Cueing and Precorrecting can help students who are unable to change because they fail to recognize when they are engaging in inappropriate behavior. Awareness is a necessary first step in learning to be responsible for behavior.

Note: Cueing and Precorrecting should be viewed as a temporary measure until the student can learn to monitor his own behavior.

Before implementing Cueing and Precorrecting

Before this intervention can be successfully implemented, be sure that you have discussed the problem and general goals for improvement with the student. Gather any relevant background information that may help in designing and implementing the intervention. In addition, contact the student's parents or guardian to discuss the problem and keep them informed of all aspects of the intervention plan.

IMPLEMENTATION STEPS
Step 1: Develop a plan.

A. Review the problem and overall goals for the student.

Defining the nature and scope of the problem provides critical information for developing a successful intervention.

Kashala, a fourth-grade student, frequently brags and puts others down. If Kashala's family buys a new car or the latest video game, she seems compelled to tell everyone about the new purchase and even the price. When Kashala does well in a recess game, she loudly announces, "I creamed everyone in four square today. I served the whole time." Kashala's comments are often hurtful and sarcastic. In class, she is often heard to say things like the following:

- "Duh. Isn't that obvious!"
- "You don't need to tell me that! I already knew."
- "Grow up, will you?"
- "You couldn't have planned anything more stupid."

Kashala's comments are clearly disruptive, irritating, and hurtful to others. Staff members indicate that Kashala is an excellent student, but she is difficult to be around.

Identify when the student is likely to have problems. This will help you recognize when the student may need a reminder about behavior:

- Does the student have more difficulty on certain days or at certain times in the day?
- Are particular activities more difficult than others?
- Does the student have greater difficulties with certain people?
- Describe specific examples of the student's behavior.

If certain situations are likely to trigger inappropriate behavior, the teacher can give the student a signal prior to the difficult time. This precorrection gives the student an opportunity to think before acting.

Mr. Caldwell: (Teacher)	I think that Kashala's sarcasm seems to be worse on Mondays. I know her parents have joint custody and that Kashala stays with her father and his new family on the weekends. She also seems to be more boastful—almost compulsively. If someone else gets attention, she has to engage in one-upmanship.
Mrs. Larson: (Interventionist)	Let's identify specific situations and the types of comments Kashala has made.

INTERVENTION

J

Notes on Kashala's comments:

- A classmate is complimented on her work.
  Kashala says, "That's simple stuff."

- A classmate tells about his new watch.
  Kashala says, "My watch does more, and it cost more."

- The teacher introduces a new activity.
  Kashala rolls her eyes and says, "Whoop-de-do."

Kashala's mother and teacher have discussed the problems and agree that the put-downs and bragging are a problem. Kashala interacts the same way at home, frequently criticizing both her mother and grandmother.

Kashala's mother and teacher collaboratively determine that they would like to help Kashala make friends and get along with others. Because Kashala's comments tend to be hurtful, they decide that their initial goal will be to help her be thoughtful of others' feelings.

With a pervasive behavior such as pencil tapping or humming that happens randomly and unpredictably, cueing may be necessary because you will have no way of knowing when to precorrect.

B. Decide whether cueing, precorrecting, or both will be used.

Determine whether you will use cueing, precorrecting, or both. Remember that a cue is used to get problematic behavior to stop, and a precorrection is provided in advance of the behavior happening. In many cases, you may elect to use both. Any time you can precorrect and prevent a behavior, cueing is rendered unnecessary, so in most situations precorrecting is best to try first. Because precorrection is a prompt for responsible behavior, it proactively sets the stage for positive feedback rather than reactively waiting and risking a potentially unnecessary or negative interaction. However, with a pervasive behavior such as pencil tapping or humming that happens randomly and unpredictably, cueing may be necessary because you will have no way of knowing when to precorrect.

Music students are often told to practice a passage so slowly that they don't make any mistakes. The short-term result is that they must play the same passage correctly, over and over, very slowly, which may seem less rewarding than playing the passage faster with more mistakes. However, the long-term result is that they can eventually play the passage correctly much more accurately and quickly than they would if they'd practiced only up to speed. It's far easier to learn to do something the right way than to unlearn something you've been doing wrong. As a teaching corollary, it's far easier to build a good habit in a student than to break an ingrained bad habit. That's the power of precorrection.

Note: The same principle is at work in the first two letters of the STOIC mnemonic. You teach and reteach your expectations and structure everything about your classroom for student success, knowing the effort will pay dividends later. An ounce of prevention is worth a pound of cure.

C. Identify possible signals that might be used to cue the student to avoid or interrupt the inappropriate behavior.

The choice of a specific signal should be worked out with the student. In advance of meeting with the student, develop a list of possible signals for the student to choose from. The signal should be reasonably private and unobtrusive, such as one of the following:

- Say the student's name quietly.
- Hold up the palm of your hand like a stop signal.
- Hold a finger to your lips.
- Touch your earlobe.
- Give a quick verbal cue such as "Think."
- Use a specific phrase: "James, I am going to give you a direction."

D. Identify what adults will do when the student either responds appropriately or fails to respond to a signal.

Identify the procedures or techniques that will be used to encourage the student when he successfully responds to the signal and indicate how he will be corrected if he neglects or is unable to respond to the signal. Ask the following questions:

- If the student successfully changes the behavior, how will the teacher let him know he is doing a great job?
- If the student ignores the signal, how will the teacher respond?

The interventionist and teacher determine that when Kashala successfully responds to the signal, the teacher will use eye contact and a nod to communicate privately to Kashala that she is being successful. The signal between the teacher and Kashala will remain confidential. Later, in private discussions, the teacher will acknowledge Kashala's success.

If Kashala does not respond to the signal occasionally or if she is heard making inappropriate comments, Kashala's teacher will provide a gentle verbal reprimand to correct the behavior. "Kashala, you need to be a better listener and think about your comments. Every idea deserves respect." To avoid embarrassing her, Mr. Caldwell will not mention Kashala's failure to respond to the signal.

For now, there will be no consequence if Kashala fails to respond to the signal. The teacher is confident that Kashala will cooperate.

E. Identify other settings to include in the plan and adults who will need training.

Habitual behaviors usually occur across settings. Cueing and Precorrecting will be more effective if other adults also use the signal in different locations.

Mr. Caldwell: (Teacher)	Since Kashala has the same problems at home, perhaps her mom could implement the same system.
Mrs. Larson: (Interventionist)	The consistency would help her break the habit faster. We should also think about including the playground aides.
Mr. Caldwell:	That's no problem. I'm on recess duty this week, so it would be easy for me to talk with them and show them how to use the signal.

F. Decide whether the student needs to be taught a replacement behavior.

If the behavior you want to cue or precorrect is not within the student's current range of abilities, you need to teach a replacement behavior, as discussed in "Intervention M: Teaching Replacement Behavior." Precorrecting a student to exhibit a certain behavior will not be effective if the preferred behavior isn't in the student's current repertoire. Likewise, cueing the student to cease a behavior won't work if the student can't easily summon an alternative behavior. Try to gauge the student's behavioral skill set.

If you frequently see the student exhibiting an acceptable or appropriate behavior that could replace the undesirable behavior, teaching another replacement behavior may not be necessary. You may need to help the student identify when to use the positive behavior instead of the negative one. You could start by praising the student for the many times you've witnessed him producing the positive behavior and then suggest that by unobtrusively cueing him at certain times, you may be able to help him switch to the more appropriate behavior. If you almost never see an appropriate behavior exhibited, pair this intervention with Intervention M.

G. Identify ways to determine whether the intervention is helping the student reach the goal.

If you have already tried "Intervention D: Data Collection and Debriefing" or other interventions, you may have already accumulated data on the problem. What you hope to see as you incorporate precorrecting or cueing is some improvement in the data you are collecting. If you aren't keeping a record of the student's progress, you need to collect some form of data to help you determine the usefulness of this (and any other) intervention. A logical type of data to collect for this intervention would be a signaling frequency count—both for cueing and precorrecting. Simply make a mark every time you have to use a signal, and then add a plus (+) or minus (–) to indicate the student's response to the signal. By keeping a frequency count with plus and minus signs, you can track how often you signal, whether you are signaling less as time goes on, and what percentage of time the student responds appropriately to your signal.

Here are some alternative choices for data collection:

- a student self-monitoring system
- a tally of appropriate and inappropriate behavior kept by the teacher
- an anecdotal log
- periodic observations
- a daily rating system, such as a 1–5 scale

A logical type of data to collect for this intervention would be a signaling frequency count

Mrs. Larson:	Because Kashala is very bright, I think she will learn rapidly—especially with everyone working together. However, her negative comments are habits. We will probably see immediate changes, but she will lapse into her old patterns if we don't keep it up. To help keep every-

	one focused, I'd like to check in with you at least every two weeks, and I'll also keep in touch with Kashala's mother.
Mr. Caldwell: (Teacher)	That's great. We get so busy with everything else, I can see how I might lose focus if Kashala's behavior improves right away.
Mrs. Larson:	We also need a procedure to determine whether Kashala's negative comments are on a downward trend.
Mr. Caldwell:	It will need to be very easy. I sometimes feel like I don't know whether I'm coming or going.
Mrs. Larson:	One possibility would be for me to schedule an observation now and then another in two weeks. During the observation, I would tally Kashala's appropriate and inappropriate comments. Then in two weeks, I can do the same thing at about the same time of day. A second option would be for you to carry a small card and pencil in your pocket. Any time you hear Kashala making inappropriate comments, you would make a quick mark on the card. That way we would have a daily record.
Mr. Caldwell:	To be honest, I don't think I can keep that up. If you can work it out, let's have you observe.
Mrs. Larson:	Sounds good. Since Mondays are Kashala's toughest days, let's schedule a time for next Monday. I would like to get initial data before we begin the intervention. When is a good time for me to come in?

H. Determine who will meet with the student to discuss and finalize the plan.

The discussion should include the primary staff person who will cue the student (more than likely this will be the classroom teacher), parents or guardians, if they wish to participate, and whoever will debrief with the student (see Step 2E). Although it may be helpful to include the other adults who will be involved, the student should not feel overwhelmed during this initial discussion.

Kashala's teacher and the interventionist decide that Kashala should meet with Mr. Caldwell and her mother for the initial discussion.

Schedule the discussion at a time when you, the student, and the student's parents are relaxed. Tell the student in private before the time of the meeting what the goal will be and who will be involved. By prearranging the meeting with the student and parents, you can communicate that the discussion is not a punishment for past behavior but an important opportunity to map out a plan for the future.

If it is difficult to find a time for a private discussion with the student, the interventionist may help by supervising the class while the teacher and student meet.

Mr. Caldwell:	Kashala, I am very glad to have you in my class this year. I periodically set up special goals for some of my students. This year I'd like to help you learn to be thoughtful of other people's feelings.
Kashala:	I don't know what the big deal is.
Mr. Caldwell:	That's OK. It's something I would like to help you with. I think you'll have a better year. I've arranged to meet with you and your mom during math. Mrs. Larson has offered to work with the class so we can meet. I'm excited that we'll have a chance to work on this. Sometimes it's hard to find time to talk with kids individually, and this will be a special opportunity. Is that OK with you?
Kashala:	I guess.
Mr. Caldwell:	Good. We'll talk more tomorrow. In the meantime, do some thinking about ways that you might be more thoughtful of other people. Tomorrow, we will figure out how we can all help you with that goal.

Step 2: Meet with the student to discuss and finalize the plan.

A. Review the problem and goals.

Involve the student in clarifying the problem and the goals.

Although Kashala's mother is scheduled to come to the meeting, she does not show up at the scheduled time. The interventionist arrives to cover the teacher's math class, so the teacher decides they should go ahead with the meeting.

Mr. Caldwell: (Teacher)	Kashala, I'm glad you and I have this time together. Your mom must have gotten held up, but we can fill her in later. This will be a special talk between you and me. I want to talk with you about being thoughtful of others. I notice that sometimes the other kids seem to be irritated with you.
Kashala:	They just don't like me.
Mr. Caldwell:	Would you like to get along better with other people? (Kashala nods.) I think that's possible, but there are things you'll need to work on. Tell me what you would like in a friend.
Kashala:	They should be nice to you.
Mr. Caldwell:	Yes, that's an important part of friendship. Do you know what being nice to someone means?
Kashala:	They play with you.
Mr. Caldwell:	Yes. They play with you, and one of the reasons they play with you is because friends are thoughtful of each other. Friends don't say things that make their friends feel bad. For example, let's say I'm a student. I get a 100% on a spelling test. I'm very proud of that, and I should share it with my parents, but I yell out to the whole class, "I got a 100%!" How do you think someone who got 80% or 90% would feel?
Kashala:	(Shrugs)
Mr. Caldwell:	Let's pretend that you get 95% on the same spelling test. How would you feel?
Kashala:	OK. It's an A.
Mr. Caldwell:	Yes, but what if I yell out, "That was easy, easy, easy. I got 100%." Now, how would you feel about your 95%?
Kashala:	(Shrugs)
Mr. Caldwell:	I don't think you would as be as happy. Kashala, can you think about things that you might do or say that make you feel good but make the other kids feel bad?

Once you establish the problem and set a goal, discuss the plan to provide cueing and precorrecting. Explain to the student that you would like to help her be aware of her own behavior by quietly signaling her when she is starting to behave inappropriately or when she has already begun to engage in the problem behavior.

> **Mr. Caldwell:** Kashala, I'd like to help you reach your goal of being careful about what you say. I'll give you a signal when you need to think about what you are saying. For example, if I hear you starting to brag, I might put my finger to my mouth. When you see that signal, you will know that you need to stop and think about other people's feelings.

B. Help the student select a signal and explain any consequences that will be used if the student fails to respond.

Present the list of possible signals developed in Step 1C, and allow the student to select a signal.

> **Mr. Caldwell:** Would you be comfortable with any of those as a signal?
>
> **Kashala:** I guess the one where you touch your ear is OK.
>
> **Mr. Caldwell:** Good. If you see me tug on my ear, it means that you should stop and think about what you are saying or are about to say.

C. Briefly demonstrate and practice using the signal through role-playing.

Once the signal and the consequences for following or not following the signal have been identified, briefly practice with the student. Set up different situations in which the student has a tendency to exhibit the problem behavior. Have the student role-play the problem behavior, and then give the signal. If the student has trouble switching to the goal behavior, model the inappropriate behavior, then the goal behavior. If the student still continues to have problems exhibiting the goal behavior, or if you previously determined that the goal behavior is not within the student's current behavioral repertoire, the structured lessons in "Intervention M: Teaching Replacement Behavior" may be necessary.

> **Mr. Caldwell:** We're going to do some role-playing to make sure we both know how this is going to work. You get to be me, and I'll be you. What are you going to do if you hear me starting to say something that would be bragging or a put-down of another student?

Once the signal and the consequences for following or not following the signal have been identified, briefly practice with the student.

INTERVENTION

J

Kashala:	I'll tug on my ear.
Mr. Caldwell: (Teacher)	Good. Let's pretend I'm just coming in from recess and you hear me loudly announcing to Erica, "That was really stupid." What will you do? (Kashala tugs her ear.) Uh oh, I may not notice. Maybe you should also say my name. Try that.
Kashala:	OK. Kashala. (She tugs her ear.)
Mr. Caldwell:	That's better. So, what should I do?
Kashala:	Stop and think.
Mr. Caldwell:	Great. Let's try another one. Pretend that Martin has just told the class that he got to see David Copperfield and I start saying, "Who cares? David Copperfield is just . . . ."
Kashala:	Kashala. (She tugs her ear.)
Mr. Caldwell:	I stop and think. What could I say instead of "David Copperfield is just a jerk. He does tricks, and you can tell how he does everything"?
Kashala:	I don't know.
Mr. Caldwell:	I might say, "I wish I could have gone. Could you tell how he did the tricks?" Of course, I wouldn't want to lie. If I didn't care about seeing David Copperfield, I might just ask whether Martin could tell how he did the tricks. That wouldn't make Martin feel bad.
Kashala:	I get it.
Mr. Caldwell:	Let's try a couple more. Would you like to be me or you?

D. Review everyone's roles and responsibilities.

Mr. Caldwell:	Kashala, my job will be to signal you by saying your name and tugging on my ear when I hear you starting to say something hurtful. I'll also use the signal when I just think you need to be cautious. Your job will be to stop and think about what you are saying or might say.

E. Set up regular meeting times to debrief with the student.

For the first two or three days of the intervention, an adult should meet with the student daily for a quick debriefing. Once the intervention seems to be working well, these meetings can be cut back to once a week. If you are collecting data, review it with the student at the meetings. Debriefing meetings are also a good time to discuss with the student any subtle aspects of the goal behavior that need work. Because this step is moderately time-consuming, debriefing may need to be assigned to the interventionist, counselor, teaching assistant, or mentor. If debriefings will be conducted by someone other than the classroom teacher, the student should know that the teacher has helped set up the plan and supports the student's efforts.

> The teacher lets Kashala know that for the first three days of the plan he would like to talk to Kashala at the end of the day to discuss the plan.
>
> **Mr. Caldwell:**   Kashala, I know that you ride the bus home, but for the next few days, I would like you to stay after class for just a few minutes. When I excuse the rest of the class, stay in the room and we will take a couple of minutes to discuss whether the signal is helping. You can let me know how you feel about our plan. The bus doesn't leave until ten minutes after the bell, and I'll make sure that you don't miss it.

F. Conclude the meeting with words of encouragement.
Make sure the student knows that she is not in trouble when the signal is given. The signal simply means that it is time to concentrate on reaching her goal.

> **Mr. Caldwell:**   Kashala, you learn very fast. I'm looking forward to working with you on this. It will be fun for me to see you grow and mature.

Step 3: Implement the plan.

A. Begin using the precorrection or cue anytime the student exhibits the inappropriate behavior.

B. Watch for opportunities to reinforce the student for responding to the signal and for not needing the signal.

Mr. Caldwell: (Teacher)	Kashala, several times today you were very thoughtful of your classmates on your own, and I didn't need to use the signal. You painted a beautiful picture. I could see you smiling, but you didn't brag to the others about it. During soccer, you made some great plays and you let the others cheer you on. When a couple of the kids made errors, you encouraged them. I even heard you congratulate Sonja. You have been thoughtful and supportive of others, and I've enjoyed watching your progress with the other students.

C. Implement evaluation and debriefing procedures.

Periodic checks with Kashala and her teacher indicate that they both perceive that Kashala's behavior is improving in the classroom.

Kashala:	Sometimes I forget and start to say something like "That was stupid." But then I hear Mr. Caldwell saying my name, and I know I need to close my mouth. It works pretty good!
Mr. Caldwell:	Kashala has worked very hard on her goal. I'm having fun watching her progress.

Objective data collected during observations by the interventionist verify that Kashala's behavior is improving. By dividing inappropriate comments by the total number of comments Kashala made in a 45-minute period, it is clear that Kashala's inappropriate comments are becoming less and less frequent.

Though Kashala's improvements at school are clear, Kashala's mother is unable to keep three school appointments. By phone, Kashala's mother indicates that nothing seems to be changing at home.

D. Make periodic revisions and adjustments to the plan as necessary.

Additional attempts to involve Kashala's mother fail; it is apparent that she will not be able to implement the plan at home. Therefore, efforts to establish consistency between school and home are put on hold while efforts to invite the mother to implement the strategies at home continue. In spite of the lack of follow-through at home, Kashala continues to make rapid improvements at school, and the teacher continues to provide progress reports to Kashala's mother.

A second revision to the plan is made to teach Kashala that it can be appropriate to share accomplishments sometimes. To help Kashala take pride in her work, Kashala and the interventionist will meet once each week to develop a scrapbook of her best work.

E. Provide continued follow-up, support, and encouragement.

Cueing and Precorrecting will automatically fade as the student becomes successful—the more successful the student is, the less signaling is used. However, once the student has begun consistently achieving the goal, it is easy to take appropriate behavior for granted. The student will have made a major change in behavior and will need continued support and attention.

Because Kashala is a quick study, her teacher is able to fade signaling fairly rapidly. However, Mondays are still difficult. Though Kashala's improved behavior is rewarded by making friends and gaining acceptance from other students, her teacher decides to make Monday a special day. He makes it a point to greet Kashala at the door and always manages to squeeze in a few minutes to give her a special job, to confer with her about her work, or to chat with her for a few moments.

Despite Kashala's success in the classroom, her interventionist also decides to keep meeting with her every other week to work on the scrapbook. Because support from home is limited, ongoing support at school is essential to help her maintain success.

Cueing and Precorrecting will automatically fade as the student becomes successful—the more successful the student is, the less signaling is used.

CONCLUSION

Once a system is set up, Cueing and Precorrecting requires little time and is relatively easy to implement. As you consider this intervention, keep in mind that even 15 or 20 signals each day take only a minute or two of actual time.

Cueing and Precorrecting helps students decrease or eliminate annoying or inappropriate behaviors. However, if inappropriate behavior is the result of many interwoven problems, Cueing and Precorrecting alone may not be sufficient. When problems are complex and varied, use Cueing and Precorrecting in combination with other interventions such as:

Intervention E: Increasing Positive Interactions (p. 257)

Intervention F: STOIC ANALYSIS and Intervention (p. 305)

INTERVENTION

J

REFERENCES

Colvin, G., Sugai, G., & Patching, B. (1993). Precorrection: An instructional approach for managing predictable problem behaviors. *Intervention in School and Clinic, 28*, 143–150.

Fagan, W. T. (1989). Empowered students; Empowered teachers. *The Reading Teacher, 42*, 572–579.

Greenwood, C. R., Delquadri, J. C., Stanely, S. O., Terry, B., & Hall, R. V. (1985). Assessment of ecobehavioral interaction in school settings. *Behavioral Assessment, 7*, 331–347.

Greenwood, C. R., Schultze, D., Kohler, F., Dinwiddie, G., & Carta, J. (1986). Assessment and analysis of ecobehavioral interaction in school settings. In R. Prinz (Ed.), *Advances in behavioral assessment of children and families* (Vol. 2, pp. 69–98). Greenwich, CT: JAI Press.

Gresham, F. M., & Nagle, R. J. (1980). Social skills training with children: Responsiveness to modeling and coaching as a function of peer orientation. *Journal of Consulting and Clinical Psychology, 48*, 718–729.

Grumpel, T. P., & David, S. (2000). Exploring the efficacy of self-regulatory training as a possible alternative to social skills training. *Behavioral Disorders, 25*(2), 131–141.

Herring, M., & Northrup, J. (1998). The generalization of social skills for a child with behavior disorders in the school setting. *Child and Family Behavior Therapy, 20*(3), 51–66.

Kauffman, J. (2001). *Characteristics of emotional and behavioral disorders of children and youth* (7th ed.). Upper Saddle River, NJ: Merrill Prentice Hall.

Kauffman, J., Mostert, M., Trent, S., & Pullen, P. (2006). *Managing classroom behavior: A reflective case-based approach* (4th ed.). Boston: Pearson Education.

Kendon, A. (1981). *Nonverbal communication, interaction, and gestures.* New York: Mouton Publishers.

Lewis, T., Colvin, G., & Sugai, G. (2000). The effects of pre-correction and active supervision on the recess behavior of elementary students. *Education and Treatment of Children, 23*, 109–121.

Marks, S. U., Schrader, C., Levine, M., Hagie, C., Longaker, T., Morales, M., & Peters, I. (1999). Social skills for social ills: Supporting the social skills development of adolescents with Asperger's syndrome. *Teaching Exceptional Children, 32*(2), 56–61.

Posavac, H. D., Sheridan, S. M., & Posavac, S. S. (1999). A cueing procedure to control impulsivity in children with Attention Deficit Hyperactivity Disorder. *Behavior Modification, 23*(2), 234–253.

Rich, H. L., & McNeils, M. J. (1988). A study of academic time on task in the elementary school. *Educational Research Quarterly, 12*(1), 37–46.

Sprague, J., & Thomas, T. (1997). The effect of a neutralizing routine on problem behavior performance. *Journal of Behavioral Education, 7*, 325–334.

Yu, M., Darch, C., & Rabren, K. (2002). Use of precorrection strategies to enhance reading performance of students with learning and behavior problems. *Journal of Instructional Psychology, 29*, 162–174.

Reproducible Materials

The following reproducible form may be used in conjunction with "Intervention J: Managing Cueing and Precorrecting." A copy is provided in the chapter and on the CD. Permission is given for individual classroom teachers to reproduce any forms labeled "Reproducible" for classroom use. Reproduction of these materials for an entire school system is prohibited without express permission of the publisher.

Step-by-Step Summary, p. 482

INTERVENTION  J

CUEING AND PRECORRECTING

Step-by-Step Summary

Following is a summary of the steps involved in Intervention J. It is important to use professional judgment, adjusting procedures to meet the needs of the situation and the individual. See the chapter "Intervention J: Cueing and Precorrecting" for a detailed description of this intervention.

STEP 1   Develop a plan.

A. Review the problem and overall goals for the student.

B. Decide whether cueing, precorrecting, or both will be used.

C. Identify possible signals that might be used to cue the student to avoid or interrupt the inappropriate behavior.

D. Identify what adults will do when the student either responds appropriately or fails to respond to a signal.

E. Identify other settings to include in the plan and adults who will need training.

F. Decide whether the student needs to be taught a replacement behavior.

G. Identify ways to determine whether the intervention is helping the student reach the goal.

H. Determine who will meet with the student to discuss and finalize the plan.

STEP 2   Meet with the student to discuss and finalize the plan.

A. Review the problem and goals.

B. Help the student select a signal and explain any consequences that will be used if the student fails to respond.

C. Briefly demonstrate and practice using the signal through role-playing.

D. Reivew everyone's roles and responsibilities.

Step-by-Step Summary (2 of 2)

INTERVENTION J

E. Set up regular meeting times to debrief with the student.

F. Conclude the meeting with words of encouragement.

STEP 3 Implement the plan.

A. Begin using the precorrection or cue anytime the student exhibits the inappropriate behavior.

B. Watch for opportunities to reinforce the student for responding to the signal and for not needing the signal.

C. Implement evaluation and debriefing procedures.

D. Make periodic revisions and adjustments to the plan as necessary.

E. Provide continued follow-up, support, and encouragement.

*Special thanks to Daniel Gulchak
for reviewing and offering helpful content to this chapter.*

Self-Monitoring and Self-Evaluation

| *The student has some motivation to change
or learn new behaviors*

PURPOSE

THIS INTERVENTION ALLOWS STUDENTS to take responsibility for and control of their behavior.

THIS INTERVENTION IS APPROPRIATE FOR:

Mild misbehavior

Habitual misbehavior
- blurting out
- complaining

Academic productivity
- off-task behavior
- careless work
- rate
- accuracy

Poor listening skills
- failure to pay attention

Inappropriate comments
- sarcasm
- criticism
- bragging

Social skills
- inappropriate interactions
- inappropriate comments

Severe misbehavior
- anger management
- aggression
- disrespect
- self-injurious behavior

Categories
- developmental delay
- learning disabilities
- attention deficit/hyperactivity disorder
- conduct disorder
- oppositional defiant disorder
- emotional and behavioral disorders
- autism/Asberger syndrome

Self-Monitoring and Self-Evaluation is an intervention that helps students become aware of their problem behavior and the improvements they are striving to make by involving them in keeping records of their own behavior. With self-monitoring, the student will observe and track certain behaviors to better understand and then change these problem behaviors. Self-evaluation is a modified form of self-monitoring in which the student will regularly evaluate and record the quality of some aspect of her behavior, using the information to improve the behavior as time goes on. Students can monitor positive behavior, such as work completion or time on task, or they can track negative behavior they wish to reduce, such as complaining or lack of self-control. The purpose of Self-Monitoring and Self-Evaluation is to increase students' awareness of a particular behavior so they can learn to take responsibility for their own behavior and control what they do.

RATIONALE

Some students with behavior problems are not aware of their own actions. Their problems arise out of impulsiveness, yet they, and often others, perceive themselves to be irresponsible, distractible, obnoxious, sloppy, or bad. These students see their problems as the result of who they are rather than the result of actions they have taken. Self-Monitoring and Self-Evaluation can help students take control of situations they believe are hopeless.

> Annie is a highly gifted first-grade student. Unfortunately, she is also a very unhappy child. She argues with other children, criticizes their work, shows off her own accomplishments, and frequently demands to be the center of attention. Annie's teacher, Mrs. Hayes, worries about her growing isolation. Though Mrs. Hayes has talked to Annie about being more sensitive to the feelings of the others, Annie does not seem to be able to help herself. She says, "The other kids don't like me because I am smart." Annie's mother also believes that her daughter isn't accepted because she is gifted. Annie's teacher senses that the bragging, showing off, and criticizing others are simply deeply ingrained habits. She gently suggests that because Annie is so bright, she can learn to be more sensitive of the other children. Mrs. Hayes suggests implementing a self-monitoring system so that Annie can learn to be more aware of her comments.

The strength of self-monitoring is that it teaches students to manage their own behavior, as opposed to having an adult do so.

Self-Monitoring and Self-Evaluation puts students such as Annie in touch with their actions and empowers them to take control. The strength of self-monitoring is that it teaches students to manage their own behavior, as opposed to having an adult do so. To monitor their actions accurately, students must learn to pay close attention to what they are or are not doing. As they count and chart their improvements, the motivation to change becomes intrinsic. Reinforcement is often as simple as the sense of accomplishment students feel as they recognize self-improvement. Self-Monitoring and Self-Evaluation is especially effective for students who seem to be motivated but are unaware of their inappropriate behavior and for those who act impulsively and have difficulty taking ownership of their behavior.

Self-monitoring can also save you time and energy because the student records the useful data that will be used for regular debriefing and evaluating intervention effectiveness.

Before implementing Self-Monitoring and Self-Evaluation

Before this intervention can be successfully implemented, be sure that you have discussed the problem and general goal for improvement with the student. Gather any relevant background information that may help in designing and implementing the intervention. Defining the nature and scope of the problem provides critical information for developing a successful intervention. In addition, contact the student's parent or guardian to discuss the problem and keep them informed of all aspects of the intervention plan.

Note: Self-Monitoring and Self-Evaluation is effective, but it can be relatively time-consuming. Remember that you should always attempt the easiest and least time-intensive interventions first. If you have not tried the Early-Stage Interventions, such as "Intervention A: Planned Discussion" or "Intervention C: Goal Setting," begin implementing one or more of these before attempting this intervention. It may also be useful to use one or more of the other interventions in this book while concurrently implementing Self-Monitoring and Self-Evaluation.

Bobby is a seventh-grade student in Mrs. Werner's language arts/social studies block. During class, Bobby participates. His class assignments are above average. He is always pleasant to have in class. Despite Bobby's strong abilities, Mrs. Werner is concerned because he is failing in English and barely passing in social studies. Bobby's problem is homework. Mrs. Werner has discussed the problem with Bobby, but the discussions have not done much good. Mrs. Werner decides to ask the counselor for assistance. She sees Bobby sliding the wrong way and hopes to find a solution before he gives up.

The counselor, Mr. Pope, looks up Bobby's elementary school records. Bobby was two when his parents divorced. They have joint custody, and Bobby switches between homes every Wednesday. Both parents are professionals with demanding careers.

INTERVENTION

K

Bobby's records indicate that homework has been a problem since the third grade. Teacher comments describe an academically capable student who is charming but chronically disorganized. Daily report cards were tried in sixth grade, with only partial success. Assignments were still frequently missing after the report card program was instituted.

Mr. Pope checks with Bobby's other teachers and finds that Bobby is doing fine in PE and photography, but he is getting D's or failing grades in all academic subjects. All of his teachers indicate that the problem is homework. Mr. Pope finds that Bobby reads with good fluency and understanding, his writing abilities are average, and he is physically and mentally able to do his homework.

In talking with Bobby's parents, Mr. Pope finds that each parent blames the other for Bobby's problems. His father says that his ex-wife is disorganized and coddles the boy. His mother says that his father is too critical and demanding. Both parents have high aspirations for their son, but beyond that they do not seem to agree. Both parents are amenable to working with Bobby but indicate that they do not want to talk with one another.

Mr. Pope decides that because less intensive interventions had no effect, Self-Monitoring and Self-Evaluation may be useful to help Bobby learn to take responsibility for his homework.

One of the most important parts of this intervention is to define the goal behavior in as much detail as possible so that it can be taught to the student.

IMPLEMENTATION STEPS
Step 1: Develop a plan.

A. Determine the behavior to be monitored and evaluated.

Begin planning by identifying the specific behavior or academic task that will be focused on. The behavior can be positive (raise hand before calling out, stay in seat during reading, complete 80 percent of math worksheet during class period) or negative (eliminate yelling at recess, stop running in the halls, avoid off-task talking in social studies class).

One of the most important parts of this intervention is to define the goal behavior in as much detail as possible so that it can be taught to the student. The language you use will vary depending on whether the intervention is intended for an elementary or high school student, but the process will remain the same. It is vitally important to describe the behavior in observable terms. For example, if the goal for the student is to "increase on-task behavior," ask yourself questions like:

- What does on-task behavior look like?

- Should the student be looking at the teacher during class lectures?

- Does this mean being in-seat, facing forward, with all chair legs on the floor?

- Should the student complete 80 percent of math questions with the correct answers, or does simply writing down a number under the problem count as complete? (You know the student will call you out on this technicality unless you define it ahead of time.)

All of these behaviors can fall under the umbrella of "on-task," but each behavior is uniquely different.

> Because Bobby's problem is relatively straightforward, Bobby's teachers and the counselor, Mr. Pope, decide that he needs to self-monitor his own homework and learn to get work done despite his inconsistent home situation. Mr. Pope agrees to set up a self-monitoring system in which Bobby will 1) write down assignments, 2) self-check to make sure he has all needed materials before leaving school, 3) stick to a prearranged homework schedule, 4) stay with the schedule until homework is done, 5) put completed homework in his notebook, and 6) get his notebook to school in the morning.

For a student to accurately monitor his own behavior, it is important to define acceptable and unacceptable behavior clearly and draw the line between the two.

B. **If necessary, identify examples of student behavior that set boundaries between responsible and irresponsible behavior.**

For a student to accurately monitor his own behavior, it is important to define acceptable and unacceptable behavior clearly and draw the line between the two. With a behavior problem such as work completion, this step is easy. The work is either done on time or it is not. However, with most behavior, the borderline between acceptable and unacceptable is fuzzy and requires definition. For example, with a behavior such as talking respectfully to adults, what defines respectful versus disrespectful talk? Is it the words? The tone of voice? Does body language play a part? Is it all of these? To draw the line between appropriate and inappropriate behavior, brainstorm several examples of possible student behavior and help the student identify whether each example as appropriate or inappropriate.

Figure K1 is an example of a student who needs to learn to speak respectfully to adults. The list was generated from the types of misbehavior the student exhibited in the past.

Figure K1: *Behavior Examples*

Responsible Behavior:	Irresponsible Behavior:
The teacher asks Joan to sit down. • Joan nods and sits down. • Joan says, "Okay," and sits down. • Joan does not respond to the teacher but immediately goes to her seat. • Joan asks in a respectful tone, "I need to sharpen my pencil. Is that okay?"	The teacher asks Joan to sit down. • Joan sits down but calls the teacher a name or says, "Why should I?" • Joan sits down, but in a sarcastic tone says, "Okay, whatever you say." • Joan does not sit down or respond. • Joan goes to sit down in exaggerated slow motion.
The teacher says "Good morning" as Joan enters the classroom. • Joan replies in a polite tone, "Good morning." • Joan says, "It hasn't been a good morning. My mom was all over my case this morning." • Joan smiles and nods.	The teacher says "Good morning" as Joan enters the classroom. • Joan responds in a sarcastic tone, "Good morning, teacher." • Joan says, "It might be good for you, but what do you know?" • Joan looks disgusted and sighs.

If the line between acceptable and unacceptable behavior is difficult to distinguish, it is important to define it through examples prior to teaching the student to self-monitor his behavior. By discussing limits before asking a student to self-monitor, you let the student know in advance what is acceptable and what is unacceptable. This greatly reduces the natural human urge to test the limits.

Boundaries between behaviors should be defined for most disruptive behaviors, out-of-control behaviors, complaining, crying, whining, and so on. For more in-depth information, see "Intervention P: Defining Limits and Establishing Consequences."

> Defining limits for Bobby is not an issue. Homework is either turned in on time and complete, or it is not.

C. Determine when the student will record behaviors.

Once you have identified the behavior that will be monitored, determine when the student will monitor his or her behavior. Behavior may be monitored:

• **Once a day at a specified time.** If a student has difficulty paying attention during the afternoon, for example, she might monitor her behavior only in the afternoon.

- **Only during certain activities.** If the student has difficulty keeping his hands and feet to himself when students line up or sit together on the floor, he might monitor his behavior only during those specific activities.

- **At specified intervals.** If the student has difficulty with work completion, she might mark the number of problems completed in a 15-minute period.

- **At random intervals.** If the student has difficulty with on-task behavior, it may be effective to have the student monitor his behavior at random intervals. This requires a cueing system, as in Step E that follows.

- **Whenever the behavior occurs.** If the student is monitoring a behavior such as hand-raising and waiting to be called on, talking respectfully to the teacher, or engaging in positive self-talk, it may be best to record the behavior as it occurs. If the student records at intervals, it might be difficult for her to judge whether she had been appropriate or inappropriate.

Bobby's self-monitoring system will be in effect from the moment he leaves his house in the morning until he packs up his materials in the evening. Mr. Pope decides that Bobby would benefit from a system in which he records all homework as it is assigned and is accountable for checking off homework as he finishes it. During each class period, Bobby will record his assignments as they are given and list the materials he will need to do his homework. At the end of the day, Bobby will determine when he will study that evening and check off all the materials he needs as he puts them in his notebook or backpack. As he is doing his homework, Bobby will check off each completed assignment. When he is finished with his homework, he will pack everything up and put his backpack by the door.

D. Develop a recording system for the student.

Once you have determined when self-monitoring will be used, design a recording system. There are numerous formats you can use for recording. The following examples are provided to help you design a recording system that is easy for the student to understand and manage and that fits the student's problem and goal.

Note: Not all Reproducible forms are shown throughout this chapter. You should skim through the forms at the back of the chapter to determine which Self-Monitoring and Self-Evaluation format is best suited to the student's needs. All forms are available on the CD as well. You may also design your own recording system.

The student makes simple tally marks on a chart each time the behavior is exhibited.

The chart shown in Figure K2 was designed for a student who will tally on-task and off-task behavior during independent work. This kind of simple tally chart may be more effective if you include specific examples of the negative and positive behavior that define "On Task" and "Off Task" to remind the student of what to work on. For example, with the student who is tallying on-task and off-task behavior, you might tailor his chart to "On Task: Eyes on work, attempting to complete assignment" and "Off Task: Out of seat, talking to peers."

Figure K2: *Behavior Tally*

On Task	Off Task
~~IIII~~ I	II

The chart in Figure K3 shows a system designed for monitoring whether a primary-level student has interacted positively with peers.

Figure K3: *Primary Tally*

Happy Face	Unhappy Face
III	I

The student uses symbols such as a plus (+) or minus (–) to record responsible and irresponsible behavior, respectively.

The monitoring system shown in Reproducible Form K1 was designed for a student learning to follow directions without complaining. The student marks a plus or minus based on how well she follows directions without complaining.

Note: Copies of this and other Self-Monitoring and Self-Evaluation forms are also provided on the CD.

The student tracks a behavior by circling a number or symbol each time a task is completed successfully.

The Happy Cat/Sad Dog diagram (Reproducible Form K2) is designed to help younger students (grades K–2) connect to the self-monitoring process. Note that the top half of the reproducible shows happy cats while the bottom half shows happy dogs, giving both cat fanciers and dog lovers among your primary-age students equal opportunity to indicate positive behavior with the animal pal of their choice.

In the example shown in Reproducible Form K3, the student circles a number each time she completes a problem or each time she completes an assignment.

The student rates his own behavior or effort.

The self-evaluation system shown in Reproducible Form K4 was designed for a student who has difficulty participating in class. After specifically identified class activities, the student rates his behavior.

Reproducible Forms K5–K7 are rating forms for self-evaluating different traits, including neatness and complaining.

The student uses a checklist for tasks that must be completed.

For example, the student who needs to improve hygiene might use Reproducible Form K8 to check a list of things to do in the morning.

A student who has difficulty with independent class work might use a Work Completion checklist (Reproducible Form K9), which includes writing down assignments, starting an assignment, finishing an assignment, and handing it in.

Reproducible Form K1: *Self-Monitoring Form: Following Directions*

Self-Monitoring Form:
Following Directions

Name _____   Week of _____

Directions: Mark a "+" for each direction followed without complaining.
Mark a "–" for each direction that led to complaining.

	+/– Count
Date _____	
Date _____	
Date _____	
Date _____	
Date _____	

Reproducible Form K2: *Happy Cat/Sad Dog and Happy Dog/Sad Cat*

Happy Cat/Sad Dog

_____   Behavior _____
Name

Each time you remember, color the smiling cat. When you forget, color the sad dog.

Happy Dog/Sad Cat

_____   Behavior _____
Name

Each time you remember, color the smiling dog. When you forget, color the sad cat.

Reproducible Form K3: *Self-Monitoring Form: Completed Problems/Assignments*

Self-Monitoring Form:
Completed Problems/Assignments

Name _____   Goal _____

Date _____

1   2   3   4   5   6   7   8   9   10

Date _____

1   2   3   4   5   6   7   8   9   10

Date _____

1   2   3   4   5   6   7   8   9   10

Date _____

1   2   3   4   5   6   7   8   9   10

Date _____

1   2   3   4   5   6   7   8   9   10

Self-Evaluation Form:
Class Participation

Name _____   Date _____

Level of Participation		
Period/Class _____	❏ I gave it my best effort.	I raised my hand, and I asked relevant questions. I volunteered information. I listened to others and thought about what they said.
	❏ I did just enough to get by.	I sat quietly and didn't interfere with others.
	❏ I didn't try.	I didn't listen. I made noises that interfered with what other people were saying. I did things that got other people to look at me.
Period/Class _____	❏ I gave it my best effort.	I raised my hand, and I asked relevant questions. I volunteered information. I listened to others and thought about what they said.
	❏ I did just enough to get by.	I sat quietly and didn't interfere with others.
	❏ I didn't try.	I didn't listen. I made noises that interfered with what other people were saying. I did things that got other people to look at me.
Period/Class _____	❏ I gave it my best effort.	I raised my hand, and I asked relevant questions. I volunteered information. I listened to others and thought about what they said.
	❏ I did just enough to get by.	I sat quietly and didn't interfere with others.
	❏ I didn't try.	I didn't listen. I made noises that interfered with what other people were saying. I did things that got other people to look at me.
Period/Class _____	❏ I gave it my best effort.	I raised my hand, and I asked relevant questions. I volunteered information. I listened to others and thought about what they said.
	❏ I did just enough to get by.	I sat quietly and didn't interfere with others.
	❏ I didn't try.	I didn't listen. I made noises that interfered with what other people were saying. I did things that got other people to look at me.
Period/Class _____	❏ I gave it my best effort.	I raised my hand, and I asked relevant questions. I volunteered information. I listened to others and thought about what they said.
	❏ I did just enough to get by.	I sat quietly and didn't interfere with others.
	❏ I didn't try.	I didn't listen. I made noises that interfered with what other people were saying. I did things that got other people to look at me.
Period/Class _____	❏ I gave it my best effort.	I raised my hand, and I asked relevant questions. I volunteered information. I listened to others and thought about what they said.
	❏ I did just enough to get by.	I sat quietly and didn't interfere with others.
	❏ I didn't try.	I didn't listen. I made noises that interfered with what other people were saying. I did things that got other people to look at me.

Neatness Evaluation Form

Neatness Evaluation Form

| Name | Assignment | Date |

Directions: Circle the number that best describes the level of neatness of this assignment. If the assignment is rated 0 or 1, it will have to be cleaned up or redone. If the teacher agrees with your rating, there may be an occasional reward.

4	The paper is whole and flat with no extra marks. The writing sits appropriately on the line. There are spaces between the words. The capitals are big and the small letters are small. The writing is all printing or all cursive. The writing is straight or at a uniform slant.
3	The paper is whole and flat with no extra marks. The writing sits appropriately on the line. There are spaces between the words. The capitals are big and the small letters are small. The writing is all printing or all cursive.
2	The paper is whole and flat with no extra marks. The writing sits appropriately on the line. There are spaces between the words.
1	The paper is whole and flat, but has extra marks/smudges.
0	The paper is torn or crumpled.

- -

Neatness Evaluation Form

| Name | Assignment | Date |

Directions: Circle the number that best describes the level of neatness of this assignment. If the assignment is rated 0 or 1, it will have to be cleaned up or redone. If the teacher agrees with your rating, there may be an occasional reward.

4	The paper is whole and flat with no extra marks. The writing sits appropriately on the line. There are spaces between the words. The capitals are big and the small letters are small. The writing is all printing or all cursive. The writing is straight or at a uniform slant.
3	The paper is whole and flat with no extra marks. The writing sits appropriately on the line. There are spaces between the words. The capitals are big and the small letters are small. The writing is all printing or all cursive.
2	The paper is whole and flat with no extra marks. The writing sits appropriately on the line. There are spaces between the words.
1	The paper is whole and flat, but has extra marks/smudges.
0	The paper is torn or crumpled.

Self-Evaluation Form:
Complaining Behavior

Name _____   Date _____

Directions: Circle the number that best describes your level of participation.

	Went to the health room	Complained about how I felt	Acted sick or tired	Was okay	Was enthusiastic
First Hour	0	1	2	3	4
Second Hour	0	1	2	3	4
Third Hour	0	1	2	3	4
Fourth Hour	0	1	2	3	4
Fifth Hour	0	1	2	3	4
Sixth Hour	0	1	2	3	4
Seventh Hour	0	1	2	3	4

Total points for the day ☐

Reproducible Form K7: *Self-Evaluation Form*

Self-Evaluation Form

Name

Time Period   Date

Rating: Each day, rate the time period and record in the boxes below.

  0 = Hands tense and moving the entire time
  1 = Hands still and relaxed a little bit of the time
  2 = Hands still and relaxed some of the time
  3 = Hands still and relaxed most of the time
  4 = Hands still and relaxed the entire time

M	T	W	Th	F

Self-Evaluation Form

Name

Time Period   Date

Rating: Each day, rate the time period and record in the boxes below.

  0 = Hands tense and moving the entire time
  1 = Hands still and relaxed a little bit of the time
  2 = Hands still and relaxed some of the time
  3 = Hands still and relaxed most of the time
  4 = Hands still and relaxed the entire time

M	T	W	Th	F

Self-Evaluation Form

Name

Time Period   Date

Rating: Each day, rate the time period and record in the boxes below.

  0 = Hands tense and moving the entire time
  1 = Hands still and relaxed a little bit of the time
  2 = Hands still and relaxed some of the time
  3 = Hands still and relaxed most of the time
  4 = Hands still and relaxed the entire time

M	T	W	Th	F

Self-Evaluation Form

Name

Time Period   Date

Rating: Each day, rate the time period and record in the boxes below.

  0 = Hands tense and moving the entire time
  1 = Hands still and relaxed a little bit of the time
  2 = Hands still and relaxed some of the time
  3 = Hands still and relaxed most of the time
  4 = Hands still and relaxed the entire time

M	T	W	Th	F

Intervention K:
Self-Monitoring and Self-Evaluation

Self-Monitoring Form:
Personal Hygiene

Name _____

	Personal Hygiene	M	T	W	Th	F
Week of _____	1. Get up at 6:30.					
	2. Shower and wash hair.					
	3. Put on deodorant.					
	4. Comb or brush hair.					
	5. Brush teeth.					
Week of _____	1. Get up at 6:30.					
	2. Shower and wash hair.					
	3. Put on deodorant.					
	4. Comb or brush hair.					
	5. Brush teeth.					
Week of _____	1. Get up at 6:30.					
	2. Shower and wash hair.					
	3. Put on deodorant.					
	4. Comb or brush hair.					
	5. Brush teeth.					
Week of _____	1. Get up at 6:30.					
	2. Shower and wash hair.					
	3. Put on deodorant.					
	4. Comb or brush hair.					
	5. Brush teeth.					
Week of _____	1. Get up at 6:30.					
	2. Shower and wash hair.					
	3. Put on deodorant.					
	4. Comb or brush hair.					
	5. Brush teeth.					

Reproducible Form K9: *Self-Monitoring Form: Work Completion*

Self-Monitoring Form:
Work Completion

Name _____   Week of _____

	M	T	W	Th	F
Period: **Subject:**					
I wrote down the assignment.					
I started the assignment.					
I finished the assignment.					
I handed in the assignment.					
Period: **Subject:**					
I wrote down the assignment.					
I started the assignment.					
I finished the assignment.					
I handed in the assignment.					
Period: **Subject:**					
I wrote down the assignment.					
I started the assignment.					
I finished the assignment.					
I handed in the assignment.					
Period: **Subject:**					
I wrote down the assignment.					
I started the assignment.					
I finished the assignment.					
I handed in the assignment.					
Period: **Subject:**					
I wrote down the assignment.					
I started the assignment.					
I finished the assignment.					
I handed in the assignment.					

I will put an "X" in any box where nothing was assigned or due during that period. When a box is successfully completed, I will initial that box.

I will meet with _____ to discuss my progress.

When/Where: _____

When I can get _____ of the boxes filled in (including Xs), I will earn _____

I also recognize that when I can get _____ to _____ boxes filled in, my grades will begin to go up and I will feel very responsible.

To assist Bobby with homework completion, Bobby's counselor decides to use a checklist (Sample Reproducible Form K10). Bobby will record his assignments and when they are due, list materials he needs to take home, write down when he will study, and check off assignments as they are completed.

Design a fairly unobtrusive system using one of the provided forms or by designing one of your own to match the student's needs. Self-monitoring can be beneficial to any student, but remember that the power of self-monitoring can be diluted if the student is embarrassed. Especially for older students, the system should involve recording behavior privately, possibly inside a notebook or folder. Younger students tend to be less concerned about embarrassment and often like having a "special system." Other students may even ask for a self-monitoring chart.

One new and exciting way to unobtrusively self-monitor academic or behavioral performance is through the use of PDAs (personal digital assistants) or handheld computers. These ubiquitous devices are small, portable, and cost efficient when compared to desktop or laptop computers. For self-monitoring, database programs such as Microsoft Access, FileMaker, and HandBase can be used to create customized charts and tables like those seen in the previous figures. There are several advantages to using digital self-monitoring records. First, there is a reduced negative stigma associated with using computers compared with using cumbersome charts and folders. Second, students are often more motivated to self-record using technology rather than "old-fashioned" pen and paper. Finally, recording data digitally enables users to easily transfer the record into digital graphs and print out or e-mail charts to the student or their parents. Students young and old can use PDAs for a self-monitoring intervention. This method for recording performance may even make other students envious and eager for a chance to record their school performance!

E. Design a cueing system to prompt the student to record.

If the student is counting specific behaviors, the behavior itself acts as a cue. "When you hear yourself saying something positive, make a tally." "When you raise your hand and wait quietly for me to call on you, make a tally." "When you complete an assignment, check it off." "When you say something positive to someone else, circle the next number on your chart."

Other cases may require an independent cueing mechanism. For example, if the student is using random intervals to monitor on- and off-task behavior, she will need a cue when it is time to record her behavior. This can be

Self-monitoring can be beneficial to any student, but remember that the power of self-monitoring can be diluted if the student is embarrassed.

INTERVENTION

K

Sample Reproducible Form K10: *Self-Monitoring Form: Homework Completion*

Intervention K:
Self-Monitoring and Self-Evaluation

Self-Monitoring Form:
Homework Completion

Bobby Ross
Name

10/15–10/19
Week of

Due	Assignment	Materials	Done
10/16	Math Pg. 16	Math book and folder	X
10/16	The Pearl Pgs. 42–60	The Pearl	
10/19	Field trip permission slip	Notebook	X

	M	U	W	H	F
Before leaving school each day, I will study from __2:30__ to __3:30__ and from __5:00__ to __6:00__ if needed.					
I have logged long-term assignments not yet finished on tomorrow's assignment sheet.					
I have organized my assignments in my notebook.	X				
I have packed all my books, materials, and notebook in my backpack.	X				
I have put my backpack by the door.					

A blank version of this form is available in the *Reproducible Materials* section at the end of the chapter.

accomplished with some sort of timing device. A low-tech way to do this is to set a timer for random intervals. When the student hears the timer go off, she records whether she was on- or off-task at that point in time. Another independent cueing mechanism is an audio recording of beeps spaced at random intervals. These intervals may be as frequent as every two minutes or as infrequent as two per hour, depending on the needs of the student and the objectives of the intervention. Train the student to record her behavior when she hears a beep. Other low-cost devices can be placed directly on a student's desk. Simple timers can be used, which feature a recording of the teacher's voice that plays at preset intervals. For instance, the student might hear, "Celinda, evaluate on your cooperation form how well you have done in the last hour." More high-tech methods are also available. For example, low-cost computer applications can be set to emit a sound at regular intervals—say, every 15 minutes—or intermittently—say, four times an hour at random intervals. One such device is the WatchMinder2, which was introduced in 2006. This wristwatch was designed by a psychologist who specializes in ADHD. A search of the Internet for timers, cueing devices, or reminder devices will yield a variety of possibilities.

These options are cost efficient and effective, but they also require that the student be near a computer, a timer, or the teacher. Some new mobile options, including PDAs, phones, and iPods or MP3 players, offer a solution to this problem; they can be operated by the student from his or her seat. PDAs, also known as handheld computers or electronic organizers, have calendar functions with alarms. These alarm reminders for appointments can be set up to beep at intervals of five minutes or more. Because many students already come to school with mobile phones or smartphones, using this technology may make the most sense. Most such phones have alarms that can be set to repeat, and they can also be set to vibrate, which is a less intrusive option for the rest of the class. Finally, portable audio players like iPods or MP3 players can download music files that you create to beep or play brief musical reminders at whatever interval is necessary. There are many free programs teachers can use to create their own interval recording. One free program is found at www.audacity.com. Students may be more motivated to participate in a self-monitoring program if the cueing system is less obtrusive and stigmatizing. These options—PDAs, phones, and music players, along with the numerous other kinds of timers and audio devices—offer appealing options to most students.

With any of these cueing systems, it is essential that the student is "on board" so that he does not feel embarrassed or offended by the system. Discuss the multiple options for cueing systems with the student and allow him to choose one that he is comfortable with.

Discuss the multiple options for cueing systems with the student and allow him to choose one that he is comfortable with.

INTERVENTION

K

F. Plan to have an adult monitor the student's behavior occasionally and compare results with the student's record.

In the early phases of the plan, an adult should monitor the student's progress frequently. Adult monitoring can consist of intermittent checks. For example, if a student is learning to stay on task, the teacher might parallel the student's monitoring at unpredictable intervals, such as at the first, third, fourth, and eighth intervals. The teacher should then check with the student to see whether their perceptions match. If both have recorded the same behavior in the same way, the student should be commended. Even if the behavior itself has not yet improved, the student is taking the first step in being responsible—by learning how to self-assess on- and off-task behaviors. Accurate self-assessment is prerequisite to being able to self-manage a behavioral change. If the student and adult records do not match, find a time to discuss the reason for the discrepancy. Is the student recording every event? Is the division between responsible and irresponsible behavior unclear?

Adult monitoring during the initial phases of self-monitoring will increase the effectiveness of the intervention. As the student demonstrates reliable self-monitoring, adult monitoring can be gradually reduced. In using self-evaluation systems, intermittent parallel adult monitoring is even more important to determine whether the student is accurately assessing the behavior. For example, if the student is rating her "cooperation" each hour, the teacher should also assess the student's behavior on the rating scale occasionally. Then the student's and the teacher's ratings can be compared and discrepancies discussed. If the ratings are consistent, even if they show minimal progress toward the goal behavior, the student should be praised for rating herself accurately. Without these checks, the student has little incentive to rate herself accurately.

Bobby's counselor, Mr. Pope, decides that Bobby will initially need frequent adult guidance as he learns to monitor his homework. For the first week, Mr. Pope decides to set up a daily after-school meeting in which Bobby will check in at the counseling office so Mr. Pope and Bobby can go over the assignment sheet and make sure Bobby has all his needed materials before he gets on the bus. If time permits, Bobby and Mr. Pope will discuss when he plans to study at home and will verbally rehearse how he will use his assignment sheet. In addition, Bobby will stop in to see Mr. Pope as soon as he gets to school for a quick review and discussion of the assignment sheet and how things went the previous evening. In the following weeks, these meetings will be faded to three times a week, then two times per week, and eventually once per week.

Before continuing with this plan, Mr. Pope discusses the plan with a parent volunteer and talks with Bobby's parents to make sure that they can work out the after-school arrangement.

G. Identify ways to determine whether the intervention is helping the student reach his goal.

The records kept by students and adults provide important information. As the data is collected, student progress should be graphed and discussed. Depending on the behavior, evaluation might also include subjective impressions from the teacher and student, grades, attendance records, office referrals, and so on.

Bobby's counselor decides to determine the effectiveness of the self-monitoring system by:

- checking with Bobby's teachers once a week to determine whether he is keeping up with his homework assignments
- charting the percentage of homework Bobby completes each week
- looking at any anecdotal notes kept by the teachers or Mr. Pope about Bobby's progress

H. Determine who will meet with the student to discuss and finalize the plan.

Use professional judgment to determine who will be present when the plan is discussed with the student. Some students will be responsive only if the teacher is present. In other cases, it will be important to include a parent, an interventionist, other teachers, or a paraprofessional or volunteer who will be working with the student.

Bobby is a very affable student who seems comfortable with adults, so Mr. Pope decides to include Bobby's language arts/social studies block teacher, Mrs. Werner. Mrs. Werner originally brought Bobby to Mr. Pope's attention and has a warm relationship with her student, and she can help add a teacher's perspective to the problem.

Though Bobby's parents have decided not to be part of the planning discussion with Bobby, Mr. Pope keeps them informed by phone and e-mail.

Step 2: Meet with the student to discuss and finalize the plan.

A. Review the problem and goal.

Begin the meeting with a quick review of the problem and goal.

Mr. Pope: (Counselor)	I'm pleased to meet with all of you today. Bobby, you know Mrs. Werner. Mrs. Werner will be helping us work on a plan to help you with homework. Can you tell us a little about your homework situation?
Bobby:	Sure. I kind of have problems getting it done. Sometimes I forget my stuff. It drives my folks nuts.
Mrs. Werner: (Teacher)	And your teachers!
Mr. Pope:	Would you like to work on this? You could make it a goal to learn how to get homework done this year.
Bobby:	I don't know.
Mrs. Werner:	Bobby, I figured out your grades in my block. If I looked only at your in-class assignments, you would have an A in social studies and a B in English. Instead you have a D in social studies and an F in English.
Bobby:	How about this? You give me the grade for my in-class work.
Mrs. Werner:	Ha ha! Very funny.
Bobby:	This stuff doesn't count. I'll pull it together when I get to high school.
Mr. Pope:	I wish that were true. Unfortunately, most of the students I know tend to have the same problems in high school that they have here. The habits you have now are the habits you will take with you to high school. Would you like to go to college?
Bobby:	Stanford . . .
Mrs. Werner:	You are fully capable of going to college and doing well—especially if you study and learn while you are here with us. But if you miss out on learning opportunities like homework while you are here, you will begin slipping behind the others. You may also develop bad habits that will be hard to break. What do you think gets in the way of getting your homework done?
Bobby:	I don't know. My dad says I just don't try. Mom thinks it's the TV.
Mr. Pope:	Let's review some of the roadblocks to getting your homework done. Then we would like to design a plan with you that may help you overcome those problems.

B. Introduce the procedures that will be followed.

1. Introduce the self-monitoring or self-evaluation system to the student.

Begin by discussing the purpose and the benefits of self-monitoring or self-evaluation. If the student seems resistant or uninterested, discuss how this intervention may assist with the student's problem and consider other interventions in addition to Self-Monitoring and Self-Evaluation. "Intervention C: Goal Setting" or "Intervention O: Structured Reinforcement Systems" may be particularly appropriate.

Mr. Pope: (Counselor)	Now that we've walked through the monitoring system, what do you think?
Bobby:	It's OK.
Mrs. Werner: (Teacher)	Do you think the system will help you?
Bobby:	I don't know. I'm already so far behind, what difference will it make?
Mrs. Werner:	I understand your doubts. But Bobby, I'm not worried about the past. I'm hoping you can make things better for the future.
Bobby:	It won't make any difference.
Mr. Pope:	Mrs. Werner, we'll have to think this through, but perhaps we could work out a system where Bobby's grades start counting from now and the past is somehow forgiven.
Mrs. Werner:	I don't think that would be fair to the other students.
Mr. Pope:	What if we worked out a system where one zero was erased for every assignment that Bobby turns in on time and complete?
Mrs. Werner:	I think I could live with that. Bobby, what do you think? It means you have a chance to get rid of all those zeroes, but you have to show us you are really making an effort.
Bobby:	Yeah, that would be OK.
Mr. Pope:	Good. You can begin with Mrs. Werner's class. I'll talk with your other teachers, and we'll see what we can do.

2. Show the student how to record his behavior.

Go over logistics of the plan—where the student's record will be kept, when and how information will be recorded, and so on.

3. Define responsible and irresponsible behavior.

Discuss several examples of responsible and irresponsible behavior to identify boundaries, as explained in Step 1B. Role-play examples and have the student identify whether the behavior is a responsible or an irresponsible example. Provide supportive and corrective feedback about the student's responses. Continue this process using a wide variety of different examples. If the student needs practice beyond the initial meeting, schedule additional practice times.

Mr. Pope: (Counselor)	Bobby, I appreciate your working with us. By putting our heads together, I know that we are going to conquer this homework thing. You deserve the chance to earn good grades and to do as well as you can. Do you understand the monitoring system?
Bobby:	(Nods)
Mr. Pope:	Good. Understanding it is the first step. I look forward to working with you. I have two boys of my own—one in sixth grade and one in ninth grade. I've worked with them on homework too. My oldest son had a terrible time learning to get organized, but he is doing great now. I think we can really make progress. This is the schedule we've set up . . .

4. Help the student identify a reward to give himself as he makes progress.

Discuss with the student possible self-rewards. Examples might include:
- using a computer to graph the record
- extra time with friends
- extra privilege in class (front of the line, homework pass, etc.)
- scheduling a special time with a parent to discuss improvements
- writing to a grandparent about improvements
- telling yourself you are doing a good job

Mr. Pope:	Bobby, you are going to be working on becoming more mature. It will not be easy, so you deserve to reward yourself for improvements. What are some things that

	you might like to do to remind yourself you are doing a good job?
Bobby:	Like get a Ferrari?
Mr. Pope:	Don't we all wish . . . . Are there special things you like to do? Let me give you an example. I hate to exercise, but I know that I need to. So I tell myself that every time I exercise, I get to watch the evening news on TV. I know that probably sounds weird, but the point is I love to watch the news but often think I don't have time. It is a reward for me. Can you think of some things that might make you feel good—not big, huge, splashy things, but things you would feel good letting yourself do?
Bobby:	Well, I like to watch TV.
Mr. Pope:	That's the idea. How about letting yourself watch a half hour of TV for every half hour you study?

C. Review everyone's roles and responsibilities.

Review the schedules and the roles and responsibilities of everyone involved.

1. Model and verbally rehearse the steps.

Have the student model and verbally rehearse the steps of the self-monitoring procedures. Make sure the student can demonstrate what he will do and explain the goal of self-monitoring.

2. Provide a list of the process steps.

If it is appropriate for the student's academic level, provide a written list of the self-monitoring steps. A short list of the process can serve as a guide for reviewing the process at periodic intervals during the first several days of the plan. (If the self-monitoring system involves a checklist, this may already be embedded in the self-monitoring process.)

3. Schedule a follow-up meeting to discuss progress.

An adult should meet with the student soon after implementing the plan to determine how things are going and whether the plan needs revision, and to provide the student with encouragement.

INTERVENTION

K

Mr. Pope: (Counselor)	Let's see. On Monday, I will get you from your seventh-period class and walk you through the process of going to your locker, picking up your materials, checking things off, and so on. Does anyone have any questions?
Bobby:	(Shakes his head)
Mr. Pope:	Good. Bobby, you and I will meet every morning for a few minutes during homeroom. We'll do that for awhile so we can see how things are going. I'll also get weekly reports from your teachers so we can see if things are going better. Mrs. Werner, you will check periodically to make sure that Bobby has recorded his assignments, and when you can, give me anecdotal notes about Bobby's progress. And then, for every new homework assignment that Bobby turns in completed and on time, you will erase one zero from your grade book. I'll talk with the other teachers and see if we can work something out.

4. Review the procedures.

Be sure everyone involved in the plan has a clear understanding of the procedures. Use a few minutes of this time to ask *what-if* questions. If various contingencies have been discussed in advance, the greater the likelihood the plan will not break down due to unforeseen events.

D. Conclude the meeting with words of encouragement.

Mrs. Werner: (Teacher)	Bobby, I am very excited about this plan. I know you have a lot of potential. I appreciate Mr. Pope's willingness to help us out. Mr. Pope, I'm glad that you can find the time to meet with Bobby.
Mr. Pope:	Bobby, I hope you realize that we are here to help you. If you have any problems or questions, you can talk to any of us.
Mrs. Werner:	Bobby, I think that you really deserve to learn how to get homework done. You are so capable. I know that you can learn to be responsible. I am looking forward to seeing you make a lot of improvement this year. I'm glad to have you in my class so that I can be part of it.

Step 3: Implement the plan.

A. Encourage student efforts.

Learning new behaviors and discarding old behaviors is very difficult for some students. Though a particular change may seem simple to an adult, to a child it can be as difficult as learning a new language or musical instrument. The student may need a lot of practice, the opportunity to make errors and adjustments, and a lot of encouragement along the way.

B. Make periodic revisions and adjustments to the plan as necessary.

During the first week of the intervention, Bobby turns in all of his assignments on time. Mrs. Werner is delighted, as are his other teachers. Mrs. Werner reports in her anecdotal record that Bobby did most of his assignments independently, but he wanted approval on assignments that required writing. Mr. Pope worries that without attention, Bobby might not complete his writing assignments when working at home. Mr. Pope discusses the concern with Mrs. Werner, and she agrees to edit Bobby's writing the day it's due and allow him to make corrections during lunch.

C. When the student demonstrates consistent success, fade the intervention.

As the student assumes ownership of a new behavior or breaks an old habit, gradually remove the monitoring system. Fading can involve increasing time intervals between monitoring. For example, if the student has been keeping track of on-task behavior and the monitoring was initially taking place all day, the system could be faded by limiting checks to certain parts of the day. Fading might also include providing less and less adult guidance. The general rule of thumb is to fade the system when the student demonstrates consistent success, but to provide the student with any support that is necessary for continued improvements. One very natural way to fade the system is to eliminate the formal self-monitoring form but continue verbal debriefing with the student once or twice a week to encourage the student to be self-reflective about her behavior. The teacher can also provide feedback on her perceptions of the student's overall performance. If the gains are being maintained, provide positive feedback on the student's maturity and self-discipline. If the student is backsliding, consider reinstituting formal self-monitoring.

The general rule of thumb is to fade the system when the student demonstrates consistent success, but to provide the student with any support that is necessary for continued improvements.

INTERVENTION

K

During the first two weeks of the intervention, Bobby's self-monitoring plan works extremely well under Mr. Pope's guidance. In the second week, Bobby meets with Mr. Pope only on Monday, Wednesday, and Friday. On Tuesday and Thursday, Bobby successfully completes his homework, and Mr. Pope calls Bobby's father and mother to let them know how well Bobby is doing. During the third week, Mr. Pope's help is provided only on Tuesday and Thursday. Wednesday night, Bobby does not complete his homework assignment. Bobby tells Mr. Pope that he didn't have time to get it done because his mother had taken him out for a special dinner with friends, and by the time they got home it was too late to study. Bobby and Mr. Pope decide that Bobby needs to complete his homework right after school. This plan seems to work.

Just as Mr. Pope and Bobby are considering cutting Mr. Pope's assistance back to once a week, Bobby receives a long-term report-writing assignment from Mrs. Werner. Mrs. Werner lets Mr. Pope know that Bobby might need extra help managing the assignment. Rather than cutting back on help, it seems likely Bobby might need special assistance for this assignment. Because Bobby views his growing independence as a sign of his improvement, Mr. Pope thinks it would be inappropriate to increase his assistance, so they decide to keep the existing schedule so that Bobby doesn't put the entire assignment off until it is too late. After problem solving with Mrs. Werner, it is decided that the long-term report writing assignment will be broken down into daily assignments that can be managed with the routines that are already in place.

D. Once the intervention has been faded, provide continued follow-up, support, and encouragement.

Once a student demonstrates consistent success, it is easy to take appropriate behavior for granted. However, the student will have made a major change in behavior and will need continued encouragement and support for his efforts.

As Bobby shows consistency in turning in completed homework assignments, his parents both provide him with tremendous support. His father calls the school to ask if he can take Bobby out of school to go on a special ski trip. After considering the consequences of Bobby's potentially falling behind in his work, it is decided that winter break might be a better option. Mr. Pope also brainstorms a list of other supportive things Bobby's father could do—giving Bobby occasional notes of encouragement and recognition, taking Bobby out for a soda, going over his work with a focus on assignments done well, having Bobby explain his assignment sheet and goals, and playing a game together.

Mr. Pope continues to meet with Bobby and check with his teachers every two weeks. Toward the end of the year, Bobby is selected to be a peer mentor for the following year.

CONCLUSION

One-to-one interventions can be time consuming and difficult to implement in a busy classroom. Therefore, systems must be designed to be as unintrusive as possible. If the plan requires an unrealistic amount of teacher time and energy, modify the plan to reduce teacher monitoring or include another adult.

Self-monitoring can be an extremely empowering process for a student. It is used by adults when they learn time-management systems or for managing diet or exercise programs. Self-monitoring teaches students that they can manage how they act and what they do, and they can grow and mature in the process.

REFERENCES

Alberto, P. A., & Troutman, A. C. (2003). *Applied behavior analysis for teachers* (6th ed.). Upper Saddle River, NJ: Pearson Education.

Amato-Zech, N. A., Hoff, K. E., & Doepke, K. J. (2006). Increasing on-task behavior in the classroom: Extension of self-monitoring strategies. *Psychology in the Schools, 43,* 211–221.

Anderson, L. M. (1989). Implementing instructional programs to promote meaningful, self-regulated learning. In Brophy, J. E. (Ed.), *Advances in research on teaching* (Vol. 1, pp. 311–341). Greenwich, CT: JAI Press.

Brown, D., & Frank, A. (1990). "Let me do it!" Self-monitoring in solving arithmetic problems. *Education and Treatment of Children, 13,* 239–248.

Cavalier, A. R., Ferretti, R. P., & Hodges, A. E. (1997). Self-management within a classroom token economy for students with learning disabilities. *Research in Developmental Disabilities, 18*(3), 167–178.

Corno, L., & Mandinach, E. (1983). The role of cognitive engagement in classroom learning and motivation. *Educational Psychologist, 18*, 88–108.

Daly, P. M., & Ranalli, P. (2003). Using countoons to teach self-monitoring skills. *Teaching Exceptional Children, 35*(5), 30–35.

De La Paz, S. (1999). Self-regulated strategy instruction in regular education settings: Improving outcomes for students with and without learning disabilities. *Learning Disabilities Research and Practice, 14*(2), 92–106.

Dunlap, G., Shelley, C., Jackson, M., Wright, S., Ramos, E., & Brinson, S. (1995). Self-monitoring of classroom behaviors with students exhibiting emotional and behavioral challenges. *School Psychology Quarterly, 10*, 165–177.

Fuchs, L. S., & Fuchs, D. (1987). The relation between methods of graphing student performance data and achievement: A meta-analysis. *Journal of Special Education Technology, 8*, 135–149.

Graham, S., Harris, K., & Reid, R. (1992). Developing self-regulated learners. *Focus on Exceptional Children, 24*(6), 3–16.

Gureasko-Moore, S., DuPaul, G. J., & White, G. P. (2006). The effects of self-management in general education classrooms on the organizational skills of adolescents with ADHD. *Behavior Modification, 30*, 159–183.

Hallahan, D. P., Marshall, K. J., & Lloyd, J. W. (1981). Self-recording during group instruction: Effects on attention to task. *Learning Disabilities Quarterly, 4*, 407–413.

Johnson, L. R., & Johnson, C. E. (1999). Teaching students to regulate their own behavior. *Teaching Exceptional Children, 31*(4), 6–10.

Kern, L., Dunlap, G., Childs, K., & Clarke, S. (1994). Use of a classroom self-management program to improve the behavior of students with emotional and behavioral disorders. *Education and Treatment of Children, 17*, 445–458.

Lloyd, J. W., Hallahan, D. P., Kosiewicz, M. M., & Kneedler, R. D. (1982). Reactive effects of self-assessment and self-recording on attention to task and academic productivity. *Learning Disability Quarterly, 5*, 216–227.

Lloyd, J. W., & Landrum, T. J. (1990). Self-recording of attending to task: Treatment components and generalization of effects. In T. E. Scruggs & B. Y. L. Wong (Eds.), *Intervention research in learning disabilities* (pp. 235–262). New York: Springer-Verlag.

Maag, J. W., Reid, R., & DiGangi, S. A. (1993). Differential effects of self-monitoring attention, accuracy, and productivity. *Journal of Applied Behavior Analysis, 26,* 329–344.

McConnell, M. (1999). Self-monitoring, cueing, recording, and managing: Teaching students to manage their own behavior. *Teaching Exceptional Children, 32*(2), 14–21.

McDougall, D., & Brady, M. P. (1995). Using audio-cued self-monitoring for students with severe behavioral disorders. *The Journal of Educational Research, 88,* 309–317.

McDougall, D., & Brady, M. P. (1998). Initiating and fading self-management interventions to increase math fluency in general education classes. *Exceptional Children, 64*(2), 151–166.

Meichenbaum, D. H. (1977). *Cognitive-behavior modification: An integrated approach.* New York: Plenum Press.

Meichenbaum, D. H. (1979). Teaching children self-control. In B. Lahey & A. Kazdin (Eds.), *Advances in child psychology* (Vol. 2). New York: Plenum Press.

Mitchem, K. J., & Young, K. R. (2001). Adapting self-management programs for classwide use: Acceptability, feasibility, and effectiveness. *Remedial and Special Education, 22,* 75–88.

Mooney, P., Ryan, J. B., Uhing, B. M., Reid, R., & Epstein, M. H. (2005). A review of self-management interventions targeting academic outcomes for students with emotional and behavioral disorders. *Journal of Behavioral Education, 14,* 203–221.

Osborne, S. S., Kosiewick, M. M., Crumley, E. B., & Lee, C. (1987). Destructible students use self-monitoring. *Teaching Exceptional Children, 19,* 66–69.

Peterson, L., Young, R., West, R., & Peterson, M. (1999). Effects of student self-management on generalization of student performance to regular classrooms. *Education and Treatment of Children, 22*(3), 357–372.

Reid, R. (1996). Research in self-monitoring with students with learning disabilities: The present, the prospects, and the pitfalls. *Journal of Learning Disabilities, 29,* 317–331.

Reid, R., & Harris, K. (1993). Self-monitoring of attention versus self-monitoring of performance. *Exceptional Children, 60*(1), 29–40.

Reid, R., Trout, A. L., & Schwartz, M. (2005). Self-regulation interventions for children with Attention Deficit/Hyperactivity Disorder. *Exceptional Children, 71,* 361–377.

Rock, M. L. (2005). Use of strategic self-monitoring to enhance academic engagement, productivity, and accuracy of students with and without exceptionalities. *Journal of Positive Behavior Interventions, 7,* 3–17.

Shapiro, E. S., DuPaul, G. J., & Bradley-Klug, K. L. (1998). Self-management as a strategy to improve the classroom behavior of adolescents with ADHD. *Journal of Learning Disabilities, 31*(6), 545–555.

Shapiro, E. S., Durnan, S. L., Post, E. E., & Levinson, T. S. (2002). Self-monitoring procedures for children and adolescents. In M. A. Shinn, H. M. Walker, & G. Stoner (Eds.), *Interventions for academic and behavior problems II: Preventive and remedial approaches* (pp. 433–454). Bethesda, MD: National Association of School Psychologists.

Shimabukuro, S., Prater, M., Jenkins, A., & Edelen-Smith, P. (1999). The effects of self-monitoring of academic performance on students with learning disabilities and ADD/ADHD. *Education and Treatment of Children, 22,* 397–414.

Sutherland, K. S., & Wehby, J. H. (2001). The effect of self-evaluation on teaching behavior in classrooms for students with emotional and behavioral disorders. *The Journal of Special Education, 35*(3), 161–171.

Swaggart, B. (1998). Implementing a cognitive behavior management program. *Intervention in School and Clinic, 33,* 235–238.

Todd, A., Horner, R., & Sugai, G. (1999). Effects of self-monitoring and self-recruited praise on problem behavior, academic engagement and work completion in a typical classroom. *Journal of Positive Behavior Interventions, 1,* 66–76.

Toney, L. P., Kelley, M. L., & Lanclos, N. F. (2003). Self- and parental monitoring of homework in adolescents: Comparative effects on parents' perceptions of homework behavior problems. *Child and Family Behavior Therapy, 25,* 35–51.

Trammel, D., Schloss, P., & Alper, S. (1994). Using self-recording, evaluation, and graphing to increase completion of homework assignments. *Journal of Learning Disabilities, 27*(2), 75–81.

Van Leuvan, P., & Wang, M. C. (1997). An analysis of students' self-monitoring in first- and second-grade classrooms. *Journal of Educational Research, 90*(3), 132–143.

INTERVENTION

K

Webber, J., Scheuermann, B., McCall, C., & Coleman, M. (1993). Research on self-monitoring as a behavior management technique in special education classrooms: A descriptive review. *Remedial and Special Education, 14*(2), 38–56.

Wong, B. Y. L., & Wong, R. (1986). Study behavior as a function of metacognitive knowledge about critical task variables: An investigation of above average, average and learning-disabled readers. *Learning Disabilities Research, 1,* 101–111.

Reproducible Materials

The following reproducible materials may be used in conjunction with "Intervention K: Self-Monitoring and Self-Evaluation." Copies are provided in this chapter and on the CD. Permission is given for individual classroom teachers to reproduce any forms labeled "Reproducible" for classroom use. Reproduction of these materials for an entire school system is prohibited without express permission of the publisher.

Reproducible Step-by-Step Summary (1 of 2)

INTERVENTION  K

SELF-MONITORING AND SELF-EVALUATION

Step-by-Step Summary

Following is a summary of the steps involved in Intervention K. It is important to use professional judgment, adjusting procedures to meet the needs of the situation and the individual. See the chapter "Intervention K: Self-Monitoring and Self-Evaluation" for a detailed description of this intervention.

STEP 1 Develop a plan.

A. Determine the behavior to be monitored and evaluated.

B. If necessary, identify examples of student behavior that set boundaries between responsible and irresponsible behavior.

C. Determine when the student will record behaviors.

D. Develop a recording system for the student.

E. Design a cueing system to prompt the student to record.

F. Plan to have an adult monitor the student's behavior occasionally and compare results with the student's record.

G. Identify ways to determine whether the intervention is helping the student reach his goal.

H. Determine who will meet with the student to discuss and finalize the plan.

STEP 2 Meet with the student to discuss and finalize the plan.

A. Review the problem and goal.

B. Introduce the procedures that will be followed.
   1. Introduce the self-monitoring or self-evaluation system to the student.
   2. Show the student how to record his behavior.
   3. Define responsible and irresponsible behavior.
   4. Help the student identify a reward to give himself as he makes progress.

INTERVENTION

C. Review everyone's roles and responsibilities.
1. Model and verbally rehearse the steps.
2. Provide a list of the process steps.
3. Schedule a follow-up meeting to discuss progress.
4. Review the procedures.

D. Conclude the meeting with words of encouragement.

STEP 3   Implement the plan.

A. Encourage student efforts.

B. Make periodic revisions and adjustments to the plan as necessary.

C. When the student demonstrates consistent success, fade the intervention.

D. Once the intervention has been faded, provide continued follow-up, support, and encouragement.

Self-Monitoring Form:
Homework Completion

Name _____   Week of _____

Due	Assignment	Materials	Done

	M	U	W	H	F
Before leaving school each day, I will study from _____ to _____ and from _____ to _____ if needed.					
I have logged long-term assignments not yet finished on tomorrow's assignment sheet.					
I have organized my assignments in my notebook.					
I have packed all my books, materials, and notebook in my backpack.					
I have put my backpack by the door.					

Self-Monitoring Form:
On-Task Behavior

Name _____   Week of _____

Date _____

Did I stay focused on my task?			
very off task	off task	mostly on task	on task; very focused
1	2	3	4

Date _____

Did I stay focused on my task?			
very off task	off task	mostly on task	on task; very focused
1	2	3	4

Date _____

Did I stay focused on my task?			
very off task	off task	mostly on task	on task; very focused
1	2	3	4

Date _____

Did I stay focused on my task?			
very off task	off task	mostly on task	on task; very focused
1	2	3	4

Date _____

Did I stay focused on my task?			
very off task	off task	mostly on task	on task; very focused
1	2	3	4

Reproducible Form K12: *Self-Monitoring Form*

Intervention K:
Self-Monitoring and Self-Evaluation

Self-Monitoring Form

Name _____   Week of _____

Date _____

| I am working on _____ |
| 1   2   3   4 |

Date _____

| I am working on _____ |
| 1   2   3   4 |

Date _____

| I am working on _____ |
| 1   2   3   4 |

Date _____

| I am working on _____ |
| 1   2   3   4 |

Date _____

| I am working on _____ |
| 1   2   3   4 |

Reproducible Form K13: *Self-Monitoring Form: On-Task Behavior*

Self-Monitoring Form:
On-Task Behavior

Name _____   Week of _____

Date _____

| Did I stay focused on my work? |
| no 1   2   3   yes 4 |

Date _____

| Did I stay focused on my work? |
| no 1   2   3   yes 4 |

Date _____

| Did I stay focused on my work? |
| no 1   2   3   yes 4 |

Date _____

| Did I stay focused on my work? |
| no 1   2   3   yes 4 |

Date _____

| Did I stay focused on my work? |
| no 1   2   3   yes 4 |

Reproducible Form K14: *Self-Monitoring Form*

Self-Monitoring Form

Name _____

Week of _____

Date _____

I am working on _____

😞 1   😐 2   🙂 3   😄 4

Date _____

I am working on _____

😞 1   😐 2   🙂 3   😄 4

Date _____

I am working on _____

😞 1   😐 2   🙂 3   😄 4

Date _____

I am working on _____

😞 1   😐 2   🙂 3   😄 4

Date _____

I am working on _____

😞 1   😐 2   🙂 3   😄 4

Reproducible Form K15: *Self-Monitoring Form*

Self-Monitoring Form

Name _____

Week of _____

Goal _____

Directions: Put a + or - after each time period.

WEEK OF:	Bus	9:00	10:00	11:00	12:00	1:00	2:00	3:00
Monday								
Tuesday								
Wednesday								
Thursday								
Friday								

WEEK OF:	Bus	9:00	10:00	11:00	12:00	1:00	2:00	3:00
Monday								
Tuesday								
Wednesday								
Thursday								
Friday								

WEEK OF:	Bus	9:00	10:00	11:00	12:00	1:00	2:00	3:00
Monday								
Tuesday								
Wednesday								
Thursday								
Friday								

WEEK OF:	Bus	9:00	10:00	11:00	12:00	1:00	2:00	3:00
Monday								
Tuesday								
Wednesday								
Thursday								
Friday								

Self-Monitoring Form

Name _____

Week of _____

Directions: Put a + under each header, where earned.

DATE	SUBJECT	Behavior	Work	In Seat	Language	TOTAL
				Total of + marks		

DATE	SUBJECT	Behavior	Work	In Seat	Language	TOTAL
				Total of + marks		

DATE	SUBJECT	Behavior	Work	In Seat	Language	TOTAL
				Total of + marks		

DATE	SUBJECT	Behavior	Work	In Seat	Language	TOTAL
				Total of + marks		

DATE	SUBJECT	Behavior	Work	In Seat	Language	TOTAL
				Total of + marks		

Reproducible Form K17: *Self-Monitoring Form*

Self-Monitoring Form

Name _____   Date _____

Directions: Put a + under each header, where earned. Calculate bonus points with tally marks in the column.

DATE:

Time	Work = Complete 8/10 reading comprehension questions using complete sentences.		
	Behavior = Eyes on own work, writing all period, staying at desk.		
	Bonus = Making positive comments to peers or teacher.		
Time	**Work**	**Behavior**	**Bonus**
9:00			
9:30			
10:00			
10:30			
11:00			
11:30			
12:00			
12:30			
1:00			
1:30			
2:00			
2:30			
3:00			
3:30			
Percent of + marks:			Total:

Intervention K:
Self-Monitoring and Self-Evaluation

Self-Monitoring Form

Name _____   Date _____

Directions: Put a + under each header, where earned. Calculate bonus points with tally marks in the column.

DATE:

Work =			
Behavior =			
Bonus =			

Time	Work	Behavior	Bonus
9:00			
9:30			
10:00			
10:30			
11:00			
11:30			
12:00			
12:30			
1:00			
1:30			
2:00			
2:30			
3:00			
3:30			
Percent of + marks:			Total:

Reproducible Form K19: *Self-Monitoring Form: Behavior*

Self-Monitoring Form: Behavior

Name _____   Date _____

Directions: Put a ✔ under each header, as appropriate.

Target Behavior					
Time		Sad		OK		Happy
8:00 to 8:15					
8:15 to 8:30					
8:30 to 8:45					
8:45 to 9:00					
9:00 to 9:15					
9:15 to 9:30					
9:30 to 9:45					
9:45 to 10:00					
10:00 to 10:15					
10:15 to 10:30					
10:30 to 10:45					
10:45 to 11:00					
11:00 to 11:15					
11:15 to 11:30					
11:30 to 11:45					
11:45 to 12:00					
12:00 to 12:15					
12:15 to 12:30					
12:30 to 12:45					
12:45 to 1:00					
1:00 to 1:15					
1:15 to 1:30					
1:30 to 1:45					
1:45 to 2:00					
2:00 to 2:15					
2:15 to 2:30					
2:30 to 2:45					
2:45 to 3:00					
3:00 to 3:15					
3:15 to 3:30					

Total of Happy ✔ [   ]

Self-Talk and Attribution Training

| *The student habitually makes negative comments about himself or others*

PURPOSE

THIS INTERVENTION IS DESIGNED to help students overcome problems associated with negative thinking and self-criticism.

THIS INTERVENTION IS APPROPRIATE FOR:

Negative attitude
- "Do we have to do that?"
- "Painting is stupid. Why do we have to do art, anyway?"

Self-putdowns
- "I can't do anything."

Poor self-esteem or self-concept
- "What do you expect? I knew I'd blow it."

Defeatist attitude
- "I'll just mess it up if I try and do that."

Self-control problems
- "I can't help it. He made me hit him."

Excessive criticism or sarcasm
- "Those are really ugly shoes."
- "Yeah, right. Sure."

Self-talk encompasses the verbal and nonverbal statements and thoughts people make about themselves and others. It's the running interior monologue that everyone engages in, even when we're barely aware of it. In a more abstract sense, self-talk can be thought of as the stories we tell ourselves about ourselves. Over time, patterns of self-talk can affect how people think about themselves and others, achievements and setbacks, success and "failure." How people feel in turn affects their self-talk, creating the conditions for a self-perpetuating cycle. There's nothing inherently wrong with that; such a cycle can often be positive. But when the cycle turns negative for more than a short period, the long-term effects can be far-reaching and destructive.

Self-Talk and Attribution Training can interrupt a potentially destructive cycle spiral by teaching students how to redirect negative thoughts and statements. This simple change can produce more positive results in their lives, which in turn affects attitude, motivation, academic achievement, and overall behavior.

> *Over time, patterns of self-talk can affect how people think about themselves and others, achievements and setbacks, success and "failure."*

Note: Be sure to involve parents in the process of deciding whether this intervention is appropriate. Some parents may have religious, philosophical, or cultural concerns about the concept of directly addressing a child's self-talk through intervention.

RATIONALE

Clearly, behavior is influenced by how we perceive ourselves. We tend to do the things we think we will be successful at and avoid endeavors we think we will fail in. (Remember the *Expectancy × Value = Motivation* formula from Intervention B.) By the same token, when our behaviors and actions result in success and achievement, we feel good about ourselves. Self-talk is an integral part of how people perceive their own successes and achievements and thus how they feel and behave. When we allow our thoughts to turn negative, we are more likely to feel bad, have difficulty accomplishing tasks, and lose touch with a positive sense of ourselves. Alternatively, when we think positively, we tend to behave positively and realize feelings of self-worth and accomplishment.

Self-talk is thus intimately tied to self-concept and image—the general perceptions people have of themselves. Behavior, for better or worse, tends to reflect these perceptions. For example, if a student's self-talk states that the student is "a failure," the student's behavior will probably include a lack of motivation, avoidance tactics, and other problem behaviors. Because educators can do little to influence a student's self-concept directly, this intervention is primarily concerned with addressing what can be monitored, modified, and positively affected—self-talk.

> Note: For the purposes of this intervention, the term *self-talk* is inclusive of self-criticism (inwardly directed negativity) and criticism of others (outwardly directed negativity), both verbalized and internal.

This intervention addresses both overt self-talk (statements made aloud or attitudes on public display) and, hopefully over time, covert self-talk (thoughts and feelings imperceptible to an outside observer). If you are concerned about a student who displays outward negativity, it is safe to assume that the student's internal self-talk follows much the same path. By working with the student to redirect verbalized statements in a more positive direction, you can help reframe the student's internal dialogue. Over time this should lead to a healthier and more accurate self-image.

> Angie is a sixth-grade student who never learned to read well. Although her reading abilities are sufficient enough for her to comprehend much of the material, Angie reads slowly and inaccurately. Because reading has always been difficult, Angie avoids reading unless it's absolutely necessary, which is resulting in her falling further and further behind her peers in all subjects. As Angie muddles through her schoolwork, she begins to feel less and less competent.

INTERVENTION

L

In fifth grade, Angie's reading difficulties began outpacing her ability to compensate, and remediation of her reading problem was initiated. By the end of the year, Angie was reading solidly at grade level. However, her other academic difficulties persisted. Although she gained the skills needed to be successful, Angie's self-concept is still bruised by years of struggling. She still approaches assignments out of habit, thinking, "It won't be fun. It's too hard. I can't do this." Angie's ingrained negative thoughts are becoming barriers to her success. Angie's counselor determines that Self-Talk and Attribution Training is an appropriate intervention for Angie, in combination with other academic assistance strategies such as those in "Intervention B: Academic Assistance."

Note: Some level of negativity and self-criticism is inevitable for anyone who is in touch with reality. Events are not always positive, and everyone has strengths and weaknesses. This intervention is not about eliminating negative statements or self-criticism, but is rather about helping an individual who is excessively negative to get out of a self-defeating or pessimistic cycle and into more healthy and optimistic patterns of overt statements and internal self-talk.

Before implementing Self-Talk and Attribution Training

Before beginning this intervention, be sure you have done the following:

- Discuss the problem with the student.

- Outline some general goals for improvement.

- Try one or more of the Early-Stage Interventions first.

- Gather background information that may be relevant and helpful in designing the intervention.

- Contact the student's parents or guardian to discuss the concern, invite them to participate in intervention selection and design, and keep them actively informed throughout the process.

IMPLEMENTATION STEPS

Self-Talk and Attribution Training is often best paired with other interventions. In Angie's example, it would be inappropriate to provide Angie with training in positive self-talk unless her academic problems are also addressed. Similarly, if a student has anger-control problems, training in positive self-talk should be coupled with an intervention that would teach the student appropriate responses to situational triggers, such as "Intervention I: Managing the Cycle of Emotional Escalation" or "Intervention M: Teaching Replacement Behavior."

Step 1: Develop a plan.

Review the problem and overall goals for the student. Defining the nature and scope of the problem provides critical information for developing a successful intervention.

Armando is a ninth grader who is easily frustrated. When he makes errors in math, he explodes. "This sucks! I can't do this!" If he misses a ball in a baseball game, he stalks off in a huff. He is often seen leaving games, and he frequently tells his teachers, "I can't do anything!"

Athletically, Armando is like most boys his age. He does not have remarkable abilities, nor does he have serious problems. Academically, Armando also seems of average ability. Results from an informal reading inventory show that he reads with good fluency and comprehends grade-level materials. His English teacher, Mr. Blake, reports that he's a capable boy, but he becomes very angry when he makes even a minor mistake.

Armando's parents are supportive of school. They see reasons for his frustration at home—Armando has an older sister who does exceptionally well in school, and Armando feels he must compete. On the other hand, it is difficult to get Armando to do his work. Armando's parents report that he huffs and puffs about having to do homework. Once he settles down, he does fine, but it is always a struggle at first.

Armando's teachers notice that Armando vacillates between frustration, anger, and not wanting to try. "I can't do this assignment. I'll just mess it up." Armando's English teacher tries to reassure him whenever he hears Armando put himself down, but he believes Armando needs help learning to value his own efforts.

Everyone agrees that Armando's negative self-talk is increasing his dissatisfaction with himself. The school counselor, acting as an interventionist, Armando's teachers, and his parents decide to help Armando restructure his self-talk and work to provide Armando with activities that will help him improve his self-concept. They decide that the goal for this intervention is to help Armando recognize his abilities through positive self-talk.

A. List the types of negative statements the student makes.

Compiling a list of negative statements will help you determine which steps to take in this intervention, and it will help the student understand how his specific negative statements—statements that are self-directed, aimed toward others, or just gripes in general—impede personal goals. As extensively as you can, document the types of negative and defeatist self-talk you hear regularly from the student. The examples you generate will define the kind of statements you want to focus on changing with the student.

As extensively as you can, document the types of negative and defeatist self-talk you hear regularly from the student.

Mr. Shuffield, the school counselor, confers with Armando's English teacher and begins making a list of Armando's negative statements:

PE
- "I hate running laps. It's stupid. I'm always last."
- "Soccer is a dumb sport, and no one wants me on their team."

Book reports
- "I can't read that whole book."
- "There is no way I will be able to write a decent persuasive essay."

Homework
- "I hate homework. I don't have time to get it all done."
- "I always forget, and I leave the work I do get done at home."

This intervention addresses two broad types of negative self-talk. The first is self-talk that is negativity directed outward—complaining about events and circumstances, criticizing other people. An outwardly negative student may appear annoyed and irritable much of the time. Negativity that is directed inward looks different; it is marked by pessimism, defeatism, or excessive self-criticism. Inward negativity is characterized by the student frequently attributing failure to himself, even with events over which the student has little or no control—"It will always be this bad because I am stupid; nothing ever works for me"—or by discounting success as a fluke or exception rather than a function of the student's own abilities and initiative. After you have completed a list of typical negative statements the student makes, begin categorizing the statements according to type. If the student's negative comments appear to be primarily directed outward, proceed to Step 1B. If inward negativity appears to be the problem, proceed to Step 1C.

B. Consider whether training in positive self-talk would be sufficient.

If the list of negative statements you developed in Step 1A is primarily oriented outward, directed toward others or external events rather than self-directed criticism, your intervention plan can be straightforward: You will teach the student how to decrease negative comments simply by substituting more positive statements. From a teaching perspective, dealing with a chronic complainer will no longer be a problem if 80 percent of what used to be complaints are replaced with positive statements.

If you are concerned that the student also has issues with self-criticism that impede his ability to see and achieve success, proceed to Step 1C, attribution training. If inwardly directed criticism is not a major concern for the student, proceed to Step 1D, constructing a positive statement bank.

C. Consider whether attribution training would be appropriate.

The student who appears to direct the bulk of negativity at himself may be more difficult to reach and create a change in his behavior. Because of this, your intervention will be slightly more complicated than the simple method of increasing positive statements, as discussed in Step 1B. You will need to expand your focus to deal with negativity that is directed inward ("I am so stupid") as well as statements that are directed outward ("This assignment is so stupid"). One method we recommend, based on the landmark work of psychologist Martin Seligman, is called *attribution retraining* or simply *attribution training*. It's based on the fundamental understanding that people attach meaning to circumstances and events—that is, they attribute—based on the way they talk and think about them. Another word for attribution in this sense is *explanation*. How students perceive and explain their successes and failures becomes the prism through which they view everything, including themselves. Attribution training involves teaching students to change the way they think and talk about their experiences—is the glass half empty or half full?

Attribution training involves teaching students to change the way they think and talk about their experiences—is the glass half empty or half full?

INTERVENTION

L

Note: Seligman's *The Optimistic Child* (1995) and *Learned Optimism: How to Change Your Mind and Your Life* (1998) are excellent resources for more on this subject.

Seligman's research on learned helplessness indicates that depressed individuals tend to attribute failures and problems to their own perceived weaknesses or shortcomings, and they attribute successes and positive events to factors outside their control. Conversely, individuals with a more healthy outlook tend to do the opposite—they attribute their successes to their own effort and determination, and they attribute occasional failures and problems to factors outside their control. That is not to say that healthy individuals make excuses, but rather that they are willing to recognize that sometimes events are outside their control. For example, it is more healthy for a student to attribute her parents' divorce to outside circumstances than to blame herself for this unhappy circumstance. Having an optimistic outlook does not mean putting on rose-colored glasses. Both the optimist and pessimist recognize their failures and are aware of bad circumstances. The difference is in how they explain or interpret events to themselves. Whether a student views the glass as half empty or half full is a personal choice with important implications.

A student who tends to discount successes ("I just got lucky that time") and wallow in mistakes, failures, and setbacks ("Everything I touch falls apart") may benefit from attribution training. Following is a brief explanation of attribution training theory. It may seem complicated at first, but it really all comes down to this: Depressed and pessimistic people explain failures as uncontrollable or insurmountable and explain successes as flukes. The aim of intervention is to turn that habituation on its head, so that in time the student may learn to view successes and failures in more empowering terms.

Explanation of Attribution Theory

Attribution has three dimensions: self, time, and scope or breadth. Happy and successful students view the good things that happen to them as being a result of internal, stable, and global factors. In other words, they chalk up the bad things that inevitably happen to external, unstable, and case-specific causes. For example, a student who has a healthy manner of attribution would view an A in math as the result of her own perseverance and skills. She might view a bad grade on one assignment as the result of not planning ahead to study and running out of time. This viewpoint does not mean the student is unaccountable for mistakes; it simply means she does not believe that most problems are insurmountable and arising from defects of character. Unhappy and negative students do just the reverse—they tend to explain away, or *attribute,* their successes to external, unstable, and case-specific causes. They blow mistakes out of proportion, attributing failure to internal, stable, and global causes. To make this clear, we can look at each of these dimensions individually. We'll call a healthy, positive approach of viewing endeavors with a high likelihood of success "optimistic attribution." A fatalistic, despairing, or defeatist approach will be called "pessimistic attribution."

Figure L1 illustrates how attribution styles can positively or negatively affect self-talk. Notice how each approach views the same circumstance through different internal or external lenses.

Following are descriptions of each of the three dimensions of attribution theory—internal versus external (self), stable versus unstable (time), and specific versus global (scope or breadth).

Figure L1: *Internal/External Attribution*

	Good Things that Happen: Success, Opportunities	**Bad Things that Happen:** Mistakes, Failures, Setbacks
Optimistic attribution 🙂	**Internal:** I got a good grade because I'm good at math and I work hard.	**External:** I got a bad grade because I had to babysit my little brother the last three nights and I did not have time to study. Next time, I should start studying for the test sooner, so if something comes up, I can still do well.
Pessimistic attribution ☹️	**External:** I got a good grade because the assignment was easy.	**Internal:** I got a bad grade on that assignment because I'm dumb.

Internal versus external attribution

In Figure L1, the optimist attributes success or positive circumstances to internal factors within the individual's control, whereas the pessimist attributes success to external factors outside the individual's control. Just the opposite is true for attribution of failure or bad events. In this, the optimist does not deny the mistake or failure (no Pollyannaish naiveté), but attributes it to external events, leaving open the possibility that in the future she might well be able to account for it. ("Next time I should start studying for the test sooner, so if I have to babysit, I can still do well.") The pessimist, meanwhile, blames her own internal inadequacies in every failure—the fault is internal, and there is no recourse for that.

Control theory states that an individual's understanding of who or what controls what happens is either internal or external. With an internal locus of control, we ascribe responsibility for events to our own actions or to factors within our control. With an external locus of control, we ascribe responsibility for things that happen to outside forces over which we have little or no control. In grade-school students, locus of control has been shown to be a good predictor of academic and extracurricular achievement. People with an internal locus of control are, on average, happier and more successful in their endeavors than those with an external locus of control. Put another way, those who "own" their actions believe they have more options and make better choices than those who assign blame everywhere else and, as a result, feel helpless in the face of everything.

Stable versus unstable attribution

The optimist attributes successes to factors that are stable over time ("I always . . .," "Most of the time I . . .," "Usually I can . . .," "With rare exceptions I . . .," "In general I do pretty well at . . ."). The optimist attributes failure to brief, transitory circumstances that will not always be present—"Whoops! I'll get it right next time. I always bounce back."

The pessimist, on the other hand, views success as a brief interruption in a long procession of failures—a blip or anomaly. ("Even a monkey will spell a word now and then if it spends enough time punching a keyboard.") The pessimist also tends to view failure as a product of stable, enduring circumstances that are unlikely to ever change. The pessimist's observations might be peppered with phrases like "always" and "never," "There's no way," "Every single time," "I can't catch a break," and "That's the story of my life." These kinds of attributions, based on stable versus unstable factors, are shown in Figure L2.

The pessimist, on the other hand, views success as a brief interruption in a long procession of failures—a blip or anomaly.

INTERVENTION

L

Figure L2: *Stable/Unstable Attribution*

	Good Things that Happen: Success, Opportunities	**Bad Things that Happen:** Mistakes, Failures, Setbacks
Optimistic attribution	**Stable:** I usually do well at jump shots.	**Unstable:** Once in awhile I am off my game.
Pessimistic attribution	**Unstable:** Not often, but once in a while, I get lucky and do okay with a jump shot.	**Stable:** I always mess up when I get the ball.

Specific versus global attribution

The final attribution type can be seen when the optimist expresses experiences of success or good fortune in broad, far-reaching, or all-encompassing (global) terms. The optimist contextualizes mistakes or misfortune, giving specificity and reasonable weight to the conditions or choices that caused them. By contrast, the pessimist tends to offer constrained, narrow explanations for success and overgeneralizes or widens the scope of perceived reasons for failure. These attributions are shown in Figure L3.

Figure L3: *Specific/Global Attribution*

	Good Things that Happen: Success, Opportunities	**Bad Things that Happen:** Mistakes, Failures, Setbacks
Optimistic attribution	**Global:** Yep, I do pretty well with drawing, and I am even better with painting.	**Specific:** I messed up that drawing because I didn't get the perspective right with my first lines. I'll do better next time.
Pessimistic attribution	**Specific:** Yeah, I can draw horses, but I can't draw anything else.	**Global:** Perspective is such a mess in everything I draw.

Allowing for some overlap, we can generalize and say that the internal/external continuum is about *self*, the stable/unstable continuum concerns *time*, and the global/specific continuum describes the *breadth* or *scope* of attribution. This is where this knowledge becomes powerful. Knowing that a student's negative self-talk is framed along these three dimensions, you can help the student learn to reframe his or her self-talk along the same dimensions.

The goal is to help the student begin to attribute successes to factors within his control (*internal*), conditions that are lasting (*stable*), and an outlook that takes the long view (*global*). At the same time, the student can learn to chalk up perceived failures or shortcomings to factors that are more transient, less generally applicable, and possibly outside of his direct control—that is, *unstable*, *specific*, and *external*.

Students with unhealthy attribution habits often do not realize that even the best-laid plans may sometimes go awry. Some things, of course, are outside of anyone's control. But instead of wallowing in situations that truly are uncontrollable, students can learn to contextualize or compartmentalize those things they can't control. For example, a student who has parents going through divorce proceedings is dealing with something a child can't control. But through attribution training, the student might learn to process and contextualize the problem and find more productive rather than destructive ways of dealing with it. Though it may seem subtle, teaching the student to say "This is tough, but it's manageable," instead of "This is tough, and it's hopeless," is a powerful lesson that can have lifelong effects.

D. Construct a "positive statements bank."

Examine the list of negative statements you have heard from the student. Generate a list of counter-statements that could serve as examples of internal, stable, or global attributions of successes or positive events. Contrast the new positive statements with each negative pronouncement. Pay particular attention to positive statements about mistakes and bad circumstances. Do not endorse statements that are clearly untrue—a student who can't dribble or shoot should not be encouraged to say, "I am the best soccer player in the world." Rather, positive statements should be realistic and cast failure as external (due to events beyond one's control), unstable (transient and unlikely to persist), or specific (not representative of one's usual performance). Encourage the student to say to himself or others, "Whenever I make a mistake, I learn from it," or "If I practice, I'm only going to get better."

Quote Bank

It may help to point out to the student that practically everyone who ever succeeded in anything (including whatever the student is struggling with) failed many times on their way to success—with experiments that failed, books that were rejected, acting roles denied, scholarships passed up, or games lost. The success story is almost always one of overcoming initial struggles and obstacles. Albert Einstein couldn't find work as a physics professor for years after publishing his theory of special relativity. Thomas Edison, himself no stranger to success, remarked during one particularly dry stretch, "I have not failed. I've just found 10,000 ways that won't work." Here are some other good quotes about success you can share:

"I find my greatest pleasure, and so my reward, in the work that precedes what the world calls success."

—*Thomas Edison*

"Success is going from failure to failure without a loss of enthusiasm."

—*Winston Churchill*

"Success is often the result of taking a misstep in the right direction."

—*Al Bernstein*

"I honestly think it is better to be a failure at something you love than to be a success at something you hate."

—*George Burns*

"I don't know the key to success, but the key to failure is trying to please everybody."

—*Bill Cosby*

"Success has a simple formula: Do your best, and people may like it."

—*Sam Ewing*

"Success is a lousy teacher. It seduces smart people into thinking they can't lose."

—*Bill Gates*

"Try again. Fail again. Fail better."

—*Samuel Beckett*

"Success is not to be pursued; it is to be attracted by the person you become."

—*Jim Rohn*

"Success usually comes to those who are too busy to be looking for it."

—Henry David Thoreau

"The only real failure in life is one not learned from."

—Anthony J. D'Angelo

"There are no secrets to success. It is the result of preparation, hard work, and learning from failure."

—Colin Powell

"Perseverance is a great element of success. If you only knock long enough and loud enough at the gate, you are sure to wake up somebody."

—Henry Wadsworth Longfellow

"Success is achieved by developing our strengths, not by eliminating our weaknesses."

—Marilyn vos Savant

"Creativity is allowing yourself to make mistakes. Art is knowing which ones to keep."

—Scott Adams

"Experience is the name everyone gives to their mistakes."

—Oscar Wilde

And in a more lighthearted vein . . .
"If at first you don't succeed, try, try again. Then quit. There's no point in being a damn fool about it."

—W. C. Fields

"If A equals success, then the formula is: A = X + Y + Z. X is work. Y is play. Z is keep your mouth shut."

—Albert Einstein

"Seventy percent of success in life is showing up."

—Woody Allen

"Success is simply a matter of luck. Ask any failure."

—Earl Wilson

"Take chances! Make mistakes! Get messy!"

—Miss Frizzle

For each item on the list of negative statements you developed, draft one or more positive alternatives and list them next to the negative thought or statement they might replace. The more extensive the list of positive alternatives you can generate, the better. In this way, when you meet with the student and parents, you can keep the tone of the meeting upbeat and positive because you will be able to counter any negative examples with at least as many positive alternatives. This list will become the foundation for a *positive statement bank* that you and the student can continue adding to.

Mr. Blake, the reading teacher, and Mr. Shuffield, the counselor, begin identifying alternative statements Armando might make.

PE

Negative:	"I hate running laps. It's stupid. I'm always last."
Alternatives:	"I can pace myself and be right with everyone else."
	"I'm going to try my best, and the sooner we finish, the sooner we can play baseball, which I'm pretty good at."
Negative:	"Soccer is dumb, and no one wants me on their team."
Alternatives:	"If I don't get mad that we have to play, people will probably be more likely to want me on their team."

Book reports

Negative:	"I can't read that whole book."
Alternatives:	"I can read a little each day. Before I know it, I will have read the whole book."
Negative:	"There is no way I will be able to write a decent persuasive essay."
Alternatives:	"Mr. Blake has offered to help me get started in class. Maybe then I can really get going."
	"At least I have the option to choose a topic. I should pick something I really feel strongly about."

Homework

Negative:	"I hate homework. I don't have time to get it all done."
Alternative:	"I need to stay on top of my homework. I can do the assignment quickly to ensure I have something to turn in. Then if there is time, I can take a second pass and try to make it better."
Negative:	"I always forget, and I leave the work I do get done at home."
Alternative:	"The new assignment sheet will help me remember to check off that all my homework is in my backpack before I leave for school."

The headings for the columns on your list will depend on the age and sophistication of the student. For a young student, you might label the categories like so:

- Success and Good Things That Happen
- Mistakes and Bad Things That Happen

With an older and more sophisticated student, headings for each column might read like this:

- Pleasant Circumstances: Successes, Opportunities, Celebrations

- Unpleasant Circumstances: Failures, Setbacks, Mistakes

E. Identify signals that might be used to prompt the student to make positive statements

Years of negative self-talk often make the transition to a more positive internal monologue difficult. You can set up a private signal to use when you or another adult notice the student encountering a trying situation, prompting the student to make a positive statement or try practiced self-talk. The specific signal, which should be developed jointly with the student, could involve:

- touching an earlobe

- raising an eyebrow

- clearing your throat

- touching the student's arm gently

See "Intervention J: Cueing and Precorrecting" for additional ideas on signaling.

F. Develop a monitoring procedure for the student's self-talk.

Because negative self-talk may be a deeply ingrained habit, it is important to help the student become aware of his own thoughts and statements. It might be useful to have the student self-monitor, using a system in which the student counts his negative and positive thoughts or statements (see Reproducible Form L1 for an example of a self-monitoring form for negative and positive statements). Along with this system, the student would be taught to make a positive statement when recording a negative statement. This results in the student making at least one positive statement for every negative statement. Self-monitoring systems need to be tailored to the sophistication of the student and may not be appropriate in some cases.

It might be useful to have the student self-monitor, using a system in which the student counts his negative and positive thoughts or statements.

INTERVENTION

L

Reproducible Form L1: *Negative Versus Positive Comments*

Intervention L:
Self-Talk and Attribution Training

Negative vs. Positive Comments

Student _____   Grade/Class _____   Teacher _____   Period/Time _____

Negative Comments	0	1	2	3	4	5	6	7	8	9	10	11	12	13	14	15
Positive Comments	0	1	2	3	4	5	6	7	8	9	10	11	12	13	14	15

Negative Comments	0	1	2	3	4	5	6	7	8	9	10	11	12	13	14	15
Positive Comments	0	1	2	3	4	5	6	7	8	9	10	11	12	13	14	15

Negative Comments	0	1	2	3	4	5	6	7	8	9	10	11	12	13	14	15
Positive Comments	0	1	2	3	4	5	6	7	8	9	10	11	12	13	14	15

Negative Comments	0	1	2	3	4	5	6	7	8	9	10	11	12	13	14	15
Positive Comments	0	1	2	3	4	5	6	7	8	9	10	11	12	13	14	15

Negative Comments	0	1	2	3	4	5	6	7	8	9	10	11	12	13	14	15
Positive Comments	0	1	2	3	4	5	6	7	8	9	10	11	12	13	14	15

Negative Comments	0	1	2	3	4	5	6	7	8	9	10	11	12	13	14	15
Positive Comments	0	1	2	3	4	5	6	7	8	9	10	11	12	13	14	15

Negative Comments	0	1	2	3	4	5	6	7	8	9	10	11	12	13	14	15
Positive Comments	0	1	2	3	4	5	6	7	8	9	10	11	12	13	14	15

Negative Comments	0	1	2	3	4	5	6	7	8	9	10	11	12	13	14	15
Positive Comments	0	1	2	3	4	5	6	7	8	9	10	11	12	13	14	15

Negative Comments	0	1	2	3	4	5	6	7	8	9	10	11	12	13	14	15
Positive Comments	0	1	2	3	4	5	6	7	8	9	10	11	12	13	14	15

If you are working on attribution retraining, an optimistic statement about a mistake or problem—"I forgot to carry the 1 on that math problem, but I can go back and fix it"—would be a positive. A statement like "I always forget to carry the 1 when I do subtraction" would be a negative.

Mr. Shuffield, the counselor, and Mr. Blake, the reading teacher, decide that Armando is sophisticated enough to self-monitor his own self-talk. To assist him, they have decided to use the chart shown in Reproducible Form L1. This chart will be kept in the front of Armando's notebook. Armando will be taught to circle a number each time he catches himself making a negative thought or comment, and to circle a number each time he makes a positive thought or comment. If Mr. Blake notices Armando marking a negative comment, he can coach him to make a positive statement at that time. Later, if the number of negative statements recorded on Armando's chart is higher than the number of positives, the adult can ask Armando to make and record positive comments until the number of positive comments exceeds the number of negative comments.

Note: Though you do want to see a reduction in the number of negative comments the student makes over time, they do not need to be eliminated. If there are more positives than negatives overall, the most important objective will have been achieved.

G. Identify an adult who can meet with the student on a regular basis.

Determine whether the teacher, the counselor, or even an administrator will meet with the student to discuss progress and practice positive self-talk. In some cases, this will be finalized at the first meeting with the student.

Armando's teacher and the counselor agree that Armando should initially work with someone five days a week in 5- to 10-minute sessions to practice and discuss increasing positive self-talk. Mr. Blake thinks Armando's mother can help out; she seems very willing and able to work patiently with him. Mr. Shuffield agrees to work on positive self-talk with Armando every Tuesday and Thursday morning as soon as Armando gets off the bus and suggests that they explore the possibility of having Armando's mother work with him on Mondays, Wednesdays, and Fridays.

H. Provide information on the plan to all the appropriate adults.

Provide information to all the adults who spend time with this student about the importance of providing positive feedback, and modeling the type of statements the student is being encouraged to make. If you are focusing on general negativity, all adults should look for opportunities in which the student uses positive comments and when the student shows restraint in negativity (e.g., the student does not complain about something he normally would have complained about). In either circumstance, the student should receive age-appropriate positive feedback.

I. Identify ways to determine whether the intervention is helping the student meet his goal.

Because behavior is difficult to change, small improvements may go unnoticed unless you can determine whether the intervention is having a positive impact. Evaluation might include some combination of charting the plus and minus marks from the student's self-monitoring forms, direct observation of the student to see whether he is practicing improved self-talk, and a subjective assessment from the teacher, parent, or student. Evaluation procedures are important to help determine whether the procedures should be revised or faded.

Armando's teacher and counselor decide to use Armando's self-monitoring and their own perceptions to provide two measures of the intervention's effectiveness. Mr. Blake agrees to keep an informal daily log of Armando's willingness to attempt tasks and his record of positive and negative talk.

J. Determine who will meet with the student to discuss and finalize the plan.

Use professional judgment to determine who will be present when the plan is discussed with the student. Some students will be more responsive to a discussion if only one adult is present. In other cases, it will be important to include parents, an interventionist, and/or an assistant who will be working with the student.

Mr. Blake and Mr. Shuffield decide that they both should be involved in the meeting and that it would be appropriate to invite both of Armando's parents.

Step 2: Meet with the student.

Begin the meeting with a quick review of the problem and goals. This is the time to discuss and finalize the plan with the student, the student's parents, and anyone else who may be involved.

Mr. Blake: (Teacher)	Armando, I am concerned that sometimes you talk yourself into not being able to do something that you really can do. We've talked a little about this, but it seems to be a very strong habit. Yesterday during writing you told me that you couldn't write, but I know that you write quite well. Today I heard you tell Addie that you hate art because you can't draw. It's OK not to like art, but I think your drawings are some of the best I've seen.
Armando's Mother:	Armando, your father and I are also concerned. You do many things well, but we often hear you saying you can't. I worry that you are very hard on yourself. We've talked about it before. Many days it seems like you are unhappy with everything you do.
Mr. Shuffield: (Counselor)	Armando, can you think of some things that you say that are put-downs to yourself?
Armando:	Not really.
Armando's Father:	Think about when we went camping.
Armando:	Well, I said I couldn't hike that far. I mean, 15 miles . . .
Mr. Shuffield:	Did you do it?
Armando:	Well, yeah.
Mr. Blake:	That's great, Armando. I think there are many times when you think you can't do something, but you really can. Let's think of some other times when you have told us, or yourself, that you can't do something or you aren't any good.

(After discussing Armando's frequent put-downs of himself, the counselor provides examples of what happens when someone gets into negative self-talk.) |
| **Mr. Shuffield:** | Let's see if we can all understand what happens when we get on a negative roll. This afternoon, I will be |

speaking to a group of 50 teachers. It's a little daunting, but I've worked hard on my presentation. I'm all ready to go, but then I start thinking, "I'm probably going to trip on my way to the front of the room. Everyone will think I look strange. No one is going to be able to understand a word I say. They will probably start booing. Maybe they will get up and leave. I can't talk in front of a group of 50 people. I just can't do it. My voice is going to crack." Armando, how do you think I will do?

Armando: You will probably make a fool of yourself.

Mr. Shuffield: That's right. In fact, I might not want to give that speech at all.

Armando: Yeah, that might be better.

(Quiet laughter from everyone as Armando nods)

Mr. Shuffield: Armando, you are funny! You are right! If all those things happened, I would make a fool of myself. What should I really be telling myself?

Armando: You could tell yourself that you would do OK.

Mr. Shuffield: Yes, in fact, I've been telling myself that I am going to do great!

A. Help the student change negative statements into positive statements.

When negative self-talk is habitual, the student may not know how to replace negative thoughts with more positive alternatives. Introduce the negative self-talk examples you have prepared and the positive alternatives listed on the positive statement bank. Next, generate other examples of negative self-talk and have the student work with you to change the negative comments into positive talk. Add the positive comments to the bank list. If you are doing attribution retraining with the student, be sure the bank has two lists—Positive Statements About Success/Good Things and a separate list of Positive Statements About Failures/Mistakes/Bad Things.

After discussing various situations where positive self-talk would be helpful, Armando's teacher provides a few examples of how to turn negative self-talk into positive talk. Other negative comments are generated, and everyone helps Armando work on changing the statements to positive, but realistic, statements.

INTERVENTION

L

Negative:
- "I can't read that whole book."
- "I hate homework. I don't have time to get it all done."
- "I'm stupid. I can't do percentages."
- "My paintings are ugly. I hate art."

Positive:
- "I can read a little bit of the book each night."
- "I need to do my homework. I will work for ten minutes after my snack and again for a half hour after dinner."
- "Percentages are hard. I can stay focused and ask questions if I don't understand."
- "I can paint. My paintings are OK, and I don't have to love art."

B. Briefly demonstrate the use of positive statements through role-playing.

Have the student actually practice using one or two of the positive statements. Initially, this may be difficult for the student, but with encouragement he may be willing to try. This sort of positive practice and role-playing of various situations will be a large part of the practice sessions.

Mr. Shuffield: (Counselor)	OK, Armando. We are going to do a little role-playing. Say it's math and your teacher assigns you page 52. In the past you might have said, "Page 52. How am I supposed to get that done in 10 minutes? There's no way!" What could you say instead?
Armando:	I don't know.
Mr. Shuffield:	You might say something like this. "Wow! That's a long page. I can work hard and finish it. I've completed tough assignments before. One problem at a time . . . ." I think you can do this. We'll set up some times to practice this later, but why don't we try another example.

If you are doing attribution retraining, be sure to include examples of successes/good things and mistakes/bad things. For both categories, include negative statements and positive statements.

C. Help the student learn to recognize and respond to a signal.

Explain to the student that changing the way he talks to himself will be a big job. No one expects him to be able to change his self-talk overnight. Because making negative comments is a habit, adults will help him remember to use positive self-talk by giving him a signal when it seems like he is going to make a negative statement. Have the student pick a signal that will not embarrass him. Once the signal has been determined, have the student practice responding to the signal.

Armando decides that a raised eyebrow would work best. Armando's mother and father will use the same prompt at home and will try to avoid getting impatient or angry if Armando is overtly negative.

Armando:	The other students probably wouldn't notice, and besides, it looks sort of funny when you try to raise only one eyebrow.
Mr. Shuffield: (Counselor)	Great. Now let's practice a little. When you see the signal, you need to try to say something positive. Let's say that it is time to do a creative project. Your teacher gives the class an assignment to make a collage. As you are getting your materials out, she comes over to you and raises her eyebrow. What might you say?
Armando:	Hi.
Mr. Shuffield:	I like your sense of humor, Armando. And what else?
Armando:	I could say, "This is an interesting assignment."
Mr. Shuffield:	Terrific! Let's try another scenario.

D. Show the student how to monitor self-talk.

If the student will be keeping records, show him the record-keeping form and work together to determine an organizational plan for keeping the form and recording the information. Work out procedures that the student agrees will not be embarrassing for him. Once a procedure has been worked out, have the student practice.

Mr. Shuffield:	Armando, here is a copy of the self-monitoring chart we will put in your notebook. Imagine that it is art class. You are to make a painting, and you have just heard yourself say, "This is stupid." What will you do?
Armando:	Put a circle around a negative.
Mr. Shuffield:	And then what?

Armando:	I need to say something more positive.
Mr. Shuffield:	Yes. What might you say?
Armando:	"I will make an interesting painting. It will be different."
Mr. Shuffield:	Great. Then what?
Armando:	I need to circle a positive.

E. Set up a schedule for practicing positive self-talk, debriefing with the student, and evaluating progress.

If negative self-talk is a persistent and chronic habit, short (5- to 10-minute) lessons in positive self-talk should probably be scheduled on a daily basis. During the practice session, have the student read through the positive statement bank and work with him to add more examples of positive statements to the list. Also encourage the student to read the positive statement bank several times each day.

Ideally, daily practice should be continued for three weeks. At the end of this time, an evaluation should be scheduled. The evaluation will help you determine when you can fade practice sessions to three times per week, then eventually once per week, every two weeks, and finally once a month.

F. Review everyone's roles and responsibilities.

It will be important for one person to summarize the plan. Go over each person's roles and responsibilities. This should include identifying who will be responsible for training other adults who will be involved in the plan but were not included in the meeting.

Encourage the student to read the positive statement bank several times each day.

Mr. Shuffield: (Counselor)	I am very happy with our plan. Armando, your job will be to work hard on talking to others and yourself more positively. You will be responsible for making an effort, responding with positive talk when an adult signals you, and using your self-monitoring chart. Your mother will work on practicing self-talk with you every Monday, Wednesday, and Friday after you finish breakfast. This will include role-playing and practicing how to turn negative self-talk into positive talk. I will help you on Tuesdays and Thursdays during attendance and morning announcements. On those days, we will go over your self-monitoring charts and talk a bit about how things are going. Since you always carry your notebook, you will have your charts handy. Your teacher will also keep a log of how you are doing. All of us will signal

> you by raising an eyebrow when we notice times that you should practice positive self-talk, and we will all work on being patient while you are learning this new behavior. Then we will meet back here on November 15 at 3 p.m. to see how things are going. Your dad will need to work that day, but you and your mom will keep him informed. I will send everyone a reminder the week before that.

G. Conclude with words of encouragement.

It is important to end the meeting by focusing on the goal and the positive nature of working together.

Mr. Blake: (Teacher)	I would like to thank everyone for working together. Armando, I know that this plan will help you recognize what you can do. I think you will be much happier at school and at home. I will enjoy working with you on your goal and look forward to getting started.

Step 3: Monitor progress and revise the plan.

Conduct daily lessons with humor and support. During lessons, help the student change negative self-talk examples into positive comments. Practice using the self-monitoring chart and role-play situations that commonly result in negative self-talk. Use the signal to prompt the student to make positive comments when appropriate, and provide the student with positive feedback when possible.

A. Evaluate, revise, and fade the plan.

Gradual improvements over a long period of time are more likely to occur than immediate and dramatic improvements. As the student begins taking ownership of positive self-talk, lengthen the time between lessons and debriefing sessions. Eventually, the student should carry more and more of the responsibility for evaluating and monitoring his own performance. When the student is able to maintain positive self-talk with only a monthly debriefing session, begin to fade out structured lessons and structured self-monitoring systems.

If these simple approaches to fostering positive self-talk and attribution retraining do not seem to be having a positive effect, they may need to be combined with "Intervention O: Structured Reinforcement Systems" or "Intervention P: Defining Limits and Establishing Consequences." If the student appears to be seriously depressed, read "Intervention R: Internalizing Problems and Mental Health" and consider seeking additional professional help for possible depression or anxiety disorders.

B. Once the intervention has been faded, provide continued follow-up, support, and encouragement.

Once the plan has been faded, continue monthly check-ins with the teacher, parents, and student for a full year, with occasional debriefings the following year. Check-ins can be accomplished through an occasional phone call or informal discussion. If the student lapses into old habits of negative self-talk, a modified plan may need to be briefly implemented to help the student get back on track.

CONCLUSION

Self-talk has a powerful influence on how students perceive themselves and direct their own behavior. This intervention can help a student make life-changing adjustments in personal attitudes and self-concept. However, progress can be slow. It may be difficult to keep adults committed to providing the necessary lessons, prompts, and debriefings. Let adults know that, at least initially, daily lessons will be required. Though the lessons may eventually be faded to a couple of times a week, cueing, precorrecting, and a continued emphasis on positive self-talk will likely be needed for several months.

Self-Talk and Attribution Training is most effective when the student is encouraged to think and speak positively in many settings. The interventionist needs to check frequently with the parents, classroom teachers, specialists, and supervisors of the playground and cafeteria to ensure that every adult who regularly comes into contact with the student is helping encourage and prompt the student. Periodic check-ins with adults will help maintain the positive focus and allow the interventionist to determine whether the student still needs practice in some situations.

Another potential roadblock may be parental reservations. Parents may view restructuring self-talk as tantamount to a religious practice. Because of this, it will be important to communicate clearly that this intervention is simply designed to help children think positively about themselves, what they do, and why they do it. If a parent does find the intervention to be inappropri-

This intervention can help a student make life-changing adjustments in personal attitudes and self-concept.

INTERVENTION

L

ate for any reason, honor the parent's wishes and find a different intervention to help the student.

Negative self-talk or excessive complaining can be a deeply ingrained habit. In the same way that nail biting is a very difficult habit for some people to break, a habit of negative thinking and talking can be very hard to change. Weighing the difficulty of this intervention against the potential rewards, however, can help you realize its value. Students who learn to direct their own actions and see themselves in a more positive light become healthier, happier individuals—in school and in life.

REFERENCES

Becker, W. (1986). *Applied psychology for teachers: A behavioral cognitive approach.* Chicago: Science Research Associates.

Brophy, J. (1998). Failure syndrome students. *ERIC Digest.* Champaign, IL: ERIC Clearinghouse on Elementary and Early Childhood Education.

Burnett, P. C. (1994). Self-talk in upper elementary school children: Its relationship with irrational beliefs, self-esteem, and depression. *Journal of Rational-Emotive & Cognitive Behavior Therapy, 12*(3), 181–188.

Burnett, P. C. (1996). Children's self-talk and significant others' positive and negative statements. *Educational Psychology, 16,* 57–67.

Burnett, P. C. (1999). Children's self-talk and academic self-concepts. *Educational Psychology in Practice, 15,* 195–200.

Burnett, P. C. (2002). Teacher praise and feedback and students' perceptions of the classroom environment. *Educational Psychology, 22*(1), 5–16.

Burnett, P. C., & McCrindle, A. R. (1999). The relationship between significant others' positive and negative statements, self-talk, and self-esteem. *Child Study Journal, 29,* 39–48.

Calvete, E., & Cardennoso, O. (2002). Self-talk in adolescents: Dimensions, states of mind, and psychological maladjustment. *Cognitive Therapy & Research, 26*(4), 473–485.

Chiu, S., & Alexander, P. A. (2000). The motivational function of preschoolers' private speech. *Discourse Processes, 30*(2), 133–152.

Corral, N., & Anita, S. D. (1997). Self-talk: Strategies for success in math. *Teaching Exceptional Children, 29,* 42–45.

Dush, D. M., Hirt, M. L., & Schroeder, H. E. (1989). Self-statement modification in the treatment of child behavior disorders: A meta-analysis. *Psychological Bulletin, 106*, 97–106.

Gillham, J. E., Shatte, A. J., & Freres, D. R. (2000). Preventing depression: A review of cognitive-behavioral and family interventions. *Applied & Preventive Psychology, 9*(2), 63–88.

Hart, L. (1993). *The winning family: Increasing self-esteem in your children and yourself*. Berkeley, CA: Celestial Arts.

Haugh, J. A., & Pawtowksi, J. (1996). Creating metacognitive experiences during written communication: Positive self-talk using the thinking mirror. *Reading Horizons, 37*(1), 75–93.

Kamann, M. P., & Wong, B. Y. L. (1993). Inducing adaptive coping self-statements in children with learning disabilities through self-instruction training. *Journal of Learning Disabilities, 26*(9), 630–638.

Lamke, L. K., Lujan, B. M., & Showalter, J. M. (1988). The case for modifying adolescents' cognitive self-statements. *Adolescents, 23*, 967–974.

Lange, A., Richard, R., Kiestra, J., & van Oostendorp, E. (1997). Cognitive treatment through positive self-verbalization: A multiple case study. *Behavioural & Cognitive Psychotherapy, 25*, 161–171.

Larson, K. A. (1984). *The efficacy of social meta cognition training for social adjustment of LD and non LD delinquent adolescents*. Unpublished doctoral dissertation, University of California, Santa Barbara.

Lodge, J., Harte, D. K., & Tripp, G. (1998). Children's self-talk under conditions of mild anxiety. *Journal of Anxiety Disorders, 12*(2), 153–176.

Martella, R. C., Leonard, I. J., Marchand-Martella, N. E., & Agran, M. (1993). Self-monitoring negative statements. *Journal of Behavioral Education, 3*, 77–86.

Meichenbaum, D., & Goodman, J. (1971). Training impulsive children to talk to themselves: A means of developing self-control. *Journal of Consulting and Clinical Psychology, 40*, 148–154.

Paris, S. G., & Cross, D. R. (1983). Ordinary learning: Pragmatic connections among children's beliefs, motives and actions. In J. Bisanz & R. Kail (Eds.), *Learning in children* (pp. 137–168). New York: Springer Verlag.

Philpot, V. D., & Bamburg, J. W. (1996). Rehearsal of positive self-statements and restructured negative self-statements to increase self-esteem and decrease depression. *Psychological Reports, 79*, 83–91.

Pressely, M. (1979). Increasing children's self-control through cognitive interventions. *Review of Educational Research, 49*, 319–370.

Ronan, K. R., & Kendall, P. C. (1997). Self-talk in distressed youth: States-of-mind and content specificity. *Journal of Clinical Child Psychology, 26*, 330–337.

Scarr, S., & McCartney, K. (1983). How people make their own environments: A theory of genotype environment correlations. *Child Development, 54*, 424–435.

Seligman, M. E. P. (1998). *Learned optimism: How to change your mind and your life* (Rev. ed.). New York: Pocket Books/Simon & Schuster.

Seligman, M. E. P., Reivich, K., Jaycox, L., & Gillham, J. (1995). *The optimistic child*. Boston: Houghton Mifflin.

Siddle, B. G. (1980). *Interpersonal problem solving training adolescents: A cognitive behavior modification approach*. Unpublished doctoral dissertation, Arizona State University.

Solley, B. A., & Payne, B. B. (1992). The use of self-talk to enhance children's writing. *Journal of Instructional Psychology, 19*, 205–213.

Wittrock, M. C. (1986). Students' thought processes. In M.C. Wittrock (Ed.), *Handbook of research on teaching* (3rd ed., pp. 297–314). New York: Macmillan.

Workman, E. A., & Williams, R. L. (1980). Self-cued relaxation in the control of an adolescent's violent arguments and debilitating complaints. *Education and Treatment of Children, 3*, 315–322.

Reproducible Materials

The following reproducible form may be used in conjunction with "Intervention L: Self-Talk and Attribution Training." A copy is provided in the chapter and on the CD. Permission is given for individual classroom teachers to reproduce any forms labeled "Reproducible" for classroom use. Reproduction of these materials for an entire school system is prohibited without express permission of the publisher.

Reproducible Step-by-Step Summary, p. 564
Reproducible Form L1: Negative vs. Positive Comments, p. 551

INTERVENTION  L

SELF-TALK AND ATTRIBUTION TRAINING

Step-by-Step Summary

Following is a summary of the steps involved in Intervention L. It is important to use professional judgment, adjusting procedures to meet the needs of the situation and the individual. See the chapter "Intervention L: Self-Talk and Attribution Training" for a detailed description of this intervention.

STEP 1 Develop a plan.

A. List the type of negative statements the student makes.

B. Consider whether training in positive self-talk would be sufficient.

C. Consider whether attribution training would be appropriate.

D. Construct a "positive statements bank."

E. Identify signals that might be used to prompt the student to make positive statements.

F. Develop a monitoring procedure for the student's self-talk.

G. Identify an adult who can meet with the student on a regular basis.

H. Provide information on the plan to all the approriate adults.

I. Identify ways to determine whether the intervention is helping the student meet his goal.

J. Determine who will meet with the student to discuss and finalize the plan.

STEP 2 Meet with the student.

A. Help the student change negative statements into positive statements.

B. Briefly demonstrate the use of positive statements through role-playing.

C. Help the student learn to recognize and respond to a signal.

INTERVENTION **L**

D. Show the student how to monitor self-talk.

E. Set up a schedule for practicing positive self-talk, debriefing with the student, and evaluating progress.

F. Review everyone's roles and responsibilities.

G. Conclude with words of encouragement.

STEP 3 Monitor progress and revise the plan.

A. Evaluate, revise, and fade the plan.

B. Once the intervention has been faded, provide continued follow-up, support, and encouragement.

Teaching Replacement Behavior

The student does not know how to meet expectations

PURPOSE

TEACHING REPLACEMENT BEHAVIOR is a way to approach modifying any recurring minor or major misbehavior.

THIS INTERVENTION IS APPROPRIATE FOR:

Poor peer relations
- being the scapegoat
- teasing
- poor interactions

Problems interacting with adults
- disrespect
- problems being corrected or accepting feedback
- not following directions

Bad habits
- nose picking
- swearing
- masturbation
- noisemaking

Chronic off-task behavior
- daydreaming
- being distractible
- having a short attention span

Aggressive behavior
- chasing others
- threatening others
- hitting
- poking

Anger management
- shouting
- inability to handle disagreements

Chronic misbehavior is often a function of the student not knowing the expectations of the teacher or other adults, not having the skills to meet those expectations, or not knowing when to exhibit the expected behavior.

Teaching Replacement Behavior is an intervention that incorporates features of behavior training that are sometimes referred to as *behavioral rehearsal*, *positive practice*, *replacement training*, or *strategy training*. This intervention is useful because a chronic misbehavior is often a function of the student not knowing the expectations of the teacher or other adults, not having the skills to meet those expectations, or not knowing when to exhibit the expected behavior. For example, many children (and some adults) do not know how to accept a compliment and may cover their discomfort in an inappropriate manner because they do not know any other way to respond.

With Teaching Replacement Behavior, students learn appropriate behavior in the same way a child learns to read, master a musical instrument, or participate in a new sport—through instruction, practice, and encouragement. This intensive, powerful intervention gives students the opportunity to succeed in ways they may never have thought possible. Daily lessons are designed to teach students a new behavior, replacement behavior, or strategy. Lessons provide students with guided practice in simulated and real-life situations. "Being responsible," "listening," "working harder," "being polite," "showing consideration," and "feeling less angry," among others, are all attainable goals.

Teaching Replacement Behavior can help students learn to use desirable behavior by ensuring that the replacement behavior is incompatible with the problem behavior—it occurs at the same time. Thus, a student will automatically phase out negative behaviors as he begins to practice positive ones. For example, the student who uses profanity may be taught to use alternative words to express displeasure or amazement. A young student who publicly rubs his genitals may be taught to do something else with his hands. Because the new behavior tends to be incompatible with problem behavior, the replacement behavior gives students positive choices when they respond to various situations.

Teaching Replacement Behavior will help you narrow the focus of your intervention plan and identify logical replacement behaviors and strategies, and it provides guidelines for structured lessons that will give students needed instruction and practice. This intervention may be used with a whole class, a small group, or in one-to-one tutorials.

RATIONALE

Students with behavior problems are often incapable of successfully exhibiting a desirable behavior because they have never learned the appropriate behavior.

Brian is a tenth-grade student who gets angry and frustrated whenever his work is corrected. Though a good student, Brian has trouble staying calm when he makes errors. Although he is basically mad at himself for making errors, he tends to take it out on the teacher. His teacher, Ms. Sugimura, characterizes Brian as difficult but not mean-spirited:

"Sometimes he raises his voice a bit, and sometimes he almost hisses at me. I know he isn't really mad at me, but his tone of voice is accusatory. Sometimes he blames the other students, and sometimes he says the assignment is stupid. The thing is, he really does quite well. I've tried telling him he doesn't have to be perfect, but Brian can't seem to help himself. These are angry responses to normal tenth-grade corrections—misspelled words, an error in computation, editing kinds of things. I worry about Brian. He could learn so much more if he didn't get so wound up. He needs to learn to be calmer and more easy-going about the learning process. So far, Brian hasn't been considered a major behavior problem. I guess that's because we all know he is basically a charming kid. I wonder what will happen when he leaves school or starts working and people no longer excuse him when he blows his top?"

Brian needs to learn how to respond more maturely when he makes mistakes and requires correction. Since the problem has not been solved with discussions, Teaching Replacement Behavior would be an appropriate intervention to help Brian learn to respond calmly and maturely to corrective feedback.

Adults frequently take appropriate behavior for granted because the majority of students have learned these skills incidentally at home or at an earlier age. Some students, however, have not learned these skills and need to be taught how to replace misbehaviors with appropriate behaviors. Brian does not know how to respond to feedback without becoming angry. He needs to be taught how to accept feedback with grace and dignity. Similarly, a student who has poor listening skills needs to be taught how to keep her attention focused on the speaker, sit reasonably still, and answer questions related to the topic. A student who shouts during a disagreement needs to learn to listen actively and talk calmly. A student who fights when problems occur needs to learn to think about choices and act responsibly. These students need to be taught skills through direct and purposeful lessons. Teaching Replacement Behavior provides students with daily lessons in the positive behaviors and strategies that will help them learn the repertoires necessary for more successful daily living.

Note that *teaching* is not the same thing as *telling*. Teaching involves repeated instruction across time until mastery is achieved. Instruction will involve modeling; creating frequent practice opportunities; providing positive and corrective feedback; combining simple, previously mastered behaviors into more complex chains of behavior; and providing context instruction (in this situation do this, but in another situation do that). Teaching also involves trying to inspire the students to exhibit these newly learned and frequently practiced behaviors. A masterful basketball coach who repeatedly drills players every day on skills and techniques is a good example of someone who is actively teaching rather than telling.

While this intervention offers general steps for improving and replacing a wide range of inappropriate behaviors, other interventions in this book offer specific and detailed examples of teaching replacement behaviors. "Intervention I: Managing the Cycle of Emotional Escalation" is designed to help the student learn to manage situations positively instead of letting them lead to angry confrontations or out-of-control behavior. "Intervention L: Self-Talk and Attribution Training" teaches students to replace negative thoughts and defeatist attitudes with more positive self-assessments. "Intervention N: Functional Communication" teaches students replacement behaviors for communication problems, and "Intervention R: Internalizing Problems and Mental Health" includes strategies for managing student stress and replacing a variety of mentally unhealthy behavior patterns with positive alternatives.

Before implementing Teaching Replacement Behavior

Before this intervention can be successfully implemented, be sure that you have discussed the problem and general goal for improvement with the student. Gather any relevant background information that may help in designing

Note that teaching *is not the same thing as* telling. *Teaching involves repeated instruction across time until mastery is achieved.*

and implementing the intervention. In addition, contact the student's parents or guardian to discuss the problem and keep the parents informed of all aspects of the intervention plan.

IMPLEMENTATION STEPS
Step 1: Develop a plan for using Teaching Replacement Behavior.

A. Review the problem and overall goals for the student.

Defining the nature and scope of the problem provides critical information for developing a successful intervention. Look at a broad range of concerns about the student. The scope of the behaviors can be based on data you have collected but also on subjective concerns. For example, you may have collected data on a student's outbursts, but you also know for a fact that the student has hygiene problems because you notice those daily. If you identify a number of different types of behaviors you would like to see change, you probably need to narrow your focus. The idea behind looking at the broad range but then narrowing the scope is that if the student has hygiene problems, disruption problems, peer relation problems, and work completion problems, you cannot work on all of those at once. You may, however, be able to identify categories of misbehavior. You're going to need to narrow the scope of the objective/purpose of the intervention to a particular category of the greatest concern about the student.

Note: If a number of students in your class lack a particular skill or have trouble with a particular behavior, it may be worth teaching group lessons to the whole class. For example, if several children have problems with bullying and victimization, an effective published prevention program can help you teach assertiveness and other related skills. If many of your students have trouble staying on task, completing work, or organizing materials, you may want to teach a study skills curriculum. If your students have trouble with basic manners and interacting with one another, consider a social skills curriculum.

Replacement Behavior Worksheet

It may be useful to have Reproducible Form M1, the Replacement Behavior Worksheet, available to make notes as you proceed through this chapter. This worksheet loosely follows the steps of this intervention and can be a useful organizational tool to help guide and focus discussions.

In the first column of the worksheet, you will list all problem behaviors. For each behavior, you will develop a hypothesis about the function of the misbehavior (see "Intervention F: STOIC Analysis and Intervention"). In the Goal column, you will identify the desired outcome of the intervention. Next you will identify several possible replacement behaviors that might address the problem and goal, and write the potential replacement behaviors in the Brainstorming column. The remaining columns will allow you to evaluate the potential efficacy of the replacement behaviors before you begin implementing this intervention. Behaviors that accomplish the following will be more useful replacements than those that do not:

- Does the proposed replacement address the function of the misbehavior and serve the student's needs?

- Does the proposed replacement capitalize on student strengths?

- Is the proposed replacement concrete, observable, and teachable?

- Is the proposed replacement within the student's repertoire—is the student physically and mentally capable of performing the desired behavior?

Note: A copy of this form and other Teaching Replacement Behavior forms are provided on the CD.

Molly is a fifth-grade student referred to the Intervention Planning Team by her classroom teacher. The Intervention Planning Team is a group of professionals who work collaboratively to design interventions for individual students who are experiencing behavioral or academic difficulties. Molly has been enrolled at Hamilton Elementary for a little more than a year, but school records and parent reports indicate she has a history of problems at other schools dating back to kindergarten. Initially, Molly's difficulties seemed directed at other students, with hitting, hair pulling, and angry outbursts when she didn't get her way. Though Molly continues to

Reproducible Form M1: *Replacement Behavior Worksheet*

Intervention M:
Teaching Replacement Behavior

Replacement Behavior Worksheet

Student _____ Grade/Class _____ Teacher _____ Date _____

Define the Problem	Consider the Function		Identify Replacement Behaviors	Does the proposed replacement ...		Is the proposed replacement ...	
		Goal	Brainstorm Ideas	Meet the need/serve the function?	Capitalize on student's strengths?	Concrete, observable, and teachable?	Within the student's repertoire?
Behavior	Awareness; ability; attention from peers; attention from adults; power/control; avoid work; avoid something else; competing reinforcers.						

struggle with peer relationships, progress is evident. In her fifth-grade year, Molly has not been referred for playground infractions, and her mother reports that she has begun playing with other children in her neighborhood.

Despite the improvements, Molly's teacher, Mrs. Baker, has concerns. Molly no longer has full-blown temper tantrums, but she has difficulty getting her classwork completed, often fails to turn in homework, and talks back to her teacher whenever she feels angry or frustrated. Mrs. Baker is worried that Molly will have a difficult time when she goes on to middle school next year.

Molly's mother reports similar difficulties at home. She promised during fall conferences to monitor Molly's homework, but she now indicates that her efforts to get Molly to do her homework result in shouting matches.

The Intervention Planning Team has helped Mrs. Baker and Molly's mother narrow their concerns to two major and related problems—failure to complete work and talking back when frustrated.

On the suggestion of the Intervention Planning Team, Mrs. Baker has checked and confirmed that classwork is of reasonable length and that Molly is capable of doing the work independently. An informal reading check as well as test scores indicate that Molly functions well within the average range. Homework expectations have been determined jointly by all the fifth-grade teachers and are thought to be reasonable for fifth-grade students at Hamilton Elementary. Mrs. Baker finds that when she works with Molly one-to-one, Molly is able to complete her work, but that she needs to have someone get her started and continual reminders to keep working.

To help Molly learn to complete her work in a timely fashion at school, Mrs. Baker has tried gentle reminders, keeping her in at recess, keeping her after school, and sending incomplete work home.

These consequences have resulted in Molly's responding very angrily and sometimes disruptively: "Why don't you just leave me alone? I don't care what you say. You can't make me do anything!"

The goals of this intervention are to help Molly learn to stay focused on her work without continual adult supervision and respond more constructively to adult corrections. The Intervention Planning Team agrees that the Teaching Replacement Behavior intervention, though time-consuming, may help Molly before she has major problems with insubordination and becomes totally discouraged with school. Mrs. Baker agrees to work with the school interventionist, Ms. Schrader, to design lessons for Molly.

B. Determine who will provide the lessons, how much time will be needed, and when and where they will be held.

Because a replacement behavior may not be in the student's current repertoire, it is important to provide frequent opportunities for practice. Five minutes of practice each day will usually get better results than 45 minutes once a week. As a rule of thumb, the greater the change you hope to effect, the more frequent lessons should be.

Another primary consideration is to schedule lessons so that the student is not embarrassed in front of his or her peers. The student must feel comfortable enough in sessions to quell any fear of failure. Lessons should provide the student with "safe" practice. Sometimes the classroom teacher can skillfully and unobtrusively find time to provide five-minute behavioral lessons while other children work independently or in small groups. With secondary students, these lessons probably need to be conducted away from peers—in an empty classroom or counselor's office, for example.

If other classmates need improvement in the same skills that are being taught to the individual student of concern, behavioral lessons can also be taught to a small group of students or the whole class. For example, if the target student needs to learn how to work independently, you could teach the class strategies such as getting help from other students, circling a problem and moving on until the teacher is free, "guesstimating" answers, or ignoring distractions. In this way, the targeted student can practice the replacement behavior along with peers, who will also benefit.

Schedule lessons so that the student is not embarrassed in front of his or her peers.

As Mrs. Baker and the interventionist continue planning, Mrs. Baker indicates that some of the less mature students in her class share Molly's problem of not getting started right away on assignments and becoming easily distracted. Mrs. Baker decides that it would be appropriate to teach the whole class about how to get papers, pencils, and other needed materials out for "quick starts" on work. Mrs. Baker decides to provide lessons to the whole class, two to three times each week in various subject areas. She thinks that she can make it a game, perhaps using a stopwatch to encour age greater efficiency in work habits. She also agrees to help her entire class focus on getting back to work quickly when a distraction occurs. She decides to have students role-play what to do when an interruption occurs.

In addition to the whole-class activities, it is agreed that Molly needs more intensive work. Though they would like to schedule 15-minute sessions five days a week, they decide that three individual lessons per week, plus the whole class lessons, are more realistic and will hopefully be sufficient.

Who will teach the initial observation and practice sessions depends on variables such as time, availability, and trust or chemistry between teacher and student. If more than one adult will be asked to teach the lessons, further planning should include each involved adult. Someone with whom the student feels relatively comfortable and enjoys working should conduct these initial practice lessons.

If more than one adult will be asked to teach the lessons, further planning should include each involved adult.

If the skill being taught is fairly simple, it may be possible for you or another classroom teacher to discuss the behavior and goal and conduct informal lessons with the student individually for a few minutes several times a week. Five minutes of time can be created, for instance, when the class is just getting started on an independent work assignment—see "Intervention A: Planned Discussion" for ideas on how to conduct short informal discussions and lessons with the student. However, if the lessons will be fairly involved and need to be practiced on a daily basis, you may not be in the best position to provide them due to time constraints. A member of the school's Intervention Planning Team, the interventionist, counselor, principal, school psychologist, or school nurse might conduct initial sessions. It might be useful to have a paraprofessional, mentor, or parent volunteer teach some of the lessons under the guidance of the interventionist. One arrangement would be to have a paraprofessional conduct the daily lessons, with the interventionist participating and observing once each week. In all cases, as the student becomes more competent, lessons will gradually be transferred to the "real" environment of the classroom as the teacher takes over active and ongoing support.

The teacher of a replacement behavior must show great patience. Behavior changes rarely come all at once. If the student senses that the teacher is becoming frustrated, impatient, and irritated, she may reflect back all of those attitudes or become discouraged and refuse to continue practicing.

Molly's interventionist offers to meet with Molly for 15-minute sessions three times a week. Though homework completion is a concern, Mrs. Baker agrees to reduce Molly's homework to three assignments per week. These assignments will be completed during the practice sessions. As Molly gains competence, her interventionist also agrees to teach Molly's mother how to help with homework.

Finding three 15-minute periods to work with Molly is not an easy task. The interventionist is generally not available either before or after school. Though recess seems to be a logical time, Mrs. Baker and the interventionist agree that it would be disruptive to separate Molly from her new friends during recesses. It is finally decided that Molly will meet for lessons immediately following lunch recess on Mondays, Wednesdays, and Fridays.

C. Determine behaviors or strategies the student can learn to replace the inappropriate behaviors.

Look at the objective of the intervention: What area of concern have you decided to focus on? Having identified particular behaviors of concern, you must next identify the *positive opposite* of those behaviors. In other words, try to name specific, observable behaviors that would not be problematic if the student were to engage in them in place of the negative behaviors. The whole notion of this intervention is that if you can successfully teach and get a student to replace problem behavior with a positive opposite that serves the same function or fulfills the same need, the problem no longer exists. A well-considered replacement behavior will bring the student more success, as it is more desirable and acceptable, and will also gradually "squeeze out" the problem behavior. Teaching students to replace problem behaviors with their positive opposite will thus resolve many problems naturally.

A good candidate for a replacement behavior will capitalize on the student's strengths. If a basketball team is having trouble with a particular aspect of the game, the coach may come up with new plays that make better use of things the team is good at—passing, fast breaks, perimeter shooting, and so on. These could be considered replacement behaviors. If the players execute new plays with some success, the new behaviors will automatically tend to replace the behaviors that were failing them before. In the same way, rechanneling a behavior with replacement behaviors can become more powerful as the new behaviors bring success and, through that success, become self-sustaining.

Figure M1: *Replacement Behavior Chart*

Problem	Goal	Replacement Behavior
Anger when work is corrected	Calmly accepting feedback	Nodding acceptance; saying "Okay, I'll fix it."
Swearing	Appropriate response or exclamation	Silence; "Shoot!"; "Shizzle!"; "Wow!"; etc.
Aggression	Calming down without aggressive acts	Deep breathing; self-imposed timeout
Oversensitivity	Responding maturely to teasing	Ignoring; use of "I" statements
Not completing work	Staying focused and on task	Ignoring distractions; returning to work quickly

When you are trying to identify a replacement behavior, also give some thought to the function or purpose of the misbehavior. Think of a context in which the student has been disruptive. If such disruptions are a function of the student demanding attention, you would teach the student alternative ways of getting attention that are prosocial and within the student's current behavioral skill set. If the student will try these new methods, she may see that her needs are met and pursue the strategies with keener interest. Your needs as a teacher are also met because the disruptive behavior doesn't occur anymore.

Figure M1 provides examples of common problem behaviors and acceptable alternatives that might be taught to help students replace the behaviors. To identify a possible replacement behavior, brainstorm a list of reasonable alternatives and then determine which might be most appropriate for the specific situation.

If the student wants to get attention, choose a replacement behavior that allows the student to get more attention, but in more positive and acceptable ways. If the problem is lack of awareness, the intervention might logically include some form of cueing, in which the cue redirects the student to exhibit the new or replacement behavior. It may be useful to combine this intervention with "Intervention J: Cueing and Precorrecting." If the student taps his pencil incessantly, an effective replacement behavior might be keeping his hands still, or picking up a Koosh ball or other stress-relieving device. In place of drumming on the desk, you've taught the student to pick up the Koosh ball and squeeze it instead.

If the function of the misbehavior is power (the student argues to engage you emotionally), then teaching a replacement behavior might be teamed with planned ignoring. First teach the student the replacement behavior—for example, how to make an appointment with you for a later time: "Mrs. Thompson, I think that's unfair. Can I schedule an appointment to speak with you later?"

Encourage the student to substitute this phrase whenever she wants to argue. Teach, practice, and rehearse variations on the phrase until it rolls off her tongue automatically. Next, explain to the student that when she tries to argue, you are going to ignore her. Continue in the same way for each subsequent replacement behavior you teach.

Perhaps the student has a hard time keeping her cool at the after-class appointment. "Instead of raising your voice to me, think about what you want to say and then keep your voice calm as you say it. Let's practice calmly telling me your concern, not demanding to get your own way." In other words, you're teaching the student that she can actually have more power by making an appointment and calmly stating her case; she actually has less power and makes less of an impact when she tries to argue and make demands. In other words, the student will learn that she is more likely to get what she wants by exhibiting the replacement behavior.

If the function of a misbehavior is to escape work that the student thinks is too difficult, teach the student how and when to ask for assistance and arrange to help the student get the needed assistance when she requests it. Think through what this kind of interaction might look like and how the student can get help in a non-embarrassing way. A replacement behavior for escapist misbehaviors should also close off less appropriate avenues for escape.

Figure M2 reflects the work of Molly's Intervention Planning Team in determining the replacement behaviors that need to be taught.

Figure M2: *Molly's Replacement Behavior Chart*

Problem	Goal	Replacement Behavior
Inability to complete classwork and homework: • *Not getting started* • *Not staying on task*	Completing work in a timely manner	• Getting started on work • Staying on task despite distractions • Getting back to work if distracted • Staying with a task until finished
Inappropriate responses to teacher correction and feedback	Responding constructively to adult feedback and criticism	• Nod acceptance • Saying "Okay"

Emphasis should be placed on why the replacement behaviors are necessary and how they can help.

D. Design lessons to teach the replacement behavior.

When you meet with the student, you will need to share a rationale for each replacement behavior, demonstrate and model the replacement behavior, practice it with the student, provide feedback, and then gradually increase the complexity of the new behavior.

1. Communicate an age-appropriate rationale for the replacement behavior—what, why, how, when, and where.

Emphasis should be placed on *why* the replacement behaviors are necessary and how they can help. Why is this important? Why will the replacement behavior you're suggesting work out better for the student and the teacher than the old behavior? How will she benefit? Will she get more attention, more power and influence, more control over her situation? If you've perceptively identified the student's underlying needs—the function of the misbehavior—your rationale should make sense to the student. The older the student, the more important your *why* rationale becomes. High school students require a more carefully explained rationale than primary students, who are on the whole more willing to practice just for the sake of practice.

This brings you to *how*. How should the student model the behavior? At this stage, you won't need to launch into a formal lesson; just give a quick, cursory demonstration of how the behavior will help her and how it looks. Then talk about *when* and *where*: "These are the times when you tend to argue. I've noticed that you seem to argue when things haven't gone your way. Now it's OK for you to try to get things to go your way. But we're going to try out some ways to get what you want more acceptably and more effectively. Does that make sense to you?" Though explaining when and where may not always be applicable, at a minimum you should convey to the student the exact behaviors you'll be encouraging her to replace, why change is important to you and to her, how the replacement behaviors will look, and when and where you'd like to see her try the new behavior.

2. Provide demonstrations and modeling.

When the replacement behavior is introduced, the student should have an opportunity to see what the new behavior looks like in action. Students you have singled out for intervention are probably quite familiar with injunctions such as "stay on task," "work harder," or "behave yourself," but they may have no understanding of how to actually put these phrases into practice. The notion behind Teaching Replacement Behavior is that many of these students don't know *how* to stay on task, work harder, or behave themselves. The recipient of this intervention will often need to see the appropriate behavior demonstrated or mirrored back to her.

You or another adult can model the replacement behavior. Even more powerful is to have a peer demonstrate the behavior. The ideal peer for this assignment is someone the target student looks up to or would like to emulate. If you have identified a willing student (who is sufficiently mature) to be a peer model, set up a time for the target student to observe the peer unobtrusively. Prompt the student to watch for specific words, actions, and behaviors that coincide with the student's problems and goals. Afterward, debrief with the student. What behavior was appropriate or inappropriate, and why? Discuss how the peer responded to challenging situations. Can the student think of other ways she might respond appropriately in the same situation?

A powerful demonstration model is to give a positive/negative/positive example. To do this, demonstrate the right way, show the wrong way (the way the student has behaved in the past), and then show the right way again. In effect, you are "sandwiching" the example of what you don't want to see between two examples of the behavior you'd like to see, helping the student make the connection without unduly stressing the "bad" behavior.

Let's break the positive/negative/positive demonstration down in more detail. First, show the student the right way to exhibit the behavior. Model it, and break it down: "Watch how I do this." "Notice what I'm saying, how I gesture, what my face is doing." Then demonstrate a negative behavior you've seen: "This is the wrong way to do it." (Though this is a good chance to practice your acting skills, be as faithful to the original as decorum permits.) Explain, "I've seen this behavior from you or other students in the past. Here's why it's not OK, and why it won't work as well for you as what I'm showing you. Now watch me do it the right way again." Always sandwich a demonstration of the wrong way in between two examples of the right way.

Note: Some models of Teaching Replacement Behavior suggest that a teacher should model only the "right way" to exhibit a behavior. Although it is preferable to keep the balance of your demonstrations positive, just as you would your ratio of interactions, the simplest, most direct way to explain how the "wrong way" looks and is problematic or ineffective is simply to show it. This show-don't-tell approach is more likely to trigger an "Oh, I recognize that" response from the student, helping the student self-identify and visualize behaviors to avoid. It will take less time, too.

If your school is equipped for it, you can set up video-based demonstrations involving peers or the target student herself. Videotape students demonstrating the right way to exhibit the behavior. As you get the student engaged in practicing the behavior, you can actually record the sessions. With this video bank of examples showing the student exhibiting a replacement behavior the right way in different contexts, you can open subsequent lessons by saying, "Now before we get started, let's take a look at how well you can do this." The student gets to watch herself actually exhibiting the positive behavior, sitting down, standing up, asking and answering questions, and so on. When using a video recording to demonstrate behavior, it's best not to show recordings of students acting out in the wrong ways—the students should see them-selves engaged in positive actions, successfully modeling replacement behaviors in different situations.

> Molly's teacher and interventionist decide that she could benefit from both an adult model and a student model. They decide that lessons will involve an adult showing Molly appropriate work habits—how to get started imme-diately, how to handle distractions, how to get back to work after a disrup-tion, and how to respond to an adult correction. Later Molly will be asked to observe a student she admires. She will observe what the student does when she gets to work, what she does while working, and how she responds to teacher comments.

3. Provide opportunities for verbal practice.

In addition to providing demonstrations and practice opportunities, les-sons should also include time for the student to rehearse verbally what she will do when faced with challenging situations. Talking through vari-ous scenarios gives a student the opportunity to "think aloud" about her behavior. By verbalizing the behavior or strategy, the student demonstrates an understanding of what she should be doing. Verbal practice also allows the student to practice a behavior before trying it, minimizing the risk of failure. If more explanation or practice in the new behavior is needed, verbal practice will help you identify areas that need more work before entering the classroom. This is especially important if the new behavior will be difficult for the student.

> Note: If the student has limited language skills or a short at-tention span, you may need to consider providing demonstra-tions and then moving directly to positive practice. As with all interventions, procedures should be tailored to the needs and sophistication of each student.

The adult working with Molly will demonstrate appropriate behavior and will also ask Molly questions so that she can verbally rehearse what she will do. The adult will ask her questions similar to the following:

- When your teacher says it's time to begin your math, what will you do?
- If another student gets up to sharpen his pencil while you are working on your math, what will you do?
- Let's pretend that Mrs. Baker has reminded you to get back to work. What will you do or say?
- Suppose your mom says, "Molly, it's time to do your homework." How will you respond?
- If you do all these things, what will happen? How will your parents feel? What will happen to your grades? How will you feel about yourself?

4. Provide positive practice and feedback.

In addition to providing positive models and opportunities for the student to discuss how she will behave, lessons must provide time for the student to rehearse the replacement behavior. This in turn will provide many opportunities to offer the student specific feedback on her performance. For sufficient structured practice, you will need to simulate situations that resemble the real settings and events that the student has had difficulty managing in the past.

As you practice, ask the student some what-why-how-when-where questions directed at the rationale for the replacement behavior. If the student has trouble answering, provide the information for her and then repeat the question.

Each time the student acts out the replacement behavior, provide positive feedback if it was done well. Point out the positive things you noticed.

If you need to point out a negative, try to come up with at least three positive aspects of the rehearsal so that your work together remains on a 3:1 positive-to-negative ratio. "Good! You talked about needing an appointment. You didn't demand that it be now. And something you did really, really well was use a very calm voice. But you got a little too close; you were a little too much in my face. Sometimes that can make people not want to listen to what you have to say. But you're saying it so well! Stand back a step or two, and let's try it again."

For every run-through in which you point out an error, run three positive trials. That is, if the student makes an error in modeling the replacement behavior, practice the very same behavior—performed appropriately—at least three more times. It's important to maintain *a bare minimum* rate of three successful trials for every error. Just as a musician practices a difficult passage correctly until it has been drilled into "muscle memory" and can be reproduced at will, Teaching Replacement Behavior is essentially skill building. Be skeptical of shortcuts.

> Because Molly has difficulty completing work and tends to backtalk when she is asked to work, simulations will be relatively easy to structure. It is decided that Molly will bring homework to her lessons and practice working on actual assignments.

5. Gradually increase the difficulty of the lessons.

As the student gains competence, gradually increase the difficulty of the lessons until the student adopts the behavior in everyday situations. In the early stages, lessons should be conducted in an environment that is relatively free of distractions. As the student becomes more successful, lessons can be conducted in more complex contexts that assume more of the characteristics of the actual setting in which the student usually has problems. Eventually the goal is to teach the student to employ the new behavior in the problematic school setting for progressively longer periods of time.

For every run-through in which you point out an error, run three positive trials.

> When Molly is able to demonstrate appropriate behavior in her practice sessions, Mrs. Baker will begin to intervene actively in classroom work according to the replacement behavior plan, and Molly's mother will be taught how to help Molly with homework.

E. **Plan to conduct the lessons in a manner and place that will not embarrass the student.**
    At-risk students often respond positively to supportive adult attention in one-to-one lessons, but conditions that cause unintended embarrassment or agitation may lead to resistance. Keep practice sessions with the student private and unobtrusive. Plan to meet periodically with the student to provide encouragement and to suggest modifications to the plan. If you encourage the student to take part in and influence the content of the lessons, the student's motivation to learn new behavior will increase.

INTERVENTION

M

Resistance to lessons can also be tempered by making sure that the student understands the real-life applicability of the practice sessions. You might also consider combining this intervention with "Intervention C: Goal Setting" or "Intervention O: Structured Reinforcement Systems."

F. Identify ways to determine whether the intervention is helping the student reach her goal.

Because behavior is difficult to change, small improvements may go unnoticed unless you have devised a way to determine whether the intervention is having a positive impact. Evaluation may be formal or informal. It might include having the student maintain a self-monitoring chart, or you may need to directly observe the student to see whether she is practicing the replacement behavior. Evaluation procedures are important, as the results will help determine whether procedures should be revised, maintained, or faded.

1. Use self-monitoring or self-evaluation procedures.

Evaluation procedures are important, as the results will help determine whether procedures should be revised, maintained, or faded.

Self-monitoring is a process that helps the student become aware of her own behavior and the progress she is making. Evaluation can be done in a number of different ways. In some cases, evaluation will involve the person who is conducting the lessons informally prompting the student to think about her progress. ("Tell me how you did today.") In other cases, the student might actually count or record behaviors. ("Let's graph how many problems you did today.") The student might also be provided with a self-evaluation system. For example, if the target student is working on staying focused and on task, she might be taught to evaluate her performance on a scale similar to that shown in Reproducible Form M2.

Each value on a self-monitoring scale must be carefully described by the behavioral coach. A student working on improving on-task behavior during sustained silent reading could be provided with the following descriptors:

4 = On task and focused
  • Book ready
  • Began reading immediately
  • Got involved in the book
  • Ignored distractions

(Chart continued on p. 588)

INTERVENTION

M

Reproducible Form M2: *On-Task Evaluation Form*

On-Task Evaluation Form

Student _____ Grade/Class _____ Teacher _____ Date _____

Did I stay focused on my task?

very off task	off task	mostly on task	on task; focused
1	2	3	4

Subject: _____

Class Period: _____

Did I stay focused on my task?

very off task	off task	mostly on task	on task; focused
1	2	3	4

Subject: _____

Class Period: _____

Did I stay focused on my task?

very off task	off task	mostly on task	on task; focused
1	2	3	4

Subject: _____

Class Period: _____

Did I stay focused on my task?

very off task	off task	mostly on task	on task; focused
1	2	3	4

Subject: _____

Class Period: _____

3 = Mostly on task
- Started slowly
- Distracted once or twice
- Read and thought about reading most of the time

2 = Somewhat off task
- Started late
- Distracted several times
- Went through the motions of reading, but didn't really pay attention

1 = Off task
- Failed to read most of the time

If a self-monitoring chart is used, the teacher and student should role-play various situations. Both the teacher and student should rate the student's behavior, comparing evaluations with each role-play example, until the student is accurately evaluating her own behavior. (See "Intervention K: Self-Monitoring and Self-Evaluation" for more examples and forms you can use to create student monitoring systems.)

2. Collect data on the student's use of replacement behaviors.

A more objective way to evaluate the effects of an intervention, of course, is to collect data. This might involve counting how many times during the day a particular behavior occurs, determining the quantity of finished work, or timing how long the student engages in a particular behavior. Older students may be able to collect this kind of information themselves. If data is plotted on a graph, it is easy for the teacher and student to see whether the student's behavior is improving, staying the same, or deteriorating. When dealing with a chronic problem that requires a long-term resolution, it is often difficult to see progress unless an objective measure has been established. An overview of possible evaluation options for common Teaching Replacement Behavior problems is provided in Figure M3. (For more detailed information on developing an evaluation plan, see "Intervention D: Data Collection and Debriefing.")

Molly's teacher and interventionist decide that she would probably respond well to a self-monitoring system for staying on task. Molly will be taught to use the On-Task Evaluation Form (Reproducible Form M2) in her simulated work sessions. Once she is successful with the system in her practice sessions, Molly will be taught to use it for her classroom work. Mrs. Baker will track work completion as part of her normal grading procedures, and she will also keep an informal record of backtalk. She decides to keep this very simple, using an index card to tally the amount of backtalk each day.

Figure M3: *Recommended Evaluation Procedures*

Problem	Goal	Replacement Behavior	Evaluation
Anger when work is corrected	Calmly accepting feedback	Nodding acceptance; saying "Okay, I'll fix it."	• Two-week check-ins with student, parent, and teacher • Frequency count kept by teacher and charted by teacher and student
Swearing	Appropriate response or exclamation	Silence; "Shoot!"; "Shizzle!"; "Wow!"; etc.	• Two-week check-ins with student, parent, and teacher • Self-count charted by teacher and student
Aggression	Calming down without aggressive acts	Deep breathing; self-imposed timeout	• Two-week check-ins with student, parent, and teacher • Frequency count of aggressive acts charted by teacher
Oversensitivity	Responding maturely to teasing	Ignoring; use of "I" statements	• Two-week check-ins with student, parent, and teacher • Frequency count charted by student
Not completing work	Staying focused and on task	Ignoring distractions; returning to work quickly	• Count of work completed (e.g., number of math problems, pages completed) • Student chart, compared to teacher grade book

G. Determine whether a reinforcement system and consequences need to be integrated into the plan.

As you determine how the student might be taught to replace and evaluate her own behavior, consider the age and sophistication of the student, the type of behavior being taught, and whether the student may need a system of extrinsic rewards to enhance motivation to exhibit the newly learned behaviors. Teaching Replacement Behavior may be more effective for some students if it is combined with "Intervention O: Structured Reinforcement Systems" and "Intervention P: Defining Limits and Establishing Consequences."

In discussing Molly's readiness to improve, Mrs. Baker says that, more than anything else, Molly wants to be like the other students. Mrs. Baker knows that Molly is embarrassed by her own behavior but seems unable to control her impulsive responses. Mrs. Baker and the interventionist believe that Molly will be motivated to improve.

Mrs. Baker and the interventionist decide not to implement a reinforcement system along with their plan, but they agree that it might be wise to look at such a system for Molly's mother to use when they begin working on Molly's ability to complete homework at home. When considering consequences, Mrs. Baker feels that backtalk can be ignored, and she agrees to turn her attention immediately away from Molly any time she talks disrespectfully. Mrs. Baker's only reaction will be to make note of the incident on an index card.

H. Identify criteria and procedures for fading the intervention.

Fading this intervention should consist of a gradual reduction in the length and frequency of the lessons and in the amount of monitoring being conducted. Any accompanying reinforcement procedures should also be faded over time. The rate at which you fade the intervention should be determined by the frequency with which the student is successful. The more the student displays the new behavior, the sooner and more rapidly the lessons can be faded. As the intervention is gradually removed and behavior shows generalization to real-life settings, continue to provide encouragement to the student about her increasing ability to manage her own behavior. The student will need continued support in recognizing the sense of power she has gained as she manages situations on her own.

If the student begins to fall back into old patterns as the program is faded, increase support by resuming more frequent lessons and continue to reinforce the student when she responds appropriately. Avoid making the student feel guilty about sliding backward, or the intervention will begin to take on negative or punitive connotations. As long as the student needs support, provide it. When the student again becomes more successful, gradually fade procedures and continue support with encouragement and positive feedback.

I. Determine who will meet with the student to discuss and finalize the plan.

Consider including the person who will work as the behavioral coach and anyone else who will be working directly with the student as she attempts to change her behavior. However, it is important to convene a group that will not overwhelm the student. If the student is likely to feel uncomfortable meeting with several adults, it may be best to select one person to meet with her.

Schedule the discussion at a time when the student and adult can be relatively relaxed. Prior to the discussion, the student's teacher should let her know in private that the meeting is coming up and the goal of the meeting. By prearranging the meeting with the student, the teacher can communicate that the discussion is important—it is not a punishment for past behavior, but an opportunity to set up a plan for the future.

Mrs. Baker: (Teacher)	Molly, I am very glad to have you in class with me this year. With some of my students, I periodically set up special goals. My goals for you this year are to help you learn to be more focused when you are doing your independent work and for you to be able to get along well with adults who want to help you with your work. I would really like to help you with this. Would that be OK?
Molly:	I guess so.
Mrs. Baker:	Good. I would like to help you with these goals because I think you will be happier with yourself. We want to help you get ready for middle school. I've asked our interventionist, Ms. Schrader, to meet with us because she will be working with us on these goals. Is this OK with you?
Molly:	I guess.
Mrs. Baker:	Good. We will all meet tomorrow morning after spelling. I am excited that we can all work together to help you with these goals.

Step 2: Meet with the student to discuss and finalize the plan.

A. Review the problem and goals.

In the initial meeting with the student, it is important to establish a sense of trust. The student should understand that this intervention is being initiated to assist in her efforts to be more successful. The student must understand the goals of the lessons, the outcome, and the benefits.

Be prepared for the possibility that the student may say, "But I already know how to do this." Consider using an example from sports, music, or dance, based on the student's interests. Knowing how to do something is not the same thing as being ready and able to do it on a moment's notice and does not reduce the need for coaching and practice.

Mrs. Baker: (Teacher)	I am glad that we could all meet. Molly, yesterday I told you that we would like to work with you on two goals that will help prepare you for middle school. Do you remember what those goals were?
Molly:	Sort of.
Mrs. Baker:	What were they?
Molly:	Getting along better and getting my work done.
Mrs. Baker:	Yes, Molly. I am glad that you remember. You have really grown up a lot since you've been at Hamilton. How do you think those goals might help you?
Molly:	I don't know.
Mrs. Baker:	Well, let's see if we can make a list. What do you think will happen if you learn to be respectful with adults and learn to get your work done?
Molly:	I won't get in trouble.
Mrs. Baker:	Yes, and you might feel happier at the end of the day if you have a pleasant day. What else?
Molly:	I probably would get better grades.
Ms. Schrader: (Interventionist)	Yes. How would you feel about that?
Molly:	Good.
Ms. Schrader:	If you could learn to talk more respectfully and get your work done, how do you think the other kids would feel about you?
Molly:	Better, I guess.
Mrs. Baker:	Yes, I think so Molly. You are making new friends this year, and that is wonderful. When you yell at me, it em-

	barrasses the other kids. If you can learn to work with me and other adults more maturely, I think the other kids would respect you more. Are these things you would be willing to work on?
Molly:	I guess.
Ms. Schrader:	That's great, Molly. I'd like to meet with you three times each week. We will work on things you can do to get your work done, and we'll also work on better ways to deal with adults.

Once the purpose of the lessons has been established in the first meeting, briefly review the student's goals at the beginning of each lesson.

B. Review everyone's roles and responsibilities.

Ms. Schrader: (Interventionist)	Molly, I am really glad that we will be able to meet together. I will come and get you every Monday, Wednesday, and Friday right after lunch. Your responsibility will be to come with me as soon as you see me.
Mrs. Baker: (Teacher)	When you have worked with Ms. Schrader for a week or so, I will begin helping you in class.

C. Conclude the meeting with words of encouragement.

Mrs. Baker:	Molly, I am happy that you will be working on this plan. I know that you and I can learn to work respectfully with each other, and I also know that you can learn to be responsible for your work. I'm looking forward to a great year. It's fun to see my students making progress.

Step 3: Implement the plan.

A. Get started with Teaching Replacement Behavior lessons.

1. At the beginning of each lesson, review the goals of the plan with the student.

Ms. Schrader: (Interventionist)	Molly, I'm glad to see you. Thanks for coming as soon as you saw me. I'm looking forward to our meetings. Do you remember what your two goals are?
Molly:	I need to get along with Mrs. Baker, and I need to get my work done.

2. Communicate an age-appropriate rationale for the replacement behavior to be learned.

Discuss the rationale for the replacement behavior that you are teaching—the what, why, how, when, and where. What will this get for the student? Why will this behavior help? The older the student, the more critical it is that you back up the proposed replacement behaviors with well-considered reasoning that will be meaningful to the student.

3. Provide demonstrations and modeling.

Ms. Schrader:	We are going to work on getting your assignments done. You can do that by getting started quickly and staying focused. Let's pretend it is math period, and Mrs. Baker has assigned you the problems on page 15 of your math book. Watch what I do. I quickly get out my paper and book. Then I turn to page 15 without stopping. Next, I pick up my pencil and begin working. I write the first problem down and figure out the answer. Then I look at the next problem and write it down. (The interventionist works two problems, exaggerating the movement of her hand as she copies and works the problems without stopping.) If someone coughs or comes into the room, I keep my eyes on my paper and my mind on my math.

4. Provide opportunities for verbal practice.

Ms. Schrader: (Interventionist)	Now it's your turn. Mrs. Baker has just asked you to get started on page 15 in your math book. What will you do?
Molly:	I need to get out my book, a pencil, and piece of paper. Then I need to start copying and working the problems.
Ms. Schrader:	That's exactly right. What should you do if the person next to you has to sharpen his pencil?
Molly:	I should keep working.
Ms. Schrader:	Yes, keep your mind on your math and your eyes on your paper.

5. Provide positive practice and feedback.

Ms. Schrader:	Let's give that a try. I'll pretend I'm Mrs. Baker. Let's see if you can work three problems without looking up.
(Molly does three problems.)	
Ms. Schrader:	Molly, that was great. You got three problems done. No sweat! Congratulations, you have already completed one-fifth of today's homework.

6. Gradually increase the difficulty of the lessons.

The difficulty of the lessons can be increased by asking the student to deal with more complex situations, by increasing the length or duration of the behavioral expectation, and by removing adult assistance.

Ms. Schrader:	Molly, in our session on Monday, you showed me that you could get to work immediately and complete three math problems without stopping. In fact, you were able to get your homework done in ten minutes. Today, I am going to make it a little harder. Do you think you can handle it?
Molly:	No problem!
Ms. Schrader:	OK. Today, I am going to ask you to do four math problems without looking up, and I am going to try to distract you. I might whistle. What will you do?

Molly:	I know. Keep my mind on my math and my eyes on my paper.
Ms. Schrader:	Yes. But I might start singing a song, or I might drop my book. Do you think I can get you?
Molly:	No!

As Molly demonstrates success, lessons are increased to include corrections from the interventionist that simulate the kinds of comments Molly might hear from her teacher or her mother. In the second lesson, Molly is taught how to self-monitor her work habits. By the second week, she will begin monitoring her ability to stay on task during math class.

7. Make a conscious effort to recognize student success outside of the practice sessions.

Providing the student with positive feedback on efforts to generalize the skill will be the means by which the student learns to incorporate the new skill into her daily life.

As the student begins to practice new behavior in her real classroom environment, it will be important for the teacher to monitor key times when the student is likely to engage in the new behavior. As the student gains competence, all adults should try to catch her exhibiting the goal behavior outside of structured lesson times. Providing the student with positive feedback on efforts to generalize the skill will be the means by which the student learns to incorporate the new skill into her daily life.

Mrs. Baker: (Teacher)	(In private) Molly, Ms. Schrader tells me you are making great progress. I am very proud of you. In fact, even though we haven't said anything about using what you are learning in class, I've noticed that you get your materials out without any reminders. You were very responsible for getting a quick start in math. In fact, we are going to begin working on this as a class. You were much more efficient than half the class!

B. Evaluate, revise, and fade the plan.

Once the plan is in operation, it is important to periodically review the evaluation information being collected. If no improvement is seen, the intervention plan may need to be altered. If things are going well, the lessons may increase in difficulty. Finally, as the student shows consistent use of the new behaviors or strategies without prompting and assistance, the plan should be faded.

Molly's teacher and the interventionist meet for their first formal meeting three weeks after the plan has been started. At this point, Molly's teacher indicates that Molly has made tremendous strides in her ability to get started and to remain on task. Records indicate that Molly has completed all in-class math assignments and her three weekly homework assignments. Though progress is noted in this area, the teacher does not see a change in the frequency of backtalk or work completion in other subjects.

Mrs. Baker and the interventionist decide to have Molly continue self-monitoring in math and to add self-monitoring during reading to begin generalizing the replacement behavior in other areas. They also decide to continue working on math homework for 10 minutes in her special lessons, and then they'll work for 5 minutes on role-playing various situations that lead to backtalk. It is also decided that Ms. Schrader will try to set up a couple of sessions with Molly's mother so she can begin helping Molly do math homework.

C. Provide continued support for maintenance.

Changing behavior is a difficult process. The teacher should continue to provide the student with positive feedback throughout the fading process. Once a student has begun achieving the goal, it is very easy to take appropriate behavior for granted. The student will have made a major change in behavior and will need continued support and attention from the teacher and periodic check-ins with the interventionist so the student knows that she has the support required for long-term success.

Molly's intervention plan is lengthy but by and large successful. By the end of the year, Molly slips occasionally into backtalk, but she has developed a positive and constructive relationship with Mrs. Baker. Throughout the year, Mrs. Baker continues providing Molly with positive feedback regarding her work and makes it a point to have a special snack with Molly every two weeks to discuss her progress. The self-monitoring chart is reintroduced twice, each time at Molly's request.

Homework continues to be challenging because Molly and her mother are unable to work out routines and have a well-established pattern of argumentative interactions. Ultimately, Molly decides to do her homework while she is at her after-school daycare program. Arrangements are made with the daycare provider to have Molly work in a quiet spot after her snack.

As Molly demonstrates her ability to interact respectfully with her classroom teacher and work efficiently on in-class assignments, weekly lessons are gradually reduced from three lessons each week to two, to one, and eventually to a brief conference with the interventionist each week.

By the end of the year, Mrs. Baker is sincere in saying that Molly will be missed as she heads off to middle school. Because Molly is still considered to be at a fragile point in her behavioral growth, the interventionist makes a special appointment with the middle school counselor to set up a transition program for Molly as she enters sixth grade.

Note: Other interventions in this book can be used to teach specific replacement behaviors, including: "Intervention L: Self-Talk and Attribution Training," "Intervention N: Functional Communication," and "Intervention R: Internalizing Problems and Mental Health."

Teaching Replacement Behavior can be powerful enough to make the difference in whether a student completes school and is able to enter society with the skills needed to be successful and independent.

CONCLUSION

Teaching Replacement Behavior is designed to help students learn behavior that will help them succeed in school, both academically and socially, and can help them succeed in other important aspects of life. However, with crowded and understaffed schools, it may be difficult to arrange lessons. With a creative use of resources, this potential barrier can usually be overcome. Sometimes the classroom teacher can provide quick lessons while other students work independently. In other cases, an interventionist—administrator, counselor, school psychologist, school nurse, classroom consultant, or at-risk coordinator—might provide lessons. Lessons may also be conducted by a trained teaching assistant, parent, or adult mentor. When those conducting the lessons are unfamiliar with behavioral training, the interventionist should demonstrate the procedures and observe lessons at least once a week until training is moving smoothly. Though time-consuming, interventions such as Teaching Replacement Behavior can be powerful enough to make the difference in whether a student completes school and is able to enter society with the skills needed to be successful and independent.

INTERVENTION

M

Given the large number of issues that teachers face each day in school, it is sometimes difficult to justify one-to-one lessons: "Why should this trouble-maker get all my time and attention? It isn't fair to the other students." Teaching Replacement Behavior must be viewed as remedial instruction, as necessary as remediation of academic concerns. If justifying the time necessary to implement this intervention is an issue, consider looking first at "Pre-Intervention: Classroom Management Strategies," "Intervention E: Increasing Positive Interactions," or "Intervention Q: Relaxation and Stress Management."

REFERENCES

Abrams, B. J., & Segal, A. (1998). How to prevent aggressive behavior. *Teaching Exceptional Children, 30*, 10–15.

Apple, A. L., Billingsley, F., & Schwartz, I. S. (2005). Effects of video monitoring alone and with self-management on compliment-giving behaviors of children with high-functioning ASD. *Journal of Positive Behavior Interventions, 7*(1), 33–46.

Babyak, A. E., Luze, G. J., & Kamps, D. M. (2000). The good student game: Behavior management for diverse classrooms. *Intervention in School and Clinic, 35*(4), 216–223.

Bandura, A. (1977a). *Social learning theory.* Englewood Cliffs, NJ: Prentice-Hall.

Bandura, A. (1977b). Self-efficacy. In V. S. Ramachaudran (Ed.), *Encyclopedia of human behavior* (Vol. 4, pp. 71–81). New York: Academic Press. (Reprinted in *Encyclopedia of mental health*, by H. Friedman, Ed., 1998, San Diego: Academic Press.)

Bandura, A. (1997). *Self-efficacy: The exercise of control.* New York: Freeman.

Beyda, S. D., Zentall, S. S., & Ferko, D. J. K. (2002). The relationship between teacher practices and the task-appropriate and social behavior of students with behavioral disorders. *Behavioral Disorders, 27*(3), 236–255.

Bornstein, M., Bellack, A. S., & Hersen, M. (1980). Social skills training for highly aggressive children. *Behavior Modification, 4*, 173–186.

Brandt, M., & Christensen, R. (2002). *Improving student social skills through the use of cooperative learning, problem solving, and direct instruction.* Master's project, St. Xavier University, Chicago, IL. (ED465929)

Carey, S. P., & Stoner, G. (1994). Contextual considerations in social skills instruction. *School Psychology Quarterly, 9*, 137–141.

Cashwell, T. H., Skinner, C. H., & Smith, E. S. (2001). Increasing second-grade students' reports of peers' prosocial behaviors via direct instruction, group reinforcement, and progress feedback: A replication and extension. *Education and Treatment of Children, 24*(2), 161–175.

Cone, J. J., Fulton, R., & Van Nieuwenhuyse, D. (2000). *Improving student behavior by teaching social skills.* Master's project, St. Xavier University, Chicago, IL. (ED444089)

Dowrick, P. (1999). A review of self-modeling and related interventions. *Applied and Preventive Psychology, 8,* 23–39.

DuPaul, G. J., & Eckert, T. L. (1994). The effects of social skills curricula: Now you see them, now you don't. *School Psychology Quarterly, 9,* 113–132.

Eddy, J. M., Reid, J. B., & Fetrow, R. A. (2000). An elementary school-based prevention program targeting modifiable antecedents of youth delinquency and violence: Linking the interests of families and teachers (LIFT). *Journal of Emotional and Behavioral Disorders, 8*(3), 165–176.

Goldstein, A. P., & Glick, B. (1994). Aggression replacement training: Curriculum and evaluation. *Simulation and Gaming, 25*(1), 2–26.

Hitchcock, C. H., Dowrick, P. W., & Prater, M. A. (2003). Video self-modeling in school-based settings. *Remedial and Special Education, 56,* 36–45.

Jones, R. N., Sheridan, S. M., & Binns, W. R. (1993). Schoolwide social skills training: Providing preventive services to students at risk. *School Psychology Quarterly, 8,* 57–80.

Kehle, T. J., Clark, E., Jenson, W. R., & Wampold, B. E. (1986). Effectiveness of self-observation with behavior-disordered elementary school children. *School Psychology Review, 15,* 289–295.

Knapczyk, D. R. (1988). Reducing aggressive behavior in special and regular classroom settings by training alternative responses. *Behavior Disorders, 14,* 27–39.

Knapczyk, D. R. (1989). An analysis of setting events and use of modeling and rehearsal in training alternatives to aggressive behavior. *Journal of Child and Adolescent Psychotherapy, 2,* 21–35.

Kratochwill, T. R., & French, D. C. (1984). Social skills training for withdrawn children. *School Psychology Review, 13,* 331–337.

Morgan, D. P., & Jenson, W. R. (1990). *Teaching behaviorally disordered students: Preferred practices.* Upper Saddle River, NJ: Prentice Hall.

Starek, J., & McCullagh, P. (1999). The effect of video self-modeling on the performance of beginning swimmers. *Sports Psychologist, 13,* 269–287.

Stillwell, B. E. (2002). Coaching behaviors to create a positive atmosphere. *Strategies, 15*(3), 11–14.

Sugai, G., & Lewis, T. J. (1996). Preferred and promising practices for social skills instruction. *Focus on Exceptional Children, 29,* 1–16.

Sulzer-Azaroff, B., & Mayer, G. R. (1986). *Achieving educational excellence: Using behavioral strategies.* New York: Holt, Rinehart, and Winston.

Wiesberg, R. P., & Gersten, E. L. (1982). Considerations for developing effective school based social problem solving (SPS) training programs. *School Psychology Review, 11,* 56–63.

Reproducible Materials

The following reproducible materials may be used in conjunction with "Intervention M: Teaching Replacement Behavior." Copies are provided here and on the CD. Permission is given for individual classroom teachers to reproduce any forms labeled "Reproducible" for classroom use. Reproduction of these materials for an entire school system is prohibited without express permission of the publisher.

INTERVENTION

Teaching Replacement Behavior

Step-by-Step Summary

Following is a summary of the steps involved in Intervention M. It is important to use professional judgment, adjusting procedures to meet the needs of the situation and the individual. See the chapter "Intervention M: Teaching Replacement Behavior" for a detailed description of this intervention.

STEP 1   Develop a plan for using Teaching Replacement Behavior.

A. Review the problem and overall goals for the student.

B. Determine who will provide the lessons, how much time will be needed, and when and where they will be held.

C. Determine behaviors or strategies the student can learn to replace the inappropriate behaviors.

D. Design lessons to teach the replacement behavior.
   1. Communicate an age-appropriate rationale for the replacement behavior—what, why, how, when, and where.
   2. Provide demonstrations and modeling.
   3. Provide opportunities for verbal practice.
   4. Provide positive practice and feedback.
   5. Gradually increase the difficulty of the lessons.

E. Plan to conduct the lessons in a manner and place that will not embarrass the student.

F. Identify ways to determine whether the intervention is helping the student reach her goal.
   1. Use self-monitoring or self-evaluation procedures.
   2. Collect data on the student's use of replacement behaviors.

G. Determine whether a reinforcement system and consequences need to be integrated into the plan.

H. Identify criteria and procedures for fading the intervention.

I. Determine who will meet with the student to discuss and finalize the plan.

INTERVENTION

STEP 2 Meet with the student to discuss and finalize the plan.

A. Review the problem and goals.

B. Review everyone's roles and responsibilities.

C. Conclude the meeting with words of encouragement.

STEP 3 Implement the plan.

A. Get started with Teaching Replacement Behavior lessons.
1. At the beginning of each lesson, review the goals of the plan with the student.
2. Communicate an age-appropriate rationale for the replacement behavior to be learned.
3. Provide demonstrations and modeling.
4. Provide opportunities for verbal practice.
5. Provide positive practice and feedback.
6. Gradually increase the difficulty of the lessons.
7. Make a conscious effort to recognize student success outside of the practice sessions.

B. Evaluate, revise, and fade the plan.

C. Provide continued support for maintenance.

Leanne S. Hawken, Ph.D.
Sarah L. Adolphson, M.A.

Functional Communication

The student cannot or will not communicate verbally

PURPOSE

FUNCTIONAL COMMUNICATION is intended to assist students whose limited communication skills prevent their needs from being met, resulting in misbehavior. Limited communication may stem from physical, learning, or mental disabilities or impairments, language barriers, or a simple lack of training.

THIS INTERVENTION IS APPROPRIATE FOR:

Aggressive behavior
- hitting
- kicking
- pinching
- hair pulling
- scratching
- biting

Disruptive behavior
- tantrums
- throwing items
- falling on floor
- knocking over tables or chairs
- yelling

Stereotypic behavior
- repetitive hand flapping
- body rocking
- finger flicking

Self-injurious behavior
- pinching or biting arm
- hitting face
- banging head on wall

Unconventional verbal behavior
- echoing another's speech
- repeating phrases excessively
- inappropriate vocal noises

Communication is a fundamental aspect of life for all individuals and is necessary for us to get our basic needs met and to express our desires. Communication can occur in many forms and does not always involve the use of speech. Changes in body or facial positions, pointing, leading an adult by the hand to a desired item, and crying are among many forms of a child's nonverbal communication. Individuals with disabilities and/or communication disorders may not always be able to express their needs or wants through typical means. Lacking the skills to engage in appropriate forms of communication, they may resort to misbehavior both to communicate and to get their needs met.

Teaching Functional Communication is a way to provide an appropriate alternative behavior for misbehaviors that serve communicative functions (i.e., gaining attention, getting a desired item, or avoiding an undesired situation or task). It involves rewarding the student for appropriate forms of communication and ignoring the misbehaviors the student is using to try to get his needs met. Functional Communication training may involve teaching students to use new ways of communicating, such as an electronic communication board, sign language, or communication with pictures. This intervention also provides individuals who have not developed typical and socially acceptable methods of communication with training in appropriate ways to make requests, often leading to a reduction of the dysfunctional behaviors that

Teaching Functional Communication is a way to provide an appropriate alternative behavior for misbehaviors that serve communicative functions.

serve the same purpose. It can also be used with English language learners (ELLs)—students who may have learned appropriate ways to communicate but are unable to get their needs met due to language barriers.

Whatever the mode of communication, the goal of the Functional Communication intervention is to provide students with alternative, appropriate ways to communicate, decreasing their need to express themselves through misbehavior. Increasing the ability of individuals with disabilities or language barriers to communicate can greatly improve their quality of life and lead to increased independence.

> Note: This is a time- and work-intensive intervention that will require the use of a multidisciplinary team. If you are considering using this intervention with any student who might benefit from any of the Early-Stage Interventions that you have not yet implemented, always remember to try the easiest intervention that has a reasonable likelihood of success first. Unlike other interventions, this intervention is targeted at students with specific communication difficulties, so it may be necessary to implement this intervention alone or in combination with other interventions to address the student's needs.

RATIONALE

Students with limited communication options may engage in a range of inappropriate behaviors—minor (screaming, tantrums) to severe (aggression toward themselves or others)—to get their needs met. It is typical for children who are able to say only a few words to use behavior to communicate. Some students may be able to say "yes" or "no" but cannot communicate more complex ideas such as "I have to go to the bathroom." These students often become frustrated when they are unable to get their point across. Functional Communication provides a way for these students to communicate needs and wants reliably, offering them more control over their environment.

What types of students benefit from communication training?

Communication training benefits students who are limited in their abilities to use appropriate forms of communication. Studies have shown that teachers frequently do not respond to students who use unconventional forms of communication. Communication training can benefit students who use facial expressions, body movement, vocal sounds, or other unusual means to express themselves.

With what populations has Functional Communication training been used?

Fairly extensive research has demonstrated that Functional Communication training can be highly effective in many settings for individuals of all ages, with and without disabilities. It has been used for people with autism, mild to severe intellectual disabilities, schizophrenia, hearing and vision impairments, emotional disabilities, and learning disabilities. Using pictures to communicate can also benefit ELL students who lack the English language skills necessary to express desires or participate in classroom activities.

Functional Communication training can be highly effective in many settings for individuals of all ages, with and without disabilities.

What are the indicators that Functional Communication is an appropriate intervention?

Misbehaviors that can be effectively reduced through Functional Communication often serve a specific communicative function. To determine whether a student is using behavior to communicate, the behavior should be observed, with specific attention paid to situations in which the behavior is likely to occur. Notice what is required before the student discontinues the inappropriate behavior— what function is the student's misbehavior serving? It is necessary to assess whether the behavior is likely to stop if the student attains the desired reward, because this will inform how you develop your intervention plan. If the student misbehaves in order to communicate a need or desire—the behavior stops when the reward is attained—then Functional Communication training will be most effective when the student is given the desired outcome or reward following use of the new, alternative form of communication. In addition, the reward should be withheld when the misbehavior occurs.

Before implementing Functional Communication

Before this intervention can be successfully implemented, be sure that you have discussed the problem and general goals for improvement with the student. Gather any relevant background information that may help in designing and implementing the intervention. In addition, contact the student's parents or guardians to discuss the problem. Be sure to keep the parents informed of all aspects of the intervention plan throughout the process.

Students with Multiple Misbehaviors Related to Communication

Some students may use several types of misbehaviors in different situations for different communicative purposes. For example, a student may fall to the floor if he is trying to communicate that he doesn't want to participate in an activity, he may become aggressive when he wants a toy or food item, and he may yell if he wants the teacher's attention. For students who use multiple forms of misbehavior (or one type of misbehavior to communicate different things), prioritize the situations and address the most important situation first. Once the student has successfully replaced the misbehavior with a new form of communication in the first situation, the next communicative behavior can be taught. If several different communicative behaviors are taught simultaneously, the student may become confused and fail to learn the appropriate forms of communication.

IMPLEMENTATION STEPS

Step 1: Decide whether an alternative form of communication is an appropriate intervention.

A. Identify the misbehavior and determine whether it is related to communication.

Prior to calling a multidisciplinary meeting, identify and define the misbehavior that needs to be modified. When does the misbehavior occur? Do any predictable events or situations occur just prior to the misbehavior? What does the teacher currently do when the student misbehaves?

Oscar Avila is in first grade in Ms. Glick's self-contained special education classroom. Ms. Glick is concerned with Oscar's behavior. He will hit other people when he is presented with a task such as matching letters or other academic tasks he finds difficult, even when he is capable of completing them. Typically, Ms. Glick will not require that Oscar complete the task but will offer him something else to do.

Oscar has been diagnosed with moderate mental retardation and is unable to communicate verbally. He does make a few sounds, such as "eeeee" or "mmm," but he does not use the sounds specifically to communicate. Ms. Glick has asked for help from the school psychologist, Mr. Baker, to work on decreasing Oscar's aggression in the classroom.

INTERVENTION

N

Use the Problem Behavior Checklist to determine whether or not the misbehaviors of concern are related to communication. Sample Reproducible Form N1 shows a record of the possible communicative intent of Oscar's misbehaviors during one day.

Note: Blank copies of this form and other Functional Communication forms are available at the end of the chapter and are also provided on the CD.

B. Determine what the student is trying to communicate with the misbehavior.

If you believe the student's misbehavior is arising because the student lacks the communicative ability to get his needs met in acceptable ways, next determine the function of the misbehavior. The first step in training a student to use an appropriate form of communication is to assess what the student is trying to communicate by engaging in misbehavior. The most common reasons that students misbehave are to gain attention from peers or adults, to get access to a desired item (e.g., a student yells and cries because he wants a snack), or to escape an undesirable situation (e.g., a student repeatedly runs from the classroom because he does not want to participate in the class lesson).

Oscar hits other people when he is presented with tasks that are difficult for him. Ms. Glick believes that because Oscar cannot express himself verbally, he gets frustrated and uses hitting as a way to communicate that he does not want to do something.

Step 2: Conduct a multidisciplinary team meeting.

A. Form or convene a multidisciplinary intervention team.

Functional Communication training is a powerful technique that allows children more control over their environment. However, if poorly implemented, this training can leave the student frustrated and confused. This intervention requires the use of a multidisciplinary team, and members should include at least one person who is familiar with

Sample Reproducible Form N1: *Problem Behavior Checklist*

Problem Behavior Checklist

Oscar Avila
Student

Special Ed
Grade/Class

Ms. Glick
Teacher

Nov. 11
Date

The box below includes sample sequences of events indicating that a student may be trying to use problem behavior to communicate. Look at each scenario and check the box if it relates to this specific student.

Antecedent *What was happening just before the misbehavior?*	Behavior	Consequence	Possible Communicative Intent of Misbehavior	Check Boxes that Apply
Student appeared to be in discomfort while sitting at the table.	Fidgeting, inattentive to teacher, trying to leave seat.	Student is required to continue activity.	Student needs to use the bathroom.	☐
Teacher is trying to help student finish class work.	Student refuses to follow instructions and screams.	Student is required to complete the task.	Student would like a break from the activity.	☒
Teacher is working with others. Student is alone at a table.	Student repeatedly makes loud and inappropriate noises.	Student is asked to work quietly, but continues to make disruptive noises.	Student would like attention.	☐
Teacher is giving a whole-group lesson just before lunchtime.	Student begins to cry and tantrum.	Separation within the classroom.	Student is hungry.	☒
Another student takes an item from student.	Student hits and bites the other student.	Student is sent to time-out.	Student would like the item.	☐
Student is working independently.	Student begins to hit herself in the forehead.	Teacher stops student and gives her another task.	Student needs help completing the task.	☒
Another student is drinking a bottle of juice.	Student pulls the other student's hair.	Student is required to leave the lunchroom.	Student needs a drink.	☐

If you checked one or more boxes, it may be indicative that problem behavior is being used for communicative purposes.

A blank version of this form is available in the *Reproducible Materials* section at the end of the chapter.

Functional Communication training, such as a behavioral consultant, school psychologist, or speech therapist. This may require hiring an outside consultant to train school personnel. Functional Communication planning should also include the student's teacher or teachers as well as the student's parents, as these people are likely to have the most insight into how the student typically communicates.

B. Discuss Functional Communication techniques and select an alternative form of communication for the student.

Once you have identified and defined the misbehavior you want to correct and its communicative function, an appropriate replacement behavior should be selected. Many different Functional Communication techniques can be used. Some students prefer sign language while others may use pictures, gestures, or an electronic communication board. The replacement behavior you will teach should be appropriate to the student's age and level of functioning. For example, a student with unintelligible speech could be taught the use of a gesture, sign, or picture exchange.

The replacement behavior you will teach should be appropriate to the student's age and level of functioning.

> Note: Basic pictures for a picture exchange are provided in Reproducible Form N4 in the *Reproducible Materials* section at the end of this chapter.

Whatever technique is chosen, the student should be able to use it consistently across settings throughout the school day. Parent and student participation is also very important, as the chosen communication technique will need to be generalized into the home. Parents are usually particular about how they want their child to communicate, and their input will help ensure "buy-in" to the intervention plan. With any student who has the ability to indicate a preference in the chosen communication technique and who may be self-conscious, be sure to design a system that will be acceptable and not embarrassing for the student. When you meet with the student, you should present several possible Functional Communication techniques and allow the student to choose one. Also strive to make the replacement behavior as similar in effort to the misbehavior as possible. If the new communicative behavior requires significantly more effort than the misbehavior, the student may lack the motivation to use it. So, for a student who typically speaks in one- to two-word utterances and screams when wanting a break from a task, an appropriate replacement behavior

INTERVENTION

may be a two-word request such as, "Break, please." A longer phrase—"I want a break, please"—may not be effective with the student if hitting has worked to get him a break in the past.

> Ms. Glick, the teacher, and Mr. Baker, the school psychologist, discuss what method of communication would be the most effective for Oscar. They believe that simple sign language is the best choice so that Oscar will be able to communicate in any setting, without needing access to pictures or an electronic device. Mr. Baker thinks that because most of Oscar's misbehavior occurs when he does not want to engage in an activity, a simple sign for "stop" might be a good starting point.

C. Determine who will conduct the Functional Communication training.

Implementing Functional Communication training should be a collaborative effort. Training sessions should be conducted in environments in which the student will be likely to use the new communicative behavior and with individuals who interact daily with the student. As previously mentioned, it is important to involve parents in the initial training. This can include having a parent come to the school to observe training sessions and then conduct training sessions at home to help generalize the behavior to the home. In the school setting, training sessions can be conducted by the child's teacher, a school psychologist or speech pathologist, or a paraprofessional (e.g., classroom assistant) who has been trained in the correct procedures for conducting training sessions. The most important consideration in deciding who will teach the student is that the individual understands how to conduct training sessions and is available to conduct sessions regularly.

> **Mr. Baker:** (School Psychologist)　Now that we have decided on a technique, let's talk about who will conduct the training. I could help on some days, but in my experience it is important for Oscar's parents to be involved in the training because this will also need to transfer to the home setting. I spoke with Ms. Avila, and she stated that she might be able to get off work early for a few afternoons while we get started with initial training. She thinks this intervention will really help reduce some of Oscar's frustration.

Ms. Glick: (Teacher)	I could also allocate 15 minutes after school if that would make it easier for Ms. Avila to be involved.
Mr. Baker:	Great! It sounds like we can conduct daily sessions for 15 minutes after school for a week, and at the end of the week see what other training needs to be done.
Ms. Glick:	My only concern is that we are teaching Oscar how to refuse to do work. Won't he try to use this new communication to get out of doing his work?
Mr. Baker:	The goal is for Oscar to learn an appropriate way to express that he does not want to engage in an activity. Initially, when we are teaching him the sign, we will allow him to get out of work every time he signs "stop." Once he uses the sign reliably to communicate disapproval, we will gradually fade in statements like, "That was nice that you told me that you didn't want to do this, but you will need to work on this task for one minute." We will then need to increase the amount of time he spends on tasks he dislikes. Most children dislike some school activity, but they need to learn that they cannot always get out of doing what they do not like. In situations where Oscar gets to choose between two activities, we will reward him for appropriately refusing one activity and choosing the other.

Functional Communication should initially take the form of frequent but brief structured lessons to teach the student the new behavior.

D. Determine how Functional Communication will be taught.

Functional Communication should initially take the form of frequent but brief structured lessons to teach the student the new behavior. Initial sessions should include between 10 and 20 trials presented rapidly to allow the student multiple opportunities to learn the new communicative behavior. As the student gains success in one-to-one training sessions with the person who initially conducts the training, the replacement behavior should be generalized to other settings. The student should begin working with other trainers and teachers on including the behavior in every setting until the student begins to use the replacement behavior spontaneously.

When the new form of communication is first introduced, the student should immediately receive the desired reward (e.g., attention, desired item, or a break from the activity) every time he communicates appropriately. In the beginning, the student may need help from the trainer to use the replacement behavior. The new behavior can be prompted by modeling the correct behavior, using a verbal cue, or by using a partial or full physical prompt. Plan to use the least intrusive prompt that helps the student respond correctly. More-intrusive prompts (partial or full physical prompts) should be systematically faded to less intrusive ones as the student demonstrates success. If the misbehavior occurs during training sessions, withhold reinforcement. For example, if the student screams because he wants to take a break, the teacher would continue working with the child until he uses the new, appropriate form of communication.

It has been found that training sessions for Functional Communication should involve multiple teaching opportunities presented to the student in a discrete trial format. The teaching sequence follows.

1. Engage the student in a situation where the misbehavior typically occurs.

Although training sessions will be conducted on a one-to-one basis, they should simulate the situations that trigger the student's misbehavior as closely as possible. Plan to engage a student with a task you are certain the student is capable of completing, but one that often causes the student to act out.

> Mr. Baker, the school psychologist, decides that Oscar will be presented with a letter-matching task during training sessions. Even though Oscar has a tendency to engage in the problem behavior frequently during letter matching, he can complete the task when the problem behavior does not get in the way. The problem behavior could be Oscar's way of communicating that he would like a break, or it could occur due to frustration with the task.

2. Help the student produce the desired communication.

Initially, the trainer may need to model and lead the student to use the appropriate form of communication by taking the student's hand and guiding him to point to a picture or make a sign, and then immediately providing the desired item or action the new behavior signifies. In other words, the trainer may initially have to help the student produce the desired communication—this is referred to as *prompting* the communicative behavior. Eventually, the student will learn which actions lead to which results. As the student begins to use the new communicative behavior, the type of prompting can be reduced to touching the student's elbow to indicate that the student should point to something. For a student who uses signs to communicate, the student would initially be prompted to sign "stop" by the teacher taking his hand and helping him produce the sign. Later, just touching his elbow may be enough to prompt him to sign that he wants to stop.

Note: Refer to "Prompting Tips" below for more detailed instructions on prompting.

---

3. When the student fails to use the appropriate form of communication, do not give the desired reward.

If the student does not use the new communicative behavior, re-engage the student in the difficult situation and prompt the student to use the appropriate behavior. Do not give the desired reward or respond to the student's expression of need until the student behaves appropriately.

Prompting Tips

When and how to prompt
- When introducing a new response, prompt more frequently.
- Prompts should always be given at the same time as or immediately following the instruction.
- Use the least intrusive prompt necessary to help the student use the appropriate response (i.e., if the student can respond with a modeling prompt, do not use a physical prompt).

Types of prompts
Least Intrusive
1. pointing (tapping or pointing to the correct picture)
2. modeling (teacher physically modeling the response)
3. verbal (verbally instructing the student about the correct response)

Most Intrusive
4. partial physical (physically guiding student but less intrusive than hand-over-hand—e.g., guiding student's elbow, but allowing student to pick up picture or signs independently)
5. physical/hand-over-hand (taking student's hand and physically guiding him through the new behavior)

Initially in training sessions, when the trainer asks Oscar to match letters, Oscar tries to hit the trainer. The trainer ignores the attempted aggression and asks Oscar to match a letter. The trainer presents the matching task, and then immediately guides Oscar to sign "stop" with a hand-over-hand prompt, thus reducing the likelihood that Oscar will get frustrated. The trainer works to demonstrate to Oscar that he can control when he needs a break by signing "stop." In the first several attempts, Oscar does not adopt the new sign; however, on the fourth try, with the trainer's physical prompt, Oscar uses the new sign for "stop."

4. Immediately provide a reward to the student for performing the appropriate behavior.

As soon as the student uses the appropriate behavior, with or without prompting, provide the desired reward. For example, if the student is learning to signal that she needs a break, give the student a short

Fading prompts
- Prompt as many times in a row as necessary to keep the student successful.
- When prompting repeatedly, systematically fade the prompts to promote more independent responses (i.e., gradually require the student to do more of the response on his own). For example, if you initially used hand-over-hand prompting, you would move to a partial physical prompt and then to a pointing prompt.
- To promote independent responses and to avoid having the student become prompt-dependent, eventually fade out all prompts. A guideline to follow is that once the student is responding correctly on 90 percent or more of the teaching opportunities, prompts may be faded to less intrusive prompts or all prompts can be discontinued. The trainer should also consider the rate of acquiring new skills for each particular student. For a student who typically acquires a new skill in a couple of days, prompts can usually be faded quickly. For a student who takes several weeks to master a new skill, the trainer should be more conservative when fading prompts and wait until the student is successful on 90 percent or more of all teaching opportunities across two to three teaching sessions.

break before resuming practice. Allow the student to do something she enjoys during these periods, so the student begins to make the connection between using the appropriate behavior and gaining something she desires. Following a one- or two-minute break, have the student return to the teaching situation and continue the training session.

> Mr. Baker and the trainer decide that Oscar should be rewarded with a break from the task whenever he performs the communicative behavior with the assistance of prompting. As he begins to use the sign for "stop" consistently with help from the trainer, prompting will be gradually faded until Oscar is making the sign for "stop" on his own. At the same time, the criteria for which he is rewarded will increase—meaning that Oscar may be told, "You can take a break very soon," and the trainer will have him perform a few more tasks after requesting a break.

As the student begins to have success with the replacement behavior, gradually fade prompting and increase the criteria for which the student is rewarded. As modeling and guiding are faded, the student may periodically slip back into the misbehavior. Reteach the appropriate behavior and continue with encouragement and practice.

> Note: The student should receive reinforcement rather than correction for misbehavior at a ratio of 4 to 1 to avoid frustration. Proactively prompting the student when first teaching a new replacement behavior can ensure that the student gains the desired reward.

E. Determine how to measure intervention effectiveness.
During training sessions, the student should be able to use the Functional Communication behavior in 90 percent of the trials presented across three consecutive days before he will be expected to generalize the new behavior to general classroom settings. Develop an evaluation system to monitor the student's progress in training sessions and in classes.

Figure N1: *Communicative Behavior Tally*

Opportunies Presented	Communicative Responses
~~IIII~~ III	~~IIII~~

$$\frac{\text{Number of Communicative Responses}}{\text{Number of Opportunities Presented}} = 5/8$$

Trainers and teachers can use a simple tally system (Figure N1) or a plus/minus coding system (Sample Reproducible Form N2) to indicate the number of opportunities in which the student could have used communicative behavior and the number of times he actually used the communicative behavior appropriately.

Before his one-on-one training sessions are discontinued, Oscar is expected to independently use his hand signal (rather than misbehavior) to request a break an average nine out of ten times over three days of practice. Furthermore, a 90 percent criterion will be used to determine whether Oscar has generalized the skill to an untrained environment. Oscar's progress will be monitored using the Functional Communication Training form (Reproducible Form N2). Once the trainer has determined that Oscar has learned to use the signal to request a break, he will be expected to use this behavior in any situation in which he would like a break.

Data should also be collected on the misbehavior you believe is serving a communicative function to see if the intervention is effective. Determine a method of counting the targeted misbehavior to track whether the behavior is being effectively reduced with this intervention. Though the student may behave inappropriately during other times of the day, acts of misbehavior that are not the focus of Functional Communication training should not be included in the frequency count. If you count all the times a student displays misbehaviors, you may believe that your intervention is not working, when in fact the student is consistently using the sign and is no longer misbehaving when presented with a nonpreferred task or activity.

Sample Reproducible Form N2: *Functional Communication Training*

Functional Communication Training

Jessamyn _____ _____ Mr. Padilla _____ 1/07 _____
Student   Grade/Class   Teacher   Date

Date	Target Communicative Response	+ / –	Prompt
1/23/07	Giving picture of eating when hungry	+	PP, Pt
↓	↓	+	Pt
		–	none
		+	PP, Pt

Communicative Response	Prompting
+ = Uses desired communicative response – = Fails to use communicative response	M = Model prompt Pt = Pointing prompt VP = Verbal prompt PP = Partial physical prompt HOH = Hand-over-hand physical prompt

A blank version of this form is available in the *Reproducible Materials* section at the end of the chapter.

Because Oscar is learning to refuse a task by using a sign for "stop," Mr. Baker, the school psychologist, expects that his aggression will decrease as he becomes more consistent with using the sign. Data will be collected by simply counting the number of times Oscar engages in aggression when presented with a task or an item he does not want to do (Reproducible Form N3, the Problem Behavior Log).

The sample of Reproducible Form N3 shows a misbehavior count for a student whose Functional Communication training is targeting her out-of-control behavior during transition periods.

Sample Reproducible Form N3: *Problem Behavior Log*

Intervention N:
Functional Communication

Functional Communication Training
Problem Behavior Log

_Jessamyn_____   _____   _Mr. Padilla_____   _2/07____
Student   Grade/Class   Teacher   Date

Date	Type of Problem Behavior	Number of Occurrences	Situation
2/10/07	Screaming and hitting	IIII III	Transition from recess to classroom

Step 3: Meet with the student and implement the plan.

A. Meet with the student and the parents to discuss the intervention.

> Ms. Glick, the teacher, and Mr. Baker, the school psychologist, meet with Oscar and his mother, Ms. Avila, in a classroom after school when the other students have gone home.
>
> | **Ms. Glick:** (Teacher) | Oscar, we know you get upset sometimes when you don't want to do your school work. But it's not OK to hit, even when you're mad. We're going to be teaching you to use sign language to tell us "stop" when you want a break. If you hit, we will keep working and you will not get a break. |
> | --- | --- |
>
> Mr. Baker explains Functional Communication training and guides Oscar and his mother through the technique that Oscar will use at home and at school to sign "stop." Ms. Avila agrees to try conducting short 15-minute training sessions at home and to continue working with Oscar until he uses the replacement behavior rather than misbehavior to convey his needs.

B. Conduct daily training sessions.

> For one week, Oscar's mother and Ms. Glick conduct training sessions after school. Each session lasts about 10 minutes, and Oscar is presented with about 15 opportunities to engage in Functional Communication (the sign for "stop"). By the end of the third day, Oscar is using the sign 90 percent of the time during training trials, and all prompting has been faded. Ms. Glick reports that he has started to sign "stop" in class without prompting.

C. Determine whether the intervention is working and consider fading or discontinuing.

When a student has successfully replaced misbehavior with an appropriate form of communication, it is important to make sure he continues to use the new form of communication over time and in other environments (e.g., at home or at locations in the school other than the classroom). When the student is using the new form of communication 90 percent of the time or more, regular training sessions may not be necessary. Training sessions can be reduced to once a week. If the student continues to use the appropriate form of communication, the frequency of training sessions can be reduced to every other week or monthly, and then discontinued. During this time, it is important to continue to collect data on the misbehavior that has been replaced.

Ms. Glick has been keeping track of the opportunities for Oscar to use sign language to communicate and the number of times he actually uses the sign for "stop." She has determined that he is using the sign in class during 85 percent of the opportunities that are presented. She has also noted that his aggression during presentation of nonpreferred activities has decreased from five times per day to once a day. Ms. Glick has scheduled a meeting to discuss Oscar's progress with the intervention plan and discuss any changes that they may need to implement.

Ms. Glick: (Teacher)	I am very pleased with the progress Oscar is making, and he has been much happier and easier to manage in my classroom
Ms. Avila: (Parent)	I agree Oscar is making good progress. He has started to sign "stop" at home when he doesn't want to get dressed or take a bath.
Ms. Glick:	One concern I still have is that while Oscar is using much less aggression in the classroom, he continues to scream or try to climb up on the counter by the shelves where the snacks are kept when he's hungry. I think it would be very helpful if we could teach Oscar to ask for a snack.
Mr. Baker: (School Psychologist)	I think that's a great idea, but I think we should hold off for another week or so until Oscar is using the sign for "stop" consistently. Right now, he is signing "stop" in about 85 percent of the teaching opportunities presented to him. We should wait until he is signing "stop" 90 percent of the time or more during teaching sessions and using the sign consistently in other situations. I am guessing that Oscar should reach that point after a few more teaching sessions. Then we could begin to teach the next response.

If the student continues to use the appropriate form of communication, the frequency of training sessions can be reduced.

If a student fails to generalize the response across trainers, it may indicate a lack of consistency among trainers (some may be inadvertently reinforcing undesired behavior or failing to reinforce the new communicative behavior), or it may simply be due to the amount of time each trainer has worked with the student. If the lack of generalization across trainers is due to inconsistency in teaching sessions, the trainer who is not observing the new communicative response should engage in a teaching session with another trainer, and they should discuss any inconsistencies they observe. If the student is using the new communicative behavior only with the trainer who spends the greatest amount of time teaching him, generalization can usually be achieved by having other trainers do additional teaching sessions.

In Oscar's case, the trainer will continue to teach Oscar to use the hand signal to request breaks in other settings until Oscar achieves mastery (uses the new behavior 90 percent of the time or more) in all settings. In addition, Oscar should generalize the new communicative response to other trainers and any other individuals involved with his instruction.

If a student begins to revert back to the misbehavior after formal teaching sessions have been discontinued, it will be necessary to begin training sessions again. Once the student is using the appropriate form of communication in 90 percent of teaching opportunities and spontaneously in other situations, the frequency of formal training sessions can be gradually reduced again.

CONCLUSION

Students who learn functional ways to communicate may be served in less restrictive environments.

Functional Communication is an intensive intervention that is very effective in reducing problem behaviors that serve communicative functions. Due to the complexity of the intervention, it is important that one member of the multidisciplinary team has experience in implementing Functional Communication training. If this is not possible, an outside consultant may need to be hired. Students who engage in severe misbehavior, such as hitting, slapping, pinching themselves, and/or aggression toward others, are at risk for being isolated from their peers and from the community. Students who learn functional ways to communicate may be served in less restrictive environments and can be integrated more readily into classroom activities and into the community at large.

Resources

Picture Exchange

Frost, L., & Bondy, A. (2002). The picture exchange communication system. Training manual (2nd ed.). Cherry Hill, NJ: Pyramid Educational Consultants.

Mayer-Johnson, www.mayer-johnson.com. This Web site is an excellent resource for creating picture exchange communication systems. Electronic communication devices may be purchased on this site.

Sign Language

Thompson, S. A. (2005). Teach your tot to sign: The parents' guide to American Sign Language. Washington, DC: Gallaudet University Press.

ASLPro.com, www.aslpro.com. This Web site provides free access to an American Sign Language online dictionary.

Electronic Communication Devices

Beukelman, D. R., & Mirenda, P. (2005). Augmentative and alternative communication: Supporting children & adults with complex communication needs (2nd ed.). Baltimore, MD: Brooks Publishing Co.

Ablenet Corporation, www.ablenetinc.com. Augmentative and alternative communication (AAC) devices are available for purchase through this Web site.

REFERENCES

Bondy, A., & Frost, L. (1994). The picture exchange communication system. *Focus on Autistic Behavior, 9,* 1–19.

Carr, E., & Durand, V. (1985). Reducing behavior problems through functional communication training. *Journal of Applied Behavior Analysis, 18,* 111–126.

Cipani, E. (1991). "Excuse me, I'll have": Teaching appropriate attention getting behavior in young children with severe handicaps. *Mental Retardation, 29,* 29–33.

Drasgow, E., Jalle, J. W., Ostrosky, M. M., & Harbers, H. M. (1996). Using behavioral indication and functional communication training to establish an initial sign repertoire with a young child with severe disabilities. *Topics in Early Childhood Special Education, 16*, 500–521.

Dyer, K., & Larsson, D. (1997). Developing functional communication skills: Alternatives to severe behavior problems. In N. Singh (Ed.), *Prevention and treatment of severe problems: Models and methods in developmental disabilities*, (pp. 121–148). Pacific Grove, CA: Brooks Cole Publishing.

Dyer, K., Williams, L., & Luce, S. (1991). Training teachers to use naturalistic communication strategies in classroom for students with autism and other severe handicaps. *Language, Speech, and Hearing Services in the Schools, 22*, 313–321.

Gerra, L. L., & Dorfman, S. (1995). Functional communication as a means of decreasing self-injurious behavior: A case study. *Journal of Visual Impairment and Blindness, 89*, 343–348.

Keen, D., Sigafoos, J., & Woodyatt, G. (2001). Replacing prelinguistic behaviors with functional communication. *Journal of Autism and Developmental Disorders, 31*, 385–398.

Layton, T., & Watson, L. (1995). Enhancing communication in nonverbal children with autism. In K. Quill (Ed.), *Teaching children with autism: Strategies to enhance communication and socialization* (pp. 73–103). Albany, NY: Delmar Publishers.

Miltenberger, R. G. (2004). Behavior modification. *Principals and procedures* (3rd ed.). Belmont: Wadsworth Publishing Company.

O'Neill, R. E., & Sweetland-Baker, M. (2001). Brief report: An assessment of stimulus generalization and contingency effects in functional communication training with two students with autism. *Journal of Autism and Developmental Disorders, 31*, 235–240.

Richmond, G., Mancil, M., Conroy, A., & Alter, J. (2006). Functional communication training in the natural environment: A pilot investigation with a young child with autism spectrum disorder. *Education and Treatment of Children, 29*, 615–633.

Schwartz, I., Garfinkle, A., & Bauer, J. (1998). The picture exchange communication system: Communicative outcomes for young children with disabilities. *Topics in Early Childhood Education, 18*, 144–159.

Sigfoos, J. (1997). Review of communication programs for people with developmental disabilities. *Behavior Change, 14*(3), 125–138.

Stoner, J. B., Beck, A. R., Jones-Bock, S., Hickley, K., Kosuwan, K., & Thompson, J. R. (2006). The effectiveness of the picture exchange communication system with non-speaking adults. *Remedial and Special Education, 27,* 154–165.

Valletutti, P., Bender, M., & Hoffnung, A. (1996). *A functional curriculum for teaching students with disabilities: Nonverbal and oral communication.* Austin, TX: PRO-ED.

Wickstrom-Kane, S., & Goldstein, H. (1999). Communication assessment and intervention to address challenging behavior in toddlers. *Topics in Language Disorders, 19,* 70–89.

Reproducible Materials

The following reproducible materials may be used in conjunction with "Intervention N: Functional Communication." Copies are provided here and on the CD. Permission is given for individual classroom teachers to reproduce any forms labeled "Reproducible" for classroom use. Reproduction of these materials for an entire school system is prohibited without express permission of the publisher.

INTERVENTION

FUNCTIONAL COMMUNICATION

Step-by-Step Summary

Following is a summary of the steps involved in Intervention N. It is important to use professional judgment, adjusting procedures to meet the needs of the situation and the individual. See the chapter "Intervention N: Functional Communication" for a detailed description of this intervention.

STEP 1   Decide whether an alternative form of communication is an appropriate intervention.

A. Identify the misbehavior and determine whether it is related to communication.

B. Determine what the student is trying to communicate with the misbehavior.

STEP 2   Conduct a multidisciplinary team meeting.

A. Form or convene a multidisciplinary intervention team.

B. Discuss Functional Communication techniques and select an alternative form of communication for the student.

C. Determine who will conduct the Functional Communication training.

D. Determine how Functional Communication will be taught.
   1. Engage the student in a situation where the misbehavior typically occurs.
   2. Help the student produce the desired communication.
   3. When the student fails to use the appropriate form of communication, do not give the desired reward.
   4. Immediately provide a reward to the student for performing the appropriate behavior.

E. Determine how to measure intervention effectiveness.

STEP 3   Meet with the student and implement the plan.

A. Meet with the student and the parents to discuss the intervention.

B. Conduct daily training sessions.

C. Determine whether the intervention is working and consider fading or discontinuing.

Reproducible Form N1: *Problem Behavior Checklist*

Problem Behavior Checklist

Student	Grade/Class	Teacher	Date

The box below includes sample sequences of events indicating that a student may be trying to use problem behavior to communicate. Look at each scenario and check the box if it relates to this specific student.

Antecedent *What was happening just before the misbehavior?*	Behavior	Consequence	Possible Communicative Intent of Misbehavior	Check Boxes that Apply
Student appeared to be in discomfort while sitting at the table.	Fidgeting, inattentive to teacher, trying to leave seat.	Student is required to continue activity.	Student needs to use the bathroom.	❏
Teacher is trying to help student finish class work.	Student refuses to follow instructions and screams.	Student is required to complete the task.	Student would like a break from the activity.	❏
Teacher is working with others. Student is alone at a table.	Student repeatedly makes loud and inappropriate noises.	Student is asked to work quietly, but continues to make disruptive noises.	Student would like attention.	❏
Teacher is giving a whole-group lesson just before lunchtime.	Student begins to cry and tantrum.	Separation within the classroom.	Student is hungry.	❏
Another student takes an item from student.	Student hits and bites the other student.	Student is sent to time-out.	Student would like the item.	❏
Student is working independently.	Student begins to hit herself in the forehead.	Teacher stops student and gives her another task.	Student needs help completing the task.	❏
Another student is drinking a bottle of juice.	Student pulls the other student's hair.	Student is required to leave the lunchroom.	Student needs a drink.	❏

If you checked one or more boxes, it may be indicative that problem behavior is being used for communicative purposes.

Reproducible Form N2: *Functional Communication Training*

Functional Communication Training

Student _____ Grade/Class _____ Teacher _____ Date _____

Date	Target Communicative Response	+ / −	Prompt

Communicative Response	Prompting
+ = Uses desired communicative response − = Fails to use communicative response	M = Model prompt Pt = Pointing prompt VP = Verbal prompt PP = Partial physical prompt HOH = Hand-over-hand physical prompt

Reproducible Form N3: *Functional Communication Training Problem Behavior Log*

Intervention N:
Functional Communication

Functional Communication Training Problem Behavior Log

Student _____ Grade/Class _____ Teacher _____ Date _____

Date	Type of Problem Behavior	Number of Occurrences	Situation

Reproducible Form N4: *Picture Exchange (1 of 6)*

BASIC NEEDS

TAKE A BREAK

BATHROOM

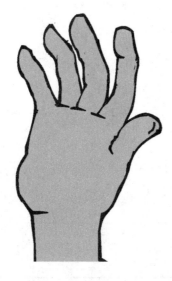

I NEED HELP

I AM COLD

Reproducible Form N4: *Picture Exchange (2 of 6)*

WASH MY HANDS

ACTIVITIES

COMPUTER

SLIDE

PUZZLE

BOOK

Reproducible Form N4: *Picture Exchange (3 of 6)*

SWING

MUSIC

BALL

FOODS

FRENCH FRIES

PRETZEL

Reproducible Form N4: *Picture Exchange (4 of 6)*

APPLE

SANDWICH

LUNCH

GRAPES

ICE CREAM

CRACKERS

Reproducible Form N4: *Picture Exchange (5 of 6)*

TREAT

COOKIE

DRINKS

JUICE

DRINK

MILK

WATER

CLASSROOM ITEMS

PENCIL

BACKPACK

SCISSORS

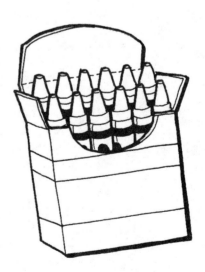

CRAYONS

Structured Reinforcement Systems

The misbehavior is a firmly established part of the student's behavioral repertoire

PURPOSE

STRUCTURED REINFORCEMENT SYSTEMS can be used to motivate students to improve their behavior through the use of external rewards. A structured reinforcement system is a highly intensive intervention that may be necessary when problems have been resistant to simpler solutions.

THIS INTERVENTION IS APPROPRIATE FOR:

Poor motivation

Work completion

Quality of work

Attendance/punctuality

Eliminating a negative behavior
- disruptions
- arguing
- swearing
- fighting
- throwing tantrums

Structured Reinforcement Systems can be used to help students increase engagement in particular skills or behavior such as amount of work completed, time on task, and positive interactions with peers. It can also assist students in reducing or eliminating the frequency of negative behavior such as using profanity, fighting, and interacting disrespectfully with adults.

With Structured Reinforcement Systems, students break deeply ingrained cycles of inappropriate behavior by working for external reinforcements or rewards. This is a temporary intervention designed to move students in more productive directions.

With Structured Reinforcement Systems, students break deeply ingrained cycles of inappropriate behavior by working for external reinforcements or rewards.

RATIONALE

Many students find natural success and encouragement in the classroom. They take pride in their accomplishments and feel a sense of satisfaction at completing a task. These students share these positive interactions and comments from the teacher at home: "Hey, Mom! Mrs. Dubach said she'd like to borrow my book. She hasn't read it yet." Feedback is taken seriously: "Mrs. Dubach said that we need to be more careful when we multiply with decimals." Corrections are made, and students are successful. These students are fueled by a sense of well-being. The motivation to cooperate and do one's best is deeply ingrained.

Other students who fail to meet expectations may be dealing with several variables that make success unattainable. Structured reinforcement may help make success a reality. Here are some examples:

Some students may not know how to be successful. If students do not have appropriate behaviors in their repertoire, they may require instruction and practice in behaviors needed for success. Consider implementing "Intervention M: Teaching Replacement Behavior." This intervention may be used alone or in combination with Structured Reinforcement Systems.

Some students may need additional motivation because learning and using new behavior requires a lot of effort. Because change is difficult, the motivation to change must outweigh the difficulty. Sometimes students

INTERVENTION

need an external motivator to overcome the challenges of ending habitual behavior problems. In the early states of learning something new or difficult, some students (particularly those who have experienced past failure) are not likely to be motivated simply by the value of learning, knowledge, or improving oneself. These students often need the boost of external reinforcement to get them started.

Some students may not value school success. Motivation to change may initially require an external reward to link school success with something worthwhile and important to the student. Some students do not initially value praise and positive attention or value learning for itself. They need an external reward to boost their interest until these values become important.

Some students may find their needs are more fulfilled when they engage in inappropriate behavior than when they behave appropriately. In this case, the motivation to change must include reinforcers that are different from those found in success and encouragement. If misbehavior has been sustained because of negative attention, the student may not value positive attention. The motivation to change may initially require an external, tangible reward. Consider combining this intervention with "Intervention E: Increasing Positive Interactions."

Scott, an eighth-grade student, exhibits many problems. Teachers find him impossible to motivate. He has a long history of tardiness and often fails to have the materials he needs for class. Though he does average or better on assignments and tests, Scott's punctuality problems and chronic disorganization take a toll on his grades. In PE, he loses points because he forgets his gym clothes and cannot suit up. He often arrives in class without his notebook, text, or other required materials. Scott has been tardy so many times that he has earned numerous consequences—including after-school detention and a full day of in-school suspension—none of which seems to have had any impact on his behavior. Scott might benefit from a structured reinforcement system that motivates him to arrive at each class on time with his required materials.

COMMON CONCERNS ABOUT USING REINFORCERS

Despite its benefits for some students, a structured reinforcement system raises several legitimate concerns that need to be addressed.

Shouldn't students behave appropriately without rewards and reinforcers?
Students should behave appropriately, and they should be motivated to be successful. However, some students need to be taught to value appropriate behavior. When less structured interventions, such as "Intervention A: Planned Discussion" and "Intervention C: Goal Setting" have not been effective, or are not likely to be effective, staff are left with two options: (a) let the student continue engaging in inappropriate behavior, or (b) provide a highly structured reinforcement system to motivate the student to change the pattern of behavior as quickly as possible. The longer misbehavior goes unchanged, the more deeply ingrained it becomes and the more likely it is to worsen.

It may be helpful to think of rewards and reinforcers as *extrinsic motivators*. Extrinsic motivation occurs when someone engages in a behavior because of the pleasant consequences that are not directly related to the essential nature of the behavior—they engage in behavior to gain a particular prize, grade, praise, and so on. These motivators differ from *intrinsic motivators*, which are the pleasant consequences of a behavior that motivate someone and are related to the essential nature of the behavior—engaging in a behavior to learn new things, relax, have fun, and so on. Some people believe that the only valid kind of motivation is intrinsic—students should want to learn simply for the value of knowledge—and teachers should not give students praise or rewards. Other people believe that motivators such as praise and good grades are acceptable, but other extrinsic reinforcement, in the form of tangible rewards, should not be used. The simple truth is that the line between intrinsic and extrinsic motivation is not as distinct as it may seem, and tangible versus intangible reinforcers are not terribly different—they all function to engage students in school. Teachers often need to use a combination of techniques to motivate their students to learn and grow. For the student who has experienced little academic success or who has had behavioral problems, you may initially need to use tangible reinforcers to spark the student's motivation. In most cases, you will need to try and enhance both intrinsic (for example, making a science lesson more engaging) and extrinsic (for example, write an encouraging note on returned homework) motivation.

The simple truth is that the line between intrinsic and extrinsic motivation is not as distinct as it may seem.

Won't students stop working as soon as the reinforcers are removed?
If Structured Reinforcement Systems are overused, students may learn to work only for tangible rewards and fail to learn the value of working hard, getting along with others, being cooperative, taking pride in a job well done, and other intrinsic rewards in school and life. However, a structured reinforcement system that assists in the initial process of making a behavioral change can be faded with carefully planned steps. If a system is removed suddenly, the student may stop working. A carefully designed system is a long, involved process that gradually teaches the student to value success.

Why should students who misbehave get extra rewards or privileges?
Students probably shouldn't get extra rewards and privileges as a result of misbehavior. In an ideal world everything would be equal and fair. However, students do not enter school as equals. Therefore, "equal" treatment cannot mean the "same" treatment when working with students of different backgrounds and abilities. Some students bring values and background knowledge that support cooperation, responsibility, and hard work. These students have already learned to value the attitudes and behaviors that bring success; reinforcement for these students is inherent within the natural school environment and in their homes without external rewards. Students with behavior problems have more to learn. They may be discouraged by or suspicious of efforts to help them change. These students may need additional incentives to learn how to behave responsibly.

Shouldn't we avoid "reinforcing" students and focus more on "encouraging" students and "facilitating" learning?
In education, we often get wrapped up in words. The distinction between *reinforcement* and *encouragement* is largely semantic. If a student is working hard and the teacher stops to engage in a friendly interaction, one person might say, "The teacher is facilitating learning by encouraging the student's interest." Another person might say, "The teacher's attention is reinforcing or rewarding the on-task behavior." In both cases, the teacher does the same thing; only the words describing the situation are different. Regardless of semantics, reinforcement procedures can be either implemented carefully to support and encourage students or implemented poorly so students do not learn to value effort and accomplishment.

> *The distinction between* reinforcement *and* encouragement *is largely semantic.*

Won't other students object?
Students expect the school system to treat them fairly and equitably. Therefore, special reinforcers for some students can cause problems with other students. It might appear that students who misbehave are rewarded, and those who behave are punished because they are denied access to the reinforcement. This can be dealt with in several different ways, depending on the situation:

- Design the reinforcement system in such a way that it is not obvious to other students.

- Discuss the reinforcement system with other students prior to implementing the system and solicit their assistance in the spirit of cooperation and support.

- Let the entire class earn a special award or privilege occasionally as a way of celebrating the target individual's success.

Isn't this bribery?

A *bribe* is defined as "offering a reward, especially money, to induce a person to do something illegal or wrong." A *reinforcement*, on the other hand, encourages a person to do something that creates success. Reinforcement thus is more akin to rewarding four years of diligent study with a college diploma.

Will students become the kind of people who always ask, "What will you give me if I do that?"

If reinforcement systems are not handled carefully, this potential drawback may become a reality. All adults involved in this intervention must carefully focus on the accomplishments that lead to the reward versus the reward itself. If adults systematically focus interactions on student accomplishments, eventually students develop a sense of satisfaction that takes the place of the actual reward.

Ms. Mayberry: (Teacher)	Scott, here is the mechanical pencil you earned. Tell me what you did to earn it.
Scott:	I read at home for 10 days.
Ms. Mayberry:	You must be exceptionally proud of yourself. You are getting to be a stronger reader because of this kind of practice. When you go home today, be sure to tell your folks how you earned that pencil.

If possible, students should be encouraged to make improvements through positive interactions and strategies that honor hard work, cooperation, kindness, and responsibility. However, there are times when less structured interventions will not be understood by some students or are not sufficient to motivate them. A high-powered reinforcement system may be necessary to get students moving in the right direction.

Caution: Structured Reinforcement Systems can help students make difficult behavioral changes. However, if the reinforcement system is not carefully structured and gradually removed, the above concerns with this approach may become realities. Be prepared for a long, involved process if you want the system to have a long-term impact on the student's ability to take responsibility.

Before implementing Structured Reinforcement Systems

Before this intervention can be successfully implemented, be sure you have discussed the problem and general goals for improvement with the student. Gather any relevant background information that may help in designing and implementing the intervention. In addition, contact the student's parents or guardian to discuss the problem and keep the parents informed of all aspects of the intervention plan.

IMPLEMENTATION STEPS
Step 1: Develop a plan.

Review the problem and overall goals for the student. Defining the nature and scope of the problem provides critical information in developing a successful intervention. Be sure you have a clear idea of the specific goals the intervention will be designed to achieve—that is, what will be different about the student's behavior after the intervention?

Take time to review previously implemented interventions and develop some hypotheses based on the collected data about why those interventions were unsuccessful. In the case of a student who is academically successful in school, you might not implement "Intervention B: Academic Assistance" because the student is completing all work with above-average performance. However, if the student's problems of chronic disruption and disrespect have not been resolved by "Intervention C: Goal Setting," "Intervention D: Data Collection and Debriefing," or "Intervention E: Increasing Positive Interactions," you may determine that a structured reinforcement system in combination with any of these interventions might motivate the student to improve behavior.

Tracy is a second-grade student who always moves extremely slowly. When the teacher, Mr. Dreyer, says "Put your things away and line up," all of the students follow instructions and are in line before Tracy has even started putting her things away. Because Mr. Dreyer cannot leave Tracy or the class unsupervised, everyone must wait for her. Even with constant reminders and peer pressure, Tracy continually keeps everyone waiting. This happens several times a day, day after day. While at recess, Tracy walks slowly about the playground or just stands in one place. Watching Tracy is like watching a very old woman, not a seven-year-old child.

The school counselor, Ms. Thompson, contacts Tracy's family and finds that her father is rarely in the home. Tracy's mother is under a doctor's care and is heavily medicated for psychiatric problems. When meeting with Tracy's mother, the counselor sees an older version of Tracy. She operates as if she is moving under water—everything slow and laborious, including speech. Although the communication is difficult, Tracy's mother does say that she hoped the school could help Tracy learn to "do things more like other little girls." She also goes on to say, "I am just too tired to help her."

Working with Tracy's mother, the counselor is able to have Tracy examined by a physician. The physician concludes that Tracy is in perfect health and that her slow behavior is not a medical problem.

Tracy's overall goal will be to move faster, especially when others are waiting for her. Because the change will be very difficult for Tracy and she will not be receiving modeling at home, Tracy's teacher and counselor decide that she will need lessons on how to move faster as well as a fairly intensive reinforcement system to get Tracy moving.

A. Identify specific behavioral objectives.

Once the overall goals have been determined, identify exactly what the student must do and/or not do to demonstrate improvement. Is the objective to increase a positive behavior or decrease a negative behavior? Is the purpose to do more of something or less of something? If work completion is a problem, the goal will be to increase work completion. In the case of swearing or throwing tantrums, the goal will be to reduce the negative behavior. In some instances, the objective will be to decrease a negative behavior and increase a positive one. For example, if a student has poor peer interactions, the goal will be to decrease negative interactions while increasing positive interactions.

In addition to determining what the student must do, you should identify when and where the student will be expected to make changes. If major changes are required, the student will need to make improvements in small increments. Change should not be expected all at once in all settings. For example, if a student has a difficult time with on-task behavior, the first five minutes of an activity may be best to target for initial focus. As the student achieves success, objectives can be gradually expanded for longer periods of time and across settings so that the new skills generalize.

The counselor and Tracy's teacher, Mr. Dreyer, decide that they should initially focus the intervention plan on helping Tracy learn to make "energetic transitions" during five critical times—going to recess in the morning and afternoon, going to lunch, going to PE each day, and going to the bus. Because of supervision issues, each of these transitions results in the class having to wait when Tracy does not move at a reasonable pace. Although other transitions occur during the day, they do not present supervision problems. These transitions will be dealt with after Tracy has learned to manage the five critical transitions. In the meantime, Mr. Dreyer will no longer wait for Tracy during transitions that do not present supervision problems.

B. If the behavior is not currently in the student's repertoire, design lessons to teach the student the appropriate behavior.

Although Structured Reinforcement Systems may be useful for just about any problem, if the student doesn't know how to exhibit the desired behavior, the intervention plan must include a plan to teach the student the appropriate behavior. See "Intervention M: Teaching Replacement Behaviors" for more on this subject.

If the student doesn't know how to exhibit the desired behavior, the intervention plan must include a plan to teach the student the appropriate behavior.

To help Tracy learn how to complete an "energetic transition," the counselor will meet with her three times a week to model, role-play, and practice putting materials away and lining up for recess, lunch, PE, and the bus.

C. Design a reinforcement system.

Once specific behaviors have been identified, set up a system to provide the student with reinforcers for successfully meeting the identified objectives. To develop an effective reinforcement system, design a method for monitoring student behaviors and counting points, identify a menu of possible rewards or privileges, and determine how many points will be required for the student to earn each reward or privilege.

1. Choose a method for monitoring student behaviors and counting points.

   Behavior can be monitored in a number of different ways:

   - counting a positive behavior
   - counting both a positive and negative behavior
   - counting the absence or reduction of a negative behavior within specific time intervals
   - rating a positive behavior on a predetermined scale
   - recording the length of time a student engages in a particular behavior
   - counting a permanent product

   "Intervention D: Data Collection and Debriefing" explains how to monitor behavior using each of these methods. A key to making a reinforcement system effective is to ensure that you have an easy and reliable way to monitor and record student behavior. This data will be used to develop a point system for earning rewards.

   The following descriptions are provided to assist in developing a monitoring/counting system that is easy to manage, age-appropriate, and best suited to the needs of the student. These descriptions also show how different types of monitoring and counting can be turned into a points system.

   Counting a positive behavior
   Counting the number of times a student engages in a positive behavior may be an effective monitoring system if the goal of the intervention is to increase the frequency of a specific discrete behavior. For example, if a shy student fails to interact with peers, you might design a system to count the number of times she interacts with peers. If a student blurts out inappropriate answers, a system might be designed to count the number of times the student raises his hand, waits to be called on, and makes reasonable contributions to a discussion.

   The monitoring system might be as simple as Reproducible Form 01. Each time the student demonstrates the desired behavior, the student circles a number.

Intervention O:
Structured Reinforcement Systems

Behavior Counting Grid

Student _____

Behavior _____   Date _____

1	2	3	4	5	6	7	8	9	10
11	12	13	14	15	16	17	18	19	20

Behavior _____   Date _____

1	2	3	4	5	6	7	8	9	10
11	12	13	14	15	16	17	18	19	20

Behavior _____   Date _____

1	2	3	4	5	6	7	8	9	10
11	12	13	14	15	16	17	18	19	20

Behavior _____   Date _____

1	2	3	4	5	6	7	8	9	10
11	12	13	14	15	16	17	18	19	20

> Note: A copy of this and other Structured Reinforcement Systems forms are also provided on the CD. Only selected reproducible forms are shown throughout this chapter—others appear only in the *Reproducible Materials* section at the end of the chapter. You should also skim through that section to determine which monitoring format is best suited to the student's needs.

Figure O1: *Positive Comments Tally*

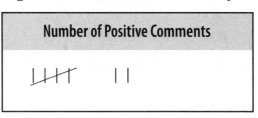

A tally system (Figure O1) or a simple graph may also be used to count positive behaviors. In any of these systems, students would earn a point for each positive behavior demonstrated. Use Reproducible Form O2 (at right) or O3 (found in the *Reproducible Materials* section at the end of the chapter) to track behavior counts over time.

Counting both a positive and a negative behavior
Counting both a positive and a negative behavior may be necessary when students need to increase a positive behavior while decreasing a related negative one. When only positive behavior is monitored, a false picture may be presented, as it will not reflect negative behaviors that are still problematic. For example, a student who has difficulty interacting in a friendly manner with adults might also have a corresponding problem of aggressive, adversarial interactions with adults. If the intervention monitors only friendly interactions, the student may appear to be more successful than he is: "Nathan engaged in five positive interactions" presents a very different picture than "Nathan engaged in five positive interactions and fifteen adversarial interactions." If the goal of the intervention is to encourage a positive behavior and reduce a negative behavior, it is preferable to use a system that monitors both the negative and positive behaviors. The monitoring system shown in Reproducible Form O4 could be used in such a case.

Reproducible Form O2: *Behavior Graph (Version 1)*

Behavior Graph (Version 1)

Student _____   Grade/Class _____   Teacher _____   Beginning Date _____

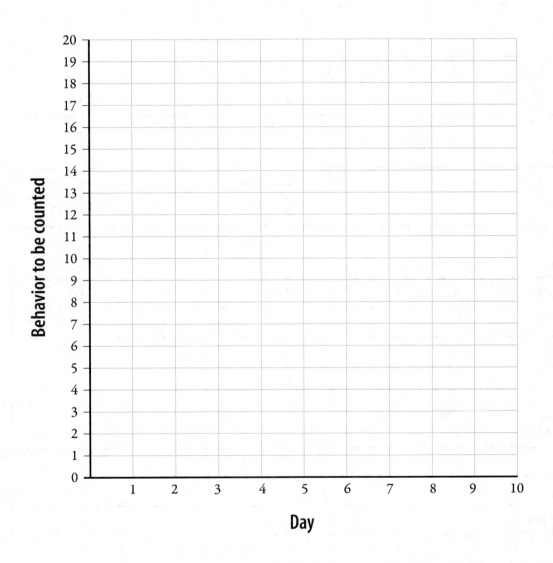

Reproducible Form O4: *Positive/Negative Behavior Scaling Form*

Positive/Negative Behavior Scaling Form

Student _____ GradeClass _____ Teacher _____ Date _____

Goal _____

Time:

Positive	0	1	2	3	4	5	6	7	8	9	10
Negative	0	1	2	3	4	5	6	7	8	9	10

Time:

Positive	0	1	2	3	4	5	6	7	8	9	10
Negative	0	1	2	3	4	5	6	7	8	9	10

Time:

Positive	0	1	2	3	4	5	6	7	8	9	10
Negative	0	1	2	3	4	5	6	7	8	9	10

Time:

Positive	0	1	2	3	4	5	6	7	8	9	10
Negative	0	1	2	3	4	5	6	7	8	9	10

Time:

Positive	0	1	2	3	4	5	6	7	8	9	10
Negative	0	1	2	3	4	5	6	7	8	9	10

In a positive and negative monitoring system, students earn points based on the ratio of positive to negative behaviors. For example, if a student has problems making negative comments to peers, the student might earn a point for every hour that her positive comments exceed negative comments. As the student becomes more successful, the ratio can be adjusted. "Mary, you are doing such a good job being respectful to other students. I would like to challenge you this week to see if you can make at least two positive comments for every negative comment."

This system is particularly useful when the goal of the intervention is to reduce but not eliminate a behavior. If the student is learning to talk more positively, the goal is not to eliminate all negative thoughts or opinions. The goal is simply to reduce the ratio of negative to positive behaviors.

Counting the absence or reduction of a negative behavior or increase of a positive behavior within specific time intervals

Many interventions are designed to help a student eliminate annoying, disruptive, or immature behaviors. Although the goal of the intervention should always be stated positively, success may actually be determined by the absence or reduction of an inappropriate behavior within a specified time interval. For example, if the student throws tantrums, the goal may be to demonstrate self-control. In this case, the monitoring system would track the number of tantrums within a specified time interval and award points for reductions in the number of outbursts.

Select time intervals that permit the student to see a high rate of success. If the student experiences difficulty in the early stages of the intervention, the reinforcement system can actually work as a disincentive. For example, if student's behavior is monitored in half-day intervals and the student has difficulty in the first half hour of school, she will have no incentive to work on successful behavior for the rest of the morning. Reduce the time between intervals so the student has an opportunity to demonstrate success.

A rule of thumb is to establish intervals that guarantee success at least 50 percent of the time without making changes in current behavior. The student who experiences success in the early stages of the intervention will be motivated to make improvements. As the student shows progress, the time intervals can be gradually adjusted.

The sample of Reproducible Form O5 shows a system that is being used to monitor a student's goal behavior in 14 half-hour intervals. This monitoring schedule is designed for a student who tends to engage in inappropriate

Although the goal of the intervention should always be stated positively, success may actually be determined by the absence or reduction of an inappropriate behavior within a specified time interval.

Sample Reproducible Form O5: *Positive/Negative Behavior Rating Form (Version 1)*

Positive/Negative Behavior Rating Form (Version 1)

Zach Turnball _____   6 _____   Ms. Howard _____   3/15 _____
Student   Grade/Class   Teacher   Week of

Treating others with dignity and respect _____
Goal

Time	Rating (+/−)				
	Monday	**Tuesday**	**Wednesday**	**Thursday**	**Friday**
8:00 – 8:30	n/a				
8:30 – 9:00	+				
9:00 – 9:30	+				
9:30 – 10:00	-				
10:00 – 10:30	+				
10:30 – 11:00	+				
11:00 – 11:30	-				
11:30 – Noon	-				
Noon – 12:30	+				
12:30 – 1:00	+				
1:00 – 1:30	+				
1:30 – 2:00	-				
2:00 – 2:30	+				
2:30 – 3:00	n/a				
Points Earned	8				

A blank version of this form is available in the *Reproducible Materials* section at the end of the chapter.

Positive/Negative Behavior Rating Form (Version 2)

Shelly Burnquist	6	Ms. Howard	3/15
Student	Grade/Class	Teacher	Week of

Self-Control
Goal

	Rating (+/–)				
Time	**Monday**	**Tuesday**	**Wednesday**	**Thursday**	**Friday**
8:00 – 10:30	+				
10:30 – 12:00	-				
12:00 – 1:30	+				
1:30 – 2:45	+				
Points Earned	3				

A blank version of this form is available in the *Reproducible Materials* section at the end of the chapter.

behavior four to six times per day. The short monitoring intervals allow the student to experience success despite the high rate of inappropriate behavior. In this system the student earns a point for every half-hour interval in which he has treated others with dignity and respect.

Sample Reproducible Form O6 shows the same monitoring system, but one in which self-control is monitored for a student who tantrums once and sometimes twice per day. Self-control is monitored in larger intervals, four times daily, to ensure that the student experiences success. The student earns a point for each interval in which the goal behavior, the absence of tantrums, is demonstrated. Reproducible Form O6 is provided at the back of this chapter with blanks for time intervals to allow for customization.

Another simple system involves recording every incidence of the misbehavior in a specified interval of time. For example, if a student speaks disrespectfully, each disrespectful comment might be counted during a specified time interval. Sample Reproducible Form O7 is an example of a

Sample Reproducible Form O7: *Positive/Negative Behavior Tracking Form*

Positive/Negative Behavior Tracking Form

Alexander Brophy
Student

6
Grade/Class

Ms. Howard
Teacher

3/15
Week of

Talking respectfully to others (less than four disrespectful comments in any half hour demonstrates
Goal
                  improvement for this week)

	Number of Misbehaviors									
Time										
8:00 – 8:30	①	②	③	④	⑤	6	7	8	9	10
8:30 – 9:00	①	②	③	④	5	6	7	8	9	10
9:00 – 9:30	①	②	③	④	⑤	⑥	⑦	8	9	10
9:30 – 10:00	①	②	3	4	5	6	7	8	9	10
10:00 – 10:30	①	②	3	4	5	6	7	8	9	10
10:30 – 11:00	①	②	③	④	5	6	7	8	9	10
11:00 – 11:30	①	2	3	4	5	6	7	8	9	10
11:30 – Noon	①	②	③	④	⑤	⑥	⑦	⑧	⑨	10
Noon – 12:30	①	②	3	4	5	6	7	8	9	10
12:30 – 1:00	①	②	③	④	⑤	6	7	8	9	10
1:00 – 1:30	①	②	③	④	⑤	⑥	⑦	8	9	10
1:30 – 2:00	①	②	③	④	5	6	7	8	9	10
2:00 – 2:30	①	②	③	④	⑤	6	7	8	9	10
2:30 – 3:00	①	②	③	4	5	6	7	8	9	10

A blank version of this form is available in the *Reproducible Materials* section at the end of the chapter.

tracking form in which a student is monitoring the number of disrespectful comments made in half-hour intervals. The student's goal is to make no more than a prespecified number of disrespectful comments during each interval. Points will be awarded each time the student keeps negative comments below the predetermined number. As the student improves, the number will be gradually adjusted.

Though this system is relatively easy to manage, the drawback is that it focuses on misbehavior. Because the system focuses on the negative behavior, the student should receive frequent feedback regarding the significance of success. "Alexander, you had only a few disrespectful interactions today, and I appreciate that you are learning to express your opinions much more respectfully."

Rating a positive behavior on a predetermined scale

Many desired behaviors are difficult to count because there is a qualitative aspect to the behavior. Initially, students may approximate the goal behavior, demonstrating only certain elements of the positive behavior. Then gradual improvements are made over time until students exhibit the full behavior. Rating scales are useful when behavior needs to improve in quality or across a number of dimensions. With a rating scale, students receive a variable number of points based on the degree to which they exhibit a particular behavior. For example, a student might receive points according to a predetermined scale based on how well she is able to follow directions: 0 = Not at all, 1 = Needed reminders, or 2 = Followed directions independently (see Sample Reproducible Form O8).

Tracy's counselor, Ms. Thomson, and teacher, Mr. Dreyer, determine that a rating scale would be an effective method of monitoring her "energetic transitions." At each of the five critical transition times, Mr. Dreyer will evaluate the quality of Tracy's behavior on the scale shown in Sample Reproducible Form O9. If Tracy moves too slowly during a transition, she will not earn a point. If she goes too fast and acts frantic or pushes someone (an unlikely event), she will not earn a point. If she handles the transition at an adequate rate, she will earn one point. If she moves enthusiastically and energetically, she will earn two points. Because this system involves a subjective rating of Tracy's transition, Mr. Dreyer and the counselor plan to teach Tracy how the quality of various transitions looks and feels through modeling and role-playing.

Sample Reproducible Form O8: *Behavior Monitoring Form*

Intervention O:
Structured Reinforcement Systems

Behavior Monitoring Form

Giselle Purdy _Following directions_ _5/12_
Student   Goal   Date

Points: *0 = Not at all*   *1 = Needed reminders*   *2 = Followed directions independently*

DAY	AM	PM	TOTAL
Monday	0 1 ②	⓪ 1 2	2
Tuesday	0 1 ②	0 ① 2	3

A blank version of this form is available in the *Reproducible Materials* section at the end of the chapter.

Recording the length of time a student engages in a particular behavior
Some behaviors are best monitored by keeping track of the amount of time a student engages in those behaviors. Generally, this is the case when the student's goal includes reducing not only the frequency of a behavior, but also the duration. For example, if a student engages in lengthy and frequent crying bouts, the goal might be to become more self-sufficient, to learn self-control, or to act more grown up. Monitoring only the number of times the student cries may not be sufficient to determine whether the student is meeting the goal. Six short sniffly incidents would appear far worse than a two-hour long sobbing bout if only frequency were recorded.

To monitor duration, start a stopwatch any time the student engages in the inappropriate behavior, stop the watch when the behavior ceases, and restart it if the inappropriate behavior begins again. If the watch is not

Sample Reproducible Form O9: *Behavior Qualifying Form*

Behavior Qualifying Form

Tracy Larson
Student

2
Grade/Class

Mr. Dreyer
Teacher

3/15
Date

Tracy's Transitions
Behavior

| Activity | Qualifiers | | | | TOTAL |
	Too slow	Too fast	Just fine (+1)	Energetic (+2)	
1. Going to AM recess	0				0
2. Going to lunch			1		1
3. Going to PE	0				0
4. Going to PM recess	0				0
5. Going to the bus				2	2
				Total Points for the Day	3

A blank version of this form is available in the *Reproducible Materials* section at the end of the chapter.

reset, the total amount of time engaged in the inappropriate behavior will be recorded cumulatively throughout the day. The student would earn points when the total time of inappropriate behavior is below a predetermined amount. Because this type of monitoring system is labor intensive, it is recommended that other methods be explored first when possible.

Counting completed work

To monitor the desired behavior, count the number of assignments or problems completed in a specified period of time. This procedure is used primarily in interventions that involve work completion.

With this monitoring system, points are generally based on the amount of work completed. The system should be set up so the student experiences success. If the student rarely completes an assignment, do not implement a system that requires getting all assignments in during the week, or even in a day. Instead, award points for each assignment completed, each half assignment completed, or for a certain number of problems completed, depending on the severity of the problem. If the system is established so the student experiences success, the student will begin to learn that success feels good. The criterion for success should gradually be increased as the student gains competency.

Because some students may focus solely on work completion and neglect quality, the system should specify that points will be earned not only for quantity of work completed, but also for quality. Your expectations need to be clear in terms of correctness and neatness. The criterion for each of these should be based on what the student can reasonably do. A copy of previous acceptable work completed by the student can be used as a model in regard to "neatness." The criterion for correctness might be 80 percent, 90 percent, or even 100 percent with opportunities to correct errors. Points are awarded for work when all errors have been corrected and the neatness criterion has been met. The fact that work will not earn any points until it has met quality expectations reduces the chance that the student will rush simply to complete the work.

Identify a menu of possible rewards and privileges tailored to the interests of the student.

2. Identify a menu of possible rewards or privileges.

Once the monitoring system has been designed, identify a menu of possible rewards and privileges tailored to the interests of the student. Two primary methods are helpful for identifying reinforcement ideas, and in most cases it is wise to use both. The first is to observe what the student likes to do. If the student gravitates to certain peers, she might want to earn time to play a game with a classmate. If the student likes certain toys, she might earn time to play with them. If the student craves adult time, she might earn time to help the teacher in the classroom. If the student is the youngest in a family, she might enjoy reading to a younger student. Anything that the student appears to enjoy is potentially a reinforcer. Include options that can be earned quickly, as well as those that might take longer to earn.

The second method of identifying possible rewards is to have the student and parent brainstorm ideas about what the student might like to earn when she is successful. This is by far the most straightforward and respectful method. Plan to set the discussion up by reviewing the cardinal rule of brainstorming: All ideas (excluding any illegal or obscene) will be listed, initially without consideration as to whether they are realistic or feasible. Write everything down. The only downside to this is that the student and parent may not have ideas about what's possible within the school setting, so it is always a good idea to enter this kind of discussion with some ideas to get the discussion flowing.

Mr. Dreyer: (Teacher)	Finding reinforcers for Tracy may be hard. She doesn't seem to be interested in anything.
Ms. Thompson: (Counselor)	Is there something you notice her watching? Is there anything she seems to like doing?
Mr. Dreyer:	She doesn't do much ever. She just sits when we have free time. I have noticed her watching when the other kids come up to my desk to get fancy pencils that they've earned by reading at home. Tracy might be interested in a fancy pencil.
Ms. Thompson:	It's worth a try. How about other things? I know Tracy doesn't have access to many of the things that other kids have.
Mr. Dreyer:	Well, the girls seem to be into those plastic bangles and keychains, and I've seen a lot of them bring some tiny little plastic ponies to school.
Ms. Thompson:	Good. How about activities she might enjoy?
Mr. Dreyer:	Oh, boy. I don't know. She is so passive, it is hard to know what she might enjoy. I doubt she has ever played a game with an adult. How about playing a game with me or another student? She might also like to spend some time on the class computer.

Within minutes Mr. Dreyer and the Ms. Thompson have a beginning list— fancy pencils, keychains, little ponies, plastic bangles, playing a game, using the computer, first in line for lunch, lunch with the teacher, and lunch with the counselor.

The list of possible reinforcers is endless, and many do not require purchasing tangible rewards. Privileges and responsibilities are often as powerful as things. Ideas for reinforcers include the following:

- giving a certificate signed by the principal

- providing a homework pass (a chance not to do one assignment)

- calling the student's grandmother with a good report

- initiating an activity at home, such as playing a game with mom
- playing a game with another student
- spending extra time on the computer
- granting five minutes to play outside
- ordering a pizza
- getting to be a messenger
- posting the student's completed assignments
- making cookies after school in the home economics room
- compiling a "Completed Work Folder"
- tutoring a younger student
- operating equipment
- taking care of a class pet
- helping with a class demonstration
- making photocopies for the teacher
- giving book covers, bookmarks, pens, pencils
- getting to take and print a digital picture

3. Determine how many points will be required for the student to earn each reward or privilege.

When determining how many points are needed to earn a reinforcer, consider the monitoring system, the amount of time and effort required of the student, the sophistication of the student, and the value of the reinforcer in terms of cost and/or adult time required. Reinforcers should be possible for the student to earn, but they should also require the student's cooperation and effort. As the details of the intervention are worked out, the following guidelines may help prevent problems often found in reinforcement systems:

Reinforcers should be quickly earned in the initial phases of the intervention. The student should view the behavior goals and the criteria for earning reinforcers as achievable. When presented with the system, the student should be thinking, "I could do that." A common error is to design a reinforcement system that requires the student to make large and fairly immediate changes in behavior. If the system is too difficult, the student may not try or may not be able to sustain the effort.

Reinforcement menus are useful so that the student has a variety of reinforcers from which to choose. However, if the student is likely to select reinforcers that will take too long to earn, structure an initial menu of only easy-to-earn reinforcers. As the student gains sophistication, more difficult reinforcers can be added to the menu.

If the student shows no interest in small reinforcers but needs fairly immediate gratification, structure a reinforcement ladder. This type of reinforcement system allows the student to earn smaller reinforcements on the way to her ultimate goal. As each reward is earned, the student does not "spend" points, but proceeds up the ladder accumulating points. Figure O2 shows a reinforcement ladder.

Avoid putting time limits on what the student must do to earn reinforcers. Allowing students to accumulate points over time is far more powerful. Systems that involve a certain number of points by the end of the

Figure O2: *Reinforcement Ladder*

Reward	Points
Pizza with the principal	100 points
Read to the kindergarten students	90 points
15 minutes game time with friend	80 points
15 minutes computer time	70 points
Choose a class job	60 points
Certificate from the principal	50 points
Pick a prize	40 points
Run off papers	30 points
Certificate from teacher	20 points
Game with teacher	10 points

Systems that involve a certain number of points by the end of the day or by the end of the week have some inherent weaknesses.

INTERVENTION

day or by the end of the week have some inherent weaknesses. First, they tend to be too inflexible. If a student must get five homework assignments completed in a week to earn a reinforcer and she completes only four assignments, she may feel discouraged by having to begin over again the next week. Credit should always be given for success the student has achieved, irrespective of the student's pace. Time limits also create problems if the student begins the day or week unsuccessfully. The student may realize early in the week that success is not possible no matter how well she does the rest of the week. Reinforcement systems must have "forgiveness" built in. A bad day or a bad hour should not overshadow positive efforts, negate previous efforts, or eliminate reinforcement for future efforts. Therefore, instead of setting up a system as "Get five points by Friday," set it up as "As soon as you earn five points, you can spend them on a reward."

Tracy's teacher and counselor look over their list of possible reinforcers and decide to ask Tracy to help brainstorm other possibilities. To help establish point values for different reinforcers, Mr. Dreyer and the counselor look at Tracy's monitoring system (refer back to Sample Reproducible Form O9) and discuss reasonable expectations for Tracy.

Mr. Dreyer: (Teacher)   Let's see. Tracy can earn five to ten points each day for transitions that range from "fine" to "energetic."

Ms. Thompson: (Counselor)   This change is going to be rough. She has been moving slowly all day, every day, for who knows how long.

Mr. Dreyer: Do you think Tracy could earn something with only four or five points?

Ms. Thompson: I'd like to see quick success.

Mr. Dreyer: If we use little prizes, will it be hard to fade later?

Ms. Thompson: I think we'll need to be careful. If we structure this so that Tracy can have a lot of success early on, later we can start getting her to focus on other transition times. We can also move her off the tangible rewards and get her to work on responsibilities. Right now, you couldn't give her any responsibilities—like passing out papers—because it would take too long.

Mr. Dreyer: Good. Then I think a fancy pencil, a keychain, or one of those small toy ponies should be worth four points. Maybe a few bangles or having lunch or playing a game with me could be ten points.

Ms. Thompson: That gives us some good guidelines. Let's put the list of reinforcers in order from low to high cost so Tracy can see how this works. We can fill in other details with Tracy.

D. Specify consequences for misbehavior if necessary.

Once a reinforcement system has been mapped out, determine whether the teacher will need to respond to possible misbehaviors. When the goal of the intervention is to encourage or increase appropriate behaviors, this step may be unnecessary. However, if the student needs to eliminate or reduce an inappropriate behavior as well as learn more responsible behaviors, the teacher may also need to implement consequences. Any consequences must be delivered calmly and consistently.

If a student has difficulties with fighting, the reinforcement system might reward the student for cooperation or self-control. At the same time, if the student engages in fighting, the teacher needs to be prepared to respond. Four major ways of responding to misbehavior are available:

- Provide corrective feedback.

- Ignore the behavior.

- Implement classroom consequences.

- Implement out-of-class consequences.

If the student is unaware of the misbehavior, does not know the behavior is inappropriate, or simply needs a reminder, respond with corrective feedback. Consider ignoring the misbehavior if it does not interfere with teaching. However, if the misbehavior cannot be ignored, implement a mild classroom consequence such as a one-minute timeout or one minute of recess time owed. (For more detailed information, see the discussion on correcting fluently with a menu of classroom-based consequences in "Pre-Intervention: Classroom Management Strategies" at the beginning of this book or "Intervention P: Defining Limits and Establishing Consequences.") If the misbehavior is highly disruptive, physically dangerous, or involves outright insubordination, implement out-of-class consequences that have been arranged in advance (see "Intervention G: Managing Physically Dangerous Behavior" and "Intervention H: Managing Severely Disruptive Behavior").

Ms. Thompson:	Since Tracy's intervention plan focuses strictly on getting her to move faster, I don't see any need to talk about consequences for misbehavior.
Mr. Dreyer:	I don't either. If we can just get her to move . . . .

E. Determine whether and how to include the parents as active participants in the system.

Invite the student's parents to be active partners in the system. The easiest and safest way to do this is to have the students earn rewards or privileges at home in addition to, but not in place of, the rewards or privileges she is earning at school. For example, in addition to a reinforcement menu of school-based rewards, develop a menu of home-based rewards. As the student earns school-based points, the parents would be informed so that the student could spend the points both at home and at school. In setting this up, make clear to the parents that if they volunteer to offer home-based rewards for school-based points, they must be prepared to follow through.

In spite of these assurances, there is a risk that if the student misbehaves at home, she will not be given the reward for the school-based points, which would defeat any positive gains of the system. At a minimum, therefore, ensure that the school-based points lead to school-based rewards—this way, if the parents wish to assist, home-based rewards are simply a nice supplement to the program.

F. Summarize the reinforcement system and review the procedures.

At this point, the intervention plan should include objectives for improved behavior, a monitoring system, possible reinforcers, point values for the reinforcers, and specification of consequences if needed. Summarize the plan and then try to anticipate any possible glitches by asking *what-if* questions.

Ms. Thompson: (Counselor)	So far, we have a very workable system. Tracy's objective will be to make improvements in the five critical transition times. I will work with her on how to make an "energetic" transition. Can I meet with Tracy from 10:00 to 10:15 on Monday, Wednesday, and Friday?
Mr. Dreyer:	Any time would be fine.
Ms. Thompson:	Good. I'll put it on my schedule, and I'll plan to pick her up. She will be able to earn one to two points for each appropriate transition during the day, and points can be traded for the various objects and privileges we identified. Now let's talk about problems that could occur.
Mr. Dreyer: (Teacher)	We might have a hard time determining what a "fine" transition is and what an "energetic" transition is.

INTERVENTION

Ms. Thompson:	Yes, that could be a problem. Let's schedule Tracy's first practice session with me when you can be there. We can practice rating with Tracy's assistance. What else?
Mr. Dreyer:	What if Tracy disagrees with my evaluation? I don't want to argue about it.
Ms. Thompson:	Actually, that does occur fairly often. We can plan for that by having a time for you to debrief with Tracy. We can let Tracy know that time has been set aside for her to discuss how things are going—both good and bad. Then, if she has a problem with one of your ratings, you can tell her that you would be happy to talk about it during your discussion time. Something else we might consider down the road is a self-monitoring system.

The more time you spend mentally rehearsing how the system will work, the greater the likelihood that glitches will be found and remedied before an otherwise strong intervention is sabotaged.

G. Identify ways to determine whether the intervention is helping the student reach her goals.

Your monitoring system will provide an ongoing record of student progress. Keep dated records so that student progress can be analyzed and the system adjusted periodically.

H. Identify procedures for increasing the sophistication of the system.

When a reinforcement system is successful, it needs to be gradually modified so the student becomes motivated by reinforcers that are part of the teacher's daily routine and inherent in the classroom atmosphere—praise, positive interactions, notes on papers, grades, self-satisfaction, and others. The most important concept in increasing the sophistication of the system is the word *gradual*. One of the most frequent errors in using a reinforcement system is to change it abruptly as soon as the student has been successful. In most cases, students quickly revert back to problem behaviors. The student must have a couple of weeks of success prior to any change in the system.

One of the most frequent errors in using a reinforcement system is to change it abruptly as soon as the student has been successful.

Mr. Dreyer: (Teacher)	I'm very excited about this plan. However, I am still a little concerned about how we might get Tracy off the plan if it does work. I've worked with a lot of kids who do fine on a reinforcement system, but who just don't want to work when we remove it.
Ms. Thompson: (Counselor)	Let's talk about some ways we can adjust the system so that Tracy will begin to accept more responsibility. We can work out the details as we go, but this will help us set some direction for ourselves.

Initially, allow the student to experience easy success (for example, for at least of couple of weeks). The student needs to feel that she's in control of the system before modifications are made. Then gradually adjust the criteria for earning reinforcers. This change can be made in several ways:

Require more points to earn the same reinforcers—that is, increase the price. Reinforcers that used to cost four points might now cost six, for example.

Ms. Thompson:	After Tracy has been successful for a couple of weeks, we can begin working on delaying the reinforcers. Let's consider taking the little four-point reinforcers off and adding other ten-point items. Maybe we ought to leave the bangles and some of the other things off the menu so we can add them later.

Change reinforcers. Reinforcers can be adjusted to reflect more and more natural reinforcers—moving the student from tangible rewards to internal ones such as taking pride in success and recognition.

Mr. Dreyer:	You also mentioned letting Tracy work for responsibilities.
Ms. Thompson:	Yes, later we can add some responsibilities—such as being a line leader or hall messenger. If we put high point values on those kinds of things, Tracy will see that responsibilities are major acknowledgments of growth and maturity.

INTERVENTION

Increase time intervals. If the student is earning points for demonstrating self-control during half-hour intervals, the intervals might be increased to 45 minutes.

Redefine expectations. For the student who aimlessly wanders around the classroom, the first expectation might be to stay in a specific work area. When the student has successfully met this expectation for a couple of weeks, the expectation might be increased to staying in her seat for specific amounts of time.

Mr. Dreyer:	I guess the other thing we will need to work on is generalizing our expectations. I get real excited about this and then I remember we're focusing on only five transition times, not the whole day.
Ms. Thompson:	I know. We are talking about trying to help Tracy with a major life change here. It is going to be slow and laborious. But, can you imagine Tracy going through life moving at the rate she moves?
Mr. Dreyer:	You are saying we need to be patient.
Ms. Thompson:	Yes. We have a lot of years of this bad habit to undo and a lot of other new repertoires to teach Tracy. Later we can add other transitions. We can look at playground behavior and her rate of speech.

I. Determine who will meet with the student.

Once the system has been carefully outlined, determine who will meet with the student to discuss her problems, goals, and the reinforcement system. This meeting may include the interventionist, the teacher, adults who will be working with the student, and the student's parents. It is important to convene a group that will not overwhelm the student. If the student is likely to feel uncomfortable meeting with several adults, it may be best to select one person to meet with her.

Schedule the discussion for a time when everyone can be relatively relaxed. Prior to the discussion, let the student know in private that the meeting is coming up and the goal of the meeting. By prearranging the meeting, the teacher can communicate that the discussion is important and that it is not a punishment for past behavior, but an opportunity to set up a plan for the future.

Mr. Dreyer and the Ms. Thompson decide to meet with Tracy together. Even though the counselor offers to take Mr. Dreyer's class, Mr. Dreyer decides that he would like the counselor's guidance as they work through the details of the reinforcement system with Tracy.

Mr. Dreyer: (Teacher)	Tracy, as you know, the class usually has to wait for you when we go to PE, lunch, recess, and the bus. We've talked a lot about your needing to move faster. I know that's really hard for you, so I've met with our counselor and we've worked out a plan that we hope will help you. I'm very excited because I know that you'll be happier if you can learn to do things like the other kids do. We'd like to meet with you during PE to discuss the plan with you and to work out the details.

Step 2: Meet with the student.

Begin by reviewing the problem and goals with an eye toward discussing and finalizing your plan with the student and other involved parties. When the reinforcement system is introduced to the student, it is important to establish a sense of trust. The student should understand that this intervention is being initiated to assist her in being more successful. The student must understand the goals of the intervention, the desired outcome, and the benefits.

Mr. Dreyer:	Tracy, I am glad that we can all meet. This morning I told you that we would like to work on a plan to help you move faster. Do you know why we would like to help you do that?
Tracy:	(Speaking very slowly) Yes. I . . . keep . . . everyone . . . waiting.
Mr. Dreyer:	Yes, Tracy that's part of it. But more importantly, I want you to be happy. I want you to feel like you are a part of my class, to work and have fun with the rest of us. Right now, you are always behind us. Would you like to work with us? (Tracy slowly moves her head and looks at Mr. Dreyer.)
Ms. Thompson: (Counselor)	Let us share what we have planned. Then you can let us know what you think about it.

A. Describe the behavioral objectives, the planned reinforcement system, and any consequences that might be used.

When explaining the system to the student, be as clear as possible. As you identify the expectations or plan objectives, model the expected behaviors and have the student role-play or verbally rehearse what she will be asked to do.

As much as possible, engage the student in helping to plan the system and invite the student to take part in the discussion. Ask her to voice suggestions, questions, or concerns. Provide suggestions for reinforcers and then brainstorm other ideas with the student. Explain to her that you want to mention as many ideas as possible when brainstorming, so it is important to list every suggestion regardless of how crazy or impossible it might seem. When the list is completed, help the student select reinforcers that are feasible. Ask her to help put point values on reinforcers. The more engaged the student is in the discussion and final planning, the greater the likelihood that she will take ownership of the plan.

Engage the student in helping to plan the system and invite the student to take part in the discussion.

Ms. Thompson:	Tracy, the first thing we would like to work on with you is getting ready and getting in line for recess, lunch, PE, and the bus. What do the other kids do when you make them wait?
Tracy:	They . . . get . . . mad.
Ms. Thompson:	Yes, they do. Would you like them to be nicer to you?
Tracy:	(No response)
Ms. Thompson:	Tracy, you are a very smart girl, and you are a nice girl. I know that a lot of things would be better for you if you could move a little faster. And I know that you can. We just need to help you change some habits you've developed. I'm going to meet with you three days a week to help you practice putting your things away and getting into line as quickly as possible.
Mr. Dreyer:	Because this will be hard for you, we would like you to be able to earn points that you can trade for different things you want. What do you think?
Tracy:	What . . . could I . . . earn?
Mr. Dreyer:	We thought of time on the computer or game time with another student or with me. Are there other things you would like?
Tracy:	A . . . million . . . dollars.
Mr. Dreyer:	Good. I'll put that down. What else?

After brainstorming for a while, Mr. Dreyer lets Tracy know that they will use the list as they work on their plan. He tells Tracy that she can work for some of the listed items as an adult—like the million dollars. Then he explains that they will pick things for now that she can earn very quickly.

Next, Mr. Dreyer and the counselor show Tracy the monitoring system. Both Ms. Thompson and Mr. Dreyer model transition behavior that is "too slow," "too fast," "just fine," and "energetic." Both adults are relieved when Tracy smiles at Mr. Dreyer's "too fast" imitation. The counselor role-plays various transitions, and Tracy and Mr. Dreyer practice rating the transitions on a monitoring form. Finally, Tracy has an opportunity to role-play various transitions as the two adults rate Tracy's performance. Mr. Dreyer is amazed that Tracy is able to engage in a "fine" transition.

Mr. Dreyer: (Teacher)	Tracy, I know you are going to be very successful. Somewhere, you learned this funny turtle behavior, and it became a habit. I look forward to seeing you learn to be a little quicker. I think you're going to enjoy it!

B. Set up a schedule for any lessons and regular debriefings with the student.

If the intervention requires that the student learn and practice a new behavior, short, regular lessons should be scheduled with the interventionist, a teacher, a trained paraprofessional, or a volunteer. The more frequently the lessons can be scheduled, the faster the student will master the new behavior. Lessons should include modeling and positive practice. See "Intervention M: Teaching Replacement Behavior" for more detailed information. Also plan to set up debriefing meetings with the student to discuss progress and any concerns.

Ms. Thompson: (Counselor)	Tracy, Mr. Dreyer has agreed to let me work with you on transitions every Monday, Wednesday, and Friday at 10:00. I think it will be fun. We will also set up time every Friday before recess so that you can periodically talk with Mr. Dreyer about how things are going and if the two of you agree on how the points system is working.

C. Review everyone's roles and responsibilities and write up the plan.

A sample plan is illustrated on the Intervention Summary Form in Sample Reproducible Form O10.

D. Conclude the meeting with words of encouragement.

> **Ms. Thompson:** Tracy, I appreciate the way you took part in this meeting. You were very grown up. I know that it won't be long before you'll be feeling very good about your accomplishments. You did great when we were practicing. I think this plan is going to be great fun.

Step 3: Implement the plan.

A. Provide continued support and encouragement.

When working with the student on a daily basis, provide positive feedback if the student demonstrates the desired behaviors—especially if it occurs without prompting. Feedback should focus on appropriate behavior. Avoid comments that remind the student of any negative behavior. Rather than saying, "Nice job, Tracy. You didn't keep the class waiting before lunch," focus on the goal behavior: "Tracy, nice job. You put your things away fairly quickly and lined up with the class. You've earned another point."

B. Meet again during the first week of the plan to make any necessary modifications.

If the system is working, celebrate the student's success and continue using the system without any changes for another week or so. If the system is not working, try to determine what the problems are and revise the system. The following questions may help pinpoint problems:

- Is the student getting too much attention from the teacher and/or peers for exhibiting the problem behaviors? If so, see "Intervention E: Increasing Positive Interactions."

- Does the student understand the system? Ask the student to explain the system or show you what must be done to earn the reinforcer.

- Does the student care about the reinforcers that have been identified? Brainstorm other alternatives with the student that she might be more motivated to earn. If the student is interested only in big reinforcers, consider a reinforcement ladder (Figure O2).

Sample Reproducible Form O10: *Intervention Summary Form*

Intervention Summary Form

Student: <u>Tracy Larson</u>   Date: <u>3/20</u>

OBJECTIVE
Tracy will learn to put her things away quickly and get into line without keeping others waiting.

RESPONSIBILITIES
Tracy's:
As soon as Mr. Dreyer says, "Class, get ready for recess (etc.)," Tracy will move quickly and steadily so that she is ready to leave the room with the rest of the class.

Mr. Dreyer's:
Mr. Dreyer will evaluate each of Tracy's efforts on the monitoring form and quietly let Tracy know how she did before leaving the room for recess, lunch, etc. They will debrief every Friday afternoon before the afternoon recess to discuss how the plan is going.

Ms. Thompson's:
Ms. Thompson will meet with Tracy from 10:00 to 10:15 on Monday, Wednesday, and Friday to practice putting things away and lining up energetically.

CONSEQUENCES
None.

POINTS
Tracy may earn one point for a "just fine" transition or two points for an "energetic" transition.

For the week of April 10-14, points may be traded as follows with Ms. Thompson or during any recess with Mr. Dreyer:
4 points = fancy pencil, small toy pony, or keychain
10 points = game with Mr. Dreyer

Later, Tracy will be able to trade points for classroom responsibilities (e.g., being a line leader or messenger).

SIGNATURES

Student Signature: _____

Teacher Signature: _____

Interventionist Signature: _____

A blank version of this form is available in the *Reproducible Materials* section at the end of the chapter.

• Is the system designed so the student has little chance of success? Check whether the reinforcers take too long to earn so that the student is not able to experience success. If so, adjust the system. Check whether the behavioral expectations require too much change at once and adjust the system accordingly.

C. Periodically evaluate and revise the plan, eventually fading the system.

Once the student has experienced success for at least two weeks, consider making gradual adjustments. The following list summarizes ways that reinforcement systems can be faded:

• Change reinforcers to reflect increasingly natural reinforcers (i.e., privileges and responsibilities).

• Require more points for the same or different reinforcers.

• Increase the amount of time the student needs to work to earn the reinforcers.

• Redefine expectations.

• Increase intervals of time between earning reinforcers by increasing the number of points required to earn more sophisticated reinforcers.

• Increase the sophistication of reinforcers.

Any time the system will be changed, the student should be informed in advance. Emphasize the student's success and sense of accomplishment. This will help her accept the changes and take pride in the fact that the system is requiring more of her.

Any time the system will be changed, the student should be informed in advance.

| Mr. Dreyer: (Teacher) | Tracy, you are doing such a great job moving energetically when it is time to line up. You should be very proud of yourself. In another week, we are going to make it just a little bit harder. I think you are getting really close to being able to move energetically to your reading group. In fact, I have already noticed you do it on your own occasionally. Would you like to add that into your system next week? |

Each time the system becomes more sophisticated, plan to increase the amount of praise and attention the student receives. Help the student recognize that she can be successful even when the expectations are increased. Positive feedback will help the student internalize the positive behavior: "Yes, I am more responsible. Yes, I am more capable. Yes, I am growing up!"

If the student's behavior deteriorates following a change in the system, the change may be too big or too abrupt. Give the student the option of going back to the previously implemented plan. Once the student has experienced two or more weeks of success, introduce another very gradual change.

Continue adjusting the system until the student is engaging in positive behavior with only reinforcers that approximate the natural reinforcers found in the classroom. Eventually, give the student the option of discontinuing the system.

Mr. Dreyer: (Teacher)	Tracy, I am so proud of you. You have made so much progress this year. Do you remember how you moved at the beginning of this year?
Tracy:	Yeah.
Mr. Dreyer:	I think you have grown so much you may not need those points anymore. You get to enjoy so many responsibilities. We'll talk tomorrow, and you can let me know whether you think you still need the old system.

If the system has been carefully designed and adjusted, students usually volunteer to go off the system. If the student isn't ready to let the system go, she may need the continued structure. The system can be continued, with more and more refinements, until the student is actually working for natural reinforcers found in the classroom environment.

Changing behavior is a difficult process. The student will need continued positive feedback throughout the fading process. Once the student has begun achieving the goals, it is easy to take appropriate behavior for granted. However, the student will have made a major change, and periodic check-ins from the interventionist let the student know that she will have the support she needs to achieve long-term success.

CONCLUSION

Setting up Structured Reinforcement Systems may be time consuming and intrusive, but if simpler solutions have been ineffective, active reinforcement has a high probability of jump-starting improvement. Initially, reinforcers work by motivating the student to earn rewards, but the sense of satisfaction the student derives from achievement may in time result in more intrinsic motivation to behave appropriately. Success tends to foster success.

REFERENCES

Adair, J. G., & Schneider, J. L. (1993). Banking on learning: An incentive system for adolescents in the resource room. *Teaching Exceptional Children, 25*(2), 30–34.

Brantley, D. C., & Webster, R. E. (1993). Use of an independent group contingency management system in a regular classroom setting. *Psychology in the Schools, 30*(1), 60–66.

Broughton, S. F., & Laltey, B. B. (1978). Direct and collateral effects of positive reinforcement, response cost, and mixed contingencies for academic performance. *Journal of School Psychology, 16*, 126–136.

Day, H.I., Berlyne, D.E., & Hunt, D. E. (Eds.), *Intrinsic motivation: A new direction in education* (pp. 113–127). Toronto: Holt, Reinhart & Winston.

Cruz, L., & Cullinan, D. (2001). Awarding points, using levels to help children improve behavior. *Teaching Exceptional Children, 33*(3), 16–23.

DuPaul, G. J., McGoey, K. E., & Yugar, J. M. (1997). Mainstreaming students with behavior disorders: The use of classroom peers as facilitators of generalization. *School Psychology Review, 26*(4), 634–650.

Higgins, J. W., Williams, R. L., & McLaughlin, T. F. (2001). The effects of a token economy employing instructional consequences for a third-grade student with learning disabilities: A data-based study. *Education and Treatment of Children, 24*(1), 99–106.

Lyon, C. S., & Lagarde, R. (1997). Tokens for success: Using the graduated reinforcement system. *Teaching Exceptional Children, 29*(6), 52–57.

Malouf, J. C. (1983). Do rewards reduce student motivation? *School Psychology, 65*, 202–210.

If simpler solutions have been ineffective, active reinforcement has a high probability of jump-starting improvement.

Manassis, K., & Young, A. (2001). Adapting positive reinforcement systems to suit child temperament. *Journal of the American Academy of Child & Adolescent Psychiatry, 40*(5), 603–605.

McGoey, K. E., & DuPaul, G. J. (2000). Token reinforcement and response cost procedures: Reducing the disruptive behavior of preschool children with Attention Deficit/Hyperactivity Disorder. *School Psychology Quarterly, 15*(3), 330–343.

O'Leary, K. D., & Drabman, R. (1971). Token reinforcement programs in the classroom: A review. *Psychological Bulletin, 75,* 379–398.

Repp, A. C., Barton, L. E., & Brulle, A. R. (1983). A comparison of two procedures for programming the differential reinforcement of other behaviors. *Journal of Applied Behavior Analysis, 16,* 435–445.

Smith, M. A., & Misra, A. (1992). A comprehensive management system for students in regular classrooms. *Elementary School Journal, 92*(3), 353–372.

Switzky, H. N. (1985). Self-reinforcement schedules in young children: A preliminary investigation of the effects of motivational orientation in instructional demands. *Reflections of Learning Research, 1,* 3–18.

Weiner, B. (1984). Principles for a theory of student motivation and their application within an attributional framework. In R.E. Ames & C. Ames (Eds.), *Research on motivation in education: Student motivation* (Vol. 1, pp. 15–38). New York: Academic Press.

Worrall, C., Worrall, N., & Meldrum, C. (1983). The consequences of verbal praise and criticism. *Educational Psychologist, 3,* 127–136.

Reproducible Materials

The following reproducible materials may be used in conjunction with "Intervention O: Structured Reinforcement Systems." Copies are provided here and on the CD. Permission is given for individual classroom teachers to reproduce any forms labeled "Reproducible" for classroom use. Reproduction of these materials for an entire school system is prohibited without express permission of the publisher.

INTERVENTION O

STRUCTURED REINFORCEMENT SYSTEMS

Step-by-Step Summary

Following is a summary of the steps involved in Intervention O. It is important to use professional judgment, adjusting procedures to meet the needs of the situation and the individual. See the chapter "Intervention O: Structured Reinforcement Systems" for a detailed description of this intervention.

STEP 1   Develop a plan.

A. Identify specific behavioral objectives.

B. If the behavior is not currently in the student's repertoire, design lessons to teach the student the appropriate behavior.

C. Design a reinforcement system.
1. Choose a method for monitoring student behaviors and counting points.
2. Identify a menu of possible rewards or privileges.
3. Determine how many points will be required for the student to earn each reward or privilege.

D. Specify consequences for misbehavior if necessary.

E. Determine whether and how to include the parents as active participants in the system.

F. Summarize the reinforcement system and review the procedures.

G. Identify ways to determine whether the intervention is helping the student reach her goals.

H. Identify procedures for increasing the sophistication of the system.

I. Determine who will meet with the student.

STEP 2   Meet with the student.

A. Describe the behavioral objectives, the planned reinforcement system, and any consequences that might be used.

B. Set up a schedule for any lessons and regular debriefings with the student.

INTERVENTION

C. Review everyone's roles and responsibilities and write up the plan.

D. Conclude the meeting with words of encouragement.

STEP 3 Implement the plan.

A. Provide continued support and encouragement.

B. Meet again during the first week of the plan to make any necessary modifications.

C. Periodically evaluate and revise the plan, eventually fading the system.

Reproducible Form O3: *Behavior Graph (Version 2)*

Intervention O:
Structured Reinforcement Systems

Behavior Graph (Version 2)

Student   Grade/Class   Teacher   Beginning Date

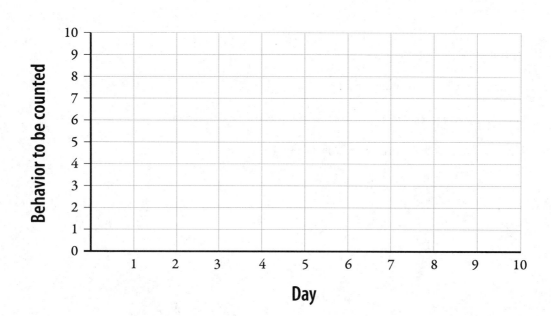

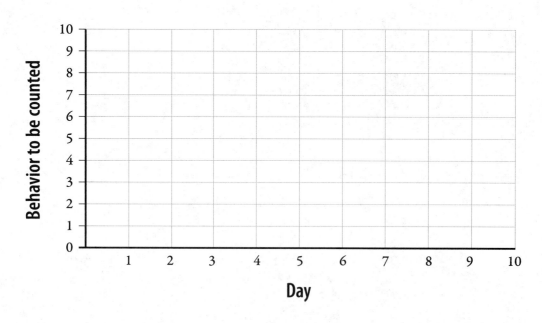

Reproducible Form O5: *Positive/Negative Behavior Rating Form (Version 1)*

Positive/Negative Behavior Rating Form (Version 1)

Student _____   Grade/Class _____   Teacher _____   Week of _____

Goal _____

Time	Rating (+/−)				
	Monday	**Tuesday**	**Wednesday**	**Thursday**	**Friday**
8:00 – 8:30					
8:30 – 9:00					
9:00 – 9:30					
9:30 – 10:00					
10:00 – 10:30					
10:30 – 11:00					
11:00 – 11:30					
11:30 – Noon					
Noon – 12:30					
12:30 – 1:00					
1:00 – 1:30					
1:30 – 2:00					
2:00 – 2:30					
2:30 – 3:00					
Points Earned					

Reproducible Form O6: *Positive/Negative Behavior Rating Form (Version 2)*

Positive/Negative Behavior Rating Form (Version 2)

Student _____ Grade/Class _____ Teacher _____ Week of _____

Goal _____

Rating (+/−)					
Time	**Monday**	**Tuesday**	**Wednesday**	**Thursday**	**Friday**
Points Earned					

Rating (+/−)					
Time	**Monday**	**Tuesday**	**Wednesday**	**Thursday**	**Friday**
Points Earned					

Rating (+/−)					
Time	**Monday**	**Tuesday**	**Wednesday**	**Thursday**	**Friday**
Points Earned					

Reproducible Form O7: *Positive/Negative Behavior Tracking Form*

Positive/Negative Behavior Tracking Form

Student _____ Grade/Class _____ Teacher _____ Week of _____

Goal _____

Time	Number of Misbehaviors									
8:00 – 8:30	1	2	3	4	5	6	7	8	9	10
8:30 – 9:00	1	2	3	4	5	6	7	8	9	10
9:00 – 9:30	1	2	3	4	5	6	7	8	9	10
9:30 – 10:00	1	2	3	4	5	6	7	8	9	10
10:00 – 10:30	1	2	3	4	5	6	7	8	9	10
10:30 – 11:00	1	2	3	4	5	6	7	8	9	10
11:00 – 11:30	1	2	3	4	5	6	7	8	9	10
11:30 – Noon	1	2	3	4	5	6	7	8	9	10
Noon – 12:30	1	2	3	4	5	6	7	8	9	10
12:30 – 1:00	1	2	3	4	5	6	7	8	9	10
1:00 – 1:30	1	2	3	4	5	6	7	8	9	10
1:30 – 2:00	1	2	3	4	5	6	7	8	9	10
2:00 – 2:30	1	2	3	4	5	6	7	8	9	10
2:30 – 3:00	1	2	3	4	5	6	7	8	9	10

Intervention O:
Structured Reinforcement Systems

Behavior Monitoring Form

Student _____ Goal _____ Date _____

Points: *0 = Not at all*   *1 = Needed reminders*   *2 = Followed directions independently*

DAY	AM	PM	TOTAL
Monday	0 1 2	0 1 2	
Tuesday	0 1 2	0 1 2	
Wednesday	0 1 2	0 1 2	
Thursday	0 1 2	0 1 2	
Friday	0 1 2	0 1 2	

DAY	AM	PM	TOTAL
Monday	0 1 2	0 1 2	
Tuesday	0 1 2	0 1 2	
Wednesday	0 1 2	0 1 2	
Thursday	0 1 2	0 1 2	
Friday	0 1 2	0 1 2	

Reproducible Form O9: *Behavior Qualifying Form*

Behavior Qualifying Form

Student _____ Grade/Class _____ Teacher _____ Date _____

Behavior _____

Activity	Qualifiers				TOTAL
Total Points for the Day					

Activity	Qualifiers				TOTAL
Total Points for the Day					

Reproducible Form O10: *Intervention Summary Form*

Intervention Summary Form

Student: _____   Date: _____

OBJECTIVE

_____

RESPONSIBILITIES

_____

_____

_____

_____

_____

CONSEQUENCES

_____

POINTS

_____

_____

_____

_____

SIGNATURES

Student Signature: _____

Teacher Signature: _____

Interventionist Signature: _____

Defining Limits and Establishing Consequences

It is difficult to be consistent with the student because it is not always clear when the student has crossed the line between appropriate and inappropriate behavior

PURPOSE

THIS INTERVENTION may help overcome chronic misbehaviors that are difficult to respond to with consistency.

THIS INTERVENTION IS APPROPRIATE FOR:

Any chronic misbehavior that necessitates the use of consequences
- sarcasm
- rudeness

Disruptive behavior
- noisemaking
- blurt-outs
- frequently out of seat
- arguing
- swearing

Disrespectful behavior
- talking back
- open hostility

Manipulative behavior
- testing limits
- getting the "last word"

Excessive behavior
- tattling
- complaining
- questioning

INTRODUCTION

Defining Limits and Establishing Consequences addresses the *C* for *Correct fluently* in STOIC. This intervention provides guidelines for correcting chronic misbehavior effectively through the judicious use of consequences. Though negative consequences in isolation are weak interventions for reducing chronic or severe misbehavior, their effectiveness can be amplified (and their use is often necessary) in combination with other procedures. Consequences are an integral part of an overall plan to teach students that some behaviors are unacceptable and unproductive, while alternative behaviors can meet their needs in a more productive and satisfying way.

Fluency is key to implementing consequences successfully. A fluent response to an incident of misbehavior is given in a manner that continues the flow of the instructional activity as much as possible. This means that what is done to correct a student's misbehavior is actually of less importance than continuing instruction. For example, if a student makes a disrespectful comment during teacher-directed instruction and the teacher matter-of-factly states, "That was disrespectful. I would like to speak to you after class. Now, class, the next paragraph states . . . ," the flow of the lesson is maintained. On the other hand, if the teacher immediately takes the student into the hall or gets into an argument about assigning detention, the flow of the lesson is lost.

Fluent corrections are important for a number of reasons. When you strive for fluency, you will be less likely to get into power struggles with students, and you will demonstrate that misbehavior will not gain your undivided attention. Keeping the momentum of a lesson can frequently reduce or even eliminate the vast majority of misbehavior. When students are busily

A fluent response to an incident of misbehavior is given in a manner that continues the flow of the instructional activity as much as possible.

INTERVENTION

P

engaged in meaningful activities, they have no time to misbehave. Within this chapter, information will be provided on how to correct fluently—how to master the *C* in the STOIC acronym (Structure for success, Teach expectations, Observe and monitor, Interact positively, and Correct fluently).

A fluent correction is performed calmly, consistently, briefly, and immediately. It is specific, direct, and, above all, respectful. As straightforward as fluency may sound, it is surprisingly difficult to achieve. You must deliberately analyze and define for yourself the sometimes fine line between acceptable and unacceptable behaviors before you encounter misbehaviors in your class. This will allow you to make the quick judgments necessary to follow through with consequences for infractions without undue strain on the flow of instruction. At the same time, predetermining boundaries will provide clues for knowing which behaviors to encourage. By carefully delineating what is and isn't acceptable behavior, you are teaching students positive expectations for their behavior and setting appropriate limits. Once limits are clarified, you can calmly and fluently implement a prearranged consequence every time the student crosses the line into unacceptable behavior.

> Note: Defining Limits and Establishing Consequences is one of the most effective interventions to use in combination with other interventions to develop a comprehensive plan. If any intervention is having limited success and the student and teacher might benefit from Defining Limits and Establishing Consequences, consider implementing this intervention concurrently to increase the effectiveness of the intervention plan.

RATIONALE

Fluency is often impossible if no clear distinction exists between acceptable and unacceptable behaviors. Spelling out the subtle distinctions between appropriate and inappropriate behaviors can be taxing for teachers and students alike. But without active identification of those limits, chronic misbehavior will be perpetuated by inconsistency and nourished by irritation.

Marco is a chronically disruptive student in Mrs. Laird's fourth-grade classroom. Mrs. Laird, who is known for her fairness and patience, says that she often doesn't know what to do with him. "Marco pushes the limits all day long. He's never really out of control, and he isn't a threat to anyone. He just does annoying things. He sings at the wrong times. He pokes other students—just kid stuff, but it's excessive to the point that I get irritated. He also plays practical jokes and makes smart remarks. I try to treat Marco like the other students, so I ignore some of it. Sometimes I encourage his jokes like I do with the other kids. I like my class to have personality. But then Marco goes too far, and by the end of the day I know I'm correcting him for things I said were OK at other times. In my attempts to be fair with Marco, I know I'm being terribly inconsistent."

Unless the line between appropriate and inappropriate behavior is clearly drawn and taught to students, teachers will find themselves implementing consequences inconsistently.

Like many chronic behavior problems, Marco's behavior is acceptable in certain contexts but inappropriate when engaged in excessively or at inappropriate times. Because the line between acceptable and unacceptable is sometimes difficult to determine, these students often receive mixed messages from adults. The student who chronically tattles will sometimes inform the teacher about another student's misbehavior that requires adult intervention, but he more often tells on other students for silly or trivial issues. The behavior itself is not the problem; its excessiveness or inappropriateness to the setting is. The class clown may be a funny kid with a good sense of humor, but her frequent and inappropriate clowning can cause undue disruption in the classroom. The distractible student gets up to sharpen his pencil, wanders to the back of the classroom, washes his hands, asks a classmate a question, and then comments on the work of his neighbor. None of these actions can be classified as misbehaviors in and of themselves; it is the combination and frequency of the behaviors that interferes with classroom work. Unless the line between appropriate and inappropriate behavior is clearly drawn and taught to students, teachers will find themselves implementing consequences inconsistently, which disrupts a teacher's ability to correct fluently and can lead to a number of other problems.

COMMON PROBLEMS WITH UNCLEAR LIMITS

It can be reinforcing—"I can make the teacher so mad she loses it."
If the line between inappropriate and appropriate behavior is unclear, as in Marco's situation, a behavior tolerated in the morning may run into a consequence late in the day when the teacher has "had enough." "He just keeps pushing, and pushing, and pushing." But implementing consequences

only when the misbehavior can no longer be tolerated can compound the problem; some students are reinforced in their mischief by their ability to upset the teacher. Knowing this, it is important to define exactly what your limits are so that when a student crosses that line, both you and the student know it—the division between acceptable and unacceptable is perfectly clear. When the line is crossed, calmly implement a predetermined consequence rather than waiting until you "can't take it anymore." Your students learn, "When I do this, the consequence is this," instead of, "When I do this, sometimes nothing happens, but sometimes I can make the teacher turn purple, raise her voice, and generally come unglued."

Students may test the limits to see what they can get away with.

Another problem with inconsistently implemented consequences is that there will always be some students who will test the limits just to see how much they can get away with. People—both children and adults—feel compelled to see how far they can go before they get caught. Think of an interstate with a speed limit of 65 miles per hour. The speed limit is clearly posted, and the consequences for violating the speed limit are known. But— surprise, surprise—most drivers do not drive 65 miles per hour or under. Depending on the state and the degree of enforcement, the average driver may cruise along the interstate at 68, 70, or 75 miles per hour. Why? Most drivers know that they are unlikely to get a speeding ticket. Therefore, they will go at the highest speed that from previous experience they believe will not result in a ticket.

The same phenomenon occurs in classrooms when consequences are implemented sporadically. When students "push it" and get away with a behavior, they may experience conscious or unconscious satisfaction. "Wow, I got away with it that time. I wonder if she'll notice if I do it again." To prevent inordinate testing of the limits, teachers need to apply consequences consistently. The limits will quickly become known and understood by students, resulting in less need for students to see what they can "get away with."

Students may perceive that consequences are unfair or have nothing to do with rules.

Consequences that are implemented with irritation or anger may also result in students feeling that consequences are "done" to them rather than "earned" by them. If teachers implement consequences inconsistently when irritated, students may conclude that consequences have nothing to do with the rules or with their behavior. Instead, students may come to believe consequences are implemented simply because the teacher is grumpy or that consequences have more to do with who they are or what they've done. Some students may think, "I get nailed because I'm bad" or "The teacher picks on me.

She gets mad when I cut in line, but she doesn't care if somebody else does it." If students perceive that consequences are arbitrarily or unfairly implemented, they will not have to take responsibility for their actions—they can blame their problems on the teacher. The message must be clear—consequences have nothing to do with the teacher's mood; with issues of race, gender, age, or personality preferences; or with who the student is. Students should know that consequences spring from their behavior, not arbitrary circumstances—when anyone misbehaves, the consequences are doled out equally.

Some behavior management problems may be occurring in your class if you often hear yourself saying or thinking the following:

- "He really knows how to push my buttons."
- "I've had it up to here with you."
- "He just doesn't know when to stop."
- "How many times do I have to tell you . . . "
- "He just doesn't listen . . . "
- "Are you going to make me call your mother?"

Before implementing Defining Limits and Establishing Consequences

Be sure that you have discussed the problem and general goals for improvement with the student. Gather any relevant background information that may help in designing and implementing the intervention. In addition, contact the student's parents or guardians to discuss the problem. Invite them to participate and keep them informed of all aspects of the intervention plan. While this intervention is laid out in a step-by-step format, it is important that you use your professional judgment, adapting procedures to the situation and the needs of the student.

IMPLEMENTATION STEPS
Step 1: Develop a plan.

Review the problem and overall goal for the student. If you are clear on what has led you to this intervention, it will help you define the nature and scope of the problem—critical information for developing a successful intervention. If you have tried any of the Early-Stage Interventions, review any forms (for example, the Discussion Record, Goal Setting forms, STOIC worksheets) and data you have collected (for example, academic assistance data such as oral reading fluency or data on frequency and duration of mis-behavior). Any data you have collected will be of assistance as you proceed to subsequent planning steps.

Carly, a student in Mrs. Parson's sixth-grade class, continually interacts with the teacher in negative ways. After a particularly difficult interaction, Mrs. Parson decides it's time for assistance. In talking with the principal, Mr. Hunter, she says, "Carly is so rude. She gets into a snit and talks back to me in front of the other kids. I sent her to you because I asked her to do something and she said, 'Who do you think you are?' I told her very calmly that she needed to watch what she said. Then she said in a very snotty tone, 'I'll need a mirror if you want me to watch what I say.' That was just the beginning. Finally, I just sent her down here. If she isn't being disrespectful, she is trying to manipulate me. She always has to get the last word in. 'Why do we have to do it? That's not fair.' And on and on and on. Eventually, Carly gets down to work, but I feel like I spend the whole day dealing with her." In talking with Carly's mother, the principal learns that she has the same problem at home and her mother doesn't know what to do. Mrs. Parson and the principal agree to do some intervention planning and then get back to Carly's mother. They decide the major goal of the intervention should be to help Carly learn to interact respectfully with adults.

A. Identify all the problem behaviors the student exhibits.

Note: You may have completed the same or a similar process prior to implementing this intervention. However, to ensure that all necessary information has been gathered, you should review or repeat this process.

Work through a typical day, identifying any problems that might occur during various activities.

Write down every behavior the student exhibits or interaction she engages in that you view as inappropriate or bordering on inappropriate. Work through a typical day, identifying any problems that might occur during various activities. Brainstorm, writing down anything that comes to mind. You will be able to organize your list later. For now, note the full range of the student's misbehavior, starting with when the student first enters the classroom to when she leaves for the day.

Think about when the student first enters the classroom. Ask yourself the following questions:

- Does the student say or do anything that bothers me?

- Does the student say or do anything that is annoying?

- Does the student say or do anything that interferes with her or others' learning?

- Does the student say or do anything that disrupts the class?

- Does the student say or do anything that wastes class time?

Mr. Hunter: (Principal)	Tell me anything that Carly says or does that is annoying, beginning with the moment she enters the classroom. We need to list everything—even things that seem petty.

Within a few minutes, Mrs. Parson has identified the following problems:

1) When Mrs. Parson says, "Good morning," Carly has responded:
   - "Good morning, Mrs. Parson," in a singsong, sarcastic tone.
   - "Oh, good. Another day with Mrs. Parsley."

2) When Carly is tardy, she:
   - tries not to be counted as tardy.
   - implies that Mrs. Parson treats her unfairly compared with other students.

3) When Mrs. Parson calls on Carly during discussions, Carly has said:
   - "Who cares? This is stupid!"
   - "No one else is interested."
   - "Why would I care?"
   - "If you don't know the answer, you're pretty stupid."

4) When Mrs. Parson gives group directions, such as "Line up for recess," or "Everyone, get cleaned up," Carly has mimicked her teacher.

5) When Mrs. Parson gives assignments, Carly has said:
   - "Why should I do it?"
   - "What a laugh. Here we go with another of Mrs. Parsley's dumb assignments."
   - "OK, I'll do it," in a sulky, obnoxious voice.
   - "No one else has to do so much."

6) Carly tries to evade assignments. She has said:
   - "I don't see why I have to do it. I already did it once."
   - "Can't I fix just one problem? I understand it."

7) Carly has to have the last word. She has said, "You always give us too much work."

> 8) When asked to clean up after some types of work, Carly has complained that Mrs. Parson never gives them enough time.
> 9) When Mrs. Parson tries to talk with Carly, Carly has:
> - walked away from her.
> - glared at her.
> - sighed (in a disgusted manner).

Continue the process, identifying as many different misbehaviors that typically occur during a school day as possible. You may not address all the misbehaviors that you identify with this intervention, but a complete list will help you define the parameters of the intervention. Here are some final questions to ask yourself as you complete this step:

- Does the student comply with instructions?
- Does the student get along with other students?
- Does the student get her work done?
- Does the student get her work done satisfactorily?
- Are there any other problems?

> Mr. Hunter and Mrs. Parson add to the list:
> - Carly sometimes forgets her homework.
> - Carly sometimes makes inappropriate noises, such as belching.
> - Carly doesn't seem to have many friends.

B. Categorize the problems.

Examine the list to determine whether the misbehaviors can be categorized. For example, if the list includes pencil tapping, chair screeching, and making animal noises, combine these behaviors into one category: "making noises." If the student tells classmates to pick their own things up, tells the teacher to watch the clock, tells other students to sharpen their pencils, and so on, combine these behaviors into a category such as "bossiness."

> **Mr. Hunter:** From the list, we need to categorize Carly's problems.
> **(Principal)** It looks like your initial concern about disrespect is a clear category.

Mrs. Parson: (Teacher)	Yes.
Mr. Hunter:	Is complaining a problem?
Mrs. Parson:	Yes, Carly complains all day long. About half the time her complaining is disrespectful, and the rest of the time it's just excessive.
Mr. Hunter:	Let's try categorizing the list using disrespect and complaining as major categories. We can adjust it as we go.

The principal and teacher categorize the list of Carly's annoying behaviors (see Figure P1).

C. Select intervention priorities.

Once the problem behaviors have been categorized, select one, two, or possibly three general behaviors as priorities for immediate intervention. Less important categories of misbehavior can be considered after the student has resolved her most pressing problems. Identify priorities based on two variables:

1. How manageable will the change be?

When selecting the misbehaviors for immediate intervention, consider that the change needs to be manageable for the student and teacher. Though many problems may exist, it is important to select the number of priorities based on the sophistication and ability of the student and manageability for the teacher. If the student is intellectually limited or a vast change is required, it may be best to select only one problem. If too many problems are selected, the teacher and the student are likely to become overwhelmed and discouraged.

2. How important is resolving the problem?

The most pervasive or disruptive problems should be dealt with first. Less intrusive problems can be handled once the student is experiencing success. Sometimes less important problems will resolve themselves as the student experiences success in other areas.

Figure P1: *STOIC—A procedural description of ABC analysis*

Misbehavior	Category
1. When Mrs. Parson says, "Good morning," Carly responds:	
• "Good morning, Mrs. Parson," in a singsong, sarcastic tone.	*disrespect*
• "Oh, good. Another day with Mrs. Parsley."	*disrespect*
2. When Carly is tardy, she:	
• tries not to be counted tardy.	*negotiating*
• implies that Mrs. Parson treats her unfairly compared to other students.	*complaining*
3. When Mrs. Parson calls on Carly during discussions, she says:	
• "Who cares about _____? This is stupid."	*disrespect*
• "No one else is interested."	*disrespect*
• "Why would I care?"	*disrespect*
• "If you don't know the answer, you're pretty stupid."	*disrespect*
4. When Mrs. Parson gives group directions like, "Line up for recess" or "Everyone get cleaned up," Carly mimics Mrs. Parson.	*disrespect*
5. When Mrs. Parson gives assignments, Carly says:	
• "Why should I do it?"	*negotiating*
• "What a laugh. Here we go with another of Mrs. Parsley's dumb assignments."	*disrespect*
• "Okay, I'll do it," in a sulky, obnoxious tone.	*disrespect*
• "No one else has to do so much."	*complaining*
6. Carly tries to evade assignments. She says:	
• "I don't see why I have to do it. I already did it once."	*complaining*
• "Can't I fix just one problem? I understand it."	*complaining*
7. Carly has to have the last word. She says, "You always give us too much work."	*disrespect*
8. When asked to clean up after some types of work, Carly has complained that Mrs. Parson never gives them enough time.	*complaining*
9. When Mrs. Parson tries to talk with Carly, Carly:	
• walks away from her.	*disrespect*
• glares at her.	*disrespect*
• sighs in a disgusted manner.	*disrespect*
10. Carly sometimes forgets her homework.	*homework*
11. Carly sometimes makes inappropriate noises, such as belching.	*inappropriate noises*
12. Carly doesn't seem to have many friends.	*friends*

Mrs. Parson: (Teacher)	I think that Carly's major problem is disrespect.
Mr. Hunter: (Principal)	I suspect that disrespect is also part of Carly's problem with making friends. How about the inappropriate noises and missing homework?
Mrs. Parson:	I've taught the class to ignore the noises. So that can be a "later" issue. As for homework, she always makes it up sometime during the day. Her academic progress is OK. Homework is a problem, but again it's something we can tackle later.
Mr. Hunter:	Is complaining a major problem? Can it be ignored, or do you need to deal with it?
Mrs. Parson:	I think it's part of the bigger issue of disrespect. Her constant negative comments tend to lead to disrespect.
Mr. Hunter:	Let's go with those two categories then—disrespect and complaining. What about negotiating?
Mrs. Parson:	Let's leave that until later. After we set up a plan for disrespect and complaining, we can decide whether or not to add in negotiating.

Figure P2: *The Strike Zone*

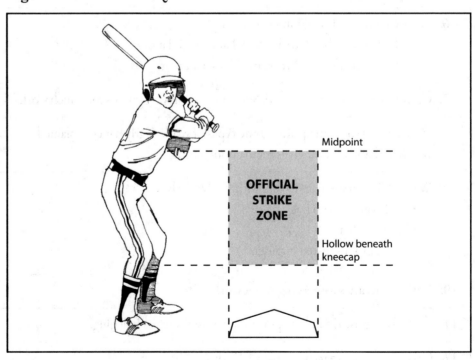

INTERVENTION

P

D. Define limits for the top intervention priorities (that is, what constitutes acceptable and unacceptable behaviors).

The process of defining limits consists of clearly identifying what is respectful and disrespectful and then communicating that information to the student. To help clarify this concept, you might think about the strike zone in baseball—a rectangle that exists in the space relative to the batter. The umpire uses this imaginary box to call each pitch a ball or a strike as the pitch travels across the plate. If the umpire did not have a clearly defined notion of the strike zone, calling each pitch objectively would be difficult—the probability of inconsistency and inadvertent bias negatively affecting both batters and pitchers would be very high. Defining the strike zone consists of deciding where the line is between a strike and a ball, or, more specifically, setting the locations of the four imaginary lines that define the rectangle of the strike zone (Figure P2). Although a precise and firm definition of what constitutes the strike zone will not always guarantee objectivity (even umpires make mistakes) or fairness (some batters are tall while others are much shorter), having such a definition will increase consistency and reduce the subjectivity inherent in making a judgment call. Only when you have clearly defined the limits in your own mind can you begin to teach the acceptable behavioral "zone" to your students.

The strike zone metaphor is particularly apt when you consider every student behavior like a pitch that you must observe and call as a strike ("Nice job, Tom, that was very respectful") or a ball ("Tom, that was disrespectful, so you will owe some time after class"). Like the umpire's call, your decisions about whether a behavior is acceptable or unacceptable must be decisive and immediate.

However, defining even seemingly clear-cut unacceptable behaviors like hitting or inappropriate language can become fuzzy when you examine them up close. Where is the line between hitting and a strong pat on the back? Is "jeez" acceptable language? How about "crap" or "damn"?

Limits for behavior are inherently difficult to define with clarity and are therefore open to inconsistent application by adults. For example, where is the line between friendly teasing and cruelty? How do you draw the line between talking back and stating an opinion? Is there a clear line between chronic tattling and social responsibility? Where is the line between sarcasm and wit?

To define limits, work with one issue at a time, beginning with the highest priority problem. Limits can be defined in at least three ways: by rule, by examples of acceptable and unacceptable behavior in particular situations, and, in some cases, in terms of quantity—how much of a behavior is acceptable.

If the umpire did not have a clearly defined notion of the strike zone, calling each pitch objectively would be difficult.

INTERVENTION

P

Figure P3: *Strike Zone Definition*

> **From the Major League Baseball official rule book:**
>
> The STRIKE ZONE is that area over home plate the upper limit of which is a horizontal line at the midpoint between the top of the shoulders and the top of the uniform pants, and the lower level is a line at the hollow beneath the kneecap. The Strike Zone shall be determined from the batter's stance as the batter is prepared to swing at a pitched ball.

1. Define limits by rule.

   One way to define limits is to develop a rule or set of rules that you can use to evaluate each behavior, like setting ground rules for a Monopoly game or legal definitions for city ordinance infractions. But behavior rules are vastly more difficult to pin down than those black and white rules of Monopoly or city ordinances—in most cases, rules are a difficult way to define limits or boundaries of acceptable and unacceptable behavior.

   For proof of this difficulty, ask yourself, "What is disruptive?" Try to come up with just a few simple rules, and you will find yourself adding more and more caveats to cover the infinite variations on themes of misbehavior that students will creatively devise to test your rules. Eventually, your list could come to look like disclaimers at a theme park—long, legalistic, and impenetrable. Neither you nor your target student is likely to be inclined to take the time to understand such a list, much less abide by it. In short, defining behavioral limits by setting rules tends to become overly complicated or too legalistic. (See Figure P3 for an example of such a definition—the official definition of the strike zone in Major League Baseball.)

   Even this previous definition would be too complicated for most students, and it remains relatively simple in comparison to many behavioral rules. Crafting a rule that can be fairly applied to the vagaries of behavior is a daunting challenge at best. As any good politician or public servant knows, you can't legislate morality. Supreme Court Justice Potter Stewart dealt with a similar situation as he tried to elucidate the limits of obscenity in movies, writing that he might never succeed in defining what he understood to be pornographic, but "I know it when I see it." Legislating behavior is similarly fraught. If defining limits by rule gets overly complicated, consider defining limits by example.

2. Define limits by example.

Another way to define the limits of a behavior is to select positive and negative examples of the behavior and use the juxtaposition of these examples to communicate where the line between them lies. In baseball, you can explain the strike zone by pointing and showing: "If the pitch is here, it would be a strike, but if the pitch is here, it would be a ball." By demonstrating similar minimal distinctions with respect to behavior, you also clarify the difference between acceptable and unacceptable behavior in your own mind. If you are defining disrespect, for example, you might tell the student it is acceptable to ask a question in a conversational voice and then model such behavior. Then explain how a snide tone of voice is disrespectful and unacceptable—demonstrate such a tone and then model the positive example again. Whenever you are modeling an unacceptable behavior, be sure to demonstrate the positive replacement both before and after the unacceptable example. This will ensure that the student sees the positive example twice for each time he sees the negative. By "sandwiching" the unacceptable between positive examples, you communicate high expectations and eliminate any risk that all the student remembers is the negative example.

Start by identifying a few typical situations that have resulted in the student misbehaving. For each situation, list ways the student might handle the situation appropriately and ways the student might handle the situation inappropriately. (By citing only the types of behaviors you have previously observed, you avoid introducing your students to new misbehaviors they may not yet have contemplated.) You do not need to include examples of everything the student might do, only the types of things the student has done or seems likely to do. You also do not need to include extreme examples. What's most important is that you describe or model examples that fall near the border between appropriate and inappropriate behavior. In the same way that a batter can easily determine that a pitch 15 feet over his head is a ball, students can determine for themselves that extreme behavior is outside the boundary of what is acceptable and appropriate. What takes real finesse, both from you in the explaining process and your students in comprehending, is understanding the behaviors that are near the boundary between a strike (appropriate) and a ball (inappropriate).
The list of situations and problems generated in Step 1A can be used, along with any other relevant examples. See Figure P4 for examples.

If limits are difficult to define, identify many situations and examples of acceptable and unacceptable behaviors. Include a sufficient number of examples so that teachers and students can easily generalize the boundaries to classroom situations.

Whenever you are modeling an unacceptable behavior, be sure to demonstrate the positive replacement both before and after the unacceptable example.

Figure P4: *Limits by Example*

If the problem is inappropriate language, the following kinds of examples might be used to define behavioral limits.

Situation: Thomas trips in the classroom.	
Acceptable responses:	*Unacceptable responses:*
"Darn!"	"D*mn!"
"Oops!"	"Sh*t!"

Situation: Thomas misses a ball in four square.	
Acceptable responses:	*Unacceptable responses:*
"Darn!"	"D*mn!"
"Shoot!"	"Sh*t!"
No comment.	"F*ck!"

If the problem is hitting, physical examples might be used to define behavioral limits.

Situation: Brenda wants to get someone's attention.	
Acceptable touching:	*Unacceptable hitting:*
Touching someone like this (tap the student's shoulder).	Touching someone like this (hit the wall to demonstrate).

If the problem is putting others down, the following kinds of examples might be used to define behavioral limits.

Situation: Someone says something that Philip already knows.	
Acceptable responses:	*Unacceptable responses:*
Nodding his head.	"Isn't that obvious?"
"I noticed that too."	"Bravo, aren't you smart!"

3. Define limits in terms of quantity (how much is too much).

While limits for most behaviors can be made plain by generating a sufficient number of examples, behavior that is unacceptable because it is excessive rather than inappropriate may necessitate a third way of defining limits. In this case, provide the student with information about how often a behavior is appropriate.

For the student who asks to have assignments clarified well beyond what is necessary, define when appropriate behavior becomes inappropriate by limiting the student to a certain number of questions each morning and afternoon. This system would be explained to the student as follows: "Arthur, I want you to keep trying your best, but I've noticed that you often ask questions when you already know the answer. Because I want you to learn to be more independent and to trust yourself, I am going to give you eight tickets to use for questions each morning. Each time you ask a question, you will give me a ticket. When you run out, I won't be able to answer your questions. This will help you think carefully about the questions you want to ask and make sure they are really important." By limiting the number of questions the student can ask, the teacher begins identifying the line between acceptable and unacceptable behavior.

Limits are especially useful for behaviors that teachers do not want to eliminate but hope to reduce. Another example would be the student who clowns around too much. "Tony, we all love your great sense of humor, but you need to learn how to curb it a bit. Your jesting is interfering with what we need to accomplish in class. Therefore, I am going to give you five 'laugh' tickets for the day. Use the tickets wisely. Once they are gone, you cannot take class time for jokes and fun comments. If you take additional time to entertain us after your tickets are gone, you will owe time after the bell."

To determine quantity-based limits, consider what would be acceptable from any student, what you can reasonably manage, and whether the student could reasonably meet the expectations. If a major change is required of the student, initially set limits that are within the range of the student's daily performance and then gradually increase your expectations to shape the student's behavior.

When you set limits for a student, you also need to stipulate additional consequences in case the student exceeds the number of behaviors you identified as acceptable. Various consequences are discussed in Step 1E.

A further complication with correcting excessiveness is that some students have this problem because they do not know when a behavior is inappropriate. If this is the case, set limits and then give examples that will demonstrate when the behavior is appropriate and when it is inappropriate. These examples can be used to actively teach the student when to engage in the behavior without affecting the limit placed on the behavior. For example, if a student asks too many questions, the teacher might allow the student ten questions each morning. When the teacher discusses the plan with the student, she would use examples of inappropriate and appropriate questions to help the student learn the best times to use the ten questions. During implementation, the teacher might help the student evaluate whether to ask a question by asking, "Diane, do you know the answer to that question? Are you sure you want to use one of your tickets for that question?" When the student asks an appropriate question, provide verbal feedback. "Diane, that was a good question. You need that information to get started." And finally, when the student has learned to make judgments, give the student corrective feedback as necessary. "Diane, you just used a question to get information that wasn't important. Think carefully before you ask your next question."

Mr. Hunter: (Principal)	Let's define limits for disrespectful interactions by looking at the list of situations you generated and defining the boundaries by example. We'll make a list of disrespectful behaviors that Carly might engage in and a list of more responsible alternative behaviors.

Mrs. Parson and Mr. Hunter make a list of disrespectful behaviors and responsible alternative behaviors (Figure P5).

Because an element of subjectivity is unavoidable in deciding whether a behavior is acceptable or unacceptable, providing examples will help you define consistent limits when faced with misbehaviors in your classroom. Once established, teach these limits to the student.

E. Select consequences for misbehavior.
Complete this step separately for each category of misbehavior.

I. Consider some guidelines for selecting consequences.

- Consistency is the most important factor.

- It is easier to consistently implement a mild consequence than a severe consequence. If the behavior occurs 18 times a day, choose a consequence that can be easily implemented 18 times a day.

- When implementing any consequence, the student must be treated with dignity and respect—belittlement has no place in the teacher's repertoire.

Figure P5: *Carly's Defined Limits*

Situation: Mrs. Parson says, "Good morning, Carly."	
Responsible behavior to encourage:	*Disrespectful behavior to correct:*
In a friendly or neutral tone, Carly says, "Good morning" or "How are you?" Carly responds with a smile or nod.	Carly says in a mocking tone, "Good morning, Mrs. Parson." Carly turns her back on Mrs. Parson.
Situation: Mrs. Parson says, "Class, line up," or gives any general class direction.	
Responsible behavior to encourage:	*Disrespectful behavior to correct:*
Carly gets in line without comment. Carly says, "I'm not finished. Do I have time to get this part done?"	Carly says, "Why should I?" Carly mimics Mrs. Parson.
Situation: Mrs. Parson gives an assignment.	
Responsible behavior to encourage:	*Disrespectful behavior to correct:*
Carly • gets busy on the assignment without comment. • asks a question to clarify what she needs to do on the assignment.	Carly • mimics, "Do problems 1–10." • says, "That's a joke." • asks, "Why should I do it?" • calls Mrs. Parson a name. • sulks.

- The student should get very little adult or peer attention when you are implementing a consequence for misbehavior.

- The consequence should be implemented as privately as possible; the student should not be "put on display."

- If the teacher stays calm when implementing a consequence, the teacher's behavior is less likely to reinforce the student.

- When possible, the consequence should have some logical association to the misbehavior, such as time owed for distracting behavior.

- The student should be informed in advance that a given behavior will lead to a given consequence.

- Consequences for misbehavior alone are not sufficient; the student should be given attention and encouragement when he is behaving responsibly.

2.   Avoid common errors when selecting consequences.

Avoid differential consequences based on the severity of the problem. Though it may seem logical to establish a set of consequences based on the severity of the misbehavior, such as a set of mild/medium/severe consequences, subjectivity may affect a teacher's ability to be consistent. For example, if a student has trouble being respectful, he might be reprimanded for a minor comment, given a timeout for a moderate incident, and sent to the office for flagrant disrespect. The problem with this type of system is that it forces the teacher to make continual judgments regarding the severity of the misbehavior. If the misbehavior occurs frequently, even the most tolerant teacher can be stressed out and nonobjective as he or she tries to make numerous judgments throughout the day, while still trying to teach.

Even if the teacher effectively implements a system of differentiated consequences, students may believe the system is spurious. "Sometimes the teacher does nothing, and other times she gets all bent out of shape and sends me to the principal." Consequences tend to be more effective when they are clear and consistent. "Each time you are disrespectful, you will go to the timeout area and write down what you did that was disrespectful."

Avoid designing sequential consequences. In a sequential plan, consequences become progressively more severe each time a student engages in misbehavior. For example, the system might dictate that the student's name be written on the board as a warning for the first infraction. For the second infraction, the student owes time after class. For the third infraction, the student is kept after school and his parents are contacted, and for the fourth infraction, the student is sent to the office.

Sequential consequences tend to be effective for students who engage in misbehavior infrequently, and they may work for a teacher who has the misbehaving student for only one period. However, sequential systems are difficult to implement when teachers have the same students throughout the day. If a student engages in frequent mild misbehavior and the teacher is consistent, the student may end up in the office by the middle of each morning for several incidents of mild misbehavior. The teacher will have to make the difficult choice

Consequences tend to be more effective when they are clear and consistent.

of being consistent or overly harsh every time the student engages in a mild misbehavior, such as making annoying noises or talking at inappropriate times.

As they are reluctant to send students to the office for minor misbehavior, many teachers opt for a second mistake—inconsistency. The first time the student misbehaves, his name goes on the board. Ten minutes later, the student engages in minor misbehavior and owes time after class. But a half hour later, the student engages in minor misbehavior—a disrespectful comment—and the teacher begins stalling. "Oh, Tim's comments weren't so bad. I don't want to have to call his parents about him being mildly sarcastic." As the student grows a little bolder, another check might go on the board and the teacher has to face a call to the parents. Now things get very tricky for the teacher. If the student is disrespectful again, according to the system, he must be sent to the office, but perhaps it is only 10:00 a.m. Because sequential consequences tend to become harsher as time goes on, they are difficult to implement with fairness or consistency.

3. Consider the many options available for consequences.

Select a consequence for each unacceptable behavior that will be the most effective in teaching the student to behave responsibly and the least intrusive to the flow of classroom activities. Consequences can be determined collaboratively. Devise and plan them with an administrator, an interventionist, or with input from the student. If you want to include the student in the process of selecting consequences, first review the list of possible consequences and select some you think would be most reasonable. Many options are available.

Note: This list of possible consequences is similar to the menu of classroom-based consequences in "Pre-Intervention: Classroom Management Strategies." See this chapter at the beginning of the book for more information on devising and implementing a menu of consequences.

INTERVENTION

P

Ignoring

When a student misbehaves to gain the teacher's attention, ignoring is the most effective consequence. When the student misbehaves, the teacher continues on as if the behavior didn't occur. By failing to respond, both verbally and nonverbally, the teacher communicates to the student, "You need to be responsible for your own behavior."

When ignoring is used as a response to misbehavior, the teacher must seek opportunities to give the student attention by interacting positively—saying "hello" to the student, engaging in friendly inter-actions, and providing positive feedback when possible. By ignoring irresponsible behavior and interacting with the student when she is behaving responsibly, the student will learn that she can get attention easily by behaving responsibly.

Caution: Ignoring is a difficult technique to implement. If a student misbehaves to get teacher attention, behavior is likely to worsen before it gets better. If the student has a long history of getting attention through negative means, she will try harder to get attention in the way she has been most successful—through misbehavior. Though difficult to deal with, worsening behavior is a sign that ignoring will eventually work. Give ignoring at least two weeks of consistent implementation before making a judgment regarding its effectiveness.

Gentle verbal reprimands

When the student does not know that a behavior is unacceptable or is unaware of when he engages in a particular behavior, provide a gentle verbal reprimand. A gentle verbal reprimand reminds the student that he is engaging (or about to engage) in inappropriate behavior. A fluent and gentle verbal reprimand, given in a neutral or supportive tone, provides the student with useful information about the nature of his behavior. "Malcolm, when I hear that edge in your voice, I know that you are starting to get argumentative. Please try that statement again, but in a less argumentative tone."

Keep the following in mind when providing a gentle verbal reprimand:

- Move to the student if possible. Reprimands from across the room tend to be ineffective.
- Calmly state what the student should be doing.
- Offer praise as soon as the student begins to exhibit more acceptable behavior.
- Avoid increasing the emotional intensity of repeated feedback if a reprimand must be repeated. The student is less likely to be reinforced for the misbehavior by a short, neutral statement than by an angry or lengthy attempt to correct his behavior.

Verbal cues and warnings

When a student's misbehavior starts to slide from appropriate behavior into inappropriate behavior, a verbal warning may be an appropriate consequence prior to a more severe consequence (such as in-class timeout or time owed). As the student's behavior begins to deteriorate, the teacher might say something like: "Ellis, your tone of voice is starting to sound impatient. You need to take a deep breath. Then lower your voice."

Delaying

When a student engages in excessive misbehavior to get teacher attention, delaying discussion or implementation of consequences may be an appropriate response, as students often find that delays are not reinforcing. If students do not get immediate gratification with attention for misbehavior, many students will give up and return to productive activities. For example, in response to complaining, the teacher might say, "Mieka, that was a complaint. We can talk about it later during your discussion time." If delaying is selected as an effective response for undue tattling, the teacher might say, "Sue, you are starting to tattle. If it is not an emergency, you need to wait until after school to tell me."

Parental contact

Parents should always be kept informed of problems and successes at school. When parents are contacted about a problem, suggest that they talk to their child. Avoid saying or implying that the parents should punish the child; consequences for misbehavior that occurs at school should be implemented at school. The purpose of parental contact should simply be to keep the parents informed while encouraging the child, by every means at your disposal, to behave more responsibly.

Having an open dialogue with parents is a vital part of any intervention plan; however, parental notification should not be viewed as an effective consequence for chronic misbehavior, and parents should generally not be put in the position of having to "enforce" classroom or school rules at home. However, if the student rarely engages in misbehavior and has firm but supportive parents, parental contact as a consequence may be an option—but be wary. It is not uncommon for the parent of a student with chronic misbehavior problems to fume in exasperation, "What am I supposed to do? My child talks back to the teacher at school, and the teacher expects me to do something about it at home? As if I don't have enough to deal with." The aftermath of this kind of contact—defensiveness, a sense of helplessness, perhaps a highly emotional confrontation with the student—will likely be at best ineffective and at worst abusive.

Time owed

When a student wastes class time by engaging in frequent misbehavior, time owed communicates to the student that the wasted class time will be repaid during a time that is valued by the student. For example, when the student engages in misbehavior, calmly say, "That was an example of _____. You owe one minute of recess."

When time owed is used as a consequence for frequent misbehavior, it is important to use only small amounts of time for each infraction. A common error is to have the student owe an entire recess or passing period for each infraction. With frequent misbehavior, you soon run out of recesses and passing periods to take away. The teacher and student end up without needed breaks, and any potential impact from the consequence is soon lost. In most cases, owing 15 seconds to one minute per infraction is more effective than owing larger amounts of time. These small amounts of time owed also allow the teacher to be consistent with every incidence of misbehavior. If the student causes 10 disruptions that waste class time, he still owes less than three minutes, which is a manageable period of time for the teacher to implement. In comparison, the teacher who implements five minutes of time owed for each infraction would face close to an extra hour with the frequently misbehaving student. This teacher will probably find himself implementing consequences inconsistently or progressively, both of which can do as much harm as good.

> *When time owed is used as a consequence for frequent misbehavior, it is important to use only small amounts of time for each infraction.*

Decide what the student should be doing during time owed. In some early cases of misbehavior, the time might be used to discuss the problem with the student. If time is owed repeatedly and frequently, the student should sit and do nothing. The more boring time owed can be made, the better, as the student will be thinking of the many other things she would rather be doing than sitting silently.

This consequence may be difficult to implement for secondary teachers and for elementary teachers who have students for only one period, such as secondary teachers, librarians, PE teachers, or music specialists, as there are fewer opportunities during the day to implement time owed. These teachers should consider in-class timeouts as an alternative.

In-class timeout

When a student engages in misbehavior frequently, an in-class timeout communicates to the student that taking part in class activities is a privilege. When the student engages in unacceptable behavior, calmly say something like, "That was an example of _____. Go to timeout and think about other ways you might have handled that situation. You may return to your seat when the timer rings." Timeout in the room may be as simple as having the student go to a chair at the side of the classroom or to a study carrel.

Decide in advance whether or not you will specify how long the student will spend in timeout. Some teachers assign specific durations. Others structure timeout as more flexible, according to the student's behavior: "Come back and join the group when you are ready." If the timeout is to be a specific length, keep it short and set a timer so that the student isn't forgotten. Time begins when the student is in the timeout area and sitting quietly. For students in sixth grade and above, five minutes would be a reasonable period of time. With older students who refuse or delay going to the timeout area, record the amount of time they take to get to timeout and explain that they will owe that time from recess or after school. For younger students, timeout should be shorter and based on the age and sophistication of the student. One-minute timeouts are appropriate for kindergarten and first-grade students, who may need to be escorted to the timeout area.

During an in-class timeout, the student should sit and do nothing. If academically capable, the student should fill out a Behavior Improvement Form (Reproducible Form P1).

Decide in advance whether or not you will specify how long the student will spend in timeout.

Behavior Improvement Form

Name   Grade/Class   Teacher   Period/Time

1. What did you do? _____

_____

_____

_____

_____

_____

2. Why did you do it? _____

_____

_____

_____

_____

_____

3. What else could you have done? _____

_____

_____

_____

_____

_____

If the student misbehaves after returning from timeout, calmly tell him to return to the timeout area and repeat the process. It is not unusual for a student to be sent to timeout 5, 10, or even 20 times in the first several days of implementing a new timeout procedure. So long as the time period is not unduly harsh and you have established that the student is capable of exhibiting the expected behavior, this high level of implementation is OK. Be calm and consistent, and with persistence and time this approach will resolve many chronic behavior problems.

Behavior Improvement Form

For a student who engages in misbehavior without thinking, it may be useful to have her fill out a Behavior Improvement Form (Reproducible P1) so that she can reflect on her actions and think about ways to avoid future problems. The Behavior Improvement Form requires that the student think about her actions, begin assuming responsibility, and learn how to take control by identifying more-acceptable ways of handling similar situations. When the student misbehaves, calmly say, "That was an example of _____. You need to think about what you did and fill out a Behavior Improvement Form." Using this form as a consequence requires that the student have sophisticated reading and writing skills and would not be appropriate for a student who struggles academically.

Note: Copies of this and other Defining Limits and Establishing Consequences forms are also provided on the accompanying CD.

Out-of-class timeout

When a student's misbehavior is too disruptive for her to remain in the classroom, an out-of-class consequence may be necessary. However, this consequence should be reserved only for behavior that is highly disruptive—overt defiance toward adults, loud and sustained noncompliance, screaming, or highly aggressive behavior such as hitting or hair pulling. (See "Intervention G: Managing Physically Dangerous Behavior" and "Intervention H: Managing Severely Disruptive Behavior" for more on ways to address highly disruptive behavior.)

INTERVENTION

P

Caution: The only occasion when an out-of-class consequence should be used is when a behavior simply cannot be tolerated in the classroom because it impedes the learning of other students or threatens the student or others. Be sure you and your school administrators are in agreement about which behaviors are at a level of severity to warrant the student's removal from class and where students whose behavior crosses the threshold should be sent.

When a behavioral episode is escalating toward a Code Red situation and one or more students' misbehavior is so severe as to warrant removal from the classroom, you must know exactly what procedures to follow. These procedures should have been set in advance, possibly on a schoolwide basis, as discussed in Interventions G and H. Before you are faced with having to handle such a disruption, take time to answer some questions for yourself:

- Which behaviors warrant removal from the classroom?
- Where will the student go for an out-of-class timeout?
- How long will the student spend in the timeout location?
- What will the student do while she is in timeout?
- Who will supervise the student while she is in timeout?
- How will the student transition back to the classroom?

Because dismissing a student from his regularly scheduled class has the potential to cause as many problems as it solves, such as escalating the student's behavior, your answers to these questions are important. If a student is not in class, where should he be? Typical out-of-class detention locations include the hallway, the office, another classroom, or a designated timeout room.

After-school or lunchtime detentions
After-school or lunchtime detentions are generally not effective for frequent or chronic misbehavior. The delay between the misbehavior

and the consequence simply dilutes the consequence's effectiveness. If Charlie misbehaves early in the day and is informed that he will have detention, the consequence can't be imposed again should the misbehavior occur a second time. The functional result is that teachers are unable to respond consistently to misbehavior.

Mr. Hunter: (Principal)	Now that we've defined disrespectful interactions and identified some respectful alternatives, let's decide on a consequence for disrespect. Some options include gentle verbal reprimands, ignoring, time owed from lunch, timeout in your classroom, the Behavior Improvement Form, timeout in another location, and some others. Any thoughts?
Mrs. Parson: (Teacher)	I have reprimanded Carly till I'm blue in the face. Ignoring doesn't seem appropriate because it might send the wrong message. I would rather not send Carly out of the room. I don't want her to think I can't handle her. Timeout in the room might be an option. Tell me more about time owed and the Behavior Improvement Form.

After discussing the various options, the principal and teacher agree that Carly should go to in-class timeout when she has been disrespectful.

F. **Define the limits and identify the consequences for any other priority problems identified in Step 1D.**

If the intervention will focus multiple misbehaviors, complete Step 1D (defining limits) and Step 1E (selecting consequences) for any additional problems that were identified as priorities.

Mrs. Parson and the principal begin work on Carly's excessive complaining. After defining limits by example, they decide that a good response to her complaining would be delaying. Because Carly is academically capable, they decide that she should write down her complaints for later discussion with the teacher. This consequence will require Carly to determine whether her complaint is important enough to write down and also provides Mrs. Parson with a consistent response.

Mrs. Parson:	I can actually see how this might work. If Carly says, "You give us stupid work," then I can say, "Carly, that's a complaint we can talk about. Write it in your log and we will discuss it during our meeting tomorrow."

Mr. Hunter: (Principal)	How should we address Carly's negotiating problem?
Mrs. Parson: (Teacher)	Couldn't I handle it the same way? I could say, "If you really want to talk about shorter assignments, write it down and we can discuss it on Tuesday."

G. Determine ways to encourage responsible behavior.

In addition to Defining Limits and Establishing Consequences, the intervention plan must include procedures that focus on helping the student learn responsible behavior. While working on eliminating or reducing inappropriate behavior through the use of consequences may be necessary, a corresponding emphasis must be placed on encouragement and support for things the student does well. Consequences alone may work in the short run, but they will work in the long run only when the student learns that it feels good to be responsible.

In some cases, encouragement, praise, and positive attention will be sufficient to change behavior (see "Intervention E: Increasing Positive Interactions"). In other cases, support and encouragement for appropriate behavior may need to be as structured as a reinforcement contract. To determine procedures for encouraging responsible behavior, consider the following options:

Brainstorm a list of ways to focus on appropriate behavior and select procedures that will be manageable. First, make a list of what the student does responsibly. Include special strengths, abilities, and activities the student likes to do. Next, generate a list of strategies that would provide the student with positive interactions. Include procedures that would highlight and encourage what the student already does well.

Emphasis must be placed on encouragement and support for things the student does well.

The principal and teacher brainstorm a list of Carly's strengths and then develop another list of strategies to keep the intervention focused on encouragement rather than consequences.

Mrs. Parson:	I get so annoyed with Carly that I forget about her good qualities. But she is a good reader, and she likes to read aloud.

Within a few minutes, the principal and teacher have brainstormed many of Carly's strengths and abilities and compiled a list of possible positive procedures (Figure P6).

INTERVENTION

P

Figure P6: *Possible Positive Procedures*

Responsible Behavior and Student Strengths	Procedures for Encouraging the Student
Reads well	Tutor to a younger student
Artistic	Special jobs—help with the bulletin board
Nice smile	Increase positive interactions (see "Intervention E: Increasing Positive Interactions")
Can be humorous	Make editorial cartoons for class news
Completes work	Special notes to her mom
Articulate	Read news bulletin

Mr. Hunter: (Principal)	Do you want to include any of these things in the plan?
Mrs. Parson:	I'd like to do it all. It's too bad there isn't more time.
Mr. Hunter:	I don't want you to feel overwhelmed. Let's look at increasing positive interactions. This procedure doesn't require a lot of extra work. It just involves you being more conscious about when and how you interact with Carly. Maybe some of the other things can be implemented intermittently.
Mrs. Parson:	That's a good idea. I think I'll go ahead and set her up as a tutor, though. She reads beautifully, and I know Mrs. Johnson has been recruiting students to read to kindergarten children. Carly might enjoy the responsibility.

Consider implementing other interventions. For some students, you may wish to set up a more intensive intervention. Reproducible Form P2, the intervention Decision Guide, includes a descriptor in the left column of the type of student that may benefit from each intervention. If this broad statement is true, it means that the intervention specified in the intervention column is worth considering. Check all interventions that may be applicable in the third column. Then choose one, two, or three interventions to create a comprehensive plan to supplement Defining Limits and Establishing Consequences.

H. Identify how to determine whether the intervention is helping the student meet her goals.

Because behavior is difficult to change, small improvements may go unnoticed unless you have an objective way to determine whether the intervention is having a positive effect. Evaluation might include a frequency count or duration record of the misbehavior. It might involve direct observation of the student to see whether she is improving, a direct count of the behavior, or a self-monitoring system. See "Intervention D: Data Collection and Debriefing" for more information on possible methods of data collection.

Reproducible Form P2: *Decision Guide*

Intervention P:
Defining Limits and Establishing Consequences

Decision Guide

Presenting Behavior	Check if true	Intervention	Date of implementation	Effectiveness (+/−)
Several or many students in class misbehave.		**Pre-Intervention:** *Classroom Management*		
The student may not know what is expected.		**Intervention A:** *Planned Discussion*		
The student may have an underlying academic problem.		**Intervention B:** *Academic Assistance*		
The student has difficulty with motivation and may not understand how to reach a goal.		**Intervention C:** *Goal Setting*		
The student's behavior appears to be chronic and resistant to simple intervention.		**Intervention D:** *Data Collection and Debriefing*		
The student gets a lot of attention from adults or peers for misbehavior or failure.		**Intervention E:** *Increasing Positive Interactions*		
The reason the behavior is occuring chronically needs to be analyzed and incorporated into the intervention plan.		**Intervention F:** *STOIC Analysis and Intervention*		
The student's escalating behavior is physically dangerous or poses a threat to physical safety.		**Intervention G:** *Managing Physically Dangerous Behavior and Threats of Targeted Violence*		
The behavior is so severe that the teacher cannot continue to teach.		**Intervention H:** *Managing Severely Disruptive Behavior*		
The student is impulsive and has difficulty maintaining emotional control.		**Intervention I:** *Managing the Cycle of Emotional Escalation*		
The student seems to be unaware of when he/she engages in inappropriate behavior.		**Intervention J:** *Cueing and Precorrecting*		
The student has some motivation to change or learn new behaviors.		**Intervention K:** *Self-Monitoring and Self-Evaluation*		
The student makes negative comments about him- or herself and others.		**Intervention L:** *Positive Self-Talk and Attribution Training*		
The student does not know how to meet expectations.		**Intervention M:** *Teaching Replacement Behavior*		
The student cannot or will not communicate verbally.		**Intervention N:** *Functional Communication*		
The misbehavior is a firmly established part of the student's behavior.		**Intervention O:** *Structured Reinforcement Systems*		
It is difficult to be consistent with the student because it is not always clear when the student has crossed the line between appropriate and inappropriate behavior.		**Intervention P:** *Defining Limits and Establishing Consequences*		
Consequences for misbehavior seem necessary but do not seem to work.				
Teacher feels anxious, worried, discouraged, or angry about one or more students.		**Intervention Q:** *Relaxation and Stress Management*		
The student seems anxious, lethargic, or depressed.		**Intervention R:** *Internalizing Problems and Mental Health*		

EARLY STAGE

When consequences are a major part of an intervention plan, it may be wise to keep anecdotal notes of any difficult situations that arise. If limits have been difficult to establish, having a record can help work out glitches over time. By recording times when you were unsure of how to respond, further clarification can be made about unclear boundaries.

Mr. Hunter: (Principal)	Let's see. We'll need to see how the plan is working. With complaining, we have a built-in system. We'll have Carly's log of complaints to look at. We can evaluate it for sheer quantity and also the quality of the complaints.
Mrs. Parson: (Teacher)	Yes, and I can also keep track of how often she's in timeout. I'll keep an index card in my pocket and make a tally mark any time I have to send her to timeout.
Mr. Hunter:	That sounds great!
Mrs. Parson:	I could also write down situations that I don't quite know how to handle. I know that there will be times when I won't know what to do.
Mr. Hunter:	Yes, then we can talk it over with Carly and determine how these situations ought to be handled.

I. Review, rehearse, and refine the plan.

To complete the planning process, revisit the problems and review the limits and consequences set for this intervention. Ask as many what-if questions as possible. For each situation, you should be able to quickly categorize the behavior as appropriate or inappropriate and identify how to respond to the situation. If you are unable to do so, review Steps 1D and 1E.

You should be able to quickly categorize the behavior as appropriate or inappropriate and identify how to respond to the situation.

Mr. Hunter:	What if Carly was in a cooperative learning group, saw you coming, and stuck her tongue out at you?
Mrs. Parson:	I'd say, "Carly that was disrespectful. You need to go to timeout for one minute to think about your behavior."
Mr. Hunter:	What if Carly said, "This assignment is stupid. Do I have to do it?"
Mrs. Parson:	I'd say, "Carly that was a complaint. If it's important, write it in your log and we will discuss it in our meeting on Tuesday."
Mr. Hunter:	What if she tries to change your mind, saying, "What if I do half the assignment and then write in my log. The assignment is too long to do both."

| Mrs. Parson: | I'd probably begin feeling frustrated, but I would tell her to do the whole assignment and write both of her complaints in the log. |
| Mr. Hunter: | Carly is very astute, so you will need to work really hard at staying physically relaxed as you go on to do other things. |

Continue rehearsing until you are consistent in categorizing behavior and identifying the corresponding procedure for responding to the behavior. This process will increase consistency and build confidence in your ability to deal with the problem. The list of misbehaviors that you brainstormed in the first steps of the planning process can be useful for this mental rehearsal. If you are unsure of any limit or consequence, this process will assist in refining the plan.

J. Determine who will meet with the student to discuss and finalize the plan.

Use professional judgment to determine who will be present when the plan is discussed with the student. Some students are more responsive to a discussion when only one adult is present. In other cases, it will be important to include the parents, an interventionist, or a teaching assistant who will be working with the student.

Mr. Hunter: (Principal)	Would meeting from 1:00 to 2:00 Thursday work? I can get someone to cover your class. I know you've spent a lot of time on this. Hopefully, it will save us all time in the long run, though.
Mrs. Parson: (Teacher)	That's fine. There's an art assignment that I can give during that time of the day. The kids go to electives part of the time. It would be easy for someone to supervise the remainder of my class, and I don't need to be there.
Mr. Hunter:	Would you like to include Carly's mother?
Mrs. Parson:	I think so. She seems to be having the same problems with Carly. If she could also use similar procedures, maybe we could create some synergy and get Carly going in a more positive direction.

Step 2: Meet with the student

At your first meeting for this intervention, review your perception of the problem and establish goals with the student in a positive, nonconfrontational way.

Mrs. Parson: (Teacher)	Carly, as you know, we are meeting today to see if we can work on a plan to make life a little happier for all of us. I hate to see us get irritated with one another. I think we can have a great year if we can iron out our problems.
Mr. Hunter: (Principal)	Carly, what do you think the problem is?
Carly:	I don't know.
Mrs. Parson:	Carly, Mr. Hunter and I went through a lot of different situations that have occurred. Let me share some of the situations with you. (Mrs. Parson shares a list of situations.)
Carly:	So?
Mrs. Parson:	We've decided that we need to help you work on being respectful to adults and on reducing complaining. We want you to be able to express your opinion, but we know that you will be a very unhappy adult if you don't learn to do it respectfully and within reasonable bounds. What do you think?
Carly:	I don't care.
Mr. Hunter:	That's OK, Carly. We care. Let's begin work on disrespect first.

A. Begin with one priority and provide instruction on the difference between acceptable and unacceptable behavior through discussion, modeling, role-playing, and verbal rehearsal.

Actively teach the concept of the limits between acceptable and unacceptable behavior through demonstration and examples. Through discussing, modeling, role-playing, and verbal rehearsal, the student can begin the process of learning the difference between goal behavior and inappropriate behavior. Think about how you might teach the concept of the strike zone to a young baseball player.

Mr. Hunter: (Principal)	What I want to do is share a situation with you and then go through some examples of behavior that would be disrespectful. Then we'll identify more responsible ways the same situation might be handled.
	What if Mrs. Parson says "Good morning" to you? If you ignore her, that would be disrespectful. If you respond in this tone of voice, (sarcastically) "Good morning," it would be disrespectful. It would be respectful to nod your head at Mrs. Parson in acknowledgment. What else could you do?
Carly:	Say "Good morning."
Mr. Hunter:	Yes. Listen to me say "Good morning" in different ways and tell me which ways were disrespectful or respectful.

Carly, the teacher, the principal, and Carly's mother continue through several situations, defining limits by listening to the tone and content of various comments Carly might make.

Mr. Hunter:	OK, Carly. Let's pretend I'm you and you are Mrs. Parson. Can you imagine me being you? I'm going to walk in the room as if I'm you and you say, "Good morning."
Carly:	(Laughs) "Good morning, Carly."
Mr. Hunter:	(Playing Carly, gives a disgusted look) OK, Carly. Was that respectful or disrespectful?

After you and the student discuss and rehearse examples that were generated in the first step of the planning process, check the student's understanding by asking questions about ways to handle different situations. This verbal rehearsal will help you determine whether the student understands how to behave more appropriately and follow the intervention plan. If discrepancies in interpretation are noted, work together to come to a common understanding.

B. Explain consequences, rehearsing various situations.
Throughout the discussion, the student should have many opportunities to provide input. Explain consequences fully. If ignoring will be used, let the student know that you will ignore some misbehaviors, but not the student. Role-play situations so the student knows exactly what will happen if she makes a mistake. The student should know that it is OK to make errors and that consequences will help her learn from her mistakes.

Make sure the student understands that each time she crosses the line into unacceptable behavior, you will implement consequences. Also let her know that when she does not cross that line, you will let her know how responsible she is.

C. Define the limits and explain the consequences for any additional problems.

D. Discuss the positive aspects of the intervention plan, such as rewards that may be earned or positive feedback that the student will receive.

E. Schedule a time to discuss progress.

F. Review the roles and responsibilities of all participants.

G. Conclude the meeting with words of encouragement.

Be sure the student understands that the plan is designed to help her manage her own behavior. Even if the student does not participate fully in the discussion, adults should keep the discussion focused on the maturity, growth, and greater independence this intervention may bring the student. Let the student know that her input is valued and that she can make suggestions about the plan during later planned discussions.

Step 3: Implement the plan.

Meet regularly to fine-tune the plan. If this intervention is in response to a chronic behavior problem, you and the interventionist should plan to meet weekly until the plan is working smoothly. Examine anecdotal records. As you work with the plan, recognize that persistent problems require some trial and error. Remember that it is impossible to have an answer for every problem, and modifications may be necessary.

Whenever a behavioral limit needs clarifying, the information should be shared with the student as soon as possible. Explain to the student, "We need to change the plan a bit. Starting today, if you do _____, then the consequence will be _____."

A. Evaluate the impact of the intervention, making revisions and adjustments as necessary.

Monitor student progress. If gradual progress does not occur within two weeks, review the procedures that are being used to encourage responsible behavior. The plan may lack a positive focus. If gradual progress still does not occur within three weeks, consider modifying the consequences and tightening the limits.

B. Once the student experiences consistent success, provide continued support, follow-up, and encouragement.

As the student begins experiencing success, misbehavior will occur less often; therefore, consequences will need to be used less frequently. This provides a natural fading process. However, even after the student is being successful, she will occasionally make mistakes. A consistent response to misbehavior should be maintained throughout the year.

CONCLUSION

When consequences for misbehavior are implemented, plans often do not adequately define the limits between desired behavior and undesirable behavior. This often results in inconsistent, emotional patterns of interaction between the teacher and the student, leading to failure of the intervention plan.

To help the student learn to behave more responsibly, the plan needs to be designed so that the student receives very clear and consistent information about the benefits of behaving responsibly and the consequences for behaving irresponsibly. To achieve this consistency, intervention plans should assist teachers in doing the following:

- defining limits
- teaching students limits
- implementing consequences calmly and consistently
- encouraging responsible behavior

When these elements are in place, intervention plans have a much greater chance of making a difference for students who need guidance and support as they make major changes in their behavior.

The plan needs to be designed so that the student receives very clear and consistent information about the benefits of behaving responsibly and the consequences for behaving irresponsibly.

REFERENCES

Baer, D. (1987). Weak contingencies, strong contingencies, and many behaviors to change. *Journal of Applied Behavior Analysis, 20,* 335–337.

Bear, G. G. (1998). School discipline in the United States: Prevention, correction, and long-term social development. *School Psychology Review, 27,* 14–32.

INTERVENTION

P

Cook, B. G., Landrum, T. J., Tankersley, M., & Kauffman, J. M. (2003). Bringing research to bear on practice: Effecting evidence-based instruction for students with emotional or behavioral disorders. *Education and Treatment of Children, 26*, 345–361.

Donnellan, A. M., & LaVigna, G. W. (1990). Myths about punishment. In A. C. Repp & N. N. Singh (Eds.), *Perspectives on the use of nonaversive and aversive interventions for persons with developmental disabilities* (pp. 33–57). Sycamore, IL: Sycamore.

Emmer, E. T., Evertson, C. M., & Worsham, M. E. (2003). *Classroom management for secondary teachers* (6th ed.). Boston: Allyn & Bacon.

Evertson, C. M., Emmer, E. T., & Worsham, M. E. (2003). *Classroom management for elementary teachers* (6th ed.). Boston: Allyn & Bacon.

Horner, R. H. (2002). On the status of knowledge for using punishment: A commentary. *Journal of Applied Behavior Analysis, 35*, 465–467.

Kauffman, J. M. (2005). *Characteristics of emotional and behavioral disorders of children and youth* (8th ed.). Upper Saddle River, NJ: Prentice-Hall.

Koestner, R., Ryan, R. M., Bernieri, F., & Holt, K. (1984). Setting limits on children's behavior: The differential effects of controlling versus informational styles on intrinsic motivation and creativity. *Journal of Personality, 52*, 233–248.

Lerman, D. C., & Vorndran, C. M. (2002). On the status of knowledge for using punishment: Implications for treating behavior disorders. *Journal of Applied Behavior Analysis, 35*, 431–464.

Magee, S. K., & Ellis, J. (2000). Extinction effects during the assessment of multiple problem behaviors. *Journal of Applied Behavior Analysis, 33*, 313–316.

O'Leary, K. D., Kaufman, K. F., Kass, R. E., and Drabman, R. S. (1970). The effects of loud and soft reprimands on the behavior of disruptive students. *Exceptional Children, 37*, 145–155.

O'Leary, K. D., & O'Leary, S. G. (1977). *Classroom management: The successful use of behavior modification* (2nd ed.). New York: Pergamon Press.

Rhode, G., Jenson, W. R., & Reavis, H. K. (1992). *The tough kid book: Practical classroom management strategies*. Longmont, CO: Sopris West.

Rosenshine, B., & Stevens, R. (1986). Teaching functions. In M.C. Wittrock (Ed.), *Handbook of research on teaching* (3rd ed., pp. 376–391). New York: Macmillan.

Spradlin, J. E. (2002). Punishment: A primary process? *Journal of Applied Behavior Analysis, 35*, 475–477.

Sprick, R. S. (2006). *Discipline in the secondary classroom: A positive approach to behavior management* (2nd ed.). San Francisco: John Wiley & Sons.

Sprick, R. S., Garrison, M., & Howard, L. M. (1998). *CHAMPs: A proactive and positive approach to classroom management.* Longmont, CO: Sopris West.

Sprick, R. S., & Howard, L. M. (1995). *The teacher's encyclopedia on behavior management: 100 problems/500 plans.* Eugene, OR: Pacific Northwest Publishing.

Wielkiewicz, R.M. (1986). *Behavior management in the schools.* New York: Pergamon Press.

Reproducible Materials

The following reproducible materials may be used in conjunction with "Intervention P: Defining Limits and Establishing Consequences." Copies are provided in the chapter and on the CD. Permission is given for individual classroom teachers to reproduce any forms labeled "Reproducible" for classroom use. Reproduction of these materials for an entire school system is prohibited without express permission of the publisher.

Reproducible Step-by-Step Summary, p. 729
Reproducible Form P1: Behavior Improvement Form, p. 714
Reproducible Form P2: Decision Guide, p. 720

INTERVENTION

DEFINING LIMITS AND
ESTABLISHING CONSEQUENCES

Step-by-Step Summary

Following is a summary of the steps involved in Intervention P. It is important to use professional judgment, adjusting procedures to meet the needs of the situation and the individual. See the chapter "Intervention P: Defining Limits and Establishing Consequences" for a detailed description of this intervention.

STEP 1   Develop a plan.

A. Identify all the problem behaviors the student exhibits.

B. Categorize the problems.

C. Select intervention priorities.
  1. How manageable will the change be?
  2. How important is resolving the problem?

D. Define limits for the top intervention priorities (that is, what constitutes acceptable and unacceptable behaviors).
  1. Define limits by rule.
  2. Define limits by example.
  3. Define limits in terms of quantity (how much is too much).

E. Select consequences for misbehavior. (Repeat for each category of misbehavior.)
  1. Consider some guidelines for selecting consequences.
  2. Avoid common errors when selecting consequences.
  3. Consider the many options available for consequences.

F. Define the limits and identify the consequences for any other priority problems identified in Step 1D.

G. Determine ways to encourage responsible behavior.

H. Identify how to determine whether the intervention is helping the student meet her goals.

I. Review, rehearse, and refine the plan.

J. Determine who will meet with the student to discuss and finalize the plan.

INTERVENTION **P**

STEP 2 — Meet with the student.

A. Begin with one priority and provide instruction on the difference between acceptable and unacceptable behavior through discussion, modeling, role-playing, and verbal rehearsal.

B. Explain consequences, rehearsing various situations.

C. Define the limits and explain the consequences for any additional problems.

D. Discuss the positive aspects of the intervention plan, such as rewards that may be earned or positive feedback that the student will receive.

E. Schedule a time to discuss progress.

F. Review the roles and responsibilities of all participants.

G. Conclude the meeting with words of encouragement.

STEP 3 — Implement the plan.

A. Evaluate the impact of the intervention, making revisions and adjustments as necessary.

B. Once the student experiences consistent success, provide continued support, follow-up, and encouragement.

Relaxation and Stress Management

The teacher feels worried, discouraged, or angry about one or more students

PURPOSE

THIS INTERVENTION, unlike others, is directed toward the classroom teacher—to help him or her implement the interventions in this book, maintain positive expectations for all students in the face of trying conditions, and deal with frustration, burnout, and out-of-control classrooms.

The hope is that this intervention will help you reduce your level of stress. Though especially helpful for teachers who are feeling burned out, irritated, or tense, Relaxation and Stress Management provides procedures that can help anyone approach the day in a less harried and more relaxed manner. Relaxation and Stress Management is especially appropriate when a student's behavior is upsetting and distracting or when it's hard to imagine doing anything more to help students improve their behavior. The six easy techniques presented in this chapter may help you feel less burdened by the pressures of teaching.

A stressed-out teacher may have unwanted recurring thoughts. If you hear yourself thinking or making any of the following statements, consider this intervention to help reduce your stress and improve your ability to interact productively with students:

- "I am always exhausted."
- "I have to admit, I just don't like this kid."
- "How can I be expected to do any more? I have 26 other students in the room."
- "They make me so mad. It's impossible to remain calm."
- "I just want that student out of my room!"
- "There isn't enough time to get anything done."

When we are overly tense, we are rarely at our best.

RATIONALE

It may at first seem odd that this intervention is geared toward you, not your students. After all, the students have the behavior problems. But working with students and implementing any of the interventions in this book requires that you be at your best—fresh, positive, optimistic, and willing to persevere as long as it takes to find an intervention plan that will help each student who needs it.

When we are overly tense, we are rarely at our best. This is true in any field. A baseball player who knows in advance that he is going to be scouted at a game may worry so much that by the time the scout arrives, he is agitated, makes unforced fielding errors, and strikes out every time he is at bat. The harder he tries, the worse things get. Everyone has probably experienced a similar situation at some time or another.

It's natural that tension can build for teachers, whether dealing with one difficult student or a roomful of them. Students who have a history of chronic behavior problems are adept at creating volatile and punishing situations at school, and teachers may suffer from these situations if they do not find an effective method of dealing with the stress. If a student comes from an environment where he has no power, he may learn to use misbehavior as a way to demonstrate his influence on adults. "Look how mad I can make the teacher. I wonder how mad I can make her tomorrow." Upsetting the teacher becomes a game. If several children in the classroom join in the game, it can become an undeclared conspiracy, with the teacher absorbing the brunt of the punishment and becoming more and more tense as the school year wears on. This is only one example of the various reasons teachers sometimes find themselves in a destructive cycle of tension, but regardless of the reason, teachers who find themselves spiraling must find ways to escape the cycle.

Mr. Mallory wakes up in the morning, dreading having to face another day with Toby. "If Toby just weren't in my class, life at school would be so different," he thinks. Going through morning routines and driving to school, Mr. Mallory imagines all the awful things that are likely to occur that day. By the time his students arrive, Mr. Mallory is already tied in knots. Jessica passes a note to Toby, and Mr. Mallory hits the ceiling, blowing the situation out of proportion and embarrassing Jessica and Toby in the process. Both students feel unfairly singled out and angry, and as a result they spend the day trying to "get back" at Mr. Mallory. Other students, seeing what is happening, join in. The war is on—teacher versus students. It becomes a vicious and destructive cycle, and unfortunately for Mr. Mallory, he's outnumbered (see Figure Q1).

Figure Q1: *Destructive Cycles of Tension*

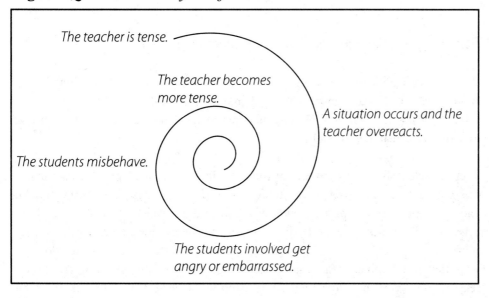

The teacher is tense.

The teacher becomes more tense.

A situation occurs and the teacher overreacts.

The students misbehave.

The students involved get angry or embarrassed.

This chapter presents six strategies you can use to break the cycle and begin to relax, enjoy teaching more, and increase your day-to-day effectiveness, especially when implementing interventions with at-risk students.

THE STRESS REDUCTION MENU: A RESOURCE FOR TEACHERS AND INTERVENTIONISTS

The following menu of stress reduction techniques provides a series of procedures to consider when you're dealing with the daily pressures of teaching. These strategies are designed to help you keep the challenges of teaching in perspective and maintain high expectations for the success of your students. For some situations, a combination of two or three techniques may be most effective.

1. Practice deep muscle relaxation.

2. Keep a confidential journal.

3. Work on a balanced lifestyle.

4. Promote positive self-talk and attribution.

5. Practice visualization.

6. Identify student strengths.

Strategies for relaxing and unwinding can also be helpful to students. "Intervention R: Internalizing Problems and Mental Health" has a relaxation script and a range of activities that can be used to help students who exhibit signs of anxiety or depression.

Strategy 1: Practice deep muscle relaxation.

Teaching can be an exhausting profession, with hard-to-teach students, large class sizes, administrative pressures, demanding parents, a shortage of materials, and/or a continual lack of time as constants. Each of these factors can lead to stress and teacher burnout.

Deep muscle relaxation is probably the most important strategy of all. Learning this physical skill is a useful way to deal with the pressures of teaching. Tension and relaxation are at opposite ends of a continuum used to describe the physical state of muscles in your body. Learning to keep your muscles in a relaxed state can help you improve your performance no matter what you are doing—activities and hobbies, teaching, or learning. Consciously focusing on staying relaxed gives you the added benefit of using less energy to accomplish the same tasks, meaning you will be less tired at the end of the day.

Though people tend to associate tension with a state of mind, it is also related to the physical state of the body. As teachers respond to the pressures of the day, muscles can become more and more tense. Physical tension can drain

Though people tend to associate tension with a state of mind, it is also related to the physical state of the body.

INTERVENTION

Q

your energy until patience wears thin and little is accomplished. As stress builds, it becomes more difficult to keep classroom problems in perspective. This carries over into the rest of life and has a major impact on general health and well-being. Statements such as following may indicate that physical tension is playing a part in a teacher's stress level:

- "I am exhausted by the end of the day."
- "I can't stay calm. I'm a nervous wreck."
- "Sometimes I find myself yelling about little things."
- "I never feel rested."
- "I can hardly wait until vacation."

These are common comments for those who are working in schools under challenging, complex circumstances. If you identify with any of these comments, consider learning deep muscle relaxation techniques. Try the following 30-second experiment:

> For about 15 seconds, as you read this passage, tense as many muscle groups as you can. Tense the muscles in both feet. Tense your legs and buttocks. Tense your torso, arms, neck, and face. While keeping your entire body tense, visualize a child engaging in an annoying behavior. Imagine how you might handle the problem. Then reverse this process. Relax all the tense muscles as deeply as possible for 15 seconds while you imagine how you might handle the same problem.

If you are like most people, little productive thought can occur when your body is too tense. Additionally, it is probably hard to imagine being patient with a student who is doing something annoying when you feel tense. Though this experiment may seem artificial, sometimes teachers are unconsciously tense in the same way you were just consciously tense. When a teacher feels a sense of emotional exhaustion or fatigue at the end of the day, this kind of excessive physical tension may have been building throughout the day.

Relaxation is not a mystical phenomenon. It simply involves knowing how to relax your muscles. However, learning this physical skill is like learning any new skill. It requires daily practice. Like learning to ride a bike, it is initially awkward and may be difficult to use during stressful interactions. However, once learned, deep muscle relaxation can be a valuable lifelong skill. Learning to relax can increase your effectiveness with students, your enjoyment of teaching, and your appreciation of each day.

Figure Q2: *Muscle Tension and Relaxation Exercise*

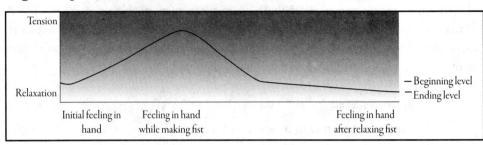

Follow these procedures to learn deep muscle relaxation.

A. Learn to tense and relax your muscles.

1. Put one hand in your lap or on a table.

2. Concentrate on how your hand feels.

3. Make a fist. Squeeze for five seconds.

4. Concentrate on how the muscles feel when they are tense.

5. Slowly unclench your fist.

6. Relax the muscles so there is no tension in your hand.

7. Concentrate on how your muscles feel.

Figure Q2 illustrates what you have just experienced. Note that the tension level goes up when you make a fist and then drops to a lower level of tension as you release the fist. In the following exercises, you will work with each muscle group in your body. By consciously tensing and relaxing your muscles, you can learn to reduce tension throughout your body.

B. Schedule daily practice sessions.

Plan to practice deep muscle relaxation at specific times of day so that you can begin to make the process more natural and beneficial. Two scripts are provided at the end of this strategy section to guide these daily practice sessions (Figures Q5 and Q6 on pages 738 and 740). These sessions should be conducted in a quiet place, as free from interruptions as possible. Try to fit in one to three sessions daily for three to five minutes each. Practice can be scheduled before school begins, during breaks, or as soon as school is out. If you tend to have hectic breaks—making copies, making phone calls, grabbing a cup of coffee, and so on—schedule a relaxation exercise during part of the break. By trying to do a million little tasks during your break, you may end up being more tense after a break than before. The graph in Figure Q3 shows the levels of tension for a teacher who has not been able to relax during breaks.

Figure Q3: *Teacher Stress Build-up*

Tension

Relaxation

— Ending level

— Beginning level

8:15	9:45-10:00	11:30-12:00	2:30	4:00
Students	Morning	Lunch	Students	End of
arrive	recess		dismissed	contract day

While this teacher who does not work on relaxing generally becomes more tense as the day progresses, a teacher who schedules three specific times to practice deep muscle relaxation will move through gentle peaks and valleys of tension following relaxation exercises (Figure Q4). By the end of the day, regardless of the stressful situations encountered, this teacher may actually be more relaxed than at the beginning of the day.

The teacher illustrated in Figure Q4 scheduled a three-minute relaxation exercise during morning recess, the lunch break, and again when the students were dismissed. The short, frequent breaks renewed the teacher's energy throughout the day. In each period after the relaxation exercises, the teacher faced challenges calmly, presented lessons with a fresh perspective, and was able to concentrate on the tasks to be accomplished.

C. Practice relaxation exercises by following a script.

You may wish to make an audio tape of the two relaxation scripts found at the end of this section (Figures Q5 and Q6). The tapes can be played during your daily practice sessions, or you may prefer to read through the scripts, following each instruction as you read it.

Script 1 teaches you to focus on each muscle group in the body by tensing a set of muscles and then gradually relaxing them. For people new to the

Figure Q4: *Teacher Tension and Relaxation*

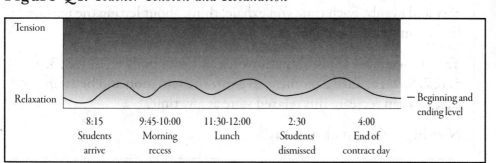

Tension

Relaxation

— Beginning and ending level

8:15	9:45-10:00	11:30-12:00	2:30	4:00
Students	Morning	Lunch	Students	End of
arrive	recess		dismissed	contract day

Figure Q5: *Muscle Tension/Relaxation, Script 1*

Think about the muscles in your feet. Slowly tense those muscles. Hold for five seconds. 1, 2, 3, 4, 5. Now slowly let those muscles relax. 1, 2, 3, 4, 5. Let the muscles release until they are more relaxed than when you started. Focus your attention on how those muscles now feel.

Now do the same thing with your calves. Slowly tense those muscles. Hold for five seconds. 1, 2, 3, 4, 5. Now slowly let those muscles relax. 1, 2, 3, 4, 5. Feel how relaxed your calves and feet are in this relaxed state.

Focus on your thighs. Slowly tense those muscles. Hold for five seconds. 1, 2, 3, 4, 5. Gradually let go of the tension. Take 10 seconds. 1, 2, 3, 4, 5, 6, 7, 8, 9, 10. Feel how relaxed your legs and feet are.

Now concentrate on your lower torso—stomach, lower back, and seat. Slowly tense those muscles. Hold for five seconds. 1, 2, 3, 4, 5. Gradually let go of the tension until there's no more tension in your lower torso. Feel how relaxed your lower body is. Pay special attention to your lower back. Let those muscles release.

Now concentrate on your hands and arms. Make fists. Tighten your biceps and triceps. Hold for five seconds. 1, 2, 3, 4, 5. Gradually release. Let the tension go. Let the muscles go until they are more relaxed than when you started.

Focus on your neck, shoulders, and chest. Gradually tense up. Hold for five seconds. 1, 2, 3, 4, 5. Release.

Concentrate on the muscles in your face. Close your eyes as tightly as possible. Scrunch up your face. Hold for five seconds. 1, 2, 3, 4, 5. Now let go. Relax those muscles. Don't frown. Don't smile. Simply relax the muscles in your face.

Now take a few moments to concentrate on your breathing. Breathe easy and evenly. Each time you exhale, think about letting the tension in your muscles dissolve away.

Take 10 seconds. Think about how relaxed your body feels. 1, 2, 3, 4, 5, 6, 7, 8, 9, 10. Take a moment to enjoy the sensation and be aware that you can recreate this relaxed state at any time.

Now begin the rest of your day.

process of deep muscle relaxation, this is the best script to start with. The contrast of feeling the muscles tensing and then relaxing is an important part of learning deep muscle relaxation. Use this exercise several times a day for a couple of weeks before using the second script. This process takes about five or six minutes.

Script 2 is designed for people who are more experienced with deep muscle relaxation. This script goes straight to steps involving relaxation of each part of the body. This process takes about three minutes, but it requires experience and practice to be as effective as the tension/release method described in Script 1.

In both scripts, the relaxation process begins with the feet and progresses up to the head. You may wish to experiment by reversing the order, going from head to feet. There is no right or correct way to practice this skill. Your objective is to learn to relax the muscles of your body—thus reducing tension.

With practice and experience, you will be able to use this skill without depending on the scripts or tapes. You can then use deep muscle relaxation while sitting in meetings, while standing in a check-out line at a store, or while waiting for your students to return from lunch. Once the skill is mastered, you will be able to achieve a relaxed state within 10 to 30 seconds.

Sit upright in a reasonably comfortable chair and begin the exercise.

Strategy 2: Keep a confidential journal.

Allocate a few minutes at the end of each day to write in a journal. Write in stream-of-consciousness mode. Include challenges, frustrations, concerns, doubts, questions, and successes. This process has many benefits:

- It can help you sort out problems. Often the process of writing has a clarifying effect. Complex situations that seem overwhelming often become clear as they are described in writing.

- It can provide an emotional release. Annoying or disturbing situations can be put to rest when you have an opportunity to express your feelings, doubts, and frustrations.

- It can help you recognize successes.

With practice and experience, you will be able to use this skill without depending on the scripts or tapes.

INTERVENTION

Q

Figure Q6: *Muscle Relaxation, Script 2*

Think about the muscles in your feet. Now slowly let those muscles relax. 1, 2, 3, 4, 5. Let all of the tension drain from those muscles. Focus your attention on how those muscles now feel.

Now do the same thing with your calves. Let those muscles relax. 1, 2, 3, 4, 5. Feel how relaxed your calves and feet are in this relaxed state.

Focus on your thighs. Gradually let go of the tension. Take 10 seconds. 1, 2, 3, 4, 5, 6, 7, 8, 9, 10. Feel how relaxed your legs and feet are.

Now concentrate on your lower torso—stomach, lower back, and seat. Gradually let go of the tension until there's no more tension in your lower torso. 1, 2, 3, 4, 5. Feel how relaxed your lower body is. Pay special attention to your lower back. Let those muscles release. (Pause.)

Now concentrate on your hands and arms. Gradually release for five seconds and let the tension go. 1, 2, 3, 4, 5. Focus on your neck, shoulders, and chest. Release. 1, 2, 3, 4, 5.

Concentrate on the muscles in your face. Now let go. Relax those muscles. Don't frown. Don't smile. Simply relax those muscles. (Pause.)

Now take a few moments to concentrate on your breathing. Breathe easy and evenly. Each time your exhale, think about letting the tension in your muscles dissolve away.

Take 10 seconds. Think about how relaxed your body feels. 1, 2, 3, 4, 5, 6, 7, 8, 9, 10. Take a moment to enjoy this sensation.

Now begin the rest of your day.

- It can give closure to the day. Once a journal entry is completed, put the school day aside for the rest of the evening. This can help you avoid churning things over and over so that you can begin the next day with a fresh start.

Journals must be confidential. A journal is not a formal record of events; it is a process for sorting through the day. You don't need to be objective, fair, consistent, or diplomatic in your writing. From time to time, you may even use the process of writing to vent frustration or anger. Because your reflections may include subjective thoughts, the journal should probably be written and stored at home. Leaving the journal where a student or colleague might read it could cause hurt feelings or have serious repercussions. For example, if you write during school hours or on a school computer, it could be argued that the document is an official record, not a personal reflection.

Strategy 3: Cultivate a balanced lifestyle.

Teaching can be an entirely absorbing profession. Boredom is rarely a problem, as it seems that there is always something more to be done. Educators often thrive on total engagement. Though this can be positive, making work more productive and fulfilling, immersion in teaching can also become an obsession. Trying to do everything all the time can result in feeling overwhelmed. When a problem occurs, it is easy to become consumed. Problems and overwork can build until worry and stress are severe and debilitating.

"I am spending virtually every waking moment working. I don't spend time with my husband. I don't even go to church anymore. There is no way I can possibly do any more."

"My students Alex and Vanessa have the entire class under their control. They clown around. They are smart-mouthed. They misbehave, and I can see them looking around for approval from the rest of the kids. I don't feel like I can teach. My stomach is in knots. I go out to dinner, and all I can think about is what happened that day, what I should have done, what I'm going to do if . . . . I go to bed thinking about this class, and I wake up thinking about it."

The concept of a balanced lifestyle is based on the idea that three aspects of life—career, relationships with others, and relationship with one's self—should be nurtured (see Figure Q7). If any one aspect becomes too consuming, it takes away from the others, potentially throwing all aspects of life out of balance. For example, if a person is so wrapped up in work that she ignores her family, this can eventually lead to strife and turmoil at home, which can

Trying to do everything all the time can result in feeling overwhelmed.

Figure Q7: *Three Aspects of a Balanced Lifestyle*

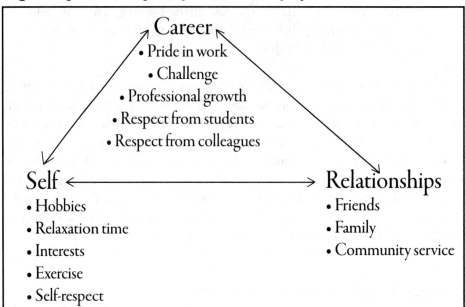

in turn affect work performance. Thus, an unhealthy commitment to work can eventually reduce effectiveness on the job.

Because stress and burnout are potential hazards of teaching, it is wise to occasionally check the balance between work and other necessary experiences in your life. Ask yourself the following questions:

- How much time do I have each day that is not devoted to teaching?
- Do I have time for interests outside of teaching?
- Do I have time to devote to important relationships in my life?

If you are concerned about any of your answers, examine the time you devote to professional responsibilities. Consider the amount of time you want to spend doing things other than teaching. Set up a schedule of your time outside of school hours. Then do yourself a favor. Put teaching aside during the time you make for yourself and for your important relationships.

Strategy 4: Promote positive self-talk and attribution.

Negative thinking is a natural response to problems, but it can perpetuate more problems and build tension. Negative thinking can turn into a self-fulfilling prophecy. Each thought provides one more piece of evidence about how hopeless a situation is. "I just got upset again. See, there is no way that I can stay calm. These situations really get to me. I can't . . . ." If you think or

Figure Q8: *Restructuring Self-Talk*

Negative Self-Talk	Positive Self-Talk
"I just don't know what to do."	"I don't know what to do, but I will find a solution."
"These kids know how to get to me."	"I am an adult, and I can stay calm."
"There is no way I can ignore Rick's behavior."	"When Rick is trying to bug me, I can pretend I don't even notice."
"Martha will never learn to be responsible for her behavior."	"Martha has to work very hard to be responsible. I will help her as long as it takes."

make statements similar to the following, you may wish to consider working on restructuring your self-talk:

- "I just don't know what to do."
- "These kids know how to get to me."
- "There is no way I can ignore Rick's behavior."
- "Martha will never learn to be responsible for her behavior."

By restructuring your self-talk, you can help yourself develop positive expectations. This procedure is a conscious effort to frame every experience, whether positive or negative, as a learning experience. By thinking positively, you can convince yourself to act in ways that will reduce tension (Figure Q8).

A positive outlook can make a tremendous difference in your ability to deal effectively with a problem situation or a particularly challenging student. To restructure your own self-talk, follow these procedures:

A. Schedule daily practice.

If you decide that restructuring your self-talk can help you establish a more positive outlook, determine specific times to make positive comments to yourself. You might want to begin each school day with one or two positive thoughts. Other natural times for structured positive self-talk include during breaks, as students are lining up, before the students return from lunch, as the day ends, and prior to going home.

If you are writing each day in a journal (see Strategy 2), you might wish to conclude each entry with two to three positive statements. If you are working on deep muscle relaxation (Strategy 1), you might want to conclude each session with two to three positive statements. A few minutes of deep muscle relaxation followed by positive self-talk can help you prepare for the next part of your day.

B. Work actively to frame problems using positive self-talk.

It is easy for educators to believe that they need to be perfect. However, when working with people on a daily basis, perfection is not a reasonable goal. When you have a problem, learn to frame it in a positive direction. For example, if you are trying to ignore a student's inappropriate behavior and have difficulty doing so, your positive self-talk might run as follows: "Even though Melissa is getting to me today, I am in charge. I can ignore her efforts to get attention negatively." Framing the situation positively helps you to think more productively about future interactions and leaves you dwelling on the positive.

> Note: Be careful to avoid falling into patterns of negativity when discussing issues and problems with colleagues. It is healthy to bring up concerns and collaboratively explore possible solutions. It is not healthy, however, to continuously vent and complain about students. In some schools, the staff room is the most negative environment in the school. If this is true, you should avoid getting sucked into these patterns for your own health and well-being.

Strategy 5: Practice visualization.

Visualization practice can be very productive at the end of the day. If you are having difficulty working with a group of students or an individual, mentally rehearse successful responses to various situations:

- Identify situations that have caused problems in the past.
- Mentally rehearse how to handle these situations in the future.
- Visualize each situation in its entirety in as much detail as possible.
- If your visualization begins to veer toward a negative outcome, "rewind" the mental image and try again.

Replay actual situations from the day. If you handled a situation as planned, pat yourself on the back. If you are disappointed in a situation, mentally reset the scene and view yourself handling the situation more effectively. For example, if a student's behavior makes you angry, picture yourself ignoring the student and calmly continuing with your lessons or quietly implementing consequences as necessary. (For more information on ignoring and implementation of consequences, see "Intervention P: Defining Limits and Establishing Consequences.")

Visualization is an efficient way to practice a new or difficult skill. Repeatedly visualizing yourself handling a complex situation well increases the likelihood that you will handle the real-life situation more effectively.

Strategy 6: Identify student strengths.

Every teacher eventually encounters a student who makes life seem miserable. Despite our best efforts, some students force adults into adversarial relationships. In extreme cases, the interactions between a student and teacher can become so hostile that it is difficult to see any positive characteristics in the student. However, a student with lots of problems cannot learn to mature and become more responsible if the teacher is merely trying to squelch problems. Student maturity and self-discipline can grow from helping students take pride in their strengths and abilities; therefore, you may need to make an active effort to help yourself identify student strengths. Only then can you be effective in helping a student build the self-confidence and pride to mature and behave appropriately. In addition, the very act of focusing on student strengths will reduce any tendency on your part to view the situation as hopeless. Feelings of hopelessness contribute greatly to stress. Simply reminding yourself of student strengths can help you realize that there are positive features within the student and the situation to build upon. These reminders can help you realize that the situation is far from hopeless.

If you have a student who is difficult to like or whose shortcomings seem to overshadow his strengths, it is important to recognize and focus periodically on that student's positive characteristics. You might set aside time to make a list of the student's positive characteristics, strengths, abilities, and good behaviors. The greater the problem, the more often you should take time to focus on positive traits.

If you have difficulty coming up with positive attributes or student strengths, ask yourself the following types of questions:

Simply reminding yourself of student strengths can help you realize that there are positive features within the student and the situation to build upon.

- What does the student do when he is not misbehaving?
- How does the student interact with other students?
- What does the student do during lunch?
- Does the student have outside interests?

If you still have difficulty identifying a student's strengths, have someone help you. It is sometimes difficult to see past a student's problems when you have to deal with the student's misbehaviors on a daily basis. Have the school interventionist, a previous teacher, the administrator, or the student's parents help you identify the student's strengths and abilities.

Note: "Intervention L: Self-Talk and Attribution Training" and "Intervention R: Internalizing Problems and Mental Health" provide other suggestions and activities that may be helpful. Although these chapters suggest interventions for students, the same techniques can be useful for adults as part of a concentrated effort to maintain mental and physical health.

CONCLUSION

Relaxation and Stress Management can help a teacher reduce the tension and anxiety of dealing with the daily pressures of the classroom. It is particularly helpful when a teacher has to deal with difficult students. Learning to relax does not guarantee that you will be a better teacher, nor will it change the problem behavior of your students. However, learning to relax may increase the probability that you can successfully implement other interventions aimed directly at helping students. Because classroom teachers are so important in the success of at-risk students, Relaxation and Stress Management may be useful in combination with other interventions.

REFERENCES

Abelson, A. G. (1986). A factor analytic study of job satisfaction among special educators. *Educational and Psychological Measurement, 46,* 37–43.

Benson, H. (1994). *Beyond the relaxation response.* Berkeley, CA: Berkeley Publishing.

Campbell, J. D. (1990). The show must go on . . . even when personal tragedy strikes. *Learning, 19*(4), 22–24.

Davis, M. D., Eshelman, E. R., & McKay, M. (2000). *The relaxation & stress reduction workbook* (5th ed.). Oakland, CA: New Harbinger Publications.

Gold, Y. (1987). Stress reduction programs to prevent teacher burnout. *Education, 107,* 338–340.

Jenkins, S., & Calhoun, J. F. (1991). Teacher stress: Issues and interventions. *Psychology in the Schools, 28*(1), 60–70.

Kalker, P. (1984). Teacher stress and burnout: Causes and coping strategies. *Contemporary Education, 56*(1), 16–19.

Keavney, G., & Sinclair, K. (1978). Teacher concerns and teacher anxiety: A neglected topic of classroom research. *Review of Educational Research, 48,* 273–290.

Kyriacou, C. (1987). Teacher stress and burnout: An international review. *Educational Research, 29,* 146–152.

Long, B. (1988). Stress management for school personnel: Stress inoculation training and exercise. *Psychology in the Schools, 25,* 314–324.

Martinez, J. G. (1989). Cooling off before burning out. *Academic Therapy, 24*(3), 271–284.

Maslach, C. (1982). *Burnout: The cost of caring.* Englewood Cliffs, NJ: Consulting Psychologists Press.

Mazur, P., & Lynch, M. (1989). Differential impact of administrative, organizational, and personality factors on teacher burnout. *Teaching and Teacher Education, 5,* 337–353.

Peterson, A. V., & Parr, G. D. (1986). Controlling stress and burnout: Self-help for educators. *Texas Technical Journal of Education, 13*(1), 41–47.

Russell, D., Altmaier, E., & Van Velzen, D. (1987). Job-related stress, social support and burnout among classroom teachers. *Journal of Applied Psychology, 72,* 269–274.

Sapolsky, R. M. (1998). *Why zebras don't get ulcers: A guide to stress, stress-related diseases, and coping.* New York: W. H. Freeman.

Schmid, K. D., Schatz, C. J., Walter, M. B., Shidla, M. C., Leone, P. E., & Trickett, E. J. (1990). Proving help: Characteristics and correlates of stress, burnout, and accomplishment across three groups of teachers. In R. B. Rutherford, Jr., & S. A. DiGangi (Eds.), *Severe behavior disorders of children and youth* (Vol. 13, pp. 115–127). Reston, VA: Council for Children with Behavioral Disorders.

Schon, D. A. (1983). *The reflective practitioner.* New York: Basic Books.

Selye, H. (1978). *The stress of life.* New York: McGraw Hill.

Slife, B. D. (1988). Coping strategies for teachers. *Academic Therapy, 24*(1), 9–19.

Sobel, D. S., & Orstein, R. (1997). *The healthy mind, healthy body handbook.* Los Altos, CA: DRx.

Sparks, D. (1983). Practical solutions for teacher stress. *Theory Into Practice, 22*(1), 33–42.

Sutton, G. W., & Huberty, T. J. (1984). An evaluation of teacher stress and job satisfaction. *Education, 105*(2), 189–192.

Weiskopf, P. (1980). Burnout among teachers of exceptional children. *Exceptional Children, 47*, 18–23.

Wyly, J., & Frusher, S. (1990). Stressors and coping strategies of teachers. *Rural Educator, 11*(2), 29–32.

 # Reproducible Materials

The following reproducible materials may be used in conjunction with "Intervention Q: Relaxation and Stress Management." Copies are provided in the chapter and on the CD. Permission is given for individual classroom teachers to reproduce any forms labeled "Reproducible" for classroom use. Reproduction of these materials for an entire school system is prohibited without express permission of the publisher.

Reproducible Step-by-Step Summary, p. 749

Reproducible Step-by-Step Summary

INTERVENTION

RELAXATION AND STRESS MANAGEMENT

Step-by-Step Summary

Following is a summary of the steps involved in Intervention Q, which provide suggestions for managing your own tensions and emotions. See the chapter "Intervention Q: Relaxation and Stress Management" for a detailed description of this intervention.

THE STRESS REDUCTION MENU: A RESOURCE FOR TEACHERS AND INTERVENTIONISTS

STRATEGY 1 Practice deep muscle relaxation.

A. Learn to tense and relax your muscles.

B. Schedule daily practice sessions.

C. Practice relaxation exercises by following a script.

STRATEGY 2 Keep a confidential journal.

STRATEGY 3 Cultivate a balanced lifestyle.

STRATEGY 4 Promote positive self-talk and attribution.

A. Schedule daily practice.

B. Work actively to frame problems using positive self-talk.

STRATEGY 5 Practice visualization.

STRATEGY 6 Identify student strengths.

Barbara A. Gueldner, Ph.D.
Ken Merrell, Ph.D.

Internalizing Problems and Mental Health

▌ *The student seems anxious, lethargic, or depressed*

PURPOSE

THIS INTERVENTION may assist students with problems associated with anxiety, lethargy, or depression.

THIS INTERVENTION IS APPROPRIATE FOR:

Depression
- feeling sad
- having no interest in everyday or enjoyable activities
- seeming irritable
- sleeping too much or too little
- physically slowing down or seeming agitated
- feeling fatigued or showing lack of energy
- feeling worthless or guilty
- having trouble concentrating and making decisions
- complaining of physical aches and pains
- being preoccupied with death

Anxiety

- feeling generally uncomfortable or fearful
- avoiding or withdrawing from situations that provoke feelings of discomfort or fear
- experiencing physiological or bodily responses such as sweating, shaking, nausea, and/or headaches
- being irritable
- panicking
- worrying about a variety of situations: taking a test, talking to a teacher about an assignment, separating from a caregiver, contracting germs or diseases, going to school, or even talking to peers
- misinterpreting common unpleasant or difficult situations so that they seem especially threatening or "catastrophic"

INTRODUCTION

Internalizing problems such as depression and anxiety are mental health concerns that are often difficult to understand and detect, particularly in children. Compared with externalizing problems such as hyperactivity, impulsive behavior, and aggression, internalizing problems are more difficult to observe and assist with because they tend to be privately experienced. Consequently, these problems are often misunderstood and underidentified among children and adolescents.

The most common internalizing problems are depression and anxiety. Statistically, it is estimated that at least one or two children in a typical classroom of 30 students—perhaps 4 to 5 percent overall—experience internalizing problems severe enough to impair their functioning and quality of life. It is likely that these students would benefit from intervention.

Not all of the characteristics of depression must be present for a diagnosis of depression, but the presence of five or more of the characteristics listed at the beginning of this chapter suggest that depression may be a significant concern, particularly if the symptoms are intense and prolonged. It is important to understand that at least one of the two hallmark characteristics of depression—feeling sad or losing interest in participating in everyday activities—must be present to meet the clinical definition of depression. With children—especially younger children—irritability is often a prominent symptom.

Internalizing problems are more difficult to observe and assist with because they tend to be privately experienced.

INTERVENTION

R

Note: If you are concerned that a student is seriously depressed, wants to harm himself, wants to harm others, or is in imminent danger of being harmed, see the "When Additional Help Is Indicated" section at the end of the chapter. A student experiencing severe and chronic mental health problems may need more comprehensive services than are offered in the typical school setting. Make sure you understand your school's policies and required practices prior to making any referrals.

Many of the characteristics of anxiety are similar to symptoms of depression, such as sleep disturbances, problems concentrating, fatigue, and irritability. In fact, anxiety and depression can and frequently do occur simultaneously. Children experiencing depression and anxiety may withdraw from interacting with peers, be paralyzed by shyness, have problems with social skills, and have unrealistic expectations for their social performance or a chronically negative perception of themselves. They may complain of physical aches and pains, symptoms that might actually be caused by emotional distress rather than a physical problem. Because children experiencing depression and anxiety symptoms may also have known or unknown medical problems, physical symptoms should not be dismissed as being related solely to their mental health—or "all in their head."

COMMON QUESTIONS ABOUT INTERNALIZING PROBLEMS

What causes internalizing problems?

A student's internalizing problems can be the product of biological or environmental factors and are often due to the interaction of both. Biological factors may include abnormalities in neurotransmitter transmission in the brain (such as with the brain chemicals serotonin and norepinephrine) as well as malfunctions in the endocrine system (such as thyroid and adrenal gland functioning), each of which have been linked to anxiety and depression. Temperament, which also has a biological basis, may influence a child's predisposition to internalizing problems. Even infants who are naturally excitable and sensitive to new stimuli may become agitated and difficult to soothe.

Environmental factors such as strained or dysfunctional family relationships, poor communication skills, and parental depression can significantly influence the development of depression and anxiety in children. For example, when parents model anxious ways of responding to stressful situations (e.g., focusing on the worst possible outcome), a child may develop similar ways of coping with life's inevitable problems. Acute and chronic exposure to stressors such as poverty, divorce, abuse, natural disasters, and hospitalization can increase the risk that a child will develop internalizing problems.

Simply being exposed to stressors or maladaptive modeling does not automatically lead to depression and anxiety. How students perceive and interpret events in their lives and the world around them strongly influences the course of their mental health. In other words, the way we think about and respond to the everyday challenges of life influences whether our challenges and vulnerabilities actually lead to the development of depression or anxiety. The goal of prevention and intervention efforts is to give children skills they can use to offset any negative effects they experience when biological factors cannot be altered and life stressors are unavoidable.

How do internalizing problems affect children in their daily lives?

Children can be anywhere from mildly to significantly affected in their daily functioning when they are depressed or anxious. There is increasing evidence that students' mental health is directly related to school performance. If a student is too depressed to get out of bed in the morning and attend school, academic performance is sure to suffer. Occasional crying spells, constant daydreaming, frequent requests for reassurance, sporadic work completion, and declining peer relationships may interfere with routine tasks. Students who are overly concerned with what others think of them may not ask for a teacher's help on assignments and may avoid activities most kids enjoy or shun social interactions with peers.

Unfortunately, when anxiety and depression go untreated, symptoms may persist and even worsen over time. For some children, these difficulties become so serious and unrelenting that going to school and doing regular activities seem like too much effort. Schoolwork is not completed, and grades drop. This can lead to a vicious cycle in which growing failure in school eventually becomes evidence of perceived internal failures and shortcomings, leading such students to a deeper belief in their inability to function in school. These students may come to believe that they really are worthless or incapable of performing any better. Beliefs such as these may eventually become self-fulfilling prophecies as these students alienate peers with their dark moods, irritability, and negativity. Alcohol and other substance abuse has also been linked to untreated internalizing problems as well as suicidal thoughts and behaviors. Ultimately, school attendance, employment, relationships, and enjoyment of life may be significantly affected if internalizing problems are not addressed.

What can be done to help children experiencing internalizing problems?

Schools are in a unique position to bolster students' resiliency—their ability to bounce back during difficult times. Because teachers are already trained in effective instructional practices, many teachers are using their expertise to teach strategies that focus on social and emotional education. There is increasing evidence that *resiliency skills* can be learned through explicit instruction and practice. Students can learn skills to cope with environmental stressors and biological predispositions. Some teachers also use packaged programs; acquiring resiliency skills through specially designed instructional programs or strategies is commonly referred to as *social and emotional learning* (SEL). SEL skills can be taught to all students as a classwide instructional activity, to small groups, or one-to-one when indicated.

RATIONALE

The most effective strategies for alleviating anxiety and depression symptoms in children focus on changing behaviors and thoughts associated with them and teaching children more about emotions in general. Behaviorally based strategies include inserting fun activities into the school day, engaging students in behaviors that are incompatible with feeling anxious (for example, deep breathing), or encouraging and reinforcing students to engage in non-depressive behaviors (for example, making eye contact). Cognitive strategies focus on helping students identify the negative thoughts and beliefs that accompany depression and anxiety and then working on challenging and replacing these maladaptive perceptions with more realistic views. A depressed or anxious child might have unwanted or intrusive thoughts such as "I'm stupid," "I feel dizzy and scared; I think I'm going crazy," "I feel like I'm going to die," and "I'll never feel better so life isn't worth living anymore." Simply educating children about their symptoms to help them better understand and talk through why they are having these thoughts and feeling is often extremely beneficial and leads to improvement in functioning.

Most often, students who are having significant mental health and behavioral problems should receive prompt services from intervention specialists

Ultimately, school attendance, employment, relationships, and enjoyment of life may be significantly affected if internalizing problems are not addressed.

INTERVENTION

R

such as school psychologists, counselors, and social workers. These students may be set up with one-to-one interventions or referred to participate in intervention groups with other students who have similar issues such as lack of social skills or anger management problems. Both of these service delivery models are good ways to assist students in need.

Increasingly, teachers and other school personnel are implementing another strategy: presenting mental health and emotional well-being ideas to entire classes and interweaving these programs throughout the usual language arts, health, or social studies curricula. By doing so, schools ensure that *all* children are learning skills that can help them cope with uncomfortable feelings, thoughts, and behaviors. By including children who are not experiencing depression and anxiety in the present moment, this strategy acknowledges and addresses the reality that virtually all students will eventually encounter life stressors that will test their coping resources, whether they are considered at-risk or not. This practice may also help positively affect those students whose symptoms have not yet been identified but who are struggling with mental health issues or internalizing problems. If these students have access to information about their problems, they may seek out more help.

IMPLEMENTATION STEPS

This section describes a variety of commonly used intervention strategies, explains how to choose an intervention for a student with internalizing problems and monitor progress, and helps you identify the resources you may need.

Step 1: Assess the situation and choose an intervention strategy.

A. Identify the problem and symptoms to be targeted.

When working with an individual student, conduct assessments to identify the problem of concern and describe it in enough detail so everyone involved in planning and implementing will understand the exact nature and scope of the problem. Internalizing problems are difficult to assess because they are often experienced privately rather than expressed outwardly. Compounding this difficulty, a thorough assessment requires that data be gathered using a variety of methods (observations, interviews, behavior rating scales) from a variety of sources (student, teacher, parent, community) and in multiple settings (different classes or times of day, at home, and in school). School personnel who are trained in social, emotional, and behavior-based assessment and data collection are probably the best resource for gathering this information. Review the collected data to determine the best course of action. The Social and Emotional Assessment Worksheet (Reproducible Form R1) can be used to organize, summarize, and analyze the assessment data and link the information to an appropriate intervention.

Note: Copies of this form and other Internalizing Problems and Mental Health forms are also provided on the CD. These reproducible forms can be used with students as part of classwide, group, or individual activities.

B. Choose an intervention.

There are several behaviorally and cognitively based interventions that can be successfully implemented one-to-one, in small groups, or in large-group settings, depending on how many students you think might benefit from the strategy. For example, if you have one or two students who might benefit, see if the counselor might be able to conduct small-group lessons with a few students from your class and a few from other classes. If you have many students who might benefit, these lessons can be conducted as whole-class activities. To develop the most effective intervention possible, review the following intervention strategies and determine whether they address the symptoms that are targeted for intervention.

Behavioral and cognitive strategies for individual, small-, and large-group interventions

Following are seven approaches commonly used to challenge and change depression and anxiety symptoms:

1. Emotional education

2. Behavior change

3. Cognitive change: cognitive therapy

4. Cognitive change: Rational Emotive Behavioral Therapy

5. Journal writing

6. Reducing stress

7. *Strong Start/Strong Kids/Strong Teens*: Social and emotional learning curricula

Reproducible Form R1 (1 of 2): *Social and Emotional Assessment Worksheet*

Social and Emotional Assessment Worksheet

_____ _____ _____ _____
Student   Grade/Class   Teacher/Counselor   Date

1. Student information

List major concerns and reason for assessment. _____

_____

_____

_____

2. Summary of assessment information

Write down the most important test scores, observations, and information from interviews or other assessment sources.

_____

_____

_____

_____

_____

3. Problem analysis

A. List major problems, concerns, diagnostic indicators, and so forth that are indicated and supported by the assessment information.

_____

_____

_____

_____

Reproducible Form R1 (2 of 2): *Social and Emotional Assessment Worksheet*

3. Problem analysis (continued)

B. List any hypotheses you have developed regarding the possible origins and functions of any problems that are indicated.

_____

_____

_____

_____

_____

C. How might these hypotheses be tested?

_____

_____

_____

_____

4. Problem solution and evaluation

List potential interventions that appear to be appropriate for the identified problems. Include tools or methods that might be useful for monitoring intervention progress and evaluating the intervention outcome.

_____

_____

_____

_____

_____

_____

_____

I. Emotional education

Emotional education essentially involves teaching students about feelings—how to identify feelings and understand how feelings are experienced physically, in thoughts, and in behaviors. Students are taught that feelings, thoughts, and behaviors are connected, and that some event usually triggers them. Emotional education is often used as part of a comprehensive behavior plan; however, simply teaching students about their thoughts and feelings can be quite helpful.

> Alexa is typically a talkative girl at home, but when she gets to school (the event that triggers her anxiety) she is very quiet. Her body feels tense, she finds it hard to breathe, and she feels like she has a rock in her stomach (the physical experience of anxiety). However much she tries, she cannot get the thought out of her mind that if she talks, she will embarrass herself because people will think her voice sounds strange (thoughts associated with anxiety). As a result, she rarely talks above a whisper (behavior associated with anxiety).

Simply teaching students about their thoughts and feelings can be quite helpful.

Several emotional education techniques can be used to help students learn about anxious thoughts and behaviors.

a. **Identify comfortable and uncomfortable feelings.**
   Common feelings can be experienced as being either comfortable or uncomfortable, but feelings will differ among individuals. Give students a list or flashcards with "feeling words" and ask them to decide whether each feeling is comfortable or uncomfortable. No two students experience all feelings in the same way. Some feelings are thought of as positive or negative, or as comfortable or uncomfortable, based on past experiences, mood, or other factors unique to each individual. "Surprised" is a feeling that some students might perceive as comfortable and enjoyable, while others feel it as uncomfortable and unwanted. The Feelings Identification form (Reproducible Form R2) may be useful for this activity to help students identify feelings and whether they are comfortable or uncomfortable. This form provides a variety of common feelings that students may experience.

b. **Use incomplete-sentence techniques.**
   The goal of an incomplete-sentence activity is to increase the student's awareness of the link between feelings and the situations

Reproducible Form R2: *Feelings Identification*

Feelings Identification

_____ _____ _____ _____
Student   Grade/Class   Teacher/Counselor Date

This activity will help you learn to identify comfortable and uncomfortable feelings.

Comfortable feelings make people feel good. They let you have fun and enjoy life. Uncomfortable feelings make people feel bad. They can also help people grow and change for the better. Uncomfortable feelings can help people notice and appreciate their comfortable feelings.

For one of the lists on this worksheet, put a plus sign (+) next to any words that you think describe comfortable feelings and put a minus sign (–) next to any words that you think describe uncomfortable feelings.

Feelings List 1

happy	lonely	scared	bored
angry	sad	upset	surprised
strong	proud	lonely	glad
shy	worried	tired	love

Feelings List 2

lonely	sorry	guilty	worried
happy	miserable	excited	proud
confused	strong	scared	loyal
crabby	surprised	upset	bored
serene	inspired	warm	angry
anxious	frustrated	thrilled	furious
compassionate	ignored	embarrassed	love

that provoke them. Provide the student with a sentence stem, such as "I was really angry when . . ." and ask her to complete the sentence. Modeling examples can be helpful for students who have difficulty with this task. Reproducible Form R3, About My Feelings, can be used for this activity. This worksheet can be used with individual students or in a group setting.

c. **Use a self-rating inventory for communicating feelings.**
Once students have learned how to identify their feelings, self-evaluating how well they can communicate these feelings can be beneficial, particularly for older children and adolescents. This activity can be used to assess areas for growth and goal setting. Ask students to rate how well they are able to express common emotions on a scale of "very easy" to "very hard." The Expressing Feelings Inventory (Reproducible Form R4) may be used for this activity. Students are asked to rate how easy it is to express certain feelings to other people. This worksheet can help older students monitor their progress with communicating feelings.

2. Behavior change

Behaviorally based strategies focus on changing behaviors that are associated with depression and anxiety. Examples include increasing the amount of time spent in purposeful, fun activities and having adults pay attention to and reward behaviors that usually occur when students feel good. When a student feels depressed and anxious, he often does not engage in typical childhood activities that can decrease stress (physical activity or peer interactions), and he misses out on fun and enjoyable activities that under other circumstances would boost his mood (avoiding social events with peers because of feeling fatigued or worrying what others think about him). To interrupt this negative spiral, introduce positive activities that lead to improved mood and behaviors that are rewarded. These activities are incompatible with depression and anxiety (e.g., smiling, making eye contact, and interacting with peers).

Following are two behavioral strategies that may be used as activities:

a. **Schedule enjoyable activities.**
Encourage students to purposefully increase the amount of time spent in enjoyable activities. Adults will need to help structure these activities, especially in the beginning, because depressed or anxious students may not have the energy or the organizational skills to do so. Activities should be simple in the beginning, and providing

When a student feels depressed and anxious, he often does not engage in typical childhood activities that can decrease stress (physical activity or peer interactions).

INTERVENTION

R

Reproducible Form R3: *About My Feelings*

About My Feelings

Student   Grade/Class   Teacher/Counselor   Date

Complete these sentences in your own words, using real examples about how you feel.

I feel afraid when _____

_____

I am really good at _____

_____

I get excited when _____

_____

Most of the time, I feel _____

_____

I feel upset when _____

_____

I am sad when _____

_____

I am calm when _____

_____

I was really mad when _____

_____

I am thankful for _____

_____

I am lonely when _____

_____

Reproducible Form R4: *Expressing Feelings Inventory*

Expressing Feelings Inventory

Student	Grade/Class	Teacher/Counselor	Date	

For each of the feeling words listed on the rating form below, think about how easy or hard it is for you to express those feelings to other people. Show whether it is very easy, somewhat easy, somewhat hard, or very hard for you to express those feelings by putting a check in the appropriate box. This exercise can help you see how much progress you have made and set goals for changes you might want to make in the future.

When I feel ...	How easy is it to express this emotion to other people?			
	very easy	somewhat easy	somewhat hard	very hard
angry				
love				
sad				
worried				
joyful				
excited				
surprised				
fearful				
embarrassed				
jealous				
bored				
confident				
lonely				

I think that I am (circle one):

very emotional	somewhat emotional	somewhat unemotional	very unemotional

reinforcers such as praise and encouragement may be necessary to increase the likelihood that the students continue to participate in changing their behavior. The Weekly Planning Form for Scheduling Positive Activities (Reproducible Form R5) is helpful when students would benefit from scheduling positive activities into their daily lives. Increasing positive activities can decrease symptoms of anxiety and depression.

b. Use operant conditioning techniques.

Operant conditioning techniques usually involve reinforcing desired behaviors, such as eye contact, to increase the likelihood that prosocial and nondepressed or nonanxious behaviors will continue. Reinforcers can be social (praise) or tangible (obtaining something that is desired or getting out of something) and should be given immediately after the desired behavior is observed. The key is to determine what the student finds reinforcing, because what is reinforcing to one person is not always reinforcing to another.

> Javon's teacher, Ms. Ramirez, is very concerned about Javon's behavior over the last several weeks. She notices that he rarely smiles, uses an irritable tone of voice with peers, and has stopped saying hello to her in the morning. She decides to try some operant conditioning techniques. First, Ms. Ramirez identifies the behaviors she will reinforce: Javon smiling at her or other people, saying hello in the morning, and talking in a pleasant or at least neutral tone of voice. Ms. Ramirez decides she will give him a "thumbs-up" signal every time she observes any of these behaviors because this is something she regularly uses with the students to let them know they are doing a good job. Ms. Ramirez talks to Javon before implementing this procedure, so he knows why she is giving this signal to him more frequently. They decide that if this signal does not help his behavior, they will find another signal that might work more effectively.

3. Cognitive change: Cognitive therapy

As compared with behavior strategies that focus on observable behaviors, cognitive strategies focus on what we cannot see: thoughts and beliefs.

As compared with behavior strategies that focus on observable behaviors, cognitive strategies focus on what we cannot see: thoughts and beliefs. To use cognitive strategies, the student must be able to engage in cognitive thinking and reasoning. For this reason, these strategies are best used with at least typically developed (i.e., having average intellectual abilities) adolescents and possibly younger students if they are bright and insightful. Young children or lower functioning students

Reproducible Form R5: *Weekly Planning Form for Scheduling Positive Activities*

Weekly Planning Form for Scheduling Positive Activities

Student _____ Grade/Class _____ Teacher/Counselor _____ Class _____

Date	Monday	Tuesday	Wednesday	Thursday	Friday	Saturday	Sunday
Goals for positive activities							
People who will be involved							
Materials or resources needed							

Adapted from: *Helping Students Overcome Depression and Anxiety: A Practical Guide to Internalizing Problems* (2nd ed.), by Kenneth W. Merrell. Copyright 2008 by the Guilford Press, New York. Adapted and included by permission of the publisher.

might better benefit from emotional education and behavioral activities, which require less developed processing. Three major steps (usually performed in sequence) are used with cognitive strategies:

1. Develop an awareness of emotional variability.

2. Detect automatic thoughts and identify beliefs.

3. Evaluate automatic thoughts and beliefs.

a. Develop an awareness of emotional variability.

Students are taught that thoughts, feelings, and behaviors are connected to one another and emotions vary in the degree to which they are experienced. The following two tools can be used to teach this idea: the Feelings Thermometer and the Emotional Pie.

Feelings Thermometer

Students look at a picture of a thermometer and discuss how emotions can be experienced in terms of degrees of intensity. Students may give examples of situations that provoke particular feelings such as anger, sadness, irritability, and excitement, and then discuss to what degree the emotion is experienced given the situation. The Feelings Thermometer (Reproducible Form R6) may be used to help students identify the level of intensity of particular emotions they have experienced. This worksheet provides a graphic measurement to help students understand that feelings can be experienced in varying degrees. This exercise can also be useful in a group setting to promote discussion.

Emotional Pie

Students are asked to draw a circle and divide the circle into a pie graph, with each slice representing the size of the emotion that is experienced as compared with other emotions. The Emotional Pie worksheet (Reproducible Form R7) can be used for this activity. Use this activity to help students understand that several feelings can be experienced at once and in varying amounts. This worksheet can be useful for individual students or in a group setting.

b. Detect automatic thoughts and identify beliefs.

When students are depressed or anxious, they often have thoughts that occur automatically, and they may not evaluate whether or not these thoughts are realistic. In actuality, the thoughts may be distorted or unrealistic. For example, a student who is depressed may automatically think "I can never do anything right" when presented

Reproducible Form R6: *Feelings Thermometer*

Feelings Thermometer

Student _____ Grade/Class _____ Teacher/Counselor _____ Date _____

Situation/Trigger _____

High

Medium

Low

Adapted from: *Strong Kids—Grades 3-5: A social-emotional learning curriculum*, by Kenneth W. Merrell, Dianna Carrizales, Laura Feuerborn, Barbara A. Gueldner, and Oanh K. Tran. Copyright 2007 by Paul H. Brookes Publishing Inc., Baltimore. Reprinted by permission of the publisher.

Reproducible Form R7: *Emotional Pie*

Emotional Pie

_____   _____   _____   _____
Name   Grade/Class   Teacher/Counselor   Date

This activity will help you describe how your feelings were divided up during a particular time frame, like a day or a week. Like a pie cut into different-sized slices, our feelings can take up different amounts of room in our life. Sometimes one feeling is bigger than another.

For the time period that you picked, divide the circle on this sheet into different-sized "slices" to show how much room different feelings took up in your life during that time. Pick at least two feelings and label the slices of the pie using the first letter of each feeling. Here are some examples.

N = normal mood, okay	H = happy	S = sad
T = tense	A = angry or mad	W = worried

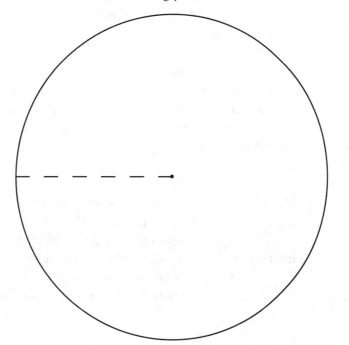

Write down the names and letters of the feelings you are including in your chart.

___ = _____   ___ = _____   ___ = _____

___ = _____   ___ = _____   ___ = _____

with a math assignment. Attached to these thoughts are beliefs about himself that can also be automatic and distorted. The student who thinks "I can never do anything right" may believe that he cannot complete the assignment because "I'm stupid and everyone else is so much smarter." Identifying these automatic thoughts and beliefs is important so that these beliefs may then be challenged. Three techniques are used to teach this idea: thought charts, cognitive replay, and hypothesizing/guessing.

Thought charts

Students are asked to keep track of their thoughts during a situation that triggers feelings and thoughts. For example, if a student is chosen last for a basketball team during PE class, he might *feel* hurt because he *believes* he is bad at everything he does. A school practitioner can help the student in this initial process by discussing his or her observations of the student's thoughts when in a particular situation or experiencing a particular emotion. The Thought Chart (Reproducible Form R8) represents one way to set up this activity. Use the chart to practice identifying automatic thoughts, feelings that are associated with the thoughts, and the situations that usually provoke these thoughts and feelings. Each student will complete his own thought chart, but the worksheet can also be used to generate a class discussion.

Cognitive replay

Instead of asking the student to chart thoughts independently, guide the student through a problem situation that happened recently, asking him to consider feelings, thoughts, and beliefs he associated with the situation.

Nicholas:	I went to the skate park last night to hang out with people from my neighborhood, but when I got there, no one said hello and nobody was skating anywhere close to me.
Interventionist:	So what were you feeling? Was it comfortable or uncomfortable? What thoughts were going through your head? What did you think about yourself?

Hypothesizing/Guessing

The teacher or interventionist offers a hypothesis or guess about the feelings, thoughts, and beliefs the student may have had in a particular situation. This strategy is particularly useful when students are having a difficult time identifying these issues.

Reproducible Form R8: *Thought Chart*

Thought Chart

Student	Grade/Class	Teacher/Counselor	Date

This exercise will help you identify some of your *automatic thoughts*—those thoughts that seem to happen without warning and without you realizing how they got there. When those thoughts are negative, they can lead to feeling depressed. Think of some situations from the past few days when you felt bad. Identify the situation and the specific feelings you had. Then, identify any automatic thoughts that seemed to go along with it.

The Situation	My Feelings	My Automatic Thoughts

Adapted from: *Helping Students Overcome Depression and Anxiety: A Practical Guide to Internalizing Problems* (2nd ed.), by Kenneth W. Merrell. Copyright 2008 by the Guilford Press, New York. Adapted and included by permission of the publisher.

c. Evaluate automatic thoughts and beliefs.

Once student's automatic thoughts and beliefs are identified, evaluate them with students to determine whether they are realistic and adaptive or useful, or unrealistic and maladaptive. Students often enjoy this part of using cognitive strategies. For many students, the idea that something could be faulty in their thinking is a new concept. The goal in this step is not to eliminate negative thoughts altogether because sometimes negative thoughts are realistic—life sometimes throws unpleasant and unexpected curveballs. Some students, however, need to learn the difference between pervasive unproductive and damaging thoughts and natural negative thoughts that may occasionally occur when something bad happens. When students can recognize automatic thoughts and beliefs and begin to evaluate them, they can cope better with life stressors and bounce back more quickly. Three strategies can assist in this process:

- identifying cognitive distortions or thinking errors

- examining the evidence

- evaluating positives and negatives

Identifying cognitive distortions or thinking errors

Cognitive distortions or thinking errors can perpetuate depression because of the way in which situations are viewed. For example, if a student tends to view *all* problems as big problems, feelings of being chronically overwhelmed and helpless tend to emerge. Challenging common thinking errors can lead to alleviation of these symptoms. In the *Strong Kids* and *Strong Teens* curricula (Merrell, et al., 2007), the following six thinking errors are used as lessons on identifying cognitive distortions: Binocular Vision, Black or White Thinking, Dark Glasses, Fortune-Telling, Making It Personal, and The Blame Game. The Common Thinking Errors worksheet (Reproducible Form R9) provides graphic representations of six common thinking errors. Use this worksheet to facilitate a discussion regarding situations that might lead students to think in unhealthy ways, leading to uncomfortable feelings and unpleasant thoughts. The form can be used as an instructional aid to illustrate this process. Students and practitioners can generate problem situations together, identify the student's feelings and thoughts, and determine whether a thinking error is present.

Reproducible Form R9: *Common Thinking Errors*

Common Thinking Errors

| Student | Grade/Class | Teacher/Counselor | Date |

Binocular Vision

Looking at things in a way that makes them seem bigger or smaller than they really are.

Black or White Thinking

Looking at things only in extreme or opposite ways (for example, good or bad, always or never, all or nothing).

Dark Glasses

Thinking about only the negative aspects of things.

Fortune-Telling

Making predictions about what will happen in the future without supporting evidence.

Making It Personal

Blaming yourself for things that are not your fault or that you have no control over.

Blame Game

Blaming others for things you should take responsibility for.

Reproducible Form R10: *Are Things Really That Bad? Three Questions*

Are Things Really That Bad?
Three Questions

Student _____   Grade/Class _____   Teacher/Counselor _____   Date _____

1. What's the evidence?

If something seems really bad, or if you are looking at something in a negative way, how much evidence is there that things are really as awful as you think they are?

_____

_____

_____

_____

2. Is there any alternative evidence?

So you are thinking that something bad is happening or might happen. Is there any evidence out there that indicates otherwise? Is there another explanation?

_____

_____

_____

_____

3. What if?

If the negative event you are thinking of really does occur, what's the worst possible thing that realistically might happen to you? Have you been through worse things before and survived? Have other people experienced a similar hardship and still survived? _____

_____

_____

_____

_____

Examining the evidence: Three questions

To determine whether thoughts and beliefs are realistic, ask three questions:

1. What's the evidence?
2. Is there any alternative evidence?
3. What if?

Reproducible Form R10, the Are Things Really That Bad? worksheet, can be used for this activity. Students are asked to find evidence for their thoughts, identify alternative evidence, and hypothesize how they would cope with the worst-case scenario. This exercise is particularly helpful for students who are feeling worried or anxious.

Soraya thinks she'll fail seventh grade if she gets a couple of failing grades in science. Soraya's teacher uses the Are Things Really That Bad? form to ask Soraya the following questions:

- What's the evidence? Ask what evidence she has to support this thought and belief.
- Is there any alternative evidence? Is there any evidence that contradicts the thought and belief?
- What if? What if it were true that she got a couple of failing grades in science? Is there anything she could do to improve the situation?

Evaluating positives and negatives

Some students become stuck thinking about the negative aspects of a situation and need reminders to consider the positive. Older children and adolescents may find it helpful to conduct a cost-benefit analysis to evaluate thoughts and beliefs, especially students who have a tendency to look at only the negative aspects of a situation. Guide students in the initial phase of using this strategy. It is OK to include negative aspects of the situation in the analysis—after all, few situations are 100 percent positive. Consider using Reproducible Form R11, Evaluating Positives and Negatives, for this activity. This exercise reminds students to consider positive aspects of a situation, especially when they are stuck on thinking about the negative. This technique works particularly well with students who are feeling sad and hopeless.

Reproducible Form R11: *Evaluating Positives and Negatives*

Evaluating Positives and Negatives

Student _____   Grade/Class _____   Teacher/Counselor _____   Date _____

Situation	Pros List the positive things about this situation.	Cons List the negative things about this situation.

4. Cognitive change: Rational-Emotive Behavior Therapy

Rational-Emotive Behavior Therapy (REBT) is a technique that is similar to cognitive therapy because a focus of REBT is challenging maladaptive thoughts. REBT is based on the assumption that symptoms of depression and anxiety develop due to irrational or mistaken thoughts, which lead to stress, feelings of guilt, low self-esteem, and difficulties solving problems. Following are some common irrational thoughts and beliefs:

- "There is something wrong with me."
- "I'll never feel better."
- "There is no point in this."
- "Nobody cares about me."

Note: If your staff or students are knowledgeable in ABC terminology regarding behavior (Antecedent, Behavior, Consequence), it may be better to avoid referring to this strategy with the ABC acronym and simply say that a three-step process can be used to find the A, *Activating event,* that leads to B, the irrational *Belief,* which then leads to C, the *Consequence* of having this irrational belief. In other words, if the ABC acronym would help people remember these steps, use it, but if it would cause confusion with existing acronyms, find another method to help staff and students remember the process.

Activating Event: Caleb tried out for the basketball team, but he didn't make the cut.

Belief: He thought, "I never get picked for anything."

Consequence: He felt worthless, ashamed, and stopped playing basketball, even though it was his favorite sport.

Once an activating event, unhealthy belief, and consequence are identified, the thought can be disputed and replaced with a more realistic way of thinking about the situation.

> **Caution:** Students sometimes have problems that are not in their complete control, and there may be some realistic justification for their thoughts and feelings. When disputing the "irrational" thought, be realistic, yet positive. For example, while a student might be upset about not making a basketball team, it is possible that his skills were not at the level it would take to make the team. You might say something like, "It's too bad you weren't picked for the team. The competition must have been pretty intense. Do you think you might still enjoy playing basketball at the rec center?"

5. Journal writing

Many students enjoy writing as a way to identify and work through their thoughts and feelings. It allows them time to reflect on their experiences and monitor their progress toward alleviating depression and anxiety. An added bonus is that journal writing helps support literacy and language development efforts in school. Expectations for journal writing should be tailored to a student's age and developmental level. A student with pre- or early writing skills may not be able to write out his thoughts in complete sentences; using story starters or artwork may facilitate communication.

Journal writing can be used alone or in conjunction with the previously described behavior and cognitive strategies. Generally, journal writing is best used on a regular basis for students to reflect on activities, thoughts, and feelings. Aim for a new journal entry at least once a week. Have students write on their own time or during the first 10 to 15 minutes of a weekly intervention session. If a student needs guidance on how to keep a journal, you might suggest any of the following ideas:

- Write about activities from the past week.
- Write about thoughts, feelings, and beliefs about a situation.
- Rate how intensely you experienced these feelings.

The Weekly Journal Entry Form with Mood Rating (Reproducible Form R12) can be used for this activity.

6. Reducing stress

Experiencing stress is part of being a student, and student reactions to stress vary. Stressors include unpleasant events (divorce, death, illness, school demands), but it is important to note that stressors can also be positive and exciting events. For example, going to prom is generally something students eagerly anticipate and look forward to, but it means that time and money will need to be spent, which can be stressful.

Chronic high stress can lead to lowered immunity as well as anxiety and depression symptoms. Common signs of stress include

- hand or body shakes
- clenching fists, teeth, and jaw
- tight muscles
- feeling like you can't do it
- fatigue
- irritability
- feeling scared, worried, or nervous

When students learn how to identify and deal with stress constructively, they dramatically improve their chances of withstanding inevitable stressors. They also get in touch with their own needs and limitations, learning what activities they can manage and when they need to slow down.

When students learn how to identify and deal with stress constructively, they dramatically improve their chances of withstanding inevitable stressors.

Mr. Hernandez, a ninth-grade history teacher, has noticed that Jose is often tired, irritable, and sometimes clenches his jaw during class. Mr. Hernandez knows Jose is going through a difficult time since transferring to a new school. One day after school, Mr. Hernandez asks to speak with Jose. He explains that stress is a normal part of life and that everyone responds to stress differently. Mr. Hernandez tells Jose that he is going to start guiding all the students through a relaxation exercise because the entire class is stressed from time to time and everyone could benefit from knowing a strategy that might help. Jose is curious about this "relaxation strategy" and relieved that the whole class will be doing this, not just him.

Reproducible Form R12: *Weekly Journal Entry Form with Mood Rating*

Weekly Journal Entry Form with Mood Rating

Student _____ Grade/Class _____ Teacher/Counselor _____ Date _____

Describe some of your thoughts over the past week about yourself, your world, and the future.

_____

_____

_____

Describe how you often felt this past week. (Happy, upset, angry, bored, depressed, excited, or something else?)

_____

_____

_____

Describe some of the activities you did this past week. What thoughts and feelings did you have during these activities?

_____

_____

_____

Write down anything else you think was important about this past week.

_____

_____

_____

Rate your usual mood for the past week (circle one):

1	**2**	**3**	**4**	**5**
Very sad or depressed	Somewhat sad or depressed	Okay, about average (normal mood)	Pretty good, happy	Great! Terrific! Very happy

Talking about ways people cope with stress can help. Discuss with students how negative coping strategies can lead to more problems. Negative coping strategies include:

- using drugs and alcohol
- becoming angry with other people
- avoiding things that are stressful
- putting off tasks that need to get done
- sleeping excessively
- chronic worrying

Some of the ways a student can cope positively with stress include:

- talking about a problem with friends or a trusted adult
- exercising or engaging in physical activity
- focusing on something that can be changed (Jose could not change the fact that he transferred schools, but he could focus on making new friends.)
- asking whether thinking errors (cognitive distortions) may be contributing to stress, and making an effort to change any that are identified

Relaxation Exercise

The following exercise can be used with students to help them learn how to relax. Consider whether the exercise is appropriate for your students, and allow students not to participate if they strongly resist or have cultural values that may prohibit this type of activity.

1. Find a place where you feel comfortable and close your eyes.
2. Listen to your breathing. Draw in a deep, full breath. Inhale, counting to five. Let the breath out slowly, count to five, and feel yourself relax as you breathe.
3. Take nine more breaths in the same way.
4. Breathe in and tighten your leg muscles. Breathe out and relax.
5. Breathe in and tighten your arm muscles. Breathe out and relax.

6. Breathe in and tighten your face muscles. Breathe out and relax. Notice how calm your body feels as you let it relax.

7. Continue breathing in and out. Take slow, deep breaths.

8. Think about being in a favorite place and being very relaxed and calm. If something is bothering you even when you are trying to relax, imagine yourself putting the thoughts of the things that bother you into a box and tying the box high up in the branches of a tree or on a high shelf. You can leave those worry thoughts there for a while.

9. Stay quiet for a few minutes.

10. Open your eyes.

7. *Strong Kids* programs: Social and emotional learning curricula

The *Strong Kids* programs may be a useful resource to teach social and emotional skills, promote resilience, and increase children's and adolescents' coping skills. The series includes four components: *Strong Start* (for children in kindergarten through second grade), *Strong Kids: Grades 3–5, Strong Kids: Grades 6–8,* and *Strong Teens: Grades 9–12.*

The *Strong Kids* programs are intended to be used for prevention of and early intervention with mental health problems. These programs do not specifically address antisocial behavior or school violence; instead, they focus on internalizing problems and promoting resilience. *Strong Kids* programs specifically target emotional education, managing anger, identifying thinking errors and changing them, thinking positively, dealing with interpersonal conflict, reducing stress, and setting and attaining goals.

The lessons are scripted and intended to be easy to use within the timeframe of one 45- to 55-minute class period over the course of 12 weeks (one lesson per week). The curricula have been used successfully with high- and typical-functioning youth, as well as at-risk youth and those who have already developed significant behavioral and emotional disorders. Successful group leaders have included general and special education teachers, school counselors, school psychologists, and other mental health professionals. These lessons have been developed to complement academic skills such as critical thinking, analysis skills, and literacy. Many schools have integrated the lessons into the course of a typical

Figure R1: *Strong Kids: Grades 3–5 Lessons*

Lesson	Title	Description
1	About Strong Kids: Emotional Strength Training	Overview of the curriculum
2	Understanding Your Feelings: Part 1	Introduction to emotions Identify emotions as comfortable or uncomfortable
3	Understanding Your Feelings: Part 2	Discussion of appropriate and inappropriate ways of expressing emotions
4	Dealing with Anger	Recognizing triggers to anger Practicing ways to change inappropriate responses
5	Understanding Other People's Feelings	Identifying others' emotions by using clues
6	Clear Thinking: Part 1	Recognizing negative thought patterns
7	Clear Thinking: Part 2	Challenging these thought patterns to think more positively
8	The Power of Positive Thinking	Promoting optimistic thinking
9	Solving People Problems	Conflict resolution strategies
10	Letting Go of Stress	Stress reduction and relaxation exercises
11	Behavior Change: Setting Goals and Staying Active	Increasing time spent in enjoyable activities and meeting goals
12	Finishing Up	Review of the lessons

language arts, health, or social studies curriculum. Figure R1 lists the lessons that are included in *Strong Kids: Grades 3–5* and a brief description of each lesson.

Several strategies have helped to implement the curricula successfully:

- Keep the pace brisk.
- Provide immediate feedback and opportunities to respond.
- Maintain a high positive to negative ratio of reinforcement.

- Maintain high student expectations.

- Ensure student participation.

- Consider using frequent rewards for participation.

- Consider small groups for activities.

- Incorporate schoolwide behavior supports.

- Allow opportunities to practice the skills.

- Find other times during the day when students can use the skills.

- Allow students to "show off" skills they have learned.

- Shorten the scripts if they are too long for your group.

Note: For more information about the *Strong Kids* programs, see the official *Strong Kids* Web site (http://strongkids.uoregon. edu) for additional information, research references, and free assessment tools. Or see www.brookespublishing.com to purchase the programs.

C. Determine whether the intervention is better used individually, in a small group, or as a classwide intervention strategy.

Once you have reviewed the possible intervention strategies and chosen the one that best suits the student or students of concern, determine whether you will teach the strategies individually, in a small group, or classwide. Most strategies for internalizing problems such as depression and anxiety can be used in a variety of settings. However, each student's problems are specific to his own unique situation, and this should be considered when choosing the setting and format for the intervention. Students dealing with issues that are best addressed in private (serious family stressors, abuse, and specific fears or phobias) would likely benefit from working individually with a school-based mental health professional or being referred to a community agency. On the other hand, many students experience common problems such as chronic worries or sadness; these students often greatly benefit from participating in a small group where they can share their experiences and be heard and understood by others who have had similar problems. The small-group format also allows the intervention to be efficiently delivered. It may also be beneficial to conduct periodic whole class lessons on mental health and emotional well-being to ensure that all students are gaining access to important information about their mental and emotional health.

D. Meet with the student.

As with any intervention, plan to meet with the student and student's parents to discuss your concerns and intervention options. If this intervention will be conducted through small-group or classwide lessons, be sure to make students' parents aware of the procedures you will be implementing, as some parents may object due to personal beliefs. You may wish to send home a letter to parents with all students who may be involved in the lessons.

Step 2: Implement the plan and evaluate student progress.

Once you have begun implementing any intervention, it is important that you evaluate whether an intervention is successful in improving a student's internalizing problems. At the completion of the intervention, common methods for assessing internalizing problems (e.g., teacher, parent, and self-report rating scales, interviews) are appropriate. This information can be compared with data collected at the time the student was first identified with internalizing symptoms. Measuring internalizing symptoms at relatively close intervals during the intervention, however, poses some challenges. (Academic progress monitoring, for example, is typically conducted once a week.) No standardized measures that have adequate psychometric properties are available for gauging depression and anxiety at brief and regular time intervals. Nonetheless, it is vital to measure how a student is progressing during intervention. Frequent progress monitoring can be accomplished either by using a weekly mood and behavior rating scale or by using selected items from behavior rating scales that target behaviors and feelings of concern, such as persistent sadness or worries. The Weekly Journal Entry Form with Mood Rating template (Reproducible Form R12) can be used to monitor feelings associated with depression and anxiety and to determine a student's progress over time.

To assess a student's depression symptoms over the course of four weeks, you develop a rating scale and ask the student questions like the following from the Sample Behavior Scale (Figure R2):

It may also be beneficial to conduct periodic whole class lessons on mental health and emotional well-being.

Figure R2: *Sample Feelings Scale*

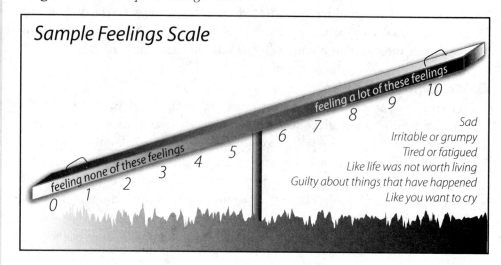

Sample Feelings Scale

feeling a lot of these feelings

feeling none of these feelings

0   1   2   3   4   5   6   7   8   9   10

Sad
Irritable or grumpy
Tired or fatigued
Like life was not worth living
Guilty about things that have happened
Like you want to cry

On a scale of 0 to 10, where 0 means feeling none of these feelings and 10 means feeling a lot of these feelings, how have you felt in the past week?

- sad

- irritable or grumpy

- tired or fatigued

- like life was not worth living

- guilty about things that have happened

- like you want to cry

WHEN ADDITIONAL HELP IS INDICATED

Sometimes students need more help than is available in a school setting. Students who experience severe and chronic mental health problems often need comprehensive services that include additional community resources for individual and family intervention services. School personnel often have many responsibilities that do not allow them to provide the extensive mental health services children may need, or they may not have the training necessary to intervene. For example, schools generally do not have psychiatrists on staff to prescribe and monitor psychiatric medications. In these instances, it may be appropriate to initiate referrals to agencies or community professionals who can provide individual and family psychotherapy as well as medication evaluations and management. School districts have widely varying policies regarding making suggestions or referrals for student assistance from outside professionals or agencies. Make sure you understand your school's policies and required practices prior to making any referrals.

Immediate response—that is, contacting community health providers such as a primary or emergency care physician, parents, and sometimes law enforcement officials—is required if there is a suspicion that a student wants to harm himself, harm others, is in imminent danger of being harmed, or appears seriously ill. Schools usually have a designated professional (such as an administrator or school psychologist) who is responsible for evaluating and responding to these concerns. In other instances where a referral for additional support is indicated but not immediately necessary, it can be helpful for school mental health professionals to have a list of referral sources available in the community. Parents should be included in this process and be made aware of the concerns that led to the referral as well as their role in following through with the plan for intervention. Often it is helpful to write a brief letter to the community resource in order to relay information that may assist this provider in fully understanding the school's concerns.

The following guidelines can be used when considering whether to make a referral for counseling, a medication evaluation, or both. School mental health professionals and administrators should be consulted before discussing the possibility of a referral with parents, students, or other school professionals. A referral for counseling is generally appropriate in the following situations:

- Problems are severe and chronic.
- Daily functioning seems to be impaired.
- There are concerns for the safety of the student or others.
- Interventions in the school did not appear to help sufficiently or school-based services are not available.
- The student would benefit from either talk-based or activity-based therapy.

A referral for a medication evaluation is generally appropriate if the above guidelines are true, in addition to any of the following:

- The student displays very bizarre and/or disorganized thinking.
- The student is seeing, hearing, and/or experiencing phenomena that others do not experience.
- Psychosocial interventions have been provided but have not produced the desired benefits for the student.

For every case in which mental health referrals are believed to be the best course of action, individual, family, and cultural issues *must* be considered. Cultural considerations can include (but are not limited to) nation of origin, regional norms, religious beliefs and practices, socioeconomic status, stage of acculturation, language, intellectual or physical disabilities, sexual orientation, and educational level and experiences. Depending on student and familial background and current status, the understanding of mental health concerns and treatment options can vary greatly. Years of racial and socioeconomic inequalities can greatly influence views on psychiatric medication as well as the ability to obtain adequate medical attention. For example, access to healthcare may be severely limited in certain communities, and individuals may be wary of taking psychotropic medication for fear of addiction. Many individuals are skeptical of psychological treatments due to prior experiences or their level of understanding of therapy and medicine, or they may possess a healthy dose of skepticism due to imperfections of the science and practice of psychology and psychiatry. Although these areas have made great gains in diagnostic and treatment issues, as with most areas in science, much remains to be learned and solved. With this in mind, school professionals must consider these perspectives, provide education and support when indicated, and consistently interact with students and their families with respect and regard for a variety of beliefs and opinions.

CONCLUSION

The emotional well-being of children is a powerful contributor to academic progress and overall healthy development across the lifespan. Without sufficient skills, children will struggle to cope with stressors that will inevitably occur in their lives. The danger is that many children will needlessly struggle, stumble, and find themselves in an undesirable situation: feeling overwhelmingly anxious, depressed, having difficulties with attending school, not engaging in enjoyable activities, and feeling hopeless that their situation may not change. Caring for children demands comprehensive attention not only to their health and educational needs, but also to their social and emotional development.

Schools of the 21st century have an important opportunity and challenge to support the relationship between social and emotional health and overall school success by serving as places where children can receive systematic instruction to promote their general development. As educators, you are the best-trained professionals in the area of instruction and can effectively use the strategies presented in this chapter. Consultation with educational colleagues can certainly support your efforts to find efficient and creative ways to implement these techniques so they are interesting and beneficial to

As educators, you are the best-trained professionals in the area of instruction and can effectively use the strategies presented in this chapter.

INTERVENTION

R

students. Many of the strategies can be easily integrated into the course of a language arts or health curriculum, whether it is a 10-minute journal-writing activity or teaching one lesson per week from a social-emotional learning program. As students learn these skills over the course of their educational career, their emotional resiliency should grow along with their academic skills and carry them through challenging times.

Note: For more information and strategies on internalizing problems, see *Helping Students Overcome Depression and Anxiety: A Practical Guide to Internalizing Problems* by Kenneth W. Merrell (www.guilford.com).

REFERENCES

Doepheide, J. A. (2006). Recognizing and treating depression in children and adolescents. *American Journal of Health Systems Pharmacology, 63*, 233–243.

Elias, M. J., Zins, J. E., Weissberg, R. P., Frey, K. S., Greenberg, M. T., Haynes, N. M., Kessler, R., et al. (1997). *Promoting social and emotional learning: Guidelines for educators.* Alexandria, VA: Association for Supervision and Curriculum Development.

Lewinsohn, P. M., Clarke, G. N., Rohde, P., Hops, H., & Seeley, J. R. (1996). A course in coping: A cognitive-behavioral approach to the treatment of adolescent depression. In E. D. Hibbs & P. S. Jensen (Eds.), *Psychosocial treatments for child and adolescent disorders* (pp. 109–135). Washington, DC: American Psychological Association.

Merrell, K. W. (2007). *Behavioral, social, and emotional assessment of children and adolescents.* Mahwah, NJ: Erlbaum/Routledge.

Merrell, K. W. (2008). *Helping students overcome depression and anxiety: A practical guide to internalizing problems* (2nd ed.). New York, NY: Guilford Press.

Merrell, K. W., Carrizales, D., Feuerborn, L., Gueldner, B. A., & Tran, O. (2007a) *Strong kids—Grades 3-5: A social and emotional learning curriculum.* Baltimore, MD: Paul H. Brookes Publishing Company.

Merrell, K. W., Carrizales, D., Feuerborn, L., Gueldner, B. A., & Tran, O. (2007b) *Strong kids—Grades 6-8: A social and emotional learning curriculum.* Baltimore, MD: Paul H. Brookes Publishing Company.

Merrell, K. W., Carrizales, D., Feuerborn, L., Gueldner, B. A., & Tran, O. (2007c) *Strong teens—Grades 9-12: A social and emotional learning curriculum.* Baltimore, MD: Paul H. Brookes Publishing Company.

Merrell, K. W., Parisi, D., & Whitcomb, S. (2007). *Strong Start—Grades K-2: A social-emotional learning curriculum.* Baltimore, MD: Paul H. Brookes Publishing Company.

Seeley, J. R., Rohde, P., Lewinsohn, P. M., & Clarke, G. N. (2002). Depression in youth: Epidemiology, identification, and intervention. In M. R. Shinn, H. M. Walker, & G. Stoner (Eds.), *Interventions for academic and behavior problems II: Preventative and remedial approaches* (pp. 885–911). Bethesda, MD: National Association of School Psychologists.

 # Reproducible Materials

The following reproducible materials may be used in conjunction with "Intervention R: Internalizing Problems and Mental Health." Copies are provided in the chapter and on the CD. Permission is given for individual classroom teachers to reproduce any forms labeled "Reproducible" for classroom use. Reproduction of these materials for an entire school system is prohibited without express permission of the publisher.

Reproducible Step-by-Step Summary

INTERVENTION R

INTERNALIZING PROBLEMS AND MENTAL HEALTH

Step-by-Step Summary

Following is a summary of the steps involved in Intervention R. It is important to use professional judgment, adjusting procedures to meet the needs of the situation and the individual. See the chapter "Intervention R: Internalizing Problems and Mental Health" for a detailed description of this intervention.

STEP 1 Assess the situation and choose an intervention strategy.

A. Identify the problem and symptoms to be targeted.

B. Choose an intervention.

BEHAVIORAL AND COGNITIVE STRATEGIES FOR INDIVIDUAL, SMALL-, AND LARGE-GROUP INTERVENTIONS

1. Emotional education
   1. Identify comfortable and uncomfortable feelings.
   2. Use incomplete-sentence techniques.
   3. Use a self-rating inventory for communicating feelings.

2. Behavior change
   1. Schedule enjoyable activities.
   2. Use operant conditioning techniques.

3. Cognitive change: Cognitive therapy
   1. Develop an awareness of emotional variability.
   2. Detect automatic thoughts and identify beliefs.
   3. Evaluate automatic thoughts and beliefs.

4. Cognitive change: Rational-Emotive Behavior Therapy

5. Journal writing

6. Reducing stress

7. *Strong Kids* programs: Social and emotional learning curricula

---

C. Determine whether the intervention is better used individually, in a small group, or a as a classwide intervention strategy.

D. Meet with the student.

STEP 2 Implement the plan and evaluate student progress.

Note that in the following chart, most of the problems indicate that Interventions A, D, and Q are appropriate for consideration. "Intervention A: Planned Discussion" is always the logical starting place for any and all problems—that is, let the student and the parents know about your concerns and try to jointly arrive at solutions.

"Intervention D: Data Collection and Analysis" is an essential component for all problems/interventions that are not solved with very simple interventions. Decisions about maintaining, modifying, and eventually fading interventions should be based on objective data.

"Intervention Q: Relaxation and Stress Management" provides suggestions for managing your own tension and emotions and is worth considering any time a student's behavior problem has you emotionally engaged—feeling anger or frustration, or even feeling sorry for the student. These emotional entanglements will reduce the chance of implementing procedures consistently and unemotionally.

Problem	Intervention																	
	Early-Stage						*Highly Structured*											
	A	**B**	**C**	**D**	**E**	**F**	**G**	**H**	**I**	**J**	**K**	**L**	**M**	**N**	**O**	**P**	**Q**	**R**
Page	71	93	185	223	257	305	335	393	425	463	485	535	567	605	639	689	731	751
Absenteeism	✓	✓		✓		✓											✓	
Academic problems	✓	✓		✓		✓											✓	
Aggression/fighting	✓			✓		✓	✓	✓	✓		✓		✓	✓			✓	
Anger or hostility	✓	✓		✓		✓		✓	✓	✓		✓					✓	
Annoying habits	✓		✓	✓		✓											✓	
Anxiety	✓			✓													✓	✓
Arguing	✓		✓	✓	✓	✓				✓					✓	✓	✓	
Assault	✓			✓			✓										✓	
Attendance/punctuality	✓	✓		✓											✓		✓	
ADHD	✓			✓							✓						✓	
Attention problems	✓	✓		✓	✓	✓			✓	✓		✓					✓	
Attention-seeking behavior	✓	✓	✓	✓	✓	✓											✓	
Bad habits	✓		✓	✓	✓	✓							✓				✓	
Being preoccupied with death	✓			✓													✓	✓
Being the scapegoat	✓			✓									✓				✓	
Biting	✓			✓										✓			✓	
Blurting out	✓		✓	✓	✓						✓					✓	✓	
Bossiness	✓		✓	✓		✓											✓	
Bragging	✓		✓		✓				✓	✓							✓	
Cheating	✓	✓		✓		✓											✓	
"Class clown" behavior	✓	✓		✓		✓											✓	
Complaining	✓	✓	✓	✓		✓			✓	✓						✓	✓	✓
Conduct disorder	✓	✓	✓	✓	✓	✓					✓						✓	
Creating excuses for every mistake	✓	✓		✓	✓	✓											✓	
Criticism	✓		✓	✓		✓					✓	✓					✓	
Daydreaming	✓		✓	✓									✓				✓	
Dependency	✓			✓		✓											✓	
Depression	✓			✓													✓	✓

Problem	Intervention																	
	Early-Stage						Highly Structured											
	A	B	C	D	E	F	G	H	I	J	K	L	M	N	O	P	Q	R
Page	71	93	185	223	257	305	335	393	425	463	485	535	567	605	639	689	731	751
Disruptive behavior	✓	✓	✓	✓	✓	✓		✓	✓					✓	✓	✓	✓	
Echoing another's speech	✓			✓										✓			✓	
Feeling generally uncomfortable or fearful	✓			✓													✓	✓
Feeling sad	✓			✓													✓	✓
Fighting	✓			✓			✓		✓						✓		✓	
Finger flicking	✓			✓										✓			✓	
Frequently out of seat	✓			✓												✓	✓	
Getting the last word	✓		✓	✓												✓	✓	
Grabbing	✓			✓			✓	✓									✓	
Habitual behaviors	✓		✓	✓						✓	✓						✓	
Hair pulling	✓			✓				✓						✓			✓	
Having no interest in everyday or enjoyable activities	✓			✓													✓	✓
Having trouble concentrating and making decisions	✓	✓		✓													✓	✓
Helplessness	✓	✓		✓	✓	✓											✓	
Hitting	✓			✓			✓					✓	✓				✓	
Hypochrondia	✓	✓		✓		✓											✓	✓
Immaturity	✓			✓		✓											✓	
Inability to handle disagreement	✓			✓								✓					✓	
Inaccurate or incomplete work	✓	✓	✓	✓		✓											✓	
Inappropriate comments/ interactions	✓			✓							✓						✓	
Insubordination	✓		✓	✓		✓		✓									✓	
Irritability	✓			✓					✓								✓	✓
Kicking	✓						✓	✓						✓			✓	
Lack of energy	✓	✓	✓	✓		✓											✓	✓
Loud, sustained disruptions	✓			✓				✓									✓	
Lying	✓	✓		✓		✓											✓	

Problem	Intervention																	
	Early-Stage						*Highly Structured*											
	A	B	C	D	E	F	G	H	I	J	K	L	M	N	O	P	Q	R
Page	71	93	185	223	257	305	335	393	425	463	485	535	567	605	639	689	731	751
Manipulative behavior	✓		✓	✓												✓	✓	
Masturbating	✓			✓						✓			✓				✓	
Minor but potentially annoying misbehavior	✓		✓	✓		✓					✓						✓	
Negotiating	✓			✓	✓	✓											✓	
Noisemaking	✓			✓									✓			✓	✓	
Nose-picking	✓			✓						✓			✓				✓	
Not following directions	✓	✓	✓	✓						✓			✓				✓	
Off-task behavior	✓	✓	✓	✓	✓	✓				✓	✓		✓				✓	
Open hostility	✓			✓				✓	✓							✓	✓	
Oppositional defiant disorder	✓	✓		✓							✓						✓	
Outbursts, verbal or physical	✓			✓			✓	✓	✓	✓							✓	
Out-of-control behavior	✓			✓			✓		✓								✓	
Panicking	✓			✓													✓	✓
Perfectionism	✓		✓	✓		✓											✓	
Physically dangerous behavior	✓			✓			✓		✓								✓	
Pinching or biting	✓			✓										✓			✓	
Poking	✓			✓									✓				✓	
Poor listening skills	✓	✓		✓		✓					✓						✓	
Poor motivation	✓	✓		✓		✓									✓		✓	
Poor peer relations	✓		✓	✓									✓				✓	
Poor self-concept/self-esteem	✓	✓	✓	✓	✓	✓						✓					✓	✓
Problems being corrected or accepting feedback	✓	✓		✓									✓				✓	
Problems interacting with adults	✓		✓	✓									✓				✓	
Put-downs	✓		✓	✓						✓							✓	
Quality of work	✓	✓		✓											✓		✓	
Questioning	✓			✓												✓	✓	
Rambunctious behavior	✓		✓	✓		✓	✓										✓	

Problem	Intervention																	
	Early-Stage						Highly Structured											
	A	B	C	D	E	F	G	H	I	J	K	L	M	N	O	P	Q	R
Page	71	93	185	223	257	305	335	393	425	463	485	535	567	605	639	689	731	751
Repeating phrases excessively	✓			✓										✓			✓	
Repetitive motions	✓			✓										✓			✓	
Repetitive, loud noises	✓			✓				✓									✓	
Rudeness	✓		✓	✓												✓	✓	
Self-control problems	✓			✓					✓			✓					✓	
Self-destructive behavior	✓			✓			✓				✓						✓	
Self-putdowns	✓			✓								✓					✓	
Shouting	✓			✓				✓					✓				✓	
Shy or withdrawn behavior	✓	✓		✓		✓											✓	✓
Sleeping too much or too little	✓			✓													✓	✓
Sloppy work	✓	✓	✓	✓		✓					✓						✓	
Stealing	✓	✓		✓		✓											✓	
Stereotypic behavior	✓			✓										✓			✓	
Swearing, cursing, yelling obscenities	✓			✓				✓	✓	✓		✓			✓	✓	✓	
Talking back	✓		✓	✓		✓										✓	✓	
Tantrums	✓	✓		✓		✓	✓			✓				✓	✓		✓	
Tardiness	✓			✓		✓											✓	
Tattling	✓		✓	✓	✓	✓										✓	✓	
Teasing	✓			✓	✓	✓							✓				✓	
Testing limits	✓		✓	✓												✓	✓	
Threats	✓			✓					✓				✓				✓	
Throwing items	✓			✓										✓			✓	
Unconventional verbal behavior	✓			✓										✓			✓	
Volatile behavior	✓			✓			✓		✓								✓	
Whining	✓			✓						✓							✓	
Work completion	✓	✓		✓											✓		✓	
Worrying	✓	✓		✓													✓	✓